MARIO PRAZ
THE ROMANTIC AGONY

Second Edition
with a Foreword
by Frank Kermode

The Romantic Agony

The
Romantic Agony

By Mario Praz

Translated from the Italian by
ANGUS DAVIDSON

SECOND EDITION

With a Foreword By
FRANK KERMODE

*'J'ai trouvé la définition du Beau, de mon Beau. C'est
quelque chose d'ardent et de triste . . . . Je ne conçois
guère un type de Beauté où il n'y ait du Malheur.'*

Oxford New York
OXFORD   UNIVERSITY   PRESS

Oxford University Press, Walton Stree, Oxford OX2 6DP

Oxford New York Toronto
Delhi Bombay Calcutta Madras Karachi
Kuala Lumpur Singapore Hong Kong Tokyo
Nairobi Dar es Salaam Cape Town
Melbourne Auckland

and associated companies in
Beirut Berlin Ibadan Nicosia

Oxford is a trade mark of Oxford University Press

ISBN 0−19−281061−8

Translated from the Italian La carne, la morte e il diavola nella letteratura
romantica, and published by arrangement with G. C. Sansoni
S.p.A., Florence

First published in English 1933 by Oxford University Press
Second edition 1951
Reissued with a new Foreword by Frank Kermode
as an Oxford University Press paperback
and simultaneiously in a hardback edition 1970
Reprinted 1978, 1979, 1983, 1985

Printed in Great Britain by
The Guernsey Press Co. Ltd.
Guernsey, Channel Islands.

FOREWORD
to the 1970 Impression

> Yet it is less the horror than the grace
> Which turns the gazer's spirit into stone,
> Whereon the lineaments of that dead face
> Are graven till the characters be grown
> Into itself, and thought no more can trace. . .

A modern reader of poetry, invited to attribute these verses to an author, would in all probability pick Yeats, thinking of 'The Statues' and perhaps other poems heavy with marble and bronze. But they come from Shelley's lines on a picture of the Medusa. Yeats's lovers, and his Irish heroes, bring 'character enough' to the 'lineaments of a plummet-measured face': his poem is obscure, the argument more wilful and portentous than Shelley's simpler assertion of 'the tempestuous loveliness of terror'. But the affinity between the poems is clear enough, and it is no more than an emblem of other affinities between great twentieth-century poets and the Romantic-Decadents; or, more generally, between the character of literary culture in the formative years of modernism and that earlier pre-occupation with the exotic, with perversities of pleasure and pain, with the establishment of a rhetoric for velleities formerly denied expression, which Mario Praz undertook to expound in his remarkable book.

The Romantic Agony is now almost forty years old, and it is surely safe to call it a classic, and not merely a classic of academic literary history—it has a brilliance much greater than needed to achieve that modest eminence—but a classic in a sense which places it among such books as have, in the depth of their insights, power to alter a reader's understanding of the history of his society, and perhaps of his own history. It is rare for a work of literary scholarship to achieve so much; and the few which have comparable scope and order fall short in curiosity, vigour, and wit. An Auerbach, though of even greater philological range, may be much more selective as to documentation; a Lukács modifies and specializes a doctrine rather than defines a new insight.

The qualities I have just attributed to Praz's book are displayed most obviously in the collection and analysis of material which lay about in all manner of unlikely places, and must often have seemed too heavy and dull to dispose of. How firmly and delicately he managed it his notes demonstrate. They are not merely a very full record of his frequently obscure sources, but a testimony to his rapid mind and his eye for the relevance of disparate observations. How happy, to take a single small instance, is note 112 in the fourth chapter, which appends to a high-falutin passage from a novel by D'Annunzio ('Love, like all divine powers, is not truly exalted except in a trinity') a dry observation of Colette's on *'le vice prétentieux qui s'intitule "harmonie ternaire de l'amour"'*! Such Burtonian breezes do much to refresh the reader after exposure to the pathological specimens Praz has to exhibit.

It is easy, in 1970, to underestimate his primary achievement, namely the identification of his subject, which is the pathology of Romanticism. Four decades have established it as a commonplace, and nobody now considers the origins of modern sensibility in ignorance of it, whether or not he has read and acknowledged Praz. This is the common fate of authors who are obviously right; but it does not alter the fact that few critics have ever been vouchsafed so brilliant an idea. Fewer still have had the industry, the acumen, and the methodological caution, to give such an idea its appropriately full and moderate expression. From the outset he was aware that the book might be misunderstood and abused, as indeed it was; he could not prevent readers determined to read it wrong from doing so, or critics who believed that the hand which dabbled in such materials ought to be subdued by what it worked in from saying that his was. All he could do was to ensure that these people were without excuse; and he did so, by carefully defining his objects and carefully controlling his tone. The intellectual skill with which he went about these tasks seems to me an index of very great civility, further evidence of which is plentifully available in his other major works and in his autobiography.

Praz speaks in his Preface of the danger that his work might be confounded—since it pivoted on the literature of the Decadents—with such contemptible exercises in 'literary nosology' as Nordau's *Degeneration*. Since he wrote there have been many other books even more likely than Nordau's to give us misleading preconceptions of *The Romantic Agony*, and we still need to remind ourselves that matters of this kind may be studied without either salacity or sanctimony. If Praz praises or condemns it is on literary grounds. Thus, writing at a time when the Marquis de Sade had been awarded the status of heroic progenitor— *'un écrivain qu'il faut placer sans doute parmi les plus grands'*—by the Surrealists, he remarks:

Let us give Sade his due, as having been the first to expose, in all its crudity, the mechanism of *homo sensualis*, let us even assign him a place of honour as a psychopathologist and admit his influence on a whole century of literature; but courage (to give a nobler name to what most people would call shamelessness) does not suffice to give originality to a thought, nor does the hurried jotting down of all the cruel fantasies which obsess the mind suffice to give a work mastery of style. . . . The most elementary qualities of a writer—let us not say, of a writer of genius—are lacking in Sade.

And throughout the book, which requires him to recount one mechanical fantasy after another, he preserves this sense of literary value and limit, as well as that independence of judgement which makes him resistant to the thought-saving generalizations characteristic of so much literary history. This latter quality is well exemplified in the pages of his Preface which comment on the habit of tracing the detailed aberrations of a literary period to some overriding metaphysical crisis. It is worth remembering that the erroneous reading of Donne, to which he casually alludes, was at the time of writing pretty well a standard one. And this may serve to remind us also that Praz is a very distinguished exponent of English seventeenth-century poetry; his range is certain to be underestimated by those who cannot read his Italian works.

The scope of this book is, obviously, enormous, from Sade to D'Annunzio (Praz was writing, we should remember, in the Rome of Mussolini) with Byron and Shelley, Gautier and Baudelaire, Swinburne and Verlaine, and hundreds of lesser figures, along the way. And for all the amplitude of the treatment, there is a constant sense that the author is decorously denying himself, that there must have been many occasions when it was difficult not to move only a little outside literature and so, in seeking to enrich it, blur the argument. There is for instance, the whole nineteenth-century history of magic, secret societies, occultism of every kind; but he is not tempted. He confines himself to the literature of many languages, and justly claims that in consequence he has been able to do what he set out to do: 'I have watched the pattern which no other critic had detected and I have described that alone.' Inferences as to the spirit of the age, prophecies as to what must follow, are the more readily made when that pattern has been demonstrated. The clarity and modesty of this programme seem to us to merit imitation by younger scholars.

So, I think, does the dryness of Praz's tone, which is of wine not dust. It enables him to cope with the most outrageous books, for example Chateaubriand's *Atala*—'the voluptuousness of incest, sacrilege and death' crammed into one sexual act, without comment other than what is required to relate it to his theme, or to call attention to a logical absurdity in Chateaubriand's heated preface to the book. He does, of course, being human, have opinions about the social consequences of this kind of thing, and he expresses them, though without censoriousness. He believes that life often imitates art; and this conviction leads him to make certain statements which English readers, who are accustomed to the same kind of thing with much more overbearing moralistic overtones, may well wish to ponder.

For example: 'Since the Romantic theory asserted that the best means of expressing passions was to begin to feel them, people sought, instead of translating spontaneous acts of life into the realm of art, to experience in actual life the monstrous suggestions of imaginations fed upon literary horrors.' This proposition has its origins in the Horatian *si vis me flere*, but as stated it is perhaps unjust to the extremely refined 'Romantic theory' we learn from Wordsworth and Coleridge, who certainly held that the communication of poetic meaning was dependent on pleasure, a pleasure which the poet himself must feel; but maintained only that this required in the *poet* a dangerously high level of organic sensibility. It is not part of the doctrine that this should be achieved by other men. That there were 'raging passions *à la* Byron, suicides *à la* Chatterton,' need not be denied; but they were surely confined to a special class of artists and aspirants. Praz offers, as a vivid illustration of life imitating decadent art, the story of a man looking with amorous sentimentality on a corpse encountered by chance in Florence, where the funerals had a specially horrid charm. But the man was Berlioz, an artist not famous for regularity of conduct and emotional balance. This is *art* imitating art.

The difficulty becomes acute when it concerns Sade. Praz thinks it probable that some Romantics and Decadents wished to translate Sade's fantasies into real life, as he did in some degree himself; and we may be left with the impression that the author does not wholly disagree with Janin, himself a writer of erotic horror stories, when he announces that '*les livres du marquis de Sade ont tué plus d'enfants que n'en pourraient tuer vingt maréchaux de Retz, ils en tuent chaque jour, ils en tueront encore, ils en tueront l'âme aussi bien que le corps.*' Allowing for some rhetorical exaggeration, this may seem a serious claim at a time when *Justine* is on sale in the newsagent's, and when child-murderers have been readers of Sade. What we have to remember is that sadistic pleasure, like *belles dames sans merci* and the rest of the decadent properties, was available in nonliterary forms in the society within which the literary conventions grew; it was a *milieu* in which nothing, from the child whore to the *vice anglais*, could seem new. Its practices needed no prompting from literature, which at worst exploited and at best examined them. The torture of children was doubtless a more habitual practice in

the schools of the rich and the houses of the poor than in the garrets
of poets, and the postures of a Byron, a Berlioz, a Petrus Borel,
even of a Wilde or a Yeats, seem not to have been widely imitated.

Praz does not, I think, argue that the obscenities he sometimes has
to deal with are in general corrupting, save in this one instance,
where he at least does not openly disagree with Janin. And it is
hardly conceivable that he would favour the suppression of any book.
The matter seems worth mentioning, however, as a point at which
the extraordinary and methodical detachment of the author may
allow the wrong inference. Perhaps Praz would simply say that any
matching of his evidence to psychologies or sociologies or moralities
that interest the reader must always be the reader's responsibility.
His own interest is literary. He collects this material (some of it
certainly dreary or detestable) for reasons which are of a serious
literary kind, and this means, of course, that finally they may be
related to the study of a whole culture and its health. The intertwined traditions he studies helped to produce great poetry, and not
only from Byron and Shelley, Baudelaire and Mallarmé, but from
great modern poets, Yeats, Eliot, Valéry. Praz remarks that he
could have continued his enquiry beyond the point when he broke
off, and it is likely enough that we have still not seen the Decadent
themes exhausted. Thus *The Romantic Agony* is more than a catalogue
of curiosities, or an aid to the study (which has grown so fashionable)
of the exotic and erotic in nineteenth-century society; it is, as I
suggested at the outset, one of the indispensable guides to the study
of our own literature and our own epoch.

London   FRANK KERMODE
1970

CONTENTS

FOREWORD TO THE 1970 IMPRESSION
by Frank Kermode . . . . *page* v

AUTHOR'S PREFACE TO THE FIRST EDITION . *page* xv

NOTE TO THE SECOND EDITION . . . *page* xxiv

INTRODUCTION. 'Romantic': an Approximate Term . *page* 1

Notes to the Introduction . . . . . *page* 17

CHAPTER I. THE BEAUTY OF THE MEDUSA . . *page* 23

1. 'Medusean' beauty in Goethe, Shelley, Keats. 2. The Beauty of the Horrid, the Beauty of Sadness, Beauty and Death, in the Pre-Romantics, in Novalis, Chateaubriand, Hugo, Baudelaire, Flaubert, D'Annunzio. 3. Precursors: Tasso, Marlowe, Webster. 4. Lyric poets of the Seventeenth Century. 5. Difference of meaning in themes of tainted beauty in Seventeenth-century writers and in the Romantics. 6. Recurrence of these themes in Baudelaire. The attraction of *faisandage*. The beauty of gloomy landscape.

Notes and Addenda to Chapter I . . . . *page* 46

CHAPTER II. THE METAMORPHOSES OF SATAN . *page* 53

1. The figure of Satan in Tasso and Marino. 2. Milton's Satan. An opinion of Taine. Supposed Satanism in Milton. Point of view of the Romantics (Schiller, Blake, Shelley). 3. Fusion of the 'noble bandit' type with that of the Miltonic Satan. Schiller's Robber. 4. Type of outlaw in the 'tales of terror'. Mrs. Radcliffe's Schedoni. Shakespearean elements. 5. M. G. Lewis, H. Zschokke. *Abellino, Jean Sbogar*. 6. Byron and the 'outlaw' type. Characteristics derived from Mrs. Radcliffe. 7. Byron and *Zeluco*. 8. Byron and Chateaubriand (*René*). 9. Biographical character of Byron. 10. The sense of sin in Byron: *le bonheur dans le crime*. 11. The Fatal Man of the Romantics: Jean Sbogar, Antony. Criminal erotism. 12. Vampirism. 13. The philanthropic outlaw in the writers of the *roman-feuilleton*. 14. Significance of vampirism. Connexion with the subject of Chapter I. A speech by Auger and an opinion of Sainte-Beuve. 'Byron et de Sade ... les deux plus grands inspirateurs de nos modernes.'

Notes and Addenda to Chapter II . . . *page* 84

CHAPTER III. THE SHADOW OF THE DIVINE MARQUIS *page* 95

1. The type of the Persecuted Woman. *Clarissa Harlowe*. Richardson's moral outlook. 2. *La Religieuse*. Diderot and the *Système de la Nature*.

3. *Thérèse philosophe*. 4. *Les Liaisons dangereuses*. Observations of Baudelaire. 5. The novels of the Marquis de Sade and his 'philosophy'. 6. Restif de la Bretonne. 7. Morbid themes in Chateaubriand. 8. Diffusion of the 'persecuted woman' theme. M. G. Lewis and his *Monk*. Success of this novel; Hoffmann, V. Hugo, G. Sand. 9. The Persecuted Woman in the novels of Mrs. Radcliffe. Recognition-scenes. 10. Female writers under the influence of the masculine point of view. Miss Wilkinson, Mrs. Shelley. 11. Shelley's Beatrice Cenci. Morbid themes in Shelley. 12. Maturin and his *Melmoth*. 13. Diffusion of the English 'tales of terror' in France. Influence on the conception of life. Anecdote of Berlioz. The Princess Belgiojoso. The 'Jeunes-France'. 14. *L'Âne mort* by J. Janin. 15. Janin as a moralist. His essay on Sade; his review of *Madame Putiphar*. 16. The *Mémoires du Diable* of F. Soulié. 17. Pétrus Borel le lycanthrope. *Champavert*; *Madame Putiphar*. 18. The literary atmosphere in which Baudelaire grew up. An observation of the Comte H. de Viel Castel. Berlioz. Musset. 19. Delacroix. 20. Baudelaire. Discovery of Poe. Baudelaire and Sade. The erotology of Baudelaire. 21. Flaubert. *La Tentation de Saint Antoine*. The feminine ideal according to Flaubert. Flaubert and *Mademoiselle de Maupin*. Exoticism. 22. Autobiographical details of Flaubert. Flaubert and Sade. Flaubert and Byron. 23. The Comte de Lautréamont and his *Chants de Maldoror*. Affinity with P. Borel.

Notes and Addenda to Chapter III   .   .   .   *page* 167

CHAPTER IV. LA BELLE DAME SANS MERCI . . *page* 197

1. Universality of the 'fatal woman' theme. Aeschylus; the Elizabethan Dramatists. 2. The type of the Fatal Woman in Romanticism. Two families. 3. Matilda in *The Monk*. 4. Velléda, Salammbô. 5. Mérimée: *Une Femme est un diable*, *Carmen*. Localization of the Fatal Woman. Exoticism and erotism. 6. Cécily in the *Mystères de Paris*. 7. Various derivations: Rosalba la Pudica, Conchita, &c. 8. Exoticism and mysticism. Anticipations of Romantic exoticism. Keats's *La Belle Dame sans merci*. Th. Wainewright. 9. Gautier, founder of exotic aestheticism. *Une Nuit de Cléopâtre*. Parabola of the sexes during the Nineteenth Century. 10. Nyssia (*Le Roi Candaule*). *La Vénus d'Ille*. *La Morte amoureuse*. 11. The synthetic Fatal Woman. Gautier's Impéria. The courtesan Marie in *Novembre* (Flaubert). The Queen of Sheba and Ennoia in Flaubert's *Tentation*. Development of this type of Fatal Woman in England. 12. Swinburne. 13. Monckton-Milnes initiates Swinburne into the writings of Sade. 14. Swinburne's algolagnia. 'The powerless victim of the furious rage of a beautiful woman.' The type of Fatal Woman in the works of Swinburne. Influence of the Pre-Raphaelites. Analogy of female type with that of Gautier and Flaubert. 15. Mary Stuart in *Chastelard*. 16. *Atalanta in Calydon* and the influence of Sade's theories. 17. *Lesbia Brandon*, *Anactoria*. 18. The Fatal Woman in *Poems and Ballads I*, *Dolores*. 19. Sublimation of

Swinburne's algolagnia: the goddess Liberty. 20. Notes by Swinburne
on certain female heads drawn by Michaelangelo. *Cleopatra*. 21. The
type of synthetic Fatal Woman culminates in Pater's Monna Lisa.
The fashion of the 'Gioconda smile'. 22. Wilde's *Sphinx*. 23. The
Swinburnian Fatal Woman in E. Nencioni's *Rapsodia Lirica*. 24. The
synthetic Fatal Woman in D'Annunzio. *Pamphila*. Influence of
Flaubert. Sonnets by Banville and D'Annunzio on Fatal Women.
Ippolita Sanzio in *Il Trionfo della Morte*. 25. Sadism in the work of
D'Annunzio. D'Annunzio's insincerity. 26. Derivation of the Super-
woman of D'Annunzio from the Fatal Woman of Swinburne. 27. La
Comnena; Basiliola; Fedra. 28. Sadistic theories in the work of D'An-
nunzio. Isabella Inghirami *philosophe*. 29. Other Fatal Women in
Rachilde, Huysmans, O. Mirbeau. La Marquise de Sade. Clara in
the *Jardin des supplices*. 30. The type of Mademoiselle Bistouri in
Decadent poetry. Humoristic evasion: Laforgue.

Notes and Addenda to Chapter IV . . . . *page* 282

CHAPTER V. BYZANTIUM . . . . . . *page* 301

1. The art of G. Moreau. 2. The Salomé of Moreau and Huysmans.
3. The Fatal Woman in Moreau. Helen among the dying. 4. The
Salomé of Wilde. The theme as treated by Heine and by Flaubert.
Banville. Laforgue. 5. Mallarmé's *Hérodiade*. Its symbolic significance.
Herodias and Salammbô. 6. 'Lasciva est nobis pagina, vita proba.'
7. Sadism and Catholicism in the French Decadents. 8. Huysmans.
The feeling for mournful landscape. Gilles de Rais. 9. Barbey d'Aure-
villy. 10. Villiers de l'Isle Adam. 11. Joséphin Péladan's *Éthopée*.
Decadent occultism. The theme of the Androgyne. Leonardo da
Vinci's Androgyne. Perverse interpretation of the Primitives. The
Russian novel. Wagner. 12. Élémir Bourges: *Le Crépuscule des dieux*.
13. Another *éthopée* of the Decadence: the novels of C. Mendès.
14. Rachilde. *Monsieur Vénus*. 15. Russian influence. Dostoievsky.
16. *Très russe*, by J. Lorrain, *Les Noronsoff*. 17. Dorian Gray and
Monsieur de Phocas. Pater and the English Decadents. *Under the
Hill*, by A. Beardsley. Lorrain and Moreau. *Buveurs d'âmes*. 18. The
perverse fairy-tale. 19. Remy de Gourmont. 20. Marcel Schwob.
21. Barrès. Mournful landscape in Barrès. 22. Gide. 23. Rops and
Satanism; Lust and Death. 24. Post-Baudelairean poetry. Rollinat.
Samain. R. de Montesquiou. Renée Vivien. Parodies. *Les Déliquescences
d'Adoré Floupette*; *The Decadent to his soul*. Verlaine. 25. The lament
over the end of Latin civilization. *Tout décade*. . . . Byzantium.
P. Adam. 26. The most monumental figure of the Decadent Movement: D'Annunzio. *Le Laudi* and the Vittoriale.

Notes and Addenda to Chapter V . . . . . *page* 404

APPENDIX. SWINBURNE AND 'LE VICE ANGLAIS' . *page* 435

1. English algolagnia. G. A. Selwyn. 2. The type of the English
sadist in French Romanticism. 3. In the *Journal* of the Goncourts.

A portrait of Swinburne by Maupassant; its influence on the character of G. Selwyn in *La Faustin*; intermixture with other real characters. 4. The scandals of London as revealed by the *Pall Mall Gazette*, 1885; an article by Villiers de l'Isle Adam. 5. Pedigree of the character of the Marquis of Mount Edgcumbe in *Il Piacere*. 6. English sadism in Toulet's *Monsieur du Paur*, in d'Aurevilly's *Diaboliques*; in *Le Jardin des supplices*, by O. Mirbeau; in *Monsieur de Phocas* and *Les Noronsoff*, by J. Lorrain; in *La Vertu suprême*, by J. Péladàn. 7. Conclusion.

Notes and Addenda to the Appendix . . . . *page* 452

INDEX . . . . *page* 459

AUTHOR'S PREFACE

to the First Edition

THE aim of the greater part of this book is a study of Romantic literature (of which the Decadent Movement of the end of the last century is only a development) under one of its most characteristic aspects, that of erotic sensibility. It is, therefore, a study of certain states of mind and peculiarities of behaviour, which are given a definite direction by various types and themes that recur as insistently as myths engendered in the ferment of the blood.

Looked at from this point of view, the literature of the nineteenth century appears as a unique, clearly distinct whole, which the various formulas such as 'romanticism', 'realism', 'decadence,' &c., tend to disrupt. In no other literary period, I think, has sex been so obviously the mainspring of works of imagination: but it is more profitable to study the historical development of such a tendency than to repeat from hearsay, and as though incidentally, the vague accusations of sensuality and perversity with which critics of that period are generally content to label the darker portions of the picture.

A student who undertakes such a discussion runs a risk of being classed with a band of writers who have made their name by a professedly scientific treatment of such subjects, such as Dr. Dühren (Ivan Bloch) or Max Nordau. Nordau's volume on *Degeneration* aims at being a literary nosology of the Decadent Movement, but it is completely discredited by its pseudo-erudition, its grossly positivist point of view, and its insincere moral tone. A writer who, adopting the method of Lombroso, classifies a degenerate tram-conductor with Verlaine, and places Rossetti among the weak-minded (or even the imbecile, as he delicately hints in parenthesis) as described by Sollier, seems hardly capable of tracing the hidden sources of Decadent 'degeneration'.

Again, it is much easier to label as monsters certain writers who were tormented by obsessions, than to discern the universal human background which is visible behind their paroxysms. The sexual idiosyncrasies which will be discussed in the following pages offer, so to speak, a distorted image of characteristics common to all mankind. The remark made by Edmond Jaloux about Lafourcade's study of Swinburne[1] is apposite: 'Pourquoi alors ne pas s'expliquer franchement sur le sadisme et ne pas vouloir accepter qu'il soit un des ferments les plus naturels de l'âme humaine? On ne l'en débusquera que plus facilement si on le connaît bien.'

[1] In the *Nouvelles littéraires*, June 14th, 1930.

To any one who may protest, therefore, that the intimate examination of an artist's life is irreverent, or worse, we may answer with
Sainte-Beuve: 'Quand on fait une étude sur un homme considérable,
il faut oser tout voir, tout regarder, et au moins tout indiquer.'[1]
We must not pay so much attention to momentary exclamations of
satisfied curiosity—such as 'Habemus confitentem', 'nous touchons
ici à la clef'—as to the more general aim of casting some light upon
the most profound instincts of humanity—an aim in which a study
like the present may perhaps, in the end, succeed.

It must, however, be stated without further delay that a study such
as the present one differs from a medico-scientific treatise in that the
recurrence of certain morbid themes in a particular period of literature
is not invariably treated as an indication of a psychopathic state in the
writers discussed. The genetic link is in this case provided by taste
and fashion; literary sources are discussed, and not—is it necessary
to mention?—resemblances due to physiological causes, so that, side
by side with writers of genuinely specialized sensibility are to be
found others who give a mere superficial echo of certain themes.
Again, this study has not even a remote connexion with the socio-
logical study or the study of collective psychology, in which case
it would have had to include documentations from police and assize
reports, scientific or pseudo-scientific works, and anonymous or
popular literary productions.[2]

The Marquis de Sade, in whom Sainte-Beuve saw 'one of the
greatest inspirers of the moderns', will be frequently mentioned in
the following pages. But an immediate word of warning is needed,
no longer (as would have been necessary a few years ago) against
the time-honoured condemnation of the author of *Justine*, but
against the reaction in his favour which a few years ago became
fashionable in certain literary circles in France.

[1] *Chateaubriand et son groupe*, vol. i, p. 102.

[2] A reviewer of the first edition of the present book (C. Pellizzi in the
review *Pègaso*, vol. iii, p. 5 (May 1931)) inclined to classify me as a follower of
the psychoanalytic method, as a somewhat belated utilizer of 'categories derived
from Freudian psychology, if one must judge by the stress on the sexual
theme', and wondered whether that school of psychology deserved to be
considered 'the most reliable, and the most up to date'. Of course the stress
on the sexual theme is not enough to cause a study to fall under the denomina-
tion of 'Freudian psychoanalysis'. That stress is in the very period which
forms the subject of this study; it is not deliberately laid from outside, and
answers so little to the Freudian method that a psychoanalyst would probably
call the present book superficial, based on remarks which anybody might
make. Indeed it would be difficult to find much in common between this
book and, for instance, Freud's essay on W. Jensen's *Gradiva* and Marie
Bonaparte's two volumes on Poe. (See my essay, 'Poe davanti alla psicanalisi',
in the volume *Studi e svaghi inglesi*, Florence, Sansoni, 1937.) [Add. 1950]

The conclusions of the present study will prove, even to those who are least well-informed, that Sade's work is a monument—not indeed, as Guillaume Apollinaire was pleased to declare, 'de la pensée humaine'—but at least of something. But that the light which his work throws upon the less mentionable impulses of the man-animal should suffice immediately to classify the author as an original thinker, or, without further ado, as a man of genius, is a conclusion only to be pardoned if the ignorance and momentary infatuation of its formulator are taken into account. Maurice Heine, in his introduction to the recent edition of the manuscript of the *Infortunes de la vertu*, declares:

> La coalition des intérêts que, pour les mieux masquer, on qualifie généralement de moraux et de spirituels, s'est livrée pendant un siècle, contre la pensée d'un homme de génie, à une agression permanente et appuyée de toutes les forces répressives. Le but escompté n'est pas atteint, ne le sera jamais. Certes, le préjudice causé au patrimoine humain par une importante destruction de manuscrits équivaut à un désastre. Mais par contre la salutaire révolte, provoquée et entretenue dans les esprits libres par une si odieuse persécution, devait aboutir au mouvement d'atten-tion et de sympathie qui, en France et à l'étranger, entoure désormais le nom de Sade. . . . Il y a . . . lieu de croire que Sade, après avoir inquiété tout un siècle qui ne pouvait le lire, sera de plus en plus lu pour remédier à l'inquiétude du suivant.

Jean Paulhan, reviewing Heine's book in the *Nouvelle Revue française* of September 1930, speaks of Sade as 'un écrivain qu'il faut placer sans doute parmi les plus grands', and discovers in his work merits of style. The recent enthusiasm of the Surrealists for Sade might well form a section of my chapter on 'Byzantium': but neither the conspiracy of silence which ended only yesterday, nor the apotheo-sis towards which there is a tendency to-day, can be accepted. Let us give Sade his due, as having been the first to expose, in all its crudity, the mechanism of *homo sensualis*, let us even assign him a place of honour as a psycho-pathologist and admit his influence on a whole century of literature; but courage (to give a nobler name to what most people would call shamelessness) does not suffice to give originality to a thought, nor does the hurried jotting down of all the cruel fantasies which obsess the mind suffice to give a work mastery of style.[1] It is true that the Surrealists, who have now made them-

---

[1] Already in 1921, R.-L. Doyon in an Appendix to his reprint of Barbey d'Aurevilly's *Le Cachet d'onyx*, p. 96, wrote of Sade: 'A l'énormité du paradoxe, s'ajoute une écriture claire, gracieuse même, à peine alourdie par les dissert-ations communes aux disciples attardés de Jean-Jacques, de telle sorte que la fortune littéraire du marquis dépravé tient à la folie, au cynisme de ses aveux, à l'étrangeté de ses histoires, à la spécialité de son genre et aussi à l'agrément de son style.' But a better judge, Marcel Schwob, in a review of a book by Remy de Gourmont in the *Mercure de France* for July 1894 (see *Œuvres complètes*

selves the champions of Sade's greatness, hold a curious theory on
the subject of 'automatic writing', as being the only kind of writing
to reveal the whole man, without hypocrisy or changes of mind;
but this theory of untrammelled self-expression is precisely an
extreme application of that very romanticism which, being so open
to Sade's influence, is on that account the least fitted to judge him
dispassionately. The most elementary qualities of a writer—let us
not say, of a writer of genius—are lacking in Sade. Though more
worthy of the title of polygrapher and pornographer than a writer
such as Aretino, his whole merit lies in having left documents
illustrative of the mythological, infantile phase of psycho-pathology:
he gives, in the form of a fantastic tale, the first systematized account
of sexual perversions.

Was Sade a 'surromantique'? No, but he was certainly a sinister
force in the Romantic Movement, a familiar spirit whispering in the
ear of the 'mauvais maîtres' and the 'poètes maudits'; actually he did
nothing more than give a name to an impulse which exists in every
man, an impulse mysterious as the very forces of life and death with
which it is inextricably connected.

Isolating, as it does, one particular aspect, fundamental though it
may be, of Romantic literature—that is, the education of sensibility,
and more especially of erotic sensibility—this study must be considered
as a monograph, not as a synthesis, and the point of view of its author
might be compared to that of some one who, in Poe's well-known
story, examined merely the crack which runs zig-zag across the
front of the House of Usher, without troubling about its general
architecture. I wish to add to the remarks on this point in the
Foreword to the Italian edition certain explanations which seem to
be called for by Benedetto Croce's criticisms of my book[1]—'Praz
seems to make out that what is called Romanticism consists in the
formation of a new sensibility, that particular sensibility which is
displayed in the various tendencies and fantasies which he so amply
expounds. But is not Romanticism, even in its "historical" sense,
and according to the current use of the word, a very much more
complex thing? Is it not rich, not only in theoretical values such as
those which are commonly called dialectics, aesthetics, history, and
the like, but also in moral values, and even in maladies and crises
which are less shameful than those which he examines?' The reply
to these questions already given in my Foreword—that is, that 'the

de M. Schwob, *Chroniques*, Paris, Bernouard, 1928, pp. 201-2), said apropos
of Sade: 'Par infortune ce mauvais écrivain est resté le meilleur représentant
de son tour d'esprit.'

[1] *La Critica*, vol. xxix, no. 2 (March 20th, 1931), pp. 133-4.

present study must be considered as a monograph, not as a synthesis', and that 'other tendencies and energies contribute to creating the atmosphere of the nineteenth century'—might be reinforced by the words of André Gide (*Les Faux-monnayeurs*, pp. 179–80): 'Toutes les grandes écoles ont apporté, avec un nouveau style, une nouvelle éthique, un nouveau cahier des charges, de nouvelles tables, une nouvelle façon de voir, de comprendre l'amour, et de se comporter dans la vie'; I might also argue that the study of one of these aspects does not attempt to deny the presence of the others, but that the way in which Croce establishes their interdependence seems to me to be questionable.

In the opinion of Croce,[1] who in any case fails to break away in this matter from the usual method of literary historians (a clever exaggeration of this process is to be found in *Le Romantisme français*, by Pierre Lasserre), the root of Romanticism *qua* moral phenomenon, of the 'mal du siècle', has to be sought in the borderland between an ancient, hereditary faith which had collapsed, and a new faith, the faith in new philosophical and liberal ideals which had as yet been only imperfectly and partially digested: 'This malady was due, not so much to breaking away from a traditional faith, as to the difficulty of really appropriating to oneself and living the new faith, which, to be lived and put into action, demanded courage and a virile attitude, also certain renunciations of bygone causes of self-satisfaction and comfort which had now ceased to exist; it demanded also, in order to be understood, discussed, and defended, experience, culture, and a trained mind. This may have been feasible to robust intellects and characters, who were able to trace back the genetic process of the new faith without being overthrown by it, and, through inner conflicts, to reach their haven, and was also feasible, in a different way, to simple, clear minds and straightforward natures who immediately understood, adopted, and practised its conclusions, captivated by the light of their goodness; but it was not within reach of feminine, impressionable, sentimental, incoherent, fickle minds, which stimulated and excited doubts and difficulties in themselves and then could not get the better of them, and which liked and sought out dangers and then perished in them.'

These feminine minds are those to which psychologists give the name 'schizoid'; and it is questionable whether the minds of all artists are not, in a greater or lesser degree, of this kind. One remembers Keats's words (in a letter to Woodhouse, October 27th, 1818): 'As to the poetical character itself . . . it is not itself—it has no self—it is every thing and nothing—it has no character—it enjoys light and shade—it lives in gusto, be it foul or fair, high or low,

[1] *Storia d'Europa* (Bari, Laterza, 1932), p. 53.

rich or poor, mean or elevated,—it has as much delight in conceiving an Iago as an Imogen. What shocks the virtuous philosopher delights the chameleon poet.' So that Croce's distinction comes, in substance, to mean that an artist could get the better of this conflict only in so far as he possessed strong ethical qualities over and above his artistic qualities (in Keats's letter just quoted Keats is contrasting himself with Wordsworth).

These minds, continues Croce, 'having lost sight of the true God made to themselves idols . . . they identified the infinite with this or that finite, the ideal with this or that perceptible'; and there resulted from this those exaggerations, usurpations, and in fact subversions of values which are more properly called perversions: 'lust and volupt-uousness put in place of ideals, cruelty and horror flavoured with sensual pleasure, a taste for incest, sadism, satanism and other amuse-ments of that kind—altogether monstrous and stupid.'[1] It was thus that 'not a few of the Romantics, having failed either to subdue or to pacify by their own strength of mind the upheaval which they had aroused in their own breasts, or to rise above it by forgetting it and returning to their humble everyday lives, went to perdition.'[2]

What could be more obvious than the attempt to trace the sources of the aberrations of a period to a metaphysical crisis? As an example of this, it will be remembered that literary historians, wishing to account for the rise in England of that peculiar poetical current which started with John Donne, attributed it to the collapse of the medieval conception of the world beneath the reiterated blows of newly-acquired knowledge, with the undermining of dogmas which resulted.[3]

Now, though I do not deny that such explanations are worthy of consideration, it seems to me that they account only very indirectly for particular tendencies of sensibility. At most they limit the screen on which the visions are projected, but they do not say why exactly those visions, and not others, appear. The course followed by currents of religious faith (including among these philosophy) is different from the course through which the education of sensibility is accomplished. The metaphysical wit which pervaded the seven-

---

[1] Croce, op. cit., p. 58.　　　　　　　　　[2] Croce, op. cit., p. 60.

[3] And there are art historians who have discovered social reasons for the variety of forms and fashions which appeared in Florentine painting during the Middle Ages and the Renaissance, and in French art at the end of the eighteenth and at the beginning of the nineteenth century in France. (F. Antal, 'Reflections on Classicism and Romanticism', in the *Burlington Magazine*, vol. lxvi (April 1935), pp. 259 ff., lxviii (March 1936), pp. 130 ff.; the same, *Florentine Painting and its Social Background*, London, Kegan Paul, 1947.) [Add. 1950]

teenth century found, certainly, a propitious soil in the shaky condition of religious dogma, but it had existed ever since the Middle
Ages, and one can trace its gradual infiltration through the school of
Petrarch. The cult of 'Medusean' beauty burst forth into a fashion
in the nineteenth century, but isolated signs of it were not lacking
even earlier, which indicate that it was a case of a sporadic germ
which at a certain moment became epidemic. The period of greatest
violence may have coincided with a religious crisis, but this only
avails to explain the intensity, not the nature of the epidemic, which
arrived at its final form by quite a different process.

If, therefore, the history of ideas and ideals during the nineteenth century constitutes a necessary frame for the picture I have
painted, it is a part which completes, rather than conditions, the
whole; there was no obligation for me to examine it afresh, nor to
deal with phenomena of other kinds, which in any case have been
fully discussed by others.

Why was it that, towards the end of the eighteenth century, people
came to consider landscape with different eyes? why did they look
for a 'je ne sais quoi' which they had not looked for before? Why,
at about the same time, did the 'beauty of the horrid' become a
source, no longer of conceits, as in the seventeenth century, but of
sensations? To such questions adequate answers are not to be found
in the history of the religious, philosophical, moral, and practical
development of the period. In this field of ideas is to be found a
confirmation of the axiom propounded by Wilde, as to Nature
imitating Art (in *The Decay of Lying*). Education of sensibility came
about through works of art; what it is therefore chiefly important
to establish is the means by which the transmission of themes from
one artist to another is effected. The mysterious bond between
pleasure and suffering has certainly always existed; it is one of the
vulnera naturae which is as old as man himself. But it became the
common inheritance of Romantic and Decadent sensibility through
a particular chain of literary influences.[1]

Croce would have me differentiate more profoundly between what
is termed Romanticism proper and what is called 'Later Romanticism'
or 'Decadence'. In the former, he says, 'besides sexual pathology,

[1] The reasons G. Lafourcade gives (in his review of the first edition of the
present book in the *Nouvelle Revue Française*, October 1st, 1934, p. 620) for
the spread of Sade's influence are: (1) the revival of the Christian tradition,
with the ensuing stress on martyrdom and the lives of the saints into which
sado-masochism strikes its deepest roots; (2) materialist philosophy, with its
study of the mechanism of sensation (Sade comes to the conclusion that
pleasure and pain act in the same way on the nerves); (3) a legitimate reaction
against the exaggerations of Richardson and Rousseau: *Justine* is a reversal of
the *Nouvelle Héloïse*. [Add. 1950]

the macabre and the diabolical, there existed ideals of liberty, of humanity, of justice and of purity which fought against the pathological interest and alternated with it'; but, as the century proceeds, there gradually makes itself felt 'the aesthetic conception of a life to be lived as passion and imagination, as beauty and poetry, which is in fact the opposite of actual life, which strives after the distinction, and with it the harmony, of all its forms and does not admit the pathological preference and supremacy of one single form over all the others, which are equally necessary each in its own particular capacity; and is also the opposite of poetry, which is an overcoming of action in cosmic contemplation, a deliberate pause in practical activity, though it may at the same time be a preparation for renewed activity'. In other words, the theory of Art for Art's sake steadily gained ground, and, by criticizing all literary inspiration that was dictated by ethical ideals as being due to intrusions of the practical, destroyed such barriers as dammed up the morbid tendencies of Romantic sensibility, thus leading to the progressive cooling of the passionate quality with which the first of the Romantics had invested even morbid themes, and finally to the crystallization of the whole of the movement into set fashion and lifeless decoration.

If there did not already exist a whole literature on the 'Art for Art's sake' movement, it would have been necessary to speak of it here. Highly characteristic examples of the progressive decay of ideals among artists occur in English literature. Byron found a means of escape by going to fight in the cause of an oppressed nation; Swinburne found it later by exalting the cause of Italian independence into poetry (the dissociation from actual life is here an accomplished fact); finally, artists such as Pater, and more especially Wilde, who were immured in a 'Palace of Art', sought in vain to resume contact with practical life by means of a religious ideal, through a return to Christianity.[1]

As it is limited in aim, so is the present study limited in extent: it is based almost exclusively on observations gathered from three

---

[1] Some have called in question the method adopted in the present volume, in so far as certain words and myths in the works of several artists are considered to have received an undue stress within the frame of their whole production. To this one could reply almost with the words of Thomas Hardy: 'As in looking at a carpet, by following one colour a certain pattern is suggested, by following another colour, another', so in this study of romanticism I have watched the pattern which no other critic had detected, and I have described that alone. By seeing under the same light and putting on the same level with Sade such different writers as Byron, Baudelaire, or Flaubert, I have not presumed to demonstrate an identity in their entire spiritual configuration; but rather that in the spiritual configuration of each of them, erotic sensibility fits into a pattern which has to be taken into account. [Add. 1950]

literatures, French, English, and Italian. Others are not mentioned except incidentally. Hence the reader will find absent names such as Strindberg, Sologub, Bryusov, Wedekind, and others whose testimony might have amplified the details (by pointing out interdependent reactions), but not changed the fundamental lines of the picture as it is presented here. Such a picture has appeared to be sufficiently imposing on its own merits to be worth confirmation by supplementary illustration. The central axis of the movement passes through Paris and London: the other related European literatures gravitate round these points like satellites. This study stops at the threshold of the twentieth century, crossing it only in order to illustrate the protracted activity of writers who were formed and matured in the Decadent period. It would have been easy to trace the course of certain currents of the Decadent period right down to the present day,[1] had there not been a risk of obscuring the clearness of the picture by discussing things which cannot yet be looked at in true proportion, because the eye sees them from too close an angle.

I have preferred to leave the reader to form, from my exposition of the subject, his own comprehensive judgement upon the period I have treated, rather than formulate it myself at the end of the book in a stiff-jointed conclusion which he might have suspected to be the result of a preconceived thesis. As this is the first time that the tendencies I have chosen for examination have been systematically treated, my best method seemed to be that of copious quotation, so that the reader might have some latitude in forming his estimate of them.

1930   MARIO PRAZ

[1] In France, for example: Bernanos, *Sous le soleil de Satan*; Kessel, *La Belle de jour*; Carco, *Perversité*; Lenormand, *La Vie secrète*; Jouve, *Paulina 1880, La Scène capitale*; Milosz, *L'Amoureuse Initiation*; Genêt, *Querelle de Brest*; for Germany, Ernst Jünger, *Auf den Marmorklippen*, &c.

NOTE TO THE SECOND EDITION

For many years the present book has been out of print, and its scarcity is responsible for many a legend. So we have happened to read in Charles Jackson's *The Outer Edges* (New York, Rinehart & Co., 1948), p. 185, that the 'best reading in God's world' for a sexual delinquent is supplied by "Mario Pratz [*sic*] and Bertold Brecht'. Mr. Wyndham Lewis, in *Men Without Art* (p. 175), spoke of the present book as a 'gigantic pile of satanic bric-à-brac, so industriously assembled, under my direction [?], by Professor Praz'. And Montague Summers, referring in his *Gothic Quest* to this opinion of Mr. Wyndham Lewis and to my letter to *The Times Literary Supplement* for August 8th, 1935, qualifying it, concluded: 'After all it does not in the least matter who is responsible for such disjointed gimcrack as *The Romantic Agony*.' Serious scholars have thought otherwise, and the term 'Romantic Agony' has become current in the meantime in literary criticism.

The present reissue, besides satisfying a steady demand, is destined to vindicate the author of the book from Montague Summers's strictures (p. 396 of *The Gothic Quest*: 'The voluble but not very reliable pages of Signor Mario Praz'). Only a very few corrections were needed to remove occasional inaccuracies, unavoidable in such a vast survey: they amount to the deletion of passages referring to Keats and Thomas Griffiths Wainewright, and to the correction of the date of issue of *The Monk*. Much new material included in the later Italian editions has been added as Appendix II.* Attention is drawn to this added material by asterisks in the text.

Rome   M.P.
August 1950

---

* PUBLISHER'S NOTE: For this 1970 impression, the chapter notes have been reset, and Appendix II eliminated by incorporating the 1950 Addenda, in their proper order, among the notes. Additions to the text, indicated by asterisks, are given in sequence, interspersed with the notes. Additional notes have been inserted as they occur and are numbered, e.g. 12A, 12B, etc. Some supplementary references added in 1950 have been silently inserted in the notes, but all substantive addenda, either to the text or to the notes, are marked '[Add. 1950]'.

THE ROMANTIC AGONY

As in looking at a carpet, by following one colour a certain pattern is suggested, by following another colour, another; so in life the seer should watch the pattern among general things which his idiosyncrasy moves him to observe, and describe that alone.

THOMAS HARDY

'ROMANTIC': AN APPROXIMATE TERM

THE epithet 'romantic' and the antithetical terms 'classic' and 'romantic' are approximate labels which have long been in use. The philosopher solemnly refuses to allow them, exorcising them with unerring logic, but they creep quietly in again and are always obtruding themselves, elusive, tiresome, indispensable; the grammarian attempts to give them their proper status, their rank and fixed definition, but in spite of all his laborious efforts he discovers that he has been treating shadows as though they were solid substance.

Like an infinite number of other words in current usage, these approximate terms have a value and answer a useful purpose, provided that they are treated at their proper value—that is, as approximate terms—and that what they cannot give—exact and cogent definition of thought —is not demanded of them. They are serviceable makeshifts, and their fictitious character can be easily proved, but if the proof of their relatively arbitrary nature should cause us to dispense with their services, I do not see that literary history would benefit by it.

The case is similar to that of literary 'genres'. Let them be abolished: soon they will crop up again in the shape of more elaborate distinctions and categories, more in accordance with the spirit of the particular moment, but no less approximate. Hence the practical necessity of empirical distinctions is recognized even by Croce, whose essay on Ariosto could never have been written without the aid of such expedients.[1] The mistake is to wish to graft aesthetic problems on to ideas which are intended only to be practical and informative, but there is nothing to prevent the same use being made of these ideas as Ampère made of the imaginary swimmer in the electric current.

There is something to be said in favour of the method used by Dante in the *Paradiso*, where the blessed souls, who all have their stand in the 'celestial rose', in which 'presso e lontano . . . né pon né leva', yet show themselves to the poet by groups in the various spheres,

> non perché sortita
> Sia questa spera lor, ma per far segno
> Della celestial c'ha men salita.

Literary criticism assumes the existence of a history of culture—the culture of a particular *milieu* or of a particular individual. If the merging of the work of art into the general history of culture results in losing sight of the individual artist, it is impossible, on the other hand, to think of the latter without recurring to the former. Tendencies, themes, and mannerisms current in a writer's own day provide an indispensable aid to the interpretation of his work. True, for the purpose of aesthetic appreciation, this work forms a unique world shut up in itself, rounded off and perfected, an *individuum ineffabile*; but this philosophical truism would leave the critic no other alternative but a mystical, admiring silence.

But there is more to it than that. If it is true that the life of a work of art is in direct ratio to its being, so to speak, eternally contemporary, or able to reflect, with a universal application, the sentiments of periods in history which are in themselves diverse and remote, it is yet true that, in separating the work of art from its own particular cultural substratum, it is easy to fall into arbitrary, fantastic interpretations which alter the nature of the work even to the extent of making it unrecognizable. How many variations on Dante and Shakespeare have not been devised by critics of creative rather than historical minds? It is enough to quote the case of *Hamlet*, a drama whose original colour has been entirely changed by the corrosive patina spread over it by the critics, ever since Goethe's Wilhelm Meister[2] interpreted the character according to his own image, changing into a *Gefühlsmensch* an Elizabethan whose strangeness appears to be due mainly to structural imperfections in the tragedy.[3] To-day the vast majority of critics agree in describing Hamlet as the type of academic, speculative man unexpectedly transported into the world of violent action and there destined to play the part of a vessel of clay, and the tragedy as the tragedy of the power-

lessness of intellect confronted with the hard facts of practical life.⁴ To uproot this long-standing conception seems
to-day an undertaking no less sacrilegious and graceless
than the desire to prove that Monna Lisa's smile is a good
deal less complicated than Walter Pater liked to think.
Yet there is little doubt that the current interpretation of
Hamlet is an arbitrary one—even though this arbitrariness
may be providential—and that, whenever one examines a
work of art at the same time divorcing it from the circumstances of its origin, one is bound to arrive at extreme
cases of this kind.

Now the use of formulas such as 'romantic', 'baroque',
&c., serves to give some guidance to the interpretation of
a work of art, or, in other words, to define the limits
within which the activity of the critic is to be confined and
beyond which lie mere arbitrary and anachronistic judg-
ments. The sole object of these formulas is to keep in mind
the character of the period in which the work was produced, in such a way as to avoid the danger of a combination of words, sounds, colours or forms becoming surreptitiously invested with ideas which are aroused in the
mind of the interpreter, but which certainly did not exist
in the mind of the artist. Similar results may arise out of
very different artistic intentions. Thus in a seventeenth-
century writer like Alessandro Adimari one finds a love-
sonnet on a beautiful lady recently buried, but one must
be careful not to see in it a manifestation of romantic
necrophily; when, elsewhere, he goes into ecstasies over a
'wounded beauty', one must refrain from imagining in
such a composition a morbid exquisiteness of feeling such
as is found in Baudelaire's *Une Martyre*; but keeping in
mind the partiality of the baroque period for every form
of wit, one must attribute the choice of these unattractive
subjects mainly to the desire of provoking astonishment
through the conceit which can be elicited from them.

So also, when one reads in Alcman: 'O maidens of
honey voice so loud and clear, my limbs can carry me no
more. Would, O would God I were but a ceryl, such as
flies fearless of heart with the halcyons over the bloom of
the wave, the Spring's own bird that is purple as the sea!'

one must not try to discern in him signs already of an aspiration similar to that which made Shelley invoke the wild spirit of the West Wind:

> If I were a swift cloud to fly with thee;
> A wave to pant beneath thy power, and share
> The impulse of thy strength, only less free
> Than thou, O uncontrollable . . .

or which made Monti exclaim, in the manner of Goethe:

> Oh perché non poss'io la mia deporre
> D'uom tutta dignitade, e andar confuso
> Col turbine che passa, e su le penne
> Correr del vento e lacerar le nubi,
> O su i campi a destar dell'ampio mare
> Gli addormentati nembi e le procelle!

or Hölderlin:

> . . . o dorthin nehmt mich
> Purpurne Wolken! und möge droben
> In Licht und Luft zerrinne mir Liebe und Leid!

because such aspirations are the property of the Romantics,[5] and Alcman is not a Romantic. Actually Alcman's artistic intention is shown by the passage from Antigonus Carystius which accompanies the quotation of the above lines: 'He says that old age has made him feeble, and unable to join the choruses in their evolutions or the maidens in the dance.' Alcman evokes the 'ceryl' as an example of those qualities which he no longer possesses—freedom of movement and spring-like youthful ardour. The image sticks closely to the situation (the halcyons corresponding to the maidens with whom the poet will never dance again), and there is no room for the vague *Stimmung*, the thirst for the infinite, which animates the lines of the Romantics. But there is nothing to prevent a modern critic who confines himself to its external values and separates it from the confines of time and mentality from distorting the fragment of Alcman to a romantic significance. And what is one to say of the qualities of a Venetian painter and—even more absurd—of an Impressionist, which have been discovered in Pindar by an eminent Greek scholar of the present day? And of the reputation of a romantic pessimist which has been acquired by Cecco Angiolieri, thanks to the seemingly ambiguous beginning (which, in any case, is a *cliché*)—'S'io fossi foco, arderei 'l mondo'—of a sonnet of which the end shows clearly its burlesque character?

A sense of the difference between the various cultural atmospheres should also serve to prevent us reading 'Era già l'ora che volge il disio' in the same spirit as Keats's

> Charmed magic casements, opening on the foam
> Of perilous seas, in faery lands forlorn.

Certainly, if one wishes to arrive at a true historical interpretation, one is forced to renounce elegant variations, which are seductive but lack authority. Lorenzo Montano, in his preface to a selection from the work of Magalotti, points out 'passages which make one think of De Foe's *Captain Singleton*, and of the exotic Romanticism which had its great beginnings not many years later'. And he quotes the passage on the Unicorn: '. . . that African solitude of *lofty mountains, from the peaks of which can be descried an immense tract of flat and wooded country*'. The passage, isolated in this way, acquires a colouring which it would be difficult to see in it in the original context. Actually the expression 'African solitude', which sets the tone of the whole, originates in Montano, whereas in Magalotti the passage is an illustration of what goes before it, rather than a piece of 'exotic Romanticism': 'This part of the country, being the farthest recess of the province of Agaes, serves in the ordinary way as a place of exile for all those from whom the Emperor wishes to protect himself, as it consists entirely of very *lofty mountains*, &c.' With a little imagination it might in the same way be possible to discover 'exotic Romanticism' in Marco Polo, by interpreting the passage about the palace of Cublai Can in the light of Coleridge's *Kubla Khan*. Except that in the time of Marco Polo this type of exoticism had not yet come into being; besides, who would be bold enough to represent Marco Polo as a Romantic *ante litteram*?

Approximate terms such as 'baroque', 'romantic', 'decadent', &c., have their origins in definite revolutions of sensibility, and it serves no purpose to detach them from their historical foundations and apply them generously to artists of varied types, according to the more or less extravagant whims of the critics. It happens only too often that the unsuccessful artist which lurks repressed in the soul of the critic seeks an outlet in the composition of a critical novel, or in projecting on to some author or other a light which is quite alien to him, which alters his appearance and brings it up to date, greatly to the detriment of the correct interpretation. For such purposes are these approximate terms used capriciously by critics, just as a clever cook uses sauces and seasonings to disguise the food. So Petrarch is found to be baroque, Tasso a Romantic, Marino to resemble D'Annunzio,

> miraturque novas frondes et non sua poma.

These terms, however, are intended merely to indicate where the accent falls, and have no meaning outside the circumference of certain historical periods. The same idea may assume quite a different significance in Petrarch, where it is used for the first time, and in Marino, who imitates it from Petrarch; for Marino invests it with a feeling of baroque which is alien to Petrarch, and also draws the reader's special attention to it. In Petrarch the idea is incidental, in Marino deliberate and essential. Hence the highly problematical value of any research into the forerunners of seventeenth-century literature, of Romanticism, and, indeed, of Futurism—a form of research which is as elegantly literary as it is generally arbitrary and inconclusive, since these empirical formulas cannot be applied to every period and every place. It is, I believe, to the neglect of this criterion that one may ascribe the discredit into which certain of these terms have fallen, particularly the antithetical terms 'classic' and 'romantic'.

These two terms, introduced, as is well known, by Goethe and Schiller,[6] have ended by being adopted as the criteria of interpretation for all periods and all literatures; in the case of literature, as well as in that of the plastic arts and music, people frequently speak of Classic and Romantic in the same way as, in politics, they speak, universally, of Conservative and Liberal, with an extension of meaning which is, quite obviously, arbitrary.

'Classical and romantic', says Grierson,[7] 'these are the systole and diastole of the human heart in history. They represent on the one hand our need of order, of synthesis, of a comprehensive yet definite, therefore *exclusive* as well as inclusive, ordering of thought and feeling and action';

and on the other hand the discovery of the finiteness, of the inadequacy of such a synthesis when confronted by new aspirations, and the revolution which is the result of this discovery. Grierson distinguishes an 'historical' meaning in the term 'classic' and also a merely qualificatory meaning; in accordance with the former he calls 'classic' any literature which is the expression of a society which has attained a perfect balance of forces. A classical literature, says Grierson, accepting to a great extent the ideas of Brunetière,

'is the product of a nation and a generation which has consciously achieved a definite advance, moral, political, intellectual; and is filled with the belief that its view of life is more natural, human, universal, and wise than that from which it has escaped. It has effected a synthesis which enables it to look round on life with a sense of its wholeness, its unity in variety; and the work of the artist is to give expression to that consciousness, hence the solidity of his work and hence too its definiteness, and in the hands of great artists its beauty. . . . The work of the classical artist is to give individual expression, the beauty of form, to a body of common sentiments and thoughts which he shares with his audience, thoughts and views which have for his generation the validity of universal truths.'

Since every 'classical' literature represents a synthesis, a balance of forces, it makes at the same time a compromise, that is, it implies exclusions and sacrifices which sooner or later come to be resented. No sooner does a resentment of this kind achieve a certain degree of intensity than the classical idea breaks up, and new forms of imagination and feeling make themselves felt and demand expression: a 'romantic' period begins. Thus 'romantic' is accepted by Grierson in a wider sense, similar to that found in Littré: 'Il se dit des écrivains qui s'affranchissent des règles de composition et de style établies par les auteurs classiques.'

Applying this antithesis to the whole of history, Grierson believes it possible to show three Romantic movements in European literature. The first comes to light in the tragedies of Euripides and the dialogues of Plato, and culminates in the revolution both in religious thought and in Greek prose introduced by Saint Paul: the second coincides with the blossoming of profane romances in the twelfth and thirteenth centuries (*Lancelot and Guinevere*, *Tristan and Iseult*, *Aucassin et Nicolette*) and was a sign of the revolt of worldly ideals against the ascetic and spiritual ideals of the ecclesiastical literature then predominant: the third is the one which generally bears the name of the Romantic Movement, the characteristics of which are in a sense opposed to those of the second, the reaction this time being against *Aufklärung* and rationalism. Analogously Alfred Bäumler has called the Dionysiac movement of the sixth century B.C. 'the Romanticism of antiquity', seeing in it a reaction of mystical and chthonic nature against the solar divinities of the Dorians.[8]

Extended in this way the terms 'classic' and 'romantic' come finally to denote, respectively, 'equilibrium' and 'interruption of equilibrium', and come very near to Goethe's definition, 'Classisch ist das Gesunde, Romantisch das Kranke'; on the one hand, there is the serene state of mind of the man who does not notice his own health precisely because he is healthy; on the other, the state of ferment and struggle of the invalid who fights to overcome his own fever, or in other words to achieve a new equilibrium. Such an extension of the terms ends by being of an apparent rather than of a real use, since, generalized in this way, they are bound finally to become identified, the one with the passionate, practical element in the artistic process, the other with the theoretical and synthetic element, in which matter is converted into form (Croce): so they lose all value as historical categories and merely indicate the process which goes on universally in every artist. This is evident, for instance, in the following passage from Paul Valéry:[9]

'*Tout classicisme suppose un romantisme antérieur*. Tous les avantages que l'on attribue, toutes les objections que l'on fait à un art "classique" sont relatifs à cet axiome. *L'essence du classicisme est de venir après. L'ordre* suppose un certain désordre qu'il vient réduire. La *composition*, qui est artifice, succède à quelque chaos primitif d'intuitions et de développements naturels. La *pureté* est le résultat d'opérations infinies sur le langage, et le soin de la *forme* n'est autre chose que la réorganisation méditée des moyens d'expression. Le classique implique donc des actes volontaires et réfléchis qui modifient une production "naturelle" conformément à une conception *claire et rationnelle* de l'homme et de l'art.'

However, if one wishes to protect the useful function of the word 'romantic' as an approximate term, one must first of all distinguish this function from that of its so-called opposite 'classic', which has become nothing more than a secondary abstract reflection of the term 'romantic': then, returning to the original use of the word, one must accept it as the definition of a peculiar kind of sensibility at a fixed historical period. The indiscriminate use of the word can only cause misunderstanding and confusion, as it does when Grierson speaks of the 'romantic thrill' one feels when reading the myths of the Cave, of Er, and of the Chariot of the Soul in the *Phaedrus*, and of the 'romantic conception' of Plato 'of an ideal world behind the visible'; here the epithet 'romantic' is surreptitiously transferred from the modern reader's impression to the Platonic conception itself, and Plato is shown as a Romantic because the reader is pleased to interpret his legends in a romantic way.

Before sketching the history of the word 'romantic', I wish to record the most curious example of arbitrary generalization to which the 'classic-romantic' antithesis has given rise: the elevation of the two terms into *Grundbegriffe* (in the manner of Wölfflin) by a German critic, Fritz Strich,[10] whose undeniable acuteness was blunted by an overwhelming love of theory. Strich notes certain tendencies which undoubtedly exist in Romantic poetry, and encouraged by distinctions such as Goethe's between poetry 'gegenständlichen und sehnsüchtigen Inhalts', or that of Schlegel between *Poesie des Besitzes* (which corresponds to 'classic') and *Poesie der Sehnsucht* (which corresponds to 'romantic'), and by contrasts such as

that of Hölderlin between *orgisch* and *aorgisch*, or that of
Nietzsche between Apollinean and Dionysiac, he does not
hesitate to build up on this foundation a tower of Babel
which is ingenious but unsubstantial as a dream. The
dream vanishes the moment Strich tries to come down to
reality, to the illustrations of his theories. These illustrations are extremely thin and prove nothing—unlike
Wölfflin's illustrations, which give a colour of truth to his
empirical ideas of linear and pictorial, of closed form and
open form and so on. Few of the poems quoted by Strich
can be upheld as exemplary works of art, and, if those of
Goethe and Hölderlin are excepted, the others peep out
from beneath his vast mass of theory like wretched little
mice produced by immense mountains. Strich, for example, puts great importance upon Kleist's *Penthesilea*, a
work which strives to give the impression that it is the
product of a mind full of obsessions and hallucinations,
but only succeeds in being pretentious and ridiculous.
As a general rule—it may be said in parenthesis—it is
always advisable to mistrust a drama when it can be seen,
from the mere look of the page, to be composed of long
speeches rather than of dialogue in which each character
takes a proportionate part: a drama consisting of long
speeches means what they call a 'lyrical' drama, which is
a flattering definition of bombastic drama. The reading of
Penthesilea fully confirms this first glance. If, instead of
limiting himself to the German Parnassus, Strich had
made use of foreign literatures, he might perhaps have
succeeded in giving a more convincing colour to his
theories, though he would not have been able to prove
them worthy of serious consideration, since what he attempts—the co-ordination of approximate terms in an
organic system—is no less desperate than an attempt to
build a house on quicksands.

Strich's book is a *reductio ad absurdum* of the 'classic-
romantic' antithesis. Nevertheless I think that Croce's
conclusion—that 'romantic' and 'classic' are moments of
the human spirit, existing in every individual man, identi-
fiable with matter and form, i.e. abstract moments of a
process which is in reality indivisible—I think that this

conclusion does justice only to the secondary meaning of these formulas, taking off from their value as useful approximate terms and indications of definite historical characteristics. Or, to be more exact, from the value of one of them—the term 'romantic', since the other—'classic'—is a derivative and has meaning only in the sense of *playing at being classical*, that is, as the definition of the programme of a school opposed to the romantic school, which, in its turn, inasmuch as it is a school, or conscious, organized manifestation, stands in relation to romantic sensibility as the chastened to the spontaneous. Classicism, then, is a phenomenon by no means alien to the romantic spirit; on the contrary, inasmuch as it seeks to revive manners and ideas belonging to the past, inasmuch as it strives longingly towards a fantastic pagan world, rather than sharing in the state of serene equilibrium proper to so-called classical works of art (which are serene without knowing it), it shares in the same spiritual travail which is usually defined as characteristically and *par excellence* 'romantic'. It is not the content which decides whether a work should be labelled 'romantic' or not, but the spirit, and, in this sense, a Hölderlin or a Keats, worshipping, as they do, a vanished world, is no less romantic than a Coleridge or a Shelley. In other words, there is such a thing as a 'Romantic Movement', and classicism is only an aspect of it. There is no opposite pole to 'romantic', merely because 'romantic' indicates a certain state of sensibility which, simply, is different from any other, and not comparable either by co-ordination or by contrast.

How can one describe the new state of sensibility which came into full flower towards the end of the eighteenth century? What does 'romantic' mean? The evolution of this word has been traced by Logan Pearsall Smith,[11] to whose lucid exposition I owe a great deal of what follows.

The word 'romantic' appears for the first time in the English language about the middle of the seventeenth century, meaning 'like the old romances', and shows how there began to be felt, about this time, a real need to give names to certain characteristics of the chivalrous and pastoral romances. These characteristics, thrown into relief by contrast with the growing rationalistic spirit which was soon to triumph in Pope and Dr. Johnson, lay in the falsity, the unreality, the fantastic and irrational nature of events and sentiments described in these romances. Like the terms 'gothic' and 'baroque', therefore, 'romantic' started in a bad sense. The shade of meaning indicated by 'romantic', at this stage of its development, is clearly evinced by the other words with which it was usually coupled, words such as 'chimerical', 'ridiculous', 'unnatural', 'bombast'. One reads of 'childish and romantic poems', of 'romantic absurdities and incredible fictions', and so on. Nature's truth is contrasted with the falsity of the romances. Everything that seemed to have been produced by a disorderly imagination came to be called 'romantic'. The contrast is well presented in a couplet of Pope's

> . . . that not in Fancy's maze he wandered long,
> But stooped to Truth, and moraliz'd his song.

But a new current in taste can be discerned right from the beginning of the eighteenth century: there is a growing tendency to recognize the importance of imagination in works of art. 'Romantic', though continuing to mean something slightly absurd, takes on the flavour of *attractive*, suited to please the imagination. 'The subject and scene of this tragedy, so *romantic* and uncommon, are highly pleasing to the imagination', wrote J. Warton in 1757. Side by side with the depreciatory use of the word in relation to the events and sentiments of the old romances, 'romantic' came to be used also to describe scenes and landscapes similar to those described in them, and, this time, without any note of scorn. As early as the middle of the seventeenth century examples are found of similar usage, especially in the case of old castles (as early as 1666 Pepys wrote of Windsor Castle, 'the most *romantique* castle that is in the world'), of mountains, forests, pastoral plains, desolate and solitary places. The two meanings are both to be found in Dr. Johnson, who, while on the one hand he speaks of 'romantic and superfluous', 'ridiculous and romantic', 'romantic absurdities and incredible fictions', on the other hand writes, without a hint of scorn, 'When night overshadows a romantic scene, all is stillness, silence and quiet', &c. In this second sense, the adjective has gradually ceased to retain its connexion with the literary *genre* (the romances) from which it was originally derived, and has come to express more and more the growing love for wild and melancholy aspects of nature.[12] It is so closely connected with certain qualities of landscape that French translators of English books of the period, when the word 'romantic' is used, often render it with 'pittoresque': which shows that the French were not yet aware of the new state of sensibility suggested by the word 'romantic'. It was not until 1776 that Letourneur, translator of Shakespeare, and the Marquis de Girardin, author of a book on landscape, deliberately use the word 'romantique', noting the reasons in favour of the adoption of this 'mot anglais'.[13] It is possible to see from their notes how these French writers had finally grasped the exact shade of meaning. 'Romantic', they say, means more than *romanesque* (chimerical, fabulous)[14] or *pittoresque* (used to describe a scene which strikes the eye and arouses admiration); 'romantic' describes not only the scene but the particular emotion aroused in the person who contemplates it. Rousseau probably came by the word from his friend Girardin, and conferred upon it full French citizenship in the well-known *Rêveries du promeneur solitaire*. In *romantique* Rousseau found the appropriate word to define that elusive and indistinct thing which hitherto he had vaguely expressed by 'je ne sais quoi': 'Enfin, ce spectacle a je ne sais quoi de magique, de surnaturel, qui ravit l'esprit et les sens' (*Nouvelle Héloïse*). In this sense, 'romantic' assumes a subjective character, like 'interesting', 'charming', 'exciting', which describe not so much the property of the objects as our reactions to them, the effects which they arouse in an impressionable onlooker. Besides, as L. P. Smith observes, Nature described as 'romantic' is seen through a veil of associations and feelings extracted from poetry and literature in general.

The term *pittoresque*, which arose at the same time,

expresses a similar phenomenon.[15] The subjective element, implicit in 'romantic', rendered this word particularly suitable to describe the new kind of literature in which suggestion and aspiration had so large a part. It is true that in England, where the word 'Romanticism' only came to be used later, the antithesis between 'romantic' and 'classic', German in its origin, was at first expressed by the contrasting of 'magical and evocative poetry' with rhetorical and didactic poetry as exemplified by Pope. *Magie der Einbildungskraft* (Magic of the Imagination) is the title of the well-known essay in which Jean Paul defines the essence of romantic sensibility. How does it come about—asks Jean Paul—that everything which exists only in aspiration (*Sehnsucht*) and in remembrance, everything which is remote, dead, unknown, possesses this magic transfiguring charm? Because—the answer is —everything, when inwardly represented, loses its precise outline, since the imagination possesses the magic virtue of making things infinite. And Novalis: 'Alles wird in der Entfernung Poesie: ferne Berge, ferne Menschen, ferne Begebenheiten. Alles wird *romantisch*'.[16]

The word 'romantic' thus comes to be associated with another group of ideas, such as 'magic', 'suggestive', 'nostalgic', and above all with words expressing states of mind which cannot be described, such as the German 'Sehnsucht' and the English 'wistful'. It is curious to note that these two words have no equivalent in the Romance languages—a clear sign of the Nordic, Anglo-Germanic origin of the sentiments they express. Such ideas have this in common, that they furnish only a vague indication, leaving it to the imagination to make the final evocation. A Freudian would say that these ideas appeal to the unconscious in us. It is the appeal of Yeats's *Land of Heart's Desire*.

The essence of Romanticism consequently comes to consist in that which cannot be described. The word and the form, says Schlegel in *Lucinde*, are only accessories. The essential is the thought and the poetic image, and these are rendered possible only in a passive state. The Romantic exalts the artist who does not give a material

form to his dreams—the poet ecstatic in front of a forever
blank page, the musician who listens to the prodigious
concerts of his soul without attempting to translate them
into notes. It is romantic to consider concrete expression
as a decadence, a contamination. How many times has the
magic of the ineffable been celebrated, from Keats,
with his

> Heard melodies are sweet, but those unheard
> Are sweeter. . . .

to Maeterlinck, with his theory that silence is more
musical than any sound!

But these are extreme cases, in which the romantic
tends to merge in the mystical. The normal is that of
suggestive expression, which evokes much more than it
states. Whenever we encounter such a method, we do not
hesitate to define the artist who makes use of it as 'romantic'. But the legitimate use of this term depends upon the
deliberate method of the artist, not upon the mere interpretation of the reader. In these lines of Dante:

> Quale ne' plenilunii sereni
> Trivia ride tra le ninfe eterne
> Che dipingon lo ciel per tutti i seni

the modern reader is inclined to detect one of the most
obvious cases of evocative magic, in virtue of their purity
of sound, of the play of diaereses, of the use of certain
words in themselves suggestive—*plenilunii*, *eterne*—and
of others which bring legends to the mind—*Trivia*, *ninfe*.
Are we to say, therefore, that Dante, in these lines, is a
Romantic? Is it not, rather, a romantic education, which
has by now become traditional, that causes the modern
reader to interpret these lines in this way? If each century
had left us a list of what, in its own opinion, were the
greatest beauties in Dante, we should be able to trace an
interesting history of taste, but would it be possible to
base on these anthologies a reconstruction of Dante's
inspiration? One line of Petrarch:

> Fior, frondi, erbe, ombre, antri, onde, aure soavi

used to send the writers of the sixteenth century into
ecstasies. 'This is the loftiest, the most sonorous, and the

fullest line to be found in modern or ancient writers,' wrote Sebastiano Fausto da Longiano. But who among us at the present day would be capable of seeing in this line all that the writers of the sixteenth century saw?

A knowledge of the tastes and preferences which belong to each period is a *sine qua non* of the interpretation of a work of art, and literary history cannot afford to dispense with approximate terms such as those we have been discussing, terms which do not claim to be more than symbols of specific tendencies of sensibility. They are intended to be empirical categories, and to condemn them as futile abstractions is as great an error as to exalt them into realities of universal import.

NOTES TO THE INTRODUCTION

¹ Cf. *Ariosto, Shakespeare e Corneille*, especially pp. 27–9.

² Cf. W. Diamond, 'Wilhelm Meister's Interpretation of Hamlet', in *Modern Philology*, August 1925.

³ Cf. T. S. Eliot, 'Hamlet and his Problems', in *The Sacred Wood* (London, Methuen, 1920). See also J. Dover Wilson, *The Manuscript of Shakespeare's 'Hamlet' and the Problems of its Transmission*, Cambridge University Press, 1934, and *What Happens in 'Hamlet'*, ib. 1936.

⁴ Cf. E. K. Chambers, *Shakespeare, a Survey* (London, Sidgwick & Jackson, 1925).

⁵ Other quotations might be added, e.g. Lamartine (*L'Isolement*):
Quand la feuille des bois tombe dans la prairie,
Le vent du soir se lève et l'arrache aux vallons;
Et moi je suis semblable à la feuille flétrie:
Emportez-moi comme elle, orageux Aquilons!

⁶ Cf. J. P. Eckermann, *Gespräche mit Goethe*, 21 März 1830.

⁷ 'Classical and Romantic', in *The Background of English Literature, and other collected Essays and Addresses* (London, Chatto & Windus, 1925).

⁸ In the introduction to the new edition of *Der Mythus von Orient und Occident, eine Metaphysik der alten Welt*, by J. J. Bachofen. See E. Seillière, *Le Néoromantisme en Allemagne*, vol. iii, *De la déesse Nature à la déesse Vie (Naturalisme et vitalisme mystiques)*, (Paris, Alcan, 1931), pp. 26–7.

⁹ 'Situation de Baudelaire', in *Revue de France*, Sept.–Oct. 1924 (vol. v, p. 224) reprinted in *Variété*, ii (Paris, Nouvelle Revue Française, 1930), pp. 155-6.

¹⁰ *Deutsche Klassik und Romantik, oder Vollendung und Unendlichkeit, ein Vergleich* (Munich, Meyer Jessen, 1922). See Croce's review of this in *Critica*, vol. xxi, p. 99.

¹¹ Cf. 'Four Romantic Words' in *Words and Idioms, Studies in the English Language* (London, Constable, 1925). On the word 'romantic' see also the letters of J. Butt in *The Times Literary Supplement* for August 3rd, 1933, of W. Lee Ustick in the same periodical for December 21st, 1933, and of C. T. Onions in the issue for January 1st, 1934.

¹² Cf. R. Haferkorn, *Gotik und Ruine in der englischen Dichtung des achtzehnten Jahrhunderts* (Leipzig, Tauchnitz, 1925); A. L. Reed, *The Background of Gray's Elegy* (New York, Columbia University Press, 1925).

¹³ Cf. the essay by A. François in *Annales de la Société J. J. Rousseau* (Paris), vol. v, 1909.

¹⁴ In his essay on 'Romantisch und Romanesk', in *Britannia, Max Förster zum sechzigsten Geburtstage* (Leipzig, Tauchnitz, 1929, pp. 218-227) M. Deutschbein has tried to make use of the two terms in order to distinguish between external romanticism, to be associated with fancy, and

inner romanticism, the product of imagination. *Romanesk* should be employed to designate certain tendencies to the strange, the exotic, the grotesque which have made their appearance many times throughout history (e.g. in the Greek romances), whereas *romantisch* ought to be used for genuine Romanticism, whose essence, according to Deutschbein, lies in a deep understanding of the harmony of the universe (he quotes in this connexion certain lines from Blake's *Auguries of Innocence*: 'To see a world in a grain of sand', &c.). Such a distinction, her emarks, had been foreshadowed by Brande in *A Dictionary of Science*, 1842 (quoted from the *O.E.D.*): 'In historical painting the romanesque consists in the choice of a fanciful subject rather than one founded on fact; the romanesque is different from the romantic because the latter may be founded on the truth which the former never is.' However, Deutschbein goes on to say, nowadays 'romantic' stands in English for both *romantisch* and *romanesk*. Deutschbein's distinction is, after all, of little utility, for every work of art worth the name is *romantisch* in the sense he gives to this word (cf. 'Das Romantische erhebt die Forderung des Gleichgewichtes aller menschlichen Funktionen: Blut—Seele—Geist. Das Romantische verlangt die Totalität von Denken, Fühlen und Anschauung', &c.).

This idea of the meaning of Romanticism seems to be shared by Lascelles Abercrombie (*Romanticism*, London, Martin Secker, 1926), who opposes to it the term 'realism' (thus curiously contradicting, without knowing it, Brande's definition just quoted: needless to say, such contradiction bears witness to the hopeless state of confusion caused by the loose way in which all these terms are used). One of the most important characteristics of Romanticism consists for this critic in a kind of retreat from the external world to an 'inner' world. Realism 'loves to go out into the world, and live confidently and busily in the stirring multitude of external things' (cf. Deutschbein's *romanesk*!). Romanticism is at least a withdrawal from these outer things into inner experience. Roughly and approximately it is a transition from 'perception' to 'conception'. Therefore, also for Abercrombie, the term 'romanticism' becomes identical with the inner urge of every artistic inspiration.

According to I. Babbitt (*Rousseau and Romanticism*, Boston and New York, Houghton Mifflin Co., 1919, p. 104) 'the so-called realism does not represent any fundamental change of direction as compared with the earlier romanticism. . . . What binds together realism and romanticism is their common repudiation of decorum as something external and artificial. . . . At the bottom of much so-called realism . . . is a special type of satire, a satire that is the product of violent emotional disillusion.' It is obvious that by 'realism' Babbitt means something quite different from Abercrombie's use of the same word. For Babbitt romanticism is a return to a hypothetical spontaneity of nature conceived as essentially good, an emancipation of (mainly sexual) impulses, a cult of emotional intensity by getting rid of the rules of discipline and decorum devised by man in the course of civilization, a substitution for ethical effort of a mere lazy floating on the stream of mood and temperament; therefore a manner of living in the stirring multitude of phenomena, of going out into the world . . . so that in a way romanticism according to Babbitt's idea (which seems convincing enough) corresponds to Abercrombie's realism. The romantic tendency is to push every emotion to an extreme, regardless of decorum, so that Babbitt inclines to see also in erotic exasperation a corollary of this general principle (see p. 215: 'Pleasure is pushed to the point where it runs over into pain, and pain to the point where it becomes an auxiliary to pleasure'). [Add. 1950]

¹⁵ The 'picturesque' (a word, as is well known, of Italian origin, meaning the point of view essentially of a painter) was elaborated as a theory in England between 1730 and 1830 ('Le Pittoresque nous vient d'Angleterre' —Stendhal) and was, in a sense, a prelude to Romanticism. If we regard the 'picturesque' period merely as the period during which this particular point of view became conscious and assumed the importance of a fashion, then undoubtedly the English poets Thomson and Dyer, with their descriptions which translate into terms of literature the pictorial manner of Claude Lorrain and Salvator Rosa, are the godfathers of the Picturesque. But it is hardly safe to date the actual *discovery* of certain aspects of landscape from the eighteenth century; and extremely risky to accept, as does Christopher Hussey in his excellent study *The Picturesque, Studies in a Point of View* (London and New York, Putnam, 1927), certain general theories on the conception of Nature in the various historical periods. He makes the specious assertion that Christianity, by identifying Nature with sin, prevented the appreciation of landscape, and on the other hand, by its anthropomorphism, concentrated attention on the representation of Man—an assertion which will not stand the test of particular cases: and there is no need to bring Dante into the question, nor even the much-praised Alpinism of Laura's immortalizer, to show how even in the Middle Ages certain qualities of Nature were appreciated, which the eighteenth century only underlined and exaggerated. When Hussey quotes the example of China to prove that urbanism brings about, by contrast, an appreciation of natural beauty, one might remind him of a similar case actually in the Western world, and as ancient as Alexandria. For it was, in fact, in the Hellenistic civilization that a pastoral poetry and a *genre* painting were elaborated, which show curious affinities with the eighteenth-century Picturesque; and it was an emperor of Hellenistic education, Hadrian, who built near Tivoli a villa which seems to reveal quite as much preoccupation with picturesque views and quite as much erudite exoticism as was shown by the eighteenth-century owners of English country-houses, with their Gothic ruins and Chinese towers. If Hussey had read the Greek romances, he would have realized how much the literature of that time sought to emulate the works of the brush (descriptions in the style of paintings, taken from the Greek romances which he imitated, are to be found in Sidney's *Arcadia*), and that the description of 'picturesquely' composed scenes was no new thing in the eighteenth century. It was the Alexandrians who worked out the formula 'Ut pictura poesis', which the Emblematists of the sixteenth century, and du Fresnoy in 1665, only repeated. (On ἐκφράσεις and on 'Ut pictura poesis' see the

long essay by W. M. Howard in *Publ. Mod. Lang. Ass. Am.*, vol. xxiv, no. 1 (March 1900), pp. 40-123, and the works quoted in the notes to pp. 170-1 of *The Greek Romances in Elizabethan Prose Fiction*, by S. Wolff; and W. Lee Rensselaer, 'Ut Pictura Poësis', in *Art Bulletin*, 1940, pp. 197 ff.)

Leaving aside these Greek precedents, however, and confining ourselves to the period for which Hussey's work is so useful, the eighteenth century in England, there remains no doubt that the fashion for the Picturesque, like many other fashions, was of Italian origin (just as Vanbrugh's conception of picturesqueness, in the realm of architecture, was also of Italian origin), deriving, on the one hand, from the landscapes of Claude and Salvator Rosa (whom the worthy English of the eighteenth century called, simply, 'Salvator') and, on the other, from the buildings of Bernini and Borromini and the etchings of Piranesi. (In this connexion see also Miss Manwaring's *Italian Landscape in Eighteenth Century England*, 1925.) The collectors who, on their return from the 'Grand Tour', filled their ancestral homes with Italian canvases, promoted the taste for the Picturesque, already heralded by the poets. Among the latter, in company with Denham in *Cooper's Hill* and Milton in *L'Allegro*, Hussey does not mention Richard Lovelace (1618-57), who posed as a connoisseur of pictures, quoted Vasari and van Mander, and declared his intention of showing to the (then) indifferent English in what esteem the fine arts should be held. Still more important, he forgets Andrew Marvell (1621-78) who, in his poems *Upon Appleton House* and *The Bermudas*, displayed so well-developed a feeling for Nature and the Picturesque that it immediately places him in close relation to the Romantics. In Marvell we can already discern that worship of the 'incognito indistinto' (as Dante would have called it) which Campbell in 1799 was to formulate explicitly in the famous lines:

> 'Tis *distance* lends enchantment to the view,
> And robes the mountain in its azure hue.

But if one wished to trace to its first stages each different 'je ne sais quoi' of Romanticism, and to analyse the complex education presupposed by a line like Campbell's on the magic of distance, it would indeed be a long business. It will therefore be more convenient to start from Burke's fundamentally important book, *Inquiry into the Origin of our Ideas of the Sublime and Beautiful* (1756), which was the first to give a clear-cut form to such axioms as 'No work of art can be great but as it deceives', 'A clear idea is another name for a little idea'. This book, with its theory of the physical basis of the aesthetic emotion, and its comparison of the sensation of Beauty with the pleasure one feels in being carried along by a swift and easy coach over a gently undulating surface, explains the vogue of the serpentine lines in Chippendale furniture and in the shapes of paths and artificial lakes in the gardens of the late eighteenth century. From the books of Burke and Reynolds we go on to those of Uvedale Price and Richard Payne Knight, of Gilpin and Alison, who complete the definition of the Picturesque in relation to the Sublime and Beautiful. Its characteristics are found to consist in dazzle and flicker of effect, in rapid succession of colours, lights, and shades, in roughness, sudden variation, irregularity. 'Counterfeit neglect'— 'sprezzatura', as Baldassare Castiglione would have called it— is recognized as another fundamental characteristic of the Picturesque.

Bacon had already expressed the idea (that Poe never tired of quoting and Baudelaire repeated after him) that 'there is no excellent beauty that hath not some strangeness in the proportion'. [Add. 1950]

There would have been no harm if the Picturesque had been confined to the preference for one kind of line and one kind of effect over another. The trouble started when theory led to practice, because the Picturesque was then found to consist in an intellectual rather than visual predilection for certain subjects. A typical example of a 'picturesque' subject is a hovel beneath a gnarled oak, with an aged gipsy, a rusty donkey, mellow tints and dark shadows. This example, together with the famous description of the picturesque charm of the old parson's daughter (her cross-eyes and uneven teeth are considered picturesque qualities), is to be found in Price's highly entertaining dialogue on *The Distinct Characters of the Picturesque and Beautiful* (1801).

A sign of the new fashion in taste is shown in the capacity to appreciate Alpine landscape (both the Alps and the English Lake District). Although this subject has already been, to a certain extent, discussed, Hussey succeeds in enriching it with new illustrations. The year 1768 is an important date in the history of the Picturesque, for the publication of a poem by Dalton and a letter by Dr. Brown had the effect of making Gray and Arthur Young visit the English Lakes. Two years later, a tour of the Lakes was the height of fashion. The Reverend Dr. Gilpin, whose volumes were illustrated with scenographically picturesque drawings (published in 1782 and the years following), was one of the high priests of the new cult. He took great care also to suit to the various landscapes expressive and appropriate figures, and is delighted when a view entirely of the horrid kind seems to call for the presence of a company of *banditti* in the manner of Salvator Rosa. Gilpin has also valuable advice to give on the subject of picturesque animals, such as 'The actions of a goat are still more pleasing than the shagginess of his coat'. Hollow tree-trunks are excellent for foregrounds, trees blasted by lightning are also very picturesque, and pines can be recommended because of their association with Roman ruins.

It was in garden-designs that the new 'picturesque' sensibility eventually ran riot. The efforts of those barbers of Nature, the celebrated designers of parks—'Capability' Brown with his special type of 'idealized' garden, and Humphrey Repton, with the 'impressionist' garden—continually border on the ridiculous, and already in 1779 Richard Graves in his *Columella, or the Distres't Anchoret*, gives a delicious caricature of the picturesque *chinoiseries* indulged in by owners of parks. Later came Peacock's caricature, *Headlong Hall*. But the best, because unconscious, caricature is the garden that Mr. Tyers had arranged for his leisure hours at Denbies, in which the paths were emblems of human life, now comfortable and flat, now rugged and steep, with here and there stones bearing moral inscriptions: and, best of all, the Valley of the Shadow of Death, with coffins instead of columns, and skulls scattered picturesquely about. Extravagances of this kind—which surpass the well-known caricature of the picturesque garden in *Bouvard et Pécuchet*—show clearly the kind of pictorial-literary taint which affected the idea of the Picturesque. The Picturesque might almost be defined as the 'paintable idea', and cannot, generally speaking, be called true painting, any more than so-called poetical ideas, or ideas which suggest poetry, can be called true poetry.

16 Quoted from Strich, p. 56. Cf. the lines by Campbell quoted in note 15.

CHAPTER I
THE BEAUTY OF THE MEDUSA

Le beau est fait d'un élément éternel, invariable, dont la quantité est excessivement difficile à déterminer, et d'un élément relatif, circonstanciel, qui sera, si l'on veut, tour à tour ou tout ensemble, l'époque, la mode, la morale, la passion. Sans ce second élément, qui est comme l'enveloppe amusante, titillante, apéritive, du divin gâteau, le premier élément serait indigestible, inappréciable, non adapté et non approprié à la nature humaine.

BAUDELAIRE, L'Art romantique.

CHAPTER I
THE BEAUTY OF THE MEDUSA

1. No picture made a deeper impression on the mind of Shelley than the Medusa, at one time attributed to Leonardo,* which he saw in the Uffizi Gallery towards the end of 1819. The poem which he wrote upon it deserves to be quoted here in full, since it amounts almost to a manifesto of the conception of Beauty peculiar to the Romantics.

It lieth, gazing on the midnight sky,
  Upon the cloudy mountain-peak supine;
Below, far lands are seen tremblingly;
  Its horror and its beauty are divine.
Upon its lips and eyelids seems to lie
  Loveliness like a shadow, from which shine,
Fiery and lurid, struggling underneath,
The agonies of anguish and of death.

Yet it is less the horror than the grace
  Which turns the gazer's spirit into stone,
Whereon the lineaments of that dead face
  Are graven, till the characters be grown
Into itself, and thought no more can trace;
  'Tis the melodious hue of beauty thrown
Athwart the darkness and the glare of pain,
Which humanize and harmonize the strain.

And from its head as from one body grow,
  As [   ] grass out of a watery rock,
Hairs which are vipers, and they curl and flow
  And their long tangles in each other lock,
And with unending involutions show
  Their mailèd radiance, as it were to mock
The torture and the death within, and saw
The solid air with many a raggèd jaw.

And, from a stone beside, a poisonous eft
  Peeps idly into those Gorgonian eyes;
Whilst in the air a ghastly bat, bereft
  Of sense, has flitted with a mad surprise
Out of the cave this hideous light had cleft,
  And he comes hastening like a moth that hies
After a taper; and the midnight sky
Flares, a light more dread than obscurity.

---

* Asterisks in the text refer throughout to addenda included (1970) with chapter notes.

'Tis the tempestuous loveliness of terror;
  For from the serpents gleams a brazen glare
Kindled by that inextricable error,
  Which makes a thrilling vapour of the air
Become a [   ] and ever-shifting mirror
  Of all the beauty and the terror there—
A woman's countenance, with serpent-locks,
Gazing in death on Heaven from those wet rocks.

' 'Tis the tempestuous loveliness of terror. . . .' In these lines pleasure and pain are combined in one single impression. The very objects which should induce a shudder—the livid face of the severed head, the squirming mass of vipers, the rigidity of death, the sinister light, the repulsive animals, the lizard, the bat—all these give rise to a new sense of beauty, a beauty imperilled and contaminated, a new thrill.*

One remembers the words of Faust and Mephistopheles on the night of the witches' Sabbath. Faust has seen, alone and apart, a pale and beautiful young girl who resembles Margaret. Mephistopheles says to him:

                    Let it be—pass on—
No good can come of it—it is not well
To meet it—it is an enchanted phantom,
A lifeless idol; with its numbing look
It freezes up the blood of man; and they
Who meet its ghastly stare are turned to stone,
Like those who saw Medusa.
    Faust.   Oh, too true!
Her eyes are like the eyes of a fresh corpse
Which no belovèd hand has closed, alas!
That is the breast which Margaret yielded to me—
Those are the lovely limbs which I enjoyed!
    Meph. It is all magic, poor deluded fool!
She looks to everyone like his first love.
    Faust. Oh, what delight! what woe! I cannot turn
My looks from her sweet piteous countenance.
How strangely does a single blood-red line,
Not broader than the sharp edge of a knife,
Adorn her lovely neck!¹

Here, one might say, through the lips of Faust speaks the whole of Romanticism. This glassy-eyed, severed female head, this horrible, fascinating Medusa, was to be

the object of the dark loves of the Romantics and the Decadents throughout the whole of the century.[2]

For the Romantics beauty was enhanced by exactly
those qualities which seem to deny it, by those objects
which produce horror; the sadder, the more painful it was,
the more intensely they relished it. 'Welch eine Wonne!
welch ein Leiden!'

In his *Philosophy of Composition* Poe explicitly admits
that 'the death of a beautiful woman is, unquestionably,
the most poetical topic in the world'. The sight of his
mother dying of consumption, when Poe was hardly three
years old, could not fail to leave in the child an indelible
impression, which later transposed itself into the figures of
Berenice, Morella, Eleonora, Ligeia.[2A] Romantic fashion
for consumptive ladies can be abundantly illustrated, from
Nodier's *Filleule du Seigneur* to Irving's *The Wife* and *The
Broken Heart*, to the American *Ode to Consumption* which
begins: 'There is a beauty in woman's decay.'

2. Such instances seem to mark the culminating point of
the aesthetic theory of the Horrid and the Terrible which
had gradually developed during the course of the eighteenth century.[3] The new sensibility had begun to take
clear form in compositions such as Collins's *Ode to Fear*
and in *The Castle of Otranto*, written by Walpole as the
whim of a dilettante medievalist; it had sought to analyse
its own origins in such essays as that of J. and A. L. Aikin
'On the Pleasure derived from Objects of Terror' and the
'Enquiry into those kinds of Distress which excite agree-
able sensations' (in *Miscellaneous Pieces in Prose*, London,
1773), and in Drake's essay 'On Objects of Terror' which
precedes the fragment of *Montmorenci*; it had received the
sanction of Goethe, who declared 'Das beste des Menschen
liegt im Schaudern'. The discovery of Horror as a source
of delight and beauty ended by reacting on men's actual
conception of beauty itself: the Horrid, from being a
category of the Beautiful, ended by becoming one of its
essential elements, and the 'beautifully horrid' passed by
insensible degrees into the 'horribly beautiful'. But the
discovery of the beauty of the Horrid cannot be considered
as belonging entirely to the eighteenth century, although

it was only then that the idea came to full consciousness. It was, after all, only a question of realizing—to use Flaubert's metaphor[4]—that

'autrefois on croyait que la canne à sucre seule donnait le sucre, on en tire à peu près de tout maintenant; il en est de même de la poésie, extrayons-la de n'importe quoi, car elle gît en tout et partout.'

Beauty and poetry, therefore, can be extracted from materials that are generally considered to be base and repugnant, as, indeed, Shakespeare and the other Elizabethans knew long before this, though they did not theorize about it. On the other hand, the idea of pain as an integral part of desire is a different matter, and has a certain novelty. The following aphorisms are taken from Novalis (*Psychologische Fragmente*): 'It is strange that the association of desire, religion, and cruelty should not have immediately attracted men's attention to the intimate relationship which exists between them, and to the tendency which they have in common.' 'It is strange that the true source of cruelty should be desire.'

Nor is Novalis the only writer to observe the intimate connexion between cruelty and desire, between pleasure and pain. Shelley's disconsolate conclusion that pain is inseparable from human pleasure inspired the line:

Our sweetest songs are those that tell of saddest thought.[5]

Musset echoes the idea:

Les plus désespérés sont les chants les plus beaux.[6]

So also, later, does André Gide: 'Les plus belles œuvres des hommes sont obstinément douloureuses.'[7] All through the literature of Romanticism, down to our own times, there is an insistence on this theory of the inseparability of pleasure and pain, and, on the practical side, a search for themes of tormented, contaminated beauty. This inseparability constitutes 'la grande synthèse', says Flaubert, whom we shall find it necessary to quote frequently in these pages as one of the chief exponents of Romantic sensibility:

'Tu me dis que les punaises de Ruchiouk-Hânem — [he writes of the Arab prostitute] — te la dégradent; c'est là, moi, ce qui m'en-chantait. Leur odeur nauséabonde se mêlait au parfum de sa peau ruisselante de santal. Je veux qu'il y ait une amertume à tout, un éternel coup de sifflet au milieu de nos triomphes, et que la désolation même soit dans l'enthousiasme. Cela me rappelle Jaffa, où en entrant je humais à la fois l'odeur des citronniers et celle des cadavres; le cimetière défoncé laissait voir les squelettes à demi pourris, tandis que les arbustes verts balançaient au-dessus de nos têtes leurs fruits dorés. Ne sens-tu pas que cette poésie est complète, et que c'est la grande synthèse? Tous les appétits de l'imagination et de la pensée y sont assouvis à la fois.'[8]

Baudelaire says the same thing in his *Hymne à la Beauté*, a hymn to that Beauty which elsewhere (in his *Causerie*) he calls 'dur fléau des âmes':

> Viens-tu du ciel profond ou sors-tu de l'abîme,
> O Beauté? Ton regard, infernal et divin,
> Verse confusément le bienfait et le crime.

> Tu marches sur des morts, Beauté, dont tu te moques;
> De tes bijoux l'Horreur n'est pas le moins charmant,
> Et le Meurtre, parmi tes plus chères breloques,
> Sur ton ventre orgueilleux danse amoureusement.

> L'amoureux pantelant incliné sur sa belle
> A l'air d'un moribond caressant son tombeau.

> Que tu viennes du ciel ou de l'enfer, qu'importe,
> O Beauté! monstre énorme, effrayant, ingénu!
> Si ton œil, ton souris, ton pied, m'ouvrent la porte
> D'un infini que j'aime et n'ai jamais connu?

Also in a passage of the *Journaux intimes*:

'J'ai trouvé la définition du Beau, de mon Beau.

'C'est quelque chose d'ardent et de triste. . . . Une tête séduisante et belle, une tête de femme, veux-je dire, c'est une tête qui fait rêver à la fois, — mais d'une manière confuse, — de volupté et de tristesse; qui comporte une idée de mélancolie, de lassitude, même de satiété, — soit une idée contraire, c'est-à-dire une ardeur, un désir de vivre, associés avec une amertume refluante, comme venant de privation et de désespérance. Le mystère, le regret sont aussi des caractères du Beau.

'Une belle tête d'homme . . . contiendra aussi quelque chose d'ardent et de triste, — des besoins spirituels, — des ambitions ténébreusement refoulées, — l'idée d'une puissance grondante et

melancholy inseparable from beauty for Baudelaire

sans emploi, — quelquefois l'idée d'une insensibilité vengeresse . . .
quelquefois aussi . . . le mystère, et enfin (pour que j'aie le courage
d'avouer jusqu'à quel point je me sens moderne en esthétique) le
malheur. Je ne prétends pas que la Joie ne puisse pas s'associer
avec la Beauté, mais je dis que la Joie est un des ornements les plus
vulgaires, tandis que la Mélancolie en est pour ainsi dire l'illustre
compagne, à ce point que je ne conçois guère (mon cerveau serait-il
un miroir ensorcelé?) un type de Beauté où il n'y ait du *Malheur*.
Appuyé sur — d'autres diraient: obsédé par — ces idées, on conçoit
qu'il me serait difficile de ne pas conclure que le plus parfait type
de Beauté virile est *Satan* — à la manière de Milton.'[9]

This is a passage which serves as an explanatory note to
the *Madrigal triste*:

Sois belle! et sois triste! . . .
. . . .
Je t'aime surtout quand la joie
S'enfuit de ton front terrassé;
Quand ton cœur dans l'horreur se noie;
Quand sur ton présent se déploie
Le nuage affreux du passé.

Je t'aime quand ton grand œil verse
Une eau chaude comme le sang;
Quand, malgré ma main qui te berce,
Ton angoisse, trop lourde, perce
Comme un râle d'agonisant.

J'aspire, volupté divine!
Hymne profond, délicieux!
Tous les sanglots de ta poitrine. . . .

The idea expressed in Keats's *Ode on Melancholy* is confirmed by Baudelaire: 'La mélancolie, toujours inséparable
du sentiment du beau.'[10] A well-known passage from the
third book of the *Mémoires d'outre-tombe* of Chateaubriand
—that forerunner of the Decadence—shows quite clearly
what sort of pleasure is evoked by a melancholy landscape:

'Le saccage des bûcherons paraissait plus tragique encore à ce
moment de l'année où tout s'apprêtait à revivre. Dans l'air attiédi
les rameaux déjà se gonflaient; des bourgeons éclataient et, coupée,
chaque branche pleurait sa sève. J'avançais lentement, non point
tant triste moi-même qu'exalté par la douleur du paysage, grisé peut-
être un peu par la puissante odeur végétale que l'arbre mourant et

la terre en travail exhalaient. A peine étais-je sensible au contraste de ces morts avec le renouveau du printemps; le parc, ainsi, s'ouvrait plus largement à la lumière qui baignait et dorait également mort et vie; mais cependant, au loin, le chant tragique des cognées, occupant l'air d'une solennité funèbre, rythmait secrètement les battements heureux de mon cœur.'[11]

But there is no end to the examples which might be quoted from the Romantic and Decadent writers on the subject of this indissoluble union of the beautiful and the sad, on the supreme beauty of that beauty which is accursed. Even Victor Hugo, in whose veins certainly did not flow the tormented blood of such as Shelley, Keats, Flaubert, and Baudelaire, nevertheless solemnly asserted, rather in Baudelaire's manner, the relationship between Beauty and Death. Baudelaire, in his *Les deux bonnes sœurs*, had said:

> La Débauche et la Mort sont deux aimables filles
>
> . . . . .
>
> Et la bière et l'alcôve en blasphèmes fécondes
> Nous offrent tour à tour, comme deux bonnes sœurs,
> De terribles plaisirs et d'affreuses douceurs.

And Hugo wrote, in a sonnet of the year 1871:[12]

> La Mort et la Beauté sont deux choses profondes
> Qui contiennent tant d'ombre et d'azur qu'on dirait
> Deux sœurs également terribles et fécondes
> Ayant la même énigme et le même secret.

In fact, to such an extent were Beauty and Death looked upon as sisters by the Romantics that they became fused into a sort of two-faced herm, filled with corruption and melancholy and fatal in its beauty—a beauty of which, the more bitter the taste, the more abundant the enjoyment.

'In thee did I find the image of the perilous Beauty which kindled me and kindles me still, . . . vessel filled with all ills, uttermost depth of anguish and guilt, remote cause of infinite strife, deathly silence where, drunk with lust and slaughter, the human monster, fed upon deceits, roars through the labyrinth of the ages. The sublime aspect of the Shadow to which my inspiration is spellbound do I recognise in thee, Hippodamia.'

Thus D'Annunzio[13] celebrates the mother of Atreus, 'her royal womb filled with terrible fruitfulness'; a Beauty which is Death (as in Hugo's lines), a fatal beauty whose attributes in D'Annunzio are the same as in the French poet—'profonde' (depth of anguish), 'terrible', 'féconde' (terrible fruitfulness), 'qui contient tant d'ombre' (sublime aspect of the Shadow. . .).

3. It would not be safe to assert that the Romantics were the first to feel, as they were certainly the first to discuss, this particular kind of beauty. Vauvenargues, in the eighteenth century, speaks of a type of libertine who finds beauty insipid unless it is flavoured 'd'un air de corruption';[14] but one may be fairly sure that the libertines of all periods have found it thus. Anticipations of this tendency are to be found in a writer in whom there are often certain surprising hints of modernity—Diderot, who wrote to Sophie Volland: 'Presque toujours ce qui nuit à la beauté morale redouble la beauté poétique. On ne fait guère que des tableaux tranquilles et froids avec la vertu; c'est la passion et le vice qui animent les compositions du peintre, du poète et du musicien.' And what else but a taste for beauty very analogous to that of the Romantics could have inspired the macabre pictures of two German painters of the first half of the sixteenth century, Hans Baldung Grien and Niklas Manuel Deutsch, pictures in which the embrace of Death with a lovely woman has all the qualities of the vampirism about which the Romantics raved? Or Magnasco's scenes of torture and flagellation?

However, let us rather turn our attention (without leaving the field of literature) to the one among the poets of previous ages whose name the Romantics adored, whom Barrès called[15] 'le plus grand du Midi'—and this praise, from such a source, is symptomatic—Torquato Tasso.

The age of Tasso, it is true, was filled with the spirit of Counter-reformation which insisted on the beauty of martyrdom for the Faith and adorned the altars of churches with gloomy, gory paintings, but it is not without significance that the poetry of Tasso should have reached some of its highest peaks in descriptions in which Beauty and Death are intimately connected. Even to his eyes pain seemed to throw beauty into relief and martyrdom to wring from it accents even more moving. It has been rightfully observed[16] that Olindo, bound to the stake beside his beloved, though ostensibly a martyr for the Faith, speaks only the language of ardent love and longing. Imminent death seems to inspire love with a new thrill, and Sofronia, her tender arms bound with cruel cords, as she gazes upon her lover with pitiful eyes, appears more beautiful and more desirable now that she is threatened with martyrdom. Olindo rejoices to be the consort of the funeral pyre:

> Ed oh mia morte avventurosa a pieno!
> Oh fortunati miei dolci martiri!
> S'impetrerò che giunto seno a seno
> L'anima mia ne la tua bocca spiri . . .[17]

Would it perhaps be rash to see in these lines the same emotion which inspired in Flaubert the more explicit words of the *Tentation*, at the point where the Saint, as he flagellates himself, is transported in imagination to the side of his beloved, Ammonaria the martyr?

'J'aurais pu être attaché à la colonne près de la tienne, face à face, sous tes yeux, répondant à tes cris par mes soupirs; et nos douleurs se seraient confondues, nos âmes se seraient mêlées. (*Il se flagelle avec furie*). Tiens, tiens! pour toi, encore! — Mais voilà qu'un chatouillement me parcourt. Quel supplice! quelles délices! ce sont comme des baisers. Ma moelle se fond! je meurs.'

There is an opportune note in the stage direction, 'L'ombre des cornes du Diable reparaît'. Flaubert had no illusions about the Christian value of Antony's act. Nor was Chateaubriand deceiving himself when he made René attribute to Céluta the words 'Mêlons des voluptés à la mort.'[18] Whether Tasso had illusions about Olindo's feelings cannot be said with certainty. Donadoni, at any rate, quite rightly observes that 'the episode shows a fundamental part of the poet's nature; it was essential for him that he should not hesitate to give expression to one of the most profound and painful instincts of his soul'. He also justly remarks upon the substantial similarity of the subject with that of Tancredi, who slays, without recognizing her, his beloved Clorinda, the sister—both lesser and greater—of Camilla in the *Aeneid*. In this episode, too, tragedy adds a more subtle pathos to beauty.

> Ma ecco omai l'ora fatale è giunta,
> Che'l viver di Clorinda al suo fin deve.
> Spinge egli il ferro nel bel sen di punta,
> Che vi s'immerge, e'l sangue avido beve;
> E la veste, che d'òr vago trapunta
> Le mammelle stringea tenera e leve,
> L'empie d'un caldo fiume. Ella già sente
> Morirsi, e'l piè le manca egro e languente.
>
> .   .   .   .   .   .
>
> Amico, hai vinto: io ti perdón . . . perdona
> Tu ancora . . .
>
> .   .   .   .   .   .
>
> In queste voci languide risuona
> Un non so che di flebile e soave
> Ch'al cor gli scende, ed ogni sdegno ammorza,
> E gli occhi a lagrimar gli invoglia e sforza.
>
> .   .   .   .   .   .
>
> D'un bel pallore ha il bianco volto asperso,
> Come a'gigli sarian miste vïole;
> E gli occhi al cielo affissa; e in lei converso
> Sembra per la pietate il cielo e'l sole:
> E la man nuda e fredda alzando verso
> Il cavaliero, in vece di parole,
> Gli dà pegno di pace. In questa forma
> Passa la bella donna, e par che dorma.[19]

The full significance of Clorinda's death becomes apparent in the light of Erminia's heartbroken longing to be killed by Tancredi. Erminia (Canto VI, stanzas 84–5) mingles the ideas of imprisonment and death with that of love, in a very characteristic manner:

> E forse or fòra qui mio prigioniero,
> E sosterria da la nemica amante
> Giogo di servitù dolce e leggiero;
> E già per li suoi nodi i'sentirei
> Fatti soavi e alleggeriti i miei.

O vero a me da la sua destra il fianco
Sendo percosso, e rïaperto il core,
Pur risanata in cotal guisa al manco
Colpo di ferro avria piaga d'Amore:
Ed or la mente in pace e'l corpo stanco
Riposariansi . . . [20]

And when Erminia at last finds Tancredi again, he
looks like a dead and bloodless corpse after his duel with
Argante (Canto XIX, stanzas 104 et seq.):

Da le pallide labra i freddi baci,
Che più caldi sperai, vuo' pur rapire;
Parte torrò di sue ragioni a morte,
Baciando queste labra esangui e smorte.

Pietosa bocca . . .
. . . .
Lecito sia ch'ora ti stringa, e poi
Versi lo spirto mio fra i labri tuoi.

Rinvenne quegli . . .
. . . .
Aprì le labra, e con le luci chiuse
Un suo sospir con que' di lei confuse. [21]

Erminia, the emotional creature drunk with tears, is, as
has been observed,[22] Tasso himself.

Elsewhere, in the *Aminta*, it is Silvia's beauty which
derives a subtler charm from the painful state to which the
satyr has reduced her. Here, too, the lover is found close
beside his unfortunate mistress, this time not to die with
her nor to kill her, but to undo the knots with which the
satyr has bound her to a tree. And, again in the *Aminta*,
there is the scene in which the shepherd, a martyr for love,
comes back to life beneath Silvia's kisses, so that his
suicide

. . . sotto
Una dolente imagine di morte
Gli recò vita e gioia. [23]

The outward aspect of these subjects—martyrdom for
the Faith (in the case of Olindo and Sofronia), ignorance
as to the real nature of the adversary (in that of Tancredi
and Clorinda), defence against the assault of the satyr (in

that of Aminta and Silvia)—may momentarily obscure the source of Tasso's inspiration which is the same in all these episodes—an inspiration which can be traced to a peculiar sense of painful pleasure closely related to that which we shall find in many of the Romantics.

> 'Tis the melodious hue of beauty thrown
> Athwart the darkness and the glare of pain,
> Which humanize and harmonize the strain.

An examination of Tasso's own life from this point of view might further confirm this theory. Perhaps he experienced pleasure at feeling himself a victim, perhaps he enjoyed his imprisonment as much as he suffered from it; and the stratagem by which he terrified his sister with the news of his own death was the act, certainly, of a disturbed mind, but may have also been the act of a man who was an epicure in pain.

In such a man as Tasso the delight in pain is obvious and characteristic: it is quite obvious also, but less clearly stated, in some of the Elizabethan dramatists, especially Marlowe and Webster, in whom it was remarked by no less competent a judge than Swinburne.[24]*

4. How much of the seventeenth-century exaltation of deformed and suffering female beauty must be ascribed to a search for new effects, how much to genuine feeling?* There is no doubt that in many cases the idea was merely a matter of intellectual *parti pris*. When Alessandro Adimari cracks a series of 'jokes and poetical paradoxes on the beauty of women who, even in their defects, are yet admirable and lovely'[25] no one can possibly imagine that his feelings are serious. Adimari's sole aim was, evidently, to astonish his readers by showing how a defect may be twisted into a merit, and his beauty competition is simply a kind of handicap race. But even if this playful spirit—which is really the same as that which inspired Berni to write some of his *capitoli* in praise of things despicable and harmful—is to be found at the bottom of all the seventeenth-century gallantries on deformed and suffering female beauty, the fact remains that in some cases the idea may have sprung from some undefined but genuine feeling, from some new kind of thrill. The subject of the beauty

el epicurismo en la pena

of maturity and actually of old age, which is at least as old
as the Greek Anthology (V, 258: 'Thy autumn excels
others' spring, thy winter is more warm than others'
summer'), is taken up by, among others, Tasso (to
Lucrezia d'Este),[26] and by John Donne (to Magdalen
Herbert),[27] and is indeed not so eccentric as to be
suspected of insincerity. No more was Achillini's well-
known sonnet on a lovely beggar-woman a mere joke or a
paradox:

> Sciolta il crin, rotta i panni, e nuda il piede
> Donna, cui fe'lo Ciel povera e bella,
> Con fioca voce, e languida favella
> Mendicava per Dio poca mercede —[28]

this sonnet was immensely popular and was also imitated
abroad.[29] Achillini even wrote a sonnet on a Beautiful
Epileptic (*Bellissima Spiritata*), in which he admires 'so
fair a countenance made lodging for Furies'; and several
poets wrote on the theme of the Whipped Courtesan,
among others A. G. Brignole-Sale in the *Instabilità del-
l'Ingegno*:[30]

> La man, che ne le dita ha le quadrella,
> Con duro laccio al molle tergo è avvolta;
> L'onta a celar, ch'è ne le guance accolta,
> Spande il confuso crin ricca procella.
>
> Su 'l dorso, ove la sferza empia flagella,
> Grandine di rubini appar disciolta;
> Già dal livor la candidezza è tolta,
> Ma men candida ancor, non è men bella.
>
> Su quel tergo il mio cor spiega le piume,
> E per pietà di lui già tutto esangue,
> Ricever le ferite in sé presume.
>
> In quelle piaghe agonizzando ei langue;
> Ma non si serba il solito costume,
> Ché'l sangue al cor, non corre il core al sangue.[31]

Three other sonnets follow this, and then he pursues
his narrative as follows:

'Carlo won praise as a courteous scourger, since those lines were
such exquisite lashes; and every one professed eagerness to be so
whipped, *for the strokes seemed to impart more beauty than pain.*'

Among English writers Lovelace wrote on the same theme, adding a sting of impiety. To the courtesan, starting on her way to do penance, he says:[32]

> And as thy bare feet blesse the Way
> The people doe not mock, but pray,
> And call thee as amas'd they run
> Instead of prostitute, a Nun.*

5. Many of these themes of tainted beauty appear in the writings of the Romantics, but what was often, in the seventeenth-century writers, a mere intellectual pose, became, in the Romantics, a pose of sensibility. In the Romantics feeling takes the place of the 'conceit' of the seventeenth century. A poet such as Adimari may indulge in a play of wit on the beauty of a hunchback, a negress, a mad woman, or a woman already buried, but one may be certain that he would never have sought to give material form to these grotesques and whimseys of his imagination. A Romantic, on the other hand, tries to translate these wanderings of the imagination into actual life, or at least to give an indication of some basis of real experience. Besides, while in the seventeenth century the appearance of these themes was sporadic and eccentric, and writers adopted them more in the way of a happy thought than from any emotional curiosity (which is clear from Adimari, with his more or less exhaustive list of defects), with the Romantics the same themes fitted naturally into the general taste of the period, which tended towards the uncontrolled, the macabre, the terrible, the strange. Marino emphasized the element of Surprise, which, he said, should be the poet's aim: he discovered new spheres of the unusual and the strange, like a mathematician who works out the results of a series of equations, and his object was simply to astonish his reader's mind. Very different is Baudelaire's tone when he enunciates an apparently similar principle:

> Plonger au fond du gouffre, Enfer ou Ciel, qu'importe?
> Au fond de l'inconnu pour trouver du nouveau.

Baudelaire does not aim at astonishing the reader's mind, but rather at shocking his moral sense, and if, often, he is like an actor reciting his part in front of a mirror, he is nevertheless an actor who is half, and sometimes more than half, convinced of his part.

I have already mentioned a sonnet by Achillini on a Beautiful Epileptic:

> Là nel mezzo del Tempio a l'improvviso
> Lidia traluna gli occhi, e tiengli immoti,
> E mirano i miei lumi a lei devoti
> Fatto albergo di furie un sì bel viso.[33]

A beautiful epileptic is also the idol of Boulay-Paty's Élie Mariaker:

> Rose et pâle soudain, la jeune fille frêle
> Qui tombe du haut mal, âme forte et corps grêle,
> Je l'aimerais surtout à l'adoration!
>
> .   .   .   .   .   .
>
> Cette beauté souffrante, oh! voilà mon envie!

When he goes into ecstasies over the 'regard enragé' of his cousin, and adores her for being

> Un démon de velours, une pensionnaire,
> Belle de deux défauts, grêle et poitrinaire;

or when Barbey d'Aurevilly, in his early tale called *Léa* (1832), describes Réginald's love for the consumptive Léa in these terms:

' "Mais si! si! ma Léa, tu es belle, tu es la plus belle des créatures! Je ne te donnerais pas, toi, tes yeux battus, ta pâleur, ton corps malade, je ne les donnerais pas pour la beauté des anges dans le ciel." Et ces yeux battus, cette pâleur, ce corps malade, il les étreignait dans tous ses rêves des enlacements de sa pensée frénétique et sensuelle.... Cette mourante dont il touchait le vêtement, le brûlait comme la plus ardente des femmes. Il n'y avait pas de bayadère aux bords du Gange, pas d'odalisque dans les baignoires de Stamboul, il n'y aurait point eu de bacchante nue dont l'étreinte eût fait plus bouillonner la moelle de ses os que le contact, le simple contact de cette main frêle et fiévreuse dont on sentait la moiteur à travers le gant qui la couvrait';[34]

both of them are far from intending a joke or a paradox in the manner of Adimari: in fact, all round them in every-day life fashionable beauties were studying in every possible way to appear adorned with those adorable

defects. Again Élie Mariaker seems almost to be copying
Donne's conceits on the subject of autumnal beauty when
he declares that he abhors fresh, chubby faces, because
'la mer s'étire et se ride quand il y a un orage'. This seems
a rampant *concetto*, but its tone is quite different from that
of a seventeenth-century conceit—different, because the
poet's appeal is not to the mind, but to the senses. It was
the fashion, then, to affect a real, genuine taste for such
beauty as was threatened with disease or actually decaying.
One would write lines upon corpses:

> Le nénuphar est beau près de ta chair bleuie,
> Livide, et que dévore un grand reptile vert,

or expatiate in these words on the beauty of approaching
death:

'De légères veines bleues marquent de leurs fines arabesques sa
peau mate, trace sombre des baisers que lui a déjà donnés la Mort,
la Mort, à qui elle appartiendra peut-être bientôt, elle que j'aime
jusqu'à l'affolement.

'Dans son visage pâle et quelquefois livide, ses yeux brillent
comme des flammes, et les lueurs phosphorescentes qui sortent de
leurs orbites décharnées ressemblent aux feux follets que par les soirs
orageux d'été l'on voit errer sur les marécages où pourrissent des
choses pestilentielles.

'Autour de sa bouche flottent des teintes nacrées et bleuâtres,
comme sur un fruit qui sentirait les premières atteintes de la décomposition. . . . Et je l'aime pour tout le mystère de mort qu'elle
recèle, pour le symbole vivant qu'elle est à mes yeux de l'universelle
destruction, je l'aime pour sa grâce funéraire, et comme une belle
amphore, effilée et gracile, placée sur un tombeau. . . .'[35]

6. Lovely beggar-maids, seductive hags, fascinating
negresses, degraded prostitutes—all these subjects, which
the writers of the seventeenth century had treated light-
heartedly and as *jeux d'esprit*, are to be found again, but
impregnated with the bitter taste of reality, in the Romantics, and especially in the poet in whom the Romantic
Muse distilled her most subtle poisons—Baudelaire.

Here is the 'mendiante rousse', remote sister of Achillini's 'bellissima mendica': she is a person who really
existed, having inspired an ode by Théodore de Banville

(*A une petite chanteuse des rues*), a portrait by de Roy (*La petite guitariste*), and this little ode by Baudelaire:

> Blanche fille aux cheveux roux
> Dont la robe par ses trous
> Laisse voir la pauvreté
> Et la beauté,
>
> Pour moi, poète chétif,
> Ton jeune corps maladif
> Plein de taches de rousseur
> A sa douceur.
>
> . . . . .
>
> Va donc, sans autre ornement,
> Parfum, perles, diamant,
> Que ta maigre nudité,
> O ma beauté!

Achillini concluded in the same manner:

> Ché se vaga sei tu d'altro tesoro,
> China la ricca e preziosa testa,
> Che pioveran le chiome i nembi d'oro.[36]

But in Baudelaire the idea had been realized in an actual experience, and the 'taches de rousseur', instead of suggesting cold mythological comparisons, as in Adimari's sonnet on the 'beautiful freckled one' (for Adimari had foreseen even this case), touch an answering chord of the emotions.

And here is Sarah Louchette, the squinting little Jewess, distant relation of the 'bella guercia' (the squint-eyed beauty) and also of the 'bella calva' (the bald-headed beauty) of the seventeenth century (these also are to be found in Adimari), who inspired in Baudelaire, then a student at the *lycée*, these lines:

> Je n'ai pas pour maîtresse une lionne illustre.
> La gueuse, de mon âme emprunte tout son lustre.
> Insensible aux regards de l'univers moqueur,
> Sa beauté ne fleurit que dans mon triste cœur.
>
> . . . . .
>
> Vice beaucoup plus grave, elle porte perruque,
> Tous ses beaux cheveux noirs ont fui sa blanche nuque,
> Ce qui n'empêche pas les baisers amoureux
> De pleuvoir sur son front plus pelé qu'un lépreux.

Elle louche et l'effet de ce regard étrange,
Qu'ombragent des cils noirs plus longs que ceux d'un ange,
Est tel que tous les yeux, pour qui l'on s'est damné,
Ne valent pas pour moi son œil juif et cerné.

Elle n'a que vingt ans, la gorge déjà basse
Pend de chaque côté, comme une calebasse,
Et pourtant, me traînant chaque nuit sur son corps,
Ainsi qu'un nouveau-né, je la tette et la mords.

   .   .   .   .   .   .

Je la lèche en silence, avec plus de ferveur
Que Madeleine en feu les deux pieds du Sauveur.

Si vous la rencontrez bizarrement parée,
Se faufilant, au coin d'une rue égarée, . . .

Messieurs, ne crachez pas de jurons ni d'ordure
Au visage fardé de cette pauvre impure
Que déesse Famine a, par un soir d'hiver,
Contrainte à relever ses jupons en plein air.

Cette bohème-là, c'est mon tout, ma richesse,
Ma perle, mon bijou, ma reine, ma duchesse,
Celle qui m'a bercé sur son giron vainqueur
Et qui dans ses deux mains a réchauffé mon cœur.

We find also in Baudelaire the 'skeleton-like beauty',
the *Nymphe macabre*:[37]

> Tu n'es certes pas, ma très chère,
> Ce que Veuillot nomme un tendron
>
>   .   .   .   .   .
>
> Tu n'es plus fraîche, ma très chère,
>
> Ma vieille infante! Et cependant
> Tes caravanes insensées
> T'ont donné ce lustre abondant
> Des choses qui sont très usées
> Mais qui séduisent cependant.
>
> Je ne trouve pas monotone
> La verdeur de tes quarante ans,
> Je préfère tes fruits, Automne,
> Aux fleurs banales du Printemps!
> Non, tu n'es pas monotone!

> Ta carcasse a des agréments
> Et des grâces part.culières;
> Je trouve d'étranges piments
> Dans le creux de tes deux salières;
> Ta carcasse a des agréments!
>
> .   .   .   .   .
>
> Tes yeux qui semblent de la boue
> Où scintille quelque fanal,
> Ravivés au fard de ta joue,
> Lancent un éclair infernal! . .

Even if Baudelaire is here seen 'pétrarquisant sur l'horrible' (as Sainte-Beuve wrote to him) in a more or less seventeenth-century strain, and even if the flavour of mystification is unmistakable in the stories of love-affairs with dwarfs and giantesses which he delighted to relate to Madame de Molènes,[38] it is yet none the less true that his sense of beauty was eminently 'Medusean'. His statements in *Choix de maximes consolantes sur l'amour* show very clearly the curious psychological process of such eccentric love-affairs, and can be generally applied to many other Romantics also:

'Je suppose votre idole malade. Sa beauté a disparu sous l'affreuse croûte de la petite vérole, comme la verdure sous les lourdes glaces de l'hiver. Encore ému par les longues angoisses et les alternatives de la maladie, vous contemplez avec tristesse le stigmate ineffaçable sur le corps de la chère convalescente; vous entendez subitement résonner à vos oreilles un air *mourant* exécuté par l'archet délirant de Paganini, et cet air sympathique vous parle de vous-même, et semble vous raconter tout votre poème intérieur d'espérances perdues. — Dès lors, les traces de petite vérole feront partie de votre bonheur et chanteront toujours à votre regard attendri l'air mysté-rieux de Paganini. Elles seront désormais non seulement un objet de douce sympathie, mais encore de volupté physique, si toutefois vous êtes un de ces esprits sensibles pour qui la beauté est la *promesse* du bonheur.[39] C'est surtout l'association des idées qui fait aimer les laides; car vous risquez fort, si votre maîtresse grêlée vous trahit, de ne pouvoir vous consoler qu'avec une femme grêlée.

'Pour certains esprits plus curieux et plus blasés, la jouissance de la laideur provient d'un sentiment encore plus mystérieux, qui est la soif de l'inconnu, et le goût de l'horrible. C'est ce sentiment, dont chacun porte en soi le germe plus ou moins développé, qui précipite certains poètes dans les amphithéâtres et les cliniques, et les femmes aux exécutions publiques. Je plaindrais vivement qui ne comprendrait pas; — une harpe à qui manquerait une corde grave! . . . Il y a des gens qui rougissent d'avoir aimé une femme, le jour qu'ils s'aperçoivent qu'elle est bête. . . . La bêtise est souvent l'ornement de la beauté; c'est elle qui donne aux yeux cette limpidité morne des étangs noirâtres, et ce calme huileux des mers tropicales.'

This passage, it has been said, throws a sufficient light on what was Baudelaire's greatest erotic adventure—with the 'beautiful negress', Jeanne Duval. Beautiful she was, it seems, at least in Baudelaire's opinion, and stupid in everybody's opinion, including Baudelaire's. The 'beautiful slave' of Marino, *nigra* and *formosa* like the woman in the *Song of Songs*—

> Nera sì, ma se'bella, o di natura
> Fra le belle d'amor leggiadro mostro;
> Fosca è l'alba appo te . . .[40]

and the beautiful negress of Adimari—

> Negra sì, ma se'bella, e chi nol crede
> Di tenebre ammantato il ciel rimiri,
> Tu con due sole stelle incendio spiri,
> Ei con molt'occhi appena arder si vede . . .[41]

seem almost to be anticipations of the one of whom Baudelaire wrote:

> C'est Elle! noire et pourtant lumineuse,[42]

and also:

> Je t'adore à l'égal de la voûte nocturne,
> O vase de tristesse, ô grande taciturne,
> Et t'aime d'autant plus, belle, que tu me fuis,
> Et que tu me parais, ornement de mes nuits,
> Plus ironiquement accumuler les lieues
> Qui séparent mes bras des immensités bleues.
>
> Je m'avance à l'attaque, et je grimpe aux assauts,
> Comme après un cadavre un chœur de vermisseaux,
> Et je chéris, ô bête implacable et cruelle!
> Jusqu'à cette froideur par où tu m'es plus belle!

There is in this poem, on the one hand, a supreme power of abstraction ('Je t'adore à l'égal de la voûte nocturne'), and, on the other, a taste for the unclean which suggests images of a subterranean world of decay ('comme après un

cadavre un chœur de vermisseaux')—the great synthesis,
as Flaubert would call it. The latter may be referred to
here for some remarks very similar to those of Baudelaire
quoted above:

'Et quand ce ne serait que le costume impudent, la tentation
de la chimère, l'inconnu, *le caractère maudit*, la vieille poésie de la
corruption et de la vénalité.'[43]

To this evidence may be added that of the Goncourts:[44]

'La passion des choses ne vient pas de la bonté ou de la beauté
pure de ces choses, elle vient surtout de leur corruption. On aimera
follement une femme, pour sa putinerie, pour la méchanceté de son
esprit, pour la voyoucratie de sa tête, de son cœur, de ses sens; on
aura le goût déréglé d'une mangeaille pour son odeur avancée et qui
pue. Au fond, ce qui fait l'appassionnement: c'est le *faisandage* des
êtres et des choses.'

Baudelaire looks upon landscape with the same feelings.
He gave the world some well-known pictures of the Paris
he loved, all hospitals, brothels, purgatory, hell, anguish
without end:

Où toute énormité fleurit comme une fleur.

Je voulais m'enivrer de l'énorme catin
Dont le charme infernal me rajeunit sans cesse . . .

Je t'aime, ô capitale infâme! Courtisanes   *ciudad*
Et bandits, tels souvent vous offrez des plaisirs
Que ne comprennent pas les vulgaires profanes.[45]

The tendency in French painting both of the last century and up to our own day, to portray aspects of landscape
which are tortured and violated by man, comes from these
same 'discoveries' of Baudelaire.

Beauty of the Medusa, beloved by the Romantics,
Beauty tainted with pain, corruption, and death—we shall
find it again at the end of the century, and we shall see it
then illumined with the smile of the Gioconda.[46]

NOTES AND ADDENDA TO CHAPTER I

* *p. 25, line 3, add:* And now to an unknown Flemish artist. [Add. 1950]

* *p. 26, line 16, add:* Later, Walter Pater wrote of the Medusa, remembering Shelley's verse: 'What may be called the fascination of corruption penetrates in every touch its exquisitely finished beauty.' ('Leonardo da Vinci', in *The Renaissance*.) [Add. 1950]

¹ Shelley's translation. Goethe's feeling for the beauty of the Medusa receives further illustration from *Italienische Reise*, Zweiter Teil, April 1788: '... ein guter alter Abguss der Medusa Rondanini; ein wundersames Werk, das, den Zwiespalt zwischen Tod und Leben, *zwischen Schmerz und Wollust* ausdrückend, einen *unnennbaren Reiz* wie irgendein anderes Problem über uns ausübt.'

² This will be explained in chapter iii.

²ᴬ All the women loved by Poe pined away while still young: 'Helen' (Mrs. Stannard) went mad, Frances Allan died of an internal disease, Virginia died of consumption.... (See M. Bonaparte, *Edgar Poe*, Paris, Denoël et Steele, 1935, pp. 131, 159, &c.; see also M. Praz, 'Poe davanti alla psicanalisi', in the volume *Studi e svaghi inglesi*, Florence, Sansoni, 1937.) [Add. 1950]

³ For symptoms of this taste for the Horrid see D. Mornet, *Le Romantisme en France au XVIIIᵉ siècle* (Paris, Hachette, 1912), chap. i, 'Les premiers remous', and chap. iii, 'Les "grands ébranlements de l'âme"'. Especially p. 8, Baculard d'Arnaud:

'Il est des voluptés de tout genre, des douleurs qui ont leurs charmes, leurs transports, leurs délices. Qu'il est de plaisirs pour les âmes sensibles! ... Que les yeux d'une amante sont ravissants, adorables, lorsqu'ils sont couverts de larmes! Le cœur s'y baigne tout entier.'

Pp. 78-9, Brissot:

'J'aime la terreur que m'inspire une forêt obscure et ces caveaux lugubres où l'on ne rencontre que des ossements et des tombeaux. J'aime le sifflement des vents qui annonce l'orage, ces arbres agités, ce tonnerre qui éclate ou gronde, et les torrents de pluie qui roulent à grands flots. . . . Il y a pour moi dans cet instant un charme horrible.'

⁴ *Correspondance*, Édition du Centenaire, vol. ii, p. 17. See also: Samuel H. Monk, *The Sublime: A Study of Critical Theories in XVIIIth-Century England*, New York, Modern Language Association of America, 1935, pp. 130, 136, 201, &c.

⁵ *To a Skylark.*   ⁶ *La Nuit de mai.*   ⁷ *L'Immoraliste*, p. 108.

⁸ *Corresp.*, vol. ii, p. 16, letter of March 27th, 1853. Certain works of 'decadent' literature, such as *Le Jardin des supplices* by Octave Mirbeau, are merely diffuse illustrations of this same mode of feeling.

⁹ *Œuvres posthumes* (Paris, Mercure de France, 1908), p. 84; *Journaux intimes*, edited by A. van Bever (Paris, Crès, 1920), pp. 18-20.

Poe also, from whom Baudelaire learned so much, has an analogous idea of beauty. Cf. especially *Ligeia* (Baudelaire's version):

'Ses traits n'étaient pas jetés dans ce moule régulier qu'on nous a faussement enseigné à révérer dans les ouvrages classiques du paganisme. "Il n'y a pas de beauté exquise", dit Lord Verulam, parlant avec justesse de toutes les formes et de tous les genres de beauté, "sans une certaine étrangeté dans les proportions".'

Cf. L. Seylaz, *Edgar Poe et les premiers symbolistes français* (Lausanne, Imprimerie La Concorde, 1923), p. 70. Baudelaire, however, goes much further than Poe in his definition.

It is curious to compare Baudelaire's idea of beauty with the neo-classicists', e.g. Winckelmann's, for whom 'complete beauty appears only in the face of those whose mind is serene and exempt of all agitation', &c. See M. Praz, *Gusto neoclassico*, Florence, Sansoni, 1940, pp. 40 ff. [Add. 1950]

[10] *Œuvres posthumes*, p. 319, on the subject of Byron.

[11] A similar feeling with regard to landscape in D'Annunzio's *Villa Chigi* (*Elegie Romane*) culminates in an obviously sadistic vision:

'But we were both startled, hearing the sound of an axe: repeated blows suddenly echoed around us. . . . She, all at once, as though wounded, burst into sobs: she burst into desperate tears and I saw her in my mind, as though in a lightning-flash, I saw her humble and bleeding, humbly gasping, prostrate in a pool of blood, and raising suppliant hands from the lake of red; and she said with her eyes, "I did you no harm".'

[12] *Toute la lyre*, 1893, v. xxvi: *Ave, Dea; moriturus te salutat*. The sonnet, dedicated to Judith Gautier, bears the date '12 juillet' (1871). It finishes with a conceit in the seventeenth-century manner:

Nous sommes tous les deux voisins du ciel, madame,
Puisque vous êtes belle et puisque je suis vieux.

It is curious to discover echoes of Baudelaire in lines written by Hugo in his old age. Thus, in the first poem in Part VI of *Toute la lyre*, from the tenderly *bourgeois* effusions of the poet to his lady:

Ô bel être créé pour des sphères meilleures,
Dis, après tant de deuils, de désespoirs, d'ennuis,
Et tant d'amers chagrins et tant de tristes heures—

we plunge all at once straight into *Spleen*:

'Qui souvent font tes jours plus mornes que des nuits.'

(Cf. 'Il nous verse un jour noir plus triste que les nuits'.) Cf. also Part II, xx, *Nuit tombante* ('Vois le soir qui descend calme et silencieux') with *Recueillement*.

The quatrain by Hugo quoted in the text was remodelled in this way by Jean Lorrain (see G. Normandy, *Jean Lorrain*, Paris, Bibl. générale d'Éditions, undated, p. 265):

La Débauche et la Mort sont deux choses profondes,
Si pleines de ténèbres et d'azur qu'on dirait
Deux sœurs également terribles et fécondes
Ayant la même énigme et le même secret.

[13] *Laus Vitae*, lines 2169-84.

[14] *Œuvres de Vauvenargues*, published by D.-L. Gilbert, 1855, t. i,

p. 246, quoted by A. Monglond, *Le Préromantisme français*, (Grenoble, Arthaud, 1930), vol. i, p. 201. As reference is made in this book to 'algolagnia' simply in so far as it has inspired works of literature, we are not taking into account anecdotes of algolagnic nature referred to by ancient authors merely as part of a chronicle. E.g. Brantôme, *Vies des dames galantes*, Discours II: 'J'ay ouy parler d'une grande dame de par le monde', &c.; Giraldi Cinthio, *Ecatommithi*, Deca V, novella x (Riccio Lagnio's typical case of sadism and necrophily).

15 *Amori ac dolori sacrum*, p. 96.

16 Donadoni, *Torquato Tasso*, vol. i, p. 234.

17 Literal translation:

'And ah! my death, fortunate to the full! Ah, happy my sweet martyrdom! If I obtain that, joined with thee breast to breast, I may exhale my soul into thy mouth. . . .'

18 See chap. iii, § 7.

19 Lit. trans.:

'But lo, now the fatal hour is arrived that the life of Clorinda must to its end. He thrusts the point of the steel into her fair bosom: it sinks deep and greedily drinks her blood; and her garment, which, embroidered with fair gold, gently and lightly enfolds her breasts, is filled with the warm stream. Already she feels she is dying, and her feet, weak and languishing, fail to support her. . . . "Friend, thou hast conquered: I pardon thee . . . pardon thou me again." . . . In these languid words echoes something mournful and sweet, which pierces to his heart, and extinguishes all resentment, and excites and compels his eyes to weep. . . . Her white face is overspread with a lovely pallor, as though violets were mingled with lilies: she fixes her gaze upon the sky; and sky and sun seem turned towards her with pity: and raising her bare, cold hand towards the knight, she gives him, instead of words, the pledge of peace. In this manner passed the fair lady, and it seemed that she slept.'

20 Lit. trans.:

'Perhaps even now he might be my prisoner here, and would sustain his loving foe's sweet and light yoke of servitude: already, through his bonds, I would feel my own made kinder and lighter. Or else, should his right hand have smitten my own side, and opened again my heart, the wound of the steel would at least have healed in such wise Love's wound: my mind and my weary body would rest at last in peace.'

21 Lit. trans.:

' "From his pale lips cold kisses, which I longed to feel more ardent, do I yet wish to snatch; I will wrest from death part of its rights by kissing these wan and bloodless lips. . . . Piteous mouth. . . . Allow me now to embrace thee and then to pour out my spirit between thy lips." . . . He came back to life . . . he opened his lips, and with eyes closed mingled a sigh with hers.'

22 Donadoni, op. cit., i, p. 260.

23 Lit. trans.: ' . . . beneath a mournful image of death brought to him life and joy.'

24 In his essay on *The Early English Dramatists* (1857) Swinburne notices in these two the presence of the 'hideous lust of pain'. It is less evident in Marlowe—'There is in Marlowe a suspicion of this fatal ten-

dency'. See my essay on 'Christopher Marlowe' in *English Studies*, vol. xiii, no. 6 (December 1931), pp. 209-23, chiefly pp. 211-13.

* *p. 36, line 21, add:* Truly Elizabethan drama abounds in horrors, and outdoes its model, Seneca's theatre, in atrocities. There is more in this, however, than a mere convention: as an indication of taste even *Titus Andronicus*, inhuman and puerile as it may appear to us, has its meaning, for traits of scenery (as the description of the loathsome pit into which Bassanius's body is thrown) show a delight in the horrid which arrests our attention more than sensational atrocities; in such cases horror seems to turn from epos to elegy. As for Marlowe, he does not feel scenes of cruelty as blood-curdling, but rather as life-enhancing; his *Tamburlaine* is from end to end a paean of cruelty; and the sudden transition, in the soul of the conqueror, from thirst of blood to the adoration of beauty (First Part, Act v, sc. 2, 66 ff.) is a personal touch to which no parallel might be found in the whole dramatic production of the Elizabethans. Marlowe's life, his indubitable attraction to the androgyne, concur to make us interpret his exaltation of slaughter as a trait which is not isolated, but rather a typical aspect of a coherent physiognomy. Speaking of English Restoration drama, a modern critic, Roswell Gray Ham (*Otway and Lee, Biography from a Baroque Age*, New Haven, Yale University Press, 1931, p. 160. See my essay on 'Restoration Drama' in *English Studies*, vol. xv, p. i, Feb. 1933), remarked that 'a certain perversion of national taste—clearly recognizable from Elizabethan times—delighted in all sorts of unnatural relations'. He goes on quoting the passion of Polydore for Monimia in *The Orphan*, and chiefly the presentation of incest as a noble ecstasy of love in Dryden's and Lee's *Œdipus*. The incest theme, which John Ford had treated apologetically in '*Tis Pity*, is again romantically envisaged in the last scene of Dryden's *Don Sebastian*: in Dryden's heroic tragedies love, or rather a night of love, is presented as an ultimate end, as a *summum bonum* (to use the title a Victorian romantic, Browning, gave to a poem whose subject is a maid's kiss). How far that treatment of the incest theme may have answered to a positive taste of the Court, may be easily inferred from what is known about its moral standards. On the other hand, it was the King himself who suggested the notorious Nicky Nacky scenes, with their ribald satire upon Shaftesbury, in *Venice Preserv'd*; a companion to those scenes is to be found in Shadwell's *Virtuoso*. Political satire goes only half-way to explain the representation of vice on the stage; a mixture of exhibitionism and *voyeur's* indulgence must be supposed at the back of the delight Restoration society took in seeing its own manners reproduced on the stage or held up to derision in the satires. Authors of these latter, it should be remembered, were first of all the rakes themselves, with Rochester in the lead. But Otway's case brings us back to the considerations we have made above on Tasso, for that dramatist shows, together with a recrudescence of the Elizabethan taste for horror (shared by Nathaniel Lee), an indulgence in the noble pleasure of tears and a general effeminacy. Otway's central theme, which he attempted in *Don Carlos* and carried through successfully in *Venice Preserv'd*, is that of a man deliberately led to sacrifice by the woman he loves. Jaffier compares himself (Act IV) to a lamb bound by the priestess and laid by her on the altar, 'yet then too hardly bleats, such pleasure's in the pain'; Jaffier's words to Pierre (Act II, 424 ff., IV, 337 ff.) are no less typical of effeminate dedition; such is the spirit of this play, that one is not surprised that a decadent artist, Hugo von Hofmannsthal, was so fired by it as to feel tempted to make it his own (*Das gerettete Venedig*, 1905). [Add. 1950]

* *p. 36, line 24, add*: How much, to use Babbitt's terms, can be ascribed to intellectual romanticism rather than to emotional romanticism? [Add. 1950]

25 *La Tersicore, o vero scherzi, ecc. Opera del Sig. Alessandro Adimari, ridotta in 50 sonetti fondati principalmente sopra l'autorità d'A. Seneca il Morale, e concatenati in un capitolo. . . .* (In Fiorenza, Massi e Landi, 1637).

26 *Rime* (Solerti), iii, p. 131.   27 *The Autumnall.*

28
    Barefoot and ragged, with neglected hair,
    She whom the Heavens at once made poor and fair,
    With humble voice and moving words did stay,
    To beg an alms of all who pass'd that way.

(Philip Ayres's translation in *Lyric Poems, made in imitation of the Italians*, &c., London, 1687.)

29 By Tristan l'Hermite, by Richard Lovelace (*The Faire Begger*), and by Philip Ayres (*On a Fair Beggar*). See my article on 'Stanley, Sherburne, and Ayres as translators and imitators of Italian, Spanish and French Poets', in *Modern Language Review*, vol. xx, nos. 3 and 4, July and October 1925, pp. 420 and 423.

30 Brignole-Sale was typical of the seventeenth century. After alternating lascivious with pious writings, when his wife died he gave himself up entirely to religion, entered the Order of the Jesuits, and practised such severe flagellations that he often had to be rebuked by his fellow-priests for his over-harsh governance of the flesh. He offers a ready subject for a *biographie romancée*, especially as Van Dyck immortalized his beautiful, melancholy features and those of his voluptuous wife in two magnificent pictures, which are now in the Palazzo Rosso at Genoa. Such a character-portrait was attempted by G. Portigliotti in *Penombre Claustrali* (Milan, Treves, 1930), pp. 205-50. What a pity Barrès did not come across this subject! All the more so, since Brignole-Sale was ambassador at Madrid, where a son of his died of an epileptic fit. As can be easily seen, no element was wanting to inspire the author of *Du Sang, de la volupté, de la mort*.

31 Lit. trans.:

'The hand which holds Love's arrows in its fingers is twisted by cruel bonds behind her tender back; to conceal the shame which has gathered in her cheeks, her tangled hair scatters its rich storm. On her back, where the pitiless whip lashes her, a scattered hail of rubies appears; already the whiteness becomes livid, but though less white it is no less lovely. Upon that back my heart spreads its wings, and, all bloodless as it now is for pity of it, takes upon itself to receive the blows. My heart languishes in the agony of those wounds; but the usual custom is not observed, by which the blood runs to the heart, not the heart to the blood.'

³² *A Guiltlesse Lady imprisoned, after penanced.*

* *p. 38, line 7, add:* The pleasure of pain was a peculiarity well known to ecclesiastical writers. François Bonal (*Le Chrétien du temps*, 1665, quoted by Bremond, *Histoire littéraire du sentiment religieux en France*, vol. i, p. 410), talking about that 'cruel romance' which in his opinion Jansenists had built on the theological idea of grace, says that some of them

'trouvent ce système fort chrétien, quoiqu'ils ne se puissent empêcher de le sentir et de l'avouer non seulement dur, mais encore horrible. Mais aussi, comme ils confondent leur langage avec celui de saint Paul, la dureté même et la terreur semblent raffiner leur dévotion et plus ils tremblent de peur, plus ils s'imaginent être transis de piété. . . . Il se trouve des yeux faits ainsi, qui ne prendront qu'un fade plaisir à voir des tableaux de paysage divertissants dans une galerie, et qui se repaîtront d'une *terrible volupté* dans les peintures des embrasements, des naufrages . . . parce que ce sont des objets plus piquants et amusants, plus ils sont funestes et tragiques.' [Add. 1950].

³³ Lit. trans.:

'There, suddenly, in the middle of the Temple, Lydia casts up her eyes and keeps them motionless, and my eyes, which adore her, wonder at so fair a face made lodging for Furies.'

³⁴ Cf. the edition quoted in note 47 of chap. v. The love of Réginald for Léa ends in a manner which, to a Romantic of 1830, must have appeared exquisitely tragic. When the young man kisses her for the first time, she dies: 'Le sang du cœur avait inondé les poumons et monté dans la bouche de Léa, qui, yeux clos et tête pendante, le vomissait encore, quoiqu'elle ne fût plus qu'un cadavre.'

³⁵ See L. Maigron, *Le Romantisme et les mœurs* (Paris, Champion, 1910) pp. 180 et seq. Maigron observes rightly that the expressions in the prose poem quoted above reflect a conception of beauty similar to that of Poe.

³⁶   Nature on thee has all her treasures spread,
    Do but incline thy rich and pretious head,
    And those fair locks shall pour down showres of gold.

                                    (Ayres's translation.)

³⁷ *Œuvres posthumes*, p. 34. There is evidence here and there of this taste for the Cadaverous even in previous periods. E.g. in the *Mémoires de Tilly* (Paris, Jonquières, 1930), ii, p. 191, there is to be found this anecdote, relating to the year 1789:

'Sir John Lambert, que tout le monde a vu banquier très opulent à Paris . . . n'aimait que les femmes d'une maigreur dangereuse, et chez qui toute absence de gorge eût pu faire révoquer leur sexe en doute. . . . J'y trouvai rangée sur ses fauteuils une collection de momies. . . . C'était tout ce qu'il y avait de plus décharné dans les ballets de l'Opéra, et de plus voisin du squelette dans le rang des courtisanes subalternes. . . . (Un seul de ses amis) partageait son goût de l'ostéologie prise sur le fait dans la nature vivante.'

³⁸ *Le Gaulois*, Sept. 30th, 1886. See A. Séché et J. Bertaud, *La Vie anecdotique et pittoresque des grands écrivains, Charles Baudelaire* (Paris, Louis-Michaud, undated), p. 126.

³⁹ The definition is Stendhal's.

⁴⁰ Lit. trans.:

'Black thou art, but beautiful, O thou, Love's charming monster among nature's Beauties; dark is the dawn near thee. . . .'

⁴¹ Lit. trans.:

'Black thou art, but beautiful, and whoever does not believe it, let him contemplate the sky clad in darkness; thou with but two stars dost breathe forth fire, the sky with many eyes can scarcely be seen to burn. . . .'

⁴² *Un Fantôme*, I, *Les Ténèbres*, version of 1861. The definitive version (1868) has: C'est Elle! sombre et pourtant lumineuse'.

⁴³ *Corresp.* ii, p. 55 (June 1st, 1853).

⁴⁴ *Journal*, iii, p. 63 (Aug. 30th, 1866).

⁴⁵ *Épilogue* of the *Petits poèmes en prose*. Cf. chap. v, § 8. Recent illustrations of this same type of feeling are to be found, for instance, in the novel by Thomas Mann, *Der Tod in Venedig* (1913), a subtle analysis of the soul of an artist, Aschenbach, who derives a painful pleasure from his impossible passion for a beautiful Polish youth, in the oppressive and deathly atmosphere of Venice smitten by cholera; also in the conclusion of *Au Coin des rues* by F. Carco (Paris, Ferenczi, 1930), under the title of *Vénus des carrefours*:

'Vénus des carrefours, efflanquée, mauvaise et maquillée, aux cheveux en casque, aux yeux vides qui ne regardent pas, mais aux lèvres plus rouges que le sang et que la langue mince caresse, tu m'as connu flairant l'ombre que tu laissais derrière toi. Me voici — comme autrefois — dévoré du tourment cruel de te rencontrer au coin de basses ruelles où la lumière fardée des persiennes coule le long des murs. . . . Tu n'aurais qu'à me citer les rues de la Ville et je te dirais qu'à tel étage de vieilles prostituées attendent l'homme qu'elles fouetteront et dont elles fouleront la chair, avec les hauts talons de leurs bottines et les langues minces et déliées d'un martinet cruel.

'Donnant sur des cours noires dont les dalles toujours mouillées blanchissent à de lointains reflets du jour, des loges étroites reçoivent des couples qui, jusqu'à la nuit, s'acharneront à souffrir . . . Vénus, ta nudité d'ivoire, vénéneuse et fleurie d'images symboliques, hante mes longs après-midis d'hiver. Que d'instants j'ai passés, devant le feu qui rougeoyait, à me rappeler ton visage et le grand rire silencieux qui te tordait la bouche. Le jour brumeux restait suspendu dans l'air et, quelquefois, le cri des remorqueurs, montant du fleuve, arrêtait ma vie. . . . Vénus, n'étais-tu pas cette poupée, sans cheveux, ni dents, peinte et sans voix ? . . . D'horribles et lentes voluptés m'ont attaché sur toi. Masque effrayant, tes yeux de plâtre avaient vieilli!'

⁴⁶ D'Annunzio in the poem *Gorgon* (published in the *Domenica Letteraria — Cronaca Bizantina* of Aug. 23rd, 1885, with the title of *Il Paradiso Perduto*, later in *Isaotta Guttadàuro*, 1886) attributes the smile of the Gioconda to a lady of typically Medusa-like beauty:

'Diffused over her face was the dark pallor which I adore. . . . Upon her mouth was the glorious, cruel smile which the divine Leonardo pursued in his paintings. This smile was in sad combat with the sweetness of the long eyes, and gave a superhuman charm to the beauty of the heads of women which the great da Vinci loved. The mouth was a dolorous flower. . . .'

CHAPTER II
THE METAMORPHOSES OF SATAN

J'ai trouvé la définition du Beau, de mon Beau. C'est quelque chose d'ardent et de triste. . . . Je ne conçois guère un type de Beauté où il n'y ait du Malheur. Appuyé sur — d'autres diraient: obsédé par — ces idées, on conçoit qu'il me serait difficile de ne pas conclure que le plus parfait type de Beauté virile est Satan — à la manière de Milton.

BAUDELAIRE, Journaux intimes.

THE METAMORPHOSES OF SATAN (on Byron)

1. Even at as late a date as the *Gerusalemme Liberata*
Satan keeps his terrifying medieval mask, like that of a
Japanese warrior:

> Orrida maestà nel fero aspetto
> Terrore accresce, e più superbo il rende;
> Rosseggian gli occhi, e di veneno infetto,
> Come infausta cometa, il guardo splende;
> Gl'involge il mento, e su l'irsuto petto
> Ispida e folta la gran barba scende;
> E in guisa di voragine profonda
> S'apre la bocca d'atro sangue immonda.
>
> Qual i fumi sulfurei ed infiammati
> Escon di Mongibello, e'l puzzo e'l tuono,
> Tal de la fera bocca i negri fiati,
> Tale il fetore e le faville sono.[1]

Satan's appearance in the *Strage degli Innocenti* of
Marino is rather similar:

> Negli occhi, ove mestizia alberga e morte,
> Luce fiammeggia torbida e vermiglia.
> Gli sguardi obliqui e le pupille torte
> Sembran comete, e lampadi le ciglia.
> E da le nari e da le labra smorte
> Caligine e fetor vomita e figlia;
> Iracondi, superbi e disperati,
> Tuoni i gemiti son, folgori i fiati.[2]

One might think that Marino was simply making a
copy, with a certain added emphasis, of Tasso's grotesque
monster. Yet he has introduced one new element. The
asphyxiating gases, the artificial fires, are borrowed from
Tasso's arsenal (the contents of which, in their turn, can
easily be traced to yet other sources); but into the eyes of
the Demon, the eyes of which Tasso had said:

> Quant'è ne gli occhi lor *terrore* e morte,[3]

there has been put a new expression:

> Negli occhi, ove *mestizia* alberga e morte.

Marino's Satan is sad because he is conscious, above all else, of being a fallen angel:

> Misero, e come il tuo splendor primiero
> Perdesti, o già di luce Angel più bello![4]

He is a sooty Narcissus, a Phaethon of the abyss. It is true that in Tasso he says:

> . . . non sono anco estinti
> Gli spirti in voi di quel valor primiero,
> Quando di ferro e d'alte fiamme cinti
> Pugnammo già contra il celeste impero.
> Fummo, io no'l nego, in quel conflitto vinti:
> Pur non mancò virtute al gran pensiero.
> Diede che che si fosse a lui vittoria:
> Rimase a noi d'invitto ardir la gloria.[5]

But Marino insists above all on this Promethean aspect of Satan:

> E se quindi il mio stuol vinto cadeo,
> Il tentar l'alte imprese è pur trofeo . . .[6]

—and on the beauty he had once possessed:

> Ah non se'tu la creatura bella,
> Principe già de'fulguranti Amori,
> Del matutino Ciel la prima stella,
> La prima luce degli alati Cori? . . .
>
> .   .   .   .   .   .
>
> Lasso, ma che mi val fuor di speranza
> A lo stato primier volger la mente?
>
> .   .   .   .   .
>
> Ma qual forza tem'io? già non perdei
> Con l'antico candor l'alta natura.[7]

2. Milton had this particular aspect of Satan in mind when he was preparing, in the First Book of *Paradise Lost*, to describe a similar 'infernal council'.[8] He knew the translation which Richard Crashaw had made of the First Canto of Marino's *Strage degli Innocenti*, and he knew the original Italian. Crashaw had rendered the passage:

> Misero, e come il tuo splendor primiero
> Perdesti, o già di luce Angel più bello!

with

> Disdainefull wretch! how hath one bold sinne cost
> Thee *all the Beauties of thy once bright Eyes?*

For Milton this 'splendor primiero' is not entirely lost. Lucifer is changed, it is true:

> ... But O how fall'n! how chang'd
> From him, who in the happy Realms of Light
> Cloth'd with transcendent brightness didst outshine
> Myriads though bright ...[9]

but nevertheless:

> ... he above the rest
> In shape and gesture proudly eminent
> Stood like a Towr; his form had not yet lost
> All her Original brightness, nor appear'd
> Less then Arch Angel ruin'd, and th' excess
> Of Glory obscur'd: As when the Sun new ris'n
> Looks through the Horizontal misty Air
> Shorn of his Beams, or from behind the Moon
> In dim Eclips disastrous twilight sheds
> On half the Nations, and with fear of change
> Perplexes Monarchs. Dark'n'd so, yet shon
> Above them all th' Arch Angel: but his face
> Deep scars of Thunder had intrencht, and care
> Sat on his faded cheek, but under Browes
> Of dauntless courage, and considerate Pride
> Waiting revenge ...[10]

Sadness and death dwell also in the eyes of Milton's Satan (lines 56–8):

> ... his baleful eyes
> That witness'd huge affliction and dismay
> Mixt with obdurate pride and stedfast hate.

He proclaims also the glory of having attempted the great enterprise, in spite of his defeat (lines 623–4):

> ... that strife
> Was not inglorious, though th' event was dire;

and does not repent of his own presumption, retaining his 'alta natura' even in the loss of his former 'candore':

> nor ... do I repent, or change,
> Though changed in outward lustre, that fixed mind,
> And high disdain ...

Milton conferred upon the figure of Satan all the charm of an untamed rebel which already belonged to the Prometheus of Aeschylus and to the Capaneo of Dante, but it must not be forgotten that Marino had preceded him in the same path; so that one cannot agree with Taine[11] when he claims that the character of Milton's Satan was typically Anglo-Saxon:

'Cet héroïsme sombre, cette dure obstination, cette poignante ironie, ces bras orgueilleux et roidis qui serrent la douleur comme une maîtresse, cette concentration du courage invaincu, qui, replié en lui-même, trouve tout en lui-même, cette puissance de passion et cet empire sur la passion sont des traits propres du caractère anglais comme de la littérature anglaise.'

With Milton, the Evil One definitely assumes an aspect of fallen beauty, of splendour shadowed by sadness and death; he is 'majestic though in ruin'. The Adversary becomes strangely beautiful, but not in the manner of the witches Alcina and Lamia, whose loveliness is a work of sorcery, an empty illusion which turns to dust like the apples of Sodom. Accursed beauty is a permanent attribute of Satan; the thunder and stink of Mongibello, the last traces of the gloomy figure of the medieval Fiend, have now disappeared.

Is the reversal of values which some critics have tried to discover really to be found in Milton? Is the justification of the ways of God to men only the seeming aim of the poem, the poet himself in reality being 'of the Devil's party without knowing it', as Blake declared?[12] Is *Paradise Lost*, as a modern psychologist maintains,[13] a product of 'inverted power', the projection into a work of imagination (that is, into a dream) of Milton's thwarted purposes, at a time when all the hopes he placed in the Commonwealth were dashed to the ground? And is Satan's cry of revolt the cry of the poet himself, whose genius, inverted, has given a positive value to what objectively stands for the negative—evil—in his poem? At any rate, without accepting so extreme a theory, it cannot be denied that 'the character of Satan expresses as no other character or act or feature of the poem does, something in which Milton believed very strongly: heroic energy'.[14]

What it is important to establish here is that the Romantics approached to Blake's point of view.[15] Schiller, in the *Selbstrecension der Räuber*, observes, on the subject of *Paradise Lost*:

'Automatically we take the side of the loser; an artifice by which Milton, the panegyrist of Hell, transforms for a moment even the mildest of readers into a fallen angel.'

Shelley, in the *Defense of Poesy*, goes further:

'Milton's poem contains within itself a philosophical refutation of that system, of which, by a strange and natural antithesis, it has been a chief popular support. Nothing can exceed the energy and magnificence of the character of Satan as expressed in *Paradise Lost*. It is a mistake to suppose that he could ever have been intended for the popular personification of evil. . . . Milton's Devil as a moral being is as far superior to his God as one who perseveres in some purpose, which he has conceived to be excellent, in spite of adversity and torture, is to one who in the cold security of undoubted triumph inflicts the most horrible revenge upon his enemy . . . with the alleged design of exasperating him to deserve new torments.'[16]

3. Towards the end of the eighteenth century Milton's Satan transfused with his own sinister charm the traditional type of generous outlaw or sublime criminal.[17] Schiller's *Räuber* Karl Moor (1781) is an angel-outlaw in the manner of Milton's and of those of his German imitator Klopstock; he had in him the stuff of a Brutus, but unfavourable circumstances had made him into a Catiline. Schiller also, following Milton's example, speaks of the 'majesty' of his Robber, of 'the honourable malefactor, the majestic monster' (*Ungeheuer mit Majestät*). In a scene which was suppressed later Karl Moor says to Spiegelberg:

'I do not know, Maurice, if you have read Milton. He who could not endure that another should be above him, and who dared to challenge the Almighty to a duel, was he not an extraordinary genius? He had encountered the Invincible One, and although in defeat he exhausted all his forces, he was not humiliated; eternally, even to the present day, he makes new efforts, and every blow falls back again on his own head, yet still he is not humiliated. . . . An intelligent mind, which neglects mean duties for a more exalted purpose, will be eternally unhappy, whereas the knave who has betrayed his friend and fled before his enemy ascends to Heaven, thanks to an opportune little sigh of repentance. Who would not prefer to roast in the furnace of Belial with Borgia and Catiline, rather than sit up above at table with that vulgar ass? It is he at whose name our gossips make the sign of the cross.'

Karl Moor is compared to 'that first wicked leader who urged thousands of innocent angels into the fire of revolt and dragged them with him into the deep abyss of damnation' (ii. 3); he proclaims himself to be (iii. 2) 'a howling Abaddon among the flowers of a happy world' (here the allusion is to Klopstock's poem *Messias*); Amalie throws herself on his neck (v. 2) crying 'Assassin! Demon! I cannot do without you, angel!',[18] and Karl exclaims, 'See, see, the sons of light weep in the arms of a weeping Demon'.[19] From crime to crime Karl rushes into the abyss of despair,[20] till finally the harmony of the moral law is re-established in the Christian ending: through pain the robber is brought back to the path of sacrifice and virtue.[21]

4. Rebels in the grand manner, grandsons of Milton's Satan and brothers of Schiller's Robber, begin to inhabit the picturesque, Gothicized backgrounds of the English 'tales of terror' towards the end of the eighteenth century. The little figures of banditti, which formed pleasing decorative details in the landscapes of the Salvator Rosa school then in fashion, came to life in the writings of Mrs. Ann Radcliffe, 'the Shakespeare of romance writers', and took on gigantic and Satanic proportions, becowled and sinister as Goya's bogeys. Montoni, the scoundrel and adventurer of the *Mysteries of Udolpho* (1794), takes pleasure in the violent exercise of his passions; the difficulties and storms of life which ruin the happiness of others stimulate and strengthen all the energies of his mind.

Mrs. Radcliffe's masterpiece is the character of Schedoni in *The Italian, or the Confessional of the Black Penitents* (1797). At that time the chief source of mysterious crimes (that source of evil actions in which the British public is forced to believe by its innate Manicheism, whether it be a Machiavellian monster, as in the Elizabethan period, or a double-dyed criminal, as in the detective novels of to-day) was to be found in the Spanish and Italian Inquisition. Illuminism had pointed to the Roman

Catholic monk as an infamy which must be crushed, and the recent campaign of the states of Europe against the Society of Jesus had disclosed a sinister background of material interests. Schedoni, therefore, is a monk; when he comes on the scene he appears as a man of unknown origin, but suspected to be of exalted birth and decayed fortunes. Severe reserve, unconquerable silence, love of solitude, and frequent penances, were interpreted by some as the effect of misfortunes preying upon a haughty and disordered spirit, by others as the consequence of some hideous crime which filled his troubled conscience with remorse.

'His figure was striking . . . it was tall, and, though extremely thin, his limbs were large and uncouth, and as he stalked along, wrapt in the black garments of his order, there was something terrible in its air; something almost superhuman. His cowl, too, as it threw a shade over the livid paleness of his face, encreased its severe character, and gave an effect to his large melancholy eye, which approached to horror. His was not the melancholy of a sensible and wounded heart, but apparently that of a gloomy and ferocious disposition. There was something in his physiognomy extremely singular, and that cannot easily be defined. It bore the traces of many passions, which seemed to have fixed the features they no longer animated. An habitual gloom and severity prevailed over the deep lines of his countenance; and his eyes were so piercing that they seemed to penetrate, at a single glance, into the hearts of men, and to read their most secret thoughts; few persons could support their scrutiny, or even endure to meet them twice.'

Certain qualities can be noticed here which were destined to recur insistently in the Fatal Men of the Romantics: mysterious (but conjectured to be exalted) origin, traces of burnt-out passions, suspicion of a ghastly guilt, melancholy habits, pale face, unforgettable eyes. Decidedly there is something of Milton's Satan in this monk, whose 'whole air and attitudes exhibited the wild energy of something not of this earth'. There is something also of Shakespeare's King John (iv. 2):

> The image of a wicked heinous fault
> Lives in his eye; that close aspect of his
> Does show the mood of a much troubled breast.

His rare smiles are as the smiles of Cassius (*Julius Caesar*, I. ii):

> Seldom he smiles, and smiles in such a sort
> As if he mock'd himself and scorn'd his spirit
> That could be mov'd to smile at any thing.

The horror he inspires is not unaccompanied by a certain degree of pity, as in the case of Richard III (v. 3):

> . . . There is no creature loves me;
> And if I die, no soul shall pity me:
> Nay, wherefore should they, since that I myself
> Find in myself no pity to myself?[22]

In other ways Schedoni is reminiscent of the Machiavellians and Jesuits who had been among the abiding features of the English theatre of the seventeenth century:[23]

'He cared not for truth, nor sought it by bold and broad argument, but loved to exert the wily cunning of his nature in hunting it through artificial perplexities. At length, from a habit of intricacy and suspicion, his vitiated mind could receive nothing for truth, which was simple and easily comprehended. . . . Notwithstanding all this gloom and austerity, some rare occasions of interest had called forth a character upon his countenance entirely different; and he could adapt himself to the tempers and passions of persons, whom he wished to conciliate, with astonishing facility, and generally with complete triumph.'

5. It is possible that the influence of *The Monk*, by Matthew Gregory Lewis, published the year before, in 1796,[23A] had also contributed towards the formation of the character of Schedoni. I shall have occasion later on to speak of this immensely successful novel; in the meantime let me point out that it has been noticed that both Schedoni and Lewis's monk Ambrosio are first seen in the full odour of sanctity, then commit the most horrible crimes, and both end as victims of the Inquisition. Lewis, in fact, did little but clothe in a monastic habit a figure which already existed—existed, indeed, actually in Mrs. Radcliffe's own repertory, for Lewis asserts[24] that he had read with enthusiasm *The Mysteries of Udolpho* on their first appearing:* now the character of Montoni in *The Mysteries of Udolpho* already foreshadowed that of the monk Ambrosio.

Lewis, on the other hand, was acquainted with the German villains put into circulation by the 'Stürmer und Dränger', following the example of Schiller's *Räuber*; in his *Bravo of Venice* (1805) he was merely translating *Aballino, der grosse Bandit*, by Heinrich Zschokke (1794). This Schilleresque romance by Zschokke—later converted into a play—played no little part (in Lamartelière's version, 1801) in making known in France the figure of the 'noble brigand'; it contained, among other things, one curious detail which Sue and other writers of the *roman-feuilleton* did not forget, that of the protagonist's double personality.

Abellino is the assumed name under which an unfortunate nobleman, Flodoardo, becomes a brigand. As Flodoardo he courts the niece of the Doge, Rosamunde, and gives up the brigands to justice; as Abellino he pretends to put himself at the service of the enemies of Venice, and gets rid of the Doge's friends and counsellors. Finally the Doge consents to give his niece's hand to Flodoardo if the latter can deliver up to him within twenty-four hours Abellino, dead or alive. At the hour agreed upon Flodoardo reveals the double part he has played, unmasks the enemies of the Republic, produces the Doge's friends safe and sound, and obtains the hand of Rosamunde. There is no happy ending, however, to *Jean Sbogar*, the novel by Charles Nodier (1818), who, following in Zschokke's footsteps, also confers double personality upon his bandit, who in many respects resembles the bandits of Byron.[25]

6. It is of these latter that we must now speak, since it was Byron who brought to perfection the rebel type, remote descendant of Milton's Satan.

Milton's type of Satan is immediately recognizable in the shrewd portrait of Byron outlined by the Earl of Lovelace in *Astarte*, the first book to throw light on the mystery of the life of his grandfather the poet.[26]

'He had a fancy for some Oriental legends of pre-existence, and in his conversation and poetry took up the part of a fallen or exiled being, expelled from heaven, or sentenced to a new avatar on earth for some crime, existing under a curse, predoomed to a fate really fixed by himself in his own mind, but which he seemed determined to fulfil. At times this dramatic imagination resembled a delusion;

he would play at being mad, and gradually get more and more serious, as if he believed himself to be destined to wreck his own life and that of everyone near him.'

This is a sketch which reproduces in dim outline the sombre portrait of his idealized self drawn by Byron in three famous stanzas of *Lara* (Canto I, xvii–xix):

> In him inexplicably mix'd appear'd
> Much to be loved and hated, sought and feared;
> Opinion varying o'er his hidden lot,
> In praise or railing ne'er his name forgot:
> His silence form'd a theme for others' prate—
> They guess'd, they gazed, they fain would know his fate.
> What had he been? what was he, thus unknown,
> Who walk'd their world, his lineage only known?
> A hater of his kind? yet some would say,
> With them he could seem gay amidst the gay;[27]
> But own'd that smile, if oft observed and near,
> Waned in its mirth, and wither'd to a sneer;
> That smile might reach his lip, but pass'd not by,
> None e'er could trace its laughter to his eye:
> Yet there was softness too in his regard,
> At times, a heart as not by nature hard,
> But once perceived, his spirit seem'd to chide
> Such weakness, as unworthy of its pride,
> And steel'd itself, as scorning to redeem
> One doubt from others' half withheld esteem;[28]
> In self-inflicted penance of a breast
> Which tenderness might once have wrung from rest;
> In vigilance of grief that would compel
> The soul to hate for having loved too well.
>
> There was in him a vital scorn of all:
> As if the worst had fall'n which could befall,
> He stood a stranger in this breathing world,
> An erring spirit from another hurl'd;
> A thing of dark imaginings, that shaped
> By choice the perils he by chance escaped;
> But 'scaped in vain, for in their memory yet
> His mind would half exult and half regret:
> With more capacity for love than earth
> Bestows on most of mortal mould and birth,
> His early dreams of good outstripp'd the truth,
> And troubled manhood follow'd baffled youth;

With thought of years in phantom chase misspent,
And wasted powers for better purpose lent;[29]
And fiery passions that had pour'd their wrath
In hurried desolation o'er his path,[30]
And left the better feelings all at strife
In wild reflection o'er his stormy life;
But haughty still, and loth himself to blame,
He call'd on Nature's self to share the shame,
And charged all faults upon the fleshly form
She gave to clog the soul, and feast the worm;
Till he at last confounded good and ill,
And half mistook for fate the acts of will:
Too high for common selfishness, he could
At times resign his own for others' good,
But not in pity, not because he ought,
But in some strange perversity of thought,
That sway'd him onward with a secret pride
To do what few or none would do beside;
And this same impulse would, in tempting time,
Mislead his spirit equally to crime;
So much he soar'd beyond, or sunk beneath,
The men with whom he felt condemn'd to breathe,
And long'd by good or ill to separate
Himself from all who shared his mortal state;
His mind abhorring this, had fix'd her throne
Far from the world, in regions of her own;
Thus coldly passing all that pass'd below,
His blood in temperate seeming now would flow:
Ah! happier if it ne'er with guilt had glow'd,
But ever in that icy smoothness flow'd!
'Tis true, with other men their path he walk'd,
And like the rest in seeming did and talk'd,
Nor outraged Reason's rules by flaw nor start,
His madness was not of the head, but heart;
And rarely wander'd in his speech, or drew
His thoughts so forth as to offend the view.

With all that chilling mystery of mien,
And seeming gladness to remain unseen,
He had (if 'twere not nature's boon) an art
Of fixing memory on another's heart:
It was not love perchance, nor hate, nor aught
That words can image to express the thought;

> But they who saw him did not see in vain,
> And once beheld, would ask of him again:
> And those to whom he spake remember'd well,
> And on the words, however light, would dwell:
> None knew nor how, nor why, but he entwined
> Himself perforce around the hearer's mind;
> There he was stamp'd, in liking, or in hate,
> If greeted once; however brief the date
> That friendship, pity, or aversion knew,
> Still there within the inmost thought he grew
> You could not penetrate his soul, but found,
> Despite your wonder, to your own he wound;
> His presence haunted still; and from the breast
> He forced an all unwilling interest:
> Vain was the struggle in that mental net,
> His spirit seem'd to dare you to forget![31]

The Corsair and the Giaour have the same characteristics. The Corsair has a pale, high forehead, and hides dark passions beneath an appearance of calm. The furrows of his face and his frequent change of colour attract the eye and at the same time leave it bewildered,

> As if within that murkiness of mind
> Work'd feelings fearful, and yet undefined.

But no one knows exactly what his secret may be.

> Too close inquiry his stern glance would quell.
> There breathe but few whose aspect might defy
> The full encounter of his searching eye.
>
> .   .   .   .   .   .
>
> There was a laughing Devil in his sneer,
> That raised emotions both of rage and fear;
> And where his frown of hatred darkly fell,
> Hope withering fled, and Mercy sigh'd farewell![32]

Finally the Giaour, the first in order of time of these Byronic heroes, shows plainly his relationship with Mrs. Radcliffe's Schedoni. The Giaour, who by his passion has indirectly caused the death of Leila, hides his sinister past beneath a monk's gown.

> 'How name ye yon lone Caloyer?
> His features I have scann'd before
> In mine own land: 'tis many a year,
> Since, dashing by the lonely shore,

I saw him urge as fleet a steed
As ever served a horseman's need.
But once I saw that face, yet then
It was so mark'd with inward pain,
I could not pass it by again;
It breathes the same dark spirit now,
As death were stamp'd upon his brow.'

' 'Tis twice three years at summer tide
Since first among our freres he came;
And here it soothes him to abide
For some dark deed he will not name. . . .'

.   .   .   .

Dark and unearthly is the scowl
That glares beneath his dusky cowl.
The flash of that dilating eye
Reveals too much of times gone by;
Though varying, indistinct its hue,
Oft will his glance the gazer rue,
For in it lurks that nameless spell,
Which speaks, itself unspeakable,
A spirit yet unquell'd and high,
That claims and keeps ascendancy;
And like a bird whose pinions quake,
But cannot fly the gazing snake,
Will others quail beneath his look,
Nor 'scape the glance they scarce can brook.
From him the half-affrighted Friar
When met alone would fain retire,
As if that eye and bitter smile
Transferr'd to others fear and guile:
Not oft to smile descendeth he,
And when he doth 'tis sad to see
That he but mocks at Misery.
How that pale lip will curl and quiver!
Then fix once more as if for ever;
As if his sorrow or disdain
Forbade him e'er to smile again.
Well were it so—such ghastly mirth
From joyaunce ne'er derived its birth.
But sadder still it were to trace
What once were feelings in that face:

Time hath not yet the features fix'd,
But brighter traits with evil mix'd;
And there are hues not always faded,
Which speak a mind not all degraded
Even by the crimes through which it waded:
The common crowd but see the gloom
Of wayward deeds, and fitting doom;
The close observer can espy
A noble soul, and lineage high:
Alas! though both bestow'd in vain,
Which Grief could change, and Guilt could stain,
It was no vulgar tenement
To which such lofty gifts were lent,
And still with little less than dread
On such the sight is riveted.

The pale face furrowed by an ancient grief, the rare
Satanic smile, the traces of obscured nobility ('a noble soul
and lineage high') worthy of a better fate—Byron might
be said to have derived all these characteristics, by an
almost slavish imitation, from Mrs. Radcliffe.

7. The relationship is less obvious between Byron's
heroes and another criminal figure, Zeluco, in the novel of
the same name by John Moore (1786), in spite of the fact
that this was one of the books of which Byron was most
fond as a child, and that in the preface to *Childe Harold* he
expressly declares that the character of Harold was intended to develop in the successive cantos like that of 'a
modern Timon', and 'perhaps' of 'a poetical Zeluco'. But
Zeluco is lacking in the fundamental characteristic of the
heroes of Schiller, Mrs. Radcliffe, and Byron—the quality
of a kind of fallen angel. Zeluco is made after the pattern,
not so much of Milton's Satan, as of the villains of Elizabethan tradition. He is an Iago who has absorbed certain
of the characteristics of Othello (his very name perhaps
recalls the word ζῆλος, Jealousy) as well as those of
Richardson's Lovelace. Jealous of Laura, the young German girl whom he has married out of revenge, he wrongly
suspects that his own son is the fruit of an incestuous love
between her and her brother, and in an access of Othello-
like rage, strangles the child with the same ease with
which, as a boy, he had squeezed to death a sparrow.

There is nothing mysterious or fatal about this villain, who moves in a conventional middle-class world, without subtleties or thrills. Zeluco has only one virtue, courage. Otherwise he is ambitious, cruel, and above all—a quality particularly repellent to Byron—a hypocrite. Sicilian by birth, Zeluco is a distant offshoot of the Elizabethan monsters produced in hatred against the Latin world by the imagination of Puritans; he does not possess that mixture of qualities which makes the villains of the 'tales of terror' on the one hand descendants of Lucifer and, on the other, precursors of the Romantic hero. It is true, however, that certain external resemblances to the circumstances of his own life must have made a profound impression on Byron, for Zeluco also had lost his father at an early age and had given precocious signs of the violence of his temper, 'as inflammable as gunpowder, bursting into flashes of rage at the slightest touch of provocation'.

8. Even if there can be no doubt of the Anglo-Germanic origin of the colours used by Byron for his portrait of the bandit-hero, it is, however, quite possible that the poet's hand was guided in his design by Chateaubriand. It is difficult to calculate exactly how much Byron owed to him. French critics, basing their judgement on the words of the *Mémoires d'outre-tombe* (repeated in the *Essai sur la littérature anglaise*), tend to exaggerate the amount of this debt. Byron's silence on the subject of Chateaubriand gives the whole question a curious similarity to that other debatable question of Chaucer's knowledge of the *Decameron*.

'S'il était vrai que René entrât pour quelque chose dans le fond du personnage unique mis en scène sous des noms divers dans Childe-Harold, Conrad, Lara, Manfred, le Giaour; si par hasard lord Byron m'avait fait vivre de sa vie, il aurait donc eu la faiblesse de ne jamais me nommer? J'étais donc un de ces pères qu'on renie quand on est arrivé au pouvoir?'

Thus, among other remarks, wrote the author of *René*.[33]

The question, at any rate, is limited to this latter work, for any attempt to see in Harold's pilgrimage an imitation of the *Itinéraire* (1811)—an idea which Chateaubriand himself suggests and which Reynaud[34] without hesitation develops—does not bear examination of the facts. Apart from the fact that the publication of the *Itinéraire* was later than Byron's own journey (which started in 1809) and the composition of the first cantos of *Childe Harold*, this journey, in spite of Byron's various plans, some more, some less ambitious, resolved itself in the end into the Grand Tour which it was the usual custom for Englishmen of rank to take for the completion of their education.[35] Therefore the argument of the similarity between Harold's and René's journey loses a good deal of its force; the latter also had wandered and meditated among the ruins of the ancient world. Even though there are many similar characteristics—ennui, love of solitude, a secret which gnaws the heart, voluntary exile[36]—it must on the other hand be remembered that some of these qualities had become the common inheritance of growing Romanticism.[37] It may sometimes be more exact to speak of a relationship of ideas arising from the same sources, rather than of actual imitation. On the subject of Chateaubriand's claim that Byron had imitated him, Sainte-Beuve remarks:[38]

'Il y a là de l'enfantillage vraiment. Ces grands poètes n'ont pas eu besoin de s'imiter l'un l'autre; ils ont trouvé en eux-mêmes et dans l'air du siècle une inspiration suffisante qu'ils ont chacun appropriée et figurée à leur manière, en y mettant le cachet de leur talent et de leur égoïsme. Tous ces types sont éclos en Allemagne, en Angleterre, en France, sous un même souffle, sous un même courant atmosphérique général qui tenait à l'état du monde à ce moment.'

It would be much easier to prove had it been possible for Byron to have seen *Les Natchez*, but this was not published until after his death. In this, much more than in *René*, Chateaubriand expatiates on the fatality which pursues his hero:

'Aimer et souffrir était la double fatalité qu'il imposait à quiconque s'approchait de sa personne. Jeté dans le monde comme un grand malheur, sa pernicieuse influence s'étendait aux êtres environnants. . . . Tout lui devenait fatal, même le bonheur.'[39]

After he is dead René threatens to become a vampire—

quite in accordance with one of the developments of the Byronic hero, of which I shall have to speak later:

'Le génie fatal de René poursuivit encore Céluta, comme ces fantômes nocturnes qui vivent du sang des mortels.'[40]

Byron never saw these passages, and if his work contains some that are similar,[41] it can only be due to the common background from which both drew their inspiration. There are some who even go so far as to say that Byron's incest with his half-sister was a plagiarism, because Byron committed in reality the crime of which René had conceived the horrible possibility.[42] But the subject of incest is by no means confined to Chateaubriand.[43] We shall see, incidentally, how important a part it played in the 'tales of terror', whose influence on Byron is obvious. Besides, Chateaubriand himself was an admirer of Milton's Satan, whom he defined as 'une des conceptions les plus sublimes et les plus pathétiques qui soient jamais sorties du cerveau d'un poète',[44] though the attitude of Satanic defiance, an important quality in Byron and in the villain-heroes of the 'tales of terror', is not to be found in René, who has a stronger affinity with Werther: he accepts his fatal quality as a misfortune, possesses the evil eye, and never ceases to ask pardon for the disasters which his presence brings.[45]

9. The Giaour, the Corsair, and Lara, therefore, derive not so much from Zeluco and René as from Mrs. Radcliffe's Schedoni. From Schedoni we can go back to Milton's Satan, from Milton's Satan to the Satan of Marino, and finally discover the charm of the terrible, demoniac eyes of all these haunted creatures contained in a nutshell in the line

Negli occhi, ove mestizia alberga e morte,

which Marino took, with slight alterations, from a line of Tasso. Is it all a mere game of literary decantation?

It is quite possible that Mrs. Radcliffe drew the figure of the sinister monk Schedoni mainly from her own study of the books which, as a literary blue-stocking, she used to read: but Byron's case is more complex. Did he not, in any case, declare that 'the Corsair was written con amore,

and much from *existence*'?⁴⁶ Given the vanity of his own
nature, what is more probable than that he should have
deliberately modelled himself upon the figure of the accursed angel? Who can be sure that he may not have
studied every detail in front of a mirror, even to the
terrible oblique look with which he frightened people,
particularly his mistresses? But however artificial the
methods by which Byron cultivated his character of Fatal
Man, he possessed by nature not only 'le physique du
rôle', but also the psychological tendency handed down to
him from a long chain of ancestors who conformed more
or less to the type of the 'noble ruffian'.

Cave a signatis: in his very physical deformity Byron
saw the sign of his destiny. To what point, as an actor, he
was convinced by his own role it is impossible to say, but
he was always sincere in feeling himself 'a marked man',
stamped with a sign among ordinary mortals, 'an outlaw'.
Does the whole Byronic legend then stand on no firmer a
pedestal than a club foot? A club foot, hence the *besoin de
la fatalité*. . . .

The question is more complicated than that. Yet,
though not denying the importance of small matters, one
would not wish to reduce Byron to the level of the man
who, having received a present of a gold-topped stick, felt
it his duty to put the rest of his costume in harmony with
it, and so ran up debts, was ruined, and finished up with
his corpse at the Morgue. Let us at any rate consider the
conclusion of du Bos as being justified:⁴⁷

'Il semble qu'il soit né blasé, et qu'il ne puisse sentir vraiment
que hors la loi. Aussi, lorsqu'on envisage comme factices, comme
conventionnels les innombrables portraits que Byron a tracés de
lui-même sous la figure de l'*outlaw*, on commet à son sujet le con-
tresens irréparable, car ces portraits émanent, remontent tous de
la couche la plus profonde de sa sincérité. Dans la loi, il n'éprouve
rien; hors la loi, il sent à fond.'

10. It was in transgression that Byron found his own
life-rhythm. Du Bos (p. 207) very aptly recalls the title of
one of the *Diaboliques* of Barbey d'Aurevilly—*Le Bonheur
dans le crime*. It suffices here to sum up the case again—
the subject is a very trite one, and to-day, since the books

of Ethel Colburn Mayne, du Bos, and Maurois, there is
no more room for controversy—by saying that Byron
sought in incest a spice for love ('great is their love who
love in sin and fear': *Heaven and Earth*, line 67),[48] and that
he required the feeling of guilt to arouse in him the
phenomena of the moral sense, and the feeling of fatality
in order to appreciate the flow of life.

'Le fonds byronien est bien cette mélancolie innée, due peut-être
à un cœur, si je puis ainsi m'exprimer, en soi statique qui, pour
percevoir ses battements, a besoin que ceux-ci s'accélèrent jusqu'à
la folie.'

I think that du Bos has here (p. 84) found the key to
Byron's character. It seems a paradox, and yet the most
genuine thing that this monster of energy—if ever there
was one—possessed, was the force of inertia. The function which violent exercise and a drastic régime fulfilled
for him physically, checking his tendency to grow fat, was
fulfilled for his moral nature, which was naturally idle, by
tumultuous emotions.[49] 'Passion is the element in which
we live: without it we but vegetate', said Byron in his
mature years to Lady Blessington[50]—much in the manner
of Vauvenargues ('une vie sans passions ressemble bien à
la mort'), and of Chamfort ('les passions font vivre
l'homme, la sagesse le fait seulement durer').[51] He had to
key up his life to such a high state of tension in order to
make it yield him anything, that when it came to the post-
mortem it was found that both brain and heart showed
signs of very advanced age: the sutures of the brain were
entirely obliterated and the heart bore signs of incipient
ossification. Yet Byron was only thirty-six. His blood had
to boil like lava for him to feel it beating in his pulses: did
not the Giaour say of his own blood

> But mine was like the lava flood
> That boils in Ætna's breast of flame?

Paroxysm became his natural atmosphere; hence the
jarring and clamorous discords which strike one in so
many of his productions. This necessity of forcing
the tones may account for Byron's behaviour during
what he called his 'treacle-moon'. His conduct towards

his wife seems to have been of a moral cruelty so exceptional as to make one for a moment doubt the reliability of the historical evidence. But one quickly comes to see that no episode in Byron's life is more true to type than this. The actual story of this episode must be read in Ethel Colburn Mayne's *The Life and Letters of Anne Isabella, Lady Noel Byron*,[52] for which Miss Colburn Mayne was enabled to consult and draw upon private records in the possession of Byron's descendants.

Byron puts forward heroic arguments in order to extract sensations from marriage. 'The great object of life is sensation, to feel that we exist, even though in pain', he had written to his future wife,[53] who, though she might have been forewarned by it, was impelled by love and protective instinct towards her ambitious and rather puerile attempt to reform the poet. The first thing Byron said to her after the wedding ceremony was that it was now too late, that Annabella could have saved him if she had accepted him the first time he had asked for her hand, but that now there was no remedy: something irreparable had happened, Annabella would realize that she had married a devil, because he could only hate her: they were a damned and accursed pair. Even this was not enough. Annabella must be made to believe that the marriage was the result of a pique, of a bet, in which the woman had been treated as a mere object. Had Annabella refused Byron's hand the first time? Byron had plotted with Lady Melbourne to punish her stubbornness. Now he held her in his power, and he would make her feel it. At the moment of going to bed, Byron asked his wife if she intended to sleep in the same bed with him: 'I hate sleeping with any woman, but you may if you choose.' After all, provided she were young, he went on, one woman was as good as another. . . . In the middle of the night Annabella heard her husband cry out: 'Good God, I am surely in Hell!' The fire in the grate shone through the red curtains of the marriage bed. Profiting by his youthful reading of *Zeluco*, John Moore's romance, Byron entertained his wife on the means employed by that monster to get rid of his own child. And he concluded: 'I shall strangle ours.' Later, when Anna-

bella was suffering the pains of childbirth, Byron told her
that he hoped she would perish together with her baby,
and when the child was born, the first thing he asked on
coming into the room was 'The child *was* born dead,
wasn't it?'

But the most subtle torture, the torture which was to
wring the most exquisite cry of anguish from its victim,
was this: Byron, by every kind of allusion and insinuation,
sought to instil into Annabella the suspicion of his incest
with Augusta, his 'terrible' secret. When Augusta was
living under the same roof, Annabella must be given to
understand that Medora was Byron's daughter, and must
be convinced that Augusta was still having intercourse
with him (which was not true). Byron felt a perverse joy
at the simultaneous presence of the two women, with all
the amusement of innuendoes and double meanings which
it afforded him, and the continual sensation of hanging
over the edge of an abyss.[54] Annabella was beside herself
with desperation, to the point of feeling herself driven to
kill Augusta:[55] the thought of imminent catastrophe filled
Byron with exultation:

> . . . There was that in my spirit ever
> Which shaped out for itself some great reverse.[56]

Compared with these moral tortures his ostentation of
physical ferocity seems a mere childish game, but Byron
used to pace through the house with ruthless steps, armed
with daggers and pistols, in imitation of the fifth Lord
Byron, the 'Wicked Lord'. Like Capaneo, like Satan,
Byron wished to experience the feeling of being struck
with full force by the vengeance of Heaven.[57] He sought
to measure the depth of his own guilt in Annabella's
anguish, in Augusta's remorse. However, the material
responded only imperfectly to the artist's intention:
Augusta was amoral and therefore proof against the sense
of sin, and his wife, that patient Griselda, was a practical
character and, although in love with him, would never
commit a folly of the kind for which Caroline Lamb,
Byron's first *maîtresse en titre*, became so celebrated.
Byron alternated brutality with blandishment and made
his tortures more agonizing by contrast; but Annabella

never rose to the pitch of despair which he desired and did not lend herself to the melodrama of fatality. She was like a sailor who persists in lowering the lifeboats instead of helping to flood the hold, as the correct playing of the part assigned to her required, and Byron strove in vain to give orders to sink the ship immediately.

There were touches of comedy in this gloomy tragedy of Byron's life, whose scene was laid in a moral torture-chamber. Byron's moral sense functioned only in the exceptional conditions of a crisis, and it was only in the painful functioning of that moral sense that he found the gratification of his particular form of pleasure—*le bonheur dans le crime*. To destroy oneself and to destroy others:

> My embrace was fatal
>
> . . . .
>
> I loved her, and destroy'd her.[58]

It may be claimed that this version of Byron's married life is based mainly on his wife's statements. But Lady Byron's truthfulness was recognized by every one, and by no one more fully and explicitly than by Byron himself. Nor were Lady Byron's statements disfigured by hatred, since Annabella never came to hate her husband; on the other hand, she sought to educate her daughter Ada to respect whatever was noble in her father. Into her account of their married relations Annabella introduced no distortion of truth except the inevitable one of her own point of view. A rather professorial and too self-conscious character, isolated in a form of narcissism different from Byron's, Annabella ended by realizing, at the age of forty, that '*not to see things as they are* is then my great intellectual defect'.[59] She saw only one side of Byron. But the poet's words and deeds during their married life, in whatever way they are regarded, do not admit of a favourable interpretation. Perhaps he wished to joke, but joking in such circumstances amounts to cruelty.

11. What Manfred said of Astarte ('I loved her, and destroy'd her'), what Byron wished to be able to say of Augusta and of Annabella (see the Incantation in *Manfred*), was to become the motto of the 'fatal' heroes of Romantic literature. They diffuse all round them the

curse which weighs upon their destiny, they blast, like
the simoon, those who have the misfortune to meet with
them (the image is from *Manfred*, iii. 1); they destroy
themselves, and destroy the unlucky women who come
within their orbit. Their relations with their mistresses
are those of an incubus-devil with his victim. Byron
realizes the extreme type of Fatal Man described by
Schiller in the *Räuber*[60] and by Chateaubriand in *René*.[61]

The following are some of the innumerable Fatal Men
who came into existence on the pattern of the Byronic
hero. Jean Sbogar, the nobleman-bandit of Charles Nodier
(1818), exercises upon Antonia the spell of an obsession.
In a dream she feels that a lost soul is prowling round her
house, and has glimpses of a cruel eye which watches her
night and day. Dumas' Antony, the most popular of the
'fatal' rebels, makes the following comment upon himself
in the lines (written in 1829) which serve as a preface to
the play:

> Que de fois tu m'as dit, aux heures du délire,
> Quand mon front tout-à-coup devenait soucieux:
> Sur ta bouche pourquoi cet effrayant sourire?
> Pourquoi ces larmes dans tes yeux?
>
> . . . .
>
> Malheur! malheur à moi que le ciel en ce monde
> A jeté comme un hôte à ses lois étranger;
> A moi qui ne sais pas, dans ma douleur profonde,
> Souffrir longtemps sans me venger!
>
> Malheur! . . . car une voix qui n'a rien de la terre
> M'a dit: Pour ton bonheur, c'est sa mort qu'il te faut!
> Et cette voix m'a fait comprendre le mystère
> Et du meurtre et de l'échafaud.
>
> Viens donc, ange du mal, dont la voix me convie,
> Car il est des instants où si je te voyais,
> Je pourrais pour ton sang t'abandonner ma vie
> Et mon âme . . . si j'y croyais!

But the worthy Dumas, who adopted the idea of the
Fatal Man at a stage when it is difficult to distinguish between the Schilleresque and the Byronic elements,[62] makes
him stab Adèle out of jealousy (as Karl Moor stabbed
Amalie in the *Räuber*): he treats as a trite subject of

ordinary passion,[63] such as any normal man can understand, that which in Byron was a subtly perverse pleasure
in destruction. For, once a fashion is launched, the
majority imitate its external aspects without understanding
the spirit which originated it.

12. The same can be said of Vampirism, and for this
fashion also Byron was largely responsible.

In *The Giaour* (1813) Byron mentions vampires;[64]
three years later at Geneva, in company with Shelley, Dr.
Polidori, and M. G. Lewis, he read some German ghost-
stories and invited his friends each to write one. Thus
Mrs. Shelley conceived *Frankenstein*, and Byron composed
part of a 'tale of terror' which he had had in mind to write
for some time (it was published in 1819 as *A Fragment*). Dr.
Polidori elaborated this sketch, weaving into it suggestions
from *Glenarvon*, the autobiographical novel in which Lady
Caroline Lamb (1816) had represented Byron as the per-
fidious Ruthven Glenarvon, who was fatal to his mistresses
and was finally carried away by the devil, who for the
occasion assumed the shape of the victims' ghosts. In
April 1819 Polidori's macabre tale, *The Vampire*, appeared in the *New Monthly Magazine* under Byron's name,
through a misunderstanding on the part of the editor of
the review, and Goethe, swallowing it whole, declared it to
be the best thing the poet had written (Goethe himself, in
the *Braut von Korinth*, 1797, had been the first to give
literary form to the fearsome vampire legends which had
arisen in Illyria in the eighteenth century).[65] The hero of
Polidori's *Vampire* is a young libertine, Lord Ruthwen,
who is killed in Greece and becomes a vampire, seduces
the sister of his friend Aubrey and suffocates her during
the night which follows their wedding.[66] A love-crime
becomes an integral part of vampirism, though often in
forms so far removed as to obscure the inner sense of the
gruesome legend. Thus in *Melmoth the Wanderer*, by
Maturin (1820), the hero, who is a kind of Wandering
Jew crossed with Byronic vampire ('ce pâle et ennuyé
Melmoth', Baudelaire called him) interrupts a wedding
feast and terrifies everybody with the horrible fascination
of his preternatural glare: soon after the bride dies and the

bridegroom goes mad. Thus also in *Smarra*, by Nodier (1821), Smarra, the incubus-devil, puts to death, after a sinister banquet, the lovers Polémon and Myrrhé; Lorenzo is accused of the crime, and his head, cut off by the executioner, 'mord le bois humecté de son sang fraîchement répandu'.

Mérimée—who, notwithstanding his classic genius, had access to the underground labyrinths of the *frénétique* Romanticism which came into fashion about 1820—conferred upon his *Vampire* (in *La Guzla*, written in 1825 or 1826) all the perverse charm of a Byronic hero. Mérimée's vampire, like Maturin's Melmoth, is a hero fatal to himself and to those around him; his love is accursed; he drags to destruction the woman to whom he becomes attached:

'Qui pourrait éviter la fascination de son regard?... Sa bouche est sanglante et sourit comme celle d'un homme endormi et tour-menté d'un amour hideux.'

The lovely Sophie, who for material motives has re-jected her betrothed and married a rich man, is attacked on the threshold of the nuptial chamber by the ghost of the betrothed, who has committed suicide and who now bites her in the throat (*La Belle Sophie*). In *Cara-Ali le vampire* the kidnapper of the maiden is killed while crossing a river; he gives her a talisman which, claiming to make her husband potent, will actually destroy him—a Romantic version of the ancient legend of Nessus and Deianeira.

'Le Vampire épouvantera de son horrible amour les songes de toutes les femmes; et bientôt, sans doute, ce monstre encore exhumé prêtera son masque immobile, sa voix sépulcrale, son œil d'un gris mort... tout cet attirail de mélodrame à la Melpomène des boule-vards; et quel succès, alors, ne lui est pas réservé!'

Nodier, in these lines, correctly interpreted the taste of the period.[67] We shall see how in the second half of the nineteenth century the vampire becomes a woman, as in Goethe's ballad; but in the first part of the century the fatal, cruel lover is invariably a man; and, apart from reasons of tradition or race (the stronger sex remained such, not only in name, till the time of the Decadence, when, as will be seen, the roles appeared to be reversed) there is no doubt that the sinister charm of the Byronic hero was an influence in this direction. The vampire—just as, previously, the noble bandit—took on a Byronic colour. Refined by the touch of Byron's hand, Schiller's Robber was eventually to become Jean Sbogar, the polyglot brigand, musician and painter, pale and melancholy, lover of solitude and cemeteries, who, as though to relieve the terrible pain which devastates him behind his lofty, disdainful brow, frequently passes his hand, 'blanche, délicate et féminine', through his fair hair. Born under an unlucky star, convinced that 'Dieu n'avait rien fait pour lui', destined to suffer in solitude his eternal punishment, this bandit, whose fascinating eye pursues Antonia even in her sleep, is a close relation to the vampire of the Romantics, who naturally has nothing whatever to do with the werewolf of the popular Serbo-Croatian legend.

13. It would be a waste of time to pass in review all the different incarnations of the Byronic Fatal Man during the Romantic period: the subject has been often discussed and offers no further interest for research. It is, however, worth remarking that, as humanitarian ideas penetrated more and more into literature, the bandit finished by definitely taking on the character already hinted at by Schiller and Zschokke—becoming, in fact, a secret benefactor, a nobleman with a dark past who devotes himself to a noble ideal, employs bandits as unconscious instruments of justice, and dreams of perfecting the world by committing crimes.

The Byronic heroes of the *romans-feuilleton* of such writers as Eugène Sue and Paul Féval are in reality, under their Satanic exterior, apostles of Good. Whether they are called Rodolphe or the Marquis de Rio-Santo, they loom gigantic in the midst of a net of intrigues which have for their object the salvation of the State—a curious popular reflection of the end of Byron's career, as the champion of Greek independence.

The following is a sort of oleograph portrait of the legendary Byron, dated as late as 1844:[68]

'C'était un homme d'une trentaine d'années, au moins en apparence, d'une taille haute, élégante et de modèle aristocratique. . . .

Quant à son visage, il offrait un remarquable type de beauté; son front haut, large, et sans ride, mais traversé de haut en bas par une légère cicatrice presque imperceptible quand sa physionomie était au repos, s'encadrait d'une magnifique chevelure noire. On ne pouvait voir ses yeux; mais, sous sa paupière baissée, on devinait leur puissance. . . . Le front du rêveur était pâle et uni comme celui d'un enfant. . . . C'était un homme tout de sensations . . . un homme capable à la fois du bien et du mal: généreux par caractère, franchement enthousiaste par nature, mais égoïste par occasion, froid par calcul, et d'humeur à vendre l'univers pour un quart d'heure de plaisir. . . . Le marquis de Rio-Santo! l'éblouissant, l'incomparable marquis! Londres et Paris se souviennent de ses équipages. L'Europe entière admira ses magnificences orientales; l'univers, enfin, savait qu'il dépensait quatre millions chaque *saison*. . . . Rio-Santo arriva de Paris, où il avait été pendant quatre ou cinq hivers de suite le roi de la mode. Il arriva suivi de son armée de laquais, de ses écuries, de ses meutes royales et de plusieurs douzaines de baronnes qui se mouraient de rêverie pour l'amour de ses cheveux noirs, de son teint pâle et de ses fulgurants yeux bleus. . . . Les jeunes filles le voyaient en songe avec un œil rêveur, un front ravagé, un nez d'aigle et un sourire infernal, mais divin. Ses cheveux, bouclés naturellement, groupaient au hasard leurs mèches gracieusement ondées. . . . "Je sais que vous êtes puissant, milord," répondit la comtesse . . . "puissant pour le mal comme l'ange déchu. . . .".'

Remembering the famous banquet of May 1809 at Newstead Abbey, Féval makes Rio-Santo preside at a sacrilegious orgy in the vaults of Sainte-Marie de Crewe. The participants are dressed as monks and disguised with false beards, and in this rather cumbersome costume dance and revel with half-naked bacchantes. In Féval, as often happens with popular writers, the minor details of the Byronic legend are enlarged to spectacular size—in just the same way as the perspective is magnified in vignettes of hotel advertisements.

14. This review of Byronic Fatal Men may conclude with Féval's highly sweetened Satan. But more interesting, because of the profound influence it was to have on the vital part of literature, is the element of vampirism which was latent in the Fatal Man Byron himself.

Writing on Goethe's *Bride of Corinth*, Madame de Staël remarked[69] upon the 'mélange d'amour et d'effroi', the 'volupté funèbre', in the atmosphere of the scene in which 'l'amour fait alliance avec la tombe, la beauté même ne semble qu'une apparition effrayante'. If this could be said of Goethe's ballad it could be repeated with even more aptness of the vampire loves of the Byronic Fatal Man. Thus we come round again to our discussion of the preceding chapter; having described there principally the aspect of beauty which attracted the Romantics, we will proceed now to an analysis of the kind of behaviour which is intimately connected with this type of beauty, to the action, real or imagined, which results from its contemplation. The *caractère maudit* of love corresponds to the *caractère maudit* of beauty, for on the one hand we read:

> 'Tis the tempestuous loveliness of terror,

and on the other, corresponding to it:

> I loved her, and destroy'd her!

In a discourse delivered in 1824 at the Institut de France, the Academician Auger made this appeal against the Byronic fashion which was then prevalent in France:

'Ayez horreur de cette littérature de cannibales, qui se repaît de lambeaux de chair humaine et s'abreuve du sang des femmes et des enfants; elle ferait calomnier votre cœur, sans donner une meilleure idée de votre esprit. Ayez horreur, avant tout, de cette poésie misanthropique, ou plutôt infernale, qui semble avoir reçu sa mission de Satan même, pour pousser au crime, en le montrant toujours sublime et triomphant, pour dégoûter ou décourager de la vertu, en la peignant toujours faible, pusillanime et opprimée!'[70]

The allusion here is certainly to Byron, as Estève remarks, but it is also to another figure whom Auger names only indirectly (the last part of the passage repeats almost word for word a sentence in Sade's preface to *Justine*: 'nous allons peindre le crime comme il est, c'est-à-dire toujours triomphant et sublime . . . et la vertu . . . toujours maussade et toujours triste, &c.'), but whom Sainte-Beuve was not ashamed to mention openly about twenty years later,[71] by which time the atmosphere was even more heavily laden with *fond de cale* exhalations:

'J'oserai affirmer, sans crainte d'être démenti, que Byron et de Sade (je demande pardon du rapprochement) ont peut-être été les deux plus grands inspirateurs de nos modernes, l'un affiché et visible, l'autre clandestin, — pas trop clandestin. En lisant certains de nos romanciers en vogue, si vous voulez le fond du coffre, l'escalier secret de l'alcôve, ne perdez jamais cette dernière clef.'

With all that is known to-day about Byron's character, the distance does not seem so great between the Divine Marquis and the Satanic Lord. Certainly the works of the one are in the hands of all, while those of the other are relegated to the *enfer* of the library; Byron was a poet and a celebrated man, Sade only a lewd 'philosopher'; but the precepts to be derived from the poems and, particularly, from the life of the one, and from the unnameable lucubrations of the other, were not so entirely different but that the French Romanticists were able to combine them and thus pave the way from the imitation of Byron to the less exalted part of Baudelaire's work and to the literature of the Decadence.

NOTES AND ADDENDA TO CHAPTER II

[1] Lit. trans.:

'Horrid majesty in his fierce aspect increases terror, and makes him more superb; his eyes are red, and their glance infected with poison dazzles like an ill-boding comet; shaggy and dense his great beard covers his chin and descends upon his hairy breast; and like a deep abyss his mouth opens, foul with dark blood.

'Just as sulphurous, flaming smoke comes forth from Mongibello, and stink and thunder, so from the fierce mouth comes forth his black breath, so are the foulness and the sparks.'

[2] Lit. trans.:

'In his eyes, where sadness and death have their abode, flames a troubled, crimson light. His oblique looks and crooked glances are like comets, like lightning-flashes his regard. And from his nostrils and from his wan lips he vomits and brings forth fog and foulness; angry, superb and desperate, his groans are thunder, his breath lightning.'

[3] Lit. trans.: 'How much is in his eyes of terror and death.'

[4] Lit. trans.: 'Wretched, and how didst thou lose thy pristine splendour, O one-time fairest Angel of light!'

[5] Lit. trans.:

'Not yet is the spirit of that pristine valour extinct in you, when girt with steel and lofty flames once we fought against the empire of Heaven. We were—that will I not deny—vanquished in that conflict: yet the great intention was not lacking in nobility. Something or other gave Him victory: to us remained the glory of a dauntless daring.'

[6] Lit. trans.: 'And even if my troop fell thence vanquished, yet to have attempted a lofty enterprise is still a trophy. . . .''

[7] Lit. trans.:

'Ah, art thou not that glorious creature, once prince of the shining Loves, first star of the morning Heaven, first light of the wingèd Choirs ? . . . Alas, but what avails it for me, hopeless, to turn my mind to my pristine state ? . . . But what force do I fear ? I did not lose, with my ancient purity, my lofty nature.'

[8] On this source of derivation of Milton's Lucifer see O. H. Moore, 'The Infernal Council', in *Modern Philology*, vol. xix (1921-2), pp. 47-64.

[9] *Paradise Lost*, i, lines 84-7.

[10] *Paradise Lost*, i, lines 589-604.

[11] *Histoire de la littérature anglaise* (ed. 1892, ii, pp. 506-7).

[12] *The Marriage of Heaven and Hell.*

[13] E. H. Visiak, *Milton Agonistes, a Metaphysical Study* (London, Philpot, 1923).

[14] E. M. W. Tillyard, *Milton* (London, Chatto and Windus, 1930), p. 277.

[15] See the discussion on this subject in H. J. C. Grierson, *Cross Currents in English Literature of the XVIIth Century* (London, Chatto and Windus, 1929), pp. 254 et seq.

[16] In *The Revolt of Islam* the serpent is the symbol of Good oppressed by Evil: Canto I, especially stanza 27:

> For the new race of man went to and fro,
> Famished and homeless, loathed and loathing, wild,
> And hating good—for his immortal foe,
> He changed from starry shape, beauteous and mild,
> To a dire Snake, with man and beast unreconciled.

[17] The type of the 'noble bandit' is of very ancient date. It was well known in the Hellenistic period. Cf. E. Rohde, *Der griechische Roman* (Leipzig, Breitkopf und Härtel, 1876), p. 357 and footnote there. Therefore the theory that the Romantic type of the magnanimous bandit is derived from *Amadis de Gaule* is somewhat naïve. Larat, for example (*La Tradition et l'exotisme dans l'œuvre de Charles Nodier*, Paris, Champion, 1923, vol. i, pp. 115-24, 'Le Thème du brigand généreux'), basing his theory upon the interpretations of I. Babbit (*Rousseau and Romanticism*) and E. Seillière (*Le Mysticisme démocratique*) says:

'C'est à *Amadis de Gaule* — roman du XVIᵉ siècle — qu'il faudrait faire remonter les manifestations littéraires de générosité dans la révolte, qui devaient aboutir aux portraits de brigands redresseurs de torts si fort en vogue dans la littérature européenne, après le succès de *Goetz de Berlichingen* et du drame de Schiller. Le brigand typique du XIXᵉ siècle serait donc en quelque sorte un don Quichotte furieux et juvénile.'

The characteristic quality of the sublime criminal of the Romantics, however, is satanism. Yet Schiller himself may at the first glance give the impression that he was repeating the traditional type, when he declares (in the *Selbstrecension*) that he had modelled his Karl Moor on Roque Guinart, the bandit in *Don Quixote* who was by nature 'compasivo e bien intencionado' (part ii, ch. lx). The difference between Karl Moor and Roque did not escape Kräger (H. Kräger, *Der Byronsche Heldentypus*, Munich, Haushalter, 1898—Forschungen zur neueren Litteraturgeschichte, vi), p. 13. Some, however, consider the influence of Milton to be secondary. Thus L. A. Willoughby (edition of the *Räuber*, London, Milford, Oxford University Press, 1922), who, however, brings forward a very superficial reason (p. 20):

'The motives for the rebellion, in one case against divine Providence, in the other against man-made law, are so different, that the influence must not be overrated.'

[18] This trait was remembered by Nodier in his Jean Sbogar (see below): 'Jean Sbogar ne fut remarqué du tribunal que par cette expression plus qu'humaine de physionomie qui était le trait caractéristique de son signalement, et qui le faisait tenir, selon l'expression de Schiller de l'ange, du démon et du dieu' (*Préliminaires*).

[19] The Miltonic colouring of the *Räuber* has already been noticed by Kräger (op. cit., especially p. 14). Kräger's study is mainly concerned with the relation between Milton, Schiller, and Byron, and ignores the importance of the 'tale of terror' in the origin of the Byronic hero. Thus (p. 45) he imagines the physical aspect of the Byronic hero to be derived from painting (Ribera, Rembrandt), whereas it is copied from Mrs. Radcliffe's villains, as will be shown.

[20] Cf. the words of the *Avertissement zu der ersten Aufführung der Räuber*: 'Unrestrained ardour and bad company ruined his heart—they dragged him from vice to vice—until he found himself at the head of a band of incendiaries, piled horror upon horror, plunged from abyss to abyss, into all the depths of desperation', with the words of Roque Guinart:

'Y como un abismo llama á otro y un pecado á otro pecado, hanse eslabonado las venganzas de manera. . . .'

[21] For the sources of the *Räuber* as well as for the vast number of imitations and derivatives from this play, see the essay in Willoughby's edition mentioned above.

[22] These parallels were noticed by E. Birkhead, *The Tale of Terror, A Study of the Gothic Romance* (London, Constable, 1921), pp. 53 et seq. The sarcastic grin which became so typical of Romantic satanism goes back therefore to Shakespeare's Cassius. E. Railo, *The Haunted Castle, A Study of the Elements of English Romanticism* (London, Routledge, and New York, Dutton, 1927), p. 372, note 238, wrongly conjectures that this grin may have been an invention of Scott (the grin of Mortham in *Rokeby*, 1813).

[23] On this subject see my study on *Machiavelli and the Elizabethans*, Annual Italian Lecture of the British Academy, 1928 (*Proceedings of the British Academy*, vol. xiii, London, Milford).

[23A] Montague Summers, in *The Gothic Quest*, London, The Fortune Press [1937], p. 297, has shown that the date 1795 given to *The Monk* by most literary historians is due to an erroneous statement in *The Life and Correspondence of M. G. Lewis*, 1839, vol. i, p. 151: 'The first and greatest era in the literary life of Lewis was the publication of "Ambrosio, or The Monk", which event took place in the summer of 1795.' The volume was actually published in 1796; cf. *Monthly Magazine or British Register*, March 1796, list of new publications. The original title was *The Monk*; the fourth and fifth editions had the title *Ambrosio; or The Monk*. [Add. 1950]

[24] *Life and Correspondence*, 1839, vol. i, p. 122. See also C. F. McIntyre, *Ann Radcliffe in relation to her Time* (New Haven, 1920, Yale Studies in English, lxii), pp. 64 et seq. Certain qualities of Mrs. Radcliffe's type are to be found in many other characters in literature previous to her. See Railo, op. cit., p. 219. Besides Shakespeare and Milton, Walpole must be remembered (the tyrant type in *The Castle of Otranto*), Beckford (Eblis in *Vathek*), &c.

* *p. 62, line 38, add:* And to have felt stimulated by that book to continue a novel of his in the style of *The Castle of Otranto* (this unfinished novel was subsequently utilized by Lewis in the drama *The Castle Spectre*); but the old inspiration was replaced by a new one and in the autumn of that very year 1794 Lewis wrote *The Monk* in a few weeks. [Add. 1950]

[25] Regarding the success of Schiller's and Zschokke's dramas in France see, besides Willoughby, op. cit., E. Estève, *Byron et le romantisme français*

(Paris, Boivin, 1929, 2nd edition), p. 31, and E. Eggli, *Schiller et le romantisme français* (Paris, Gamber, 1927), vol. ii, pp. 323-37, and vol. i, pp. 137 et seq.

²⁶ *Astarte*, by Ralph Milbanke, Earl of Lovelace, revised and expanded edition by the Countess of Lovelace (London, Christophers, 1921).

It seems strange, after so many studies on the origins of the Byronic hero, that L. Pearsall Smith should declare (*Milton and his Modern Critics*, London, Oxford University Press, 1940, p. 42): 'If I may interpolate a whim of my own—at least I have not met it elsewhere—I should like to suggest that something of the Satan of *Paradise Lost* is to be found in Byron's heroes, in Childe Harold, in Cain, in Lara, in the Giaour, and above all in Manfred, &c.' [Add. 1950]

²⁷ Cf. Radcliffe, *The Italian*, apropos of Schedoni:

'notwithstanding all this gloom and austerity, some rare occasions of interest had called forth a character upon his countenance entirely different; and he could adapt himself to the tempers and passions of persons whom he wished to conciliate, &c.'

²⁸ It is the smile of Shakespeare's Cassius (*Julius Caesar*, i. ii, lines 202–4):

> Seldom he smiles, and smiles in such a sort
> As if he mock'd himself, and scorn'd his spirit
> That could be mov'd to smile at any thing.

²⁹ Cf. Schiller, *Die Räuber*, Vorrede:

'Ein merkwürdiger, wichtiger Mensch, ausgestattet mit aller Kraft, nach der Richtung, die diese bekommt, nothwendig entweder ein Brutus oder ein Catilina zu werden. Unglückliche Conjuncturen entscheiden für das Zweite . . .'

³⁰ See stanza v:

> That brow in furrow'd lines had *fix'd* at last,
> And spoke of *passions*, but of passions past:
> The pride, but not the fire, of early days,
> Coldness of mien, and carelessness of praise;
> A high demeanour, and a *glance* that took
> Their *thoughts* from others by a *single* look.
>   .   .   .   .   .
> And some deep feeling *it were vain to trace*
> At moments lighten'd o'er his *livid face*.

Cf. the following passage from Mrs. Radcliffe, op. cit.:

'. . . the *livid* paleness of his *face*. . . . There was something in his physiognomy extremely singular, and *that cannot easily be defined*. It bore the traces of many *passions*, which seemed to have *fixed* the features they no longer animated. . . . His eyes were so piercing, that they seemed to penetrate, at a *single glance*, into the hearts of men, and to read their most secret *thoughts*.'

It is clear that it is a case of parallels, not only of ideas, but of actual words.

³¹ A similar fascination is exercised by the sinister monk Schedoni in Mrs. Radcliffe's novel. Railo (op. cit., pp. 222 et seq.) sees in Scott's

rather Radcliffean character of Marmion a connecting link between Mrs. Radcliffe's villain and the Byronic hero:

'To my mind, the romantic admiration displayed for Marmion, which is expressed with the utmost clarity and even infects the reader, is in the first place something novel when compared with his predecessors, while in the second place it is exactly what Byron aimed at in his own sombre hero. Marmion thus becomes, in a quite special sense, a bridge between two stages of development.'

It must, however, be noticed that the element of admiration was already present in the case of Milton's Satan; and that in any case Byron was guided by a spontaneous inversion of values to identify himself with the Schedoni type. The connecting link of Scott is therefore superfluous.

[32] Railo (op. cit., p. 372, note 242) is of opinion that the Corsair is a pirate after the manner of Mortham in Scott's *Rokeby*.

[33] According to Chateaubriand, Byron wrote to him immediately after the publication of *Atala*:

'Au surplus, un document trancherait la question si je le possédais. Lorsque *Atala* parut, je reçus une lettre de Cambridge, signée G. Gordon, lord Byron. Lord Byron, âgé de quinze ans, était un astre non levé: des milliers de lettres de critiques ou de félicitations m'accablaient; vingt secrétaires n'auraient pas suffi pour mettre à jour cette énorme correspondance. J'étais donc contraint de jeter au feu les trois quarts de ces lettres, et à choisir seulement, pour remercier ou me défendre, les signatures les plus obligatoires. Je crois cependant me souvenir d'avoir répondu à lord Byron; mais il est possible aussi que le billet de l'étudiant de Cambridge ait subi le sort commun. En ce cas mon impolitesse forcée se sera changée en offense dans un esprit irascible; il aura puni mon silence par le sien. Combien j'ai regretté depuis les glorieuses lignes de la première jeunesse d'un grand poète!'

Now *Atala* came out in 1801; Byron did not go to Cambridge till October 1805. In 1801 Byron was a thirteen-year-old schoolboy at Harrow. But Chateaubriand's assertion can be proved wrong even without falling back upon external argument. How, actually, could the letter of an obscure student have been remembered particularly among so many thousands of other letters? And if it had impressed Chateaubriand why should he have destroyed it? It is therefore probable that the author of *Atala* may have confused, or, on the most favourable supposition, have believed that he could identify, with Byron a Cambridge correspondent whose name he had forgotten. In this connexion see Sainte-Beuve, *Chateaubriand et son groupe*, &c., vol. ii, p. 79: 'Chateaubriand était fort distrait sur les noms propres qu'il savait le mieux'. Commenting upon the passage in the *Mémoires d'outre-tombe*, Sainte-Beuve wrote (op. cit., p. 193 n.):

'Mais ce qui est plus fort que tout, énumérant les prétendues injustices et les omissions jalouses dont il aurait été l'objet de la part de lord Byron et des autres, il reproche à Mme de Staël de ne l'avoir pas nommé dans son livre de la *Littérature*: "Un autre talent supérieur a évité mon nom dans un ouvrage sur la *Littérature*." Et proclamant à l'instant son enthousiasme pour Mme de Staël comme pour lord Byron, il se donne les honneurs de la générosité. Il oublie tout à fait que Mme de Staël ne pouvait le nommer dans ce livre publié *avant* qu'il se fût donné à connaître, et il paraît encore moins se souvenir que son premier acte de publicité en France fut d'attaquer ce même livre où il s'étonne naïvement de ne point figurer.'

The case of the letter which he claimed to have received from Byron must belong to the same category. See also as well, *ad abundantiam*, on the subject of the truthfulness of Chateaubriand in general, Sainte-Beuve's book, vol. i, pp. 93, 279–80; ii, p. 385.

³⁴ L. Reynaud, *Le Romantisme, ses origines anglo-germaniques*, (Paris, Colin, 1926), p. 187.

³⁵ Things were different in France.

'René ne fait autre chose que tracer ici (et c'est sa gloire d'avoir été le premier à le concevoir et à le remplir) l'itinéraire poétique que tous les talents de notre âge suivront; car tous, à commencer par Chateaubriand lui-même qui n'exécuta que plus tard ce qu'il avait supposé dans *René*, ils parcourront avec des variantes d'impressions le même cercle, et recommenceront le même pèlerinage: l'Italie, la Grèce, l'Orient.'

Thus Sainte-Beuve, op. cit., vol. i, p. 378.

³⁶ Compare especially, *Childe Harold*, i, st. 4:

> Then loathed he in his native land to dwell,
> Which seem'd to him more lone than Eremite's sad cell.

René: 'Je me trouvai bientôt plus isolé dans ma patrie que je ne l'aurais été sur une terre étrangère.'

Childe Harold, id., st. 5:

> . . . he loved but one,
> And that loved one, alas! could ne'er be his.

René: 'c'était [his sister] la seule personne au monde que j'eusse aimée'.

On the other hand, the passage (stanza 9) 'And none did love him . . .' takes us back to Richard III and the villains of the 'tales of terror', as does also, to the latter, the description of Harold's impious revels—a characteristic quite lacking in *René*.

³⁷ See Monglond, op. cit., i, pp. 236 et seq., especially 255.

³⁸ i, p. 371. See the 14th and 15th lectures (vol. i) for René's connexion with similar and related types.

³⁹ Édition Garnier, vol. iii, pp. 297 and 357.

⁴⁰ Ibid., p. 506.

⁴¹ For instance the allusion to the vampire in *The Giaour*:

> But first, on earth as Vampire sent,
> Thy corse shall from its tomb be rent:
> Then ghastly haunt thy native place,
> And suck the blood of all thy race;
> Then from thy daughter, sister, wife,
> At midnight drain the stream of life, etc.

⁴² Reynaud, op. cit., pp. 187 n., 188–90.

⁴³ See E. Colburn Mayne, *Byron* (London, Methuen, 1924), p. 252; H. Richter, *Lord Byron* (Halle, Niemeyer, 1929), pp. 288-9, both of

which bear witness of the extent to which the subject of incest was in the air at that time. See also chap. viii of Railo's book already quoted, *Incest and Romantic Eroticism*. Monglond (op. cit., vol. i, p. 258): 'Pour la "criminelle passion", on renonce à l'interpréter comme une confidence autobiographique, quand on sait de quelle abondante littérature elle n'est que le reflet littéraire'. See also the study to which Monglond alludes in a note. Love between brother and sister was a favourite subject of the German Sturm und Drang; e.g. *Die Braut von Messina*.

44 *Génie du Christianisme*, Deuxième Partie, iv. 9. On Milton and Chateaubriand see the thesis of J. M. Telleen, *Milton dans la littérature française* (Paris, Hachette, 1904), chap. vii; and H. M. Miller, *Chateaubriand and English Literature* (Baltimore and Paris, 1925; The Johns Hopkins Studies in Romance Literatures and Languages, vol. iv).

45 This attitude is already to be found in the novels of the Abbé Prévost, especially in *Cleveland*. See B. M. Woodbridge, 'Romantic Tendencies in the Novels of the Abbé Prévost', in *Publications of the Modern Languages Assn. of America*, New Series, vol. xxvi (1911), p. 327; and Monglond, op. cit., vol. i, pp. 244 et seq.

46 *Letters and Journals*, vol. ii., p. 382.

47 Ch. du Bos, *Byron et le besoin de la fatalité* (Paris, Au Sans Pareil, 1929), p. 158.

48 Cf. Kräger, op. cit., p. 136, note 24:

'Byron wished to test the overwhelming power of passion by the overcoming of obstacles which he put in its path. Even in the simplest of his works, *Sardanapalus*, he obstructs the course of love by means of a prohibition, since Myrrha is an Ionian slave, and as a republican and a Greek must recoil from the king and the barbarian, Sardanapalus. But her inclination towards him is increased by this very opposition and by the hatred which her duty demands from her. In *The Deformed Transformed* the love between Polixena and Achilles is steeped in blood, since the maiden loves the man who has killed her brother. Byron had an almost morbid predilection for such conflicts of feeling—the love for that from which one ought to flee. Straightforward sensations were not enough for him: he was never so satisfied as when he saw shadows of death blighting a marriage-bed.'

49 The only love, apart from a mere temporary excitement of the senses, which Byron was able to feel, was for a being who already closely resembled him, tuned, so to speak, to the same key, exactly as his half-sister was (cf. *Manfred*, Act II, sc. 2: 'She was like me in lineaments, &c.') In the case of other women, the obstacles of a difference of temperament which had to be overcome in order to attain to a spiritual unison were too great for a nature as tightly shut up within itself as Byron's. Shelley, another egocentric, presents a similar case (contrast his conduct towards Harriet with his sentiments of abstract universal love). His feminine ideal, as described in *Alastor*, is a mere projection of himself:

> He dreamed a veilèd maid
> Sate near him, talking in low solemn tones.
> Her voice was like the voice of his own soul
> Heard in the calm of thought, etc.

See also my remarks on Poe, chap. iii, § 20.

Maurois, *Byron* (Paris, Grasset, 1930, and London, Cape, 1930), maintains that Byron's incest was an imaginary crime, because Augusta was only a half-sister and Byron did not know her until they were both quite grown-up. An imaginary crime, possibly, but Byron from the first sought to represent it as a crime, and what counts is not the actual incest but the consciousness of committing it.

50 *Journal of the Conversations of Lord Byron*, by the Countess of Blessington, 1834, p. 317.

51 For the 'apologie des passions' on the part of the 'Encyclopédistes', see Monglond, op. cit., vol. i, pp. 189 et seq.

52 London, Constable, 1929. See especially chaps. xi et seq.

53 Letter to Miss Milbanke, Sept. 6th, 1813.

54 On this particular source of sensations, see Du Bos, op. cit., pp. 117 n., 311, and 321.

55 Annabella confessed that 'there were moments when she could have plunged a dagger in Augusta's heart'.

56 *Marino Faliero*, Act V, sc. 2, line 11.

57 Certain passages of *Cain* (Lucifer's description of the Divinity, Act I, sc. 1, the haughty prayer of Cain, Act III, sc. 3) and of *Heaven and Earth* (the chorus of mortals threatened by the waters) reveal the same attitude towards the Divinity as the fourth chorus of Swinburne's *Atalanta in Calydon*; Lord Houghton actually cites Byron as the inspirer of this chorus, though he could not have been ignorant of its real source, the Marquis de Sade (see chap. iv, § 16). Read for example Lucifer's discourse:

> Souls who dare look the Omnipotent tyrant in
> His everlasting face, and tell him that
> His evil is not good! If he has made,
> As he saith—which I know not, nor believe—
> But, if he made us—he cannot unmake:
> We are immortal! nay, he'd *have* us so,
> That he may torture:—let him! He is great—
> But, in his greatness, is no happier than
> We in our conflict: Goodness would not make
> Evil; and what else hath he made? But let him
> Sit on his vast and solitary throne,
> Creating worlds, to make eternity
> Less burthensome to his immense existence
> And unparticipated solitude;
> Let him crowd orb on orb: he is alone
> Indefinite, indissoluble tyrant;
> Could he but crush himself, 'twere the best boon
> He ever granted: but let him reign on,
> And multiply himself in misery!
> Spirits and Men, at least we sympathize—
> And, suffering in concert, make our pangs
> Innumerable more endurable,
> By the unbounded sympathy of all

> With all! But *He*! so wretched in his height,
> So restless in his wretchedness, must still
> Create, and re-create——
>
>   .   .   .   .   .   .
>
>   The Maker—call him
> Which name thou wilt: he makes but to destroy.

Is not this the same theological conception as was at the root of *Anactoria* and of Chorus IV of *Atalanta*? Is not this the same cruel God, 'the supreme evil, God', as

> With offering and blood-sacrifice of tears
> With lamentation from strange lands ...
>
>   .   .   .   .   .   .
>
> With sorrow of labouring moons, and altering light
> And travail of the planets of the night,
> And weeping of the weary Pleiads seven,
> Feeds the mute melancholy lust of heaven
>
>   .   .   .   .   .   .
>
> Who hath made all things to break them one by one ...
>
>   .   .   .   .   .   .
>
> Is not his incense bitterness, his meat
> Murder?   (*Anactoria*)

And is not His creatures' cry of rebellion the same?

> Because thou art cruel and men are piteous,
> And our hands labour and thine hand scattereth ...
>
>   .   .   .   .   .   .
>
> At least we witness of thee ere we die
> That these things are not otherwise, but thus;
> That each man in his heart sigheth, and saith,
>   That all men, even as I,
> All we are against thee, against thee, O God most high.

                                        (*Atalanta*, Chorus IV.)

But, as Swinburne explicitly declared, this is exactly the theology of Sade, for whom the author of the universe is the most malignant of all beings, He who creates only to destroy (see chap. iii, § 5). A similar conception of a cruel, vindictive God is expounded in the words of Ahasuerus, the Wandering Jew of Canto VII of Shelley's *Queen Mab*.

⁵⁸ *Manfred*, Act II, sc. 1 and 2. Actually the remarks of the London newspapers at the time of the scandal of Byron's separation were not so very far from the truth. Byron was represented as 'a wretch whose organs, blunted by the habits and excesses of the most monstrous debauchery, could no longer find any means of excitement or stimulation except in the images of terror, suffering and destruction with which a crime-stained soul furnished him only too easily' (Estève, op. cit., p. 73).

' "Il a toujours voulu se détruire, ce Byron": c'est sur ce mot que, dans *La Mort de Venise*, s'achève l'évocation que fait Barrès de l'ombre byronienne parmi celles "qui flottent sur les couchants de l'Adriatique", et parce qu'à telles heures de sa vie lui-même avait été si sensible à la volupté de se détruire, nul mieux que Barrès n'était qualifié pour prononcer' (Du Bos, op. cit., p. 213).

The sketch of Byron at Venice in the *Cahiers* of Barrès is worth notice (vol. ii, Paris, 1930, p. 268):

'Byron, le plus grand poète et le plus grand philosophe. Son *Don Juan* est la plus haute philosophie. Il fut un scélérat et un merveilleux poète. Tous les Byrons sont des scélérats; il n'y a pas de crime que n'aient commis son père et sa mère. Quand il mourut, son cerveau, un cerveau formidable, supérieur, je crois, à celui de Cuvier, était une masse affreuse, détruite, en bouillie, par l'alcool, l'opium, tous les abus destructeurs, un cloaque. Il a fait souffrir, torturé tout autour de lui. Comme il avait une émotivité formidable, il a aussi exprimé les plus hautes, les plus nobles idées. C'est très naturel qu'il y soit sensible; les communards furent, en même temps que des bandits, les êtres les plus accessibles aux grandes causes généreuses et seuls susceptibles de se faire tuer pour elles. . . . Il a toujours voulu se détruire, ce Byron.'

[59] Ethel Colburn Mayne, *Lady Byron*, op. cit., p. 334.

[60] Byron noted in his diary, Feb. 20th, 1814: 'Redde *The Robbers*. Fine—but *Fiesco* is better'. *The Corsair* had already been finished, Dec. 13th, 1813.

[61] In this respect at any rate the influence of Chateaubriand is secondary to that of Byron. See Estève, op. cit., p. 42:

'Qui pouvait-on, en France, mettre en comparaison avec lui ? . . . Chateaubriand, certes, fait grande figure dans le monde littéraire, mais ce n'est qu'un prosateur de génie, et, depuis 1814, il a versé dans la politique. René, pair de France, ambassadeur et ministre, a perdu l'auréole de la solitude et du malheur.'

See also pp. 517–18.

[62] See Eggli, op. cit., vol. ii, p. 335. Eggli is right in observing that 'les données essentielles du drame sont visiblement apparentées à celles des *Brigands*'. As for the derivations of the Byronic hero in England, see W. C. Phillips, *Dickens, Reade and Collins, Sensation Novelists*, New York, Columbia University Press, 1919, pp. 155 ff. Chiefly Bulwer-Lytton gave a tame version of that hero in *Paul Clifford* and *Eugene Aram*. Byron had represented the Corsair as a heroic outlaw with a thousand vices and one virtue; Bulwer-Lytton strove to multiply the one virtue of the type, to cast on his crime a light which did not prevent, rather invited, compassion and regret on the part of the reader. Thus the Byronic hero became adapted to the bourgeois age, and offered a means to attack the way in which justice was administered in England. Against the kind of novel written by Bulwer-Lytton and the so-called Newgate School, Thackeray reacted with *Catherine* (1839–40), *Barry Lyndon* (1844), and *George de Barnwell* (1847), where the figure of the noble outlaw is held up to ridicule.

[63] Cf. for example *La Nouvelle Héloïse*, Troisième Partie, Lettre XVI, from Saint-Preux:

'J'aime mieux te perdre que te partager . . . avant que ta main se fût avilie dans ce nœud funeste abhorré par l'amour et réprouvé par l'honneur, j'irais de la mienne te plonger un poignard dans le sein. . . . Je voudrais que tu ne fusses plus; mais je ne puis t'aimer assez pour te poignarder.'

[64] See the passage quoted in note 41 of this chapter.

⁶⁵ This ballad by Goethe inspired Gautier's poem *Les Taches jaunes*, and particularly the story *La Morte amoureuse*. (See chap. iv, § 10.)

⁶⁶ For the success of this tale and on vampirism in general see V. M. Yovanovitch, *La Guzla de Prosper Mérimée, étude d'histoire romantique* (Paris, Hachette, 1911); and S. Hock, *Die Vampyrsage und ihre Verwertung in der deutschen Literatur* (Berlin, Duncker, 1900: Forschungen für neueren Litteraturgeschichte, xvii). See also Estève, op. cit., pp. 76 et seq. Krafft-Ebing, in *Psychopathia Sexualis* (zwölfte Auflage, Stuttgart, Enke, 1903, p. 99) connects the vampire legend with sadism.

⁶⁷ *Mélanges de littérature et de critique* (Paris, 1820), vol. i, p. 417.

⁶⁸ *Les Mystères de Londres*, by P. Féval (1844).

⁶⁹ *De l'Allemagne*, Deuxième Partie, ch. xiii.

⁷⁰ Related by Estève, op. cit., p. 130.

⁷¹ 'Quelques vérités sur la situation en littérature', in the *Revue des deux mondes*, 1843, vol. iii, p. 14; republished in *Portraits contemporains*, tome iii, p. 415.

CHAPTER III
THE SHADOW OF THE DIVINE MARQUIS

Et ces regards insolites!
Il y en a sous la voûte desquels on assiste à l'exécution d'une vierge dans
une salle close.

MAETERLINCK, Regards (Serres chaudes).

En achevant de relire ce recueil, je crois voir pourquoi l'intérêt, tout
faible qu'il est, m'en est si agréable, et le sera, je pense, à tout lecteur d'un
bon naturel: c'est qu'au moins ce faible intérêt est pur et sans mélange de
peine; qu'il n'est point excité par des noirceurs, par des crimes, ni mêlé du
tourment de haïr. Je ne saurais concevoir quel plaisir on peut prendre à
imaginer et composer le personnage d'un scélérat, à se mettre à sa place tandis
qu'on le représente, à lui prêter l'éclat le plus imposant. Je plains beaucoup
les auteurs de tant de tragédies pleines d'horreurs, lesquels passent leur vie
à faire agir et parler des gens qu'on ne peut écouter ni voir sans souffrir.
Il me semble qu'on devrait gémir d'être condamné à un travail si cruel; ceux
qui s'en font un amusement doivent être bien dévorés du zèle de l'utilité
publique. Pour moi, j'admire de bon cœur leurs talents et leurs beaux génies;
mais je remercie Dieu de ne me les avoir pas donnés.

ROUSSEAU, *marginal note to* La Nouvelle Héloïse.

Talma gehört nun ganz eigentlich der neusten Welt an. . . . Wir selbst
waren Zeuge, mit welchem Glück er sich in eine Tyrannenseele einzugeisten
trachtete; eine bösartige, heuchlerische Gewalttätigkeit auszudrücken gelang
ihm am besten. Doch war es ihm zuletzt am Nero nicht genug; man lese, wie
er sich mit einem Tiber des Chénier zu identifizieren suchte und man wird
ganz das Peinliche des Romantizismus darin finden.

GOETHE, Französisches Haupttheater.

THE SHADOW OF THE DIVINE MARQUIS

1. In the year 1842 Louis Reybaud (in *Jérôme Paturot à la recherche d'une position sociale*, vol. i, p. 149) presented the writers of *romans-feuilleton* with a mock receipt to the following effect:

'Vous prenez, môsieur, par exemple, une jeune femme, malheureuse et persécutée. Vous lui adjoignez un tyran sanguinaire et brutal, un page sensible et vertueux, un confident sournois et perfide. Quand vous tenez en main tous ces personnages, vous les mêlez ensemble, vivement, en six, huit, dix feuilletons, et vous servez chaud.'

The unfortunate, persecuted maiden! The subject is as old as the world,[1] but was refurbished in the eighteenth century by Richardson with his very celebrated heroine Clarissa Harlowe, that young lady of great virtue and beauty who, ensnared and seduced by the libertine Lovelace and persecuted by her implacable parents, becomes ill with grief and fades slowly away amid the funeral pomps of an exemplary death. This is how the author expresses himself upon the cruel fate of this innocent girl, in the words of Mr. Belford, Lovelace's correspondent:[2]

'What a fine subject for tragedy, would the injuries of this lady, and her behaviour under them, both with regard to her implacable friends, and to her persecutor, make! What a grand objection as to the moral, nevertheless,[3] for here virtue is punished! Except indeed we look forward to the rewards of HEREAFTER, which, morally, *she* must be sure of, or who can? Yet, after all, I know not, so sad a fellow art thou, and so vile an husband mightest thou have made, whether her virtue is not rewarded in missing thee: for things the most grievous to human nature, when they happen, as this charming creature once observed, are often the happiest for us in the event.'

A comparison of this heroine with the one in Nicholas Rowe's *The Fair Penitent* shows how much more suitable the title is to Clarissa. Hers was indeed a penitence, hers a true Christian piety!

With the declared purpose of enlightening parents and marriageable girls, Richardson makes his readers, through a good eight volumes, spectators of the slow Calvary of pious Clarissa, displays her, pitiful little lamb among greedy wolves, in a disorderly house and a debtors' prison, and finally on her deathbed, imparting her last wishes, forgiving every one, and even ordering devices for her coffin, which she makes them bring into her room in order that she may use it as a writing-desk. Thus Miss Clarissa Harlowe languishes, wastes away, and dies of grief in the blossom of her youth and beauty, Clarissa Harlowe 'who, her tender years [she was nineteen] considered, has not left behind her her superior in extensive knowledge and watchful prudence; nor hardly her equal for unblemished virtue, exemplary piety, sweetness of manners, discreet generosity and true Christian charity. . . .'[4]

Virtue is persecuted in this world, but will triumph ultimately in Heaven; in fact Lovelace actually dreams[5] that he sees the angelic figure of Clarissa, clad all in white, ascending with choirs of angels to the region of the Seraphim, while an abyss opens in the ground at the feet of her seducer, who falls headlong into a bottomless chasm—almost exactly as was to happen in the case of the most celebrated of all the persecuted maidens, Margaret in *Faust*.[6] Another dream, anticipating the future calamities of Clarissa,[7] seems also to anticipate the wild and sinister developments of the 'persecuted woman' theme. Clarissa dreams that Lovelace, 'seizing upon her, carries her into a churchyard; and there, notwithstanding all her prayers and tears, and protestations of innocence, stabs her to the heart, and then tumbles her into a deep grave ready dug, among two or three half-dissolved carcases; throwing in the dirt and earth upon her with his hands, and trampling it down with his feet'.

It has repeatedly been remarked that the unctuous pietism of Richardson's novels succeeds in covering only in appearance their sensual, turbid background. Certainly the art of Richardson, founded, as it was, upon accurately observed manners, could not well avoid certain contradictions in its effort to conciliate morality with the unbridled

sensuality of the period. Clarissa gets herself abducted by
Lovelace and at the same time writes to her sister—whose
betrothed she has just stolen—to send her books of
morality. Lovelace boasts of his wicked conduct, gives
himself the airs of an unscrupulous libertine (Diderot[8]
found in him 'les sentiments d'un cannibale', 'le cri d'une
bête féroce'), shuts up Clarissa in a house of ill fame, drugs
and violates her, and at the same time professes his love for
her and declares that he wishes to marry her.

Whether this contradiction of intention and result was
an inevitable consequence of the author's realistic attitude,
which brought him to accept the facts as shown him in his
surroundings, or whether it was simply an effect of his own
individual psychological situation (Richardson, in consequence of the materialistic philosophy then predominant,
was at bottom a supporter of the instinct against whose
manifestations he preached in the name of a virtue which
he estimated also by materialistic standards),[9] the fact remains that his moralizing reveals itself fully for what it was
—namely, little more than a veneer—in his French imitators, who sought in the subject of the persecuted woman
chiefly an excuse for situations of heightened sensuality.

2. This fact is sufficiently obvious in Diderot's *Religieuse*, a novel which, although based on a scandal which
really happened,[10] adopts the scheme of Richardson's
novels,[11] and offers a detailed picture of physical and
moral tortures, ostensibly intended for the object of anti-
clerical propaganda, but revealing in effect, on the part of
the author, a certain complaisance which shortly afterwards was to take its name from another French writer,
the Marquis de Sade. The manner in which Diderot
proclaims incessantly the virtue of his heroine gives the
impression, every now and then, of being only meant to
add a sharper spice to the cruelty of her persecution. It is
an anticipation of *Justine*.

Diderot, in fact, is one of the greatest exponents of that
Système de la Nature which, carrying materialism to its
logical consequences and proclaiming the supreme right
of the individual to happiness and pleasure in opposition
to the despotism of morality and religion,[12] paves the way

to the justification, in the name of Nature, of sexual perversions.[12A] His *Supplément au Voyage de Bougainville*,
written in 1772, with the intention of showing 'l'inconvénient d'attacher des idées morales à certaines actions
physiques qui n'en comportent pas', digresses on the subject of the customs of the blessed inhabitants of Tahiti,
who are ignorant of the notions of fornication, incest, and
adultery. Sade, too, culled information from certain
travellers' books in order to corroborate the most exceptional erotic fantasies by means of lists of the customs of
savage peoples. In the *Rêve de d'Alembert* (written in
1769) Diderot makes d'Alembert say:

> 'L'homme n'est qu'un effet commun, le monstre qu'un effet rare;
> tous les deux également naturels, également nécessaires, également
> dans l'ordre universel et général.'

In the same way Sade,[13] on the subject of Gilles de Rais
and other monsters, writes:

> 'C'étaient des monstres, m'objectent les sots. Oui, selon nos
> mœurs et notre façon de penser; mais relativement aux grandes
> vues de la nature sur nous, ils n'étaient que les instruments de ses
> desseins; c'était pour accomplir ses lois qu'elle les avait doués de
> ces caractères féroces et sanguinaires.'

3. Though it would be absurd to make any comparison,
from an aesthetic standpoint, between a psychological
novel such as Richardson's *Clarissa* and a coarse piece of
pornographic fiction such as the *Thérèse philosophe* of
Darles de Montigny (which appeared in 1748, the year
after the publication of *Clarissa*), it is not unsuitable to
speak of them together with regard to their social setting
and customs. And we know that the two books might
easily have been found, in France at any rate, in the library
of the same lady—except that the binding of one of them
would have been blank. To get an idea of how this 'livre
galant' was esteemed by its contemporaries, the opinion of
the Président de Brosses is sufficient:[14]

> 'J'ai lu "Thérèse philosophe" qui m'a donné de l'amusement
> de toute manière. Cela est joli et assez bien fait, d'une plaisante
> singularité. Je voudrais seulement qu'on en eût retranché: 1º. les
> estampes; 2º. les ordures qui y sont presque toujours des hors

d'œuvre. Il suffirait que le livre fût licencieux pour le but de l'auteur qui est original et certainement la philosophie y domine.'

What, indeed, was the original philosophy of this book, which Sade, later, proclaimed as 'l'unique qui ait agréablement lié la luxure à l'impiété'?[15] That virtue leads to misery and ruin, vice to prosperity—the exact principle of which Sade himself became champion:

' "Vous ne serez heureuse", me disait-on, "qu'autant que vous pratiquerez les vertus chrétiennes et morales; tout ce qui s'en éloigne est le vice; le vice nous attire le mépris, et le mépris engendre la honte et le remords qui en sont une suite." Persuadée de la solidité de ces leçons, j'ai cherché de bonne foi, jusqu'à l'âge de vingt-cinq ans, à me conduire d'après ces principes: nous allons voir comment j'ai réussi.'

As long as she remains of this persuasion, things go badly with Thérèse; but then, gradually, the 'truth' makes headway in her mind, that is, that the passions implanted by nature in man are the work of God:

'Quel excès de folie de croire que Dieu nous a fait naître pour que nous ne fassions que ce qui est contre Nature, que ce qui peut nous rendre malheureux dans ce monde; en exigeant que nous nous refusions tout ce qui satisfait les sens, les appétits qu'il nous a donnés!'

Thus Thérèse, anticipating Rousseau, becomes convinced that 'tout est bien, tout est de Dieu', and even that 'il est faux que l'Antipnysique soit contre nature, puisque c'est cette même nature qui nous donne le penchant pour ce plaisir...'

And so, taking her stand upon these metaphysical truths, Thérèse abandons herself to the most dissolute wantonness, to her great profit and satisfaction.[16]

4. If virtue does not lead to happiness, at least appearances are saved by the final punishment of triumphant vice in *Les Liaisons dangereuses* (1782), the novel which in a sense may be called the *Clarissa* of France—with more right than *La Nouvelle Héloïse*.

The Vicomte de Valmont is killed in a duel, like his English predecessor Lovelace, and the Marquise de Merteuil, whose Machiavellian mind[17] has ensnared both innocent and guilty in its meshes, suffers not only the moral

humiliation of a scandal, but an actual physical disfigurement which makes her face an outward emblem of her
soul: the smallpox, opportune ally of morality, takes upon
itself to lay waste her beauty and, *particulièrement*, to make
her lose an eye. And worse is in store for her; only Laclos
contents himself with merely giving a glimpse of her *en
route* for Holland and refrains from a full description of the
'sinistres événements qui ont comblé les malheurs ou
achevé la punition de Madame de Merteuil'. This would
seem to be the conclusion: 'Si on était éclairé sur son
véritable bonheur, on ne le chercherait jamais hors des
bornes prescrites par les Lois et la Religion.'[18]

From a religious point of view, the fate of oppressed
virtue in *Les Liaisons dangereuses* may be considered as
fortunate. The Présidente de Tourvel, who not without
reason had chosen as her breviaries the *Pensées chrétiennes*
and *Clarissa*,[19] dies quite like Richardson's heroine, from
grief, and more or less surrounded with a halo of sanctity.
Mlle de Volanges, the *ingénue* perverted by the false Valmont, leaves the world for the cloister, while her simple
admirer Danceny adopts the usual popular geographical
solution to his troubles. 'J'irai enfin chercher à perdre,
sous un ciel étranger, l'idée de tant d'horreurs accumulées,
et dont le souvenir ne pourrait qu'attrister et flétrir mon
âme.' He leaves for Malta, where he intends religiously to
respect the vows which will separate him from the wicked
world.

The novelty of the *Liaisons*, however, does not consist
in the moral aspect of the story, which is inspired by the
story of *Clarissa*; it lies, rather, in the analysis of vice,
which in fact is triumphant throughout three-quarters of
the book. This was certainly felt at the time. The following is the opinion of Alexandre de Tilly, who remarks in
his *Mémoires* that the side of virtue is represented in the
book only by the character of the Présidente de Tourvel:

'Le reste est une conception coupable ... et enfin, le rôle de cette
innocente [Mlle de Volanges], qui fait tout ce que feraient les plus
scélérates, qui donne à sa mère tous les ridicules, aux jeunes filles
tous les mauvais exemples, est le dernier coup de pinceau de ce
tableau composé avec un art trois fois coupable .... Ce sont des vices

monstrueux à la réflexion, qui paraissent tout simples à la lecture....
En un mot, c'est l'ouvrage d'une tête de premier ordre, d'un cœur
pourri et du génie du mal.'

A confirmation of how far the analysis of evil in the
Liaisons had been made *ab experto*, and of the importance
of its influence on later writers, may be seen in Baudelaire's brief notes:[20]

'A propos d'une phrase de Valmont (à retrouver):
'Le temps des Byrons venait.
'Car Byron était *préparé*, comme Michel-Ange.
'Le grand homme n'est jamais aérolithe. Chateaubriand devait
bientôt crier à un monde qui n'avait pas le droit de s'étonner:
' "Je fus toujours vertueux sans plaisir; j'eusse été criminel sans
remords."
'Caractère sinistre et satanique.
'Le satanisme badin.'

On the phrase in Valmont's Letter VI to Madame de
Merteuil—'J'oserai la ravir au Dieu même qu'elle adore',
Baudelaire makes the comment: 'Valmont Satan, rival de
Dieu', and quotes the passage:

'Quel délice d'être tour-à-tour l'objet et le vainqueur de ses remords! Loin de moi l'idée de détruire les préjugés qui l'affligent!
ils ajouteront à mon bonheur et à ma gloire. Qu'elle croie à la
vertu, mais qu'elle me la sacrifie; que ses fautes l'épouvantent sans
pouvoir l'arrêter; et qu'agitée de mille terreurs, elle ne puisse les
oublier, les vaincre que dans mes bras. Qu'alors j'y consens, elle
me dise: "Je t'adore".'[21]

And the passage in Letter XXI—'J'oubliais de vous
dire que, pour mettre tout à profit, j'ai demandé à ces
bonnes gens de prier Dieu pour le succès de mes projets'—
is followed by the comment 'Impudence et raffinement
d'impiété'. An example of a similar refinement is to be
found in the passage quoted by Baudelaire from Letter CX:

'Cet enfant [Mlle de Volanges] est réellement séduisant! Ce contraste de la candeur naïve avec le langage de l'effronterie, ne laisse
pas de faire de l'effet; et, je ne sais pas pourquoi, il n'y a plus que
les choses bizarres qui me plaisent.'[22]

Baudelaire lays particular stress upon those qualities in
Valmont which he finds in himself, in fact he remodels
the figure of the French Lovelace to the shape which it

presents from the Baudelairean point of view; he quotes
a phrase of Mme de Merteuil (whom he calls 'une Ève
satanique') upon which a note more ample than his brief
reference to 'George Sand et autres' would have been of
great interest: 'Ma tête seule fermentait; je ne désirais pas
de jouir, je voulais SAVOIR.'

Projected against a Baudelairean background, this
phrase immediately assumes a depth of meaning which it
certainly does not possess in its own context. For it was precisely in this 'savoir' which Baudelaire emphasizes that his
own personal tragedy lay: ferment of the brain, *exacerbatio
cerebri*, this was Baudelaire's form of sensuality; the desire
for the forbidden fruit because forbidden, in order to
'know'—in which theologians see the supreme sin against
the Holy Ghost.

On the other hand, the general observation which
Baudelaire makes upon the French 'littérature galante' of
the eighteenth century, the spirit of which he contrasts
with that of a certain type of literature of his own time,
gives the clue to the piety of Baudelaire which is so much
emphasized nowadays:

'En réalité, le satanisme a gagné. Satan s'est fait ingénu. Le
mal se connaissant était moins affreux et plus près de la guérison
que le mal s'ignorant. G. Sand inférieure à de Sade.'

5. The Marquis de Sade, in fact—and here was his
originality—reversed the convenient ethical theory of
Thérèse philosophe, which was actually the same as that of
Jean-Jacques. 'Everything is good, everything is the
work of God' becomes in him 'Everything is evil, everything is the work of Satan'. It is therefore necessary to
practise vice because it conforms to the laws of nature
(Rousseau's 'les plus pures lois de la nature'!) which insists upon destruction.[23] Evil is the axis of the universe:

'Je me dis: il existe un Dieu, une main a créé ce que je vois,
mais pour le mal; elle ne se plaît que dans le mal; le mal est son
essence; tout celui qu'elle nous fait commettre est indispensable à
ses plans. . . . Ce que je caractérise mal est vraisemblablement un très
grand bien relativement à l'être qui m'a mis au monde. . . . Le mal
est nécessaire à l'organisation vicieuse de ce triste univers. Dieu est
très vindicatif, méchant, injuste. Les suites du mal sont éternelles;

c'est dans le mal qu'il a créé le monde, c'est par le mal qu'il le
soutient; c'est pour le mal qu'il le perpétue; c'est impregnée de
mal que la créature doit exister; c'est dans le sein du mal qu'elle
retourne après son existence.... La vertu étant mode opposé au
système du monde, tous ceux qui l'auront admise sont sûrs d'en-
durer d'effroyables supplices par la peine qu'ils auront à rentrer
dans le sein du mal, auteur et régénérateur de tout ce que nous
voyons.... Je vois le mal éternel et universel dans le monde. Le mal
est un être moral non créé; éternel, non périssable; il existait avant
le monde, il constituait l'être monstrueux qui put créer un monde
aussi bizarre. L'auteur de l'univers est le plus méchant, le plus
féroce, le plus épouvantable de tous les êtres. Il existera donc après
les créatures qui peuplent ce monde; et c'est dans lui qu'elles rentre-
ront toutes, pour recréer d'autres êtres plus méchants encore....'[24]

'La nature... marche d'un pas rapide à son but, en prouvant
chaque jour à ceux qui l'étudient qu'elle ne crée que pour détruire
et que la destruction, la première de toutes ses lois, puisqu'elle ne
parviendrait à aucune création sans elle, lui plaît bien plus que la
propagation, qu'une secte de philosophes grecs appelaient avec
beaucoup de raison, le résultat des meurtres.'[25]

'Qui doute... que le meurtre ne soit une des lois les plus pré-
cieuses de la nature? Quel est son but quand elle crée? n'est-ce
pas de voir bientôt détruire son ouvrage? Si la destruction est une
de ses lois, celui qui détruit lui obéit donc!'[26]

'Il n'y a aucun être dans le monde... qui par une action quelque
étendue qu'elle soit, quelque irrégulière qu'elle paraisse, puisse em-
piéter sur les plans de la nature, puisse troubler l'ordre de l'univers.
Les opérations de ce scélérat sont l'ouvrage de la nature comme la
chaîne des événements qu'il croit déranger.... C'est... un véritable
blasphème que d'oser dire qu'une chétive créature comme nous
puisse, en quoi que ce soit, troubler l'ordre du monde ou usurper
l'office de la nature.... Peut-elle s'offenser de voir l'homme faire à
son semblable ce qu'elle lui fait elle-même tous les jours?... Il est
démontré qu'elle ne peut se reproduire que par des destructions....
Il faut que l'équilibre se conserve; il ne peut l'être que par le crime.'[27]

'Quand vous avez vu que tout était vicieux et criminel sur la
terre, leur dira l'Être suprême en méchanceté, pourquoi vous êtes-
vous égarés dans les sentiers de la vertu?... Et quel est donc l'acte
de ma conduite où vous m'ayez vu bienfaisant? Est-ce en vous
envoyant des pestes, des guerres civiles, des maladies, des tremble-
ments de terre, des orages? est-ce en secouant perpetuellement sur
vos têtes tous les serpents de la discorde, que je vous persuadai que
le bien était mon essence? Imbécile! que ne m'imitais-tu pas?'[28]

'La vertu ne conduit qu'à l'inaction la plus stupide et la plus
monotone, le vice à tout ce que l'homme peut espérer de plus délicieux sur la terre.[29] Douter que la plus grande somme de bonheur
possible que doive trouver l'homme sur la terre ne soit irrévocable-
ment dans le crime, certes, c'est douter que l'astre du jour soit le
premier mobile de la végétation. Oui, mes amis, ainsi que cet astre
sublime est le régénérateur de l'univers, de même le crime est le
centre de tous les feux moraux qui nous embrasent.'[30]

Here, therefore, Clarissa is deprived of the support of
her faith and her certainty of a future reward.

'C'est, nous ne le déguisons plus, pour appuyer ces systèmes, que
nous allons donner au public l'histoire de la vertueuse Justine. Il
est essentiel que les sots cessent d'encenser cette ridicule idole de
la vertu, qui ne les a jusqu'ici payés que d'ingratitude, et que les
gens d'esprit, communément livrés par principe aux écarts délicieux
du vice et de la débauche, se rassurent en voyant les exemples
frappants de bonheur et de prospérité qui les accompagnent pres-
qu'inévitablement dans la route débordée qu'ils choisissent. Il est
affreux sans doute d'avoir à peindre, d'une part, les malheurs ef-
frayants dont le ciel accable la femme douce et sensible qui respecte
le mieux la vertu; d'une autre, l'affluence des prospérités sur
ceux qui tourmentent ou qui mortifient cette même femme; mais
l'homme-de-lettres, assez philosophe pour dire le VRAI, surmonte
ces désagréments, et cruel par nécessité, il arrache impitoyablement
d'une main les superstitieuses parures dont la sottise embellit la
vertu, et montre effrontément de l'autre à l'homme ignorant que
l'on trompait, le vice au milieu des charmes et des puissances qui
l'entourent et le suivent sans cesse. C'est en raison de ces motifs
que... nous allons... peindre le crime comme il est, c'est-à-dire
toujours triomphant et sublime, toujours content et fortuné, et la
vertu comme on la voit également, toujours maussade et toujours
triste, toujours pédante et toujours malheureuse.'[31]

It is not necessary to mention here the picaresque adventures related in *Justine, ou les malheurs de la vertu* and
its sequel *Juliette, ou les prospérités du vice*.[32] The Marquis
de Sade empties his world of all psychological content except the pleasures of destruction and transgression, and
moves in an opaque atmosphere of mere matter, in which
his characters are degraded to the status of instruments for
provoking the so-called divine ecstasy of destruction.

'La multitude la plus étendue des lésions sur autrui, dont il ne doit physiquement rien ressentir, ne peut pas se mettre en compensation avec la plus légère des jouissances achetées par cet assemblage inouï de forfaits.... Quel est l'homme raisonnable qui ne préférera pas ce qui le délecte à ce qui lui est étranger ?'[33]

However 'obscures et ténébreuses' may be the means pursued to heighten this ecstasy, the butcheries of Sade are hardly different from experiments in a chemical laboratory:

'Et voilà donc ce que c'est que le meurtre: un peu de matière désorganisée, quelques changements dans les combinaisons, quelques molécules rompues et replongées dans le creuset de la nature qui les rendra dans quelques jours sous une autre forme à la terre; et où donc est le mal à cela?'[34]

Well may one of his libertines declare:

'Oh! quelle action voluptueuse que celle de la destruction... je n'en connais pas qui chatouille plus délicieusement; il n'est pas d'extase semblable à celle que l'on goûte en se livrant à cette divine infamie. . . .'[35]

The cycle of possible chemical disaggregations which constitute his tortures is soon exhausted, because, as Proust remarks,[36] nothing is more limited than pleasure and vice, and—to make a play upon words—it may be said that the vicious man moves always in the same vicious circle. The sense of the infinite, banished from human relationships by the suppression of any spiritual meaning, takes refuge in a sort of cosmic satanism:

'C'est elle [la nature] que je voudrais pouvoir outrager. Je voudrais déranger ses plans, contrecarrer sa marche, arrêter le cours des astres, bouleverser les globes qui flottent dans l'espace, détruire ce qui la sert, protéger ce qui lui nuit, édifier ce qui l'irrite, l'insulter en un mot dans ses œuvres.'[37]

In this there is a *reductio ad absurdum* of Sade's 'philosophy', since, if it is admitted that Nature's aim is destruction and that no act of destruction can irritate or insult her (even Sade recognizes that 'l'impossibilité d'outrager la nature est selon moi le plus grand supplice de l'homme'),[38] the supreme insult which can be laid upon her, and from which the sadist should legitimately derive the greatest pleasure of transgression, would be precisely—the practice of virtue! And the supreme joy of sadism should in fact be the joy of remorse and expiation: from Gilles de Rais to Dostoievsky the parabola of vice is always identical.

While the persecutions of Clarissa and of Madame de Tourvel follow a psychological course, those of Justine, developing on a physical plane, offer no more spiritual interest than a series of chemical experiments. Everything is seen externally;[38A] so that a strange abuse is made of the word 'soul' in the introduction to *Justine*:

' Quant aux tableaux cyniques, nous croyons, avec l'auteur, que toutes les situations possibles de l'âme étant à la disposition du romancier, il n'en est aucune dont il n'ait la permission de faire usage.'

Even the death of Justine is a meteorological event. In order to show that Nature is irritated against her virtue, Sade has her struck by a thunderbolt, after Noirceuil has said 'Mes amis, un orage terrible se forme; livrons cette créature à la foudre; je me convertis si elle la respecte'.[39]

It was the Romantics, profiting by the theories of the Divine Marquis, and especially Baudelaire, who gave a psychological turn to the refinements of perversity; the length to which this method could go was expressed in one of the latest of the Decadents, Remy de Gourmont.[40]

In the inversion of values which is at the basis of sadism, vice represents the positive, active element, virtue the negative and passive. Virtue exists only as a restraint to be broken.

'Les freins qu'elle lui fait rompre, ou les vertus qu'elle lui fait mépriser, deviennent comme autant d'épisodes voluptueux.'[41]

'Il ne faut pas s'imaginer que ce soit la beauté d'une femme qui irrite le mieux l'esprit d'un libertin; c'est bien plutôt l'espèce de crime qu'ont attaché à sa possession les lois civiles ou religieuses; la preuve en est que plus cette possession est criminelle, et plus nous en sommes irrités.'[42]

So, naturally, the existence of virtue comes to be a condition of sadistic pleasure, just as in orthodox morality it is necessary to have some obstacle to overcome and some evil to conquer.

'Ta douce vertu (Justine) nous est essentielle; ce n'est que du mélange de cette qualité charmante et des vices que nous lui opposerons que doit naître pour nous la plus sensuelle volupté.'[43]

Were it not for Lovelace and Valmont, Clarissa and Madame de Tourvel would not be adorned with the haloes of saints; without a Justine to oppress and torture, no sadistic amusement would be possible. The success of the persecuted beauty as a subject in the novel of the nineteenth century owes more to the motives which dictated the work of the Divine Marquis than to those which caused Richardson to write *Clarissa*.

Moreover, if the sadist refuses to believe in traditional religion he deprives himself of an inexhaustible source of pleasure: the pleasure of profanation and blasphemy. Hence the lamentable contradiction in an outburst like this:[44]

'Ô toi qui, dit-on, a créé tout ce qui existe dans le monde; toi dont je n'ai pas la moindre idée; toi que je ne connais que sur parole... être bizarre et fantastique que l'on appelle Dieu; je déclare formellement, authentiquement, publiquement, que je n'ai pas dans toi la plus légère croyance, et cela pour l'excellente raison que je ne trouve rien, ni dans mon cœur, ni dans mon esprit qui puisse me persuader une existence absurde dont rien au monde n'atteste la solidité.'

And then, what pleasure can he get from trampling on crucifixes, from the 'faire des horreurs avec des hosties', what savour from the Black Mass, unless he is convinced of the truth of transubstantiation? Sade's retort is that the pleasure is derived from thinking of the horror which these acts inspire in believers, from the moral tórture, in fact, inflicted in imagination upon the believer:

'Les trois quarts de l'Europe attachent des idées très religieuses à cette hostie...à ce crucifix, et voilà d'où vient que j'aime à les profaner; je fronde l'opinion publique, cela m'amuse; je foule aux pieds les préjugés de mon enfance, je les anéantis; cela m'échauffe la tête.'[45]

6. Restif de la Bretonne sought to react against Sade's theories in his *Anti-Justine, ou les délices de l'amour* (1798). Restif had already given, ten years before, in *Les Nuits de Paris*, a melodramatically exaggerated version of the part which 'l'affaire Keller' had played in Sade's actual life.[46] And in *Monsieur Nicolas, vᵉ époque*, he threw out this hint, in speaking of licentious books:

'Mais je connais un livre encore plus dangereux que ceux que

j'ai nommés: c'est JUSTINE; il porte à la cruauté: DANTON le lisait
pour s'exciter.'

In the same book he spoke with horror of the sadistic
pastimes of the aristocracy. But he himself handed on certain suggestions which were anything but edifying to
later writers, suggestions which were more insidious in
their sentimental falsetto than the ghastly shrieks of Sade.
What distinction, for example, can be made between the
sentiment shown in the following passage and the sadistic
pleasure in humiliation?

'Je trouve au dernier degré du vice un certain repos, une certaine
satisfaction . . . semblable sans doute à celle des Diables, s'il y en
avait. . . . C'est comme lorsque avec des habits de pauvre je descends
au plus bas étage des conditions humaines. J'ouvre devant moi une
carrière immense, je trouve des plaisirs nouveaux, que je ne connaissais pas, au sein du cynisme et de la crapule; avec des habits
semblables à ceux des bourgeois, leurs filles et leurs femmes ne me
paraissent rien; en habit de mendiant, elles sont au-dessus de moi,
elles me font illusion et se confondent à mes yeux avec les princesses;
je les envie, je voudrais les *humilier*; moi, qui suis poli, tendre même
pour leur sexe, sous mes mauvais habits je change d'inclination; si
je vois une jolie femme le soir, je l'insulte et l'entretiens de propos
grossiers. D'où vient cela?'[47]

Restif goes into ecstasies over the good heart of the
young prostitute Zéphire (in *Monsieur Nicolas*, *v^e époque*),
who is an innocent sinner in the manner of Laclos' Mlle
de Volanges:

'Cette enfant m'est attachée, malgré son état! . . . Son état ne lui
a pas ôté l'âme aimante qu'elle a reçue de la nature! . . . Mon *ami*
lecteur! cette fille perdue, cette prostituée m'ennoblit assez à mes
propres yeux pour que je te redonne le nom d'*ami*! tu l'adoreras
comme moi; tu la pleureras comme moi; et . . . bientôt . . . tu frémiras,
comme j'ai frémi! . . .

'Loiseau était déiste et très pieux: Il se mit à genoux et remercia
l'Être suprême: "Père de tout ce qui est!" s'écria-t-il, "sois béni. . . .
Tu as laissé pour elle de la vertu jusque dans la prostitution: ainsi,
jadis les prêtresses de Vénus, qui t'honoraient sous le nom de cette
déesse de la beauté, n'étaient pas moins vertueuses, en faisant ce
qui est aujourd'hui le comble de la turpitude".'

This theme of the prostitute regenerated by love, expounded by Prévost, following De Foe's example, in *Manon*

Lescaut, by Rousseau in the *Confessions* (Zulietta),* by
Goethe in the ballad *Der Gott und die Bajadere*, by Schiller
in *Kabale und Liebe* (Lady Milford, the favourite), was
destined, with the Romantics, to become one of the chief
points of their cult of tainted beauty. How many times
shall we find it again, from Musset in *Rolla* ('N'était-ce
pas sa sœur, cette prostituée?') to the Italian 'poeta
crepuscolare', Guido Gozzano—this type of 'purity in
prostitution'—the Fleur-de-Marie of Sue, D'Annunzio's
Mila di Codro!48

Nicolas, Zéphire's lover, also commits incest, because
Zéphire—who, according to the habit of these unfortunate
young women, dies in the flower of her youth—is his own
daughter by Nannette. (Sue's Fleur-de-Marie obviously
derives straight from here.)* And before this, Prévost's
Cleveland had fallen in love with Cécile, whom he later
discovered to be his own daughter.

7. Incest itself also, ennobled already by Prévost in
Cleveland (1731) thanks to the principle of the 'divine
right' of passion, became a theme dear to the Romantics,
and in a special way to Chateaubriand, who invested incestuous love between brother and sister with poetic
charm and sentimental dignity, elaborating certain events
of his own life—though to what extent cannot be verified.49
In *Atala* he makes the lovers' passion culminate in the discovery of bonds of spiritual brotherhood, of 'amitié fraternelle', 'cette amitié fraternelle qui venait nous visiter et
joindre son amour à notre amour'.

Chateaubriand is also full of longing for the 'état de
nature' idolized by the Encyclopédistes, in which he
imagined it possible to realize his sensual ideal, notwithstanding certain theoretical remarks in the first preface of
Atala.50 He speaks with an exile's regret of the 'mariages
des premiers-nés des hommes, ces unions ineffables,
alors que la sœur était l'épouse du frère, que l'amour et
l'amitié fraternelle se confondaient dans le même cœur et
que la pureté de l'une augmentait les délices de l'autre'
(*Atala*). It is an absurd regret, because the relationship of
lovers between brother and sister only fascinated him
inasmuch as he felt it through the consciousness of sin; and

since the possibility of the latter is lacking in the primitive natural state, that particular relationship could have no different savour from a relationship between strangers.

Not content with making Atala a quasi-sister, he shows her also as a virgin who has made vows of chastity, so that to the thrill of incest is added that of sacrilege. Moreover, this love kills Atala, 'la Vierge des dernières amours'; sexual pleasure is crowned with death.[51] There is the same mingling of incest and sacrilege in *René*, when René, as sponsor of Amélie's monastic vows, hears from her lips the confession of her 'criminelle passion' and disturbs the ceremony by embracing her upon the bier of her symbolic death: 'Chaste épouse de Jésus-Christ, reçois mes derniers embrassements à travers les glaces du trépas et les profondeurs de l'éternité, qui te séparent déjà de ton frère.' All the voluptuousness of incest, sacrilege, and death is condensed into this short phrase.

An idyllic background in the manner of Bernardin de Saint-Pierre, added to the charm of primitive Christianity, invests the turbid and sensual subject-matter of Chateaubriand with a halo of innocence. To him, too, may be applied Baudelaire's already quoted remark ('Le satanisme a gagné, Satan s'est fait ingénu', &c.), and even the latter part of it ('*Chateaubriand* inférieur à de Sade') if one takes into account, for instance, certain phrases of René's letter to Céluta:

'Le sein nu et déchiré, les cheveux trempés de la vapeur de la nuit, je croyais voir une femme qui se jetait dans mes bras; elle me disait: "Viens échanger des feux avec moi, et perdre la vie! mêlons des voluptés à la mort! que la voûte du ciel nous cache en tombant sur nous...." Je vous ai tenue sur ma poitrine au milieu du désert, dans les vents de l'orage, lorsque après vous avoir portée de l'autre côté d'un torrent, j'aurais voulu vous poignarder pour fixer le bonheur dans votre sein et pour me punir de vous avoir donné ce bonheur.'[52]

8. But to return to the theme of the persecuted woman. At a distance of only a few years—we are considering these works simply as psychological manifestations, and quite apart from any question of literary merit—there came into being Gretchen in Germany,[52A] Justine in France, in Eng-

land Antonia and Agnes, in the celebrated novel by M. G. Lewis, *The Monk* (1796). Not that all these victim-characters were conceived in the same spirit: we should not wish even in jest to compare a real aristocrat such as the Herr Geheimrat Johann Wolfgang von Goethe with a *ci-devant* of sinister reputation such as Louis-Donatien Aldonze, Marquis de Sade. Yet, to consider only certain outward vicissitudes, all these unhappy daughters of the ill-starred Clarissa suffered the same kind of outrages and terrors, languished in the depths of horrible prisons, and died or risked a violent death.[53]

Lewis, bearing in mind, perhaps, the 'terrible' German novel *Das Petermännchen*, by Christian Heinrich Spiess (1791), in which the hero-villain is responsible for the death of six women, is not content with only one victim. There is not only Antonia, who is seduced by the perverted monk Ambrosio (who then turns out to be her brother), who awakes, like Shakespeare's Juliet, in a fearful crypt among decayed corpses, who is made the object of a loathsome love among these emblems of death, and is finally stabbed.[54] There is also, chained in an *in-pace* of the same convent dungeons, another victim, a young girl who has been compelled to become a nun,[55] Agnes, who, being with child, has been condemned to a slow and hideous death together with her offspring. Lewis delights in describing the most disgusting graveyard horrors:

'Sometimes', says Agnes, 'I felt the bloated toad, hideous and pampered with the poisonous vapours of the dungeon, dragging his loathsome length along my bosom. Sometimes the quick cold lizard roused me, leaving its slimy track upon my face, and entangling itself in the tresses of my wild and matted hair. Often have I at waking found my fingers ringed with the long worms which bred in the corrupted flesh of my infant. . . .'[55A]

These are details which the 'frénétique' Romanticism of a later date remembered and developed insistently.[56] Of the principal plot of *The Monk* we shall have more to say later. Let it suffice here to mention that Hoffmann took his inspiration from this romance for *Die Elixire des Teufels*, in which Medardus corresponds to Ambrosio, Euphemia to Matilda, and to Antonia Aurelia, the pure young girl beloved by Medardus and slain by the mysterious spectre in which resides the other part of Medardus's double personality; that Grillparzer took from it the plot of *Die Ahnfrau*;[57] that Walter Scott, in *Ivanhoe*, derived from *The Monk* the idea of the tragic love of the Knight Templar Bois-Guilbert for the beautiful Jewess Rebecca; that Victor Hugo drew upon Lewis's romance (and upon Scott's) for the character of the persecuted Esmeralda and for that of the infamous priest Claude Frollo, and George Sand for those of Lélia and the priest Magnus (in the first version Magnus, unable to overcome the resistance of the young woman, strangles her).[58]

9. Mrs. Ann Radcliffe, who shares with Lewis and Maturin the honour of having invented that most successful branch of literature, the 'tale of terror',[58A] makes the persecuted woman a regular type in her horrifying stories. Now it is the Marchesa di Mazzini, in the *Sicilian Romance* (1790), imprisoned by a cruel husband in a horrible dungeon;[59] now it is Emily de Saint-Aubert, a lovely and virtuous orphan girl, shut up by the cruel Montoni in the sinister castle of Udolpho (*The Mysteries of Udolpho*, 1794); now it is Adeline, in *The Romance of the Forest* (1791), persecuted and tormented in another gloomy castle; now again the wretched Ellena, in the best of all Mrs. Radcliffe's novels, *The Italian, or the Confessional of the Black Penitents* (1791).

Victim of the machinations of the shameful Schedoni, carried off by villains and transported in a coach to a lonely convent in the mountains of the Abruzzi, threatened with imprisonment by the Abbess, rescued by Vivaldi but recaptured just as she is about to be married to him, Ellena is finally imprisoned in a sinister cottage on a deserted point of the Adriatic coast, in order to be murdered by the villain Spalatro;[60] there Schedoni comes to her, and, as the assassin refuses to carry out his work, approaches the girl's bedside at night (in a scene similar to the one in *The Monk* in which Ambrosio surprises the sleeping Antonia) and is on the point of killing her himself when he discovers on her breast a medal which shows her to be his own daughter.

For—let it be stated once and for all—the old recognition-scene of the Greek romances[61] became one of the mainstays of the 'tales of terror', as it was to be of Romanticism in general. Parents who rediscover their children in the most dramatic circumstances—this was the mainspring of the plays and novels of about 1830. Buridan who finds that Gaultier and Philippe are his own sons by Marguerite de Bourgogne—they are Marguerite's sons and also her lovers (Dumas' *La Tour de Nesle*); Gennaro, the incest-born son of Lucrezia Borgia, who believes himself the object of a hateful love on the part of the monstrous woman whom, later, he discovers to be his mother and whom he kills (Victor Hugo's *Lucrèce Borgia*); Rodolphe, who without knowing it rescues his own daughter, La Goualeuse (in the *Mystères de Paris*): these are some of the best-known examples of a formula which also found favour in the eyes of the Romantics on account of the flavour of incest which could be extracted from it. In Mrs. Radcliffe's *The Italian*, even though the recognition-scene between Schedoni and Ellena is afterwards found to be due to an error, there is still a genuine recognition in the discovery of the nun Olivia that Ellena, whom she has helped to escape from the gloomy convent of San Stefano, is really her long-lost daughter.

10. Like Mrs. Radcliffe, other authoresses also adopted the persecuted woman as a character; but there may be nothing more in this than another of the many manifestations of feminine imitativeness. As the literary tradition has been the monopoly of man, at any rate up till the present, it is natural that women writers should slavishly adopt in their works the masculine point of view.

In Miss Wilkinson's *The Priory of St. Clair* (1811) Julietta is shut up in a convent against her will, is drugged and conveyed as a corpse to the sinister Gothic castle of the Count of Valvé; she comes to life only to be slain before the high altar, and avenges herself after her death by haunting the Count regularly every night.

In Mrs. Shelley's *Frankenstein* (1817) we find an innocent woman accused of murdering a child, thanks to the infernal guile of a sort of satanic Homunculus manufactured by Frankenstein; and the innocent woman, imprisoned, tried and executed, is called—by an odd coincidence—Justine, like Sade's unhappy virtuous heroine. In *Valperga, or the Life and Adventures of Castruccio, Prince of Lucca*, also by Mrs. Shelley (1823), Beatrice ends her days in the prisons of the Inquisition (Castruccio, beloved by her, is the usual type of satanic hero, 'a majestic figure and a countenance beautiful but sad, and tarnished by the expression of pride that animated it').

11. All Mrs. Shelley did was to provide a passive reflection of some of the wild fantasies which, as it were, hung in the air about her. But there was a different significance in her husband's choice of the story of Beatrice Cenci as the subject of the most powerful of his dramas, in which Swinburne, as expert a judge as any one, traced the imprint of the Divine Marquis. Indeed the elder Cenci speaks very like one of Sade's villains:

> I do not feel as if I were a man,
> But like a fiend appointed to chastise
> The offences of some unremembered world.
> My blood is running up and down my veins;
> A fearful pleasure makes it prick and tingle;
> I feel a giddy sickness of strange awe;
> My heart is beating with an expectation
> Of horrid joy.[62]

'Nous sommes des dieux', declared Sade's characters. The perverse Saint-Fond in *Juliette* spoke just like Cenci, when he boasted that there was no ecstasy like that 'que l'on goûte en se livrant à cette divine infamie'. Nor was the behaviour of Sade's 'heroes'[63] towards their relations so very different from the threats of Cenci against his daughter, which he obviously uttered with the intention of feeling 'délicieusement chatouillé' by breaking laws which men consider sacred. Cenci wishes to poison and corrupt his daughter's soul:[64]

> I will drag her, step by step,
> Through infamies unheard of among men;
> She shall stand shelterless in the broad noon
> Of public scorn, for acts blazoned abroad,
> One among which shall be . . . What? Canst thou guess?

She shall become (for what she most abhors
Shall have a fascination to entrap
Her loathing will) to her own conscious self
All she appears to others; and when dead,
As she shall die unshrived and unforgiven,
A rebel to her father and her God,
Her corpse shall be abandoned to the hounds;
Her name shall be the terror of the earth;
Her spirit shall approach the throne of God
Plague-spotted with my curses. I will make
Body and soul a monstrous lump of ruin.

Then he goes on, with voluptuous delight, to this sacrilegious prayer, which echoes, but with very different significance, the maledictions of King Lear (Act II, sc. iv, lines 165 et seq., 224 et seq.):

                    . . . God,
Hear me! If this most specious mass of flesh,
Which Thou hast made my daughter; this my blood,
This particle of my divided being;
Or rather, this my bane and my disease,
Whose sight infects and poisons me; this devil
Which sprung from me as from a hell, was meant
To aught good use; if her bright loveliness
Was kindled to illumine this dark world;
If nursed by Thy selectest dew of love
Such virtues blossom in her as should make
The peace of life, I pray Thee for my sake,
As Thou the common God and Father art
Of her, and me, and all; reverse that doom!
Earth, in the name of God, let her food be
Poison, until she be encrusted round
With leprous stains! Heaven, rain upon her head
The blistering drops of the Maremma's dew,
Till she be speckled like a toad; parch up
Those love-enkindled lips, warp those fine limbs
To loathèd lameness! All-beholding sun,
Strike in thine envy those life-darting eyes
With thine own blinding beams!

The tortures described by Beatrice are of the kind which Sade's Justine suffered:[65]

                    . . . Do you know
I thought I was that wretched Beatrice

> Men speak of, whom her father sometimes hales
> From hall to hall by the entangled hair;
> At others, pens up naked in damp cells
> Where scaly reptiles crawl, and starves her there,
> Till she will eat strange flesh.

Remember the description of the Medusa quoted in Chapter I, and the joy which Shelley took in the spectacle of that tormented beauty. Remember also the minute description of the passing from beauty and life to decay and death in *The Sensitive Plant*, and the insistence with which Shelley uses in his poems such words as 'ghost', 'charnel', 'tomb', 'dungeon', 'torture', 'agony', &c. Horror, pity, and hatred against tyrants are the springs of inspiration in *The Cenci*; but the attraction which the poet felt for the subject seems to arise from another source, a troubled one. 'Incest', he wrote, with regard to Calderón's *Cabellos de Absalón*,[66] 'is, like many other incorrect things, a very poetical circumstance.' In the first version of *The Revolt of Islam* (*Laon and Cythna*) the lovers Laon and Cythna were brother and sister. Cythna, the symbol of devotion, is raped by Othman, the symbol of tyranny, and the lovers suffer tortures and are finally bound to the same stake, like Tasso's Olindo and Sofronia, and die exchanging 'looks of insatiate love'—symbol of the martyrdom of free-thinkers. The symbolic matter does not prevent the poet from lingering upon vivid descriptions of the victims' painful experiences. In *Rosalind and Helen* Rosalind tells her story, over which broods the shadow of incest, in a highly romantic spot where once a brother and sister had loved and been put to death—she, killed by the multitude, he, condemned by the priests to be burnt alive.[67]

12. But the majority of English writers of this period do not seem to have realized the nature of their predilection for cruel and terrifying spectacles. Maturin, for example, who in *Melmoth the Wanderer* (1820) produced the masterpiece of the 'tales of terror' school, and who professed to 'depict life in its extremities, and to represent those struggles of passion when the soul trembles on the verge of the unlawful and the unhallowed', puts into the

mouth of one of his characters this analysis of the feelings of 'amateurs in suffering':[68]

'It is actually possible to become *amateurs in suffering*. I have heard of men who have travelled into countries where horrible executions were to be daily witnessed, for the sake of that excitement which the sight of suffering never fails to give, from the spectacle of a tragedy, or an *auto-da-fé*, down to the writhings of the meanest reptile on whom you can inflict torture, and feel that torture is the result of your own power. It is a species of feeling of which we never can divest ourselves,—a triumph over those whose sufferings have placed them below us, and no wonder,—suffering is always an indication of weakness,—we glory in our impenetrability. . . . You will call this cruelty, I call it curiosity,—that curiosity that brings thousands to witness a tragedy, and makes the most delicate female feast on groans and agonies.'[69]

As is to be expected, there appears also in *Melmoth* the figure of the maiden born beneath an unlucky star; but she is a younger sister of Goethe's Margaret rather than a direct descendant of Clarissa, just as in *Melmoth* also the Byronic type ends by becoming confused with the Mephistopheles of the German master. Balzac, Baudelaire, and Rossetti, among others, were admirers of Maturin, which should suffice to justify a longer analysis of the novel than economy of space will permit. We shall limit ourselves to the points which are most relevant to the present discussion.

Melmoth has made a bargain with Satan, by which, in exchange for his soul, his life is to be prolonged; but he can still escape damnation if he succeeds in finding some one to share his fate. He wanders thus for more than a hundred years from country to country, spreading terror with his eyes, which no one would wish ever to have seen, for, once seen, it was impossible to forget them. Wherever there is a man reduced to desperation, there appears Melmoth to haunt him, in the hope of persuading him to entrust him with his fate: he explores the asylum, the prison, the frightful dungeons of the Inquisition, the houses of the wretched. Like a tiger in ambush, he peers in search of evil and sin; he has something of Goethe's Mephistopheles, something of the Byronic hero, something of the Wandering Jew, something of the vampire:

'Melmoth, as he spoke, flung himself on a bed of hyacinths and tulips. . . . "Oh, you will destroy my flowers," cried she. . . . "It is my vocation—I pray you pardon me!" said Melmoth, as he basked on the crushed flowers, and darted his withering sneer and scowling glance at Isidora. "I am commissioned to trample on and bruise every flower in the natural and moral world—hyacinths, hearts, and bagatelles of that kind, just as they occur." '[70]

Here it is Mephistopheles who speaks, but in the following passage it is the mocking grin of a brother of Schedoni or Lara:

'The stranger appeared troubled, an emotion new to himself agitated him for a moment, then a smile of self-disdain curled his lip, as if he reproached himself for the indulgence of human feeling even for a moment. Again his features relaxed, as he turned to the bending and averted form of Immalee, and he seemed like one conscious of agony of soul himself, yet inclined to sport with the agony of another's. This union of inward despair and outward levity is not unnatural. Smiles are the legitimate offspring of happiness, but laughter is often the misbegotten child of madness, that mocks its parent to her face.'[71]

The central episode of the novel (which is made up of several stories one inside the other, like the *Thousand and One Nights* or the masterpiece of Cervantes, works which Maturin quotes) consists of the love-affair of Melmoth, who here conforms to the type of the enamoured fiend in Oriental tales, with a girl who has been brought up in the primitive simplicity of a tropic isle: a creature who begins life with the name of Immalee and a character like that of Haidée in Byron's *Don Juan*, and finishes it with the name of Isidora and a destiny which relates her to Goethe's Margaret. Beside Immalee, the innocent child of Nature, the accursed wanderer feels as though relieved of the weight of his horrible destiny; he is on the point of confiding to her his ghastly secret; but then his hatred for all forms of life seizes upon him again, and he torments the pure virgin with threats, peals of Satanic laughter, and other Byronic-Mephistophelian terrors. Immalee, now become Isidora and transplanted to Spain, consents to unite her fate with Melmoth's; the lovers are joined in matrimony at dead of night by the spectre of a monk, among the ruins of an ancient monastery. Meanwhile Isidora's father imposes upon her a betrothed chosen by himself, and the girl, who already carries in her womb the fruit of her guilt, flies with Melmoth; her brother Fernan pursues and is killed in a duel by Melmoth, as Valentin was by Faust. Melmoth is recognized by the spectators, Isidora flings herself, desperate, upon her brother's body and refuses to follow her demon lover; she is shut up in the prisons of the Inquisition—as could be foreseen—and the infant girl who is born in the meantime is destined for the cloister. Finally the child is found dead in its mother's arms, and the mother dies of a broken heart after refusing for the last time the offer of Melmoth, who has visited her in prison and conjured her to accept liberty at a terrible price (a scene parallel to the one in Margaret's prison; Isidora's last cry is also for her wretched lover: 'Paradise!' she says to Fra José who attends her in her last moments, '*will he be there?*'). Melmoth, after wandering the earth for a hundred and fifty years, returns to his ancestral castle, and there is seized upon by devils who hurl him into the sea; in fact he has the classic end of those who are possessed of the Devil—Marlowe's Doctor Faustus, Byron's Manfred, Lewis's Monk.

The novel abounds in frightful descriptions of tortures both physical and moral. There is a long story of a forced monastic vow derived from Diderot's *Religieuse*[72] and elaborated with a subtlety of penetration into the terrors of the soul such as is elsewhere only found in Poe; there is a parricide who recognizes his own sister in the woman whom he has been pleased to starve to death with her lover; there is a mother who pretends that her son is the fruit of an adulterous union, in order to avoid his marrying a poor cousin whom he is thus persuaded to think is his sister; there is a trial of the Inquisition, a mysterious personage being present, as in Mrs. Radcliffe's *The Italian*; there is a whole family reduced to desperation and hunger through the avarice of the priests, and a youth who sells his own blood to support them. As for the latter, he is found one night in a pool of blood caused by the imperfect ligature of a vein, and the author paints this picture of cadaverous beauty:[73]

'. . . a kind of corse-like beauty, to which the light of the moon gave an effect that would have rendered the figure worthy of the pencil of a Murillo, a Rosa, or any of those painters, who, inspired by the genius of suffering, delight in representing the most exquisite of human forms in the extremity of human agony. A St. Bartholomew flayed, with his skin hanging about him in graceful drapery—a St. Laurence, broiled on a gridiron, and exhibiting his finely-formed anatomy on its bars, while naked slaves are blowing the coals beneath it,—even those were inferior to the form half-veiled, half-disclosed by the moonlight as it lay.'

Already, in another passage,[74] Maturin had lingered over the description of the tortures inflicted upon an extremely beautiful young monk, and had declared the group of torturers and victim to be worthy of Murillo: 'A more perfect human form never existed than that of this unfortunate youth. He stood in an attitude of despair—he was streaming with blood. . . . No ancient sculptor ever designed a figure more exquisite and perfect than that they had so barbarously mangled.'

13. The English 'tales of terror' were at once translated and had a widespread popularity in France,[75] where they found the ground already prepared by the French 'monastic' drama, which dealt with similar vicissitudes of fortune.[76] They had an influence on the development of melodrama and the popular novel (which later became the *roman-feuilleton* in the hands of Sue and Dumas *père*).[77] Their subjects became interwoven with kindred themes of German importation (Räuber-, Ritter-, and Schauer-romantik), and finally penetrated into the higher spheres of literature, thanks to Byron and Scott who were brought up on them.

Balzac and Hugo began their careers with novels of the 'frénétique' type. The monstrous *Han d'Islande* (1823), for instance, has in his veins the wild blood of half a dozen villains from the other side of the Channel.[78] We shall not linger over the innumerable examples of the 'persecuted heroine' type, except to make one observation. In 1797

it was possible for the critic of the *Magasin encyclopédique*[79]
to praise Mrs. Radcliffe for having set out to show that
vice, if sometimes able to oppress virtue, rejoices only in a
passing triumph and meets with certain punishment,
while virtue comes forth victorious from all its misfortunes;
as, however, subjects of cruelty and terror gradually gained
ground in France, the moral purpose was lost sight of and
interest was almost entirely concentrated on the description of ghastly and horrifying scenes. But more and
worse was to come. Since the Romantic theory asserted
that the best means of expressing passions was to begin to
feel them, people sought, instead of translating spontaneous
acts of life into the realm of art, to experience in actual
life the monstrous suggestions of imaginations fed upon
literary horrors.

And so there were raging passions *à la* Byron, suicides
à la Chatterton, and so on. The following is an example
of *delectatio morosa* attempting to translate itself into
reality. One evening in Florence Berlioz came upon the
funeral procession of a young woman who had died in
giving birth to her first child. One knows what a sinister
effect is produced by Florentine funerals even to-day, as
they move along in the evening by the smoky light of
torches, with files of hooded brethren of the Miseri-
cordia. Imagine what an impression it must have made on
a Romantic with his head full of the gloomy fancies of the
'tales of terror'. Berlioz, at the sight of the procession,
'pressent des sensations'. It seems that he succeeded in
getting the coffin opened and in remaining close to the
corpse in order to abandon himself to a delicious flow of
gloomy meditations. He stooped over the dead woman
and took her hand: 'Si j'avais été seul je l'aurais embrassée!'

But the Princess Belgiojoso went even farther than
Berlioz. During a search by the Austrian police in 1848
there was found in a cupboard in the villa at Locate belonging to the Princess the embalmed corpse of her young
secretary and lover Gaetano Stelzi, who had died of consumption a short time before. Instead of the corpse, a
tree-trunk had been buried (or, according to others,
some stones).[80] The Princess, incidentally, was the perfect

incarnation of the type of 'Medusean' beauty dear to the Romantics, and her visit to Paris left an indelible impression on the artists of the time.

'Pâle, maigre, osseuse, les yeux flamboyants, elle jouait aux effets de spectre ou de fantôme. Volontiers elle accréditait certains bruits qui, pour plus d'*effet*, lui mettaient à la main la coupe ou le poignard des trahisons italiennes à la cour des Borgia.'

Thus—not without malice—Madame d'Agoult describes her in her *Souvenirs* (Paris, Calmann Lévy, 1877, p. 357). The strange funereal furnishings of the Princess Belgiojoso's rooms in Paris suggested to Gautier their comparison with 'une vraie série de catafalques'. Madame d'Agoult described her bedroom as follows:

'Une chambre à coucher tendue de blanc, avec un lit de parade rehaussé d'argent mat, tout semblable au catafalque d'une vierge. Un nègre enturbanné, qui dormait dans l'antichambre, faisait en vous introduisant dans toute cette candeur un effet mélodramatique.'

On the episode of the corpse in the cupboard A. Augustin-Thierry writes:

'Stendhal, s'il n'était point mort trop tôt, eût aimé recueillir la trop romanesque aventure pour la prêter à quelque héroïne des *Chroniques italiennes*, Hélène de Campireali ou la duchesse de Palliano. Il s'agit bien d'un véritable accès vésanique, de la nécrolatrie exaspérée d'une amante voulant à tout prix conserver près de soi le corps du bien-aimé.'

The extravagances of the 'Jeunes-France' are too well known for it to be necessary to emphasize them here; any one who wishes to get a full account of them has only to turn the pages of *Le Romantisme et les mœurs*, by Maigron. It will suffice to illustrate Sainte-Beuve's assertion quoted at the end of the preceding chapter by giving examples from some of the most characteristic writers and books.

14. One of the most characteristic of all is *L'Âne mort et la femme guillotinée*, by Jules Janin (1829), well described by Arsène Houssaye as a 'chef d'œuvre étrange qui est à la fois l'âme et la raillerie de la littérature romantique'.[81] The multiplicity of motives which went to the inspiration of this work is reflected in the ambiguity of its character. It contains a polemic against the prudishness

of censorship and of the type of criticism then prevailing, and at the same time a parody of the *roman-charogne*, of which Gautier wrote, a few years later (1834), in the preface to *Mademoiselle de Maupin*:

'A côté du roman moyen-âge verdissait le roman-charogne. . . . Littérature de morgue ou de bagne, cauchemar de bourreau, hallucination de boucher ivre et d'argousin qui a la fièvre chaude! . . . Le siècle était à la charogne, et le charnier lui plaisait mieux que le boudoir.'

The aim of Janin is to arrive at certain bitter truths by means of an exaggeration of the methods of the horror-school. His book is a satire on society and the human heart—on a society which honours vice when it is powerful and brazen and condemns it when weak and cringing, and on the foolish feminine heart which values the craze for luxury and personal vanity above real affection. The heroine, Henriette, a country girl who takes to a loose life, is honoured by every one as long as she conforms to the type of 'laideur morale' in which Janin ironically sees the height of horror—a horror much more intense than the physical horror described in the *roman-charogne*:

'Chaque jour je me trouvais possédé davantage de je ne sais quel épouvantable désir de pousser l'horreur à bout, de savoir enfin si je pouvais la vaincre ou bien si je serais vaincu par elle: or pour moi l'horreur n'existait que là où était Henriette; cette nature si vide et si fausse, cet abîme d'égoïsme et de faiblesse, cet être qui n'avait rien de l'homme moral.'[82]

(Observe that Janin here anticipates Baudelaire's conception of woman.)

But when Henriette, in a flash of conscience—and it is the only time that any passion enters her heart or any remorse troubles her soul—kills the man who had been the first to seduce her and who now comes, drunk, to buy her body in the brothel to which she has been reduced—when Henriette commits this crime which is 'la seule action courageuse et juste de cette fille', society punishes her by condemning her to death. Janin sees the world as governed by evil, in the same way as Sade:

'On a fait beaucoup de traités sur la nature morale qui ne prouvent rien; on s'est arrêté à d'insignifiantes apparences quand on

aurait dû creuser jusqu'au tuf. Que me font vos mœurs de salon
dans une société qui ne vivrait pas un jour si elle perdait ses
mouchards, ses geôliers, ses bourreaux, ses maisons de loterie et
de débauche, ses cabarets et ses spectacles? Ces agents principaux
de l'action sociale...'[83]

If one disregards for a moment the topical and polemical
motives to examine simply the way in which Janin behaves
in relation to the terrifying spectacles which he describes,
one can easily discover a fundamentally serious concern
under the superficial appearance of satire or parody. It
is a similar attitude to that of P. J. Toulet in *Monsieur du Paur* (1898), in which the author, describing 'le
vice anglais', sticks so close to scabrous details that any
possible smile which he may have wished to arouse dies
on the reader's lips. Janin is far removed from the
humoristic evasion of a morbid obsession such as moved
De Quincey to write his essay on *Murder as one of the
Fine Arts*.[84]

Janin, moreover, holding up to ridicule the horrors of
the modern drama, says:

'Où donc avez-vous eu plus de drames qu'à Rome? Quelle fable
égyptienne ou grecque, inventée, imaginée, faite à plaisir, pouvait
émouvoir à l'égal d'un combat de gladiateurs, à l'égal de cette
tragédie sanglante, où chaque scène était une blessure, où chaque
acte était une mort? Et quels acteurs encore! Ils étaient jeunes,
ils étaient beaux, il étaient nus! Le sang coulait rouge et fumant
sur leur poitrine.... A votre sens, ces soupirs et ces larmes répandues
sur du vrai sang et sur de vrais cadavres sont-ils à comparer à ce
que nous savons en fait de tragédie? Non, regardez le cirque
sanglant, voilà le drame vrai, terrible, palpitant, effroyable; fi de vos
vers, de votre prose, de vos tréteaux, de vos poignards à ressort, du
sang de vos acteurs acheté à la boucherie, de vos tragédies royales
aux aristocratiques douleurs! deux tigres, je ne dis pas deux Ger-
mains, qui se battent, sont plus dramatiques que tout Racine....'[85]

The teller of the story of *L'Âne mort* follows Henriette
in her career as a courtesan, first in luxury, then in the
hospital (there is a description of a surgical operation on
her beautiful body: 'quand l'opérateur en eut fini avec le
fer il employa le feu; il brûla impitoyablement, regardant
par intervalle son ouvrage avec la complaisance d'un jeune
peintre qui achève un paysage': here Janin seems to antici-

pate De Quincey, but is really echoing Diderot);[86] then in a brothel, then in prison. He gloats over the sight of the prisoner; putting his head through a slit in the back of a romantically mouldy, mossy bench in the courtyard of the prison so as not to cast a separate shadow, he watches every day through the air-hole of her cell 'les mouvements de sa captive'. The eternal feminine is not dead in the unfortunate woman, who looks at herself in a metal button filched from the warder. Then—height of horror—in order to obtain a postponement of her sentence (Henriette has been condemned to death after a trial which provides material for more satire) the prisoner makes the repulsive warder get her with child.[87] The narrator feels himself fainting with voluptuous horror at this sight, and experiences a similar feeling when, later, he sees the carpenter making love to his sweetheart actually on the guillotine destined for Henriette's execution. Last act: the narrator, by bribing the executioner, gets the victim's body handed over to him for honourable burial. Romantic irony is very evident in the bill presented by the executioner, and also in the conclusion: the corpse is pilfered by night for the lecture-room of the School of Medicine and the fine linen shroud stolen by some low-class women to make themselves dresses. The story—faithful to the precepts of the *roman-charogne*—begins with the description of a slaughter-house and ends with the violation of a tomb.

It was said of *L'Âne mort* (by the critic of the *Mercure de France au xix* siècle*, September 1831) that the author had combined the manner of Sterne with that of Diderot. If this be true of the style, the responsibility of the subject-matter must be credited to a different name—that of the Marquis de Sade.

15. It may therefore be surprising to find Janin, a few years later, in 1834, denouncing the horrors of Sade in a review article.[88] One can hardly believe that this is the author of *L'Âne mort*; and one may even go so far as to guess that this assumed moral tone is a pose. For Janin's article, conceived in the style of the popular preacher, has the same effect as the parody of articles of this sort which

occurs in the preface to *Mademoiselle de Maupin*; and it is
doubtful whether the author's intention was not actually
to encourage the reading of Sade's books, so much does he
exaggerate the corrupting influence of that unreal world
of monotonous butchery. We learn, in fact, that thanks to
this article and that of the Bibliophile Jacob there was an
awakening of interest in Sade. But to get rid of the idea
that Janin was acting the moralist simply as a joke one
has only to read his review of Borel's *Madame Putiphar*,
written in 1839,[89] which is conceived in the same pompous
style of rhetorical indignation and fits him for the application of Nietzsche's aphorism, 'There is no greater liar than
an indignant man.'[90] Janin's insincerity went so far as to
make him reprove in Borel the exact form of complaisance
that he himself had shown in *L'Âne mort*:

'On reste confondu quand on songe que l'auteur s'est donné à
lui-même cet affreux courage. Une fois dans l'horrible cachot où
s'accomplit son drame, il résiste à toutes les tentations d'en sortir.
Il reste accroupi la nuit et le jour sur sa victime. Il suit d'un œil
curieux la décomposition de ce cadavre.... Pour ma part, je ne
comprends pas cette obstination funeste d'un romancier, qui, après
tout, est le maître absolu de son conte.'

When—as we shall have occasion to mention soon—
Borel imagines his hero meeting the Marquis de Sade in
prison, and speaks in defence of the latter, Janin explodes:

'Et voyez où vous mène le paradoxe! C'est du marquis de Sade
que l'auteur a pitié! Oui, cet atroce et sanglant blasphémateur, cet
obscène historien des plus formidables rêveries qui aient jamais agité
la fièvre des démons, le marquis de Sade, il se montre dans cette
histoire comme l'intéressante victime des lettres de cachet!... *Un
martyr!* Un martyr celui-là! Mais si jamais les lettres de cachet
ont pu être justifiées, etc.... Un martyr! un martyr! le marquis de
Sade un martyr!'

This is exactly the tone that Janin had used in his essay
on Sade five years before. In any case it is probable that
the reading of Sade made a strong impression on the
Romantics, who took certain morbid fantasies so seriously
that they wished to translate them into real life. Both
Romantics and Decadents asked nothing better than to have
their minds poisoned. How much of Baudelaire's madness

was due to this receptive state of mind? The humoristic catharsis of a Mérimée or a De Quincey was by no means possible to every one.

'Acceptez ces pages', says Janin, preparing to give his estimate of the biography of Sade, 'comme on accepte en histoire naturelle la monographie du scorpion ou du crapaud.... Mais par où commencer et par où finir? Mais comment faire cette analyse de sang et de boue? Comment soulever tous ces meurtres? où sommesnous?... Ô quel infatigable scélérat!... Le tremblement vous saisit rien qu'à ouvrir ses pages.... Comme c'est déjà une horrible punition pour le malheureux qui souille ses yeux et son cœur de cette horrible lecture, de se voir poursuivi par ces tristes fantômes et d'assister, timide, immobile et muet, à ces lugubres scènes, sans pouvoir se venger qu'en lacérant le volume ou en le jetant au feu! Croyez-moi, qui que vous soyez, ne touchez pas à ces livres, ce serait tuer de vos mains le sommeil, le doux sommeil, cette mort de la vie de chaque jour, comme dit Macbeth....'

Why therefore should Janin have read the works of Sade? The following hardly constitutes a satisfactory reply:

'C'est justement parce que nous avons tous été assez lâches pour parcourir ces lignes fatales, que nous devons en prémunir les honnêtes et les heureux qui sont encore ignorants de ces livres.... Car, ne vous y trompez pas, le marquis de Sade est partout; il est dans toutes les bibliothèques, sur un certain rayon mystérieux et caché qu'on découvre toujours; c'est un de ces livres qui se placent d'ordinaire derrière un saint Jean Chrysostome, ou le *Traité de morale* de Nicole, ou les *Pensées* de Pascal.'

After this preamble, Janin, like a good preacher, passes on to examples; and to prove what becomes of an 'homme ignorant, timide et frêle, à la lecture d'un livre qui suffirait à ébranler les organisations les plus solides', he tells the pathetic story of a youth who became hysterical on reading *Justine*. This is his peroration:

'Les livres du marquis de Sade ont tué plus d'enfants que n'en pourraient tuer vingt maréchaux de Retz, ils en tuent chaque jour, ils en tueront encore, ils en tueront l'âme aussi bien que le corps.'

Any comparison between a genuine Bluebeard like Gilles de Rais and a mental Bluebeard like Sade was considered by Anatole France to be unsuitable, but according to the documents published by Bourdin, Sade, it must be admitted, did his best to live up to his lecherous imaginings.[91] And if, when the Revolution broke out, Sade declared himself an opponent of the death penalty (in *Justine*[92] he had written, 'Il n'y a que les lois qui n'ont pas ce privilège' [of disposing of human life]), it must be remembered that Saint-Just also, before he held supreme power in his hands, declaimed against the punishments of the law.[93]

The conclusion of Janin's essay is in a more humorous style:

'Cet homme était de fer. Vous l'enfermiez dans un cachot, il se racontait à lui-même des infamies. Vous le laissiez libre dans sa chambre, il vociférait des infamies par les barreaux de sa fenêtre. Se promenait-il dans la cour, il traçait sur le sable des figures obscènes. Venait-on le visiter, sa première parole était une ordure, et tout cela avec une voix très-douce, avec des cheveux blancs très beaux, avec l'air le plus aimable, avec une admirable politesse; à le voir sans l'entendre, on l'eût pris pour l'honorable aïeul de quelque vieille maison qui attend ses petits enfants pour les embrasser.'

The disciples of Gall flung themselves upon the skull of the Marquis, almost before he was dead, in the hope of finding there the key of the mystery:

'Mais cette tête... est petite, bien conformée, on la prendrait pour la tête d'une femme, au premier abord, d'autant plus que les organes de la tendresse maternelle et de l'amour des enfants y sont aussi saillants que sur la tête même d'Héloïse, ce modèle de tendresse et d'amour....'

16. About 1830, people were so convinced of the virulence of Sade's writings that Frédéric Soulié, in the *Mémoires du Diable* (1837), made Captain Félix put a copy of *Justine* into the hands of Henriette Buré, who had been shut up alone in a dungeon by her family, with the idea that reading it would drive her mad.

Soulié also professed the greatest loathing of 'ce frénétique et abominable assemblage de tous les crimes et de toutes les saletés' which constituted the work of Sade, and, embittered by his previous lack of success, launched out into an invective against Paris in the same manner as Janin, who had said in *L'Âne mort*: 'Paris corrupteur de toutes les innocences, qui fane toutes les roses, qui flétrit toutes les beautés, insatiable débauché.' 'Do not come to Paris', warns Soulié, 'if you are possessed by an ambition for pure glory.' Because in Paris:

'vous verrez le public, ce vieux débauché, sourire à la virginité de votre muse, la flétrir d'un baiser impudique pour lui crier en-suite: Allons, courtisane, va-t-en, ou amuse-moi; il me faut des astringents et des moxas pour ranimer mes sensations éteintes; as-tu des incestes furibonds ou des adultères monstrueux, d'effrayantes bacchanales de crimes ou des passions impossibles à me raconter? Alors parle, je t'écouterai une heure, le temps durant lequel je sentirai ta plume âcre et envenimée courir sur ma sensibilité calleuse ou gangrénée; sinon, tais-toi, va mourir dans la misère et l'obscurité. La misère et l'obscurité, entendez-vous, jeunes gens?... Vous n'en voulez pas, et alors que ferez-vous, jeunes gens? vous prendrez une plume, une feuille de papier, vous écrirez en tête: *Mémoires du Diable*, et vous direz au siècle: Ah! vous voulez de cruelles choses pour vous en réjouir; soit, monseigneur, voici un coin de ton histoire.'

Actually, as we shall now see, Soulié's novel contains 'de cruelles choses'; but to save appearances the novelist hastens to add:

'Que Dieu nous garde toutefois de deux choses que le monde pourrait nous pardonner, mais que nous ne nous pardonnerions pas: qu'il nous garde de mensonge et d'immoralité!... Ce que nous vous dirons sera donc vrai et moral; ce ne sera pas notre faute si cela n'est pas toujours flatteur et honnête.'

The book hinges on the axiom of Sade: *prospérités du vice* and *malheurs de la vertu*. Soulié illustrates the axiom mainly in the moral sphere (the 'laideur morale' of Janin) but is not the less concerned, on this account, with sadism. His satire, like that of *L'Âne mort*, is directed against con-temporary society, which honours vice (provided it is powerful and at the same time hypocritical) and oppresses virtue. Duels, poisonings, murders, parricides, adulteries, incests, condemnations of the innocent, follow each other thick and fast in Soulié's pages, which contain the material for several short stories such as d'Aurevilly, and novels such as Mendès, wrote in the second half of the century. The ghastly phantasmagoria is dominated by the figure of a dandyish Beelzebub with his 'hideux sourire' and his 'fauve regard de cannibale, contemplant la victime qu'il va dévorer'. (Something of the same kind is to be found in Mrs. Shelley's *Frankenstein*, though Soulié's devil is descended from the *Diable boiteux* of Le Sage.)[94]

Virtuous women (is it necessary to add?) languish in prisons and asylums, or kill themselves in desperation, while prostitutes and murderesses pass for paragons of virtue in the eyes of the world; and the hero, the Baron Armand de Luizzi, over whose destiny brood the consequences of a horrible tragedy which befell his family in the Middle Ages (a period no less infested with incests and adulteries than the modern age in which Soulié is writing), proves fatal, against his own will, through the evil arts of the devil, to all those whom he loves or approaches. Caroline, Luizzi's virtuous sister, victim of every possible outrage and reduced to beggary, arrives, with the object of saving her brother, at the place which Juliette, the wicked sister, had once left to enter upon a career of vice, and where Luizzi meets her in all the pomp of luxury. It is obvious that Soulié is retracing the outlines of Sade's Justine and Juliette.[94A] There is a spectacular finale— not unlike that of *The Monk*—in which Luizzi, having lost in his game with the devil, is swallowed up in an abyss together with his sinister ancestral castle; and the three martyred women— obviously to justify to some extent the moral purpose of the book—are exalted to higher spheres. Soulié, as we have seen, maintained that he gave free rein to his cruel imagination in order to attract the public, and there are not wanting here and there in the course of the book hints of irony in accordance with the taste of the period, as in *L'Âne mort*. But, like Janin, Soulié also, though affecting to scorn horrors, plunges into them with the greatest delight:

' "Un inceste!" s'écria Luizzi. "Mon cher, vous êtes stupide!" dit le Diable avec emportement, "vous n'avez pas la moindre idée des ressources de la vie; vous êtes de la littérature de votre époque d'une manière effrénée, vous faites tout de suite un drame abominable d'une chose qui me paraît très divertissante." '[95]

' "J'ai profité de mon habit séculier, qui ne pouvait lui dire qui j'étais (says the priest who has told Luizzi of the terrible medieval tragedy in his family) pour lui montrer jusqu'à quelle triste férocité

on pouvait pousser cette manie littéraire qui ne vit plus que d'inceste, de meurtre et de sang, et je lui ai raconté cette légende." '96

Perhaps this taste for the horrible can be attributed to
the period more than to Soulié himself. At any rate the
book had an immense success and influenced considerably
the supreme example of the *roman-feuilleton*, the *Mystères
de Paris*. In his other novels, which were soon forgotten,
Soulié also had regular recourse to the arsenal of the 'tales
of terror'.97

17. A more serious concern with horror than that of
Soulié and many others (we know that *bons vivants* such as
Dumas and Gautier cultivated the macabre and the horrible
as a fashionable pose) is shown in the work of Pétrus
Borel, whom the facetious Théo called the most perfect
example of the Romantic ideal, and who was a kind of
minor Baudelaire *ante litteram*.

Certainly Pétrus Borel, the *lycanthrope* who flaunted a
waistcoat *à la* Robespierre and an ogre's beard, and missed
no opportunity of displaying his superb feline teeth, was a
dandy in the style of the Terror, a *fumiste*. But in him this
playing with violent sensations became intenser and more
serious: he depicted his hero Champavert as killing himself in circumstances both macabre and grotesque (he is
found in a horse-knacker's yard—such as Janin loved—
with a huge knife planted like a stake in his breast); and
he finished by committing suicide himself, apparently, by
letting himself die of sunstroke, in 1859.

'Chanter l'amour!... — he says — Pour moi l'amour c'est de la
haine, des gémissements, des cris, de la honte, du deuil, du fer, des
larmes, du sang, des cadavres, des ossements, des remords — je n'en
ai pas connu d'autre.' *Pétrus Borel*.

The frontispiece which Adrien Aubry designed later
for Borel's *Champavert, contes immoraux* (1833) shows
quite clearly the sort of spectacle that may be looked for if
once one enters the peepshow of horrors that the book contains. In the middle is a medallion with the effigy of the
author looking like a sinister Jesuit; on the left a guillotine, a dark lantern, a skull; on the right a boatman who
with a pole is violently pushing under water a woman with
her breast uncovered and her arms tied behind her back;

the grim outline of a Gothic castle is to be seen on the river bank.

The first story, *Monsieur de l'Argentière, l'accusateur*, presents us with one of the infinite variations of the persecuted maiden. The progressive degradation of Apolline is followed with the same minute attention to unpleasant detail as has been noticed in *L'Âne mort*. Apolline is raped by an unknown man on a dark night;[98] reduced to extreme misery, she abandons her new-born child in a cesspool and goes through the same stages as Janin's Henriette: the Hospice de la Bourbe, the Prison de la Force, 'dans un cachot étroit et sombre,' and finally the Place de la Grève. The chief responsibility for her being condemned to death lies with the Public Prosecutor, in whom Apolline recognizes the man who raped her. 'It is he, that man who is speaking! It was he whom I saw by the light of the moon, with his sallow face, his red hair, and those deep-set eyes!' Monsieur de l'Argentière pushes his sadistic inclinations to the point of being present at the execution, which takes place amid the morbid curiosity of the crowd:

'Quand le coutelas tomba, il se fit une sourde rumeur; et un Anglais, penché sur une fenêtre qu'il avait louée 500 fr., fort satisfait, cria un long *very wel* [sic] en applaudissant des mains.'

We shall come across this Englishman again several times during the second half of the nineteenth century.[99]

Jaquez Barraou, le charpentier is the next story. It is an extremely horrible tale of the criminal jealousy of two negroes over a beautiful mulatto woman; the scene is Havana. Then there is *Don Andréa Vésalius l'anatomiste*. The anatomist drugs his wife's lovers and uses their bodies for his experiments; his wife, at the sight of the jars in which are preserved in spirits the remains of her last lover, dies of horror, and the indefatigable scientist cuts up her beautiful body also; the scene is Madrid. Baudelaire recalled at least one detail of this story:

'Sur la porte était appendu un squelette, qui, lorsqu'elle était agitée, bruissait comme ces bougies de bois que les chandeliers suspendent pour enseigne, quand elles sont remuées par la bise.'

For in the *Métamorphoses du vampire* we read:

A mes côtés.   .   .   .   .   .

.   .   .   .

Tremblaient confusément des débris de squelette
Qui d'eux-mêmes rendaient le cri d'une girouette
Ou d'une enseigne, au bout d'une tringle de fer,
Que balance le vent pendant les nuits d'hiver.

From Madrid we pass on to Jamaica, to the loves of
Three-fingered Jack, l'Obi: nor are horrors and corpses
lacking here either. In placing his scene among the
negroes of the Antilles Borel was only following in the
footsteps of Hugo in *Bug-Jargal*. In the last three stories
we return to France. *Dina la belle juive* [100] has for her
motto the litanies of the Virgin: 'Rosa mystica, Turris
Davidica', &c. One thinks immediately of Baudelaire's
Franciscae meae laudes. Dina, in her anxiety for the fate of
Aymar, behaves in the way already indicated in Keats's
Ode to Melancholy ('Then glut thy sorrow on a morning
rose . . . or on the wealth of globèd peonies . . .') and in
the manner later adopted by the disciples of Baudelaire
and Huysmans' des Esseintes:

'Dépravée par la douleur, elle recherchait ardemment tout ce qui
irritait ses nerfs, tout ce qui titillait et éveillait son apathie; elle se
chargeait des fleurs les plus odorantes; elle s'entourait de vases pleins
de syringa, de jasmin, de verveines, de roses, de lys, de tubéreuses,
elle faisait fumer de l'encens, du benjoin; elle épandait autour d'elle
de l'ambre, du cinnamome, du storax, du musc.'

A Saône boatman rapes and murders Dina in the manner
illustrated in the frontispiece, and then—behaving like
Monsieur de l'Argentière—pretends to have fished up her
corpse, in order to earn the two pistoles reward. Romantic
irony—for since Dina is a Jewess, the boatman has no
right to the money for his pretended discovery.

The following is the story of *Passereau l'écolier*. A
medical student who suspects his mistress of infidelity
causes her to fall into a well, the top of which is level with
the ground: he covers her over with the coping-stones,
then challenges her lover to a duel, with the agreement
that the lady shall belong to the survivor. Before firing,
Passereau advises his opponent to go next morning and

have a look at the well. Baudelaire did not merely make use of this situation in the *Vin de l'assassin*:

> Je l'ai jetée au fond d'un puits,
> Et j'ai même poussé sur elle
> Tous les pavés de la margelle....

but also took from it the main idea of a play, *L'Ivrogne*.[101]

Passereau's request to the executioner, whom he went to find expressly for the purpose, remained famous: 'Je désirerais que vous me guillotinassiez.'

The last story, *Champavert le lycanthrope* (the pseudonym of Borel himself), completes the museum of horrors with the story of the macabre circumstances of the last days of Champavert. He makes a misanthropic will, disinters the little corpse of his own and Flava's child, kills Flava, and ends his life among the carcasses of the horses slaughtered at the Buttes de Montfaucon.

Even the tale *Gottfried Wolfgang* which Borel plagiarized from Irving (*The Adventure of the German Student*) is typical for the conclusion.[101A] In it a German student, given to Swedenborgian speculations and subject to hallucinations, is tormented by the memory of a beautiful woman of whom he has caught a glimpse in a dream. One night, roaming the streets of Paris during the Terror, he stumbles against the guillotine, and in a flash of lightning sees a figure bending down, with dishevelled hair, which he recognizes as the woman of his dream. He takes her home, and notices that she has round her neck a ribbon of black velvet. The student declares to her his passion, and the woman tells him that she has been urged towards him by a supernatural impulse. In the morning he finds her cold: at his cries the police rush in and recognize the woman as a victim of the guillotine. Gottfried removes the black ribbon from her neck and sees beneath it the cut of the axe. This tale, which is worthy of Poe, is claimed to have been found in the possession of an innkeeper at Boulogne, to whom it had been given by a strange, taciturn young Englishman.

No less frantic than *Champavert*, the novel called *Madame Putiphar* (1839) deliberately piles horror upon horror, in a style in which mystification is interwoven with sincerity in a decidedly curious manner. Certain pages are anticipatory of the grotesque method of Lautréamont—as, for instance, the beginning of the eighteenth chapter of the sixth book:

'Ma tâche est triste; mais puisque je me suis engagé à dire ces malheurs, je l'accomplirai. Je m'étais cru l'esprit plus fort, le cœur plus dur ou plus indifférent; j'avais cru pouvoir toucher à ces infortunes et en sculpter le long bas-relief avec le calme de l'artisan qui façonne une tombe; combien je me suis abusé! A mesure que j'avance dans cette vallée de larmes, mon pied soulève un tourbillon de mélancolie qui s'attache à mon âme comme la poussière s'attache au manteau du voyageur. Pas un outrage dont j'aie donné le spectacle qui n'ait allumé en moi une colère véritable; pas une souffrance que j'aie peinte qui ne m'ait coûté des pleurs. Courage, ma muse! encore quelques pages, et toutes ces belles douleurs ramassées par toi avec un soin si religieux, toutes ces belles douleurs jusqu'à ce jour ignorées du monde, étouffées, perdues, comme de petites herbes sous les gerbes de faits éclatants et sans nombre qui jonchent le sol de l'histoire, auront trouvé leur dénouement et revêtu une forme qui ne leur permettra plus de mourir, de mourir dans la mémoire des hommes.'

When the highly unfortunate Patrick—younger brother of Byron's Prisoner of Chillon—is released from the Bastille on February 27th, 1784, he falls in with two other prisoners, one of whom is 'une des gloires de la France — un martyr':

'Ce que j'entends par cette gloire de la France, s'il faut le dire, c'était l'illustre auteur d'un livre contre lequel vous criez touts [*sic*] à l'infamie, et que vous avez touts dans votre poche, je vous en demande bien pardon, cher lecteur; c'était, dis-je, très haut et très puissant seigneur, monsieur le comte de Sade [*sic*], dont les fils dégénérés portent aujourd'hui parmi nous un front noble et fier, un front noble et pur.'

Borel acquits Napoleon of the horrible cruelty of having persecuted Sade: 'C'eût été mal d'ailleurs de la part de l'empereur corse d'accommoder ainsi un empereur romain.' This is an example of romantic mystification (but then Borel took a genuine pleasure in spectacles of cruelty). Another romantic mystification is the recantation inserted by the author into the twenty-third chapter of the seventh book, in which, declaring that light had dawned upon him, he proclaims that it is not true that the good pay for the wicked, and that if this sometimes seems to be so, it is because the good are either only good in appearance, or are expiating the wrongs of their race:

'Je me suis efforcé tout le long de ce livre à faire fleurir le vice, à faire prévaloir la dissolution sur la vertu; j'ai couronné de roses la pourriture; j'ai parfumé de nard la lâcheté; j'ai versé le bonheur à plein bord dans le giron de l'infamie; j'ai mis le firmament dans la boue; j'ai mis la boue dans le ciel; pas un de mes braves héros qui ne soit une victime; partout j'ai montré le mal oppresseur et le bien opprimé. . . . — Et tout cela, toutes ces destinées cruelles accumulées, n'ont abouti après tant de peines qu'à me donner un démenti!'

Each of the unhappy lovers, Déborah and Patrick, is descended from an accursed race. Borel, like Soulié, makes an effort to save his face, and finishes by evoking a picture of social nemesis. 'Car Dieu et le peuple, ces deux formidables ouvriers, vont se mettre à la besogne! — et car leur besogne comme eux sera terrible!'

In connexion with Janin's violent article, of which we have already spoken, we are given this peep behind the scenes: [102]

' "Si je parle de votre livre", dit-il à Pétrus Borel qui lui demandait un article, "je le comparerai tout simplement aux œuvres du marquis de Sade". "Comparez!" dit Pétrus. Jules Janin ne se le fit pas dire deux fois. Lorsque M. Bertin vit l'article en question, "Holà! Jules", dit-il au critique, "tu veux donc que nous ayons un procès?" ".Nous n'aurons pas de procès", répondit Jules Janin. "L'auteur le veut ainsi". "Étrange auteur!" fit M. Bertin.'

But even if *Madame Putiphar* had only a moderate success, it at least called forth the praise of Baudelaire for 'la peinture des hideurs et des tortures du cachot, qui monte jusqu'à la vigueur de Mathurin'.[103]

The verse of the *Rhapsodies* is in no way to be distinguished from the usual productions of the followers of Byron. But, according to Baudelaire, Borel played a not unimportant part in the history of his century. Without him, he says, there would be a gap in the course of Romanticism. And he concludes:

'Pour moi, j'avoue sincèrement, quand même j'y sentirais un

ridicule, que j'ai toujours eu quelque sympathie pour ce malheureux
écrivain dont le génie manqué, plein d'ambition et de maladresse,
n'a su produire que des ébauches minutieuses, des éclairs orageux,
des figures dont quelque chose de trop bizarre, dans l'accoutrement
ou dans la voix, altère la native grandeur. Il a, en somme, une
couleur à lui, une saveur *sui generis.* . . .'

'Sa spécialité fut la *Lycanthropie*', he had already said.
After all, lycanthropy is only another name for sadism.

18. There is no need of further examples to show how
vitiated was the atmosphere in which Baudelaire grew up.
Books such as *L'Âne mort* and *Champavert* indicate the
trend of a whole literature; nor was it only such writers as
Eugène Sue, Paul Lacroix ('Bibliophile Jacob'), Roger de
Beauvoir, and Frédéric Soulié who had 'un fond de Sade
masqué, mais non point méconnaissable', as Sainte-Beuve
expressed it;[104] nor only the obscure *bohèmes* of Murger,
successors of the 'Jeunes-France', who delighted in morbid
extravagances.[105] Even allowing for exaggeration in the
following denunciation delivered by the Comte Horace
de Viel Castel,[106] one cannot deny that it is on the whole
justified:

'On ne sait pas assez tout le mal produit par les œuvres monstrueuses du marquis de Sade (*Justine* et *Juliette*). Je ne parle pas
seulement des tristes résultats produits par la lecture de ces ignobles
romans, mais de l'influence qu'ils ont eue sur toute la littérature
du XIX.ᵉ siècle. Hugo dans *Notre Dame de Paris*, Jules Janin
dans l'*Âne mort*, Théophile Gauthier [*sic*] dans *M.lle de Maupin*,[107]
M.me Sand, E. Sue,[108] de Musset, etc. etc., Dumas dans son
Théâtre, tous sont parents de Sade, tous jettent un morceau de sa
débauche dans leurs productions.'

Moreover, it was not merely the desire for money, as
Sainte-Beuve tries to make out, which drove writers to put
into their work 'un raffinement d'immoralité et de dé-
pravation', in order to 'exploiter fructueusement les mauvais penchants du public.' This may be true of such
writers as Soulié and Sue, but what is to be said when one
realizes that the source of inspiration has this same quality
even in the great artists? What is to be said when one sees
a Berlioz giving such great prominence in his operas to
macabre, obscene, and ferocious subjects, in *Harold en
Italie* combining debauch with blasphemy and slaughter

(*Orgie des brigands*), in the *Francs-Juges* translating into
music the feeling of terror aroused by the ferocity of the
secret tribunal (*Ouverture*), and, in the *Symphonie fantastique*, going from a *Marche au supplice* to the Black Mass
of the *Songe d'une nuit du sabbat*? Is there not also, perhaps, in the work of Musset, an obvious insistence on the
painful aspect of love, on the *voluptas dolendi*?[109] The *Confession d'un enfant du siècle* (1836) is a document no less
symptomatic of 'méchanceté dans l'amour' than the *Liaisons dangereuses* (Octave, also, meditated upon the 'caté-
chismes du libertinage' of the eighteeneth century). There
is mention of the libertine's sensation of 'terreur mêlée de
volupté' (IIe Partie, chap. 2), of the 'curiosité du mal,
maladie infâme qui naît de tout contact impur' (Ve Partie,
chap. 4); of real and veritable hair-shirts (Octave fixed the
medallion on which was the portrait of his mistress on the
'plaque hérissée de pointes' of a 'discipline' and wore it on
his chest so as to feel it pierce his flesh); and also of moral
hair-shirts, the latter consisting in continual scenes of
jealousy which were sought after with the thirst of a martyr. Octave, the 'libertin colère et cruel', behaved towards
the virtuous Brigitte in much the same way as Valmont
towards Madame de Tourvel, except that this time the
libertine is not content with inflicting tortures upon others,
but is 'toujours avide de souffrir' himself.

'Sa cervelle ressemble à ces cachots de l'Inquisition où les
murailles sont couvertes de tant d'instruments de supplice, qu'on
n'en comprend ni le but ni la forme et qu'on se demande en les
voyant si ce sont des tenailles ou des jouets.'

On the influence of the *Confession* there is to be found
the following note (dated 1871) in the *Journal* of the
Goncourts:

'En lisant *La Confession d'un enfant du siècle*, je suis frappé de
l'action que certains livres exercent sur certains hommes, et comme
ces hommes, chez lesquels le père n'a pas imprimé une marque de
fabrique, sortent tout entiers des entrailles d'un bouquin. Toute la
méchanceté trouble de ce livre, je l'ai sentie, je l'ai touchée chez
quelques jeunes gens, mais encore accrue, développée, mise en
pratique fielleuse par une basse naissance. Alors je me demandais
curieusement, si ces jeunes tiraient tout cela de leur propre fonds.

Aujourd'hui je m'aperçois que cette méchanceté n'était qu'un plagiat, un plagiat littéraire, qui, avec l'aide de détestables instincts, est devenu à la fin un tempérament. En sorte que l'Octave de la fiction a vraiment fait, comme dans une matrice humaine, des tas de petits Octaves, en chair et en os.'[110]

Leaving aside Dumas and Hugo, authors who were substantially sane in spite of their affectation of contemporary fashions, let us consider Delacroix, Baudelaire, Flaubert.

19. 'Delacroix, lac de sang hanté de mauvais anges . . .' —a line as vividly descriptive as are the essays which Baudelaire wrote on his favourite painter, and of which I should much prefer to quote the most important passages, rather than make a paraphrase of them which is necessarily pale and enfeebled by the remoteness of our changed tastes. For actually to-day the tendency is to apply to Delacroix a criticism which was intended as praise by Gautier when he made it, whereas to us it gives, rather, an impression of censure: 'S'il exécutait en peintre, il pensait en poète, et le fond de son talent est fait de littérature.'[111] It is symptomatic of Baudelaire's state of mind that he should appreciate particularly those painters and musicians who were most steeped in literature, such as Delacroix and Wagner, who combined intellectualism with a turbid sensuality.

This painter Delacroix, described as 'cannibale', 'molochiste', 'doloriste', with his untiring curiosity for slaughter, fire, rapine, *putrideros*, illustrator of the darkest scenes of *Faust* and of the most satanic poems of his adored Byron; with his love of the feline (what a vast number of studies he made of biting beasts!) and of violent, hot countries, Spain, Africa; with his enthusiasm for frenzied action; lamented that 'son âme a énervé ses feux, ses vingt-cinq ans sans jeunesse, son ardeur sans vigueur', and made this confession:[112]

'Ce matin, Hélène est venue. Ô disgrâce... je n'ai pu.'
'La fille est venue ce matin poser. Hélène a dormi ou fait semblant. Je ne sais pourquoi je me crus obligé de faire mine d'adorateur pendant ce temps, mais la nature n'y était point. Je me suis rejeté sur un mal de tête; au moment de son départ, et quand il n'était plus temps... le vent avait changé. Scheffer m'a consolé

le soir, et il s'est trouvé absolument dans les mêmes intentions. Je me fais des peurs de tout, et crois toujours qu'un inconvénient va être éternel....

'Je suis toujours comme ça.... Mes résolutions s'évanouissent toujours en présence de l'action. J'aurais besoin d'une maîtresse pour mater la chair d'habitude. J'en suis fort tourmenté et soutiens à mon atelier de magnanimes combats. Je souhaite quelquefois l'arrivée de la première femme venue. Fasse le ciel que vienne Laure demain! Et puis, quand il m'en tombe quelqu'une, je suis presque fâché, je voudrais n'avoir pas à agir; c'est là mon cancer....'

Hence the 'vieux levain', the 'fond tout noir à contenter' which he felt within himself,[113] was forced to find some outlet, and found it in his paintings. Perhaps the malarial fever which attacked him in 1820 and slowly devastated him is sufficient to explain the reason of the 'hymne terrible composé en l'honneur de la fatalité et de l'irrémédiable douleur', as Baudelaire described his work?[114] Can the fever explain the sort of cannibalism which reddens as with blood the gloom of his canvases? Or must we trace there too the influence of the prevailing taste, of the cruel studies of physical torment by Géricault, painter of madmen and corpses?

'All these violent works are the result of an exhausted blood', declared Dargenty.[115] 'Je n'ai point d'amour. . . . Je n'ai que de vains rêves qui m'agitent et ne satisfont rien du tout'[116]—this is the painful mystery that Baudelaire felt to be celebrated in Delacroix' melancholy pictures, the expression of the wild interior world of his imagination. The troubled springs of his inspiration and his unsatisfied desires account, as in the similar case of Swinburne, for the hyper-Dionysiacal type of expression, the quivering nervousness of style, which almost make one think of a pictorial rendering of a piece of music, of the 'soupir étouffé de Weber' (just as some critic felt in Swinburne's verse a kind of virtual music).[117] Both the poet and the painter seem to have spasmodic yearnings towards something beyond mere artistic expression: starting from darkness, their desire is lost in darkness. 'Limbes insondés de la tristesse.' . . . 'Fanfares étranges . . .' Not without reason was Delacroix the object of a veritable cult

on the part of Maurice Barrès. 'Du sang, de la volupté, *ver*
de la mort' might well be the motto of his work.

Tortured, sick women, the beautiful prisoner bound
naked on a horse in the *Massacre de Scio*, the lovely concu-
bines slaughtered on Sardanapalus' funeral bed, as in one
of the orgies described, but without the faintest breath of
art, by Sade (in his first sketch Delacroix showed the slave,
who on the right of the picture is being stabbed, as being
beheaded); the woman who has been raped and murdered,
stretched on the steps in a disordered attitude, and the
other, the blond patrician, who, defiled and exhausted,
bends over the livid face of her dead mother, in the *Prise
de Constantinople*; drowned Ophelia, whose image haunted
Delacroix all his life; the shade of Margaret appearing to
Faust (a demon holds up by the hair the pale corpse with
the bosom immodestly uncovered); Angelica and Andro-
meda chained to the rock, Olindo and Sofronia bound to
the stake, the Indian woman seized by a tiger, Rebecca   *ver*
ravished, the other young woman dragged off by pirates
to their boat, the livid beauty of the woman's corpse in the
Apollon triomphant . . . it is a whole harem of ghastly
phantoms that move in funereal file across the canvases of
Delacroix. There is Medea possessed by her mad vengeance, who with the movement of a lioness clasps the two
babes to her marble bosom: in her hand she holds a
dagger; a shadow falls like a mask over her eyes. There
is the bloody corpse of the beautiful youth Saint Sebastian, from which a woman's delicate fingers are plucking
the arrows; and that of another youthful martyr, Saint
Stephen, from whose brow a woman also wipes the blood
of his wounds; the tortured body of young Foscari upon
which his mother and his bride abandon themselves weeping; the bishop of Liège massacred in an orgy. . . . Finally
there is the ceiling of the Palais Bourbon in Paris, where
the painter's gloomy conception seems to embrace the
whole history of humanity, and a kind of philosophy of
sadism, pronouncing the changeless cruelty of Nature, is
distilled from the episodes portrayed—Pliny destroyed by
Vesuvius, Archimedes stabbed by an ignorant soldier,
Seneca committing suicide at the will of a tyrant, Saint

John the Baptist beheaded for a woman's whim, the Israelites exiled and enslaved at Babylon, Italy trampled by the fierce hordes of Attila. The whole universe is suffering and pain, as in Swinburne's *Anactoria*: not only do the bodies of men strain in violent action or twist in pain or fall exhausted in agony, not only does the flesh tremble with nerves stretched beyond bearing, or languish in mortal pallor: but beasts and plants seem to vibrate with the same shudder of pain, and the sky is dyed with a strange lymph like gall, and bends, veiled with soot, over feverish waters, or over an implacable sea.

> Delacroix, lac de sang hanté de mauvais anges,
> Ombragé par un bois de sapins toujours vert,
> Où, sous un ciel chagrin, des fanfares étranges
> Passent, comme un soupir étouffé de Weber.

These lines take us from the paintings of Delacroix to the sinister House of Usher, with its gloomy pool on which weighs an atmosphere of fatality and its maniac who delights in funereal improvizations, among which is 'une certaine paraphrase singulière, — une perversion de l'air déjà fort étrange, de la dernière valse de von Weber.'[118] A contact between Delacroix and Poe had become established in the mind of Baudelaire. In 1856 he sent a copy of his translation of the *Tales of Mystery and Imagination* (*Histoires extraordinaires*) to Delacroix, who made this comment in his diary:[119]

'Baudelaire dit dans sa préface "que je rappelle en peinture ce sentiment d'idéal, si singulier et si plaisant dans le terrible". Il a raison...'

20. 'Vous dotez le ciel de l'art d'on ne sait quel rayon macabre. Vous créez un frisson nouveau'—here it is Victor Hugo writing to Baudelaire.[120] At present there is a tendency to isolate all that is sanest and of most universal import in the poetry of Baudelaire. The 'femmes damnées' are easily forgotten for the 'petites vieilles', the black Venus for the golden-hearted servant-maid, and the dandy of ecclesiastical cut, perfumed with sulphur rather than incense, which Baudelaire strove to appear, is on the way to being canonized seriously as a saint.[121] But the 'frisson nouveau' which his contemporaries felt in him is not to

be found in the poems which the readers of to-day prefer; the Baudelaire of his own age was the satanic Baudelaire, who gathered into a choice bouquet the strangest orchids, the most monstrous aroids from among the wild tropical flora of French Romanticism. His contemporaries saw in him the poet who had gone to seek his materials—the words are Sainte-Beuve's[122]—'à l'extrémité du Kamtchatka littéraire', in order to build the strange pavilion called 'Baudelaire's Folly'. Baudelaire himself claimed to have chosen an unexplored province, to have sought to 'extraire la beauté du mal'; but as to horrors, it can be seen from what I have already shown how little there remained for Baudelaire to invent. He sent a wave of electricity through the shapeless *putridero* which had been gathering into a mass since 1820, and, galvanized by it, the phantoms took on an appearance of life. Now they have returned to the cemetery of the Past, these ghouls, vampires, and incubi, but the Danse Macabre was prolonged till after the dawn of the present century.

It may be claimed that these are mere external appearances, from which Baudelaire should be defended as though from a false self. It will be repeated that there was a great deal of affectation and deliberate mystification in certain of his attitudes; that Baudelaire's satanism fulfilled chiefly the function of a barrier which an extremely tormented and delicate soul had erected in defence of its own jealous inner self: a kind of hard and gorgeously coloured carapace to protect the profounder vein of shy confession that might otherwise have evaporated into inexpressiveness; so that even the crudest among his extravaganzas should be interpreted by way of symbol and metaphor. Just as nobody would take seriously a witticism of his about the taste of a new-born baby's brain, or the fact that he dyed his hair green, so we are advised to consider all the wildest manifestations of his mind as awkward instinctive devices, if not as mere deplorable child's play, to which no importance must be attached. However, since we are here aiming not at an aesthetic judgment but at a psychological documentation, it is necessary to insist even on the transient aspects of Baudelaire as a man.

First of all must be remembered: 'J'ai cultivé mon hystérie avec jouissance et terreur.' And, with regard to that convenient little word 'ennui', which literary historians generally employ as the 'Open Sesame' of Romanticism, certain qualifying lines of Baudelaire may be quoted:

> C'est l'Ennui! — L'œil chargé d'un pleur involontaire,
> Il rêve d'échafauds en fumant son houka.
>
> *(Les Fleurs du Mal:* 'Au lecteur')

> Il me conduit ainsi, loin du regard de Dieu,
> Haletant et brisé de fatigue, au milieu
> Des plaines de l'Ennui, profondes et désertes,
>
> Et jette dans mes yeux pleins de confusion
> *Des vêtements souillés, des blessures ouvertes,*
> *Et l'appareil sanglant de la Destruction!*
>
> *(Id.,* 'La Destruction')

Ennui is only the most generic aspect of the *mal du siècle*; its specific aspect is—sadism.[123]

A passage from Poe's *The Black Cat* is also worthy of mention. Baudelaire quotes it in full (from his own translation) in his essay on his brother-in-art, in the *Revue de Paris* (March and April, 1852), with a modest word of introduction: 'Ce passage mérite d'être cité':

'Et puis vint, pour me conduire à une chute finale et irrévocable, l'esprit de PERVERSITÉ. De cette force, la philosophie ne tient aucun compte. Cependant, aussi fermement que je crois à l'existence de mon âme, je crois que la perversité est une des impulsions primitives du cœur humain, l'une des facultés ou sentiments primaires, indivisibles, qui constituent le caractère de l'homme. — Qui n'a pas cent fois commis une action folle ou vile, par la seule raison qu'il savait devoir s'en abstenir? N'avons-nous pas une inclination perpétuelle, en dépit de notre jugement, à violer ce qui est la loi, seulement parce que nous savons que c'est la loi? Cet esprit de perversité, dis-je, causa ma dernière chute. *Ce fut ce désir insondable que l'âme éprouve de s'affliger elle-même*[124] — de violenter sa propre nature, — de faire le mal pour le seul amour du mal, — qui me poussa à continuer, et enfin à consommer, la torture que j'avais infligée à cette innocente bête. Un matin, de sang-froid, j'attachai une corde à son cou, et je le pendis à une branche d'arbre. — Je le pendis en versant d'abondantes larmes et le cœur plein du remords le plus amer; — je le pendis, *parce que* je savais qu'il m'avait aimé et *parce que* je sentais qu'il ne m'avait donné aucun sujet de colère,

— je le pendis, parce que je savais qu'en faisant ainsi je commettrais un crime, un péché mortel qui mettrait en péril mon âme immortelle, au point de la placer, si une telle chose était possible, hors de la sphère de la miséricorde infinie du Dieu très miséricordieux et très terrible.'

It is Poe speaking, but it might equally well be Baudelaire (see below, *Le mauvais vitrier*) or Dostoievsky; or, indeed, if he had been an artist and not merely a pornographer, the Marquis de Sade.

Baudelaire's discovery of Poe was, as it were, a revelation of his own hidden self: 'J'ai vu, avec épouvante et ravissement, non seulement des sujets rêvés par moi, mais des *phrases*, pensées par moi, et écrites par lui, vingt ans auparavant.' This surprise showed itself as a paramnesia. The tales of Poe, as D. H. Lawrence observed,[125] are always a symbolical, mythological translation of the same thirst for unrealizable love (so it is not quite true that 'dans les nouvelles de Poe, il n'y a jamais d'amour', as Baudelaire said![126]) and of the desire for that complete fusion with the beloved being which ends in vampirism. It is a nervous ecstasy, which becomes localized in actual genuine obsessions—the eyes of Ligeia, the teeth of Berenice; a yearning for the absolute knowledge which coincides with annihilation and death. In *The Oval Portrait* the vampire obsession is symbolized by the absorption of the model into the picture:

'Les couleurs qu'il étalait sur la toile étaient tirées des joues de celle qui était assise près de lui..... "En vérité, c'est la *Vie* elle-même!" il se retourna brusquement pour regarder sa bien-aimée: — elle était morte!' (Baudelaire's translation.)

Poe's lovers resemble each other, and are related by blood (Poe married his own cousin); their nervous systems are already attuned, and sensitized by disease. It is as if their nerves had been laid bare to be ligatured like veins. Intercourse, in such circumstances, is incest, murder: the couple are consumed in a blaze in which ecstasy and horror are identical.[127]

'Tout enfant, j'ai senti dans mon cœur deux sentiments contradictoires, l'horreur de la vie et l'extase de la vie. C'est bien le fait d'un paresseux nerveux:'

we read in Baudelaire's *Mon cœur mis à nu*.[128] And again, in a spirit of 'scherzo ma non troppo':

'Aimez bien, vigoureusement, crânement, orientalement, férocement, celle que vous aimez. . . . Chez les Incas on aimait sa sœur; contentez-vous de votre cousine.'

This might almost be a definition of Poe's type of love, with a touch of Luther's 'Pecca fortiter'. One more remark of Baudelaire may be quoted to conclude this part of our discussion:

'Il faut toujours en revenir à de Sade, c'est-à-dire à l'homme naturel, pour expliquer le mal.'

One sees how much Baudelaire had learned from the Divine Marquis. For him, as for Sade, sin is the normal state of nature, virtue the artificial reaction of human reason. Only Baudelaire was too subtle a logician not to see where the mistake lay:

'La plupart des erreurs relatives au beau naissent de la fausse conception du dix-huitième siècle relative à la morale. La nature fut prise dans ce temps-là comme base, source et type de tout bien et de tout beau possibles. La négation du péché originel ne fut pas pour peu de chose dans l'aveuglement général de cette époque. . . . C'est (la nature) qui pousse l'homme à tuer son semblable, à le manger, à le séquestrer, à le torturer; car, sitôt que nous sortons de l'ordre des nécessités et des besoins pour entrer dans celui du luxe et des plaisirs, nous voyons que la nature ne peut conseiller que le crime. C'est cette infaillible nature qui a créé le parricide et l'anthropophagie, et mille autres abominations que la pudeur et la délicatesse nous empêchent de nommer. . . . Passez en revue, analysez tout ce qui est naturel, toutes les actions et les désirs du pur homme naturel, vous ne trouverez rien que d'affreux. Tout ce qui est beau et noble est le résultat de la raison et du calcul. Le crime, dont l'animal humain a puisé le goût dans le ventre de sa mère, est originellement naturel. . . .'[129]

It is true that Baudelaire is here putting forward this principle with the absurd object of justifying women's use of make-up; but it is also true that what survives in his art survives because it conforms to this principle—which, indeed, is the starting-point of the Christian religion, or, perhaps, of the Manichean heresy. And, to invert Blake's remark about Milton, Baudelaire may be said to have been of God's party without knowing it. In practice, he had 'made himself into a devil', as Sainte-Beuve said in writing to him: 'he had sought to snatch their secret from the demons of night'. He made use of religious conviction only in order to deny it, in order to enjoy the bitter taste of blasphemy (the continual profanation of liturgical phraseology is one of the most striking things about his work), as can be seen in the passage quoted above from Poe's *Black Cat*, or in his own *Mauvais vitrier*:

'... Un autre allumera un cigare à côté d'un tonneau de poudre, *pour voir, pour savoir, pour tenter la destinée*, pour se contraindre lui-même à faire preuve d'énergie, pour faire le joueur, pour connaître les plaisirs de l'anxiété, pour rien, par caprice, par désœuvrement.

'C'est une espèce d'énergie qui jaillit de l'ennui et de la rêverie; et ceux en qui elle se manifeste si opinément sont, en général, comme je l'ai dit, les plus indolents et les plus rêveurs des êtres. . . .

'J'ai été plus d'une fois victime de ces crises et de ces élans, qui nous autorisent à croire que des Démons malicieux se glissent en nous et nous font accomplir, à notre insu, leurs plus absurdes volontés.

'(Observez, je vous prie, que l'esprit de mystification qui, chez quelques personnes, n'est pas le résultat d'un travail ou d'une combinaison, mais d'une inspiration fortuite, participe beaucoup, ne fût-ce que par l'ardeur du désir, de cette humeur, hystérique selon les médecins, satanique selon ceux qui pensent un peu mieux que les médecins, qui nous pousse sans résistance vers une foule d'actions dangereuses ou inconvenantes.). . .

'Ces plaisanteries nerveuses ne sont pas sans péril, et on peut souvent les payer cher. Mais qu'importe l'éternité de la damnation à qui a trouvé dans une seconde l'infini de la jouissance?'

It was evidently the same 'imp of the perverse' that dictated to the poet these lines addressed to his mother:

'Ta candeur, ta facilité à être dupe, ta naïveté, ta sensibilité, me font rire. Crois-tu donc que, si je le voulais, je ne pourrais pas te ruiner et jeter ta vieillesse dans la misère? Mais, *je me retiens*, et, à chaque crise nouvelle, je me dis: "Non, ma mère est vieille et pauvre; il faut la laisser tranquille".'

His soul feels an indomitable desire to afflict and torture itself. The lustful pleasure in contamination, in the idea of the soul's damnation, seems more profound than any reasoning, in this poet of the 'plaisirs plus aigus que la glace et le fer'.

'Moi, je dis: la volupté unique et suprême de l'amour gît dans la certitude de faire le *mal*. Et l'homme et la femme savent, de naissance, que dans le mal se trouve toute la volupté.[130]

> L'Amour dans sa guérite,
> Ténébreux, embusqué, bande son arc fatal.
> Je connais les engins de son vieil arsenal:
> Crime, horreur et folie!
>
> (*Les Fleurs du Mal*, 'Sonnet d'Automne'.)

'La femme est *naturelle*, c'est-à-dire abominable.'[131]

'Il y a dans l'acte de l'amour une grande ressemblance avec la torture ou avec une opération chirurgicale.[132]

'Quant à la torture, elle est née de la partie infâme du cœur de l'homme, assoiffé de voluptés. Cruauté et volupté, sensations identiques, comme l'extrême chaud et l'extrême froid.[133]

'Je crois que j'ai déjà écrit dans mes notes que l'amour ressemblait fort à une torture ou à une opération chirurgicale. Mais cette idée peut être développée de la manière la plus amère. Quand même les deux amants seraient très épris et très pleins de désirs réciproques, l'un des deux sera toujours plus calme, ou moins possédé que l'autre. Celui-là ou celle-là, c'est l'opérateur ou le bourreau; l'autre, c'est le sujet, la victime. Entendez-vous ces soupirs, préludes d'une tragédie de déshonneur, ces gémissements, ces cris, ces râles? Qui ne les a proférés, qui ne les [a] irrésistiblement extorqués? Et que trouvez-vous de pire dans la question appliquée par de soigneux tortionnaires? Ces yeux de somnambule révulsés, ces membres dont les muscles jaillissent et se roidissent comme sous l'action d'une pile galvanique, l'ivresse, le délire, l'opium, dans leurs plus furieux résultats, ne vous donneront certes pas d'aussi affreux, d'aussi curieux exemples. Et le visage humain, qu'Ovide croyait façonné pour refléter les astres, le voilà qui ne parle plus qu'une expression de férocité folle, ou qui se détend dans une espèce de mort. Car, certes, je croirais faire un sacrilège en appliquant le mot "extase" à cette sorte de décomposition.'[134]

> Deux guerriers ont couru l'un sur l'autre; leurs armes
> Ont éclaboussé l'air de lueurs et de sang.
> — Ces jeux, ces cliquetis du fer sont les vacarmes
> D'une jeunesse en proie à l'amour vagissant.

Les glaives sont brisés! comme notre jeunesse,
Ma chère! Mais les dents, les ongles acérés,
Vengent bientôt l'épée et la dague traîtresse.
— Ô fureur des cœurs mûrs par l'amour ulcérés!

. . . .

Ce gouffre, c'est l'enfer . . .
Roulons-y sans remords, amazone inhumaine, *qu'on ôte*
Afin d'éterniser l'ardeur de notre haine!

('Duellum'.)

'Il serait peut-être doux d'être alternativement victime et bourreau.'[135]

Sometimes Baudelaire appears in the guise of executioner:

. . . pour mêler l'amour avec la barbarie,
Volupté noire! des sept Péchés capitaux,
Bourreau plein de remords, je ferai sept Couteaux
Bien affilés, et, comme un jongleur insensible,
Prenant le plus profond de ton amour pour cible,
Je les planterai tous dans ton Cœur pantelant,
Dans ton Cœur sanglotant, dans ton Cœur ruisselant!

('A une Madone'.

and particularly in the lines 'A celle qui est trop gaie':[136]

Ainsi, je voudrais, une nuit,
Quand l'heure des voluptés sonne,
Vers les trésors de ta personne
Comme un lâche ramper sans bruit,

Pour châtier ta chair joyeuse,
Pour meurtrir ton sein pardonné,
Et faire à ton flanc étonné
Une blessure large et creuse,

Et, vertigineuse douceur!
A travers ces lèvres nouvelles,
Plus éclatantes et plus belles,
T'infuser mon venin, ma sœur!

But there is very little doubt as to which of the two, the black Venus Jeanne Duval, or her lover, was the real victim. 'Quaerens quem devoret'—Baudelaire wrote under Jeanne Duval's portrait, remembering the verse in the First Epistle of St. Peter (v. 8): 'Be sober, be vigilant; because your adversary the devil, as a roaring lion, walketh about, seeking whom he may devour.' Jeanne is a tigress

('Les Bijoux', 'Le Léthé'), a 'bête implacable et cruelle' ('Je t'adore à l'égal . . .'), a 'machine aveugle et sourde, en cruautés féconde', a drinker of blood ('Tu mettrais l'univers . . .'), a demon without pity, a 'Mégère libertine' ('Sed non satiata'), a frigid idol, sterile and unfeeling ('Avec ses vêtements . . .'),[137] a vampire who pierces the poet's heart like a dagger and invades his humiliated soul with the violence of a band of demons ('Le Vampire'), an inhuman Amazon 'Duellum').[138] And the poet is a

> Martyr docile, innocent condamné,
> Dont la ferveur attise le supplice . . .
>
> ('Le Léthé'.)[139]

sadism

It is essential for him to believe his mistress a monster:

> Infâme à qui je suis lié
> Comme le forçat à la chaîne . . .
>
> ('Le Vampire'.)

> La grandeur de ce mal où tu te crois savante
> Ne t'a donc jamais fait reculer d'épouvante,
> Quand la nature, grande en ses desseins cachés,
> De toi se sert, ô femme, ô reine des péchés,
> — De toi, vil animal, — pour pétrir un génie?
>
> Ô fangeuse grandeur, sublime ignominie!
>
> ('Tu mettrais l'univers . . .')

A comment on these lines is provided by one of the *Maximes consolantes sur l'amour*,[140] in which, hinting at love for a woman who has reached the last depths of perdition, as in *L'Âne mort*, and seeking the reason of it, he concludes:

'Dites hardiment, et avec la candeur du vrai philosophe: "Moins scélérat, mon idéal n'eût pas été complet. Je le contemple, et me soumets; d'une si puissante coquine la grande Nature seule sait ce qu'elle veut faire. Bonheur et raison suprêmes! Absolu! *résultante* des contraires! Ormuz et Arimane, vous êtes le même!"'

This necessity of believing the lover to be a monstrous creature is a characteristic of sadism. Baudelaire insisted upon it more than once. Now, in a major key, he evokes his 'rouge idéal' ('L'Idéal'):

> Ce qu'il faut à ce cœur profond comme un abîme,
> C'est vous, Lady Macbeth, âme puissante au crime,
> Rêve d'Eschyle éclos au climat des autans;

and now, in a more discursive tone:[141]

'Quelle horreur et quelle jouissance dans un amour pour une espionne, une voleuse, etc. La raison morale de cette jouissance.

'Il faut toujours en revenir à de Sade, c'est-à-dire à l'homme naturel, pour expliquer le mal. Débuter par une conversation sur l'amour, entre gens difficiles. Sentiments monstrueux de l'amitié ou de l'admiration pour une femme vicieuse.'

After all that has been said, the reason of Baudelaire's erotic exclusiveness will be understood, and of his strange conduct towards Madame Sabatier,[142] and it can be seen why some people gave credit of truth to the rumour reported by Nadar.[143] Perhaps what he said of Poe may be applied in part to Baudelaire himself also:[144]

'Quant à l'ardeur avec laquelle il travaille souvent dans l'horrible, j'ai remarqué chez plusieurs hommes qu'elle était souvent le résultat d'une très grande énergie vitale inoccupée, quelquefois d'une opiniâtre chasteté, et aussi d'une profonde sensibilité refoulée.'

The case of Baudelaire, indeed, was not very different from that of Delacroix: perhaps it had some affinity with that of Swinburne.[144A] His inexhaustible need to be occupied with macabre and obscene subjects, his desire to terrify and shock people (there was, for example, the episode of the blond woman whom he pictures in the position of Juno punished by Jupiter)[145]—these are traceable to one and the same source. 'L'escalier secret de l'alcôve' in this case is only to be opened with that one particular key which Sainte-Beuve recommended should not be forgotten.

These are the titles of some of the novels which he had planned to write ('Il faut peindre les vices tels qu'ils sont', he remarked, like all the other writers of the 'frénétique' school): *Les Enseignements d'un monstre*, *La Maîtresse vierge*, *Le Crime au collège*, *Les Monstres*, *Les Tribades*, *L'Amour parricide*, *Une infâme adorée*, *La Maîtresse de l'idiot*, *L'Entreteneur*, *La Femme malhonnête*, *Jeanne et l'automate* (which was to contain 'tous les libertinages'): one seems to be reading the title-pages of the books which are (or were) sold in certain kiosks. Mendès collected these succulent morsels from the Baudelairean table, and retailed them, towards the end of the century, in *Zo'har*, *La première maîtresse*, *Méphistophéla*, &c., adopting somewhat clumsily the moral tone of *Mademoiselle Bistouri*. And like Mendès, what a number of other 'pétrarchistes de l'horrible' there have been! Baudelaire also gave Mendès[146] the idea of a long poem on modern India, with its misery, its tortures, its plagues and oppressions, its languors of love, and forms blurred by the unbearable light:

    ' "Je dirai", scandait-il, "la lamentable beauté de l'éternel Midi, et les splendeurs squameuses des lèpres dans l'adorable et exécrable coruscation du jour!"'

Mirbeau's China, in *Le Jardin des supplices*, was derived from this Baudelairean India.

He had also planned poems on *L'Autel de Moloch*, *Le séduisant croquemort*, *La Salle des martyrs*, *Le Choléra à l'Opéra ou 'au bal masqué'*, the latter obviously following Poe's example (*The Masque of the Red Death*).

Baudelaire merely sowed the seed of the tropical flora of fleshy, monstrous, putrescent plants which were destined to spring up in the hothouses of the *fin de siècle*; but of these 'flowers of evil' there now remains, among many withered orchids, nothing more than, here and there, a magnificent thorny rose—a rose of the kind that will always smell sweet.

21. 'Baudelaire en vers et Flaubert en prose', said Péladan in 1885:[147] the analogy could not be juster and is to-day taken for granted.[148] Baudelaire and Flaubert are like the two faces of a Herm planted firmly in the middle of the century, marking the division between Romanticism and Decadence, between the period of the Fatal Man and that of the Fatal Woman, between the period of Delacroix and that of Moreau.

Dumesnil[149] warns us not to take too literally the professed admiration of Flaubert for the Marquis de Sade. This admiration, we are told, was often a question of pose and arose out of the somewhat free conversations which took place in a 'milieu artiste', between people who were friends or at any rate supposedly so; nor could Flaubert foresee that among the guests at the Dîners Magny was sitting a Judas, ready with pencil and note-book to take down jokes and trifles which were to be divulged in due course in that least generous of all books of memoirs, the *Journal* of the Goncourts.

'*Dimanche, Novembre* 1858. Flaubert, une intelligence hantée par de Sade, auquel il revient comme à un mystère et à une turpitude qui l'affriolent. . . .

'*29 Janvier* 1860. Causerie sur de Sade auquel revient toujours, comme fasciné, l'esprit de Flaubert: "C'est le dernier mot du catholicisme", dit-il. . . .'

But we need not have recourse to the testimony of the Goncourts, nor to that of another dangerous friend, Sainte-Beuve[150] (who, as Croce remarks, 'had a fine nose in such cases'), nor even to elaborate psycho-analytical theories like that of Reik,[151] who is not without penetration even though he does indulge in the usual ingenuities of psycho-analysts. Flaubert's works speak quite clearly, his youthful manuscripts and volumes of letters even more clearly; indeed the documentary evidence is so abundant that, were it not for the *fin de non-recevoir* of those who think like Dumesnil, I should be ready to accept Flaubert's sadistic obsession as proven.

Let us consider his various books.—Madame Bovary, in order to excite her imagination, felt the necessity of reading 'des livres extravagants où il y avait des tableaux orgiaques avec des situations sanglantes' (an obvious allusion to Sade). And the relish which the author feels 'in laying bare every wound of Emma's soul, in refusing her any glimmer of moral virtue, and in the enjoyment of the agony which assails her when she is harassed and crushed by the impostures in which she has become embroiled, like a mouse caught in a trap',[152] is of the same kind as the relish which Janin took in telling the story of his lovely but infamous heroine who ended on the guillotine (it is hardly necessary to repeat again that there is not the least intention of comparing the two works on artistic grounds, even though *L'Âne mort* is not without merit).

Salammbô is a picture in the manner of Delacroix, except that instead of the beautiful female slaves agonizing under the ferocious eye of Sardanapalus, we have the beautiful male slave suffering unspeakable tortures under the eye of his goddess-like beloved; [153] for with Flaubert we have entered the dominion of the Fatal Woman, and sadism appears under the passive aspect which is usually called masochism (as though the active and passive aspects were not usually both present in sadism, and a mere change of proportions really justified a change of name).

In the *Légende de saint Julien l'hospitalier* Julian, according to Flaubert's conception of him, is credited with a new characteristic which is not found in the traditional account—'la passion voluptueuse du sang'. When, as a boy, he kills a pigeon by strangling it, 'les convulsions de l'oiseau faisaient battre son cœur, l'emplissaient d'une joie tumultueuse et sauvage. Au dernier raidissement, il se sentit défaillir.'[154]

But it is particularly in the *Tentation* that the clearest proofs of Flaubert's obsession may be found, for the *Tentation*, in which Flaubert, as has been remarked, put his whole self into the person of the Saint, is from beginning to end an orgy *à la* Sade—with as much sublimation as is compatible with the subject.

'Au milieu du portique, en plein soleil, une femme nue était attachée contre une colonne, deux soldats la fouettant avec des lanières; à chacun des coups son corps entier se tordait . . . et belle . . . prodigieusement. (*Il se passe les mains sur le front.*) Non! non! je ne veux pas y penser! . . .'

'Les Juifs tuèrent tous leurs ennemis. . . . La ville, sans doute, regorgeait de morts! Il y en avait au seuil des jardins, sur les escaliers, à une telle hauteur dans les chambres que les portes ne pouvaient plus tourner! . . . Mais voilà que je plonge dans des idées de meurtre et de sang!'

It would take too long to quote all the obvious passages of this kind—the Saint's vision when he pictures himself in the act of slaughtering the Arians at Alexandria, wading in the blood of slain women and children and shuddering with joy at the feel of it on his limbs; his religious flagellation which turns into algolagnia;[155] the minute description (as of a sadistic *voyeur*) of the penitent woman baring her feet and whipping herself (in the 1849 version); the episode of Priscilla and Maximilla flogged by the eunuch Montanus (the appearance of the two women, as described by Flaubert, is an example of the 'Medusean' type of

beauty); the *tableaux vivants* of the Valesians and the Cir-
concelliones; the funeral orgy in the catacombs; Ennoia,
she who had been the Fair Helen, who now bears in her
countenance the traces of bites and on her arms the marks
of blows, worn and degraded, prostituted to the whole
world[156]—a typical example of sadistic beauty; the stories
of vampires related by Apollonius; the horrible tortures
employed by exotic religions; sacred prostitution; the
mutilations of the Corybantes; Adonis and Osiris torn to
pieces, nymphs groaning and bleeding beneath the axes
of the woodcutters; the monster Martichoras; and finally
the identification of Lust with Death, till the two are
united in a single image which makes one think of Baudelaire's *Les deux bonnes sœurs*[157] and *Les Métamorphoses du
vampire*, or of an etching by Rops:

'Antoine aperçoit au milieu des ténèbres une manière de monstre
devant lui. C'est une tête de mort, avec une couronne de roses.
Elle domine un torse de femme d'une blancheur nacrée. En dessous, un linceul étoilé de points d'or fait comme une queue; — et
tout le corps ondule, à la manière d'un ver gigantesque qui se
tiendrait debout.'

Profanation is the inevitable companion of cruelty.
First of all, there is the profanation of the image of the
Madonna, which Flaubert seems to have derived from
Lewis's *Monk*;[158] then there are the sacrilegious and obscene practices of the innumerable sects, some of which
(such as that of the Ophites) are Black Masses pure and
simple; the allurements of Apollonius ('J'arracherai devant
toi les armures des dieux, nous forcerons les sanctuaires,
je te ferai violer la Pythie!'); and the necrophilistic visions
(especially, in the version of 1849, the temptation beside
the corpse of Martiallus' daughter).

In other works of his, the imp of the perverse takes on
the same forms as in Poe (*The Black Cat*), in Baudelaire
(*Le mauvais vitrier*), and in Dostoievsky. It is thus in the
Légende de saint Julien l'hospitalier, which can be compared with the anecdote of the moujik who, after profaning
the Host, has a vision and is converted (in Dostoievsky's
Diary of an Author).

Flaubert's feminine ideal is, naturally, a woman of

infamous character, a prostitute, an adulteress. Examples of this can be seen in *Mémoires d'un fou* (1838) and *Novembre* (1842), which, like all Flaubert's early works, although often of an indifferent artistic merit, reveal some fundamental traits of his soul. (Among these works there are some, such as *Rêve d'enfer* (1837) or *La Peste à Florence* (1836), which fail to rise above the standard of a macabre-lecherous fantasy by Soulié; others, such as the *Dernière scène de la mort de Marguerite de Bourgogne* (1835 or 1836), or *Un Parfum à sentir* (1836),[159] are almost on a level with Janin—or even with Borel, as for instance the frenzied *Quidquid volueris* (1837). Others, again, make us think of Barbey d'Aurevilly—particularly *Passion et vertu*, in which the heroine, who contains in embryo certain of Madame Bovary's qualities, learns in Paris 'tout ce qu'il y avait de large et d'immense dans le vice, et de voluptueux dans le crime', and behaves like the most diabolical of the 'Diaboliques'.) Take for example the study of the courtesan Marie in *Novembre*: she speaks with Flaubert's own voice, she whose countless loves have left their traces upon her, stamping her with a 'majesté voluptueuse': 'la débauche la décorait d'une beauté infernale':

'Il y eut dès lors pour moi un mot qui sembla beau entre les mots humains: adultère, une douceur exquise plane vaguement sur lui, une magie singulière l'embaume; toutes les histoires qu'on raconte, tous les livres qu'on lit, tous les gestes qu'on fait le disent et le commentent éternellement pour le cœur du jeune homme, il s'en abreuve à plaisir, il y trouve une poésie suprême, mêlée de malédiction et de volupté.'

These were tastes which Flaubert had in common with the other Romantics, with Barbey d'Aurevilly, for instance, who, in his youthful *Le Cachet d'onyx* (1831),[160] which was an anticipation of the *Diaboliques*, had spoken of the 'délices qu'il y a dans la trahison et dans l'adultère', and with Pétrus Borel, who wrote in the introduction to *Rhapsodies*, 'Heureusement que pour se consoler de tout cela il nous reste l'adultère!' In common with Borel, too, and with Gautier, Delacroix, and many others (it was, after all, the fashion), Flaubert also had a taste for the Orient, the lecherous, blood-stained Orient, and for the ancient world, full of immense vices and magnificent crimes. And just like Borel—who had exclaimed[161] 'Si j'ai rêvé une existence, c'est chamelier au désert, c'est muletier andalou, c'est Otahitien'—Flaubert dreamed of being an Andalusian muleteer or a *lazzarone* at Naples or a postilion between Rome and Marseilles,[162] and his letters and early works have passages which might almost have been taken bodily from the letters of d'Albert in *Mademoiselle de Maupin*:

'Je n'ai pas dans ma vie un seul coin d'ombre où m'abriter du soleil: je souffre toutes les ardeurs de la passion sans en avoir les extases et les délices ineffables; j'en connais les tourments, et n'en ai pas les plaisirs.'

'Je suis aussi las que si j'avais éxécuté toutes les prodigieusités de Sardanapale, et cependant ma vie a été fort chaste et tranquille en apparence: c'est une erreur de croire que la possession soit la seule route qui mène à la satiété. On y arrive aussi par le désir, et l'abstinence use plus que l'excès.'

'Je suis attaqué de cette maladie qui prend aux peuples et aux hommes puissants dans leur vieillesse: — l'impossible. Tout ce que je peux faire n'a pas le moindre attrait pour moi. Tibère, Caligula, Néron, grands Romains de l'empire, ô vous que l'on a si mal compris, et que la meute des rhéteurs poursuit de ses aboiements, je souffre de votre mal et je vous plains de tout ce qui me reste de pitié! Moi aussi je voudrais bâtir un pont sur la mer et paver les flots; j'ai rêvé de brûler des villes pour illuminer mes fêtes; j'ai souhaité être femme pour connaître de nouvelles voluptés. — Ta maison dorée, ô Néron! n'est qu'une étable fangeuse à côté du palais que je me suis élevé; ma garde-robe est mieux montée que la tienne, Héliogabale, et bien autrement splendide. — Mes cirques sont plus rugissants et plus sanglants que les vôtres, mes parfums plus âcres et plus pénétrants, mes esclaves plus nombreux et mieux faits; j'ai aussi attelé à mon char des courtisanes nues, j'ai marché sur les hommes d'un talon aussi dédaigneux que vous. — Colosses du monde antique, il bat sous mes faibles côtes un cœur aussi grand que le vôtre, et, à votre place, ce que vous avez fait je l'aurais fait et peut-être davantage. Que de Babels j'ai entassées les unes sur les autres pour atteindre le ciel, souffleter les étoiles, et cracher de là sur la création! Pourquoi donc ne suis-je pas Dieu, — puisque je ne puis être homme? Oh! je crois qu'il faudra cent mille siècles de néant pour me reposer de la fatigue de ces vingt années de vie.'[163]

Here one might be reading the *gueulades* of Flaubert, but

instead, the speaker is Gautier's d'Albert, a sort of Flaubert *ante litteram* who dreams of happiness in the form of an Arabian palace, where he sits motionless and silent beneath a magnificent baldaquin, using as a footstool the naked breast of a young slave-girl, and smoking opium in a great jade pipe.[164]

In Flaubert these romantic tastes had a more corrosive quality and drew forth a new kind of virulence from the depths of his being. D'Albert, for instance, says:

'J'ai perdu complètement la science du bien et du mal. . . . Je verrais de sang-froid les scènes les plus atroces, et il y a dans les souffrances et dans les malheurs de l'humanité quelque chose qui ne me déplaît pas. . . .

'Voilà où se réduisent toutes mes notions morales. Ce qui est beau physiquement est bien, tout ce qui est laid est mal. — Je verrais une belle femme, que je saurais avoir l'âme la plus scélérate du monde, qui serait adultère et empoisonneuse, j'avoue que cela me serait parfaitement égal et ne m'empêcherait nullement de m'y complaire, si je trouvais la forme de son nez convenable.'[165]

To Flaubert, on the other hand (and the same argument might be repeated in the case of Baudelaire), it would not be at all 'parfaitement égal'; the woman's baseness would be the principal cause of her charm, and the 'scènes atroces' would arouse more than the mere timid approval of Gautier. And so, while the worthy Théophile's ideal country is a serenely shining pagan world, a Hellas made of gold, marble and purple, 'éclat, solidité, couleur' ('Je suis un homme des temps homériques . . .'),[166] for Flaubert—who realizes quite sincerely 'Hélas non! je ne suis pas un homme antique; les hommes antiques n'avaient pas de maladies de nerfs comme moi!'[167]—the ideal is a barbaric and savage Orient, with gold, marble, and purple, certainly, but also with blood and corruption and horrible decays and miasmas.

'Oh! se sentir plier sur le dos des chameaux! devant soi un ciel tout rouge, un sable tout brun, l'horizon flamboyant qui s'allonge… le conducteur vient de finir sa chanson, on va, on va, etc.… Sudan… oh! allons toujours, je veux voir le Malabar furieux et *ses danses où l'on se tue; les vins donnent la mort comme des poisons, les poisons sont doux comme les vins*; la mer, une mer bleue remplie de corail et de perles, retentit du bruit des orgies sacrées qui se font dans les

antres des montagnes, il n'y a plus de vague, l'atmosphère est vermeille, le ciel sans nuage se mire dans le tiède Océan, les câbles
fument quand on les retire de l'eau, *les requins suivent le navire et
mangent les morts.*'[168]

Both India and China are portrayed in the pages of
Novembre: side by side with enchanting scenes there are
glimpses of tigers seizing their prey, savages in canoes of
which the prows are decorated with bloodstained scalps,
poisoned arrows which bring an agonizing death, cannibal
women . . .; and the final conclusion is 'Puissé-je périr en
doublant le Cap, mourir du choléra à Calcutta ou de la
peste à Constantinople!'

In Gautier there is only a hint of this contrast, which
was to become for Flaubert the supreme synthesis.
Mademoiselle de Maupin says:[169]

'Dans ma frêle poitrine habitent ensemble les rêveries semées
de violettes de la jeune fille pudique et les ardeurs insensées des
courtisanes en orgie: mes désirs vont, comme les lions, aiguisant
leurs griffes dans l'ombre et cherchant quelque chose à dévorer. . . .
C'est un étrange pays que mon âme, un pays florissant et splendide
en apparence, mais plus saturé de miasmes putrides et délétères que
le pays de Batavia: le moindre rayon de soleil sur la vase y fait
éclore les reptiles et pulluler les moustiques; — les larges tulipes
jaunes, les nagassaris et les fleurs d'angsoka y voilent pompeusement
d'immondes charognes.'

Here one seems to be reading a metaphorical moralist
such as Daniello Bartoli, rather than a vision of a
'jardin des supplices', as were the majority of Flaubert's
visions.

22. Being a ruthless self-analyst, Flaubert can scarcely
have had any illusions as to the real significance of his
longing to travel to strange and monstrous countries. It
was a means of providing an outlet for the 'fond noir à
contenter' which troubled him no less than it troubled
Delacroix.[170] That indefatigable painter might well have
repeated with Flaubert,[171] 'J'aime mon travail d'un amour
frénétique et perverti, comme un ascète le cilice qui lui
gratte le ventre', for their cases offer curious analogies.
The following melancholy lines from Flaubert to Louise
Colet, written at the end of October 1851,[172] afford a

parallel to the confession of Delacroix which I have already quoted:

'Ce n'est pas un homme vieilli comme moi dans tous les excès de la solitude, nerveux à s'évanouir, troublé de passions rentrées, plein de doutes du dedans et du dehors, ce n'est pas celui-là qu'il fallait aimer.'

Another letter to Louise Colet (July 7th–8th, 1853)[173] throws light on this 'fond noir' and on certain impressions of childhood which may have first stirred it:[174]

'La première fois que j'ai vu des fous, c'était ici, à l'hospice général, avec ce pauvre père Parain. Dans les cellules, assises et attachées par le milieu du corps, nues jusqu'à la ceinture et toutes échevelées, une douzaine de femmes hurlaient et se déchiraient la figure avec les ongles.

'J'avais peut-être à cette époque six à sept ans; ce sont de bonnes impressions à avoir jeune, elles virilisent; quels étranges souvenirs j'ai en ce genre! l'amphithéâtre de l'Hôtel-Dieu donnait sur notre jardin; que de fois, avec ma sœur, n'avons-nous pas grimpé au treillage et, suspendus entre la vigne, regardé curieusement les cadavres étalés: le soleil donnait dessus, les mêmes mouches qui voltigeaient sur nous et sur les fleurs allaient s'abattre là, revenaient, bourdonnaient! . .

'Quand on a son modèle net, devant les yeux, on écrit toujours bien, et où donc le vrai est-il plus clairement visible que dans ces belles expositions de la misère humaine? elles ont quelque chose de si cru que cela donne à l'esprit des appétits de cannibale. Il se précipite dessus pour les dévorer, se les assimiler. . . . Comme j'ai bâti des drames féroces à la Morgue, où j'avais la rage d'aller autrefois. . . . Je crois du reste qu'à cet endroit j'ai une faculté de perception particulière; en fait de malsain, je m'y connais. . . *La folie et la luxure sont deux choses que j'ai tellement sondées, où j'ai si bien navigué par ma volonté, que je ne serai jamais (je l'espère) ni un aliéné ni un de Sade. Mais il m'en a cuit par exemple. Ma maladie de nerfs a été l'écume de ces petites facéties intellectuelles.*[175] Chaque attaque était comme une sorte d'hémorragie de l'innervation. C'était des pertes séminales de la faculté pittoresque du cerveau, cent mille images sautant à la fois, en feux d'artifice.'

With the passage which is here given in italics may be compared a passage from another letter, to Mlle Leroyer de Chantepie, dated May 18th, 1857:[176]

'En d'autres fois, je tâchais, par l'imagination, de me donner facticement ces horribles souffrances. J'ai joué avec la démence

et le fantastique comme Mithridate avec les poisons. Un grand
orgueil me soutenait et j'ai vaincu le mal à force de l'étreindre
corps à corps.'

The 'fantastique' (that is, *delectatio morosa* of the
sadistic type) was, therefore, a sort of neuralgic area
round which Flaubert's mind crystallized.   Again, in
Novembre: [177]

'Toutes les passions entraient en moi et ne pouvaient en sortir,
s'y trouvaient à l'étroit; elles s'enflammaient les unes les autres,
comme par des miroirs concentriques: modeste, j'étais plein d'orgueil; vivant dans la solitude, je rêvais la gloire; retiré du monde,
je brûlais d'y paraître, d'y briller; chaste, je m'abandonnais, dans
mes rêves du jour et de la nuit, aux luxures les plus effrénées, aux
voluptés les plus féroces. Ma vie que je refoulais en moi-même
se contractait au cœur et le serrait à l'étouffer. . . . N'usant pas de
l'existence, l'existence m'usait, mes rêves me fatiguaient plus que
de grands travaux.'

In the *Tentation*, this situation is mirrored in the dialogue between Hilarion and Antony:

'*Hilarion* — Cette vie à l'écart des autres est mauvaise.

'*Antoine* — Au contraire! L'homme, étant esprit, doit se retirer
des choses mortelles. Toute action le dégrade. Je voudrais ne pas
tenir à la terre, — même par la plante des pieds!

'*Hil.* — Hypocrite qui s'enfonce dans la solitude pour se livrer
mieux au débordement de ses convoitises! Tu te prives de viandes,
de vin, d'étuves, d'esclaves et d'honneurs; mais comme tu laisses ton
imagination t'offrir des banquets, des parfums, des femmes nues et
des foules applaudissantes! Ta chasteté n'est qu'une corruption plus
subtile, et ce mépris du monde l'impuissance de ta haine contre lui. . . .

'*Ant.* (*éclate en sanglots*)—Assez! assez! tu remues trop mon cœur!'

Here again Baudelaire's observation is to the point:
'Quant à l'ardeur avec laquelle il travaille souvent dans
l'horrible . . .'[178]

Flaubert defended himself very feebly against Sainte-
Beuve's allusion to the 'pointe d'imagination sadique',[179]
a.id Dumesnil, taking this defence literally, said[180] that
Flaubert 'se piquait pour la galerie d'une pointe de sadisme',
that he 'prétendait admirer prodigieusement le divin Marquis', but that it was simply a matter of pose and of *boutade*.
On the other hand, from the passages I have just quoted

there is clear evidence that sadism was by no means only a superficial tendency in Flaubert's temperament, but rather an inseparable part of the very nucleus of his inspiration.[181]

In an early letter (to E. Chevalier, July 15th, 1839)[182] Flaubert wrote:

'Lacenaire, qui faisait de la philosophie aussi à sa manière, et une drôle, une profonde, une amère de philosophie! quelle leçon il donnait à la morale, comme il la fessait en public, cette pauvre prude séchée, comme il lui a porté de bons coups, comme il l'a traînée dans la boue, dans le sang. J'aime bien à voir des hommes comme ça, comme Néron, comme le Marquis de Sade. . . . Ces monstres-là expliquent pour moi l'histoire, ils en sont le complément, l'apogée, la morale, le dessert; crois-moi, ce sont de grands hommes, des immortels aussi. Néron vivra aussi longtemps que Vespasien, Satan que Jésus-Christ.'

and in the first version of the *Éducation sentimentale*:[183]

'Jules alla jusqu'au bout, jusqu'à la fin; il passa par la sensualité étroite de Faublas . . . il lui préféra cent fois les monstruosités de *Justine*, cette œuvre belle à force d'horreur, où le crime vous regarde en face et vous ricane au visage, écartant ses gencives aiguës et vous tendant les bras; il descendit dans ces profondeurs ténébreuses de la nature humaine, prêta l'oreille à tous ces râles, assista à ces convulsions et n'eut pas peur. Et puis la poésie n'est-elle pas partout — si elle est quelque part. — Celui qui la porte en lui la verra sur le monde, pareille aux fleurs, qui poussent sur le marbre des tombeaux et sur les plus fraîches pelouses; elle s'exhale vers vous du cœur de la vierge et du sommeil de l'enfant, comme de la planche des échafauds et de la lumière des incendies.'

On the subject of Byron, the reading of whose poems had so much excited him in his youth, Flaubert wrote:[184]

'Il ne croyait à rien, si ce n'est à tous les vices, à un Dieu vivant, existant pour le plaisir de faire le mal.'

The teaching of Sade fitted in with that of Byron, for Flaubert also—'volupté du crime', 'joies de la corruption',[185] 'le sublime d'en bas'.[186] These two writers were the greatest sources of inspiration for the moderns, said Sainte-Beuve, in 1843; and even if, in 1843, Sade was still described as a 'secret' source of inspiration, he became less and less so during the years which followed. If Sainte-

Beuve had been writing at the end of the century he would have had no need to give the warning 'Ne perdez jamais cette dernière clef'. For this key, which might have escaped the inattentive eye of 1843, had by then become fully evident, 'more than papal',[187] to the eyes of all. The majority, however, preferred to shut their eyes.

23. As *cul-de-lampe* to this chapter may be quoted a late but extreme case of cannibalistic Byronism, which the words of Auger, related at the end of the preceding chapter, would have fitted amazingly well.[188] The case is that of the *Chants de Maldoror*, written (in 1868) under the pseudonym of 'Comte de Lautréamont'[189] by that 'poète maudit' Isidore Ducasse, who was born at Montevideo in 1846.[190] In a letter written in 1870 Ducasse, whom the Surrealists have hailed as a forerunner of themselves,[191] defined his prose poems as follows: 'Quelque chose dans le genre du Manfred de Byron et du Konrad de Mickiewicz, mais, cependant, bien plus terrible.' And in another letter, in 1869, he made a profession of faith similar to that of Baudelaire:

'J'ai chanté le mal comme ont fait Mickiewicz, Byron, Milton, Southey, A. de Musset, Baudelaire, etc. Naturellement, j'ai un peu exagéré le diapason pour faire du nouveau dans le sens de cette littérature sublime qui ne chante le désespoir que pour opprimer le lecteur, et lui faire désirer le bien comme remède.'

With sinister humour (a remote inheritance from Byron's *Don Juan*) and with absurdities worthy of Burchiello, Ducasse relates in minute detail his homosexual and sadistic fantasies,[192] inveighing against the Creator. 'Ces plaisanteries nerveuses ne sont pas sans péril, et on peut souvent les payer cher'—Baudelaire, who knew a good deal about the macabre-grotesque, had remarked. Ducasse, the description of whom has come down to us as of a strange being of strange habits, died mysteriously at the age of twenty-four.

Among the many and various writers, great or less great, whose names have been introduced in order to explain Lautréamont's particular type of genius, I do not find recorded the one who, in my opinion, displays the most noteworthy affinities with him—Pétrus Borel. A lycanthrope in the manner of Borel, a macabre humorist in whom it is impossible to distinguish where sincerity ends and mystification begins,[193] Lautréamont justifies his Muse in these words:

'Moi, je fais servir mon génie à peindre les délices de la cruauté!... Le génie ne peut-il pas s'allier avec la cruauté dans les résolutions secrètes de la Providence?'

NOTES AND ADDENDA TO CHAPTER III

1 In his essay on the *Novella della figlia del re di Dacia* (Pisa, Nistri, 1866, p. xi) Wesselowsky says: 'Among the symbolic types in which the medieval imagination delighted there was none which was more sympathetic or enjoyed greater popularity than that of the *persecuted maiden* ... Crescenzia and Uliva, Genoveffa and Hirlanda, Florencia and Santa Guglielma, the daughter of the King of Dacia and the Queen of Poland, Cinderella and Marion de Bosch in the Piedmontese tale—all these were varieties of the same type.' Wesselowsky traces the type to a cosmogonic myth. For a modern treatment of the legend of Santa Uliva, see p. 282 of this book, note 95.

2 *Clarissa Harlowe*, vol. v, Letter xxxxiv (ed. Leslie Stephen, London, 1883).

3 At this point the author remarks:

'Mr. Belford's objection, That virtue ought not to suffer in a tragedy, is not well considered: Monimia in the Orphan, Belvidera in Venice Preserved, Athenais in Theodosius, Cordelia in Shakespeare's King Lear, Desdemona in Othello, Hamlet (to name no more), are instances that a tragedy could hardly be justly called a tragedy, if virtue did not temporarily suffer, and vice for a while triumph. But he recovers himself in the same paragraph; and leads us to look up to the FUTURE for the reward of virtue, and for the punishment of guilt: and observes not amiss, when he says, He knows not but that the virtue of such a woman as Clarissa is rewarded in missing such a man as Lovelace.'

4 Vol. v, Letter cii.

5 Vol. v, Letter xxxviii.

6 For the points of resemblance between the heroine of *Faust* and Richardson's Clarissa and Pamela, see Reynaud's volume already quoted, pp. 172–3.

7 Vol. ii, Letter vii.

8 *Éloge de Richardson*, in *Œuvres complètes*, éd. Assézat et Tourneux (Paris, Garnier, 1875–9), vol. v, p. 225.

9 Reynaud, op. cit., p. 69. Reynaud, however, exaggerates when he maintains that 'la liberté de certains passages de ces romans "moraux" est inimitable'.

10 See *Œuvres complètes*, vol. v, pp. 177–8.

11 Reynaud, op. cit., p. 93. Cf. the words of Diderot in the *Éloge*, op. cit., p. 221; 'Plusieurs fois j'ai commencé la lecture de *Clarisse* pour me former'.

12 On the development of these ideas see the two first chapters of Reynaud's book already quoted, especially pp. 56–7 and 94; the book is well informed, but must be read with caution because of its tendenciousness. Reynaud's theory is that Romanticism represents an Anglo-Germanic impurity in the pure French literary tradition. But does a 'pure French literary tradition exist? That same French theatre, in which Reynaud sees the palladium of this tradition, might easily, if approached from a different point of view, be classed as an impurity brought about by the Italian criticism of the Renaissance (Castelvetro).

12A The genesis of Sade's work is thus traced by Foscolo in the *Gazzettino del Bel-mondo* (*Opere*, Florence, Le Monnier, *Prose letterarie*, vol. iv, p. 28):

'I have left blank the title and the name of the author of a novel whose sparks smouldered for seventy years under European corruption, after having been lit by the scandalous reports of the Regency of the Duke of Orleans. Then that fire was imprudently stirred by Richardson's Lovelace. Later a courtier of the Duke of Orleans-Égalité, with both the new Lovelaces, male and female, of the *Liaisons dangereuses*, approached a pair of very insidious bellows to the fire. Meanwhile the customs of the French nobility, and the systems of Nature and of Universal Morals of the either wicked or ill-advised metaphysicians brought wood to the imminent flame—until it broke out irresistibly among the torrents of blood of the guillotine which, far from quenching, quickened that fire;—and such is this fire, that even men hardened in vice watch it aghast; and no one may read even a few pages without being horrified at the thought of the shame which that book will contribute to bring on our century—because Tiberius, Caligula, and the other monsters who fed their lust with the sight of human victims, seem shy virgins in comparison.—I happened to see this book in the year 1804 in a small town between France and Flanders, in the house of a poor printer who was preparing its twentieth or maybe thirtieth clandestine edition for a Paris bookseller; he was being helped to correct the proofs by a daughter of his aged perhaps eighteen or twenty.'

The novel alluded to by Foscolo must be the *Nouvelle Justine*, which went through several clandestine editions. The sentence 'raccoglievano vigore alle loro libidini' (fed their lust) echoes a passage in Parini's ode *A Silvia*: 'Vigor da la libidine La crudeltà raccolse.' The same passage from Parini is quoted by Foscolo apropos of Count Prina's gruesome assassination, in *Lettera apologetica* (*Opere*, *Prose politiche*, p. 562). Evidently the impression received from Sade's book crystallized in Foscolo's mind round Parini's passage. The episode of the printer's daughter would have offered a welcome hint to a Jules Janin. One might imagine a parallel story to Hawthorne's *Rapaccini's Daughter*: this latter tended the poisonous flowers in the garden of the physician her father, just as the printer's daughter revised the proofs of a poisonous book. [Add. 1950]

13 *Juliette*, ed. 1797, vol. ii, p. 127; also *Justine*, vol. ii, p. 111.

14 *Lettres inédites du Président de Brosses à Ch. C. Loppin de Germeaux* (Paris, Firmin-Didot, 1929), p. 234, Letter of Feb. 24th, 1749.

15 *Juliette*, vol. iii, p. 90.

16 In his projected novel, *The Life of a Great Sinner*, Dostoievsky intended to give an important place to the teaching of *Thérèse philosophe*. The principal character was to have owed his degeneration to the reading of it. Even the saintly bishop Tikhon, who considered himself, at his age, to be free from temptations, was troubled by *Thérèse*. E. Halpérine-Kaminsky in his commentary (*La Confession de Stavroguine*, Paris, 1922), not knowing that *Thérèse philosophe* was a book, and being unable, from Dostoievsky's summary notes, to discover that it was, imagined that he was dealing with a real person and made the very awkward remark:

'Il n'est fait, précédemment, qu'une seule fois une obscure allusion à Thérèse Philosophe (feuille 16) où il est question du gamin qu'elle corrige et auquel elle confisque un livre [?]. Sans doute avait-elle joué un rôle dans l'éducation de l'enfant'.

[17] Cf. Goncourt, *Journal*, vol. iii, p. 190 (Feb. 8th, 1868), where he is dealing with the life of Gavarni:

'Quel chasseur de femmes! . . . Et quelquefois, je ne sais quoi de noir et de machiavélique, une méchanceté de *Liaisons dangereuses*, curieuse d'expériences cruelles, un jeu amer avec les faiblesses de la femme'.

Madame de Merteuil, of whom Valmont is an imperfect pupil, may be considered as the forerunner of those who treated love as an intellectual problem, as a field for interesting experiments—Stendhal's Julien Sorel, the Seducer of S. Kierkegaard, the Disciple of Bourget, and in certain respects Maurice Barrès and André Gide (of the latter see especially *Les Faux-monnayeurs*).

[18] Lettre CLXXI.

[19] Lettre CVII. Valmont, too (Lettre CX), quotes *Clarissa*:

'La difficulté ne serait pas de m'introduire chez elle, même la nuit, même encore de l'endormir et d'en faire une nouvelle Clarisse'.

[20] *Œuvres posthumes*, p. 176 et seq.

[21] On the subject of the widespread diffusion of this desire for profanation during the eighteenth century, cf. Monglond, op. cit., vol. i, p. 201.

[22] Baudelaire might well have taken from the same letter also a passage which refers to Madame de Tourvel: 'Non, elle n'aura pas *les plaisirs du vice et les honneurs de la vertu*. Ce n'est pas assez pour moi de la posséder, je veux qu'elle se livre'. Here the phrase in italics, taken from the *Nouvelle Héloïse* (Première Partie, Lettre IX: 'les plaisirs du vice et l'honneur de la vertu') might well be the point of departure for the twin titles of Sade's volumes.

[23] Of course, if things are thus according to the logical issue of the theory, the inverse process is true on the psychological plane. That is to say, Sade's satanic theory is merely a projection of his sexual attitude. E. de Goncourt remarked, apropos of *Justine* (*Journal*, vol. vi, p. 334):

'L'originalité de l'abominable livre, elle n'est pas pour moi dans l'ordure, la cochonnerie féroce, je la trouve dans la punition céleste de la vertu, c'est-à-dire dans le contrepied diabolique des dénouements de tous les romans et de toutes les pièces de théâtre'.

[24] *Juliette*, vol. ii, pp. 341–50.

[25] *Justine*, vol. i, pp. 95–6. Also p. 322.

[26] *Justine*, vol. ii, p. 249.

[27] *Justine*, vol. i, pp. 216–21.

Sade's idea seems to represent the extreme development of the ancient teaching of Empedocles, according to whom strife was not only a destructive principle, but also the origin of everything, except the Unique One. [Add. 1950]

[28] *Juliette*, vol. ii, p. 347.

[29] *Justine*, vol. i, p. 299.

30 *Justine*, vol. iii, p. 117.

31 *Justine*, vol. i, pp. 3–4.

32 The first editions of the two works were published in 1791 and 1796 respectively. The definitive and complete edition was published in 1797, 'en Hollande', with the title: *La nouvelle Justine, ou les malheurs de la vertu* (4 vols.), *suivie de l'histoire de Juliette, sa sœur, ou les prospérités du vice* (6 vols.). The first version of *Justine* has been re-exhumed by M. Heine: *Les Infortunes de la vertu*, texte établi sur le manuscrit original autographe et publié pour la première fois avec une introduction par Maurice Heine (Paris, Éditions Fourcade, 1930). A critical edition of *Justine* was announced as in preparation by the Société du Roman philosophique. In 1933 M. Heine issued in three volumes *Œuvres choisies et pages magistrales du Marquis de Sade*, Paris, Aux Éditions du Trianon.

33 *Justine*, vol. i, p. 106.

34 *Juliette*, vol. iii, p. 12.

35 *Juliette*, vol. ii, p. 63.

36 *Le Temps retrouvé*, vol. i, p. 182.

37 *Justine*, vol. iv, pp. 40–1.

38 *Justine*, vol. i, p. 112.

38A The mechanization of facts whose ultimate essence is spiritual took grotesque shapes during the eighteenth century. Just think of the armchair described by Casanova, *Mémoires*, vol. vi, ch. 1, destined to break a woman's resistance:

'Ce fauteuil est monté sur cinq ressorts qui jouent à la fois dès qu'une personne y a pris place. Deux de ces ressorts retiennent les bras, deux autres écartent les jambes, et enfin le cinquième élève le siège à la commodité du sacrificateur.' [Add. 1950]

39 *Juliette*, vol. vi, p. 346. In the original plan of *Justine* as made out by Heine (op. cit., pp. xviii–xix), the incident of the striking by lightning was treated in a very different, and quite conventional, manner. In this version Justine's sister exclaims:

'Ceci est trop fort et trop singulier, il n'est pas naturel que la providence punisse aussi cruellement et avec aussi peu de justice un être qui ne servit jamais que la vertu; ça ne m'en impose pas, c'est indirectement que la colère du ciel me frappe, et c'est à moi que tous ces coups s'adressent, à moi seule qui les ai mérités.

'Et sur cela elle quitte le monde et son amant et va finir ses jours dans un couvent après avoir donné tout ce qu'elle avait aux pauvres et y meurt fort âgée, le modèle et l'exemple de la maison.'

It is obvious that, at the time of this version, Sade was anxious, no less than Laclos, to give an impression of the honest intention of his work. Later, with the relaxation of morals under the Directoire, he considered it possible to express himself freely.

One can easily imagine the compunction with which Sade wrote, in the introduction to the version published by Heine (p. 14):

'Cette prospérité du crime n'est qu'apparente; indépendamment de la providence qui doit nécessairement punir de tels succès, le coupable nourrit au fond de son cœur un ver qui le rongeant sans cesse, l'empêche de jouir de cette lueur de félicité qui l'environne et ne lui laisse au lieu d'elle que le souvenir déchirant des crimes qui la lui ont acquise. A l'égard du malheur qui tourmente la vertu, l'infortuné que le sort persécute a pour consolation sa conscience, et les jouissances secrètes qu'il retire de sa pureté le dédommagent bientôt de l'injustice des hommes.'

Richardson could not have put it better.

⁴⁰ See especially *Le Fantôme*; cf. chap. v, § 19.   *ver .*

⁴¹ *Juliette*, vol. i, p. 160.

⁴² *Justine*, vol. iv, p. 191.

⁴³ *Justine*, vol. iii, p. 306.

⁴⁴ *Juliette*, vol. ii, p. 318.

In his review of the first edition of the present book in *Hippocrate* for December 1933, M. Heine tries to clear Sade from the taunt of Satanism by showing that the sentences which give colour to it are put into the mouth of one of Sade's characters, the Satanist Saint-Fond, whereas the atheistical quotation now given in the text would mirror Sade's own point of view, Sade being extolled by the surrealists as the 'champion idéal de l'athéisme matérialiste'. It seems to me, however, that we must not try to find in Sade's work such an objectivity of presentation as to allow for a distinction between the author and his characters, who fall ultimately into two, and two only, rudimentary categories: executioners and victims. Even though the former may be called Saint-Fond, or Madame d'Esterval, or Almani, their disguise is transparent, and Heine's subtle distinctions seem to me to deserve the title of 'love's labour's lost'. All Sade's characters preach in the same manner: their ravings are evidently the outpourings of Sade himself. [Add. 1950]

⁴⁵ *Juliette*, vol. iv, p. 79.

⁴⁶ See on this subject the *Correspondance inédite du Marquis de Sade*, edited by P. Bourdin (Paris, Librairie de France, 1929).

M. Heine defined the 'affaire Keller' (or the 'affaire d'Arcueil') 'une fessée intempestive', and the one of Marseille (on which he wrote an article in *Hippocrate*, no. 1, March 1933: 'L'Affaire des bonbons cantharidés du marquis de Sade') 'une expérience pharmaceutique mal conçue et plus mal exécutée'. Actually Sade's attempts to put into practice the suggestions of his obsessions appear extremely tame. [Add. 1950]

⁴⁷ *Le Paysan perverti*, quoted by Monglond, op. cit., vol. ii, p. 326. The well-known fetichism of Restif for the feet and shoes of women is considered by psycho-pathologists to be a vicarious form of masochism. See on Restif: A Tabaraut, *Le Vrai Visage de Rétif de la Bretonne*, Paris, Montaigne, 1936; and B. Croce, 'Intorno a Rétif de la Bretonne', in *La Critica* for January 20th, 1942.

* *p. III, line 1, add:* And in *Les Amours de Milord Édouard Bomston* at the end of the *Nouvelle Héloïse* (Lauretta Pisana). [Add. 1950]

⁴⁸ On this subject see Maigron, op. cit., pp. 259 et seq., 381, 387.

* *p. III, line 15, add:* Another derivation is possibly that pathetic Massimina in Valle-Inclán's *Sonata de invierno*. [Add. 1950]

⁴⁹ Sainte-Beuve writes about this in *Chateaubriand et son groupe*, op. cit., p. 96 note.

'Une question qu'on voudrait repousser se glisse malgré nous: René est bien René, Amélie est bien Lucile [Chateaubriand's beloved sister]; qu'est-ce donc? et qu'y a-t-il eu de réel au fond dans le reste du mystère? Poète, comment donner à deviner de telles situations, si elles ont eu quelque chose de vrai? Comment les donner à supposer, si elles sont un rêve?'

See also the remark of Monglond, vol. i, p. 258, quoted here in chap. ii, note 43.

⁵⁰ Sainte-Beuve, op. cit., vol. i, p. 197. Judging society from the point of view of a state of nature Chateaubriand makes his character Chactas say (*Les Natchez*, ed. cit., p. 264) 'Les galériens et les femmes comme toi [courtesans like Ninon de Lenclos] me semblent avoir toute la sagesse de ta nation'. This sentence seems to contain an echo of Restif and an anticipation of Sue.

⁵¹ Chateaubriand loves to dwell upon spectacles in which beauty is associated with death. A beautiful young woman, for example, holds in her hand a skull (*Les Natchez*, p. 368):

'Mila . . . échauffait contre son sein l'effigie pâle et glacée: les beaux cheveux de la jeune fille ombrageaient en tombant le front chauve de la mort. Avec ses joues colorées, ses lèvres vermeilles, les grâces de son adolescence, Mila ressemblait à ces roses de l'églantier qui croissent dans les cimetières champêtres et qui penchent leurs têtes sur la tombe.'

While in Venice in 1833 Chateaubriand felt roused by the sight of 'adolescentes déguenillées' in the poorer districts, just as at Hohlfeld he had been in seeing a pretty 'petite hotteuse', 'jambes et pieds nus, jupe courte, corset déchiré' (see M. Levaillant, *Chateaubriand*, *Madame Récamier et les Mémoires d'Outre-tombe d'après des documents inédits*, Paris, Delagrave, 1936, pp. 192 and 188): poverty adds a spice to eroticism, as it constantly happens with the decadents. [Add. 1950]

⁵² On the subject of René, Sainte-Beuve says (op. cit., vol. i, p. 386 note): 'Ce Jupiter se plaisait à consumer toutes les Sémélés.' He repeats also the vivid and very just figure of speech used by Chênedollé: 'Dans *René* Chateaubriand a caché le poison dans l'idée religieuse; c'est empoisonner dans une hostie.' On the 'méchanceté dans l'amour' in Chateaubriand see also chapter vi ('La Splendeur du faux') of Book II in the second part of *Le Romantisme français* by Pierre Lasserre (Paris, Mercure de France, 1907).

Babbitt, *Rousseau and Romanticism*, op cit., p. 229, quotes Atala's description of her emotions when torn between her religious vow and her love for Chactas, and remarks: 'Longing is here pushed to a pitch where it passes over, as in Wagner's *Tristan and Isolde*, into the desire for annihilation.' [Add. 1950]

⁵²ᴬ Also Lessing's *Emilia Galotti* (1772) deals with the subject of the persecuted maiden, under the influence of *Clarissa* and of Livy's account of Virginia's death. [Add. 1950]

⁵³ Gretchen's tragedy is the supreme artistic expression of a theme dear to the 'Stürmer und Dränger', the theme of the seduced girl abandoned

to her sad destiny by the father of her child. Cf. for instance Jakob Lenz's dramas *Der Hofmeister*, *Die Soldaten*, and the story *Zerbin*. In this latter the victim, Marie, the infanticide, 'stood erect on the scaffold like one of those early Christian martyrs who, for love of their faith, faced shame and death with composure'. The theme of the persecuted woman crops up at intervals throughout the nineteenth century. Hawthorne's *The Scarlet Letter*, Wilkie Collins's *The Woman in White*, J. S. Le Fanu's *Uncle Silas*, Hardy's *Tess of the D'Urbervilles* contain remote but still recognizable echoes of it. On the subject of Collins's novels Swinburne observed (*Studies in Prose and Poetry*, 1894):

'And the suggested or implied suffering of such poor innocent wretches, the martyrdom of perpetual terror and agony inflicted on the shattered nerves or the shaken brain of a woman or a girl, is surely a cruel and a painful mainspring for a story or a plot.'

Railo (op. cit., pp. 280–1) is the only writer to point out the sexual abnormality that the subject seems to suggest.

[54] Among the antecedents of this situation may be quoted a novel printed at The Hague in 1739, entitled *Intrigues monastiques ou l'Amour encapuchonné*, in which a confessor dishonours and then murders a girl, and also *Les Victimes cloîtrées*, a play by Monvel (1791), in which a wicked priest, Père Laurent, has a young girl, Eugénie, whom he is desirous of raping, shut up in a convent. Lewis knew this play, as is evident from a letter to his mother, dated Sept. 7th, 1791—a letter which shows him as a passionate admirer of the French revolutionary theatre. He speaks of 'at least twenty French operas, which, if translated, would undoubtedly succeed'. Among these he mentions, *Camille, ou le Souterrain*, by Marsollier, 'where a woman is hid in a cavern in her jealous husband's house; and afterwards, by accident, her child is shut up there also, without food, and they are not released till they are perishing with hunger'. *Les Victimes cloîtrées* 'is another which would undoubtedly succeed'. See Railo, op. cit., pp. 85 and 89. The situation described in *Le Souterrain* is derived from Mrs. Radcliffe's *Sicilian Romance*. See also E. Estève, *Études de littérature préromantique* (Paris, 1923, pp. 113-19). Lewis adapted Monvel's drama for the stage, in *Venoni, or the Novice of St. Mark's* (1808) (Railo, pp. 124–5). It is possible that Mrs. Radcliffe also went to *Les Victimes cloîtrées* for the plot of *The Italian* (Railo, p. 355, note 151). In the story of the hermit Barsisa which appeared in No. 148 of the *Guardian* in 1713, and which is given by Lewis as his source, Satan, alarmed at the excessive holiness of Barsisa, sends him the daughter of a king to heal, and thus tempts him, first to sin, and then to kill his victim. Barsisa is arrested; in his danger he acknowledges Satan as his god, and Satan in return promises to save him, but betrays him.

M. Heine, *Le Marquis de Sade et le roman noir*, Paris, Nouv. Revue Française, 1933 (offprint from the *Nouvelle Revue Française* for August 1933), advances the supposition that Lewis while in Paris obtained a copy of Sade's *Justine*, whose third edition appeared just then in Cazin's celebrated collection. Sade's influence on Lewis seems probable to Heine, but Mrs. Radcliffe, for this critic, would not have known him: rather, the reverse is possible, although before 1797 there were no French translations of Mrs. Radcliffe's novels. In his *Idée sur les romans*, which precedes *Les Crimes de l'Amour* (1800), Sade thinks Lewis's *Monk* 'supérieur, sous tous les rapports, aux bizarres élans de la brillante imagination de Radcliffe [*sic*]'. One may doubt, however, whether Sade spoke of Mrs. Radcliffe more than by hearsay. Anyhow it is curious to see how Sade, in his *Idée sur les romans*, tried to account for the tale of terror:

'Ce genre . . . devenait le fruit indispensable des secousses révolutionnaires, dont l'Europe entière se ressentait. Pour qui connaissait tous les malheurs dont les méchants peuvent accabler les hommes, le roman devenait aussi difficile à faire, que monotone à lire: il n'y avait point d'individu qui n'eût plus éprouvé d'infortunes en quatre ou cinq ans que n'en pouvait peindre en un siècle le plus fameux romancier de la littérature: il fallait donc appeler l'enfer à son secours, pour se composer des titres à l'intérêt, et trouver dans le pays des chimères, ce qu'on savait couramment en ne fouillant que l'histoire de l'homme dans cet âge de fer. Mais que d'inconvénients présentait cette manière d'écrire! L'auteur du *Moine* ne les a pas plus évités que Radcliffe; ici nécessairement des deux choses l'une, ou il faut développer le sortilège, et dès lors vous n'intéressez plus, ou il ne faut jamais lever le rideau, et vous voilà dans la plus affreuse invraisemblance.'

What is chiefly to be noticed is that Lewis, Mrs. Radcliffe, and Sade belong to the same mental climate; that climate which, as we have said above, produced so many incarnations of the theme of the persecuted maiden, and found its chief expression in painting in Goya: see on this latter the essay on 'Goya amaro e feroce' in E. Mottini's *L'anima e il colore, saggi d'arte*, Rome–Milan, Augustea, 1929; G. Malraux, *Saturne, Essai sur Goya*, Paris, Galerie de la Pléiade, 1950. [Add. 1950]

55 Connected with the story of Agnes is that of the Bleeding Nun, which was to have such a success among the Romantics. The Bleeding Nun was the ghost of a woman who was forced by her parents to become a nun, but who did not resist the impulses of her own 'warm and voluptuous character' and abandoned herself to all sorts of excesses, committed murder, and was herself murdered. This is a type which is found in Manzoni's Nun of Monza, who, however, was inspired by Ripamonti and by the *Mémoires pour servir à l'histoire de Port-Royal et à la vie de la Révérende Mère Marie-Angélique de Sainte-Madeleine Arnauld*, Utrecht, 1742 (see P. P. Trompeo, *Col Manzoni tra Monza e Port-Royal*, in *Rilegature Gianseniste*, Milano–Roma, La Cultura, 1930). The vicissitudes of the forced monastic vow were very popular with the free-thinkers of the eighteenth century; the subject provided plots for several plays (at least five between 1790 and 1796), as well as for Diderot's *Religieuse* which, though written in 1760, was not published until 1796, and therefore could not have had any influence on the 'monastic' theatre (see Estève, *Études* cit., p. 90, note 4). See also note 72 of this chapter.

55A Lewis might have justified himself by invoking no meaner authority than Shakespeare's (*Romeo and Juliet*, Act. iv, sc. 1, 76 ff.):

O . . . rather than marry Paris
    . . . bid me lurk

> Where serpents are; chain me with roaring bears
> Or shut me nightly in a charnel-house,
> O'er-cover'd quite with dead men's rattling bones,
> With reeky shanks, and yellow chapless skulls;
> Or bid me go into a new-made grave
> And hide me with a dead man in his shroud . . . .

Such Shakespearian hints had been already developed by Otway, e.g. in *The Orphan*, Act. 1, 209 ff., 446 ff. Chiefly:

> When in some Cell distracted, as I shall be,
> Thou seest me lye; these unregarded Locks,
> Matted like Furies Tresses; my poor Limbs
> Chain'd to the Ground, &c.

See my essay on 'Restoration Drama' in *English Studies*, vol. xv, February 1933. [Add. 1950]

56 Cf. *Justine*, vol. vi, p. 138, where the dungeons of a scandalous convent are mentioned: 'Quelquefois on vous enchaîne dans ces cachots; on y place avec vous des rats, des lézards, des crapauds, des serpents, &c'.

57 Cf. G. O. Arlt, 'A Source of Grillparzer's *Ahnfrau*', in *Modern Philology*, vol. xxix, no. 1 (Aug. 1931). pp. 91–100.

58 See F. Baldensperger, '*Le Moine* de Lewis dans la littérature française' in *Journal of Comparative Literature*, vol. i, no. 3 (July–Sept. 1903) pp. 201–19; also Estève, *Études*, ed. cit., pp. 127–9; Railo, op. cit., chap. iv; G. Bortone, *Fra il Voto e l'Amore; note critiche sul Monaco del Lewis, sul Templaro dello Scott, sull' Arcidiacono dell' Hugo, sull' Abate dello Zola, sullo Scorpione del Prévost* (Naples, Detken e Rocholl, 1908). Bortone's essay, though of little importance, nevertheless points out very justly how much Hugo derived from the story of *Ivanhoe* (pp. 81–2).

58A The vastness of the literature of this type will become evident to the reader of Montague Summers's *The Gothic Quest*, London, The Fortune Press [1939], a book crammed with farraginous and in many cases useless erudition. See also M. Sadleir, *The Northanger Novels, a Footnote to Jane Austen*, London, Milford, 1927 (Pamphlet no. 68 of the English Association); W. Whyte Watt, *Shilling Shockers of the Gothic School*, Harvard Univ. Press, Cambridge, Mass., 1932. [Add. 1950]

59 Precedents can be found for many of the situations in the 'tales of terror'. For example, in the *Comtesse d'Alibre*, by Loaisel de Tréogate (The Hague and Paris, 1779), the sinister count throws his unfaithful wife and her bastard into an underground dungeon; both succumb, the wife after opening her veins to nourish the dying child. See Mornet, op. cit., Première Partie, chap. iii.

60 The popularity of Mrs. Radcliffe's romance explains how it was that certain situations in the *Promessi Sposi* turned out remarkably like those of *The Italian*. Manzoni was such a diligent reader of the 'tales of terror' that in his youth he planned to write a 'romanzo fantastico', according to his stepson Stampa (*Alessandro Manzoni, la sua famiglia, i suoi amici*, Milan, 1885–9, vol. ii, p. 183). Manzoni's masterpiece is like a magnificent garment thrown over a mannered and worn-out lay figure. Another Italian novelist, F. D. Guerrazzi, also came strongly under the influence of Mrs. Radcliffe (see chap. iv, note 80).

Italian echoes of the theme of the persecuted maiden are Giulio Carcano's *Angela Maria*, Antonio Ranieri's *Ginevra o l'orfana della Nunziata* (both publ. 1839); see Gino Raya in the daily paper *La Sicilia* for March 2nd, 1948.

61 The Greek novel, in fact, had anticipated the 'tale of terror' even in the type of its incidents. In the Βαβυλωνιακά of Iamblichus (2nd century B.C.) King Garmos, having fallen in love with the beautiful Sinonis, binds her in chains of gold and has her lover Rhodanes crucified. However, the lovers contrive to get free and fly from their persecutors, pretending to be ghosts; there follows a series of extraordinary scenes among tombs, in caverns, in robbers' dens, until finally Rhodanes, nominated as a general of King Garmos, defeats the King of Syria and wins Sinonis.

62 *The Cenci*, Act iv, sc. 1.

In his preface to Tola Dorian's French version of *The Cenci*, Paris, Lemerre, 1883 (a preface reprinted in the Bonchurch edition of Swinburne's *Works*, vol. xv, pp. 319–29), Swinburne, while defending Old Cenci, actually pleads for his own case: 'Est-ce sa faute à lui si ses sens émoussés ne prennent plus plaisir aux voluptés mielleuses dont s'abreuvait sa jeunesse? Vraiment, il faut être d'une impudence bien endurcie pour venir reprocher à un homme ses goûts particuliers.' [Add. 1950]

63 Cf. this with *Juliette*, vol. ii, p. 93: Saint-Fond 'sodomise' his own daughter in the presence of his father whom he has poisoned, and exclaims:

'Quelle jouissance pour moi! J'étais couvert de malédictions, d'imprécations, je parricidais, j'incestais, j'assassinais, je prostituais, je sodomisais!'

64 *The Cenci*, Act iv, sc. 1.

65 *The Cenci*, Act iii, sc. 1.

Beatrice Cenci haunted also Herman Melville. See the footnote on p. 133 of his *Journal up the Straits*, New York, The Colophon, 1935. Her alleged portrait by Guido Reni exerted upon him an almost obsessional fascination; see *Pierre*, Book XXVI: 'that sweetest, most touching, but most awful of all feminine heads—the Cenci of Guido', &c.; and *Clarel*, vol. ii:

> He wore that nameless look
> About the mouth—so hard to brook—
> Which in the Cenci portrait shows. . . .
> A trembling over of small throes
> In weak swollen lips, which to restrain
> Desire is none, nor any rein.

The editor of the *Journey up the Straits* points out that both quotations appear in very morbid contexts. As for Melville's acquaintance with the tales of terror, see Newton Arvin, 'Melville and the Gothic Novel', in *The New England Quarterly*, vol. xxii, no. 1, March 1949. [Add. 1950]

66 *Prose Works*, ed. H. Buxton Forman, vol. iv, p. 143.

On the vogue of the incest theme in the novels and plays of the end of the eighteenth century see M. Summers, *The Gothic Quest*, p. 391.

[67] See Railo, op. cit., pp. 276 et seq.; also notes 43 and 49 to chap. ii of the present volume.

[68] Vol. ii, p. 62 of the 1892 London edition (R. Bentley and Son).

[69] Sade's explanation of this phenomenon may be found in a note to vol. iv of *Justine*:

'Nos places publiques ne sont-elles pas remplies chaque fois que l'on y assassine juridiquement? Ce qu'il y a de fort singulier c'est qu'elles le sont presque toujours par des femmes; elles ont plus de penchants que nous à la cruauté et cela parce qu'elles ont l'organisation plus sensible. Voilà ce que les sots n'entendent pas.'

[70] Vol. ii, p. 309.

[71] Vol. ii, p. 243.

[72] The story of Alonzo de Monçada as told in *The Tale of the Spaniard* is copied from that of Marie-Suzanne Simonin in the convent of Longchamp. Alonzo is destined by his parents for the cloister because of his irregular birth; Suzanne because she is the child of an adulterous union. Both resist the will of their parents, both are inveigled and threatened by priests in the same way and finally yield, after a moving scene with their respective mothers. Both seek an annulment of their vows from the civil tribunal, and make use of the same stratagem to obtain the paper on which to write their petition. They suffer the same cruel persecutions, are examined, as being possessed of an evil spirit, by a special ecclesiastical commission, and found innocent; but they lose their cases, and for the same reason. All these incidents, as well as many secondary details, were taken by Maturin from the *Religieuse*, often with the same words, and always with exaggerations and amplifications for the purpose of 'darkening the gloomy' and 'deepening the sad', as was the usual practice of this anti-Catholic and 'terrible' writer. A more detailed analysis of the relation between the two works was given by me in *The Review of English Studies* of Oct. 1930. Any one who wishes to examine some of the passages in which Maturin's imitation really becomes plagiarism, should compare pp. 284 et seq. of vol. i of *Melmoth* with pp. 80 et seq. of the *Religieuse*, in *Œuvres complètes*, ed. cit., vol. v (the episode of the visit of the bishop is the counterpart of the visit of the 'grand vicaire' in Diderot). The episode of the imprisonment in the dungeons of the Inquisition, of the escape and the taking refuge in the Jew's house derives partly from Godwin's *St. Leon*; see N. Idman, *Charles Robert Maturin, his Life and Works (a Dissertation)* (Helsingfors, Centraltryckeri, and London, Constable, 1923), pp. 230–1. For the analogies between *The Tale of the Indians* and *Faust*, see W. Müller, *Ch. Rob. Maturin's Romane 'The Fatal Revenge' und 'Melmoth the Wanderer', Ein Beitrag zur Gothic Romance* (Weida, 1908), pp. 98–9.

On Maturin see also W. Scholten, *Charles Robert Maturin, the Terror-novelist*, Amsterdam, H. J. Paris, 1933 (dissertation).

[73] Vol. iii, p. 120.   [74] Vol. i, p. 179.

[75] See A. M. Killen, *Le Roman 'terrifiant' ou roman 'noir' de Walpole à*

Anne Radcliffe et son influence sur la littérature française jusqu'en 1840 (Paris, Champion, 1915, in the Bibliothèque de la 'Revue de Littérature Comparée'.)

⁷⁶ See R. W. Hartland, *Walter Scott et le roman 'frénétique': contribution à l'étude de leur fortune en France* (Paris, Champion, 1928, in the Bibliothèque quoted above); especially chap. iv.

⁷⁷ See N. Atkinson, *Eugène Sue et le roman-feuilleton, thèse* (Nemours, Imprimerie André Lesot, 1929).

⁷⁸ For the pedigree of Han, see Hartland, op. cit., pp. 168, et seq.

⁷⁹ Vol. xiv, p. 529.

⁸⁰ See R. Barbiera, *La Principessa Belgiojoso* (Milan, Treves, 1902), pp. 324, et seq., pp. 115 et seq. Cf. also pp. 244, 281, and 397–8 of the present volume. The oddities of the Princess were not due to a mere pose; she was, as Tommaseo said, 'a cracked vessel', and suffered from profound nervous disorders (epilepsy). An anecdote which is characteristic, but which should be accepted with reserve, may be read in *Souvenirs du Marquis de Floranges*, published by M. Boulenger (Paris, Ollendorff, 1906), p. 78, and quoted by A. Augustin-Thierry, *Une Héroïne romantique, la Princesse Belgiojoso* (Paris, Plon, 1926), p. 20, note. See also this latter book for her relations with Stelzi, upon which the Princess's letters to Augustin Thierry throw light: pp. 52, 53, 59, 109, 110, 120, 122, 134, 141, 148–52. In the letter from Locate dated June 1848, the Princess tells of Stelzi's death and says:

'Je l'ai apporté ici, dans un tombeau qui est dans l'enceinte même de ma maison, de façon que Mrs. Parker et moi, nous avons la triste satisfaction de l'orner de fleurs et d'entretenir ce lieu comme une chambre plutôt que comme un sépulcre.'

The necrophilistic episode of the Princess Belgiojoso is reminiscent not only of Stendhal (the conclusion of *Le Rouge et le Noir*, when Mathilde 'avait placé sur une petite table de marbre, devant elle, la tête de Julien, et la baisait au front'—the head which was afterwards buried in a grotto among the mountains, sumptuously decorated), but also of the end of Rachilde's *Monsieur Vénus* (cf. pp. 332 et seq. in the present volume): Raoule keeps in her house a wax statue which represents her dead lover, of which certain parts (teeth, nails, and hair) were actually taken from the corpse.

The character of Laura Piaveni in Meredith's *Vittoria* (1867) is supposed to have traits of the Princess. See A. Luzio, 'Il romanzo della Principessa di Belgiojoso', in the vol. *Garibaldi, Cavour, Verdi*, Turin, Bocca, 1924, p. 443. A. Malvezzi, in *Cristina di Belgiojoso*, Milan, Treves, 1937, vol. iii, pp. 164–72, makes an attempt to discredit the report of the necrophilia of the Princess. She was not the only one to pursue such a course. Albert Denison narrates in his *Wanderings in Search of Health*, London, 1849 (privately printed), that Sophie de Barbé-Marbois, having the misfortune to lose her daughter while travelling in the East, caused the body to be embalmed, purposing that it should be interred with herself, and she kept it in her own room; her house catching fire, she offered a very large reward to those who would save the body, but in vain, the case was too heavy for removal. [Add. 1950]

[81] *Les Confessions, souvenirs d'un demi-siècle, 1830–1880* (Paris, Dentu, 1885), vol. iv, p. 339. Houssaye, in dedicating to Janin (in 1872) *Le Chien perdu et la femme fusillée*, a novel obviously inspired by *L'Âne mort*, said of the latter:

'C'était un livre immortel; vous ne le saviez pas: ainsi va le génie humain. Voltaire ne croyait écrire qu'une gaminerie en écrivant *Candide*; l'abbé Prévost ne signait *Manon Lescaut* qu'avec inquiétude'.

Houssaye places the scene of his novel in the Paris of the Commune: there is a woman who stabs herself like Lucretia and another who falls riddled with bullets . . . but they both of them revive, the second, however, only to throw herself finally into the sea after the ship which carries her lover to exile has disappeared. This Angéline Duportail is a superficial reflection of various Romantic *clichés*, as is shown farther on in the present study:

'Je ne sais pas si elle était née pour le bien, mais elle faisait le mal avec une fort jolie désinvolture. Pour qu'elle fût contente dans sa vie passionnée et passionnante, il fallait qu'elle fît souffrir son monde, elle aimait les larmes—celles des autres. Tous les désastres plaisaient à son âme. Elle comprenait Néron jouant du luth sur Rome incendiée. Mais Héliogabale et Tibère n'étaient pas ses hommes; ce qu'elle aimait, c'était le massacre des sentiments.

For a certain similarity between *L'Âne mort* and *Marthe* (1876), by J.-K. Huysmans, see H. Trudgian, *L'Esthétique de J.-K. Huysmans*, Paris, Conard, 1934, pp. 161, 165.

[82] The quotations from *L'Âne mort* are taken from the text of 1829. Later the author introduced considerable modifications into the style of the book and omitted the second part of the title. See the preface to the 1841 edition.

[83] In *Honestus* (1831) Janin carried this paradox even farther, showing how a fanatical young man's propaganda for virtue brought about such desolation and such apathy in the world, that there was nothing for the rash man to do but re-establish vice in order to restore to men their alacrity and happiness. Cf. Sade, *Juliette*, vol. i, p. 343:

'Ce n'est qu'à force de mal que la Nature réussit à faire le bien; ce n'est qu'à force de crimes qu'elle existe, et tout serait détruit si la vertu seule habitait la terre.'

[84] It is curious that De Quincey, in the 'Society for the Encouragement of Murder', should afford a humoristic parallel to Sade's 'Société des Amis du Crime' (*Juliette*). But De Quincey's humoristic evasion did not free him from his obsession, if it is true that, in his old age, he always showed a morbid interest in certain criminal trials.

To such an extent was algolagnia a paramount trait of his character that one wonders whether his game of hide-and-seek with his (actually threatening) creditors was not due to a craving for persecution. This surmise is well supported by a letter of his daughter, Mrs. Baird-Smith: 'It was an accepted fact among us that he was able when saturated with opium to persuade himself and delighted to persuade himself (the excitement of terror was a real delight to him) that he was dogged by dark and mysterious foes.' See H. A. Eaton, *Thomas De Quincey*, New York, Oxford University Press, 1936, p. 374. Even his disconsolate conviction, in the last years of his life, of being nothing better than a journalist, seemed to give him a not unpleasing sense of humiliation. All this would seem to countenance De Quincey's continental reputation as a fore-runner of the decadents. On the other hand, De Quincey's personality was deliberately in keeping with the bourgeois tendencies of his age (see my article on De Quincey in the review *Popoli*, vol. i, no. 16 (Dec. 1st, 1941)). [Add. 1950]

85 *Barnave* (1831), chap. xiv. Gautier derived from this passage in his preface to *Mademoiselle de Maupin* (cf. R. Jasinski, *Les Années romantiques de Th. Gautier*, Paris, Vuibert, 1929, pp. 214-15) and in the *Voyage d'Espagne*, where, speaking of bull-fights, he says that the situation of the *matador* face to face with the bull 'vaut tous les drames de Shakespeare'.

86 *Le Neveu de Rameau*:

'Je commençais à supporter avec peine le présence d'un homme qui discutait une action horrible, un exécrable forfait, comme un connaisseur en peinture ou en poésie examine les beautés d'un ouvrage de goût'.

87 It is to this episode that Baudelaire refers in his *Choix de maximes consolantes sur l'amour*, in *Œuvres posthumes*, op. cit., p. 359. See also below, in the text, § 20.

88 In the *Revue de Paris* of 1834, vol. xi, p. 333. Reproduced in a small pirated volume: *Le Marquis de Sade*, by J. Janin; *La Vérité sur les deux procès criminels du Marquis de Sade*, by Le Bibliophile Jacob (i.e. Paul Lacroix) (Paris, chez les Marchands de Nouveautés, 1834. This is a wrong date, because the article by Lacroix appeared for the first time in the *Revue de Paris* of 1837, vol. xxxviii, pp. 135-44). Flaubert wrote to his friend Chevalier (letter of July 15th, 1839, in *Correspondance*, op. cit., vol. i, p. 41) that Janin's article 'm'a révolté, sur le compte de Janin, bien entendu, car il déclamait pour la morale, pour la philanthropie, pour les vierges dép. . . .'

89 *Journal des Débats*, June 5th, 1839.

90 *Jenseits von Gut und Böse*, 26.

91 The opinion of Anatole France may be seen in his introduction to *Dorci, ou la bizarrerie du sort, conte inédit*, par le M. de Sade (Paris, Charavay, 1881), pp. 21-2. *Correspondance inédite du M. de Sade*, op. cit., Bourdin concludes (p. xlviii):

'Malgré Keller et les bonbons cantharidés, les filles de Lyon et de Vienne, Nanon, Justine, les jeunes secrétaires, les pèlerins de la Coste, les petites feuilles et les révélations de Marais, je n'arrive pas à le prendre au sérieux. Ses vices sont trop semblables à une maladie de peau; il est trop dépourvu de contrôle sur lui-même, d'inquiétude dans le mal, d'ambition dans la révolte, son esprit est trop ingénument pervers, sa littérature trop ennuyeuse. Tout est faute chez lui, c'est-à-dire manquement ou faillite.' See above, note 46 and addition.

92 Vol. i, p. 214.

93 See Sainte-Beuve, *Causeries du Lundi*, vol. v, pp. 334 et seq., especially 338 and 343.

94 Among the antecedents of Soulié may also be mentioned *Auswahl aus des Teufels Papieren*, by Jean Paul Richter (1789), and *Mittheilungen aus den Memoiren des Satan*, by Wilhelm Hauff (1826).

94A A plot based on a couple of girls of whom one, addicted to vice, has a life of pleasure, while the other, who is virtuous, goes through painful experiences, is found also in a novel whose pedigree is not in the 'tale of terror', but rather in the lucid novels of the eighteenth century, Thackeray's *Vanity Fair* (1847–8). Here, too, misfortunes of virtue and prosperity of vice: the author, should he be only a Soulié, or no less than Thackeray, traces all human actions to impure motives, and indulges in pitiless dissections. A parallel between Thackeray's novel and Soulié's could not be pushed further than that vague similarity of framework and of cynical analysis, but it is certain that the English author knew Soulié's work, as is shown by the articles on French literature he contributed to newspapers. In an article appearing in *Fraser's Magazine* for September 1843 (reprinted in *Critical Papers in Literature*, London, Macmillan, 1911, pp. 232 ff.) apropos of *Jérôme Paturot, with Considerations on Novels in general*, Thackeray shows himself well read in contemporary French fiction, although he disapproves the predominant taste for horrors. He blames among others Balzac, Dumas, Soulié. What strange opinion, he remarks, posterity would form about the France of his day from the books of those worthies!

'Did all married people, we may imagine they will ask, break a certain commandment? They all do in the novels. Was French society composed of murderers, of forgers, of children without parents, of men consequently running the daily risk of marrying their grandmothers by mistake, of disguised princes, who lived in the friendship of amiable cut-throats and spotless prostitutes, &c.?'

Already ten years earlier, in a correspondence in the *National Standard* for June 22nd, 1833 (reprinted in the volume *Burlesques, From Cornhill to Grand Cairo, and Juvenilia*, in the same Macmillan edition quoted above), he had denounced the vogue of tales of horror, the taste for minute descriptions of the anatomical peculiarities attending a crime, and had quoted as a typical instance Pétrus Borel's *Champavert*, calling attention, in a review of the book, to all its macabre aspects, and keeping an account of all the murders, adulteries, suicides. [Add. 1950]

95 *Les Mémoires du Diable*, vol. i, p. 242 (Calmann-Lévy edition of 1888).

96 Id., vol. iii, p. 150.

97 For a general account of Soulié's work, see Hartland, op. cit., pp. 205–38.

98 This circumstance, together with the condemnation to death for infanticide, has a parallel in *L'Histoire d'Hélène Gillet*, in the *Contes de la veillée* (1832), which Nodier took from a chronicle of the seventeenth century. Nodier's Hélène had been drugged, like so many other victims who are to be met with in Romantic literature, beginning with Clarissa.

'Entraînée chez une fausse amie apostée pour sa perte, sous le prétexte de quelque action de charité chrétienne, elle y fut fascinée, comme les victimes du vieux des Sept-Montagnes, par un breuvage narcotique'.

99 See the chapter farther on, entitled 'Swinburne and "le vice anglais"'. The passage is quoted from the Brussels reprint of 1872. Claretie (op. cit. note 102) has:

'Quand le couteau tomba, il se fit une sorte de rumeur, et un Anglais penché sur une fenêtre qu'il avait louée cinq cent francs, fort satisfait, cria un long *very well* en applaudissant des mains.'

¹⁰⁰ In 1824 had appeared, published by Sanson, *Dina ou la fiancée juive* (traduit de l'hébreu par Samuel Danson, et publ. par Marie Aycard).

¹⁰¹ See *Œuvres posthumes*, pp. 152 et seq. Other elements in this play are derived from Poe (*The Black Cat, The Imp of the Perverse*). See Seylaz, op. cit., pp. 54 et seq., and Baudelaire, *Lettres* (Paris, Mercure de France, 1907), pp. 60–1.

¹⁰¹ᴬ W. A. Reichart, who has found out the derivation from Irving ('Washington Irving as a Source for Borel and Dumas', in *Modern Language Notes*, June 1936, pp. 388–9), notices how Irving, in his turn, took the idea from Thomas Moore, who had taken it from Horace Smith, and how finally Dumas took the story over from Borel in *La Femme au collier de velours*. [Add. 1950]

¹⁰² See J. Claretie, *Pétrus Borel le Lycanthrope; sa vie—ses écrits—sa correspondance, poésies et documents inédits* (Paris, Pincebourde, 1865; Bibliothèque originale), p. 107. On Borel's epithet, see L. Cons, 'Pétrus Borel: pourquoi "le lycanthrope"?' in *The Romanic Review*, vol. xxiii, p. 4 (1932).

¹⁰³ *L'Art romantique; réflexions sur mes contemporains*, vol. v. A complete edition of the works of Borel, edited by Aristide Marie, began to appear in 1922, printed by 'La Force française' (500 numbered copies), but it did not go beyond the third volume (vol. i, Biography and Bibliography; vol. ii, Rhapsodies; vol. iii, Champavert).

On Borel and Baudelaire see F. Porché, *Baudelaire et la Présidente*, Geneva, Éditions du Milieu du monde, 1941, pp. 74–8; Barraou, one of Borel's heroes, whose tastes are evidently shared by the author, admits 'la propension sympathique qui toujours l'entraîne aux femmes de couleur' (in the same way Baudelaire felt attracted to Jeanne Duval). [Add. 1950]

¹⁰⁴ *Quelques vérités*, &c., op. cit.

¹⁰⁵ See the sketches of some of the eccentrics of the period of Baudelaire in E. Raynaud, *Ch. Baudelaire* (Paris, Garnier, 1922), pp. 103 et seq., especially the sketch of Lassailly, whose novel *Les Roueries de Trialph, notre contemporain avant son suicide*, published in 1833, shows the same taste for the grotesque and the horrible as we have already seen in the *Contes immoraux*. A contemporary critic (Charles Monselet) saw 'la beauté du diable' in Lassailly's book. With regard to the surroundings in which Baudelaire came to maturity, see also the remarks of Martino in *Revue d'histoire littéraire de la France*, 30ᵉ année (1923), p. 568 (review of Raynaud's book).

¹⁰⁶ *Mémoires du comte Horace de Viel Castel sur le règne de Napoléon III (1851–1864)* (Paris, chez tous les Libraires, 1883), vol. i, pp. 107 et seq. (March 29th, 1851).

¹⁰⁷ The Comte de Viel Castel uses the term 'sadism' in too wide a sense; hence the inclusion in his list of authors to whom this term cannot be applied. *Mademoiselle de Maupin* was responsible, on the other hand, for the fashion for the Androgyne, which assumed alarming proportions only

in the second part of the century. In the worthy Théo the casual allusion
to dreadful subjects is merely an affectation, but there was more than
affectation in his feeling for the equivocal charms of Lesbos.

108 On Eugène Sue, whom Viel Castel detested for political reasons,
see also vol. iii of the *Mémoires*, p. 212. Moreover, if what he says is true
—that Sue said to him one day: 'Venez me voir, nous ferons de bonnes
orgies!' it is quite probable that the novelist was pulling his leg. On Sue,
see especially Sainte-Beuve's note in *Portraits contemporains*, vol. iii,
pp. 115–17. See also the chapter 'Eugène Sue romancier mondain' in
J. Boulenger's *Les Dandys*, Paris, Calmann-Lévy, 1932.

109 This characteristic aspect of the work of de Musset has been analysed
with great penetration by P. Lasserre (op. cit., pp. 284 et seq.), and was
ascribed to masochism by J. Charpentier (*La Vie meurtrie d'Alfred de
Musset*, Paris, Piazza, 1928, p. 58 and also pp. 79, 83, 84).

I. Babbitt, *Rousseau and Romanticism*, op. cit., p. 215, apropos of
Musset's *voluptas dolendi* remarks that this perversion was not unknown
to classical antiquity, and quotes Seneca, *To Lucilius*, ep. xlix: 'Quid
turpius quam captare in ipso luctu voluptatem, et inter lacrymas quoque,
quod juvet, quaerere?' [Add. 1950]

Musset was directly and slavishly imitating Sade himself if he was really
the author of the vulgar pornographic composition called *Gamiani, ou Deux
Nuits d'excès*, By Alcide, Baron de M***, which is full of Lesbian lecheries,
bestialities, and sadistic pleasures. This naughty little volume was printed
in 1833, in 1835 (ostensibly at Venice), etc. (altogether 41 editions
between 1833 and 1928); in 1864 in Paris by Barraouel, with the
false indication 'Amsterdam, 1840', and with a frontispiece and a few
other illustrations by Rops, as well as reproductions of the illustrations
in the previous editions, some of which were extremely coarse (the
illustrations by Rops come under the numbers 464–8 in the catalogue
of the works of Rops in *La Plume*, June 15th, 1896). Rops' frontispiece
confirms the attribution to Musset, since it has written on a scroll: 'C'est
toi pâle Rolla'. The editor of the 1864 edition declares that it was printed
from 'une des copies manuscrites prises par les amis de notre jeune poète
à la suite du souper dans un des plus brillants restaurants du Palais-Royal'
a short time after the Revolution of 1830. He also quotes some lines,
'Chantez, chantez encore, rêveurs mélancoliques', which might have been
suggested by circumstances analogous with those of Musset's love for Mme
Groisellier (see L. Séché, *Alfred de Musset*, Paris, Mercure de France,
1907, vol. ii, p. 13). Some critics say that the Countess Gamiani is a
satirical portrait of George Sand, but this theory, apart from anything
else, would not agree with the date generally attributed to the book. The
attribution to Musset is reasserted by L. Perceau (*Bibliographie du roman
érotique au XIXe siècle*, Paris, Foudrinier, 1930, vol. i, p. 66), who, however, says: 'Mais il faut avouer qu'aucune preuve matérielle de cette
paternité ne peut être produite.'

110 *Journal*, vol. iv, p. 281 (Apr. 28th, 1871). On the influence of
the *Confession* in Russia, see chap. v, p. 351

[111] Essay on Delacroix in *Histoire du Romantisme* (édition Charpentier, 1877, p. 205).

[112] Passages from the *Journal*, April 13th and 20th, June 12th, 1824, quoted by R. Escholier, *Delacroix* (Paris, Floury, 1926–8), vol. i, pp. 86 et seq.

[113] *Journal*, vol. i, p. 113, quoted by Escholier, op. cit., vol. i, p. 118.

[114] Baudelaire, 'L'Œuvre et la vie d'Eugène Delacroix', in *L'Art romantique*:

'La moralité de ses œuvres, si toutefois il est permis de parler de la moralité en peinture, porte aussi un caractère molochiste visible. Tout, dans son œuvre, n'est que désolation, massacres, incendies; tout porte témoignage contre l'éternelle et incorrigible barbarie de l'homme. Les villes incendiées et fumantes, les victimes égorgées, les femmes violées, les enfants eux-mêmes jetés sous les pieds des chevaux ou sous le poignard des mères délirantes; tout cet œuvre, dis-je, ressemble à un hymne terrible composé en l'honneur de la fatalité et de l'irrémédiable douleur.'

Baudelaire's other essay on Delacroix, in *Salon de 1846*, is to be found in the volume of *Curiosités esthétiques*. See chap. iii, 'Baudelaire critico d'arte', in G. Macchia, *Baudelaire critico*, Florence, Sansoni, 1939.

[115] G. Dargenty, *Eugène Delacroix par lui-même* (Paris, Rouam, 1885).

[116] Quoted from Escholier, op. cit., vol. i, p. 56.

[117] See my article 'Swinburne', in *Cultura*, Oct. 15th, 1922 (vol. i, no. 12), pp. 536–53. (Reprinted in the volume *Ricerche anglo-italiane*, Rome, 1944.)

[118] The English text has:

'Among other things, I hold painfully in mind a certain singular perversion and amplification of the wild air of the last waltz of Von Weber.'

In the *Salon de 1846*:

'Cette haute et sérieuse mélancolie brille d'un éclat morne, même dans sa couleur, large, simple, abondante, en masses harmoniques, comme celle de tous les grands coloristes, mais plaintive et profonde comme une mélodie de Weber.'

In 1858 Baudelaire wrote to A. Fraisse: 'En 1846 ou 1847 j'eus connaissance de quelques fragments d'Edgar Poe.' So that the comparison between Delacroix and Weber must have been made before Baudelaire read *The Fall of the House of Usher*. The stanza in *Les Phares*, however, does not appear in the original version of the essay on Delacroix in the article 'Exposition universelle de 1855', *Le Pays*, June 3rd, 1855 (*Les Fleurs du mal*, éd. Crépet, 1922, p. 413).

[119] Escholier, op. cit., vol. ii, pp. 175–6. In Baudelaire's preface to the *Histoires extraordinaires* he says:

'Comme notre Eugène Delacroix, qui a élevé son art à la hauteur de la grande poésie, Edgar Poe aime à agiter ses figures sur des fonds violâtres et verdâtres où se révèlent la phosphorescence de la pourriture et la senteur de l'orage.'

[120] Letter of Oct. 6th, 1859, quoted from E. Crépet, *Charles Baudelaire, Étude biographique revue et mise à jour par J. Crépet* (Paris, Vanier, 1906), p. 377.

[121] On Baudelaire's religious opinions see the very just remarks of P.

Flottes, *Baudelaire, l'homme et le poète* (Paris, Perrin et Cie, 1922), pp. 58–71, 193–6, 217–18, 221–3.

122 *Causeries du Lundi*, vol. xv, pp. 350–2.

123 'Le Sadisme chez Baudelaire' was the subject of an article by Doctor Cabanès (in the *Chronique médicale*, IXe Année, no. 22, Nov. 15th, 1902, pp. 725–35), in which, however, the documentation is not complete, nor always reliable; Cabanès, for example, makes a point of such declarations of Baudelaire as that of his passion for giantesses and dwarfs, which were made 'pour épater le bourgeois'. The passage which C. Lombroso devoted to Baudelaire in his *Uomo di Genio* is completely devoid of value, badly informed, and stupidly contemptuous. More recently Doctor René Laforgue has attempted a psycho-analytical study of Baudelaire in his book *L'Échec de Baudelaire* (Paris, Éditions Denoël et Steele, 1931). Chapter vi, 'Le Sado-masochisme dans la poésie de Baudelaire', is little more than an anthology of significant passages. But in any case, as J. Royère remarks in 'L'Érotologie de Baudelaire', in *Le Mercure de France* of June 15th, 1920, p. 624 (reprinted in the volume *Poèmes d'amour de Baudelaire, le génie mystique*, Paris, Michel, 1927), there is no point in insisting on Baudelaire's algolagnia, 'car là-dessus tous les lecteurs s'accordent'. Anatole France, in the introduction (op. cit.) to Sade's *Dorci*, remarks (p. 25):

'Mais comment ne pas noter sur ces feuillets de nosologie littéraire le penchant irrésistible de l'auteur des *Fleurs du mal* à associer le crime et la volupté, en sorte qu'on ne sait plus s'il chante, dans ses strophes d'un sombre éclat, le crime de la volupté ou la volupté du crime? La peste sadique n'a pas tué ce poète magnifique et singulier, mais elle l'a atteint, comme elle a atteint plusieurs autres en ce temps-ci:

   Ils ne mouraient pas tous, mais tous étaient frappés'.

124 The italics here are mine. Compare this with what Poe wrote about the origin of *The Raven*: 'The lover . . . propounds queries . . . half in superstition and half in that species of despair which delights in self-torture . . . he experiences a frenzied pleasure in so modelling his questions as to receive from the *expected* "Nevermore" the most delicious, because the most intolerable, of sorrow'. Cf. also, in Baudelaire's essay on *Richard Wagner et Tannhäuser à Paris*: 'Le sentiment presque ineffable, tant il est terrible, de la joie dans la damnation', and in *Réflexions sur mes contemporains*, vol. vii, p. 359 of *L'Art romantique*, in the edition of the *Œuvres complètes* of J. Crépet (Paris, Conard, 1925).

125 D. H. Lawrence, *Studies in Classic American Literature* (London, Secker, 1924), vol. vi. Especially:

'*Ligeia* is the chief story. [Ligeia is Virginia, Poe's wife.] It is a tale of love pushed over a verge. And love pushed to extreme is a battle of wills between the lovers. . . Which shall first destroy the other, of the lovers ? . . . Ligeia is the old-fashioned woman. Her will is still to submit. She wills to submit to the vampire of her husband's consciousness. Even death. . . . What he wants to do with Ligeia is to analyse her, till he knows all her component parts, till he has got her all in his consciousness. . . . It is easy to see why each man kills the thing he loves. To *know* a living thing is to kill it. You have to kill a thing to know it satisfactorily. For this reason, the desirous consciousness, the SPIRIT, is a vampire. . . .

Every sacred instinct teaches one that one must leave her (i.e. the woman one loves) unknown. You know your woman darkly, in the blood. To try to *know* her mentally is to kill her. . . . It is the temptation of a vampire fiend, is this knowledge. . . . Poe wanted to know—wanted to know what was the strangeness in the eyes of Ligeia. She might have told him it was horror, horror at his probing, horror at being vamped by his consciousness. But she wanted to be vamped. She wanted to be probed by his consciousness, to be *known*. She paid for wanting it, too. Nowadays it is usually the man who wants to be vamped, to be KNOWN. . . . Poe and Ligeia sinned against the Holy Ghost that bids us all laugh and forget, bids us know our own limits. And they weren't forgiven.'

[126] He adds, however:

'Du moins *Ligeia, Eleonora*, ne sont pas, à proprement parler, des histoires d'amour, l'idée principale sur laquelle pivote l'œuvre étant tout autre'.

[127] Perhaps the following opinion of Baudelaire is more appropriate than the one quoted above:

'Dans ses articles, il parle quelquefois de l'amour, et même comme d'une chose dont le nom fait frémir la plume.'

[128] *Œuvres posthumes*, p. 124; *Journaux intimes*, ed. Van Bever, p. 92.

[129] *L'Art romantique, Le Peintre de la vie moderne*, xi.

[130] *Œuvres posthumes*, p. 78; *Journaux intimes*, p. 8.

[131] Id., p. 101; *Journ. int.*, p. 48.

[132] Id., p. 87; *Journ. int.*, p. 24.

[133] Id., p. 107; *Journ. int.*, p. 59.

[134] Id., p. 77; *Journ. int.*, pp. 6–8.

[135] Id., p. 100; *Journ. int.*, p. 46. Cf. *L'Héautontimorouménos* and the passage of Swinburne's *Lesbia Brandon* quoted in chap. iv, § 17.

[136] Cf. also *Madrigal triste* quoted in chap. i, and the *delectatio morbosa* of *Une Martyre*.

[137] It may be noted that in his famous sonnet on Beauty Baudelaire touches upon the subject of the *Belle Dame sans merci* with which I shall deal in the next chapter:

> Je suis belle, ô mortels! comme un rêve de pierre,
> Et mon sein, où chacun s'est meurtri tour à tour,
> Est fait pour inspirer au poète un amour
> Éternel et muet ainsi que la matière.
>
> Je trône dans l'azur comme un sphinx incompris;
> J'unis un cœur de neige à la blancheur des cygnes;
> Je hais le mouvement qui déplace les lignes,
> Et jamais je ne pleure et jamais je ne ris.

[138] I am following the arrangement suggested by Prince Alexander Ourousoff in *Le Tombeau de Charles Baudelaire*, and approved by Crépet (op. cit., p. 62 note).

[139] In a sonnet (*Œuvres posthumes*, p. 60), written when Baudelaire was at the Collège Louis-le-Grand, he had already compared himself to one of the fakirs who throw themselves beneath the car of Juggernaut:

> . . . sur mon sein brûlant, je crois tenir serrée
> Quelque idole terrible et de sang altérée,
> A qu les longs sanglots des moribonds sont doux;
> Et j'éprouve, au milieu des spasmes frénétiques,
> L'atroce enivrement des vieux Fakirs Indous,
> Les extases sans fin des Brahmes fanatiques.

[140] *Œuvres posthumes*, p. 359; *Journaux intimes*, pp. 126–7.

[141] *Œuvres posthumes*, p. 408.

[142] Baudelaire's impotence, generally admitted in this case, is denied by Flottes (op. cit., p. 130) on the basis of a letter of Baudelaire of Aug. 31st, 1857, in which he professes to see a proof of effective possession. According to Flottes, it was a case of rapid repugnance. This view is shared by Pierre Dufay, in his study of Madame Sabatier contained in *Autour de Baudelaire* (Paris, Au Cabinet du Livre, 1931): 'Son rêve s'était évanoui dans la tiédeur de ses bras.' However, a passage in that very letter of Aug. 31st, 1857: 'Et si, par malheur pour moi, j'acquiers le droit d'être jaloux!' seems to imply that no possession had taken place, for possession would have given the poet the right of being jealous. On Baudelaire's relations with Madame Sabatier see F. Porché, *Baudelaire et la Présidente*, op. cit.

[143] Nadar, *Ch. Baudelaire intime, le poète vierge* (Paris, Blaizot, 1911). Nadar's opinion is accepted by Raynaud (op. cit., pp. 249 et seq.), and discredited by Flottes (op. cit., pp. 110 and 136). In any case the theory of his virginity does not fit in with the venereal disease which Baudelaire contracted at the beginning of his erotic experience, and which eventually led to his death. Royère (op. cit., p. 625) notes certain probabilities 'très fortes' in support of the theory of virginity. According to J. Mouquet, *Ch. Baudelaire, vers retrouvés* (Paris, Émile-Paul, 1929, p. 35), the legend of his virginity was an immense mystification on the part of the poet himself.

[144] *Œuvres posthumes*, p. 234. In the definitive preface to the *Histoires extraordinaires* the text of this passage appears with certain variants of minor importance.

[144A] Erotic imagination finds frequently a very mild counterpart in the ordinary life of many of these sex-obsessed romantic artists. See on this point J. L. Vaudoyer, *Alice Ozy ou l'Aspasie moderne*, Paris, Éditions M.-P. Trémois, 1930, where, in the memoirs of the actress Ozy, whose real name was Julie-Justine (a name which oddly enough has an involuntary sadistic ring) Pilloy, Gautier appears as a platonic worshipper for whom it was enough to see the actress naked and to caress her foot; also Paul de Saint-Victor's ardours were purely of the brain: 'Un rien lui suffisait. Si dans la loge, au théâtre, je me laissais déchausser et je lui abandonnais, durant la représentation, un pied dans sa main, il était au trente-sixième ciel. . . .' It is worth noticing that Paul de Saint-Victor went to the theatre in the capacity of a dramatic critic! [Add. 1950]

[145] Séché-Bertaud, quoted in note 38 of chap. i, pp. 79 and 126; Crépet, op. cit., pp. 65–6, note.

[146] See *Le Figaro*, Nov. 2nd, 1900.

[147] *Curieuse!* 1886 edition, p. 69.

[148] See also Croce in his essay on 'Flaubert', which originally appeared in *La Critica*, vol. xviii (1920). Flaubert himself recognized the affinity; cf. *Correspondance*, édition Conard, vol. iii, pp. 301 and 346.

[149] R. Dumesnil, *Flaubert, son hérédité — son milieu — sa méthode* (Paris, Société française d'Imprimerie et de Librairie, n.d. but 1905), pp. 88–9.

[150] *Nouveaux Lundis*, vol. iv, p. 71.

[151] T. Reik, *Flaubert und seine 'Versuchung des heiligen Antonius', ein Beitrag zur Künstlerpsychologie* (Minden, Bruns, 1912).

[152] Croce, op. cit., p. 196.

[153] Cf. among others, the passage:

'Ils se penchaient pour le voir [le corps de cette victime], les femmes surtout. Elles brûlaient de contempler celui qui avait fait mourir leurs enfants et leurs époux; et au fond de leur âme, malgré elles, surgissait une infâme curiosité, le désir de le connaître complètement, envie mêlée de remords et qui se tournait en un surcroît d'exécration.'

[154] Cf. the essay by M. Schwob, 'Saint Julien l'Hospitalier', in *Spicilège* (*Œuvres complètes*, vol. iv).

[155] Quoted above, chap. i, p. 33.

[156] D'Annunzio derived from this both *Pamphila* and an episode in *Maia*, 'La vecchiezza di Elena' (see chap. iv, § 24).

[157] Cf. chap. i, p. 31.

[158] This temptation, which appears in slightly different forms in the versions of 1849 and 1856, does not appear at all in the final text. Reik (op. cit., pp. 84–5 and 183) maintains that Flaubert suppressed it because it revealed to him his own subliminal incestuous desire for his mother. But there may be a much simpler reason for its suppression: this scene was not original. In *The Monk*, Ambrosio's first temptation was provoked precisely by the image of the Madonna, after a suggestion taken from Schiller's *Geisterseher* (Railo, op. cit., pp. 261–2). This is the passage:

'"Should I meet in that world which I am constrained to enter, some lovely female—lovely as you—Madona—!" As he said this, he fixed his eyes upon a picture of the Virgin, which was suspended opposite to him; this for two years had been the object of his increasing wonder and adoration. He paused, and gazed upon it with delight. "What beauty in that countenance!" he continued, after a silence of some minutes; "how graceful is the turn of that head! what sweetness, yet what majesty in her divine eyes! how softly her cheek reclines upon her hand! Can the rose vie with the blush of that cheek? can the lily rival the *whiteness of that hand?* Oh! if such a creature existed, and existed but for me! were I permitted to twine round my fingers *those golden ringlets*, and press with my lips the treasures of that snowy bosom! gracious God, should I then resist the temptation? Should I not barter for *a single* embrace the reward of my sufferings for thirty years? Should I not abandon—Fool that I am! Whither do I suffer my admiration of this picture to hurry me? *Away, impure ideas!*"'

Cf. *Tentation* (1849):

'Il ouvre son missel et regarde l'image de la Vierge . . .: "Oh, que je t'aime!" Il contemple l'image de plus en plus. . . . *La voix*: "Qu'elle est belle la mère du Sauveur! qu'ils sont doux ses longs *cheveux blonds* épanchés le long de son pâle visage! etc. Regarde donc ses cils fins abaissés, qui font sur sa joue les ombres d'un réseau! . . . Et *ses mains plus blanches* que les hosties! etc. Les longs cheveux . . . les longs cheveux d'or. . . . Elle *te serrera dans ses bras*, elle te plongera dans ses regards . . ." *Antoine*: "*Démons de mes pensées, arrière!*" '

Flaubert makes the image of the Madonna come to life before the eyes of Antony, and even accomplish acts 'comme les courtisanes des carrefours'. Something similar happens in *The Monk*:

'Sometimes his dreams presented the image of his favourite Madona . . . the eyes of the figure seemed to beam on him with inexpressible sweetness; he pressed his lips to hers, and found them warm; the animated form started from the canvas, embraced him affectionately, and his senses were unable to support delight so exquisite. Such were the scenes on which his thoughts were employed while sleeping: his unsatisfied desires placed before him the most lustful and provoking images, and he rioted in joys till then unknown to him.'

Towards the end of the novel the Devil reveals to Ambrosio that he has tempted him through the image of the Madonna, which is none other than a portrait of Matilda, drawn by Martin Galuppi, 'a celebrated Venetian'. Lewis was writing from the Protestant point of view. Baldensperger, in the study already quoted on the influence of *The Monk* in France, does not mention this as being one of Flaubert's sources. As regards that which the Voice whispered to Antony, apropos of the Madonna: 'Ce ne serait pas la première fois, va! elle a couché avec Panthérus, qui était un soldat romain à la barbe frisée . . . elle aime tout le monde, etc.', cf. Sade, *Juliette*, vol. iii, p. 152, '. . . les soldats de la garnison de Jérusalem par qui la bougresse s'en faisait donner tous les jours . . .'

[159] Janin might well have put his name to the following passage of *Un Parfum à sentir*:

'Une maison de jeu . . . avec toute sa prostitution hideuse, un de ces taudis où parfois, le lendemain, on trouve quelque cadavre mutilé entre les verres brisés et les haillons tout rouges de sang. . . . Quelques femmes à moitié nues se promenaient paisiblement autour d'eux, et plus loin, dans un coin, deux hommes armés, debout devant une jeune fille couchée sur le pavé et liée avec des cordes, tiraient à la courte paille. Vous frémissez peut-être, aimable lecteur, à la peinture de cette moitié de la société, la maison de jeu? L'autre, c'est l'hôpital, c'est la guillotine.'

[160] Cf. below, chap. v, § 9, and note 47. In the same story he says: 'Ellé eut de l'amour pour Dorsay comme en durent avoir les filles des hommes pour les anges, quand les anges s'imaginèrent qu'il y avait plus de paradis dans l'adultère que dans les cieux.'

Provincial echoes of this low kind of romanticism are to be found in Italy in the work of Alfredo Oriani, for instance in *Al di là* (1875) (edition *Opera omnia*, Bologna, Cappelli, 1934; vol. i, pp. 128 ff.), which betrays a childish infatuation with adultery ('Adulterio! scrivo questa armoniosa parola, che mi accarezza l'orecchio come una musica . . .'), with the pleasure of evil-doing, with Lesbian love, and any form of accursed love. [Add. 1950]

[161] 'Notice sur Champavert' in *Contes immoraux*. In a letter of 1853 (*Corresp.*, vol. ii, p. 171) Flaubert says, apropos of Borel, whom he was

re-reading at the time: 'Je trouve là mes vieilles phrénésies de jeunesse'.

162 *Corresp.*, vol. i, p. 89, Oct. 29th, 1842; *Novembre*, p. 241.

163 *Mademoiselle de Maupin*, édition Charpentier, pp. 61, 154. Sade had said, on the subject of Nero (*Juliette*, vol. v, p. 291): 'Ô Néron, laisse-moi vénérer ta mémoire!'

That Nero deserved this cult can be shown by some of his refinements of cruelty, like the *tableaux vivants* of which Renan speaks in his article 'Les Dircés chrétiennes', in *Gazette des Beaux-Arts*, 1873, vol. ii, pp. 385–9. [Add. 1950]

Flaubert's work is full of regrets for the Rome of the Caesars. Cf. *Corresp.*, vol. i, p. 114: 'Aussi j'admire Néron: c'est l'homme culminant du monde antique! etc.' (in the *Danse des morts*, 1838, in *Œuvres de jeunesse*, vol. i, p. 451: 'Néron, ce fils chéri de mon cœur, le plus grand poète que la terre ait eu'); p. 152: 'J'ai vécu à Rome, c'est certain, du temps de César ou de Néron . . .'; p. 467; *Mémoires d'un fou* (*Œuvres de jeunesse*, vol. i, p. 491):

'Mais c'était Rome que j'aimais, la Rome impériale, cette belle reine se roulant dans l'orgie, salissant ses nobles vêtements du vin de la débauche, plus fière de ses vices qu'elle ne l'était de ses vertus. Néron! Néron, avec ses chars de diamant volant dans l'arène, ses mille voitures, ses amours de tigre et ses festins de géant.'

Smarh (*Œuvres de jeunesse*, vol. ii, p. 97); *Rome et les Césars* (1839):

'Néron ne vient-il jamais reprendre les rênes de son char splendide, qui vole sur le sable d'or et dont les roues broient des hommes? ses orgies titaniques, aux flambeaux humains, sont-elles bien finies? . . . Vous ne rêverez rien de si terrible et de si monstrueux que les dernières heures de l'Empire, c'est là le règne du crime, c'est son apogée, sa gloire; il est monté sur le trône, il s'y étale à l'aise, en souverain; il se farde encore pour être plus beau, à aucune époque vous le verrez pareil; Alexandre VI est un nain à côté de Tibère, et les imaginations de dix grands poètes ne créeraient pas quelque chose qui vaudrait cinq minutes de la vie de Néron. . . . Le monde étant à un seul homme, comme un esclave, il pouvait le torturer pour son plaisir, et il fut torturé en effet jusqu'à la dernière fibre. . . . Le crime est une volupté comme les autres . . . Néron disait aux bourreaux: "Faites en sorte qu'ils se sentent mourir", et penché en avant sur les poitrines ouvertes des victimes, il regardait le sang battre dans les cœurs, et il trouvait, dans ces derniers gémissements d'un être qui quitte la vie, des délices inconnues, des voluptés suprêmes, comme lorsqu'une femme, éperdue sous l'œil de l'empereur, tombait dans ses bras et se mourait sous ses baisers. Oh! les cœurs atroces! oh! les âmes sublimes dans le crime! Chaque jour ils redoublent, chaque jour ils inventent, leur esprit est un enfer qui fournit des tortures au monde, ils insultent à la nature dans leurs débauches. . . . L'histoire alors est une orgie sanglante, dans laquelle il nous faut entrer, sa vue même enivre et fait venir la nausée au cœur.'

Novembre (*Œuvres de jeunesse*, vol. ii, pp. 182 and 185):

'J'aurais voulu anéantir la création . . . que ne me réveillé-je à la lueur des villes incendiées! J'aurais voulu entendre le frémissement des ossements que la flamme fait pétiller, traverser des fleuves chargés de cadavres, galoper sur des peuples courbés et les écraser des quatres fers de mon cheval, être Gengiskan, Tamerlan, Néron, effrayer le monde au froncement de mes sourcils'.

Éducation sentimentale (1845) (*Œuvres de jeunesse*, vol. iii, p. 160):

'L'amour romain . . . se ramifiant à toutes les folies, s'élargissant dans toutes les
lubricités, tour à tour égyptien sous Antoine, asiatique à Naples avec Néron,
indien avec Héliogabale, sicilien, tartare et byzantin sous Théodora, et toujours
mêlant du sang à ses roses, et toujours étalant sa chair rouge sous l'arcade de son
grand cirque où hurlaient les lions, où nageaient les hippopotames, où mouraient
les chrétiens.'

On Flaubert's Orient, see also L. F. Benedetto, *Le Origini di 'Salammbô'*
(Florence, Bemporad, 1920), pp. 21 et seq. Useful observations on the
subject of Romantic exoticism, together with a plentiful documentation,
are to be found in F. Brie, *Exotismus der Sinne, Eine Studie zur Psychologie
der Romantik* (Heidelberg, Winter, 1920). Flaubert is discussed on p. 51
et seq. There is a hint of Romantic exoticism, a genuine anticipation of
Flaubert's lecherous, cruel Orient, in Marlowe's *Tamburlaine the Great*,
on which see my essay in *English Studies*, vol. xiii, no. 6 (Dec. 1931).
With Marlowe, just as with the French Romantics about 1830, the exploration of the soul of a powerful tyrant living in a cruel and magnificent
age became tantamount to the exploration of the sources of his own 'desire,
lift upward and divine'.

Also in Gautier's *Fortunio* (1838) (previously appearing in the *Figaro*
of 1837 with the title *L'Eldorado*) the plot, the loves of Fortunio and
Musidora, offers merely a pretext for the description of scenes of Oriental
and Venetian luxury, of whims worthy of satraps, of orgies and cruelties.
'Un des plus grands plaisirs qu'il [Fortunio] eût c'était de mélanger la vie
barbare et la vie civilisée, d'être à la fois un satrape et un fashionable,
Brummel et Sardanapale' (*Nouvelles*, Paris, Charpentier, 1912, p. 137).
The windows of Fortunio's enchanted palace looked towards dioramas
which created the most complete illusion of the world's pleasure-cities,
so that his valet could ask him in the morning: 'Quel pays voulez-vous qu'on
vous serve aujourd'hui?' Huysmans was to remember such inventions
for his Des Esseintes. Moreover Fortunio 'se plongeait délicieusement dans
cet abrutissement voluptueux si cher aux Orientaux, et qui est le plus
grand bonheur qu'on puisse goûter sur terre' (p. 141). 'Il était assez de
l'avis du sultan Schariaz, rien ne lui paraissait plus agréable que d'acheter
une jeune fille vierge et de lui faire couper la tête la première nuit' (p. 143).
'Soudja-Hari pouvait avoir treize ans . . . elle était de la race de ces terribles
Javanaises, de ces gracieux vampires qui boivent un Européen en trois
semaines et le laissent sans une goutte d'or ni de sang' (p. 144; compare
this Javanese with the Creole vamp in Sue's *Mystères de Paris*, see foll.
chap.). [Add. 1950]

Flaubert derived from Gautier a certain laconic descriptive style which
is used especially in the *Tentation*. Cf. for instance, in *Mademoiselle de
Maupin*, p. 212:

'La cigale crie et chante, l'épi craque, l'ombre vaincue et n'en pouvant plus de
chaleur, se pelotonne et se ramasse au pied des arbres; tout rayonne, tout reluit,
tout resplendit. . . .'

We have occasional glimpses of Gautier's and Flaubert's type of exoticism in Chateaubriand, e.g. *Mémoires d'outre-tombe*, vol. i:

'Il serait trop long de raconter quels voyages je faisais avec ma fleur d'amour; comment, main en main, nous visitions les ruines célèbres, Venise, Rome, Athènes, Jérusalem, Memphis, Carthage; comment nous franchissions les mers; comment nous demandions le bonheur aux palmiers d'Otahiti, aux bosquets embaumés d'Amboine et de Tidor; comment, au sommet de l'Himalaya, nous allions réveiller l'aurore; comment nous descendions les *fleuves saints*, dont les vagues épandues entourent les pagodes aux boules d'or; comment nous dormions aux rives du Gange, tandis que le bengali, perché sur le mât d'une nacelle de bambou, chantait sa barcarolle indienne.'

164 *Mademoiselle de Maupin*, p. 222. Cf. Flaubert, *Corresp.*, vol. i, p. 60:

'J'étais né pour être empereur de Cochinchine, pour fumer dans des pipes de 36 toises, pour avoir six mille femmes et 1400 bardaches, etc.'

165 *Mademoiselle de Maupin*, pp. 197 and 221.

166 Id., p. 211.

167 *Corresp.*, vol. i, p. 173, letter of Aug. 13th, 1846, to Louise Colet.

168 *Novembre*, pp. 239 et seq. The italics are mine. See also *Corresp.*, vol. i, p. 78.

Late echoes of this kind of exoticism can be found at the beginning of our century in Ramón del Valle-Inclán (*Sonata de estío*). [Add. 1950]

169 *Mademoiselle de Maupin*, p. 269. Cf. *Novembre*, p. 180:

'J'étais, dans la variété de mon être, comme une immense forêt de l'Inde, où la vie palpite dans chaque atome et apparaît, monstrueuse ou adorable, sous chaque rayon de soleil; l'azur est rempli de parfums et de poisons, les tigres bondissent, les éléphants marchent fièrement comme des pagodes vivantes, les dieux, mysté-rieux et difformes, sont cachés dans le creux des cavernes parmi de grands monceaux d'or; et au milieu, coule le large fleuve, avec des crocodiles béants qui font claquer leurs écailles dans le lotus du rivage, et ses îles de fleurs que le courant entraîne avec des troncs d'arbres et des cadavres verdis par la peste.'

170 An expression which is found in a letter of 1857 to Jules Duplan is rather revealing. Flaubert, speaking of the composition of *Salammbô*, says:

'Ce n'est pas que je sois inspiré le moins du monde, mais j'ai envie de voir ça, c'est une sorte de curiosité et comme qui dirait un désir lubrique sans érection.'

See also *Corresp.*, vol. ii, p. 159, apropos of *Madame Bovary*.

171 *Corresp.*, vol. i, p. 433 (Apr. 24th, 1852).

172 *Corresp.*, vol. i, p. 406.

173 *Corresp.*, vol. ii, pp. 84 et seq.

174 One must remember what Baudelaire wrote about E. Poe (*Œuvres posthumes*, p. 195):

'Le caractère, le génie, le style d'un homme est formé par les circonstances en apparence vulgaires de sa première jeunesse. Si tous les hommes qui ont occupé la scène du monde avaient noté leurs impressions d'enfance, quel excellent dictionnaire psychologique nous posséderions!'

175 Cf. Baudelaire, *Le mauvais vitrier*: 'Ces plaisanteries nerveuses ne sont pas sans péril, etc.'

176 *Corresp.*, vol. ii, p. 283.

177 pp. 179 et seq.

178 See above, p. 153. Cf. also *Corresp.*, vol. i, p. 131, letter of May 26th, 1845:

'C'est une chose singulière comme je suis écarté de la femme. J'en suis repu comme doivent l'être ceux qu'on a trop aimés. Je suis devenu impuissant par ces effluves magnifiques que j'ai trop sentis bouillonner pour les voir jamais se déverser. Je n'éprouve même vis-à-vis d'aucun jupon le désir de curiosité qui vous pousse à dévoiler l'inconnu et à chercher du nouveau.'

[179] *Corresp.*, vol. ii, p. 533.

[180] *Op. cit.*, p. 88.

[181] Without entering into a detailed analysis as we have done here, Croce, in his essay already quoted, comes to the same conclusion.

[182] *Corresp.*, vol. i, p. 41. The passage that I quote concludes:

'Ô mon cher Ernest, à propos du Marquis de Sade, si tu pouvais me trouver quelques-uns des romans de cet honnête écrivain, je te les payerais leur pesant d'or.'

[183] *Œuvres de jeunesse*, vol. iii, p. 162.

[184] *Œ. de jeunesse*, vol. i, pp. 25–6, *Portrait de Lord Byron.*

[185] *Mémoires d'un fou*, in *Œ. de jeun.*, vol. i, p. 498.

[186] *Corresp.*, vol. i, p. 190 (Sept. 4th–5th, 1846).

[187] The expression used by me is found in De Quincey, *Suspiria de profundis* (*Levana*): 'keys more than papal . . . which open every cottage and every palace.'   [188] See chap. ii, § 14.

[189] The name is derived from a novel by Sue, *Latréaumont* (1838), in which that popular author represents the adventurer Latréaumont, the villain of the conspiracy of the Chevalier de Rohan against Louis XIV, as a satanical cynic who, under torture, hurls forth words'of defiance and mockery. Discussing these words, Gustave Planche wrote (*Portraits littéraires*, 1848, vol. ii, p. 116):

'Je ne pense pas que ces paroles servent à dessiner le caractère de Latréaumont, et je suis sûr qu'elles exciteront un dégoût universel. Il n'y a là rien de tragique, rien qui émeuve, qui effraye; c'est tout simplement une grimace sanglante.'

This criticism may well be repeated in the case of the poems of the modern Lautréamont.

[190] The complete edition of the *Chants de Maldoror* was supposed to be published in 1869, but was not put on sale by the publisher. A few copies appeared in 1874 at a Belgian bookseller's. In 1890 the book came out in Paris, and has recently been re-exhumed by the Surrealists (edited by Blaise Cendrars in 1920 and by Philippe Soupault in 1927).

[191] According to the Surrealists Lautréamont was the first to practise 'écriture automatique', a method of composition in which the control of reason is suppressed, thanks to a swiftness of writing which allows the subconscious to display itself in full; thus the text is 'pure' and final; any correction is a hypocrisy. This theory is a *reductio ad absurdum* of the Romantic idea of 'inspiration'. Although he does not show that he shares the theory of the Surrealists, L. Pierre-Quint, in a little book which bears the high-sounding title of *Le Comte de Lautréamont et Dieu* (Marseilles, Les Cahiers du Sud, 1930; Collection Critique, no. 8), goes so far as to say that in the *Chants de Maldoror* 'un buisson ardent a parlé, comme dans la Bible', and compares Lautréamont to the moderns, finding in him the following aspirations (p. 12):

'La vieille révolte prométhéenne transformée en révolte pure, fureur de vivre; l'amour caricaturé jusqu'à la frénésie sadique; le mysticisme devenu l'ennemi de tous les dogmes; la passion de la vérité, associée à un humour prodigieusement féroce et seule raison d'exister devant "l'inutilité théâtrale et sans joie de tout".'

Pierre-Quint also asserts:

'La jeune poésie moderne se tourne vers lui avec ferveur et terreur à la fois. Pour André Breton et son groupe, pour beaucoup de jeunes gens aujourd'hui, la place de Lautréamont n'est pas dans la littérature. Ses révélations ont tellement bouleversé leur vie qu'il devient pour eux une sorte de personnage sacré et qu'il faudrait placer en dehors des atteintes du grand public. Telle est l'invraisemblable destinée historique de cet ouvrage. C'est avec le retard d'un demi-siècle qu'il apparaît comme le grand livre contemporain de la révolte.'

The chapter in Pierre-Quint's little book entitled 'Le sadisme et l'amour' may also be referred to.

Quite different is the opinion of other writers; see, for instance, L. Bloy, *Le Désespéré*, Paris, Soirat, 1886 (1930 edition, p. 38): 'L'un des signes les moins douteux de cet acculement des âmes modernes à l'extrémité de tout, c'est la récente intrusion en France d'un monstre de livre, presque inconnu encore, quoique publié en Belgique depuis dix ans: les *Chants de Maldoror*', &c. See also Maurice Blanchot, *Lautréamont et Sade*, Paris, Les Éditions de Minuit, 1949.

If we turn to the surrealists, we shall find that sadistic themes loom large in their works: there is in Max Ernst's *collages* (*La femme 100 têtes*, *Une semaine de bonté*) an abundance of corpses, pinioned women, &c., all the paraphernalia of the tales of terror combined with elements of a totally different character, according to Lautréamont's poetics, whose chief principle seems the formula: the chance meeting of a sewing-machine and an umbrella on a dissecting-table. A sadistic strain can be traced in such works as Julien Gracq's *Au Château d'Argol* (Paris, Corti, s.a.), André Pieyre de Mandiargues's *Dans les années sordides* (Monaco, 1943), &c. [Add. 1950]

192 The following macabre recipe *à la* Gilles de Rais may serve as a specimen of many others (*Œuvres complètes du Comte de Lautréamont* (Isidore Ducasse) . . . *Étude, commentaire et notes* par Philippe Soupault, Paris, Au Sans Pareil, 1927, pp. 64 et seq.):

'On doit laisser pousser ses ongles pendant quinze jours. Oh! comme il est doux d'arracher brutalement de son lit un enfant qui n'a rien encore sur la lèvre supérieure, et, avec les yeux très ouverts, de faire semblant de passer suavement la main sur son front, en inclinant en arrière ses beaux cheveux! Puis, tout à coup, au moment où il s'y attend le moins, d'enfoncer les ongles longs dans sa poitrine molle, de façon qu'il ne meure pas; car, s'il mourait, on n'aurait pas plus tard l'aspect de ses misères. Ensuite on boit le sang, etc. . . . Bande-lui les yeux, pendant que tu déchireras ses chairs palpitantes; et, après avoir entendu de longues heures ses cris sublimes . . . alors, t'ayant écarté comme une avalanche, tu te précipiteras de la chambre voisine, et tu feras semblant d'arriver à son secours. . . . Comme alors le repentir est vrai! L'étincelle divine qui est en nous, et paraît si rarement, se montre; trop tard! Comme le cœur déborde de pouvoir consoler l'innocent à qui l'on a fait du mal. . . . 'Adolescent, pardonne-moi; c'est celui qui est devant ta figure noble et sacrée, qui a brisé tes os et déchiré les chairs qui pendent à différents endroits de ton corps. Est-ce un délire de ma raison malade, est-ce un instinct secret qui ne dépend pas de mes raisonnements, pareil à celui de l'aigle déchirant sa proie, qui m'a poussé à commettre ce crime; et pourtant, autant que ma victime, je souffrais! Adolescent, pardonne-moi. Une fois sortis de cette vie passagère, je veux que nous soyons entrelacés pendant l'éternité; ne former qu'un seul être, ma bouche collée à ta bouche. Même, de cette manière, ma punition ne sera pas complète. Alors, tu me déchireras, sans jamais t'arrêter, avec les dents et les ongles à la fois. Je parerai mon corps de guirlandes embaumées, pour cet holocauste expiatoire; et nous souffrirons tous les deux, moi, d'être déchiré, toi, de me déchirer . . . ma bouche collée à ta bouche. . . .' Après avoir parlé ainsi, en même temps tu auras fait du mal à un être humain, et tu seras aimé du même être; c'est le bonheur le plus grand que l'on puisse concevoir. . . . Ô toi, dont je ne veux pas écrire le nom sur cette page qui consacre la sainteté du crime, je sais que ton pardon fut immense comme l'univers. Mais, moi, j'existe encore!'

Cf. E. Bossard, and R. de Maulde, *Gilles de Rais* (Paris, Champion, 1886), pp. 190–1.

[193] The last of the songs of Maldoror, compared by Pierre-Quint (p. 117) to 'un véritable récit rocambolesque, parfois une bouffonnerie, la caricature des histoires d'Eugène Sue', is particularly reminiscent of the first chapters of *Madame Putiphar*.

CHAPTER IV
LA BELLE DAME SANS MERCI

I saw pale kings, and princes too,
  Pale warriors, death-pale were they all;
Who cry'd— 'La belle Dame sans merci
  Hath thee in thrall!'

KEATS, La Belle Dame sans merci.

CHAPTER IV
LA BELLE DAME SANS MERCI

1. This chapter must begin, like an article in an encyclopedia, with an extremely obvious and bald statement. There have always existed Fatal Women both in mythology and in literature, since mythology and literature are imaginative reflections of the various aspects of real life, and real life has always provided more or less complete examples of arrogant and cruel female characters. There is no need, therefore, to go back to the myth of Lilith,[1] to the fables of Harpies, Sirens, and Gorgons, of Scylla and the Sphinx, or to the Homeric poems. Nevertheless, as a reminder that the type was produced so frequently, even in classical antiquity, that it became almost an obsession, there is the first Chorus of the *Choephorae* of Aeschylus:

> Many woes, strange and dire,
> Many terrors earth has bred;
> And the sea's vast embrace far and wide
> Teems with baleful monsters;
> While from the interspace there flash
> Fiery lightnings that destroy
> The birds and the four-footed beasts: of the hurricane wrath
> Of winds too, marvels might be told.
>
> But of man's overbold
> Pride of spirit none may tell,
> Nor of how passion's wild, reckless power,
> Fraught with human ruin,
> Rules o'er woman's stubborn mind.
> When perverse rebellious love
> Masters the feminine heart, then destroyed is the union
> Of mated lives for beast or man.[2]

The Chorus is telling of the fatal determination of such women as Althæa who murdered her own son; Scylla, murderess of her father; Clytemnestra, who, like the women of Lemnos, murdered her husband. . . .

Similar companies of Fatal Women are to be found in the literatures of every period, and are of course more numerous during times in which the springs of inspiration were troubled. Dante confines himself merely to giving the names of these accursed ones:

> La prima di color . . .
>
> .   .   .   .   .
>
> Fu imperadrice di molte favelle.
> A vizio di lussuria fu sì rotta,
> Che libito fe' licito in sua legge,
>
> .   .   .   .   .
>
> Ell'è Semiramis, di cui si legge
> Che succedette a Nino, e fu sua sposa;
> Tenne la terra che'l Soldan corregge.
>
> .   .   .   .   .
>
> Poi è Cleopatràs lussuriosa.
> Elena vidi, per cui tanto reo
> Tempo si volse. . . .

In the Elizabethan period, however, dramatists took their inspiration from the unbridled manners of Renaissance Italy, and figures such as Vittoria Corombona, Lucrezia Borgia, and the Comtesse de Challant—'white devils' and 'insatiate countesses'—proclaimed from the stage their reckless passions, their lecherous loves which spread ruin and perdition among men.

> For you *Vittoria*, your publicke fault,
> Joyn'd to th' condition of the present time,
> Takes from you all the fruits of noble pitty.
> Such a corrupted triall have you made
> Both of your life and beauty, and bene stil'd
> No lesse in ominous fate then blasing starres
> To Princes . . .   (III. ii. 266–72, Lucas's text.)

In Webster's lines, as in those of Aeschylus, the Fatal Women shine with all the dark splendour of comets: they are like λαμπάδες πεδάοροι, like 'blasing starres'.

2. It is natural that a period like the Romantic, which reproduces to the point of frenzy some of the characteristics of the Elizabethan age, should have its own Alcinas and Armidas as well as its Fleurdelys and its Erminias, its Vittoria Corombonas as well as its Duchesses of Malfi; for actually, whenever it happens that a writer feels admiration for the passionate energy—particularly if this energy have fatal results—of two types of women such as

are described below by Sainte-Beuve, it is always the diabolical Madame R. who ends by occupying the whole stage and causing her angelic rival, Madame de Couaën, to appear a mere frail shadow:

'J'appris d'abord, dans mes courses lascives, à discerner, à poursuivre, à redouter et à désirer le genre de beauté que j'appellerai funeste, celle qui est toujours un piège mortel, jamais un angélique symbole, celle qui ne se peint ni dans l'expression idéale du visage, ni dans le miroir des yeux, ni dans les délicatesses du souris, ni dans le voile nuancé des paupières; le visage humain n'est rien, presque rien, dans cette beauté; l'œil et la voix, qui, en se mariant avec douceur, sont si voisines de l'âme, ne font point partie ici de ce qu'on désire: c'est une beauté réelle, mais accablante et toute de chair, qui semble remonter en ligne droite aux filles des premières races déchues, qui ne se juge point en face et en conversant de vive voix, ainsi qu'il convient à l'homme, mais de loin plutôt, sur le hasard de la nuque et des reins, comme ferait le coup d'œil du chasseur pour les bêtes sauvages: oh! j'ai compris cette beauté-là. J'appris aussi comme cette beauté n'est pas la vraie; qu'elle est contraire à l'esprit même; qu'elle tue, qu'elle écrase, mais qu'elle n'attache pas. . . .'[3]

During the first stage of Romanticism, up till about the middle of the nineteenth century, we meet with several Fatal Women in literature,[3A] but there is no established type of Fatal Woman in the way that there is an established type of Byronic Hero. For a type—which is, in actual fact, a *cliché*—to be created, it is essential that some particular figure should have made a profound impression on the popular mind. A type is like a neuralgic area. Some chronic ailment has created a zone of weakened resistance, and whenever an analogous phenomenon makes itself felt it immediately confines itself to this predisposed area, until the process becomes a matter of mechanical monotony.

Nevertheless a line of tradition may be traced through the characters of these Fatal Women, right from the beginning of Romanticism. In this pedigree one may say that Lewis's Matilda is at the head of the line: she develops, on one side, into Velléda (Chateaubriand) and Salammbô (Flaubert), and, on the other, into Carmen (Mérimée), Cécily (Sue), and Conchita (Pierre Louÿs). . . . This is an arbitrary arrangement, certainly, but it enables one to make some general remarks which are not without significance in the history of taste and manners.

3. Only a bare mention is necessary in the case of a frivolous forerunner of Matilda—although the book found favour with the French Romantics—*Le Diable amoureux*, by Cazotte (1772), in which Biondetta, dressed up as a page (Biondetto), tries to make Don Alvare fall in love with her, and, when his resistance is finally vanquished, reveals the fact that she is the Devil and leaves him a prey to grotesque visions. We shall take Matilda, the witch in Lewis's *The Monk*, as our starting-point. Lewis denied having read *Le Diable amoureux*, but certain exactly parallel passages seem to prove the contrary.[4]

In the assumed guise of a novice, Matilda—who, at the end of the book, turns out to be simply an instrument of Satan, though throughout almost the whole of it she enlists the sympathy of the reader for the humanity of her passion—succeeds in entering Ambrosio's monastery and in confessing her love to the monk, who till then had had the reputation of a saint. Repulsed, she bares her beautiful bosom and makes as if to plunge a dagger into it. Lewis's pen was not skilled in voluptuous suggestion, and the passage of the monk's temptation is not without a certain awkward naïveté:

'She had torn open her habit, and her bosom was half exposed. The weapon's point rested upon her left breast: and, oh! that was such a breast! The moon-beams darting full upon it enabled the monk to observe its dazzling whiteness: his eye dwelt with insatiable avidity upon that beauteous orb: a sensation till then unknown filled his heart with a mixture of anxiety and delight; a raging fire shot through every limb; the blood boiled in his veins, and a thousand wild wishes bewildered his imagination. "Hold!" he cried, in an hurried, faltering voice; "I can resist no longer! Stay then, enchantress! Stay for my destruction!"'

As regards her 'diabolical beauty', it must be admitted that Matilda still tends too much towards the type of the Alcinas and the Armidas; 'a chin, in whose dimples seemed to lurk a thousand Cupids'—like the beauties in the epigrams of the Greek Anthology and the pastoral scenes of Boucher. But the monk cannot resist Matilda's eighteenth-century graces, with the result that every morning he 'rose from the syren's luxurious couch, intoxicated with pleasure'. But the character of the 'Syren' soon becomes imperious, and her graces are veiled with gleams of sinister, hellish light when, upon Ambrosio's falling in love with the innocent Antonia, Matilda promises to aid him with her magical arts. Her magic frightens the monk, and she rebukes him for his superstition and bigotry. The vision of Antonia undressing to bathe, which the witch causes to appear in a mirror, as in *Faust*, succeeds in overcoming the reluctance of Ambrosio, who again gasps: 'I yield!...Matilda, I follow you! Do with me what you will!' So he follows the witch into the crypt; she clothes herself in 'a long sable robe, on which was traced in gold embroidery a variety of unknown characters: it was fastened by a girdle of precious stones, in which was fixed a poniard. Her neck and arms were uncovered; in her hand she bore a golden wand; her hair was loose, and flowed wildly upon her shoulders; her eyes sparkled with terrific expression; and her whole demeanour was calculated to inspire the beholder with awe and admiration.'

The witch fashions spells with various ingredients, among which is 'an *agnus Dei*, which she broke in pieces. She threw them all into the flames. She appeared to be seized with an access of delirium . . . and drawing the poniard from her girdle, plunged it into her left arm'. The blood spurts beyond the magic circle. The Devil appears in the form of a very beautiful young man, his features overcast with melancholy—as is suitable for a fallen angel of the Miltonic school (with a touch, also, of Eblis in *Vathek*). Lucifer gives the witch 'a silver wand, imitating myrtle', whose touch opens all doors. Further on in the story, Matilda becomes ruthless and inhuman; she commands the monk to do away with Antonia and, when he hesitates, 'Matilda darted upon him a look of scorn. "Absurd!" she exclaimed, with an air of passion and majesty which impressed the monk with awe'. Ambrosio and Matilda fall into the hands of the Inquisition, but Matilda escapes, thanks to her magic arts, and, dressed in splendid garments, visits Ambrosio's prison-cell:

'In her right hand she held a small book: a lively expression of

pleasure beamed upon her countenance—but still it was mingled
with a wild imperious majesty, which inspired the monk with awe.
... "I have renounced God's service, and am enlisted beneath the
banners of his foes! ... Abandon a God who has abandoned you,
and raise yourself to the level of superior beings!" '

She gives him the magic book and disappears, like
Medea, 'in a cloud of blue fire'.

4. Chateaubriand was in London in 1795, the year of
the publication of *The Monk*, which he read and appreciated: he met Lewis twice.[5]

Velléda, in *Les Martyrs*, is a patriotic witch. As a
patriot who preaches resistance against the foreigner, she
can boast among her antecedents Virgil's Camilla and
Tasso's Clorinda; with the latter she has also in common
her love-affair with a warrior of the enemy camp. A
similar, but isolated case (which we need only just mention
here, since we are dealing with works from the point of
view of their popularity and of the illustration they offer
of a dominant taste) is shown in the frenzied *Penthesilea* of
Kleist,[6] which was contemporary with *Les Martyrs*. If as
patriot and warrior Velléda is reminiscent of the heroines
already mentioned, as a witch she is particularly reminiscent
of Lewis's Matilda. This Druidess of Brittany also puts on
a black sleeveless tunic and performs horrible sacrifices:

'Velléda devait égorger le vieillard . . . elle s'était assise sur un
triangle de bronze, le vêtement en désordre, la tête échevelée, tenant
un poignard à la main, et une torche flamboyante sous ses pieds.'

She falls in love with Eudore and offers him power:
'Veux-tu l'empire? Une Gauloise l'avait promis à Dio-
clétien, une Gauloise te le propose. . . .' She waits for her
beloved among the rocks:

'Mon bonheur à moi [says Eudore] ressemblait au désespoir,
et quiconque nous eût vus au milieu de notre félicité nous eût pris
pour deux coupables à qui l'on vient de prononcer l'arrêt fatal. Dans
ce moment, je me sentis marqué du sceau de la réprobation divine . . .
le langage de l'enfer s'échappa naturellement de ma bouche . . .'

The seduction of Eudore by the pagan Velléda is a
parallel case with the seduction of Ambrosio by the witch
Matilda. On her father's death, Velléda kills herself with
a golden sickle; here Chateaubriand leaves the English

writer and approaches nearer to Virgil and Tasso. His particular type of sensual feeling demands the death of the heroine:

> 'Aussitôt elle porte à sa gorge l'instrument sacré: le sang jaillit. Comme une moissonneuse qui a fini son ouvrage et qui s'endort fatiguée au bout du sillon, Velléda s'affaisse sur le char . . .'

The family likeness between Matilda and Velléda escaped Baldensperger in the essay which has already been quoted more than once; but the connexion between Chateaubriand's heroine and Flaubert's Salammbô was noticed by Sainte-Beuve and has been made quite obvious by Benedetto,[7] to whose observations no addition is needed. In order, however, to illustrate the admiration which Flaubert professed for the story of Velléda ('quelle belle chose, quelle poésie!' he said in one of his letters), attention may perhaps be drawn to certain traits in the character of Julietta in his early work, *Rêve d'enfer* (1837), in which the girl falls in love with the unfeeling Arthur d'Almaroës, 'd'un amour déchirant, entier, satanique. C'était bien un amour inspiré par l'enfer'. Julietta, certainly, is a sister of Margaret in *Faust*, but her waiting for her beloved among the rocks, the way in which she implores, and then surrenders herself to, an unfeeling man, have the colouring of Chateaubriand and the sharp flavour of his sensual feeling. Julietta, in any case, is not a Fatal Woman, nor indeed could she be, in a period in which the Byronic superman—which is exactly the type of Arthur— was dominant. In *Salammbô*, on the other hand, the atmosphere is changed; it is the woman who becomes frigid, unfeeling, fatal, idol-like; the man pines with passion and falls at her feet like a fakir at the feast of Juggernaut.

5. Mérimée satirized the episode of the seduction of Ambrosio by Matilda in the comedy *Une Femme est un diable* (in the *Théâtre de Clara Gazul*, 1825). 'Mon âme est tout entière à cette femme. Sûrement Satan prit cette figure pour tenter mon bienheureux patron', says the monk Antoine, who has been troubled, during his convalescence from a dangerous illness, by the sight of Mariquita.[8] Mariquita, a burlesque anticipation of Carmen and of Esmeralda in *Notre-Dame de Paris* (1831), is brought

before the tribunal of the Inquisition to be tried by Antoine as a witch ('une sorcière, une femme qui a fait un pacte avec le diable'). When the monk asks her what her profession is, 'Diable!' she replies, 'je ne sais trop que vous dire . . . je chante, je danse, je joue des castagnettes, etc., etc.' Mariquita is in love with a Scottish corporal—a character which obviously suggested that of Phœbus in *Notre-Dame*. The scene of the tribunal, with the scarecrow background of the torture-chamber, is conceived in the spirit of a ballet; Mérimée does not allow himself to take these things seriously or to be sentimental about them, and he skims humorously over the real attraction he must have felt for the subject. The soliloquy of the lovesick monk is pure parody. The effigy of the Madonna he thinks to be that of Mariquita (see above, p. 180). 'J'élèverai une famille pieuse,' the monk promises, 'et cela sera aussi agréable à Dieu que la fumée de nos bûchers.' The farce reaches its climax when Antoine is surprised and rebuked by Fray Rafael, who, also, is prompted by intentions which are anything but holy. Antoine overcomes Rafael, who dies with a derisive laugh, 'Mes prières! . . . ha, ha, ha! . . . m'y voilà!' and Mariquita concludes: 'En voyant cette fin tragique vous direz, je crois, avec nous qu'UNE FEMME EST UN DIABLE.'

A much more formidable she-devil, and one who was destined for immortal fame, is Mérimée's other gipsy-girl (and, of course, 'sorcière'), Carmen. 'Tu es un diable', says Don José to her, as she kisses him. To which she replies with a 'Oui' which is a masterpiece of categorical irony. Though Mérimée confessed, in a letter of May 16th, 1845, to the Comtesse de Montijo, that he had taken the character of Don José from a certain 'Jaque de Malaga qui avait tué sa maîtresse', whose story the Countess had told him fifteen years before, he added: 'Comme j'étudie les Bohémiens depuis quelque temps, avec beaucoup de soin, j'ai fait mon héroïne Bohémienne.'

Although related in many respects to Mariquita (here the Inquisitorial threat of torture for witchcraft has become a threat of imprisonment for brawling; Antoine kills Rafael and then escapes with Mariquita, Don José kills

the officer and escapes with Carmen; 'En une heure je suis
devenu fornicateur, perjure, assassin', says the monk;
'C'est pour toi que je suis devenu un voleur et un meurtrier', says the bandit to Carmen), Carmen has only a
vague affinity of type with the original Matilda; for the
relations with the infernal powers are substituted 'les
affaires d'Égypte', and on the whole, apart from diabolical
feminine fascination ('Je te l'ai dit que je te porterais
malheur') and a violence of passion which makes the man
lose all regard for his own social position, the two stories
develop in very different ways.

It was Mérimée who localized in Spain the type of the
Fatal Woman which towards the end of the century came
to be placed more generally in Russia: the exotic and the
erotic ideals go hand in hand, and this fact also contributes
another proof of a more or less obvious truth—that is, that
a love of the exotic is usually an imaginative projection of
a sexual desire.[9] This is very clear in such cases as those
of Gautier and Flaubert, whose dreams carry them to
an atmosphere of barbaric and Oriental antiquity, where
all the most unbridled desires can be indulged and the
cruellest fantasies can take concrete form.

6. Cécily, the diabolical creole of the *Mystères de Paris*,
'cette grande créole à la fois svelte et charnue, vigoureuse et souple
comme une panthère, était le type incarné de la sensualité brûlante
qui ne s'allume qu'aux feux des tropiques. Tout le monde a entendu parler de ces filles de couleur pour ainsi dire *mortelles* aux
Européens, de ces vampires enchanteurs qui, enivrant leur victime
de séductions terribles, pompent jusqu'à la dernière goutte d'or et
de sang,[9A] et ne lui laissent, selon l'énergique expression du pays, que
ses larmes à boire, que *son cœur à ronger*. Telle est Cécily . . . Au
lieu de se jeter violemment sur sa proie, et de ne songer, comme ses
pareilles, qu'à anéantir au plus tôt une vie et une fortune de plus,
Cécily, attachant sur ses victimes son regard magnétique, com-
mençait par les attirer peu à peu dans le tourbillon embrasé qui
semblait émaner d'elle; puis, les voyant alors pantelantes, éperdues,
souffrant les tortures d'un désir inassouvi, elle se plaisait, par un
raffinement de coquetterie féroce, à prolonger leur délire ardent;
puis, revenant à son premier instinct, elle les dévorait dans ses
embrassements homicides.

'Cela était plus terrible encore . . .'

The simile used by Sue at this point is so very common-place that it is easily recognizable as a stock detail of the traditional description of the Fatal Woman:

'Le tigre affamé, qui bondit et emporte la proie qu'il déchire en rugissant, inspire moins d'horreur que le serpent qui la fascine silencieusement, l'aspire peu à peu, l'enlace de ses replis inextricables, l'y broie longuement, la sent palpiter sous ses lentes morsures, et semble se repaître autant de ses douleurs que de son sang.'

Sue's creole had already played all sorts of pranks in Germany, to such an extent as to have deserved perpetual imprisonment; she had displayed 'une corruption digne des reines courtisanes de l'ancienne Rome'. And yet her black soul can be moved by the misfortunes of Louise (who was raped in her sleep by Jacques Ferrand and then arrested for infanticide—an episode analogous to Nodier's *Histoire d'Hélène Gillet* and to Borel's *Monsieur de l'Argentière*),[10] through one of those humanitarian sentimentalisms so dear to the heart of Sue. Cécily swears to avenge Louise, and succeeds, disguised as a chambermaid, in gaining admission to the lawyer's house (is this perhaps a reminiscence of Matilda effecting her entrance into the monastery dressed as a novice?).

'Les femmes de l'espèce de Cécily exercent une action soudaine, une omnipotence magique sur les hommes de sensualité brutale tels que Jacques Ferrand. Du premier regard ils devinent ces femmes, ils les convoitent; une puissance fatale les attire auprès d'elles, et bientôt des affinités mystérieuses, des sympathies magnétiques sans doute, les enchaînent invinciblement aux pieds de leur monstrueux idéal; car elles seules peuvent apaiser les feux impurs qu'elles allument.'

In the lawyer's house there take place those 'scènes priapiques' which finally alienated Sainte-Beuve from the work of Sue.[11] Cécily's sole aim is to inflame the lawyer's passion without satisfying it; she has with her a poisoned dagger with which to defend herself. She incites the elderly libertine to be as fierce as a tiger, in order to please her; she exasperates him by singing creole airs with passionate words ('. . . Ceux que j'aime comme je t'aime . . . je les tue'). As a proof of his love the lawyer promises to reveal a secret which, if known, would bring him to the gallows: 'Ma tête pour tes caresses, veux-tu?' 'Ah! voilà

donc de la passion enfin!' exclaims Cécily, who asks him
repeatedly whether it is really true that he has committed
crimes. After he has told her about them ('Je serai ton
tigre, s'écria-t-il, et après, si tu le veux, tu me déshonoreras,
tu feras tomber ma tête....'), Cécily exclaims: 'Oh! démon
... d'enfer ... tu m'épouvantes et pourtant tu m'attires ...
tu me passionnes.... Quel est donc ton pouvoir?' Ferrand
also gives Cécily a pocket-book containing the proof of his
guilt, and she, having thus accomplished her humanitarian
purpose, escapes by the window. The lawyer becomes a
victim of satyriasis and dies, after frightful hallucinations:
the influence of the *Mémoires du Diable* is obvious here.

'Parti de Rétif et même de de Sade, M. Sue est en voie d'aboutir
au Saint Vincent de Paul en passant par le Ducray-Duminil.'

So speaks a critic quoted by Sainte-Beuve. The humanitarian purpose does nothing more than gild the pill, the
pill in this case being an aphrodisiac of the grossest
kind.

7. The type of the fatal *allumeuse* was very widespread,
and though it may be too arbitrary to try always to trace it
to literary models such as Matilda, Carmen, or even
Cécily—for, after all, it is a type of which examples are not
so very rare even in actual life—it is, on the other hand,
quite easy to discover elements of these characters in such
figures as Rosalba 'la Pudica' (Barbey d'Aurevilly, *A un
dîner d'athées*), in Conchita (who is Carmen and Cécily
rolled into one),[12] and in the innumerable other creations
of the lower grades of Romanticism (e.g. the androgynous
Princess d'Este in Péladan's *Vice suprême* (1884), with
her murderous chastity—'bourreau de marbre', Barbey
d'Aurevilly calls her; the perverse Eliana in *Piccolo veleno
color di rosa*, by Corrado Govoni (1921), and so on). It is a
type, as we have already said, which, Spanish or creole in
origin, ends by modelling itself on the women of Dostoievsky, among whom Nastasia Filippovna is the most characteristic example. For instance, in the recently published
Ariane, jeune fille russe, by Claude Anet, one can recognize
a Russianized Conchita. And in any case Conchita herself,
with her enigmatic nature, is already influenced by the

psychology of the Slav woman. Again, while the sadistic Clara of Mirbeau's *Jardin des supplices* is, according to the recipe of the period,[13] an Englishwoman, we find that in Maurice Dekobra's *Madone des sleepings* the role of Clara is sustained by a Russian, 'Irina Mouravieff, la Marquise de Sade de la Russie rouge'.[14]

In Fatal Women of this kind, however, we shall not always find such characteristics as make reference to a *cliché* indisputable;[14A] but such characteristics are certainly to be found in a type of Fatal Woman which is more highly penetrated with aestheticism and exoticism, the type which arose with Gautier and Flaubert, which had its full development in Swinburne, and which then passed to Walter Pater, to Wilde, to D'Annunzio—to quote only a few of the most representative names.

8. We have already referred to the significance of exoticism, and repeat here the just remark made by Brie,[15] to the effect that there is a certain resemblance between the exoticist and the mystic. The latter projects himself outside the visible world into a transcendental atmosphere where he unites himself with the Divinity; the former transports himself in imagination outside the actualities of time and space, and thinks that he sees in whatever is past and remote from him the ideal atmosphere for the contentment of his own senses:

'Il se berce dans quelque inexprimable rêverie orientale toute pleine de reflets d'or, imprégnée de parfums étranges et retentissante de bruits joyeux; il y développe des sentiments d'élégance, de fierté et de sensualité, et, au lieu de se dire que par leur nature même de tels états demeurent intérieurs, il pense qu'il les trouvera réalisés dans d'autres lieux.'

Thus Barrès.[16] Actually it is a question of starting from the same sensual basis and arriving at opposite points; for, while true mysticism tends to the negation both of expression and of art, exoticism, of its own nature, tends to a sensual and artistic externalization. The first culminates in a world which cannot be described, the second succeeds to such an extent in making itself concrete in an atmosphere remote in time or space (or both) that it gives the artist the illusion of an actual former existence in the atmosphere he loves. I do not share the theory of Bremond, according to which poetry is an imperfect form of mysticism, a phenomenon of the same nature as ecstasy, or rather ecstasy itself arrested in its course. But between the mystic who denies the world of the senses and the exoticist who affirms its existence, between the mystic who empties his universe of all material content and the exoticist who invests remote periods and distant countries with the vibration of his own senses and materializes them in his imagination, there is certainly a similarity of purpose; both transfer the fulfilment of their desires to an ideal, a dream world; both, in order to bring about the necessary conditions for the intense realization of their dream, generally resort to stimulants, such as fasts and vigils in the case of the mystic, opium or other narcotics in the case of the exoticist.

Every artist is, in a certain general and provisional sense, an exoticist, inasmuch as he projects himself in imagination outside the immediate present. However, I do not wish to speak here of this generic exoticism, which can be documented in all periods and all literatures, but rather of the specific exoticism which feeds upon a particular cultural atmosphere, and, in this type of exoticism (of which a conspicuous example occurred in Humanism), only of that which flourished in the Romantic period.[16A] Brie notes the first signs of it in Heinse (*Ardinghello*, 1787) and in Beckford (*Vathek*, 1782; *Dreams, Waking Thoughts and Incidents, in a Series of Letters*, 1783);[16B] he does not quote Wackenroder (*Herzensergiessungen eines kunstliebenden Klosterbruders*, 1797) and Keats.

Keats is especially noteworthy, because in him are to be found the seeds of various elements which were to be developed later by the Pre-Raphaelites and which, through them, were to pass into French Symbolism. Keats wrote:

'According to my state of mind I am with Achilles shouting in the trenches, or with Theocritus in the vales of Sicily. Or I throw my whole being into Troilus, and repeating those lines, "I wander like a lost soul upon the Stygian banks staying for waftage", I melt into the air with a voluptuousness so delicate that I am content to be alone.'

This sort of ecstasy (if one may use in a wider sense a term which in the language of mysticism has a precise technical meaning) is the ecstasy of the exoticist; the exoticist, who is an 'ecstatic'—an exile from his own present and actual self—is also endowed with a sort of metaphysical intuition which discerns, behind the complex outward appearances of things, the permanence of a unique essence:

Keats
Ruisins

Thou wast not born for death, immortal Bird!
No hungry generations tread thee down;
The voice I hear this passing night was heard
In ancient days by emperor and clown:
Perhaps the self-same song that found a path
Through the sad heart of Ruth, when, sick for home,
She stood in tears amid the alien corn;
The same that oft-times hath
Charm'd magic casements, opening on the foam
Of perilous seas, in faery lands forlorn.

We find a similar intuition in De Quincey, when, in describing the Mater Lachrymarum (in *Levana and Our Ladies of Sorrow*, 1845) he imagines this allegorical figure present in Rama, where there is heard the lamentation of Rachel weeping for her children; at Bethlehem, among the massacred Innocents; in the chamber of the Tsar, and so on:

'By the power of the keys it is that our Lady of Tears glides a ghostly intruder into the chambers of sleepless men, sleepless women, sleepless children, from Ganges to the Nile, from Nile to Mississippi. . . . Her eyes are swift and subtle, wild and sleepy, by turn, oftentimes rising to the clouds, oftentimes challenging the heavens. She wears a diadem round her head.'

The magical, metaphysical meaning which Keats found in the song of the nightingale (*Ode to a Nightingale*) was applied by the aesthetes, from Gautier downwards, to female beauty, as we shall see shortly. Keats himself gave a hint of a similar application of it in *La Belle Dame sans merci*, a poem which in the magical, painful mystery it expresses (the subject is obviously that of Tannhäuser) contains in embryo the whole world of the Pre-Raphaelites and the Symbolists, from Swinburne's *Laus Veneris* to certain pictures by Moreau.

> I saw pale kings, and princes too,
> Pale warriors, death-pale were they all;
> Who cry'd—'La belle Dame sans merci
> Hath thee in thrall.'

In the *Laus Veneris* Swinburne is merely embroidering variations upon the theme of the Eternal Feminine disguised as Fate, who, as in one of Petrarch's *Trionfi*, drags, chained to her chariot, heroes of all times and all lands. There are no more than hints of this attitude to be found in Keats and Coleridge[17]—who were, above all, true poets, not sensation-collectors as real exoticists generally are. In the previous edition I introduced at this point the figure of Thomas Griffiths Wainewright, based on Wilde's interpretation in the essay *Pen, Pencil and Poison*; this interpretation, according to which Wainewright is caused to appear as a forerunner of Wilde himself, has been challenged by J. Curling (in *Janus Weathercock, The Life of Thomas Griffiths Wainewright, 1794–1847*, London, Nelson, 1938, p. 78).[18] That Wainewright had the soul of an artist and a voluptuous dilettante is shown, however, by the description of his rooms which can be seen on pp. 207–17 of Curling's volume: those rooms were decorated with all the refinement of an aesthete.

9. Théophile Gautier is the true and genuine founder of exotic aestheticism—one might almost say, of the school of exotic aestheticism, for the exoticists during the whole course of the century can be seen coming back to him, directly or indirectly, for their inspiration.

I shall deal here with exoticism only in relation to the subject of this chapter, and therefore refer my readers to Brie's volume for a fuller treatment; nevertheless, besides the passages from *Mademoiselle de Maupin* (1835–6) and from *Fortunio* (1838), some others must also be added from *Une Nuit de Cléopâtre* (1845), in which, against an exotic background, minutely described as though in an inventory, stands out the figure of *La Belle Dame sans merci*, the Fatal Woman:

'Notre monde est bien petit à côté du monde antique, nos fêtes sont mesquines auprès des effrayantes somptuosités des patriciens romains et des princes asiatiques ... Nous avons peine à concevoir, avec nos habitudes misérables, ces existences énormes, réalisant tout ce que l'imagination peut inventer de hardi, d'étrange et de plus monstrueusement en dehors du possible ...

'Aujourd'hui, privé de ce spectacle éblouissant de la volonté toute-puissante,[19] de cette haute contemplation d'une âme humaine dont le moindre désir se traduit en actions inouïes, en énormités de granit et d'airain, le monde s'ennuie éperdument et désespérément; l'homme n'est plus représenté dans sa fantaisie impériale ... Le spectacle du monde antique est quelque chose de si écrasant, de si décourageant pour les imaginations qui se croient effrénées et les esprits qui pensent avoir atteint aux dernières limites de la magnificence féerique, que nous n'avons pu nous empêcher de consigner ici nos doléances et nos tristesses de n'avoir pas été contemporain de Sardanapale, de Teglath Phalazar, de Cléopâtre, reine d'Égypte, ou seulement d'Héliogabale, empereur de Rome et prêtre du Soleil.

'Nous avons à décrire une orgie suprême, un festin à faire pâlir celui de Balthasar, une nuit de Cléopâtre. Comment, avec la langue française, si chaste, si glacialement prude, rendrons-nous cet emportement frénétique, cette large et puissante débauche qui ne craint pas de mêler le sang et le vin, ces deux pourpres, et ces furieux élans de la volupté inassouvie se ruant à l'impossible avec toute l'ardeur de sens que le long jeûne chrétien n'a pas encore matés?'[20]

Cleopatra was one of the first Romantic incarnations of the type of the Fatal Woman—thanks to a short passage in the *Liber de viris illustribus* (86,2): 'Hæc tantæ libidinis fuit, ut sæpe prostiterit, tantæ pulchritudinis ut multi noctem illius morte emerint.' Cleopatra, in fact, did what Semiramis had done,[21] what Marguerite de Bourgogne did later:

> la royne
> Qui commanda que Buridan
> Fuct gecté en ung sac en Saine[22] —

she massacred in the morning the lovers who had passed the night with her. Gautier had already said, in *Mademoiselle de Maupin*:[23]

'Ah! Cléopâtre, je comprends maintenant pourquoi tu faisais tuer, le matin, l'amant avec qui tu avais passé la nuit. — Sublime cruauté, pour qui, autrefois, je n'avais pas assez d'imprécations! Grande voluptueuse, comme tu connaissais la nature humaine, et qu'il y a de profondeur dans cette barbarie!'

Cleopatra combined a fabulous Oriental background with a taste for algolagnia, which, as we have seen in the previous chapter, seemed to be in the very air of the Romantic period. So much in the air was it that even the worthy Dumas made use of the theme of a massacre of lovers in the *Tour de Nesle* (1832), though in an innocent enough fashion. So much in the air was it that even in distant Russia, whither the currents of Romanticism had already penetrated, Pushkin, as early as 1825, had published as a fragment a description of a 'night of Cleopatra'. Three men, a Roman warrior, an Epicurean philosopher, and a youth, respond to the Queen's offer to prostitute herself for the price of a man's life: the plan of the story was that the first two should be put to death but the third spared. Pushkin included this fragment in his *Egyptian Nights* (1835), putting it into the mouth of an Italian *improvvisatore*, with the title (in Italian) of *Cleopatra e i suoi amanti*.

In Gautier's story Cleopatra grants the enjoyment of this particular night to the extremely beautiful young lion-hunter, Meïamoun; she dances for him, and is on the point of preventing him from drinking the cup of poison when the arrival of Mark Antony seals the young man's fate. Certain elements of the story should be noticed. The young man is beautiful, wild, and chaste, and falls in love with Cleopatra because she is unattainable; Cleopatra is suffering from ennui; she is a 'reine sidérale' of irresistible charm ('chaque regard de ses yeux était un poème supérieur à ceux d'Homère ou de Mimnerme'),[24] and the knowledge of her body is an end in itself, beyond which life has nothing to offer; Cleopatra, like the praying mantis, kills the male whom she loves. These are elements which were destined to become permanent characteristics of the type of Fatal Woman of whom we are speaking. In accordance with this conception of the Fatal Woman, the lover is usually a youth, and maintains a passive attitude; he is obscure, and inferior either in condition or in physical exuberance to the woman, who stands in the same relation to him as do the female spider, the praying mantis, &c., to their respective males: sexual cannibalism is her monopoly. Towards the end of the century the perfect incarnation of this type of woman is Herodias. But she is not the only one: Helen, the Helen of Moreau, of Samain, of Pascoli (*Anticlo*), closely resembles her. The ancient myths, such as that of the Sphinx, of Venus and Adonis, of Diana and Endymion, were called in to illustrate this type of relationship, which was to be so insistently repeated in the second half of the century. The following point must be emphasized: the function of the flame which attracts and burns is exercised, in the first half of the century, by the Fatal Man (the Byronic hero), in the second half by the Fatal Woman; the moth destined for sacrifice is in the first case the woman, in the second the man. It is not simply a case of convention and literary fashion: literature, even in its most artificial forms, reflects to some extent aspects of contemporary life. It is curious to follow the parabola of the sexes during the nineteenth century: the obsession for the androgyne type towards the end of the century is a clear indication of a turbid confusion of function and ideal. The male, who at first tends towards sadism, inclines, at the end of the century, towards masochism.

The character of Herodias, moreover, is already suggested in Gautier's Cleopatra:

'Cléopâtre elle-même se leva de son trône, rejeta son manteau royal, remplaça son diadème sidéral par une couronne de fleurs, ajusta des crotales d'or à ses mains d'albâtre, et se mit à danser devant Meïamoun éperdu de ravissement. Ses beaux bras arrondis comme les anses d'un vase de marbre, secouaient au-dessus de sa tête des grappes de notes étincelantes, et ses crotales babillaient avec une volubilité toujours croissante. Debout sur la pointe vermeille de ses petits pieds, elle avançait rapidement et venait effleurer d'un baiser le front de Meïamoun, puis elle recommençait son manège et voltigeait autour de lui, tantôt se cambrant en arrière, la tête renversée, l'œil demi-clos, les bras pâmés et morts, les cheveux débouclés et pendants comme une bacchante du mont Ménale agitée par son dieu; tantôt leste, vive, rieuse, papillonnante, infatigable et plus capricieuse en ses méandres que l'abeille qui butine. L'amour du cœur, la volupté des sens, la passion ardente, la jeunesse inépuisable et fraîche, la promesse du bonheur prochain,[25] elle exprimait tout.'

10. It is not only in the *Nuit de Cléopâtre*,[26] among Gautier's works, that woman both proposes and disposes. Nyssia, in *Le Roi Candaule*, is a kind of oriental Lady Macbeth; and that Gautier had the Scottish virago in mind is proved by this reminiscent passage:

'— J'aurais beau, dit-elle en laissant tomber les tissus humides et en renvoyant ses suivantes, verser sur moi toute l'eau des sources et des fleuves, l'Océan avec ses gouffres amers ne pourrait me purifier. Une pareille tache ne se lave qu'avec du sang.'[27]

Nyssia is a Fatal Woman. This is the effect produced upon Gyges by the sight of her:

'Il avait été plutôt ébloui, fasciné, foudroyé en quelque sorte, que charmé par cette apparition surhumaine, par ce monstre de beauté.... La perfection portée à ce point est toujours inquiétante, et les femmes si semblables aux déesses ne peuvent qu'être fatales aux faibles mortels; elles sont créées pour les adultères célestes, et les hommes, même les plus courageux, ne se hasardent qu'en tremblant dans de pareilles amours.... Si une seule fois elle traversait les rues de Sardes le visage découvert, vous auriez beau tirer vos adorateurs par le pan de leur tunique, aucun d'eux ne retournerait la tête.... Ils iraient se précipiter sous les roues d'argent de son char pour avoir la volupté d'être écrasés par elle, comme ces dévots de l'Indus qui pavent de leurs corps le chemin de leur idole.'

Her eyes are fabulous: some maintain that she has double pupils to each eye, like those of the fatal hero in *Maxime et Zoé*, one of the ballads in Mérimée's *La Guzla*:

'Pour un de ces regards on eût trempé les mains dans le sang de son hôte, dispersé aux quatre vents les cendres de son père, renversé les saintes images des dieux et volé le feu du ciel comme Prométhée, le sublime larron. Cependant leur expression la plus ordinaire, il faut le dire, était une chasteté désespérante, une froideur sublime, une ignorance de toute possibilité de passion humaine, à faire paraître les yeux de clair de lune de Phœbé et les yeux vert de mer d'Athéné plus lubriques et plus provoquants que ceux d'une jeune fille de Babylone sacrifiant à la déesse Mylitta dans l'enceinte de cordes de Succoth-Benolh. — Leur virginité invincible paraissait défier l'amour.'

Nyssia, to avenge the outrage committed against her by her husband, who has betrayed her secrecy to the eyes of Gyges, insists upon the death of one of the two men and imposes upon Gyges, who is an ordinary captain of the

King's guard, either to kill Candaules or to prepare himself
for death:

'Ce sera toi ou Candaule, je te laisse maître du choix. Tue-le,
venge moi, et conquiers par ce meurtre et ma main et le trône de
Lydie. . . . Pense que je te ferai roi de Sardes et que . . . je t'aimerai
si tu me venges. Le sang de Candaule sera ta pourpre et sa mort te
fera une place dans ce lit.'

In vain Gyges implores her clemency:

'— Si tu parlais à un Sphinx de granit dans les sables arides de
l'Égypte, tu aurais plus de chances de l'attendrir. . . . Un cœur
d'airain habite ma poitrine de marbre. . . . Meurs ou tue!'

The man submits, and she conducts him to the place
where he is to kill her husband:

'La main qui tenait celle de Gygès était froide, douce et petite;
cependant ces doigts déliés la serraient à la meurtrir comme eussent
pu le faire les doigts d'une statue d'airain animée par un prodige.'

These 'doigts d'une statue d'airain' recall immediately
the fierce *Vénus d'Ille* of Mérimée (1837), also a Fatal
Woman, who suffocated in her arms of bronze the young
bridegroom, who—according to an old legend of the
Middle Ages—had committed the imprudence of placing
a wedding-ring on her finger.[27A] Mérimée gave the old
legend the colour of those cruel vampire stories which he
had already told in *La Guzla*, and depicted Venus with all
the attributes of the Fatal Woman:

'Tous les traits étaient contractés légèrement, les yeux un peu
obliques, la bouche relevée des coins, les narines quelque peu
gonflées. Dédain, ironie, cruauté, se lisaient sur ce visage, d'une
incroyable beauté cependant. En vérité, plus on regardait cette
admirable statue et plus on éprouvait le sentiment pénible qu'une
si merveilleuse beauté pût s'allier à l'absence de toute sensibilité.

'— Si le modèle a jamais existé, dit-je à M. de Peyrehorade, et
je doute que le ciel ait jamais produit une telle femme, que je plains
ses amants! Elle a dû se complaire à les faire mourir de désespoir.
Il y a dans son expression quelque chose de féroce, et pourtant je
n'ai jamais vu rien de si beau.

'— C'est Vénus tout entière à sa proie attachée! s'écria M.
Peyrehorade, satisfait de mon enthousiasme.'

In *La Morte amoureuse* Gautier also told the story of a

vampire, drawing his chief inspiration from Goethe's *Braut von Corinth*:

'I am urged forth from the grave to seek the joy which was snatched from me, to love again the man I once lost and to suck his heart's blood. When he is ruined, I must pass on to others, and young men shall succumb to my fury.'

In Gautier the vampire woman is the lovely courtesan Clarimonde, who falls in love with a young priest; his kiss upon her corpse has the same effect as the ring in the *Vénus d'Ille*, restoring to life the courtesan, who has died 'à la suite d'une orgie qui a duré huit jours et huit nuits', according to the words of the Abbé Sérapion, who adds:

'Ç'a été quelque chose d'infernalement splendide. On a renou-velé les abominations des festins de Balthasar et de Cléopâtre. . . . Il a couru de tout temps sur cette Clarimonde de bien étranges histoires, et tous ses amants ont fini d'une manière misérable ou violente. On a dit que c'était une goule, un vampire femelle; mais je crois que c'était Belzébuth en personne. . . . Ce n'est pas, à ce qu'on dit, la première fois qu'elle est morte.'

The character of Clarimonde is strongly reminiscent of Beatrice de las Cisternas, the Bleeding Nun of Lewis, whose orgies 'vied in luxury with Cleopátra's'.

The priest leads a double life: a priest by day, he be-comes by night the lover of Clarimonde at Venice.[28] But Clarimonde languishes and is about to die, when, Romuald having by accident cut his finger,

'le sang partit aussitôt en filets pourpres, et quelques gouttes rejail-lirent sur Clarimonde. Ses yeux s'éclairèrent, sa physionomie prit une expression de joie féroce et sauvage que je ne lui avais jamais vue. Elle sauta à bas du lit avec une agilité animale, une agilité de singe ou de chat, et se précipita sur ma blessure qu'elle se mit à sucer avec un air d'indicible volupté.'

'Mêlons des voluptés à la mort', said Chateaubriand.

11. The fascination of beautiful women already dead,[29] especially if they had been great courtesans, wanton queens, or famous sinners, the idea which suggested to Villon the ballad of the *dames du temps jadis*, suggested to the Romantics, probably under the influence of the vampire legend,[30] the figure of the Fatal Woman who was successively incarnate in all ages and all lands, an

archetype which united in itself all forms of seduction, all
vices, and all delights. Gautier alludes to this figure in his
study upon the hand of the courtesan Imperia, in *Émaux
et camées* (1852):

> A-t-elle joué dans les boucles
> Des cheveux lustrés de Don Juan,
> Ou sur son caftan d'escarboucles
> Peigné la barbe du Sultan,
>
> Et tenu, courtisane ou reine,
> Entre ses doigts si bien sculptés,
> Le sceptre de la souveraine
> Ou le sceptre des voluptés?
>
> . . . . . .
>
> Impériales fantaisies,
> Amour des somptuosités;
> Voluptueuses frénésies,
> Rêves d'impossibilités,
>
> Romans extravagants, poèmes
> De haschisch et de vin du Rhin,
> Courses folles dans les bohèmes
> Sur le dos des coursiers sans frein;
>
> On voit tout cela dans les lignes
> De cette paume, livre blanc
> Où Vénus a tracé des signes
> Que l'amour ne lit qu'en tremblant.[31]

In *Novembre*,[32] Flaubert is conscious of this fullness of
sensual experience in the courtesan Marie, who, stretched
naked beside him, suggested to him, in the lines of her
body, 'je ne sais quelle forme souple et corrompue de serpent et de démon', and who pressed her mouth upon his
neck 'y fouillant avec d'âpres baisers, comme une bête
fauve au ventre de sa victime':

'Comme elles [les violettes fanées], en effet, malgré leur fraîcheur
enlevée, à cause de cela peut-être, elle m'envoyait un parfum plus
âcre et plus irritant; le malheur, qui avait dû passer dessus, la
rendait belle de l'amertume que sa bouche conservait, même en
dormant, belle des deux rides qu'elle avait derrière le cou et que le
jour, sans doute, elle cachait sous ses cheveux. A voir cette femme
si triste dans la volupté et dont les étreintes mêmes avaient une joie
lugubre, je devinais mille passions terribles qui l'avaient dû sillonner
comme la foudre à en juger par les traces restées, et puis sa vie

devrait me faire plaisir à entendre raconter, moi qui recherchais dans l'existence humaine le côté sonore et vibrant, le monde des grandes passions et des belles larmes.'

The courtesan speaks as follows:

'Dandys et rustauds, j'ai voulu voir si tous étaient de même; j'ai goûté la passion des hommes, aux mains blanches et grasses, aux cheveux teints et collés sur les tempes; j'ai eu de pâles adolescents, blonds, efféminés comme des filles, qui se mouraient sur moi; les vieillards aussi m'ont salie de leurs joies décrépites, et j'ai contemplé au réveil leur poitrine oppressée et leurs yeux éteints. Sur un banc de bois, dans un cabaret de village, entre un pot de vin et une pipe de tabac, l'homme du peuple aussi m'a embrassée avec violence; je me suis fait comme lui une joie épaisse et des allures faciles; mais la canaille ne fait pas mieux l'amour que la noblesse, et la botte de paille n'est pas plus chaude que les sofas. Pour les rendre plus ardents, je me suis dévouée à quelques-uns comme une esclave, et ils ne m'en aimaient pas davantage; j'ai eu, pour des sots, des bassesses infâmes, et en échange ils me haïssaient et me méprisaient, alors que j'aurais voulu leur centupler mes caresses et les inonder de bonheur. Espérant enfin que les gens difformes pouvaient mieux aimer que les autres, et que les natures rachitiques se raccrochaient à la vie par la volupté, je me suis donnée à des bossus, à des nègres, à des nains; je leur fis des nuits à rendre jaloux des millionnaires, mais je les épouvantais peut-être, car ils me quittaient vite. Ni les pauvres, ni les riches, ni les beaux, ni les laids n'ont pu assouvir l'amour que je leur demandais à remplir; tous, faibles, languissants, conçus dans l'ennui, avortons faits par des paralytiques que le vin enivre, que la femme tue, craignant de mourir dans les draps comme on meurt à la guerre, il n'en est pas un que je n'aie vu lassé dès la première heure. Il n'y en a donc plus, sur la terre, de ces jeunesses divines comme autrefois! plus de Bacchus, plus d'Apollons, plus de ces héros qui marchaient nus couronnés de pampres et de lauriers! J'étais faite pour être la maîtresse d'un empereur, moi; il me fallait l'amour d'un bandit, sur un rocher dur, par un soleil d'Afrique; j'ai souhaité les enlacements des serpents, et les baisers rugissants que se donnent les lions. A cette époque je lisais beaucoup; il y a surtout deux livres que j'ai relus cent fois: *Paul et Virginie* et un autre qui s'appelait *les Crimes des Reines*. On y voyait les portraits de Messaline, de Théodora, de Marguerite de Bourgogne, de Marie Stuart et de Catherine II. "Être reine, me disais-je, et rendre la foule amoureuse de toi!" Eh bien, j'ai été reine, reine comme on peut l'être maintenant . . . je dominais tout par l'insolence de ma beauté. . . .'

Flaubert concludes:

'Agrandie tout à coup à des proportions que je lui prêtais, sans doute, elle me parut une femme nouvelle, pleine de mystères ignorés... toute tentante d'un charme irritant et d'attraits nouveaux. Les hommes, en effet, qui l'avaient possédée avaient laissé sur elle comme une odeur de parfum éteint, traces de passions disparues, qui lui faisaient une majesté voluptueuse; la débauche la décorait d'une beauté infernale. Sans les orgies passées, aurait-elle eu ce sourire de suicide, qui la faisait ressembler à une morte se réveillant dans l'amour?'

Flaubert follows Gautier in that he worships in Cleopatra the perfect incarnation of antique desire:[33]

'Il adorait la courtisane antique, telle qu'elle est venue au monde un jour de soleil, la femme belle et terrible, qui bâtit des pyramides avec les présents de ses amants, devant qui se déploient les tapis de Carthage et les tuniques de Syrie, celle à qui l'on envoie l'ambre des Sarmates, l'édredon du Caucase, la poudre d'or du Sennahar, le corail de la mer Rouge, les diamants de Golconde, les gladiateurs de Thrace, l'ivoire des Indes, les poètes d'Athènes; il y a à sa porte, attendant qu'elle s'éveille, le satrape du roi de Perse, l'ambassadeur des Scythes, les fils de sénateurs, les archontes, consuls, et des peuples venus pour la voir. C'est la créature pâle, à l'œil de feu, la vipère du Nil qui enlace et qui étouffe; elle bouleverse les empires, mène les armées à la guerre et s'évanouit sous un baiser; elle connaît les philtres qui font aimer et les boissons qui font mourir, les mères en épouvantent leurs fils et les rois languissent pour elle d'amour.'

This figure takes definite form in the *Tentation* with the Queen of Sheba and, particularly, with the pathetic character Ennoia. The Queen of Sheba says to Saint Antony:

'Toutes celles que tu as rencontrées, depuis la fille des carrefours chantant sous sa lanterne jusqu'à la patricienne effeuillant des roses du haut de sa litière, toutes les formes entrevues, toutes les imaginations de ton désir, demande-les! Je ne suis pas une femme, je suis un monde. Mes vêtements n'ont qu'à tomber, et tu découvriras sur ma personne une succession de mystères!'[34]

This is the description of Ennoia:

'Elle a été l'Hélène des Troyens, dont le poète Stésichore a maudit la mémoire. Elle a été Lucrèce, la patricienne violée par les rois. Elle a été Dalila, qui coupait les cheveux de Samson. Elle a été cette fille d'Israel qui s'abandonnait aux boucs. Elle a aimé l'adultère, l'idolâtrie, le mensonge et la sottise. Elle s'est prostituée à tous les peuples. Elle a chanté dans tous les carrefours. Elle a baisé tous les visages. A Tyr, la Syrienne, elle était la maîtresse des voleurs. Elle buvait avec eux pendant les nuits, et elle cachait les assassins dans la vermine de son lit tiède. . . . Innocente comme le Christ, qui est mort pour les hommes, elle s'est dévouée pour les femmes. . . . Elle est Minerve! elle est le Saint-Esprit!'

It was not in France, however, but in England, that this type of Fatal Woman found its most complete form, thanks to the particular sensibility of one who was a partial disciple of Gautier (but in many ways superior to his master)—Algernon Charles Swinburne. And since Swinburne demonstrated in his own person a most characteristic incarnation of the particular sexual attitude which formed, as it were, the 'fond de cale' of Romantic literature, and since the various continental literatures took back again from him and from his English successors (Pater, Wilde) the themes which had previously been elaborated by the French Romantics, it seems opportune here to give some description of the poet's personality.

12. The case of Swinburne presents certain analogies with that of Baudelaire, except that in the Englishman it is easier to distinguish between sincerity and affectation. If in the viciousness of Baudelaire there was a good deal that was deliberately acquired, Swinburne, on the other hand, was placed by nature in a special kind of sexual category. Hence his relative innocence. His gradual crystallization after he came to years of maturity was merely a result of his congenital incapacity to feel in the same way as the general run of mankind. This crystallization was no more than an instinctive defence against the pain of feeling himself to be different. The sense of the artificiality of his own life which never ceased to torment Flaubert did not make itself acutely felt to Swinburne, whose artistic personality was never rent with conflicting tendencies.

'Swinburne has hitherto been fortunate in his biographers. For it would indeed have been regrettable if the life-story of one who, although surpassingly strange, was yet so exquisite a gentleman, had been marred from the outset by any ungentle handling.' With these words

Harold Nicolson opens his study of the poet, written in 1926.[35] However, he adds immediately afterwards: 'There will be those, doubtless, who will one day explore the intricacies and causes of his non-existent sexual repressions, and will trace depressing and essentially erroneous analogies to Dr. Masoch or the Marquis de Sade.' That day was not far off. In the same year, 1926, was published the revised edition of the study by T. Earle Welby,[36] which aimed at dealing 'with what was morbid or eccentric in him rather more plainly than has hitherto been done'. Welby, it is true, hastened to add that, after all and notwithstanding all, the poet 'was a very great man and a very great gentleman'. Swinburne's sexual 'speciality', however, was made into the central point of Welby's study, in a less explicit but no less conclusive manner than in the monumental thesis of Georges Lafourcade, published in 1928.[37]

The customary British reserve, rendered even more circumspect by the existence of an authoritative, sacred, anodyne biography like that of Gosse, had prevented any adequate treatment of the thing which, when all is said and done, was the principal source of inspiration to Swinburne in his youth—which was, indeed, the greater Swinburne. In this way was passed over, more or less in silence, all that Swinburne produced at an earlier date than those works which, in 1865 and 1866, made him famous at one stroke; and any awkwardness in respect of certain poems which were unequivocally perverse was smoothed over by the contention that they were founded on literature rather than on life, and that they had been written with the object of shocking Victorian society. A veil having thus been drawn over the most scabrous portion of the poet's character, it was the custom to keep off dangerous ground and invent some respectable label for him which would be acceptable to all. Swinburne was displayed as the bard of liberty—without, however, any real explanation being sought for the transition from *Poems and Ballads* to *Songs before Sunrise*. Welby, and to an even greater extent Lafourcade, have on the other hand taken into proper account the period of preparation and also certain documents from

the poet's secret archives in the possession of the bibliophile, T. J. Wise. In less respectful and less prudent hands
the exhumation of these archives might have had an effect
analogous with that of the opening of the famous pornographic trunk of the Abbé Jules, in Octave Mirbeau's
notorious novel. As an example of *delectatio morosa*, it
suffices to say that among these documents there is to be
found an unprintable epic poem on the subject of flagellation, *The Flogging-Block*, which the poet composed, not to
indulge the whim of a moment, but obviously with studied
care, at intervals between 1861 and 1881; and that in
mature years he resorted to the practice of 'ordering' drawings of scenes of flagellation he previously described in
detail.[38] As to the question of Swinburne's experiments
in algolagnia, Welby allows us to read between the lines,
while Lafourcade expressly states: 'Nous *savons* que, de
1867–68 à 1895 du moins, il satisfaisait dans des établissements spéciaux les tendances que nous venons de si-
gnaler.'[39] In any case all this was quite well known to his
contemporaries. But I shall discuss in a separate chapter[40]
the sinister legend which, during the French Decadence,
grew up round the name of the author of *Anactoria*.

13. It was Monckton-Milnes who introduced the
young poet, in 1860, to the writings of the Marquis de
Sade; but this highly amiable and cynical gentleman did
no more in this case than he was accustomed to do in
social intercourse: he brought into contact two kindred
temperaments. There are spiritual intermediaries who
delight in bringing about the encounter of minds
which seem destined to fertilize each other, and Milnes
loved to exercise this function—which in many cases
is both useful and noble—with a sting of Mephisto-
phelian malice. He used to gather round him the most
incompatible characters in order to watch them clash, or
else he set to work to bring to light affinities of perversion.
He used his friends, in fact, as instruments, in order
to put together some strange, weird comedy, from which
he, as spectator, would derive the greatest possible enjoyment, nor did he much care whether the spiritual wel-
fare of the actors gained anything from it. The youthful

Swinburne, as will be seen, showed the promise of abnormal tendencies; Milnes, to satisfy his mind, opened to the poet the *enfer* of his library—and a very rich *enfer* it was, with a European reputation.[41]

But Milnes, whom Swinburne gratified with the honourable but sinister title of 'guide of my youth' (a Virgil guiding him through the Inferno of a library), did no more than reveal to Swinburne the existence of companions in erotic singularity. The singularity was inborn.

14. At twelve years old Swinburne interpreted as religious fervour a certain ecstasy of adoration which came over him at the moment of receiving the Eucharist. He wrote a play with a Christian theme, *The Unhappy Revenge* (1849), in which the characters exalt the voluptuous pleasures of martyrdom;[42] quite soon his special tendency became more precise, and he identified himself with Frank, the whipped page of the courtesan Imperia (in *Laugh and Lie down*, 1859),[43] the precociously depraved boy (the ambiguity of disguise adopted by Frank and his twin brother Frederick, who, at Imperia's beck, appear dressed now in a male, now in a female garb, is symptomatic), who cries to the woman of mature sensual experience:

> . . . I would so fain be hurt
> But really hurt, hurt deadly, to do good
> To your most sudden fancy.

Again, he identifies himself with Tebaldeo Tebaldei, the chronicler of Lucrezia Borgia, who theorizes on the subject of algolagnia (*The Chronicle of Tebaldeo Tebaldei*, 1861),[44] associating pleasure and pain in the same way as Baudelaire (though Baudelaire was at this time unknown to the English poet):

'Knowest thou not . . . that a nerve may quiver and be convulsed with actual pain while the blood is dancing and singing for joy like a nymph drunken? that to be pinched and torn by the lips and teeth and fingers of love is a delight enduring when one is past kisses and when caresses have no sting or savour left in them? that the ache and smart of the fleshly senses are things common alike to pleasure and to pain?'

Again, Swinburne is Arthur, the young chorister who

bears on his body 'the stripes of last red week' and sings in Latin the praises of the beautiful but impure Rosamond;[45] he is Chastelard, who burns to be a martyr for love of Mary Stuart. Lafourcade has studied all these works so minutely from the same point of view as that of this present study, that it only remains for me to refer the reader to the French critic's volume. Nor shall I stay to discuss the considerable influence which Gautier's descriptive passages may have had on certain of Swinburne's (for instance, the passage where he describes Lucrezia Borgia naked,[46] which looks very like an amplification of certain passages in *Mademoiselle de Maupin* and in the *Nouvelles*). I shall rather attempt to point out the peculiarities in the position of men in relation to women in Swinburne's work, and the characteristics of his female type.

As regards the former, it suffices to record the concise formula used by Swinburne himself: man, in his work, aspires to be 'the powerless victim of the furious rage of a beautiful woman';[47] his attitude is passive, his love a martyrdom, his pleasure pain. As for the woman, whether she be Fredegond or Lucrezia Borgia, Rosamond or Mary Stuart, she is always the same type of unrestrained, imperious, cruel beauty. One might trace in detail the gradual development of this type in Swinburne, but the documentation would be so copious and withal so very obvious in its interpretation that it will be better to limit ourselves here to the main points, referring to Lafourcade's book for greater detail. Besides, given the very limited experience that Swinburne had of the opposite sex, it is natural that the women described by him should all conform to one type which is a mere projection of his own turbid sensuality: they have a good deal of the idol about them—in fact of the εἴδωλον, the phantom of the mind rather than of the real human being. The greatest effort made by the poet in the study of the feminine soul is the character of Mary Stuart, and it must be admitted that he managed it with notable success.

Swinburne's conception of woman was undoubtedly influenced not a little by the example of the Pre-Raphaelites,

by Morris in his early work (*Early Poems*) and by
Rossetti. In Rossetti there is to be found a conspicuous
preference for the sad and the cruel; the Middle Ages, to
him, are a legend of blood; beside his Beata Beatrix stand
magical, evil creatures. His Sister Helen (in the ballad of
the same name) is a cruel, fatal woman, destroying the
man whose destiny lies in her power. (Sidonia von Bork,
also, the heroine of the archaistic 'tale of terror' by the
German clergyman Wilhelm Meinhold (1847), whom
Rossetti admired and caused the Pre-Raphaelites to admire, is a cruel, fatal woman, who for vengeance casts a
spell upon the family of the Dukes of Pomerania, making
them sterile by means of her witchcraft.) And the medieval conception of the 'martyrdom of love', illustrated as
it is in sonnets like those in *Willowwood*, comes very near
to algolagnia. The type of beauty idolized by Rossetti is
the dolorous, exquisitely Romantic beauty; a spectral halo
seems to radiate from his figures, as it radiates also round
certain episodes in his life, in particular that of his
marriage, which might have been taken bodily from the
tales of Poe. The influence of the crime-stained Renaissance of the Elizabethan dramatists, of the gory Middle
Ages of the Pre-Raphaelites, and, shortly afterwards,
of Gautier's orgiastic Antiquity and Baudelaire's grim
Modernity; finally the Ate of Greek Tragedy, the implacable doctrine of the Old Testament, and the cruel nihilistic
hedonism of Sade—all these were sources which flowed
easily into one single stream and found a natural bed in a
mind such as Swinburne's, which was predisposed to receive them.

In his attraction towards a type of tainted beauty, Swinburne was not only very closely related to the French
Romantics, but also to the Pre-Raphaelites. The lovely
Rosamond, for instance, the 'Rosa mundi, non Rosa
munda', concubine of Henry II of England, inspired both
Rossetti and Burne-Jones to paint pictures, and Swinburne, in his youth, to write a play (1858–60). In this
play the sinful heroine says:

> Yea, I am found the woman in all tales,
> The face caught always in the story's face:

> I Helen, holding Paris by the lips,
> Smote Hector through the head; I Cressida
> So kissed men's mouths that they went sick or mad,
> Stung right at brain with me; I Guenevere
> Made my queen's eyes so precious and my hair
> Delicate with such gold in its soft ways
> And my mouth honied so for Launcelot . . .

This feminine figure tallies in almost every point with those of Gautier and Flaubert. And these are the feelings which she inspires in men:

> God help! [says Henry] your hair burns me to see like gold
> Burnt to pure heat; your colour seen turns in me
> To pain and plague upon the temple vein
> That aches as if the sun's heat snapt the blood
> In hot mid-measure; I could cry on you
> Like a maid weeping wise, you are so fair
> It hurts me in the head, makes the life sick
> Here in my hands . . .
> Your beauty makes me blind and hot, I am
> Stabbed in the brows with it.

Here one can see, carried to the point of paroxysm, the sentiment of mixed adoration and terror which Gautier had already given to the lovers of Cleopatra, of Nyssia, and of the courtesan Clarimonde. In *Queen Mother* (1859–60) the love of the feeble but violent monster Charles IX and Denise has hints of cruelty which anticipate *Anactoria*;[48] and the Nero-like complacency with which the poet describes the massacre of St. Bartholomew recalls a similar characteristic in Flaubert. But it is in *Chastelard* (1860–3) that the type of sensual passion celebrated by Swinburne finds its most intense and, at the same time. most artistically valuable, expression.

15. The character of Mary Stuart as it appears at the end of the trilogy dedicated to her by Swinburne (the dates of publication were: *Chastelard*, 1865, *Bothwell*, 1874, *Mary Stuart*, 1881) had lost a good deal of the rigidly fatal quality it has in the first play; there are surprises and contradictions in it, and the heroine, although she remains 'fatal' to all the men who love her, yet appears inconsistent and full of life, a poetical creation, in fact, studied with the interest of a psychologist, and no longer

seen merely through the lyrical despair of Chastelard, lovesick and athirst for martyrdom. Unfortunately, in the two last parts of the trilogy the gems are scattered over an arid waste of metrical exercises in which the poet strives to combine the techniques of various Elizabethan dramatists and often succeeds only in achieving the involved diffuseness of a Chapman, without possessing the profound metaphysical sense of the universe which, in the latter, is an excuse for many defects. Few people can boast of having read the whole of this trilogy; but *Chastelard* had its moment of popularity among connoisseurs.

The Mary Stuart of *Chastelard* is the Fatal Woman *par excellence*, a type drawn from the poet's own intimate sensual nature and without reference to historical truth. For one must contrast the historical words of the dying Chastelard—'Adieu la plus belle et la plus cruelle princesse du monde'—with Brantôme's comment—'Jamais cette reyne ne fut cruelle, elle estoit de tout bonne et très douce'; and then it can be seen that the 'cruelty' attributed by the real Chastelard to his beloved should not be taken literally, any more than the usual phraseology of the school of Petrarch. But in the play Mary Stuart is what Chastelard—that is, Swinburne portraying himself in the character of Chastelard—wishes her to be; she is precisely the monster to whom can be symbolically applied the passage from Mandeville which Swinburne adopted as a motto:

'Another Yle is there toward the Northe, in the See Occean, where that ben fulle cruele and ful evele Wommen of Nature: and thei han precious Stones in hire Eyen; and thei ben of that kynde, that yif thei beholden ony man [with wratthe, *omitted by Swinburne*], thei slen him anon with the beholdynge, as dothe the Basilisk.'

Mary Stuart is cold, she cannot weep (Act I, sc. i)—rather she enjoys the spectacle of suffering, she is a vampire. Chastelard strives to obtain her surrender at the price of his own life, as though she were Semiramis, Cleopatra, or Marguerite of Burgundy (II. i):

> He would have given his body to be slain,
> Having embraced my body. Now, God knows,
> I have no man to do as much for me

> As give me but a little of his blood
> To fill my beauty from, though I go down
> Pale to my grave for want—I think not. Pale—
> I am too pale surely—

Behind such words as these one catches a glimpse of the figures of Gautier's Fatal Women, of Cleopatra, of Clarimonde, the vampire-woman. Note also the pallor. The typical Fatal Woman is always pale, just as the Byronic hero was pale. One imagines the very sight of Mary Stuart to be formidable, as was Gautier's Nyssia. One of her future victims, Darnley, says to the Scottish Queen, when she speaks of pity (IV. i):

> I say that looking with this face of yours
> None shall believe you holy; what, you talk,
> Take mercy in your mouth, eat holiness,
> Put God under your tongue and feed on heaven,
> With fear and faith and—faith, I know not what—
> And look as though you stood and saw men slain
> To make you game and laughter: nay, your eyes
> Threaten us unto blood. What will you do
> To make men take your sweet word? pitiful—
> You are pitiful as he that's hired for death
> And loves the slaying better than the hire.

Chastelard aspires to be the victim of this cruel sphinx: he seeks pain as a pleasure, and in one passage, which Lafourcade quite rightly says is 'perhaps the most introspective that Swinburne ever wrote', he says to his beloved (III. i):

> . . . No, by God's body.
> You will not see? how shall I make you see?
> Look, it may be love was a sort of curse
> Made for my plague and mixed up with my days
> Somewise in their beginning; or indeed
> A bitter birth begotten of sad stars
> At mine own body's birth, that heaven might make
> My life taste sharp where other men drank sweet;
> But whether in heavy body or broken soul,
> I know it must go on to be my death.

For a moment Chastelard dreams of dying with his beloved; of killing her and killing himself; but then he finds a more refined method of satisfying his algolagnia. It is essential that the cause of his death should be his beloved's own wish, that he should be sent to the scaffold because of her and by her order. So he makes his way into the Queen's room and remains there till he is discovered, enjoying the foretaste of seeing 'his blood shed out about her feet'; his 'heart feels drunken when he thinks ... that her sweet lips and life will smell of his spilt blood'. Chastelard's act is, as it were, a grim rite performed at the feet of a blood-thirsty idol (v. ii):

> For all Christ's work this Venus is not quelled,
> But reddens at the mouth with blood of men,
> Sucking between small teeth the sap o' the veins,
> Dabbling with death her little tender lips—
> A bitter beauty, poisonous-pearlèd mouth. . . .
>   . . . Ah, fair love,
> Fair fearful Venus made of deadly foam,
> I shall escape you somehow with my death.

Chastelard tears up the reprieve, and reaches the summit of his rapture when the Queen comes to visit him in prison (v. ii):

> I know not: men must love you in life's spite;
> For you will always kill them; man by man
> Your lips will bite them dead; yea, though you would,
> You shall not spare one; all will die of you . . .
>
> .   .   .   .
>
> Stretch your throat out that I may kiss all round
> Where mine shall be cut through: suppose my mouth
> The axe-edge to bite so sweet a throat in twain
> With bitter iron, should not it turn soft
> As lip is soft to lip?

Lafourcade remarks:[49]

'Dans cette dernière entrevue la cruauté sensuelle de l'inspiration atteint les extrêmes limites jusqu'auxquelles l'art peut s'aventurer sans les dépasser toutefois. ... Swinburne était à l'époque où il écrivait ces vers plongé dans la lecture des œuvres du Marquis de Sade; mais il est absolument inutile de voir ici une influence directe de ce dernier. Cette influence exista, mais fut surtout intellectuelle. Swinburne ne puise l'inspiration qui anime les magnifiques tirades de Chastelard que dans ses propres tendances et dans ses propres désirs. Aucune œuvre de Swinburne n'est plus profondément sensuelle et physique que celle-ci; les idées générales n'y ont pas de place; mais Chastelard est une aspiration vers un idéal déguisé.'

16. Whereas *Chastelard*, in some respects, is the poem of sadism in the act, Swinburne's other great play, *Atalanta in Calydon* (1863–4, published 1865), may be called the poem of sadistic philosophy, to such an extent did the theories of the Divine Marquis colour Swinburne's conception of the Greek world. The theories of Sade appear in this play mixed not only with the traditional Greek and Hebrew doctrines but also with the ideas of William Blake, upon a study of whom Swinburne was engaged at the same time (1862–6). In this study, after stressing the importance of Blake's tendency towards the 'holy insurrection' (the rebellion of man against God, thanks to which man will become god on earth),[50] and after tracing this tendency in various forms of religion, Swinburne gives in a note a 'paraphrase or "excursus" on a lay sermon by a modern pagan philosopher of more material tendencies; but given to such tragic indulgence in huge Titanic dithyrambs'.[51] As Lafourcade points out,[52] this is nothing else but a paraphrase of various passages from *Justine* and *Juliette*, in which Sade puts forward his doctrine which regards crime and destruction as universal laws of nature.

'Nature averse to crime? I tell you, nature lives and breathes by it; hungers at all her pores for bloodshed, aches in all her nerves for the help of sin, yearns with all her heart for the furtherance of cruelty. Nature forbid that thing or this? Nay, the best or worst of you will never go so far as she would have you; no criminal will come up to the measure of her crimes, no destruction seem to her destructive enough. We, when we would do evil, can disorganise a little matter, shed a little blood, quench a little breath at the door of a perishable body; this we can do, and can call it crime. Unnatural is it? Good friend, it is by criminal things and deeds unnatural that nature works and moves and has her being; what subsides through inert virtue, she quickens through active crime; out of death she kindles life; she uses the dust of man to strike her light upon; she feeds with fresh blood the innumerable insatiable mouths suckled at her milkless breast; she takes the pain of the whole world to sharpen the sense of vital pleasure in her limitless veins: she stabs and poisons, crushes and corrodes, yet cannot live and sin fast enough for the cruelty of her great desire. Behold, the ages of men are dead at her feet; the blood of the world is on her hands; and her desire is continually toward evil, that she may see the end of things which she hath made. Friends, if we would be one with nature, let us continually do evil with all our might. But what evil is here for us to do, where the whole body of things is evil? The day's spider kills the day's fly, and calls it a crime? Nay, could we thwart nature, then might crime become possible and sin an actual thing. Could but a man do this; could he cross the courses of the stars, and put back the times of the sea; could he change the ways of the world and find out the house of life to destroy it; could he go into heaven to defile it and into hell to deliver it from subjection; could he draw down the sun to consume the earth, and bid the moon shed poison or fire upon the air; could he kill the fruit in the seed and corrode the child's mouth with the mother's milk; then had he sinned and done evil against nature. Nay, and not then: for nature would fain have it so, that she might create a world of new things; for she is weary of the ancient life: her eyes are sick of seeing and her ears are heavy with hearing; with the lust of creation she is burnt up, and rent in twain with travail until she bring forth change; she would fain create afresh, and cannot, except it be by destroying: in all her energies she is athirst for mortal food, and with all her forces she labours in desire of death. And what are the worst sins we can do—we who live for a day and die in a night? a few murders. . . .'

Swinburne ends this paraphrase by remarking 'how the mystical evangelist and the material humorist[53] meet in the reading of mere nature and join hands in their interpretation of the laws ruling the outer body of life: a vision of ghastly glory, without pity or help possible'. This last formula is a metaphysical reflection of the other: 'the powerless victim of the furious rage of a beautiful woman'. Swinburne's macrocosm is the exact counterpart of his microcosm.

In Chrous IV of *Atalanta*, and particularly in one passage of *Anactoria* ('Is not his incense bitterness, his meat—murder?') which belongs to the same period, the doctrine of Sade which Swinburne paraphrased in prose influenced the actual inspiration of the lines. Lord Houghton (i.e. Monckton-Milnes) had seen in this chorus the influence of Byron, but Swinburne objected:

'I only regret that in justly attacking my *Charenton* you have

wilfully misrepresented its source. I should have bowed to the
judicial sentence if instead of "Byron with a difference" you had
said "De Sade with a difference". The poet, thinker and man of
the world from whom the theology of my poem is derived was
a greater than Byron. *He*, indeed, fatalist or not, saw to the bottom
of Gods and men.'[54]

Milnes's 'misrepresentation' indirectly confirms the
opinion of Sainte-Beuve as to the 'two greatest inspirers of
the moderns' and the illustrations I have given in support
of it.

Swinburne took from Sade the idea that God smites
equally the just and the unjust, and perhaps the former
rather more than the latter; also the other idea that pain
and death are everywhere in Nature, that crime is Nature's
law; and the conception of God as a Being of supreme
wickedness ('the supreme evil, God'), and the revolt of
man against the divinity he disowns.

> All we are against thee, against thee, O God most high.
> (*Atalanta*)

> Him would I reach, him smite, him desecrate,
> Pierce the cold lips of God with human breath,
> And mix his immortality with death. (*Anactoria*)

In *Atalanta* the sadistic streak is at first sight less obvious; yet is not Meleager's death due to the fault of
Atalanta, whom he loves? Have we not, in a more
allusive and mythical form, the same sexual situation as
in *Chastelard*? The woman is a frigid virgin, it is true,
but she is also

> . . . the strange woman, she the flower, the sword,
> Red from spilt blood, a mortal flower to men,
> Adorable, detestable.

She answers therefore to the usual type of Fatal Woman;
and there is a certain analogy between the situations of
Atalanta and of *Salammbô*. The man dies under the eyes
of a frigid woman, devoted to the cult of the Moon, herself an idol, and his death is her involuntary act. Mâtho,
lacerated by torture, speaks not a word but gazes at the

woman with terrible eyes; Meleager, spent like the fatal torch, he, too, 'a woman's offering', implores the virgin:

> . . . touch me with thy rose-like hands,
> And fasten up my eyelids with thy mouth,
> A bitter kiss. . . .
> . . . hide my body with thy veil,
> And with thy raiment cover foot and head,
> And stretch thyself upon me and touch hands
> With hands and lips with lips.

The voluptuousness of pain is the ending alike of *Atalanta* and of *Chastelard*. There are also mixed with it suggestions of necrophily—one of the classic variations of sadism— such as the poet had already indicated quite plainly in *The Leper*[55] and *Les Noyades*. The man who is condemned by the Terror to be drowned together with the young woman he loves rejoices in his 'happy martyrdom', to use the words of Tasso's Olindo:

> I shall drown with her, laughing for love; and she
> *Mix* with me, touching me, lips and eyes.

And the leper-woman's lover is happy that she is dead, so that he may pour out upon her the tenderness of his morbid passion.[56]

17. This algolagnic desire, with all its subtle ramifications, found its boldest expression in *Lesbia Brandon*, the novel Swinburne wrote between 1864 and 1867, in which it is accompanied by incest and hermaphroditism (after the manner of Gautier's *Mademoiselle de Maupin* and Balzac's *La Fille aux yeux d'or*). If Swinburne put something of himself into the character of Lesbia, the modern Sappho (and the poet's sympathy with this type of anomaly is owing, as Lafourcade remarks,[57] to a common feeling of isolation caused by sexual emotions radically different from the rest of mankind), he put even more of himself into certain outbursts on the part of Bertie and of Denham—outbursts in which the algolagnic element already illustrated recurs insistently. This is Bertie with his sister:

'Her perfume thrilled and stung him; he bent down and kissed her feet . . . which he took and pressed down upon his neck. "Oh! I should like you to tread me to death, darling. . . . I wish you would kill me some day; it would be so jolly to feel you killing me. Not like it? Shouldn't I! You just hurt me and see." She pinched him so sharply that he laughed and panted with pleasure. "I should like being swished even I think, if you were to complain of me or if I knew you liked it."'

In Denham the impulses of active and passive sadism are intertwined. He might well say, like Baudelaire's *Héautontimorouménos*:

> Je suis la plaie et le couteau!
> Je suis le soufflet et la joue!
> Je suis les membres et la roue,
> Et la victime et le bourreau!

'Denham looked her in the face, shaken inwardly and throughout by a sense of inevitable pain. . . . Rage rose in him again like a returning sea. . . . He would have given his life for leave to touch her; his soul for a chance of dying crushed down under her feet; an emotion of extreme tenderness, lashed to fierce insanity by the circumstance passed into a passion of vehement cruelty. Deeply he desired to die by her if that could be; and more deeply, if this could be, to destroy her; scourge her into swooning and absorb her blood with kisses; caress and lacerate her loveliness, alleviate and heighten her pains; to feel her foot upon his throat, and wound her own with his teeth; submit his body and soul for a little to her lightest will and satiate upon her the desperate caprice of his immeasurable desire; to inflict careful torture on the limbs too tender to embrace; suck the tears off her laden eyelids, bite through her sweet and shuddering lips.'

This passage is only a prose version of the inflamed accents of *Anactoria*, in which can be seen, on the one hand, the cannibalistic elements of sadism, and, on the other, sadism permeating the whole universe ('the mute melancholy lust of heaven': heaven merely reflects the 'mute melancholy lust' of the poet himself):[58]

> I would my love could kill thee; I am satiated
> With seeing thee live, and fain would have thee dead.
>
> .   .   .   .
>
> I would find grievous ways to have thee slain,
> Intense device, and superflux of pain;
> Vex thee with amorous agonies, and shake
> Life at thy lips, and leave it there to ache;
> Strain out thy soul with pangs too soft to kill,
> Intolerable interludes, and infinite ill;

Relapse and reluctation of the breath,
Dumb tunes and shuddering semitones of death.

. . . .

That I could drink thy veins as wine, and eat
Thy breasts like honey! that from face to feet
Thy body were abolished and consumed,
And in my flesh thy very flesh entombed!

. . . . O that I

Durst crush thee out of life with love, and die,
Die of thy pain and my delight, and be
Mixed with thy blood and molten into thee!
Would I not plague thee dying overmuch?
Would I not hurt thee perfectly? not touch
Thy pores of sense with torture, and make bright
Thine eyes with bloodlike tears and grievous light?
Strike pang from pang as note is struck from note,
Catch the sob's middle music in thy throat,
Take thy limbs living, and new-mould with these
A lyre of many faultless agonies?

Many expressions from *Anactoria* were to pass into the
work of D'Annunzio, to whom belongs the following
remark:

'A. Swinburne, author of *Laus Veneris* and of *Anactoria*, in
whom there seems to live again, with incredible violence, the
criminal sensuality which fills primitive dramas with wild cries and
desperate slaughters.'59

18. But the time has come to turn our attention again
to the type of Fatal Woman which became firmly established in Swinburne's work. There remains to be discussed, from this point of view, the First Series of *Poems
and Ballads*, which is completely dominated by the figure
of the bloodthirsty, implacable idol. There is the Venus of
Tannhäuser, in *Laus Veneris*, in which the subject of
Keats's *Belle Dame sans merci* is treated more profoundly
and elaborated with all the resources of a grim and satanic
Pre-Raphaelite medievalism; Venus who was 'the world's
delight', now fallen, in Christian times, to the level of a
sinister vampire, 'de l'antique Vénus le superbe fantôme',
she whom the poet evoked again later in the ode on the

death of Baudelaire (*Ave atque.Vale*, in the Second Series
of *Poems and Ballads*):

> And one weeps with him in the ways Lethean,
> And stains with tears her changing bosom chill:
> That obscure Venus of the hollow hill,
> That thing transformed which was the Cytherean,
> With lips that lost their Grecian laugh divine
> Long since, and face no more called Erycine;
> A ghost, a bitter and luxurious god.
> Thee also with fair flesh and singing spell
> Did she, a sad and second prey, compel
> Into the footless places once more trod,
> And shadows hot from hell. . . .

In *Laus Veneris* the beautiful, cruel idol dominates a
whole vast panorama of slaughter:

> Ah, not as they, but as the souls that were
> Slain in the old time, having found her fair;
> Who, sleeping with her lips upon their eyes,
> Heard sudden serpents hiss across her hair.
>
> Their blood runs round the roots of time like rain;
> She casts them forth and gathers them again;
> With nerve and bone she weaves and multiplies
> Exceeding pleasure out of extreme pain.
>
> Her little chambers drip with flower-like red,
> Her girdles, and the chaplets of her head,
> Her armlets and her anklets; with her feet
> She tramples all that winepress of the dead.
>
> Her gateways smoke with fume of flowers and fires,
> With loves burnt out and unassuaged desires;
> Between her lips the steam of them is sweet,
> The languor in her ears of many lyres.
>
> Her beds are full of perfume and sad sound,
> Her doors are made with music, and barred round
> With sighing and with laughter and with tears,
> With tears whereby strong souls of men are bound.
>
> There is the knight Adonis that was slain;
> With flesh and blood she chains him for a chain;
> The body and the spirit in her ears
> Cry, for her lips divide him vein by vein.
> Yea, all she slayeth. . . .

There is the Empress Faustine (*Faustine*), created by

Satan as though for a challenge to God, or sent by God upon earth to scourge the sins of men with a scourge of scorpions, raised from the tomb, a thirst-raging vampire:

> She loved the games men played with death,
> > Where death must win;
> As though the slain man's blood and breath
> > Revived Faustine.

Like Venus, Faustine also is eternal, a sort of indestructible 'love-machine with clockwork joints of supple gold':

> You have the face that suits a woman
> > For her soul's screen—
> The sort of beauty that's called human
> > In hell, Faustine.

There is the cruel Eternal Feminine incarnate in the procession of wanton Oriental queens with strange names, in the *Masque of Queen Bersabe*—Herodias, Aholibah, Cleopatra, Abihail, Azubah, Ahinoam, Atarah; Semiramis:

> I am the queen Semiramis.
> The whole world and the sea that is
> In fashion like a chrysopras,
> The noise of all men labouring,
> The priest's mouth tired through thanksgiving,
> The sound of love in the blood's pause,
> The strength of love in the blood's beat,
> All these were cast beneath my feet
> And all found lesser than I was.

Hesione, Chrysothemis, Thomyris, Harhas, Myrrha, Pasiphae, Sappho; Messalina:

> I am the queen of Italy.
> These were the signs God set on me;
> A barren beauty subtle and sleek,
> Curled carven hair, and cheeks worn wan
> With fierce false lips of many a man,
> Large temples where the blood ran weak,
> A mouth athirst and amorous
> And hungering as the grave's mouth does
> That, being an-hungred, cannot speak.

Amestris:

> In Shushan toward Ecbatane
> I wrought my joys with tears and pain
> My loves with blood and bitter sin.

Ephrath; Pasithea:

> I am the queen of Cypriotes.
> Mine oarsmen, labouring with brown throats
> Sang of me many a tender thing.
> My maidens, girdled loose and braced
> With gold from bosom to white waist
> Praised me between their wool-combing.
> All that praise Venus all night long
> With lips like speech and lids like song
> Praised me till song lost heart to sing.

Alaciel; Erigone:

> I am the queen Erigone.
> The wild wine shed as blood on me
> Made my face brighter than a bride's.
> My large lips had the old thirst of earth,
> Mine arms the might of the old sea's girth
> Bound round the whole world's iron sides.
> Within mine eyes and in mine ears
> Were music and the wine of tears,
> And light, and thunder of the tides.

Last, but by no means least, there is Dolores, Our Lady
of Sensual Pain, whom the poet invokes in a litany which
is a complete example of sadistic profanation:

> Cold eyelids that hide like a jewel
> Hard eyes that grow soft for an hour;
> The heavy white limbs, and the cruel
> Red mouth like a venomous flower;
> When these are gone by with their glories,
> What shall rest of thee then, what remain,
> O mystic and sombre Dolores,
>   Our Lady of Pain?
>
> Seven sorrows the priests give their Virgin;
> But thy sins, which are seventy times seven,
> Seven ages would fail thee to purge in,
> And then they would haunt thee in heaven.
>
> .   .   .   .   .
>
> O garment not golden but gilded,
> O garden where all men may dwell,
> O tower not of ivory, but builded
> By hands that reach heaven from hell;

O mystical rose of the mire,
O house not of gold but of gain,
O house of unquenchable fire,
    Our Lady of Pain!

.   .   .   .   .

We shift and bedeck and bedrape us,
Thou art noble and nude and antique;
Libitina thy mother, Priapus
Thy father, a Tuscan and Greek.
We play with light loves in the portal,
And wince and relent and refrain;
Loves die, and we know thee immortal,
    Our Lady of Pain.

Fruits fail and love dies and time ranges;
Thou art fed with perpetual breath,
And alive after infinite changes,
And fresh from the kisses of death;
Of languors rekindled and rallied,
Of barren delights and unclean,
Things monstrous and fruitless, a pallid
    And poisonous queen.

At the touch of her lips men change

    The lilies and languors of virtue
    For the raptures and roses of vice.

This couplet, which is so much derided for its apparent silliness, is simply a poetical transcription of Sade's idea of contrasting active, triumphant vice with apathetic, down-trodden virtue. The shade of the Divine Marquis soon dominates the scene, as we shall now see.

    Those [the lilies] lie where thy foot on the floor is,
    These [the roses] crown and caress thee and chain,
    O splendid and sterile Dolores,
        Our Lady of Pain.

    There are sins it may be to discover,
    There are deeds it may be to delight.
    What new work wilt thou find for thy lover,
    What new passions for daytime or night?
    What spells that they know not a word of
    Whose lives are as leaves overblown?
    What tortures undreamt of, unheard of,
        Unwritten, unknown?

Ah beautiful passionate body
That never has ached with a heart!
On thy mouth though the kisses are bloody,
Though they sting till it shudder and smart,
More kind than the love we adore is,
They hurt not the heart or the brain,
O bitter and tender Dolores,
     Our Lady of Pain.

. . . . . .

Shall no new sin be born for men's trouble,
No dream of impossible pangs?

. . . . . .

Ah, where shall we go then for pastime,
If the worst that can be has been done?

. . . . . .

I adjure thee, respond from thine altars,
     Our Lady of Pain.

At this point, as Lafourcade has remarked,[60] there begins to appear, amid the dithyrambic fury of the lines, a hint of the real Black Mass, as described by Sade:

I have passed from the outermost portal
To the shrine where a sin is a prayer;
What care though the service be mortal?
O our Lady of Torture, what care?
All thine the last wine that I pour is,
The last in the chalice we drain,
O fierce and luxurious Dolores,
     Our Lady of Pain.

Through a veil of poetry can be seen allusions to the profanation of the sacred vessels, the libation from a chalice filled with blood, and even human sacrifice. The profanation embraces all the most sacred ties, for the poet calls Dolores 'sister, spouse and mother'.

For the lords in whose keeping the door is
That opens on all who draw breath
Gave the cypress to thee, my Dolores,
     The myrtle to death.

And they laughed, changing hands in the measure,
And they mixed and made peace after strife;
Pain melted in tears, and was pleasure;
Death tingled with blood, and was life.

Like lovers they melted and tingled,
In the dusk of thine innermost fane;
In the darkness they murmured and mingled,
         Our Lady of Pain.

In a twilight where virtues are vices,
In thy chapels, unknown of the sun,
To a tune that enthrals and entices,
They were wed, and the twain were as one.

The shade of the high priest of lustful cruelty, the Marquis de Sade, appears on the scene:

Thy life shall not cease though thou doff it;
Thou shalt live until evil be slain,
And good shall die first, said thy prophet,
         Our Lady of Pain.

Did he lie? did he laugh? does he know it,
Now he lies out of reach, out of breath,
Thy prophet, thy preacher, thy poet,
Sin's child by incestuous death?
Did he find out in fire at his waking,
Or discern as his eyelids lost light,
When the bands of the body were breaking
         And all came in sight?

Had not Sade, asks Lafourcade, had not Sade, 'prophet, preacher, poet', actually shown Good, in the person of Justine, struck by the angry lightning of Heaven, while Evil, in the person of Juliette, continued to live in prosperity?

Observe also how the vision of pagan antiquity, colossal and bloodstained, makes an accompanying *leit-motiv* to Swinburne's evocations of lustful pleasure, as it does to those of Gautier and Flaubert:

Dost thou dream, in a respite of slumber,
In a lull of the fires of thy life,
Of the days without name, without number,
When thy will stung the world into strife;
When, a goddess, the pulse of thy passion
Smote kings as they revelled in Rome;
And they hailed thee re-risen, O Thalassian,
         Foam-white, from the foam?

When thy lips had such lovers to flatter;
When the city lay red from thy rods,
And thine hands were as arrows to scatter
The children of change and their gods;
When the blood of thy foemen made fervent
A sand never moist from the main,
As one smote them, their lord and thy servant,
  Our Lady of Pain.

   · · · · ·

[Sands] red from the print of thy paces,
Made smooth for the world and its lords,
Ringed round with a flame of fair faces,
  And splendid with swords.

There the gladiator, pale for thy pleasure,
Drew bitter and perilous breath;
There torments laid hold on the treasure
Of limbs too delicious for death;
When thy gardens were lit with live torches;
When the world was a steed for thy rein;
When the nations lay prone in thy porches,
  Our Lady of Pain.

When, with flame all around him aspirant,
Stood flushed, as a harp-player stands,
The implacable beautiful tyrant,
Rose-crowned, having death in his hands;
And a sound as the sound of loud water
Smote far through the flight of the fires,
And mixed with the lightning of slaughter
  A thunder of lyres.

Dost thou dream of what was and no more is,
The old kingdoms of earth and the kings?
Dost thou hunger for these things, Dolores,
For these, in a world of new things?

   · · · · ·

What ailed us, O gods, to desert you
For creeds that refuse and restrain?
Come down and redeem us from virtue,
  Our Lady of Pain.

   · · · · ·

Thy skin changes country and colour,
And shrivels or swells to a snake's.
Let it brighten and bloat and grow duller,
We know it, the flames and the flakes,

Red brands on it smitten and bitten,
Round skies where a star is a stain,
And the leaves with thy litanies written,
  Our Lady of Pain.

  .   .   .

But the worm shall revive thee with kisses;
Thou shalt change and transmute as a god,
As the rod to a serpent that hisses,
As the serpent again to a rod.

  .   .   .

Though the heathen outface and outlive us,
And our lives and our longings are twain—
Ah, forgive us our virtues, forgive us,
  Our Lady of Pain.

  .   .   .

They were purple of raiment and golden,
Filled full of thee, fiery with wine,
Thy lovers, in haunts unbeholden,
In marvellous chambers of thine.
They are fled, and their footprints escape us,
Who appraise thee, adore, and abstain,
O daughter of Death and Priapus,
  Our Lady of Pain.

The poet who wrote this hymn of enthusiastic surrender to vice and to the sadistic law of universal cruelty was, no doubt, exaggerating,[61] but there is in it an undeniable foundation of sincerity, as though a reaction from the aching disappointment expressed in *The Triumph of Time*.[62]

19. The poet had made, in 1862, an effort to break the magic circle of his own peculiar sensibility. His love for Jane Faulkner in a certain sense marks the critical moment of Swinburne's emotional life. Rejected by her, he wrote *The Triumph of Time*, a pathetic farewell to the normal life of which he had caught a glimpse ('What should such fellows as I do?' he asks, echoing the words of Hamlet),[63] and abandoned himself to the Black Mass of *Dolores*. 'What could be done *with* and *for* Algernon?' his friends were wondering. In 1867 Rossetti endeavoured to entangle Swinburne in a liaison with a lady of athletic accomplishments, the circus-rider Adah Menken,[64] with a view to

setting him straight. Swinburne's eagerness in advertising his liaison (he rather unwisely circulated photographs of Menken and himself taken together, with the consequence that they were publicly exhibited for sale in the windows of several shops) was not matched with a proportionate success in the actual love-affair, notwithstanding the very active part assumed by the lady. (It is said that she returned to Rossetti, as unearned, the ten pounds he had given her to conquer Swinburne's affections.) Gosse, on the authority of Lord Carlisle, speaks of a sort of *conseil de famille* which was supposed to have invited Mazzini, about the same time, to give his help, and to be a spiritual father to the poet. Lafourcade does not believe that this *conseil de famille* actually took place; be that as it may, Karl Blind arranged a meeting between Mazzini and Swinburne, and the young poet was solemnly invested with the mission of becoming the Bard of Liberty. This mentioning of Mazzini almost in the same breath with a buxom female acrobat may appear cynical; but in reality, the fact that Italy could count among foreigners her most enthusiastic poet was partly due to the desire, both of the poet himself and of his intimate friends, to give a saner aim to his energies by encouraging the potential sublimation of feeling which was discernible in him. In fact, the poet's interest in the cause of liberty and Italy was of early date: as early as October 1866 he had spontaneously turned from 'Rossetti and his followers in art (l'art pour l'art)' to Italy and Mazzini, and thought of writing a 'not inadequate expression of love and reverence towards him'. But the goddess Liberty whom the poet adored was only a sublimation of his own feminine type, a divinity intolerant of restraint or law (substitute for the woman of uncontrolled morals), fatal and cruel in exacting the sacrifice of human life (substitute for algolagnia). The anarchical theories of Sade and Blake provided Swinburne with a philosophical substratum. Even as the adorer of the Mater Dolorosa and Mater Triumphalis which Liberty represented to him, Swinburne is always, fundamentally, 'the powerless victim of the furious rage of a beautiful woman'. His Liberty, like the Liberty in the picture by Delacroix (*La Barricade*), is the Liberty of the *Iambes* of Barbier, described thus in the *Curée*:

> C'est une forte femme aux puissantes mamelles,
>   A la voix rauque, aux durs appas,
> Qui, du brun sur la peau, du feu dans les prunelles,
>   Agile et marchant à grands pas,
> Se plaît aux cris du peuple, aux sanglantes mêlées,
>   Aux longs roulements des tambours,
> A l'odeur de la poudre, aux lointaines volées
>   Des cloches et des canons sourds,
> Qui ne prend des amours que dans la populace,
>   Qui ne prête son large flanc
> Qu'à des gens forts comme elle, et qui veut qu'on l'embrasse
>   Avec des bras rouges de sang.

She is the Liberty which Carducci, influenced by Barbier, portrayed as follows (in the *Vigesimo Anniversario dell' VIII Agosto 1848*):

> Dura virago ell'è, dure domanda
> Di perigli e d'amor pruove famose:
> In mezzo al sangue de la sua ghirlanda
>   Crescon le rose.[65]

Both Welby and Nicolson agree that Swinburne's idea of Liberty should be interpreted in this way, and Lafourcade's conclusion is unexceptionable:

'Dans la sensibilité de Swinburne est, je le crois du moins, la clef de l'énigme d'une nature très complexe. Nous avons signalé la précoce et troublante sensualité de son tempérament; mais ce n'est pas seulement son attitude sexuelle qui est ainsi expliquée, c'est aussi son double et contradictoire penchant à la soumission et à la révolte, les enfantillages de son caractère, le mélange de perversités les plus inquiétantes avec une certaine virilité foncière, une dignité et un équilibre proprement masculins.'

As regards this last point one reservation may be permitted. Nicolson has quite rightly pointed out in Swinburne a 'virility complex', an anxious desire to appear masculine, and an extreme susceptibility on this point. The origins of such a fixation are to be sought primarily in the years of his infancy, when his little girl cousins, so it seems, used to make a joke of the delicate build of the boy whom they called 'Cousin Hadji'. It seems also that these little girls used to bully him, but it may be super-fluous to attempt to see in this the origins of an erotic peculiarity which was undoubtedly developed by certain methods of discipline at Eton. Swinburne gave a well-known instance of his desire to assert his own virility when, his family having refused their consent to his joining the army, he undertook the dangerous ascent of Culver Cliff. A less well-known and less attractive instance was his re-action to the reading of the love-letters of Keats to Fanny Brawne, published by H. Buxton Forman in 1878.[66] Swinburne actually reproved Keats for not having known how to love and die like a man and a gentleman. Obviously Watts-Dunton, whose ascendancy over Swinburne was at that time steadily increasing, had a say in this criticism; on the other hand, the retort might have been made to Swinburne that if by 'loving like a gentleman' he meant loving in the ways approved by such exquisite gentlemen as the Maréchal Gilles de Rais and the Marquis de Sade, then Keats was certainly not a gentlemanly lover.

20. As regards the influence of Swinburne's conception of the Fatal Woman on English literature in general, the importance of the works so far discussed is perhaps not so great as that of one page of prose and one secondary poem which I shall now quote.

The page of prose comes from the *Notes on Designs of the Old Masters in Florence*, notes which were taken on the occasion of Swinburne's visit to Florence in 1864 and which were published in the *Fortnightly Review* in July 1868, and afterwards in *Essays and Studies* (1875). He is speaking of certain studies of female heads by Michael-angelo:[66A]

'But in one separate head there is more tragic attraction . . .: a woman's, three times studied, with divine and subtle care; sketched and re-sketched in youth and age, beautiful always beyond desire and cruel beyond words; fairer than heaven and more terrible than hell; pale with pride and weary with wrong-doing; a silent anger against God and man burns, white and repressed, through her clear features. In one drawing she wears a head-dress of eastern fashion rather than western, but in effect made out of the artist's mind only; plaited in the likeness of closely-welded scales as of a chrysalid serpent, raised and waved and rounded in the likeness of a sea-shell. In some inexplicable way all her ornaments seem to partake of her fatal nature, to bear upon them her brand of beauty fresh from hell; and this through no vulgar machinery of symbolism, no serpentine or otherwise bestial emblem: the bracelets and rings are innocent enough in shape and workmanship; but in touching her flesh they have become infected with deadly and malignant meaning. Broad bracelets divide the shapely splendour of her arms; over the nakedness of her firm and luminous breasts, just below the neck, there is passed a band as of metal. Her eyes are full of proud and passionless lust after gold and blood; her hair, close and curled, seems ready to shudder in sunder and divide into snakes.[67] Her throat, full and fresh, round and hard to the eye as her bosom and arms, is erect and stately, the head set firm on it without any droop or lift of the chin; her mouth crueller than a tiger's, colder than a snake's, and beautiful beyond a woman's. She is the deadlier Venus incarnate:

$$\pi o \lambda \lambda \grave{\eta} \ \mu \grave{\epsilon} \nu \ \grave{\epsilon} \nu \ \theta \epsilon o \hat{\iota} \sigma \iota \ [sic] \ \kappa o \grave{\upsilon} \kappa \ \grave{\alpha} \nu \acute{\omega} \nu \upsilon \mu o s$$
$$\theta \epsilon \acute{\alpha} \cdot \qquad \qquad \text{(Eur. } Hipp. \ \text{1-2.)}$$

for upon earth also many names might be found for her: Lamia re-transformed, invested now with a fuller beauty, but divested of all feminine attributes not native to the snake—a Lamia loveless and unassailable by the sophist, readier to drain life out of her lover than to fade for his sake at his side; or the Persian Amestris, watching the only breasts on earth more beautiful than her own cut off from her rival's living bosom; or Cleopatra, not dying but turning serpent under the serpent's bite; or that queen of the extreme East who with her husband marked every day as it went by some device of a new and wonderful cruelty.[68] In one design, where the cruel and timid face of a king rises behind her, this crowned and cowering head might stand for Ahab's, and hers for that of Jezebel. . . . There is a drawing in the furthest room at the Buonarroti Palace which recalls and almost reproduces the design of these three. Here also the electric hair, which looks as though it would hiss and glitter with sparks if once touched, is wound up to a tuft with serpentine plaits and involutions; all that remains of it unbound falls in one curl, shaping itself into a snake's likeness as it unwinds, right against a living snake held to the breast and throat. This is rightly registered as a study for Cleopatra; but notice has not yet been accorded to the subtle and sublime idea which transforms her death by the aspic's bite into a meeting of serpents which recognise and embrace, an encounter between the woman and the worm of Nile, almost as though this match for death were a monstrous love-match, or such a mystic marriage as that painted in the loveliest passage of *Salammbô*, between the maiden body and the scaly coils of the serpent and the priestess alike made sacred to the moon; so closely do the snake and the queen of snakes caress and cling. Of this idea Shakespeare also had a vague and great glimpse when he made Antony murmur, "Where's my serpent of old Nile?" mixing a foretaste of her death with the full sweet savour of her supple and amorous "pride of life". For what indeed is lovelier or more luxuriously loving than a strong and graceful snake of the nobler kind?'

It is hardly necessary to point out how little Swinburne's imagination sticks to the drawings he is discussing: Michaelangelo is translated into terms of Gautier. Even less regard for the original (an insignificant drawing by Frederick Sandys) is shown in the poem *Cleopatra*, published in the *Cornhill Magazine* in 1866.[69] The type of 'fatal' beauty was to such an extent fixed in the mind of Swinburne, that in criticizing another drawing by Sandys shown at the Academy in 1868, the poet made use of the same terms that we have already seen him use in the case of Michaelangelo:

'A woman's face . . . of rich, ripe, angry beauty; she draws one warm long lock of curling hair through her full and moulded lips, biting it with bared bright teeth, which add something of a tiger's charm to the sleepy and couching passion of her fair face.'

'Angry' is an inevitable epithet for this Fatal Woman, since the poet imagines himself in front of her as a 'powerless victim'. Behind the irate countenance of the beautiful Fury rises up the prosaic face of the Eton schoolmaster who was the first to initiate the little boy—but oh, how innocently!—into the delights of flagellation.

Cleopatra has been defined by Welby as a 'minor masterpiece of decadent poetry', in spite of the opinion of Meredith, who, seeing in it nothing but a farrago of the commonplaces of Swinburne's poetical style, persuaded the poet not to reprint it.

> Her mouth is fragrant as a vine,
> A vine with birds in all its boughs,
> Serpent and scarab for a sign
> Between the beauty of her brows
> And the amorous deep lids divine. . . .

Under those low large lids of hers
She hath the histories of all time;
The fruit of foliage-stricken years;
The old seasons with their heavy chime
That leaves its rhyme in the world's ears.

She sees the hand of death made bare,
The ravelled riddle of the skies,
The faces faded that were fair,
The mouths made speechless that were wise,
The hollow eyes and dusty hair. . . .

Dank dregs, the scum of pool or clod,
God-spawn of lizard-footed clans,
And those dog-headed hulks that trod
Swart necks of the old Egyptians,
Raw draughts of man's beginning God;

The poised hawk, quivering ere he smote,
With plume-like gems on breast and back;
The asps and water-worms afloat,
Between the marsh flowers moist and slack;
The cat's warm black bright rising throat. . . .

She holds her future close, her lips
Hold fast the face of things to be;
Actium, and sound of war that dips
Down the blown valleys of the sea,
Far sails that flee, and storms of ships;

The laughing red sweet mouth of wine
At ending of life's festival;
That spice of cerecloths, and the fine
White bitter dust funereal
Sprinkled on all things for a sign.

For Swinburne, too, Cleopatra is an impersonation of the supreme feminine ideal, as she was for Gautier, who described her as 'la femme la plus complète qui ait jamais existé, la plus femme et la plus reine, un type admirable, auquel les poètes n'ont pu rien ajouter, et que les songeurs trouvent toujours au bout de leurs rêves'.[70]

21. There remained nevertheless one thing still to be added to this type of beauty, a thing at which Gautier had just hinted in *Études de mains*:

> On voit tout cela dans les lignes
> De cette paume. . . .   (*Impéria*)

Tous les vices avec leurs griffes
Ont, dans les plis de cette peau,
Tracé d'affreux hiéroglyphes. . . .
                              (*Lacenaire*)

It was Walter Pater who made the great discovery, who traced the history of the Fatal Woman in the already celebrated smile of the Gioconda, 'the unfathomable smile, always with a touch of something sinister in it, which plays over all Leonardo's work'.[71] A letter from Swinburne[72] shows quite clearly the origin of Pater's famous 'piece' about Monna Lisa. He wrote on April 11th, 1873, to Lord Morley:

'I admire and enjoy Pater's work [i.e. *Studies in the History of the Renaissance*, 1873] so heartily that I am somewhat shy of saying how much, ever since on my telling him once at Oxford how highly Rossetti as well as myself estimated his first papers in the *Fortnightly*, he replied to the effect that he considered them as owing their inspiration entirely to the example of my own work in the same line.'

The following is the celebrated passage from Pater's study of Leonardo:

'The presence that rose thus so strangely beside the waters, is expressive of what in the ways of a thousand years men had come to desire. Hers is the head upon which all "the ends of the world are come",[73] and the eyelids are a little weary. It is a beauty wrought out from within upon the flesh, the deposit, little cell by cell, of strange thoughts and fantastic reveries and exquisite passions. Set it for a moment beside one of those white Greek goddesses or beautiful women of antiquity, and how would they be troubled by this beauty, into which the soul with all its maladies has passed! All the thoughts and experience of the world have etched and moulded there, in that which they have of power to refine and make expressive the outward form, the animalism of Greece, the lust of Rome, the mysticism of the Middle Age with its spiritual ambition and imaginative loves, the return of the Pagan world, the sins of the Borgias. She is older than the rocks among which she sits; like the vampire, she has been dead many times, and learned the secrets of the grave; and has been a diver in deep seas, and keeps their fallen day about her; and trafficked for strange webs with Eastern merchants; and, as Leda, was the mother of Helen of Troy, and, as Saint Anne, the mother of Mary; and all this has been to her but as the sound of lyres and flutes, and lives only in the delicacy with which it has moulded the changing lineaments, and tinged the eyelids and the hands. The fancy of a perpetual life, sweeping together ten thousand experiences, is an old one; and modern philosophy has conceived the idea of humanity as wrought upon by, and summing up in itself, all modes of thought and life. Certainly Lady Lisa might stand as the embodiment of the old fancy, the symbol of the modern idea.'

The family likeness between this portrait and the Fatal Women of Gautier, Flaubert, and Swinburne strikes one immediately. Monna Lisa, like Swinburne's Faustine, is a vampire; she, too, like Dolores, Cleopatra, and the anonymous figure drawn by Michaelangelo, has accumulated in herself all the experiences of the world; and there are details of comparison which prove her Swinburnian origin. For instance, the passage 'and all this has been to her but as the sound of lyres and flutes' is reminiscent of *Laus Veneris*, 'the languor in her ears of many lyres'.

Pater's description popularized the Fatal Woman type (with its perspective in time and space and its Gioconda smile) to such an extent that, during the years round about 1880, it became the fashion among the *allumeuses* in certain circles in Paris to affect the enigmatic smile. The face of the Principessa di Belgiojoso, as described in the *Confessions* of Arsène Houssaye,[74] was 'un pur chef d'œuvre de Joconde inassouvie'. The Fatal Woman in *Le Vice suprême*, by Péladan (1884), who was partly modelled on the Principessa di Belgiojoso, adopted the habit of cutting short a declaration of love with 'un sourire à la Lise'; and Lorrain, evoking memories of those times in *Monsieur de Phocas*, speaks of the 'vices d'enseigne' employed by courtesans 'pour amorcer le client', and exclaims:

'Dire que j'ai aimé, moi aussi, ces petites bêtes malfaisantes, ces fausses *Primavera*, ces *Joconde* au rabais des ateliers de peintres et de brasseries d'esthètes, ces fleurs en fil d'archal de Montparnasse et de Levallois-Perret!'

The following composition, supposed to be translated from the Provençal and put into the mouth of one of the

characters in *Le Vice suprême*, brings out all the elements
of the *cliché*:

RITTRATTO MULIEBRE

I. Plus pâle que l'aube d'hiver, plus blanche que la cire des
     cierges,
Ses deux mains ramenées sur sa poitrine plate,
Elle se tient très droite dans sa robe, rouge
Du sang des cœurs qui sont morts à saigner pour elle.
La perversité niche aux coins de sa bouche;
Ses sourires sont empennés de dédain;
Dans ses yeux pers, diamants céruléens
Qui fixent des lointaines chimères,
Sa pensée file le rouet des impossibilités.

II.
Ils sont morts damnés; elle est restée pâle,
Les lèvres fermées sur son secret.
L'Amour qui n'est que l'amour, la vertu dans le crime,
Elle n'en a pas voulu.
César Borgia et Saint-François d'Assise en un, elle eût aimé;
Mais le monstre n'est pas venu et sa pensée a continué
A filer le rouet des impossibilités.

III. Dans l'attente du Bien-Aimé, elle n'a point eu d'amants.
Elle l'eût pressé, étouffé peut-être, sur sa poitrine plate.
La grenade eût fleuri à ses joues, sa lèvre se fût ouverte au
     baiser,
Si Saint Michel eût pu être aussi Satan, si Satan eût été Saint
     Michel.
Léonard, le maître subtil, l'a éternisée sur ce panneau. . . .

Fidèle à ton vice monstrueux, O Fille du Vinci, Muse
Dépravante de l'esthétique du mal, ton sourire peut s'effacer
     sur la toile,
Il est facsimilé dans mon cœur. . . .

Chimère, ta vue m'altère de cette soif du Beau Mal,
Que tu est morte sans savoir.
Ô sœur de la Joconde, ô sphinx pervers, je t'aime!

This lyrical effusion is thus commented upon by another
character in the novel:

'C'est d'un sentiment moderne exquis et raffiné. On dirait du
Pétrarque d'une poésie dont Baudelaire serait le Dante.'

But I do not intend to trace here the history of the Gioconda smile, down to Aldous Huxley's parody of it ('The Joconda Smile' in *Mortal Coils*);[75] more curious, perhaps, is the change of appearance which the Fatal Woman underwent in a poem by Wilde, *The Sphinx* (published in 1894 in an *édition de luxe* with decorations by Charles Ricketts).

22. As always—and this is especially true of his poetry —Wilde irresistibly reminds one of his sources.[76]

The Sphinx. . . . The poet's elegant, languid sphinx is a cat, half woman, half animal—see the *Fleurs du Mal*, where the cat is a *senhal* of the black Venus beloved by the poet (*Viens, mon beau chat* . . . and *Dans ma cervelle se promène* . . .). But Wilde inflates his cat to the proportions of Cleopatra:

A thousand weary centuries are thine . . .
But you can read the Hieroglyphs on the great sandstone obelisks,
And you have talked with Basilisks, and you have looked on Hippogriffs.
O tell me, were you standing by when Isis to Osiris knelt?
And did you watch the Egyptian melt her union for Antony?. . .
And did you mark the Cyprian kiss white Adon on his catafalque?
. . . Sing me all your memories!
Sing to me of the Jewish maid who wandered with the holy child.

.   .   .   .

Sing to me of that odorous green eve when couching by the marge
You heard from Adrian's gilded barge the laughter of Antinous.

.   .   .   .

The ivory body of that rare young slave with his pomegranate mouth!

.   .   .   .

Who were your lovers? . . .

Then we plunge all at once right into the middle of *Dolores*:

. . . Who were they who wrestled for you in the dust?
Which was the vessel of your lust? What Leman had you, every day?
Did giant Lizards come and crouch before you on the reedy banks?
Did Gryphons with great metal flanks leap on you in your trampled couch?
Did monstrous hippopotami come sidling towards you in the mist?

Here the model is Swinburne's *Cleopatra*, but there is

no point in pursuing the recital of the Sphinx's amorous couplings with dragons, with chimaeras, and finally with Leviathan, Behemoth and Tragelaphos of the ivory horns. . . . Wilde ransacks the dictionary for fabulous monsters. But now we come to the point—the Gioconda smile:

How subtle-secret is your smile! Did you love none then? Nay, I know
Great Ammon was your bedfellow! . . .
With blood of goats and blood of steers you taught him monstrous miracles.
White Ammon was your bedfellow! Your chamber was the steaming Nile,
And with your curved archaic smile you watched his passion come and go.

Wilde cannot resist endowing Ammon with eyes so blue that 'The seas could not insapphirine the perfect azure of his eyes'; no more can he resist, when he has named a precious stone, naming several others also, in the manner of the thorough aesthete, and bringing in Oriental merchants as well (Pater's Gioconda, too, had trafficked with Eastern merchants). Then comes the inevitable hymn to Paganism, with its Keats-like exclamation: 'Away to Egypt!'

Away to Egypt! Have no fear. Only one God has ever died.
Only one God has let his side be wounded by a soldier's spear.
But these, thy lovers, are not dead. . . .

He invites the Sphinx-cat, if she is weary of all the dead deities whom he has so cunningly passed in review, to take as her lover a lion, or a tiger, and to strike him with her jasper claws or crush him against her agate breasts.

Why are you tarrying? Get hence! . . .

. . . .

Your pulse makes poisonous melodies, and your black throat is like the hole
Left by some torch or burning coal on Saracenic tapestries.

. . . .

What snake-tressed fury fresh from Hell, with uncouth gestures and unclean,
Stole from the poppy-drowsy queen and led you to a student's cell?

Having begun with reminiscences of Baudelaire's *Chat*,

this poetical medley concludes with the accents of Poe's *Raven*:

What songless tongueless ghost of sin crept through the curtains of
    the night,
And saw my taper burning bright, and knocked, and bade you
    enter in?

Observe how the rhythm resembles that of *The Raven*:

Get hence, you loathsome mystery! Hideous animal, get hence!
You wake in me each bestial sense . . .
False Sphinx! False Sphinx! . . . leave me to my crucifix,
Whose pallid burden, sick with pain, watches the world with
    wearied eyes,
And weeps for every soul that dies, and weeps for every soul in vain.

Wilde gives a similar picture of the eternal prostitute in *The New Helen*:

> Where hast thou been since round the walls of Troy
> The sons of God fought in that great emprise?
> Why dost thou walk our common earth again?

This poem is, as usual, a tissue of reminiscences (Keats, Swinburne, &c.).

This would be an opportune moment to introduce Wilde's incarnation of the Fatal Woman—Salome. But before leaving the subject of Swinburne we must observe how his particular type of Fatal Woman served as a model to D'Annunzio.

23. There is a story that, when the first of D'Annunzio's plagiarisms came to light, Enrico Nencioni rebuked his young friend for resorting to such expedients, as being unworthy of a great poet. I do not know whether the title of 'Rhapsody' is in itself a justification for the introduction of non-original themes, but it is certain that Nencioni's own *Rapsodia Lirica*, published in the April–June 1896 number of the *Convito* (Book VIII), is a frank mixture of passages from Swinburne. And since the subject of this *Rapsodia* is the synthetic Fatal Woman whose portrait I have been gradually unfolding, let us see what is Nencioni's idea of her.

The starting-point of the poem is supplied by Edgar Poe, as the author himself indicates, but after a few rather discursive bars he timidly introduces Swinburnian material.

The worthy Nencioni does not risk entering upon an *excursus* of the former incarnations of the Fatal Woman without resorting to the feeblest of all expedients, the dream. His guide here must have been chapter xix of Heine's *Atta Troll* (of which Nencioni imitates the metre), where, from the witch Uraka's window, are seen coming forth three famous beauties, Diana, the fairy Abunde, and Salome. The ingenuous Italian treats Swinburne's scabrous poety in a *bourgeois* fashion, and in making it thus respectable takes away from it all virulence and transforms the synthesis of voluptuousness into a provincial portrait gallery of famous female sinners, as some worthy writer of the seventeenth century might have done. 'When sacred night stretches her veil over the Earth', says Nencioni (then he slips in an echo of Shelley's *Summer Evening Churchyard*: 'like thick, dusky hair over a pale face'), 'then in a dream I see thy face, thy hair, thine eyes, and with the dream appear to me lovely forms of antique beauty.'

He sees Hesione. Swinburne, in *The Masque of Queen Bersabe*, had said that the body of Hesione was 'as fire that shone'; Nencioni, however, contents himself with saying that she is 'white' and has 'snowy feet'. Swinburne had said that Hesione had 'the summer in her hair', and that 'all the pale gold autumn air—Was as the habit of her sense'; Nencioni says, 'the golden hair which covers thee all, like a mantle of gold'.

In the next verse Nencioni attaches himself to the more familiar Carducci: Helen, 'the perfect beauty, smiles to Homer and to Goethe'—one is left to imagine—with the convivial cheerfulness so typical of Carducci. Then he continues with a shy hint at Swinburne's sadistic Phaedra —who was destined to receive less summary treatment at the hands of D'Annunzio—giving her nevertheless the lines that Swinburne gives to Myrrha in the *Masque*: 'As tears upon the eyes, as fire upon dry logs, so clinging sin feeds upon her divine form; her blood burns, the hurricane convulses it like the waves.'

> As tears on eyes, as fire on wood,
> Sin fed upon my breath and blood,
> Sin made my breasts subside and swell

The poet looks next at Semiramis, who has 'rough,
thick hair . . . like that of a Barbary mare' (*Laus Veneris*,
'her hair most thick . . . deep in the mane . . . like a steed');
at Faustina, '. . . with temples large and burning, a mouth
athirst and hungering and dumb, like the grave's mouth',
just as Swinburne had described not Faustina, but Messalina in the *Masque*;[77] however, Nencioni goes back to
Faustine for his next verse, on the 'dying gladiator'. Then
he describes Sappho, who, however, is not made to change
habit with any other of the Swinburnian ladies: 'Her face
is pale like dying fire; but love beats in her veins like hot
wine. Sappho sings—intolerable desire consumes her.'

> The intolerable infinite desire
> Made my face pale like faded fire.
>
> .   .   .   .   .   .
>
> My blood was hot wan wine of love,
> And my song's sound the sound thereof . . .

But the dream ends: 'Thou appearest—and the visions
all vanish—and thy black Oriental fairy-eyes shine alone
amid the darkness.'

The visions vanish, but not the reminiscences: *Anactoria*,
Phaedra . . ., to finish, in the fifth part, with *The Garden
of Proserpine*. I do not insist on comparisons, and merely
remark that familiarity with the sinister creatures of Swinburne did not prevent Nencioni ('Omnia munda mundis'!)
from concluding with the most blandly Pre-Raphaelite
image: 'Over thy head the angels flutter, beneath thy feet
twinkle the stars.'

I should like to record here the remark of Brie,[78] a
foreigner who cannot be suspected of partiality: 'In Italy
the unsophisticated attitude of the national character towards life and towards the world of the senses was not
naturally receptive of such tendencies as *ennui* and exoticism.' An objection might perhaps be made to this remark
on the grounds of the long-established reputation of the
Italians for extreme refinement in erotic invention,[79] so it
must be supposed that all this great quantity of sensual
effervescence found its outlet in the strictly practical field,
without ever degenerating into cold and morbid indulgence (except in extremely rare cases—among which must

be counted that of F. D. Guerrazzi, whose delight in dwelling upon spectacles of horror was by no means matched with a corresponding artistic skill in describing them).[80] In this sense it is possible to say that the Italian attitude to the world of the senses continued to be genuine and instinctive, even in spite of freedom of morals.

The case of the worthy Nencioni may serve as an illustration: the morbid themes of Swinburne become, in his hands, innocuous, even insipid. In Angelo Conti also, the aesthete who served D'Annunzio as model for Daniele Glàuro in *Il Fuoco*, the signs of decadence are barely visible. An admirer of Schopenhauer, of Wagner, and of Pater, in his study on Giorgione (1894) he sees what he calls the 'tristezza della voluttà' in Giorgione's work: he describes him as 'il poeta del tormento e della bizzarria entro cui si nasconde lo spasimo' ('the poet of anguish and of strangeness in which pain is hidden'.) But these are only passing hints; his interpretation of the smile of the Gioconda (p. 56 of the study already quoted) is enough to show how little he was affected by Decadent influences:

'It is the likeness of a smile which transcends all other expressions of the human smile. It is a movement, a light, which passes from the woman's lips and eyes into the winding rivers of the landscape, broadening and invading the whole landscape and becoming the smile of Nature herself. The miracle of a perfect harmony between man and things is accomplished.'

It was quite otherwise in the case of D'Annunzio, who, let it be said at once, was the first to introduce the Italians to the Anglo-French Byzantium of the end of the century.[81]

24. D'Annunzio (in the *Mattino* of January 18th–19th, 1893, and later in the *Poema Paradisiaco*, in the same year) was the first to bring to the notice of Italian readers the Fatal Woman who united in herself the whole sensual experience of the world—Pamphila, reincarnation of Helen and Sappho:

'Possessed by all men, from the beggar to the lord, covered with immemorial kisses, thy last descendant, O Helen, still surrounded with ancient mystery. . . .

'This is the woman I shall love. Upon her impure limbs I shall gather all earthly desire, I shall know all the love of the world; in her eyes I shall pursue shadows of things obscure; beneath her arid breast I shall hear the deep beat of her heart.

'I shall kiss her hands, her hands of ripe experience . . . in whose musical fingers, perhaps, a lyre sounded in ancient times among the breezes of Lesbos over her native Aegean, where the rose-groves of Mytilene, dear to the secret maid-companions of violet-haired Sappho, wafted their scent. . . .

'. . . I shall learn all the sweetest and most ardent names which, in sigh or cry, she has given to a thousand lovers; I shall drink, drop by drop, all the perfumes of the most distant forests, distilled in her liquid breath. . . .'

A comparison of the whole poem with the passages of Flaubert already quoted (pp. 210 et seq.) will prove the paternity of this synthetic courtesan of D'Annunzio, who used the *Tentation de Saint Antoine* as a perennial source of inspiration. Thovez[82] noticed certain analogies with the passage from *Novembre* I have mentioned, which was published in 1886 in *Par les champs et par les grèves*. But it was again the passage from the *Tentation* on Hélène-Ennoia that suggested to D'Annunzio the lines on the old age of Helen in the first book of *Le Laudi*. It was from a similar point of view that Stelio Effrena felt the charm of La Foscarina, in *Il Fuoco*:[83]

'And a heavy sadness urged him into the last embrace of the lonely, wandering woman, who seemed to him to carry in herself, mute and gathered into the folds of her garments, the frenzy of distant crowds in whose dense bestiality she had stirred the divine lightning-flash of art, with a cry of passion, a pang of pain, or the silence of death; an impure yearning forced him towards this experienced, desperate woman, in whom he believed he could trace the marks of all pleasures and all pain, towards this body no longer young, softened by every caress, but still, to him, unknown.'

In the autumn of 1893 there appeared in the *Mattino* the cycle of sonnets on Adulteresses, which was afterwards included in the *Intermezzo* of 1894. The poetry of the seventeenth and eighteenth centuries affords numerous examples of similar sonnet-cycles, but others had been written in more recent times in France, by Théodore de Banville (in *Les Exilés*, 1867, and *Les Princesses*, 1874). Banville's procession of wanton queens is like that in the

Masque of Queen Bersabe, except that the 'Parnassien', instead of making his princesses speak in the first person, describes them at the culminating moment of their careers, as in the sonnet-pictures of the eighteenth-century writers. D'Annunzio does the same thing with his adulteresses. The spirit of these evocations is clearly expressed in Banville's introductory sonnet. When the poet recalls the dead to life

> On revoit dans un riche et fabuleux décor
> Des meurtres, des amours, des lèvres ingénues,
> Des vêtements ouverts montrant des jambes nues,
> Du sang et de la pourpre et des agrafes d'or.
>
> . . . .
>
> Et leurs lèvres s'ouvrir comme des fleurs sanglantes.

D'Annunzio had already given a prose portrait of a cruel, fatal woman in the *Trionfo della Morte* (1894; the first edition appeared in the *Tribuna Illustrata* in 1890, with the title of *L'Invincibile*). Giorgio Aurispa, an intellectual who represents the phenomenon of decayed will-power, is contrasted with Ippolita Sanzio, who represents obstinate sexual will-power becoming a sort of carnal doom:

' "Cruelty lurks hidden in her love", he thought. "There is something destructive in her, which becomes the more evident the more violent her orgasm. . . ." And he saw again in memory the terrific, almost Gorgon-like vision of her as she had often appeared to him, when, convulsed by a spasm or inert in final exhaustion, he had looked at her through half-closed eyelids.'[84]

At one moment the figure of the woman becomes gigantic, and attains an almost mythological scale: there are united in her 'the sovran virtues of the women who are destined to rule the world with the scourge of their impure beauty':[85]

'All this time she had not moved. This prolonged immobility in one attitude, which sometimes took on the appearance of a trance and became almost terrifying, was not unusual in her. In this state she no longer wore a youthful, merciful aspect such as she showed towards plants and animals, but the aspect of a silent, unconquerable being in whom is concentrated the whole strength of the passion of love, which isolates, excludes, and destroys. The three divine qualities of her beauty—her forehead, her eyes, her mouth—had perhaps never attained to such a degree of intensity in their symbolic expression of the very principle of eternal feminine fascination. The calm night seemed to favour this sublimation of her form, releasing her true, ideal essence and allowing her lover a complete perception of her, with an acuteness not of eye but of thought. The summer night, laden with moonlight and with all dreams, with stars pale or invisible and with the most melodious voices of the sea, seemed the natural background for this supreme figure. Just as a shadow sometimes enlarges out of all proportion the body which produces it, so, against this infinite background, the fatality of love made the figure of Ippolita taller and more tragic in the eyes of the man who watched, and in whom the power of prescience became every moment more lucid and more terrible.'[86]

On another occasion Ippolita seems no more than a brutal love-machine, like Swinburne's Faustine; she also is 'the pale, voracious Roman, unexcelled in the art of breaking the loins of men'.[87]

> You seem a thing that hinges hold,
>   A love-machine
> With clockwork joints of supple gold—
>   No more, Faustine.

'Her very mouth, her elastic, sinuous mouth, at whose contact her lover had so often felt a kind of instinctive, undefinable terror, now seemed deprived of its spell and to be reduced to the physical aspect of a common brute organ with which even the idea of a kiss was associated as a mechanical action devoid of all nobility.'[88]

Introspection is a painful pleasure to Giorgio Aurispa; his whole being yearns for death ('Death, in fact, attracts me'); in his supreme disgust at the woman, the Enemy, he kills both her and himself. Reading between the lines of the novel one can see that the reason devised by Giorgio Aurispa for getting rid of the woman—that she was the obstacle to his spiritual life—is only a noble and avowable excuse for a more profound reason, the same that drove Giorgio to torment himself—his deep-seated, instinctive sadism. One does not understand, when one comes upon explanations such as the following, how the author can himself have failed to realize the motive of the final catastrophe:

'Hereditary lust burst forth once more, with invincible fury, in this delicate lover who liked to call his mistress his sister and who was greedy for spiritual communion.'[89]

And

' "How her beauty becomes spiritualized in sickness and in weakness!" thought Giorgio. "I like her better when she is thus broken. I recognize the unknown woman who passed by me that February evening, the woman *without a drop of blood in her veins*. I think that in death she will attain to the supreme expression of her beauty." '[90]

25. Andrea Sperelli, the protagonist of *Il Piacere*, professed the greatest horror for sadism, but was he honest with himself? Is not the Chimaera, in his fictitious *Re di Cipro*, made to evoke the typically Flaubertian combination of 'slaughter-lust'?

'Dost thou wish to fight? to kill? to see rivers of blood? great heaps of gold? herds of captive women? slaves? and other, still other spoils? Dost thou wish to bring marble to life? to build a temple? to compose an immortal Hymn? Dost thou wish (hear me, young man, hear me!) dost thou wish to love divinely?'

Even if Sperelli was not honest with himself, this at any rate is not true of Tullio Hermil in *L'Innocente* (1891–1892):

'Inquisitive and perverse, it seemed to me that the feeble life of the convalescent woman burned and melted beneath my kiss; and I thought that this voluptuousness had almost a flavour of incest. "What if she were to die of it?" I thought. Certain words of the surgeon came back to my memory, with sinister meaning. And, with the cruelty which lies concealed in all sensual men, the danger did not frighten, but attracted, me. I lingered over the examination of my feelings with a sort of bitter complacency, mingled with disgust, such as I brought to the analysis of all interior manifestations which seemed to me to furnish a proof of the fundamental wickedness of humanity. "Why has man in his nature this horrible faculty of rejoicing more keenly when he is conscious of doing harm to the being from whom he derives his happiness? Why is there the germ of this most execrable sadistic perversion in every man who loves and desires?" '[91]

D'Annunzio, at any rate, made his own attitude clearer and clearer to his readers. And the influence of Swinburne's *Poems and Ballads* helped to hasten this explanation. But the 'libido' of D'Annunzio has been adequately studied by Borgese, and later by Flora,[92] so that a few remarks will be sufficient here.

It must be observed, to begin with, how transparent the content of *La Gioconda* (1899) becomes when one reads one particular page of *Il Trionfo della Morte* and two stanzas of the poem *Le Mani* (in *Poema Paradisiaco*, from the *Corriere di Napoli* of November 29th–30th, 1891). This page of *Il Trionfo della Morte* describes the moment when Giorgio Aurispa imagines he is chopping off the hands of Ippolita at the wrists:

'He placed the two wrists side by side and again made the movement of chopping them through at one stroke. The image rose up in his mind as vivid as if it were real.—On the marble threshold of a door full of shadow and expectancy appeared the woman who was destined to die, holding out her bare arms, at the extremities of which throbbed two red fountains gushing from the severed veins of her wrists,' &c.[93]

In the poem we read:

'Other (or perhaps the same?) alabaster hands, but stronger than a snake's coil, inspired me with jealous fury, with mad anger; and I longed to cut them off. (In a dream stands, enticing, the mutilated woman. In a dream, erect and motionless, lives the terrible woman with the severed hands. And beside her two pools are red with blood, and within them are her hands, still living, but unstained by a single drop.)'

It is obvious that D'Annunzio, in this poem, derives from Maeterlinck, but in the Belgian poet's *Attouchements* (in *Serres chaudes*)[94] the following is the only hint of blood to be found, and that an extremely innocent one:

Mais ayez pitié des mains froides!
Je vois un cœur saigner sous des côtes de glace!

This, however, was enough to make D'Annunzio insert yet another reminiscence into his poem.[95] It is not for nothing that, in the fourth act of *La Gioconda*, the poem that La Sirenella sings to the mutilated heroine is the translation of a Swinburne ballad, *The King's Daughter*. One might almost say that the very smell of blood was enough to call up the presence of the Divine Marquis's great poet-disciple.

Nevertheless D'Annunzio seemed determined not to

look closely into the morbid nature of his inspiration; hence the equivocal flavour of his books and the bewilderment of the public. Leonardo in *La Città Morta* (1898), who (like Umbelino who killed Pantea, in *Le Vergini delle Rocce*)[96] killed his own sister for whom he had conceived an incestuous passion, and then declared himself to be 'pure'—he also is a victim of the same pitiful illusion as Giorgio Aurispa, and his last speech, from beginning to end, is a disagreeable lie which he tells to himself. Swinburne may sound shameless, but not false; D'Annunzio, through lack of sincerity towards himself, sounds hopelessly false.

Both Tullio Hermil and Giorgio Aurispa have intercourse with women who are scarcely convalescent from diseases of the womb. Elena gives herself to Sperelli when she is ill. In Ippolita Giorgio possesses an epileptic, and Paolo Tarsis, in Isabella Inghirami, a lunatic.[97] Sterility also, a characteristic of D'Annunzio's women, acts as a sadistic stimulus. 'She is sterile. Her womb is accursed. . . . The uselessness of her love seemed to him a *monstrous transgression* against the supreme law' (*Trionfo della Morte*, p. 361). Giorgio Aurispa is especially attracted by the bodily defects of Ippolita: 'The most vulgar features had an irritating attraction for him' (p. 360). Stelio Effrena is excited by the *faisandage* of La Foscarina. A 'transgression' from the normal, in fact, seems to be a *sine qua non* of D'Annunzio's love stories.

In the *Sogno d'un Mattino di Primavera* (1897) a woman who has held her murdered lover a whole night in her arms sees herself, in her madness, perpetually covered with his blood; in the *Sogno d'un Tramonto d'Autunno* (1898) the harlot Pantea (whom we shall mention again shortly) is burnt alive through an incantation placed upon her by her rival (this has some similarity to Rossetti's *Sister Helen*) together with her Bucentoro, while all round her men are fighting to the death. D'Annunzio dwells with especial delight upon this idea of a woman burnt alive, as for instance in *La Figlia di Iorio* and in *La Nave*. A variant of the woman burnt alive is La Pisanella, the harlot suffocated beneath a heap of roses. There is also the description

of the crime of the shepherd of Fondi, who burned alive
the woman whom he loved, in *Forse che sì*. In this last case
the author's *delectatio morbosa* is doubled—both at the
horror of the deed and at the contamination which its recital brings upon the young girls who are listening to it.

'The girls trembled at this savage vision of implacable love. . . .
Each thought she felt a rough hand laid upon her delicate body,
each became a prey and a victim. And they palpitated, offering
themselves to the passion which was to devastate them.'⁹⁸

In *La Gloria* (1899) a Fatal Woman 'capable of setting
the world on fire', the last Comnena, 'pale, impure, wicked,
voracious, consumed with pride, full of revenge, greedy
for power and gold', a figure that might have been taken
bodily from Péladan's *Décadence latine*, brings to perdition all the men who approach her, and ends by bestow-
ing death, together with her last kiss, upon the cowardly
Ruggero Flamma. A frenzied, murderous virgin, reincarnation of Electra, appears in *Il Ferro*. The death of two
incestuous lovers, which is the theme of *Francesca*, is presented in the manner of a genuine algolagnic outburst in
La Parisina: 'The two heads shall be upon the same block,
beneath the same axe, and the two fountains of blood shall
make but one pool.'⁹⁹

In *Le Martyre de Saint Sébastien* the delights of martyrdom are expressed with unambiguous accents, nor is there
much difference between these accents and those of the
prisoners shot with arrows by Basiliola. The stage direction of *La Nave* runs: 'She hearkens to these madmen,
because she is now totally swayed by a longing to look
upon bloodshed, a longing which torments the obscure
bestial nature of human females.'

This feeling, which D'Annunzio describes in *La Nave*
as the 'contagio della frenesia funebre' ('contagion of
funereal frenzy'), surely also inspired the pages of *Gli
Idolatri* (*Nouvelle del Pescara*), and the scenario of *Cabiria*,
and many passages which deal with war. And did not the
poet also write apropos of *La Gloria*: 'There is always
something carnal, something resembling carnal violence,
a mixture of cruelty and intoxication, which accompanies
the act of generation of my brain'?

Here at any rate he seems to be honest with himself. But again in 1913 (*La Leda senza Cigno*)—that is, after he had already rivalled even Swinburne in evocations of morbid sensuality, both in plays and novels—we again see D'Annunzio recoiling, as though from something alien to him, from a spectacle of 'ignominious sensuality' like that offered by the Marquis of Mount Edgcumbe to Andrea Sperelli. Such a lack of coherence and clear-sightedness makes one think of the case of Baudelaire's Mademoiselle Bistouri.

26. Plagiarism means implicit adherence and acceptance. D'Annunzio, by infusing into his work Swinburne's type of 'criminal sensuality', admitted as a consequence an affinity with Swinburne and recognized himself in him, as he recognized himself also in Nietzsche—another of Sade's disciples—and in Wagner;[100] somehow he accepted a responsibility.

The Fatal Woman as imagined by Swinburne became grafted on to D'Annunzio's own intuition and completed it; and all that a critic can do is to deplore the suppleness of the latter's mind—a suppleness which caused him to recognize an adequate rendering of his own feelings in the writings of others, when, with a little more concentration, he might have been more original. One may agree with the following remark of Gargiulo,[101] provided one bears in mind that its scope is limited by D'Annunzio's plagiarism in the case in question:

'There appears, in the *Sogno d'un Tramonto d'Autunno*, a female character, Pantea, who might well be called a "superwoman". Now Ippolita Sanzio, protagonist of *Il Trionfo della Morte*, assumes with a certain success, towards the end of the novel, the character of the woman who is simply and solely Woman, beautiful, instinctive, perverse, fascinating. Pantea is the translation of Ippolita into a superhuman world: she is the "superwoman", absolute beauty, absolute instinct, absolute perverseness, absolute charm. . . . One sees with a sense of pain, in the poet's recent productions, what has become of certain intuitions of psychological reality of a sensual description, which, in part at all events, he had achieved a long time before.'

This 'dominant image of a superwoman, which originates

in a frenzied artificiality and abstraction', as Gargiulo calls it, is derived from the First Series of *Poems and Ballads*; but in the *Sogno d'un Tramonto d'Autunno* nothing but its vague outline is to be seen, nor can much more be discerned of the young lover than a vague outline, though the small amount visible is enough to show his resemblance to the type of man we have already met in Swinburne:

'And she touched lightly with her naked feet and with the winglets upon them the full goblets and the young man's hair; and at last she placed her heel upon his temple and held it thus pressed down; then he closed his eyes, and truly he was as pale as the linen cloth.'

We have already seen in Swinburne[102] what such an act signifies. We may add to the passages from an unpublished work of Swinburne already quoted the following passage from *The Triumph of Time* in *Poems and Ballads*:

But if we had loved each other—O sweet,
Had you felt, lying under the palms of your feet,
The heart of my heart, beating harder with pleasure
To feel you tread it to dust and death . . .

The speeches of the Dogaressa Gradeniga, also, are a tissue of passages from *Phaedra*, *Laus Veneris*, *Anactoria*, *Dolores*, *Hesperia*, *The Masque of Queen Bersabe*, *At Eleusis*. D'Annunzio used the French version by G. Mourey, which came out in Paris in 1891, as is proved by certain exactly parallel expressions. For example, where Swinburne has 'a manifold flower', D'Annunzio puts 'un fiore numeroso', following Mourey ('une fleur nombreuse'). In another place, in *La Nave* (p. 84), in the stage direction, which is taken from *Aholibah* (*Poems and Ballads*), we read: 'on the broad border of whose garment the art of the Greek embroiderer has wrought the transfiguration of plants and animals as in a visible dream'. Swinburne has:

The cunning of embroiderers
That sew the pillow to the sleeve,
And likeness of all things that *live*.

and further on:

All these had on thy garments wrought
The shape of beasts and creeping things.

Owing to a misprint Mourey's version reads as follows
(p. 336): 'la semblance de tous les êtres qui *rêvent*'.
Hence D'Annunzio's 'visible dream'.[103] Although D'Annunzio had already been introduced to the English poet's
work through his friend Nencioni, he was unable to make
use of it until it became accessible to him in the French
translation.

27. The 'superwoman', of whom we caught only a
distant glimpse in *Sogno d'un Tramonto d'Autunno*, steps
into the limelight in *La Gloria*, *La Nave*, and *Fedra*. This
is how La Comnena, last descendant of the Byzantine
Emperors, is described by her victims:

'Thou wast trailed like a bait through all the sloughs of vice;
thou wast steeped in the foam of all corruptions; there was nothing
vile or desperate that thou didst not know. . . . Centuries of pomp,
of perfidy and plunder have gone to thy making, thou blood of
traitors and usurpers, murderous offspring. Wherever thou didst
touch, wherever thy fiendish flesh clung, there was destined to be
a wound without hope of healing. Thou wast damnation, torture,
certain perdition. . . . She has longed to satiate her ancient soul
with the crimes of vanished ages. . . .'[104]

La Comnena is the synthetic courtesan of Anglo-
French importation. It is worthy of remark that, just as
the Byronic hero's origin was often said to be mysterious
and extremely noble, so, too, was the origin of the Fatal
Woman. And, like the Byronic superman, the superwoman also assumes an attitude of defiance to society.
Well might all these Fatal Women repeat, with Swinburne's Phaedra:

> Man, what have I to do with shame or thee?
> I am not of one counsel with the gods.
> I am their kin, I have strange blood in me,
> I am not of their likeness nor of thine:
> My veins are mixed, and therefore am I mad,
> Yea therefore chafe and turn on mine own flesh,
> Half of a woman made with half a god.

The adventuress Comnena is descended from the last
Emperor of Trebizond; Basiliola, in *La Nave*, comes of a
more complicated pedigree:

'. . . Storm is above her head. Dost thou see her? dost thou see her attitude as she stands? It seems as though she could trample the world with a metal heel. Surely there is something in her which is eternal and beyond Fate or Death, something which cannot be tamed by man. Think'st thou to have stricken her race? She comes of a different stock. She lived upon the mountains where grow medicinal herbs, in the palaces where panthers roam; with her accursed hand she gave cups of smoking juices to her guests, and, changing their form, shut them into the pigsty. She was Byblis, who ran raging after her brother; she was Myrrha, who issued pregnant from her father's bed; she was Pasiphae who was possessed by the bull, and the adulteress of Greece who stained towers and ships with blood for ten years. She was Delilah, who cut her lover's hair upon her knee and took his strength from him, Jezebel who wallowed her naked shame in the blood of the prophets, Hoglah who bore the brunt of a goat. She knew all incests and the couplings of beasts, the lusts which bleat and low, the deceits which corrupt the seed, the spasms against which the bones cry out. Everywhere she made public her beddings. She placed her couch in the public square and at the head of the street, along the quay and beneath the portico, in the tavern and the camp. Murderers knew her pillow, robbers her coverlet, mercenaries her lewdness. Whence did she come to thee? Didst thou not sniff in her hair odours of barbarians? The sallow Hungarian, the Moor of Numidia, the Hun of the Ister and the Sarmatian of the Tanais, have they not all left their traces upon her?'

It has been remarked[105] that there is a certain likeness between this invective which D'Annunzio put into the mouth of the monk Traba, and a passage of Baronius on Theodora which was transcribed to serve as a preface to an edition of the *Historia Arcana* of Procopius, to which D'Annunzio went for information about the Byzantine court:

'So much evil did this guilty woman do that she might be called a second Eve . . . a new Delilah, who with fraudulent art sought to take Samson's strength from him; another Herodias, thirsting for the blood of holy men. . . . But it is not enough to condemn her by such names, for she surpassed all other women in wickedness. Rather should Hell bestow upon her the name which fable gave to the Furies,' &c.

Probably D'Annunzio had seen this passage (compare 'levar le forze a Sansone' of Baronius with D'Annunzio's 'troncò . . . la forza del chiomato'), but actually it was Pamphila, deriving from Flaubert, and Swinburne's

Phaedra,[106] who were the direct forebears of this harlot of universal experience. Baronius speaks of 'a second Eve', 'a new Delilah', 'another Herodias'; whereas the idea of agelong experience united in one person, of the vampire-woman, is, as we have seen, essentially Romantic. D'Annunzio's effort to draw forth the innermost soul of this type of superwoman results in the very opposite of profundity: what he gives us is mere idle enumeration of the picturesque kind—the menagerie of Circe, the pageant of great female sinners—as showy as film stars—bandits, soldiers, murderers, the sallow Hungarian, the Moor, the Hun, &c.—a scrap-heap of countries and climates, a kaleidoscope which can be twirled round *ad infinitum* and as one best likes. It is just as in Wilde's *Sphinx*. One can recognize, though in a mist of metaphysical exaggeration, the apotheosis of 'eternal feminine charm' which is celebrated in the *Trionfo della Morte*:[107]

'Lo! from the top of my forehead to the toe of my foot I am the music of the stars. The two tides alternate in my breast. The rush of rivers beats against my pulses. The melody of the world dwells in me.'[107A]

Men behave in her presence like the youthful lover of Pantea, like the desperate lovers of Swinburne: they burn with masochistic desire. It will suffice to quote the beginning of Gauro's prayer, in the scene of funereal priapism which is enacted in the Fossa Fuia:

'Come, Basiliola! My breast is bared, my throat uncovered. Come, take the two-edged sword and strike the fatal blow. Strike here, between rib and rib. Plunge the blade in right up to the gold (I am Gauro, he who hates and loves thee), right up to the gold of the hilt (I am the stone-cutter . . .) . . . strike, plunge in the whole blade, right up to the jewels of its handle!'

In this passage. D'Annunzio is merely restoring to the mouth of a man the words which Swinburne had placed in the mouth of a woman—of Phaedra—but which, from what we know of Swinburne's sensual nature, sound much more suitable on the lips of a man:

If he will slay me, baring breast and throat,
I lean toward the stroke with silent mouth
And a great heart. Come, take thy sword and slay;

·   ·   ·   ·   ·   ·   ·

Nay, but be swift with me;
Set thy sword here between the girdle and breast,

. . . .

O whatsoever of godlike names thou be,
By thy chief name I charge thee, thou strong god,
And bid thee slay me. Strike, up to the gold,
Up to the hand-grip of the hilt; strike here;
For I am Cretan of my birth; strike now;
For I am Theseus' wife; stab up to the rims,
I am born daughter to Pasiphae.

Further on, he puts into the mouth of Marco Gratico the expressions of Swinburne's Sappho (*Anactoria*).[108] Marco Gratico, posing as the precursor of the new Italy, kills his brother, in imitation of Romulus: Basiliola is the Fury who spurs on the two rivals to the conflict. In D'Annunzio the Fatal Woman offers power and empire to the man who is fascinated by her: so it is also in *La Gloria*, in *La Nave*, and in *Fedra*. (Similarly, in the *Martyre de Saint Sébastien*, the Emperor tempts the Saint with visions of apotheosis and empire: 'Moi vivant, je te léguerai—l'empire. Tu seras le maître.') With D'Annunzio lust is closely connected with the desire for power: in this also he resembles Flaubert in the *Tentation*.

D'Annunzio, therefore, intensifies the idea of feminine superiority: woman represents the active principle not only in the giving of pleasure, but also in the ruling of the world. The female is aggressive, the male vacillating.[109] Apart from this accentuation of contrast, D'Annunzio's *Fedra* presents nothing new when compared with Swinburne's *Phaedra*; it is simply an amplified paraphrase of it, decorated with the usual garland of expressions gathered, here and there, from *Poems and Ballads*. So, for example, when D'Annunzio causes Fedra to say (Act III), 'Sad love turned to ambiguous frenzy, which tries to wrest a rag of pleasure from between the teeth of guilt', he is merely echoing the line from the poem *In the Orchard*:

Pluck thy red pleasure from the teeth of pain.

28. In concluding these remarks on D'Annunzio we may observe that a complete documentation of all the well-known manifestations of sadism is to be found in his work,

from incest and sacrilege (for which, see the corresponding chapters of Flora's book)[110] to the apologia of crime as the fundamental principle of all spiritual exaltation.

Among D'Annunzio's characters Isabella Inghirami, in *Forse che sì forse che no*, is the most obviously sadistic—and that in a novel which is completely transfused with sadism:[111] and so the duty of theorizing on the subject naturally falls to her. She reflects as follows on the painful joys of incest:

'The love that I love is that which is never tired with repeating: Hurt me more, hurt me still more. . . . The crime of which you accuse me [incest with her brother], I have committed; and I do not wish to excuse myself. I have committed it for love of love, because it is not true that the perfection of love lies in the joining of two persons; and this men know but dare not confess. Love, like all divine powers, is not truly exalted except in a trinity.[112] This, in me, is not a perverse doctrine, it is not a game of deceit, but a truth testified by martyrdom and by the most painful shedding of my heart's blood. Such love disdains happiness for an unknown but infinitely higher good, towards which the soul aspires, charmed continually by the purest of all kinds of pain, the pain of despair, whereas an ordinary pair of lovers submits to the yoke and is weighed down always by it, and bent by it to the dust or the mud, and controlled, inevitably perhaps, by the miserly ploughman. Ah, when at last will the lover be no longer a stupid enemy, but a thoughtful, wanton brother? I know, I know: you will never be able to understand. It is easier for you to touch the stars in flight than to draw near to my mystery. No word, no tear will ever avail to persuade you that I yielded, not to ugly vice, but to the divine sense of suffering which I bear within me. I have neither sought nor given pleasure; but in my trembling hand I have taken another trembling hand, to descend in search of the bottom of the abyss, perhaps of the subterranean temple. I have accomplished not an act of the flesh, but an act of sad initiation. And for you too, silent one who does not speak except to offend or to rave, for you too I represent knowledge: I do not represent happiness or misfortune, but stern knowledge. . . . Nothing is certain except cruelty and the hunger of the heart, and blood and tears, and the end of all things; and yet one does not know when is the time of weeping. But perhaps there is still some more remote pain to be discovered. . . . Hurt me again, my sweet love, hurt me still more until you resemble me; because there is nothing in which we can resemble each other except in cruelty, but you cannot be my equal in enduring it.'[113]

The 'subterranean temple' which is alluded to in this passage is the same which is spoken of in Swinburne's *Dolores*, in which the Black Mass is celebrated. Sade, at least, was never ambiguous, so that, in comparing D'Annunzio with him, one can repeat, with a change of names (reading: D'Annunzio, instead of: G. Sand), the opinion of Baudelaire which has already been quoted—that is, that with D'Annunzio satanism has gained ground, that the evil which is recognized as evil, and therefore as ugliness, is more easily cured than the evil which is ignorant of itself and seeks to cloak itself in mystical heroism and beauty; and that therefore, from the moral and Christian point of view, D'Annunzio is inferior to Sade.[114] It is true that Sade's criminals also boasted of being divine ('Nous sommes des dieux'), but there was no possibility of doubt as to their psychopathic state.

D'Annunzio speaks of the 'divine agony which cries out with the cry of a beast', he makes Parisina exclaim 'Shame is the light—of my sin', and he asks, in the preface to *La Vita di Cola di Rienzo*: 'Have you ever thought that to become a brute may in a certain sense be a way of becoming a god?' In *Laus Vitae* (lines 1901–4) he comes very near to Sade's and Swinburne's concept of the Divinity: 'O Zeus, greatest of Tyrants, thou art laden with crimes and with outrages, thou art encumbered with spoils, thou alone art lofty Innocence.'[115] Crime is natural, and therefore innocent.

The following is from the long *apologia* that precedes *Più che l'amore*:[116]

'The tragedy interprets with unusual boldness the myth of Prometheus—the necessity of crime which weighs upon the man who is intent on raising himself to the condition of a Titan; it confers a kind of savage and pathetic ardour both upon the reiterated efforts of each single will to reach the universal, and upon the mad desire to break the shell of the individual and to feel oneself as the unique essence of the Universe.'

This is the exact description of the process illustrated in Swinburne's *Anactoria*: sadism, 'abolition of obstacles', revolt against the Divinity, and, finally, 'Pan-like intoxication' (see the passage in *Anactoria*: 'Like me shall be the shuddering calm of night', &c.). It has been aptly observed[117] that the Promethean attitude is characteristic of sadists—think of Byron, of Swinburne, and of the satanics in general[118]—and the 'Pan-like' inspiration is no less characteristic. Certainly a comparison between Flaubert, Swinburne, and D'Annunzio would lead to the same conclusion, that sensuality in their cases gets clarified into 'Pan-like' feeling and is, in a way, 'rapita fuor de' sensi' ('dragged free of the senses').[119] All the sea-poetry of Swinburne and the entire book of *Alcione* are illustrations of this final passage of the *Tentation*:

'Je voudrais . . . me diviser partout, être en tout, m'émaner avec les odeurs, me développer comme les plantes, couler comme l'eau, vibrer comme le son, briller comme la lumière, me blottir sur toutes les formes, pénétrer chaque atome, descendre jusqu'au fond de la matière, — être la matière!'

29. Isabella Inghirami, nevertheless, does not, like Anactoria, go through all the stages of the process we have described, and she finishes in a lunatic asylum. With her we are no longer on the mythical plane of women such as Pamphila, Pantea, Fedra, or Basiliola, but are faced with a type of Fatal Woman which has been studied more or less from life—the type hinted at in Baudelaire's *Mademoiselle Bistouri* and found again in *Les Diaboliques* (1874) by Barbey d'Aurevilly (Madame de Stasseville in *Le Dessous de cartes*), in the *Marquise de Sade* by Rachilde (1886), in Huysmans's *Là-bas* (1891), in *Le Jardin des supplices* by Octave Mirbeau (1898-9)—the type which eventually crystallized round Salome's grisly passion, and still continues to find favour with novelists (it is found again, for example, in the recent *Sous le soleil de Satan*, by Bernanos), the hysterical woman of exasperated desire, in whose hands man becomes a submissive instrument.[120]

The Marquise de Sade[121] talks a little like the courtesan in Flaubert's *Novembre*:

'Elle allait toujours, espérant trouver dans un coin inexploré et moins voulu que les autres la vision de la Rome terrible se disputant les sexes sous des voiles de sang. . . . Où était le mâle effroyable qu'il

lui fallait, à elle, femelle de la race des lionnes?.... Il était ou fini
ou pas commencé.... Du reste, quel plaisir l'assouvirait, maintenant
que les hommes avaient peur de ses morsures? Ah! ils la faisaient
rire avec leur *décadence*, elle était de la décadence de Rome et non
point de celle d'aujourd'hui, elle admettait les joûtes des histrions
dans le cirque, mais ayant, assis près d'elle, sur la pourpre de leurs
blessures, le patricien, son semblable, applaudissant avec des doigts
solides, riant avec des dents claires et vraies.'

She dreams of the 'idéale volupté' which the agony of
one of these 'mâles déchus' of her own period would give
her, and she drags one of them on a pilgrimage through
places of ill repute, 'qu'on lui vantait comme endroits
récélant de fortes horreurs, capables, en ébranlant ses
nerfs, d'étancher sa soif de meurtre'.

Hyacinthe (*Là-bas*) initiates Durtal into the Black Mass,
and then, in her lust for sacrilege, gives herself to him in
the 'abominable couche' of an 'ignoble bouge'; Clara (*Le
Jardin des supplices*) initiates her lover into the ghastly
spectacle of a Chinese prison, as a prelude to sleeping with
him in a brothel ('Et comme je vous aimerai mieux ce
soir . . .'); both, like Isabella Inghirami, 'took in their
trembling hand another trembling hand, to descend in
search of the bottom of the abyss, or perhaps of the subterranean temple'. In the *Trionfo della Morte* the spectacle
of the physical horrors of the pilgrimage to Casalbordino
serves the same purpose as the visit to the Chinese prison
in Mirbeau's novel.[122]

Clara undertakes her 'sad initiation' with almost the
same words as Isabella:

'Elle dit d'une voix plus basse, presque rauque: — Je t'apprendrai
des choses terribles . . . des choses divines . . . tu sauras enfin ce que
c'est que l'amour! Je te promets que tu descendras, avec moi, tout
au fond du mystère de l'amour . . . et de la mort!... L'amour est une
chose grave, triste et profonde. . . . L'Amour et la Mort, c'est la
même chose. . . . Voyons, dans l'acte d'amour, n'as-tu donc jamais
songé, par exemple, à commettre un beau crime? C'est-à-dire à
élever ton individu au-dessus de tous les préjugés sociaux et de
toutes les lois, au-dessus de tout, enfin?'[123]

Both in *Forse che sì* and in *Le Jardin des supplices* the
man feels horror for the woman and at the same time an

attraction which is part of his sense of horror; and when, in exasperation, he showers abuse upon her, she abandons herself to him with a delight which is all the greater precisely because of his insults. The cruel coition-scene in D'Annunzio's novel[124] is analogous to that of Mirbeau,[125] when, hearing her lover say to her:

'J'ai envie de vous tuer, démon!... je devrais vous tuer, et vous jeter ensuite au charnier, charogne! —

'Clara n'eut pas un mouvement de recul, pas même un mouvement des paupières.... Elle avança sa gorge, offrit sa poitrine.... Son visage s'illumina d'une joie inconnue et resplendissante.... Simplement, lentement, avec une douceur infinie, elle dit: — Eh bien!... tue-moi, chéri.... J'aimerais être tuée par toi, cher petit cœur!...'

The similarity between the passions in the two novels is repeated in the landscape: the inferno-like scenery of Volterra, the gloomy desert of ashes, lit by a sun which bleeds 'as though through the lips of an immense wound', corresponds to the scene of infinite desolation round the Chinese prison, a naked land which is the colour of dried blood.[126] D'Annunzio's novel ends with Isabella's madness, Mirbeau's with Clara's frightful attack of hysteria.[126A]

30. There was a tendency, towards the end of the century, to substitute a hospital background for the background of Oriental lust, cruelty, and magnificence against which the superwomen of Gautier had been painted. The following poem by Ivan Gilkin (from the volume entitled *La Nuit*, 1897) presents a sort of *non plus ultra* of the Fatal Woman type. His mannerisms are typical of the tendency of the whole period.

Amour d'Hôpital

Ô Reine des Douleurs, qui rayonnes de sang
Comme un rubis royal jette une flamme rouge,
Le forceps, qui t'a mise au monde dans un bouge,
D'un signe obscène doit t'avoir marquée au flanc.

Dans ton œil, où voyage un reflet satanique,
Le meurtre se tapit sous un velours de feu,
Ainsi qu'au fond d'un ciel amoureusement bleu
Dans les vents parfumés flotte un mal ironique.

Tu t'es faite, ô ma sœur, gardienne à l'hôpital,
Pour mieux repaître tes regards d'oiseau de proie
Du spectacle écœurant, cruel et plein de joie
De la chair qui se fend sous le couteau brutal.

Dans le grouillis rougeâtre et gluant des viscères,
Des muscles découpés, des tendons mis à nu,
Des nerfs, où vibre encore un vouloir inconnu,
Des glandes qu'on incise et des flasques artères,

Tu plonges tes deux bras polis, avidement,
Tandis qu'erre un divin sourire sur tes lèvres,
Et que sur son chevet, où bondissent les fièvres,
Le moribond t'appelle et parle doucement.

Car ton visage, pur comme un marbre, te donne,
Sous ta coiffe de toile et ton noir chaperon,
Ô vierge au bistouri, vierge au cœur de Huron,
Le resplendissement serein d'une Madone.

Sur ton sein, les stylets, les pinces, les ciseaux,
La spatule, la scie équivoque et les sondes,
Bijoux terrifiants et breloques immondes,
Comme un bouquet d'acier étoilent leurs faisceaux.

Tes doigts fins, à tremper dans les pus et les plaies,
En ont pris le tranchant affilé des scalpels;
Et l'odeur de ton corps suave a des rappels
De putréfactions rances, dont tu t'égaies.

Car ton âme de monstre est folle des gaîtés
Cocasses de la couche où le mourant se cabre
Dans les convulsions de la danse macabre,
Et la Mort a pour toi d'hilarantes beautés.

Qui nous expliquera ta funèbre hystérie,
Pauvre femme, produit de ce siècle empesté?
On dit que ton baiser trouble la volonté
Et communique aux os une lente carie.

Mais de ton mâle cœur monte un puissant amour.
Comme un vin orgueilleux, plein de rouges prestiges,
Sa riche odeur de sang évoque les vertiges
Et ronge les cerveaux mieux qu'un bec de vautour.

Et c'est pourquoi, vaincu par la coquetterie
De ta forme divine et de tes noirs instincts,
En toi j'adore, enfant des sinistres Destins,
L'Horreur fascinatrice et la Bizarrerie.

'L'Horreur fascinatrice'—the beauty of the Medusa. 'Un divin sourire sur tes lèvres'—the Gioconda smile. 'Reine des douleurs'—Dolores. 'Ô vierge au bistouri'— Mademoiselle Bistouri. The final metamorphosis both of the Fatal Man and of the Fatal Woman can be seen in Baudelaire's *Métamorphoses du vampire*.

Even here there remains the possibility of humoristic evasion; and this is indicated by Laforgue in the *Miracle des roses* (1887) (in *Moralités légendaires*), in which the consumptive woman, haunted by the idea of blood (like the heroine of the *Sogno d'un Mattino di Primavera*), casts the evil eye on all who approach her, so that there springs up in her *via crucis* a crop of more or less grotesque suicides.

There is unintentional humour, on the other hand, in the poem by R. Le Gallienne (in *English Poems*, 1892) entitled *Beauty Accursed*, in which the Fatal Woman attracts irresistibly towards herself not only men, but even 'strange creatures', even cows, toads, and snails!

> Strange creatures leer at me with uncouth love,
> And from the grass reach upward to my breast,
> And to my mouth lean from the boughs above.
>
> The sleepy kine move round me in desire
> And press their oozy lips upon my hair,
> Toads kiss my feet and creatures of the mire,
> The snails will leave their shells to watch me there.
>
> But all this worship, what is it to me?
> I smite the ox and crush the toad in death:
> I only know I am so very fair,
> And that the world was made to give me breath.
>
> I only wait the hour when God shall rise
> Up from the star where he so long hath sat,
> And bow before the wonder of my eyes
> And set *me* there—I am so fair as that.

NOTES AND ADDENDA TO CHAPTER IV

¹ Cf. M. Rudwin, *The Devil in Legend and Literature* (Chicago–London, The Open Court Publishing Co., 1931), chap. ix, 'The Legend of Lilith', pp. 101–2:

'The fatal power of Lilith is not limited to new-born infants. She offers a greater danger to men, particularly in their youth. In Eastern tradition, Lilith, as princess of the *succubi*, is primarily a seductress of men. "Lilith", says Langdon (Stephen H. Langdon, *Tammuz and Ishtar*, Oxford University Press, 1914, p. 74), "is the Semitic name for the beautiful and licentious unmarried harlot who seduces men in streets and fields".'

² From *The Oresteia of Aeschylus*, translated by R. C. Trevelyan (The University Press of Liverpool, 1922), p. 98.

³ *Volupté*, ed. 1834, vol. i, pp. 209–10.

³ᴬ Among the Fatal Women of this period, mention should be made of Countess Adelaide in the first version of Goethe's *Götz von Berlichingen*. [Add. 1950]

⁴ *Le Diable amoureux* appeared in an English translation in 1791. Railo (op. cit., p. 261) quotes a passage from Cazotte in which Biondetta's habit 'discovered part of her bosom, and the moonbeams darting full upon it, enabled me to observe its dazzling whiteness', and compares it with the following from Lewis: 'The moonbeams darting full upon it [Matilda's bosom] enabled the monk to observe its dazzling whiteness'. See also other anticipations of Matilda quoted by Railo, ibid.

Lewis, who was a homosexual (see Montague Summers, *The Gothic Quest*, pp. 263–4) must have been struck by Biondetta's disguise as Biondetto. [Add. 1950]

⁵ *Mémoires d'outre-tombe*, ed. 1849, vol. iii, p. 229. In another place he remarks that Lewis's *Monk* and Godwin's *Caleb Williams* would survive.

⁶ Croce rightly remarks in his essay on Kleist (published first in *Critica*, vol. xviii, no. 2 (March 1920), p. 71, later reprinted in the volume *Poesia e non poesia*:

'Penthesilea . . . filled with the sole desire to subdue and bind to herself Achilles whom she loves, when she sees that she does not succeed in subduing him, murders him in her raging madness and lacerates with dagger and tooth the corpse of the man she both hates and loves. Kleist did not write this, as might have been the case with other authors saturated with literature, out of love of the lecherous, the cruel, and the horrible, for the original source of his inspiration sprang from his vague yearning after an extremely high ideal and from his despair at not having been able to achieve it. But the theme remains symbolical and almost allegorical, and has a meaning beyond the gross sensual cloak of its outward rendering, in which a process of hysterical fury is developed.'

Even if it is possible to trace signs of sadism in the work of Kleist (e.g. in *Erdbeben in Chile*, 1808) his case remains isolated and without following in German literature.

7 *Le Origini di 'Salammbô'*, op. cit., p. 69. See also Benedetto's remarks (pp. 56 et seq.) on the 'fatal' character of Salammbô and on her identification with Flaubert's type of Oriental woman (Cleopatra).

8 In Zola's *Faute de l'Abbé Mouret*, also, temptation comes after the young priest's serious illness.

9 Cf. Mallarmé, *Brise marine*:

La chair est triste, hélas! et j'ai lu tous les livres.
Fuir! là-bas fuir! je sens que des oiseaux sont ivres
D'être parmi l'écume inconnue et les cieux!

.   .   .   .

Je partirai! Steamer balançant ta mâture
Lève l'ancre pour une exotique nature!
Un Ennui, désolé par les cruels espoirs,
Croit encor à l'adieu suprême des mouchoirs!

9A The derivation from the Javanese in Gautier's *Fortunio* is evident (see note 163 of the preceding chapter): 'elle était de la race de ces terribles Javanaises, de ces gracieux vampires qui boivent un Européen en trois semaines et le laissent sans une goutte d'or ni de sang'. [Add. 1950]

10 The physical type of Jacques Ferrand also corresponds to that of Borel's Public Prosecutor. He has a 'masque fauve et terreux, sa figure plate comme une tête de mort; son nez camus et punais et ses lèvres si minces, si imperceptibles, que sa bouche semblait incisée dans sa face'.

11 See the note in *Portraits contemporains*, vol. iii, pp. 115–17.

12 Pierre Louÿs, *La Femme et le pantin* (1898), pp. 57–8:

'Si vous n'avez pas encore éprouvé jusqu'à l'extrême la folie qu'elle peut engendrer et maintenir dans un cœur humain, n'approchez pas cette femme, fuyez-la comme la mort. . . .'

Don Mateo makes the acquaintance of Concha in circumstances similar to those of *Carmen* (a women's quarrel); both the women are cigar-makers; both prostitute themselves in act or in appearance to the English (*Carmen*, ed. Calmann-Lévy, 1883, p. 76; *La Femme et le pantin*, pp. 185 et seq.).

Also, the 'inventions cruelles' used by Conchita in order to excite the man without yielding herself are the same as those of Cécily (*La Femme et le pantin*, pp. 149–50, 213 et seq.); Conchita also (p. 228) defends herself with a dagger, but Don Mateo strikes her and she exclaims: 'Que tu m'as bien battue, mon cœur! Que c'était doux! Que c'était bon! . . . Pardon pour tout ce que je t'ai fait!'—and then she tells lies in order to get beaten again.

'Quand je sens ta force, je t'aime, je t'aime; tu ne peux pas savoir comme je suis heureuse de pleurer à cause de toi' — 'Mateo, tu me battras encore? Promets-le moi: tu me battras bien! Tu me tueras! Dis-moi que tu me tueras!' 'Ne croyez pas, cependant, que cette singulière prédilection fût la base de son caractère. Non; si elle avait le besoin du châtiment, elle avait aussi la passion de la faute. Elle faisait mal, non pour le plaisir de pécher, mais pour la joie de faire mal à quelqu'un. Son rôle dans la vie se bornait là: semer la souffrance et la regarder croître'.

Conchita takes other lovers simply in order to stimulate Mateo's passion. Apropos of Louys' *Aphrodite* (1896) Remy de Gourmont wrote (*Le Livre des masques*, vol. i, pp. 185–6):

'Mais aussi qu'une telle littérature est fallacieuse! Toutes ces femmes, toutes ces chairs, tous ces cris, toute cette luxure si animale et si vaine, et si cruelle! Les femelles mordillent les cervelets et mangent les cervelles; la pensée fuit éjaculée; l'âme des femmes coule comme par une plaie; et toutes ces copulations n'engendrent que le néant, le dégoût et la mort.

M. Pierre Louys a bien senti que ce livre de chair aboutissait logiquement à la mort; *Aphrodite* se clôt par une scène de mort, par des funérailles.

C'est la fin d'*Atala* (Chateaubriand plane invisible sur toute notre littérature) ... à l'idée de la mort vient se joindre l'idée de la beauté; et les deux images, enlacées comme deux courtisanes, tombent lentement dans la nuit'.

13 See the chapter 'Swinburne and "le vice anglais" '.

14 See also at the end of this chapter, § 29.

14A Thus the type of 'woman-vampire' which dominates in Strindberg's work is a very personal projection of the algolagnia of that writer. [Add. 1950]

15 Op. cit., p. 8.

Babbitt, op. cit., p. 251, on the other hand, maintains that 'the infinite of nostalgia [a name by which he calls the phenomenon defined by us as exoticism] has nothing in common with the infinite of religion'. He admits, however, that there is a similarity with the type of religion which took shape with neo-Platonism, that is with mysticism in the current sense of the word. [Add. 1950]

16 'La Mort de Venise', in *Amori et Dolori sacrum*, p. 85.

16A Babbitt, *Rousseau and Romanticism*, pp. 92–3, calls 'nostalgia' this kind of exoticism. [Add. 1950]

16B Beckford's exoticism is witnessed not only in his published works, among which special mention should be made of the *Recollections of an Excursion to the Monasteries of Alcobaca and Batalha*, 1835 (see on this point S. Sitwell, *Beckford and Beckfordism*, London, Duckworth, 1930), but also in his effusive letters to Alexander Cozens, for instance in one on the charm of the farthest North, which belongs to the Morrison Collection (*Morrison Autographs*, vol. i, p. 198, no. 50). The relations with Cozens, and other circumstances, leave little doubt as to the 'decadent' nature of Beckford's sensibility. See Guy Chapman, *Beckford*, London, Cape, 1937, chiefly p. 182 et seq. on the scandal in connexion with William Courtenay, apropos of which Chapman strangely concludes (p. 188): 'The link is not, I believe, homosexual passion.' The allusions to the pleasures indulged in by the trio Beckford–Louisa–William Courtenay breathe the atmosphere of *Justine*, or at least of the *Liaisons dangereuses*. [Add. 1950]

17 In the interlude *Love* intended for the *Ballad of the Dark Ladie*, 1799), are the lines:

> There came and looked him in the face
> An angel beautiful and bright;
> And that he knew it was a Fiend,
> This miserable Knight!

·   ·   ·   ·   ·

And that she nursed him in a cave;
And how his madness went away,
When on the yellow forest-leaves
A dying man he lay.

Coleridge's poem, with the title *Introduction to the Tale of the Dark Ladie*, appeared in the *Morning Post* of Dec. 21st, 1799. It is obvious that Keats took his inspiration from this for his *Belle Dame sans merci* (1819). It may be noted that Coleridge's poem began thus:

O leave the Lily on its stem;
O leave the Rose upon the spray. . . .

which seems to have suggested to Keats the following:

I see a lilly on thy brow

. . . . .

And on thy cheek a fading rose. . . .

On the other hand Keats's image: 'I saw pale kings, and princes too . . .' is a reminiscence of Canto V of the *Inferno*. See J. Middleton Murry, *Keats and Shakespeare* (Oxford University Press, 1925), p. 124. See also Murry's remarks on the subject of the Belle Dame as a symbolic transference of Keats's betrothed, Fanny Brawne; and also on Keats's conception of love as pain. Pleasure and death are intertwined in Keats's poems, *The Eve of St. Agnes, Lamia, Isabella*. With regard to a young Anglo-Indian girl whom he met at the house of some friends, Keats wrote:

'She is not a Cleopatra, but she is at least a Charmian. She has a rich eastern look. . . . When she comes into a room she makes an impression the same as the Beauty of a Leopardess. . . . I should like her to ruin me. . . .'

(quoted from Murry, pp. 100–1).

[18] *Janus Weathercock, The Life of Thomas Griffiths Wainewright, 1794–1847*, London, Nelson, 1938, p. 78.

[19] A similar nostalgia for an ancient world in which energy could be freely expressed is to be found in Stendhal who, in his fragmentary *Filosofia Nova* (cf. appendix to the *Journal* of Stendhal, ed. of *Œuvres complètes*, Paris, Champion, vol. ii, 1932) also enunciates a maxim *à la* Marquis de Sade: 'Tous les grands hommes grecs étaient libertins; cette passion dans un homme indique l'énergie, qualité sine qua non genius.' But Stendhal looked towards the past, and wrote the *Chroniques italiennes*, because he saw examples of energy there. He was indifferent to curiosities of cultural surroundings, and cannot therefore be called a true and proper exoticist. The true and proper exoticist hankers after a country of his own imagining, his Orient, his Rome, &c., partake of the nature of a mirage (the remark is Brie's, op. cit. p. 10–11), whereas Stendhal was satisfied with the present when he found in it the qualities which he valued in life. His ideal moral world was the Renaissance—but among the Italians of his own time he found sufficient 'virtù' (in the Machiavellian sense) to make him decide to live among them and to call himself Milanese. Like Byron, Stendhal gave more attention to the soul of a period or a country than to its exterior aspect, whereas the real exoticist gives primary importance to pageantry, and is contemplative rather than active. If one is going to give

the name of exoticism to the nostalgia of Byron and Stendhal, then Machiavelli's complaint of the decline of the pagan world must also be called exoticism.

One is reminded of Stendhal when seeing Mérimée's admiration for the vehement passions of the Renaissance and the type of humanity represented by Colomba, or hearing his regret at the thought that murder is no longer admitted by our custom. W. Pater remarked in his 1890 essay collected in *Miscellaneous Studies*: 'It is as if there were nothing to tell of in this world, but various forms of hatred, and a love that is like lunacy; and the only other world, a world of maliciously active, hideous, dead bodies.' Also R. del Valle-Inclán (*Sonata de estío*) finds it very sad that in an age like our modern one in which souls are tamer, the spiritual brothers of the *conquistadores* should find no other outlet for their energy than brigandage. [Add. 1950]

²⁰ *Une Nuit de Cléopâtre*, chap. vi.

²¹ Diodorus Siculus, ii, 13, 4.

²² Villon, *Ballade des dames du temps jadis.*

²³ p. 244.

²⁴ Cf. chap. iii, note 85.

²⁵ See chap. i, note 39.

²⁶ Cleopatra frequently inspired the Romantic poets: Victor Hugo (*Zim-Zizimi*); Louis Bouilhet in the third canto of the poem *Mélænis* (1851):

> Cléopâtre! encore toi! voluptueux génie!
> Type éternel de grâce et de virilité!
> Non, non, tu n'aimais pas, c'est une calomnie
> Que jettera sur toi la médiocrité.
> Sous le bois odorant qui couvre ta momie,
> Ton cœur n'est pas plus froid qu'au temps de ta beauté!

> Assise au bord du Nil, ô courtisane blonde,
> Tu tendais aux vainqueurs ton filet captieux;
> Tu les endormis tous d'une ivresse profonde,
> Et tu les vis tomber, tes amants glorieux!
> Sans qu'ils aient eu jamais, en échange du monde,
> Une larme d'amour échappée à tes yeux!

Théodore de Banville (*Les Princesses*, 1874, xi) shows Cleopatra sleeping naked in the moonlight:

> Et tandis qu'elle dort, délices et bourreau
> Du monde, un dieu de jaspe à tête de taureau
> Se penche, et voit son sein où la clarté se pose.

> Sur ce sein, tous les feux dans son sein recélés
> Étincellent, montrant leur braise ardente et rose,
> Et l'idole de jaspe en a les yeux brûlés.

In two sonnets by Albert Samain (in the volume *Au Jardin de l'Infante*), the queen exhibits herself naked on the terrace of her palace in order to intoxicate the whole world with her beauty:

Elle veut, et ses yeux fauves dardent l'éclair,
Que le monde ait, ce soir, le parfum de sa chair. . . .
Ô sombre fleur du sexe éparse en l'air nocturne!

Et le Sphynx, immobile aux sables de l'ennui,
Sent un feu pénétrer son granit taciturne
Et le désert immense a remué sous lui.

[27] Cf. *Macbeth*, Act v, sc. i, line 57.

[27A] The legend of the Roman nobleman who, while playing at a ball-game, places his ring on the statue's finger, is related by William of Malmesbury and through him spreads everywhere. Also Pater (*Hippolytus Veiled*, 1889, collected in *Greek Studies*) took from that source the idea of making Hippolytus place on the finger of Diana's image the ring which Phaedra had given him. [Add. 1950]

[28] The idea of the double personality of the priest goes back to Lewis's *Monk*. Cf. Railo, op. cit., pp. 183 et seq. and 306-7.

[29] A typical illustration of this Romantic fantasy is given by Heine in 'Florentinische Nächte' (*Salon*, iii, 1837), where Maximilian professes his love for representations of women in sculpture (especially Michaelangelo's *Night*) and in paintings, and also for women already dead. He falls in love in this way with the little Very, seven years after she is dead; and he tells of his passion for Mademoiselle Laurence, who was called 'das Totenkind' because of the strange circumstances of her birth (her mother had been buried; robbers had violated the tomb and found her in the pains of child-birth, so had taken the baby and re-buried the mother): 'She was so slim, so young and lovely—this lily born of the tomb, this daughter of death, this ghost with the face of an angel and the body of a *bayadère*.'

Balzac's Jane la Pâle was born in similar circumstances. Her adoptive father tells the story (ed. Brussels, Méline, 1836, vol. i, p. 262):

'On donnait à Londres un de mes opéras lorsque la salle de Drury-Lane brûla. Mistriss Jenny Duls, danseuse célèbre, éprouva une telle frayeur à l'aspect de l'incendie, qu'elle mourut dans mes bras. Elle était grosse; ne trouvant pas de chirurgien au milieu du tumulte, j'eus le courage de pratiquer l'affreuse opération qui sauva cette chère enfant. Par un phénomène inexplicable, la pâleur de la mère avait passé sur le visage de la fille, et c'est pour cela que vous m'entendez souvent la nommer Chlora ou Chlore, ce nom doit lui rappeler sans cesse qu'elle a été conquise sur la mort.'

The exquisite Jane is of 'une pâleur effrayante, et son visage ressemblait exactement à celui d'une statue' (p. 237). Salviati says of her: 'Voilà comme je me représente le vampire dont nous a parlé ce jeune Anglais à Coppet' (p. 236). The lips of the fatal Jane were like 'deux branches de corail'. It is easy to see the affinity between Balzac's conception and that of his friend Heine.

[30] In his famous description of the Monna Lisa, where the poetical fantasy of which we are speaking finds its culminating point, Pater says: 'Like the vampire, she has been dead many times, and learned the secrets of the grave.'

[31] Similar themes recur in other poems by Gautier: *Études de mains*, ii,

Lacenaire; *Symphonie en blanc majeur*; *Le Château du souvenir*; *Cærulei oculi*. See the study by B. Fehr in *Archiv für das Studium der neueren Sprachen und Literaturen*, vol. cxxxv, pp. 80–102: 'Walter Paters Beschreibung der Mona Lisa und Théophile Gautiers romantischer Orientalismus'. Among the first indications of the theme of the synthetic Fatal Woman must be mentioned a sonnet by Ernest Prarond to his friend Baudelaire (Oct. 5th, 1852), in which, recounting an adventure of the latter with 'une femme belle, et de naissance juive', he goes on:

> Elle vous fit toucher, sur sa chair toute vive,
> Du vice et de l'amour les secrets monstrueux.
>
> Elle eût enivré Loth au fond d'une caverne,
> Tenu comme Judith le sabre d'Holopherne,
> Et frappé du marteau le front de Sisara.

Brie (op. cit., p. 77, note) remarks that this poem comes very near to Pater. But it must be noticed that Prarond uses the conditional (she *would have*'), so that there is no question of re-incarnation, which makes all the difference.

[32] *Œuvres de jeunesse*, vol. ii, pp. 196 et seq.

[33] *L'Éducation sentimentale*, 1845 version. *Œ. de jeun.*, vol. iii, pp. 160–1.

[34] Cf. Gautier, *La Morte amoureuse*:

'Avoir Clarimonde, c'était avoir vingt maîtresses, c'était avoir toutes les femmes, tant elle était mobile, changeante et dissemblable d'elle-même; un vrai caméléon! Elle vous faisait commettre avec elle l'infidélité que vous eussiez commise avec d'autres, en prenant complètement le caractère, l'allure et le genre de beauté de la femme qui paraissait vous plaire'.

The idolization of an identical woman through her various incarnations was the chief thread of Gérard de Nerval's tragical life. That shadow usually took shape in the form of the Queen of Sheba. See A. Marie, *Gérard de Nerval*, Paris, Hachette, 1914, pp. 100, 107, 175, 200, 231, 294, 323. On the Queen of Sheba see A. Chastel, 'La Légende de la Reine de Saba', in *Revue de l'histoire des religions*, tomes cxix–cxx (1939), and the drama *Belkiss, rainha de Saba, d'Axum e do Hymiar* (1894) of the decadent Portuguese poet Eugenio de Castro. [Add. 1950]

[35] H. Nicolson, *Swinburne* (London, Macmillan, 1926; 'English Men of Letters').

[36] T. Earle Welby, *A Study of Swinburne* (London, Faber & Gwyer, 1926).

[37] G. Lafourcade, *La Jeunesse de Swinburne (1837–1867)* (Paris, Les Belles Lettres, 1928, 2 vols.; Publications de la Faculté des Lettres de l'Université de Strasbourg). See also: Lafourcade, *Swinburne, a literary biography* (London, Bell, 1932). (The former work is quoted here as: Lafourcade; the latter as: Lafourcade, *Swinburne*.)

[38] Lafourcade, *Swinburne*, p. 258.

[39] Vol. i, p. 265, note 109. It might perhaps also be proved that the cessation of Swinburne's erotic inspiration dates from the time that he

started to frequent those *établissements spéciaux*, which according to Lafourcade, would be from 1867 onwards. Cf. also Lafourcade, *Swinburne*,
p. 196: 'On July 28th, 1868, (he) wrote from London in the following
terms: 'My life has been enlivened of late by a fair friend who keeps a
maison de supplices à la Rodin—There is occasional balm in Gilead.'
His *libido*, having found a real outlet, would cease to evoke fantasies of
lechery. This, in fact would constitute a confirmation of the view that the
erotic details in *Poems and Ballads, First Series* 'were mainly the fruits of
his fertile imagination and not memories of actual experiences' (*Hardman
Papers*, S. M. Ellis' note, p. 327).

40 See the chapter 'Swinburne and "le vice anglais" '. On the subject
of erotic flagellation, which seems to have been traditionally held in honour
among the English, see Dr. E. Dühren, *Das Geschlechtsleben in England*,
vol. ii (Berlin, Lilienthal, 1903), chap. vi, 'Die Flagellomanie', which contains very full documentation.

41 Lafourcade, vol. i, pp. 178–9; *Swinburne*, pp. 92 et seq. *The Hardman
Papers*, ed. and annotated by S. M. Ellis (London, Constable, 1930), p. 91,
apropos of the mode of flogging women in Jamaica: 'The whipping of
women would have gratified the senses of Lord Houghton (Monckton
Milnes) and would probably have culminated in his asking to be similarly
castigated himself!'

42 Lafourcade, vol. ii, pp. 114–20.

43 Ibid., pp. 128–34. It is perhaps a mere coincidence that the whipped
page in *Laugh and Lie down* should be called Frank, like the young man
who is the subject of one of the epigrams of Sir John Davies which were
printed together with Marlowe's version of Ovid's elegies:

> When Francus comes to solace with his whore
> He sends for rods, and strips himself stark naked, etc.

44 Lafourcade, vol. ii, pp. 85–90. Among the sources of this work La-
fourcade cites Dumas's *Les Grands Crimes de l'Histoire*. *The Chronicle of
Tebaldeo Tebaldei* has been published for the first time by the Golden
Cockerel Press, London, 1943, edited by Randolph Hughes.

45 Lafourcade, vol. ii, pp. 235–246.

46 Quoted by Lafourcade, vol. ii, pp. 89–90.
On a possible influence of the *Hypnerotomachia*, see M. Praz, 'Some
Foreign Imitators of the Hypnerotomachia Poliphili', in the review
Italica, vol. xxiv, 1 (March 1947).

47 *Whippingham Papers*. See Lafourcade, vol. ii, p. 132. The complete
passage is: 'One of the great charms of birching lies in the sentiment that
the floggee is the powerless victim of the furious rage of a beautiful woman.'
Cf. the well-known passage in the *Confessions* of Rousseau, quoted in
psychopathological treatises as an illustration of masochism: 'Être aux
genoux d'une maîtresse impérieuse, obéir à ses ordres, avoir des pardons
à lui demander, étaient pour moi de très douces jouissances.'

48 Lafourcade, vol. ii, pp. 258–61.

49 Op. cit., vol. ii, p. 282.

50 Certain conformities of thought between Blake and Sade, between Dostoievsky and Nietzsche and Blake, derive from the fact that these writers were all, in greater or lesser degree, sadists. This accounts for the discovery of a twin mind—of Swinburne in Sade, of D'Annunzio in Swinburne and Nietzsche, of Gide in Nietzsche, Dostoievsky and Blake.

51 *William Blake, a Critical Essay* (London, Hotten, 1868), p. 158 note.

On Sade's 'philosophy' see G. Gorer, *The Revolutionary Ideas of the Marquis de Sade*, with an introduction by J. B. S. Haldane, London, Wishart, 1934.

52 Op. cit., vol. ii, pp. 354 et seq. Cf. the passages of Sade quoted in chap. iii.

53 Swinburne's attitude towards the works of Sade is a double one; on the one hand, he finds in the Divine Marquis a source of macabre burlesque, apt to *épater le bourgeois*; on the other, 'a valuable study to rational curiosity'. See Lafourcade, vol. i, pp. 264–5. Swinburne's attitude towards the 'frénétique' school of French literature is similar. In his essays on the imaginary Ernest Clouet and Félicien Cossu (1861 and 1862), which were destined to scandalize the readers of the respectable *Spectator*, Swinburne uses for humorous purposes the macabre obscenities of French 'bas romantisme', which, however, he also took seriously, as is shown by *Poems and Ballads, First Series*. The same may be said of him as of Janin, of Toulet, and of all the writers who treat certain gruesome subjects humorously— humoristic treatment being an evasion which presupposes attraction to the subject.

54 Letter of August 1865, quoted by Lafourcade, vol. ii, p. 401. Cf. note 57 of chap. ii. See Lafourcade, especially vol. ii, pp. 401–3, for the influence of Sade's theories on the theology of *Atalanta*. A source of Chorus IV which seems to have escaped the notice of the French critic is the speech of Almani, in *Justine* (vol. iii, pp. 63–4), on the cruelty of Nature, a speech which makes use of the same arguments which were afterwards made use of by Leopardi in *Dialogo della Natura e di un Islandese*.

55 A poem which D'Annunzio used for the second act of the *Crociata degli Innocenti*.

56 A first version of *The Leper*, entitled *The Vigil*, lays particular stress on the erotic attraction of the dead woman's naked feet. It is well known that this form of fetishism is closely connected with sadism. Baudelaire, when he frightened the blonde woman with his sadistic fantasies (Séché-Bertaut, op. cit., p. 126; Crépet, p. 65), concluded: 'Alors je me mettrais à genoux et je baiserais vos pieds nus.' And in the sadistic vision of the fair penitent in the 1849 version of Flaubert's *Tentation* (p. 221 in the edition of the *Œuvres complètes*):

'Elle essaie, elle s'enferme, elle défait sa chaussure au nœud vermeil qui passe entre son pouce et se rattache à la jambe; elle la quitte, elle ne la portera plus; ce pied, dont on polissait le talon avec la lave des volcans, dont on teignait les ongles avec le jus des coquillages et que les hommes en joie appuyaient contre leurs lèvres . . . il trébuchera sur les cailloux, il s'enfoncera jusqu'à la cheville dans l'urine des mulets, il se déchirera au tranchant des éclats de marbre, et les os passeront à travers la peau qui sera comme des guenilles. . . .'

Psychopathologists quote a passage from Barrès's *Ennemi des lois* (ed. 1893, p. 49) where he makes the Russian 'petite princesse' say:

'Quand j'avais douze ans . . . j'aimais, sitôt seule dans la campagne, à ôter mes chaussures et à enfoncer mes pieds nus dans la boue chaude. J'y passais des heures, et cela me donnait dans tout le corps un frisson de plaisir'.

57 Vol. ii, p. 312.

58 For its particular type of sensuality, this passage may be compared with *Justine*, vol. iv, pp. 270–1.

59 *Convivio*, vol. viiii, p. 654. Maupassant, in his introduction to the translation by G. Mourey of the *Poèmes et Ballades de Swinburne* (Paris, Savine, 1891), used by D'Annunzio, says (p. xiv):

'Swinburne a compris et exprimé cela [ces appels irrésistibles et tourmentants de la volupté insaisissable] comme personne avant lui, et peut-être comme personne ne le fera plus, car ils ont disparu du monde contemporain, ces poètes déments épris d'inaccessibles jouissances.'

And O. Wilde, in an open letter in French, to Edmond de Goncourt, in *L'Écho de Paris* for December 19th, 1891:

'Il y a aujourd'hui plus de vingt-cinq ans, M. Swinburne a publié ses *Poèmes et Ballades*, une des œuvres qui ont marqué le plus profondément dans notre littérature une ère nouvelle. Dans Shakespeare et dans ses contemporains Webster et Ford, il y a des cris de nature. Dans l'œuvre de Swinburne on rencontre pour la première fois le cri de la chair tourmentée par le désir et le souvenir, la jouissance et le remords, la fécondité et la stérilité.' [Add. 1950]

To which dramas D'Annunzio is especially referring may be seen from a passage in the *Faville del Maglio* (published in the *Corriere della Sera* of March 17th, 1912):

'Something similar to what I may call "carnality of thought" is to be found in certain tragic poets who were predecessors of Shakespeare, such as Christopher Marlowe, John Webster, John Ford.'

Since D'Annunzio is here speaking of himself, the identification of 'carnality of thought' with 'criminal sensuality' is a logical consequence of a comparison of the two passages. If one wished to be pedantic, one might point out to D'Annunzio that neither Webster nor Ford were 'predecessors' of Shakespeare. Very likely D'Annunzio was misled by Taine's *Histoire de la littérature anglaise*, Book II, chap. iii, 1:

'Lorsqu'une civilisation nouvelle amène un art nouveau à la lumière, il y a dix hommes de talent qui expriment à demi l'idée publique autour d'un ou deux hommes de génie qui l'expriment tout à fait: . . . Ford, Marlowe, Massinger, Webster, Beaumont, Fletcher autour de Shakespeare. . . .'

In Chap. ii Taine had dealt with these lesser Elizabethan dramatists, before dealing with Shakespeare in Chap. iv.

60 Vol. ii, pp. 434–5.

[61] Apropos of this see the postscript to a letter of 1865 to Ch. Aug. Howell (ed. Gosse and Wise, London, 1918, letter xiv):

'Since writing the above I have added ten verses to *Dolores—très infâmes et très bien tournés*. "Oh! Monsieur, peut-on prendre du plaisir à de telles horreurs ?" '

[62] Lafourcade, vol. i, p. 204.

[63] *Hamlet*, Act III, Sc. i, line 130.

[64] On Adah Menken see *Hardman Papers*, pp. 322 et seq., and B. Falk, *The Naked Lady*, *A Biography of Adah Isaacs Menken*, London, Hutchinson, 1934 (chap. xvi, 'Swinburne as Lover', full of curious information). That her ways were calculated to attract Swinburne can be judged by the following passage in Francis Burnand's *Records and Reminiscences*, quoted on pp. 324–5 of the *Hardman Papers*. Burnand found her in his box terrorizing a man who had slighted her in America:

'She had closed the door with a bang, and was standing in front of it barring the way with a shining dagger in her hand. . . . Her eyes flashed more brilliantly than her dagger, they gleamed murderously. . . . Losing all control of herself she raised her dagger, took one step back, in order to spring forward, like an angry tigress, &c.'

She appears to have been a passionate woman, 'somewhat careless and prodigal, it is true, but ever unselfish'—to use the words of a contemporary (H. B. Farnie). See also Lafourcade, *Swinburne*, pp. 188–93.

It is worth remembering that the role in which the fair Amazon excelled was that of Mazeppa: she appeared fastened to the back of 'the fiery steed of Tartary', her statuesque limbs encased in tight fleshings, and covered with a Greek tunic—a costume which may not appear very bold to us, but could not fail to strike the imagination of the repressed Victorians. See my essay, 'Cleopatra in crinolina', in the volume *Studi e svaghi inglesi*. [Add. 1950]

[65] Lit. trans.:

'A stern virago is she, stern and public tests does she require of danger and of love: the roses of her garland grow in the midst of blood.'

[66] See *Swinburne's Hyperion and Other Poems*, with an Essay on Swinburne and Keats, Thèse complémentaire présentée à la Faculté des Lettres de l'Université de Strasbourg par G. Lafourcade (London, Faber & Gwyer, 1928).

[66A] Berenson attributes them to Andrea di Michelangelo in *The Drawings of the Florentine Painters*, Amplified Edition, Chicago, The University of Chicago Press, 1938, nos. 1626 and 1655, plates 781 and 787; see also the review *L'Arte*, July 1935, p. 253. Morelli ascribed no. 781 to Bacchiacca. There was in the collection of the Marchese Carlo Camillo Visconti Venosta a small sixteenth-century oil painting which repeats the subject of the drawing no. 787, and seems actually very close to Bacchiacca. [Add. 1950]

[67] Cf. Gautier, *Le Roi Candaule* (p. 418):

'Nyssia dénoua ses cheveux . . . Gygès . . . crut . . . voir . . . leurs boucles s'allonger avec des ondulations vipérines comme la chevelure des Gorgones et des Méduses'.

See also the passage from *Laus Veneris* quoted above, p. 239.

[68] The allusion here is probably to the cruelty of the Chinese Emperor Kiè and his wife, recorded in *Justine*, vol. iv, p. 198.

[69] See E. Welby, op. cit., pp. 222–3; and *The Victorian Romantics*, by the same author (London, Howe, 1929), p. 76.

[70] *Une Nuit de Cléopâtre*, p. 325.

[71] The Gioconda smile had already for some time been puzzling people's brains. Thomas Griffiths Wainewright (see J. Curling, *Janus Weathercock*, op. cit. (in note 18)), in his essay 'The Delicate Intricacies' which appeared in the *London Magazine* for July 1822 (a parody of the dandy style in novel-writing), imagines Miss Nina L. lost in a reverie in front of a copy of the Gioconda:

'She gazed on the wily eyes of Gioconda, she knew not why. The light of the lamp mingled strangely with the light of dawn: the eyes looked at her altogether painfully, and the corners of the mouth curled slightly upwards. . . . Could it be that the imaged lips were indued with the power of evoking like phantoms? For, lo! they move; and the eyes, closing up narrower and narrower, leer amorously at a masculine head which appeared over her shoulder, &c.' [Add. 1950]

See the *Journal* of the Goncourts (vol. i, p. 317), dated March 11th, 1860:

'Femme au délicat profil, au joli petit nez droit, à la bouche d'une découpure si spirituelle, à la coiffure de bacchante donnant aujourd'hui à sa physionomie une grâce mutine et affolée, femme aux yeux étranges qui semblent rire, quand sa parole est sérieuse. Toutes les femmes sont des énigmes, mais celle-ci est la plus indéchiffrable de toutes. Elle ressemble à son regard qui n'est jamais en place, et dans lequel passent, brouillés en une seconde, les regards divers de la femme. Tout est incompréhensible chez cette créature qui peut-être ne se comprend guère elle-même; l'observation ne peut y prendre pied et y glisse comme sur le terrain du caprice. Son âme, son humeur, le battement de son cœur a quelque chose de précipité et de fuyant, comme le pouls de la Folie. On croirait voir en elle une Violante, une de ces courtisanes du XVIᵉ siècle, un de ces êtres instinctifs et déréglés qui portent comme un masque d'enchantement, *le sourire plein de nuit de la Joconde.*'

This last expression occurs again in *La Faustin*, where the smile of Bonne-Âme, the 'allumeuse', is described as 'un sourire plein d'une obscure nuit'.

And in the volume on *Prudhon* (1861), apropos of the face of Mademoiselle Mayer: 'Amoureuse, moqueuse, sentimentale, ardente, pensive, voluptueuse, passionnée, telle est cette tête mystérieuse et fascinatrice dans sa mutinerie, où l'on retrouve l'énigme du sourire de la Joconde': for the technical secret of the Gioconda smile, see M. H. Goldblatt, in the *Connoisseur* for May 1950. [Add. 1950]

[72] *Letters*, vol. i, pp. 124–5.

On Swinburne's influence on Pater's description of the Gioconda, see W. Gaunt, *The Aesthetic Adventure*, London, Cape, 1945, p. 54.

[73] The expression is from the First Epistle to the Corinthians.

[74] Paris, 1885, vol. ii, book vi, chap. i, p. 10. Heine (*Florentinische Nächte*, i) had said of the Princess: 'I shall never forget that face. It was

of those which seem to belong more to the fantastic realm of poetry than to the rude reality of life; contours which reminded one of Leonardo da Vinci, etc.' On the Princess Belgiojoso see also pp. 123, 178, 254, and 415–16 of this book.

75 Barrès, in his *Visite à Léonard de Vinci* (*Trois Stations de psychothérapie*, 1891) imagines one of Leonardo's ambiguous faces ('jeune fille, jeune homme?') as conveying the following message in its smile:

'Parce que nous connaissons les lois de la vie et la marche des passions, aucune de vos agitations ne nous étonne, rien de vos insultes ne nous blesse, rien de vos serments d'éternité ne nous trouble . . . Et cette clairvoyance ne nous apporte aucune tristesse, car c'est un plaisir parfait que d'être perpétuellement curieux avec méthode. . . . Mais nous sourions de voir la peine que tu prends pour deviner ce qui m'intéresse.'

In Hofmannsthal's *Der Tor und der Tod*, Claudio addresses these lines to an ancient portrait of the Italian school:

> Gioconda, du, aus wundervollem Grund,
> Herleuchtend mit dem Glanz durchseelter Glieder,
> Dem rätselhaften, süssen, herben Mund,
> Dem Prunk der träumeschweren Augenlider:
> Gerad so viel verrietest du mir Leben,
> Als fragend ich vermocht dir einzuweben!

E. Dowden has these Keatsian lines on *Leonardo's Monna Lisa*:

> Make thyself known, Sibyl, or let despair
> Of knowing thee be absolute: I wait
> Hour-long and waste a soul. What word of fate
> Hides 'twixt the lips which smile and still forbear?
> Secret perfection! Mystery too fair!
> Tangle the sense no more, lest I should hate
> The delicate tyranny, the inviolate
> Poise of thy folded hands, thy fallen hair.
> Nay, nay,—I wrong thee with rough words; still be
> Serene, victorious, inaccessible;
> Still smile, but speak not; lightest irony
> Lurk ever 'neath thine eyelids' shadow; still
> O'ertop our knowledge; Sphinx of Italy
> Allure us and reject us at thy will!   [Add. 1950]

76 For a detailed study of Wilde's sources, see B. Fehr, *Studien zu Oscar Wildes Gedichten* (Berlin, Mayer und Müller, 1918; Palaestra, 100). Fehr remarks, among other things, that almost all the rare words which occur in rhyme in *The Sphinx* are taken from Flaubert's *Tentation*.

77 See above, p. 240.

78 Op. cit., p. 18.

79 See for example Cellini, *Vita*, II. xxix, xxx; and Diderot, *Les Bijoux indiscrets*, chap. xli, where the 'bijou' of Callipyge says: 'On dit que mon rival aurait des autels au delà des Alpes'; and chap. xlix where Sélim learns from the Italian ladies 'les modes du plaisir': 'Il y a dans ces raffinements du caprice et de la bizarrerie.'

Should we lay much stress on the Senecan horrors of certain Italian tragedies of the sixteenth century, should we find with Neri (*La tragedia italiana del Cinquecento*, Florence, Galletti e Cocci, 1904, pp. 142 and 145) in Adriano Valerini's *Afrodite* (1578) 'a hardly disguised voluptuous thrill mixed together with the pitiless research of criminal episodes', and that in all the tragedies of that school, as a rule, 'love was not tragical by itself, in its earnest and deep and human greatness, but because of the reckless excitement, and the most troubled instinct—revealing transparently its cruel essence'? We do not seem to perceive sure indications of sensibility through the thick rhetorical crust of those dramas, in which horror verges on caricature. Second-hand monstrosities, echoes of decadent cadences are surely to be found also in Italy (e.g. the character of Asteria in Boito's *Nerone*, certain lines of Camerana and certain novels of Alfredo Oriani, *Al di là*, *No*, in which, on the tracks of the French writers, the pleasure of evil-doing is exalted in a naïvely perverse and therefore grotesque manner, artificial paradises, reckless and sinful passions are described); but these currents have been outside the main stream of Italian literary production, so that it is possible to say that the Italian attitude to the world of the senses continued for a long time to be genuine and distinctive, even in spite of freedom of morals. See B. Croce, *La letteratura della nuova Italia*, vol. i, Bari, Laterza, 1929, p. 270: Asteria 'the martyr of her sensuality . . . she who dreams as a supreme delight to be torn to pieces by the monster'. Boito causes her to say: 'Horror attracts me like a lover. . . . I live in the ecstasy of violent dreams . . . drunken with tears.' As for Camerana, see the same volume by Croce, pp. 279–80: 'Camerana feels attracted to these spectacles; he loves them because they horrify him, he dwells on them with painful delight. Even the type of woman who appears in his verse is like one of those sights. It is the woman with dark hair and eyes, pale, mysterious, perhaps criminal, &c.' Croce quotes among others these lines: 'She is blackness become live flesh for our supreme delight and torment. . . . Who are you, made of darkness and velvet like a coffin?'; other lines, inspired by Flaubert, make us aware of 'the transition from certain aspects of romanticism to corresponding forms of the decadence, in which the heroic turns into the wild and the cruel, and beauty becomes a torment for the senses'. For further illustration of Oriani, it will be enough to compare Elisa di Monero's artificial paradise in *Al di là* (Bologna edition, 1934, p. 90), or the interior described in *No* (p. 332 et seq.) with the Eldorado in Gautier's *Fortunio*; or the sayings of Ottone di Banzole (*Al di là*, p. 225), such as 'I am a pagan of the times of Alcibiades and Aspasia', or certain utterances of Ida in *No* (p. 242: 'There are gladiators still; you'll see how the virgins die') with those of Albert in *Mademoiselle de Maupin*. D'Annunzio's rhetoric seems to be anticipated by certain cadences of Oriani; e.g. *No*, p. 379: 'La sua voce piena di sonorità lontane aveva degli stridori di vento e degli echi cavernosi' (His voice full of distant sonorities reminded one of the shrieking of the wind and the echoes of caverns). [Add. 1950]

[80] A morbid attraction for cruel deeds, for the sight of physical and moral tortures, is extremely evident in all the novels of Guerrazzi, and

culminates in *Beatrice Cenci* (1854, written in 1850), into which the author said (*Lettere*, Turin, 1891, vol. i, p. 716) that he had 'poured the waves of his own soul'. This morbid attraction must certainly have been increased by the cruel disciplinary methods which were in use at the school of Don Agostino which Guerrazzi attended as a child (see *Note Autobiografiche* by F. D. Guerrazzi, with a preface by R. Guastalla, Florence, Le Monnier, 1899, pp. 38 et seq.), and also by reading, at a tender age, the novels of Mrs. Radcliffe:

> 'The *Mysteries of Udolpho*, *A Castle in the Pyrenees*, *Granville Abbey*, affected my mind profoundly: and above all *The Confessional of the Black Penitents*: from that time onwards I have never looked at them, and yet I seem to have them always in front of my eyes; this could not have happened unless they contained in a very high degree something to stir and terrify one. . . . Such means of stirring the mind are truly tragic, nor can they be compared with grotesques.' (*Note Autob.*, pp. 55–7).

Byron also left a deep impression on his imagination. Guerrazzi's novels illustrate the more trivial aspects of the current of horrific Romanticism which, in Belgium, inspired the work of that turbid follower of Rubens, Antoine Wiertz (1806–65).

Huysmans ('Le Carnet d'un voyageur', in the *Revue des Deux Mondes* for November 15th, 1876) judged Wiertz's work 'grandiose et puérile à la fois; il a du génie par endroits, de l'insanité par autres!' Guerrazzi kept to the last an interest in shocking and disgusting deeds, which he delighted to comment upon with a heavy moralistic sarcasm; his posthumous novel, *Il secolo che muore* (written about 1870, published 1885), makes one think of the rant of the *frénétique* novelists (Soulié, Borel). [Add. 1950]

[81] Naturally, once the fashion for certain 'decadent' themes had been introduced, examples of literary sadism were to be found also in Italy.

That the atmosphere was ripe for a D'Annunzio may be shown by third-rate novels like *L'ultima notte* by Leandro (Giustino Ferri), Rome, Sommaruga, 1884, where we find a 'demoniacal' Russian lady, Vera, who persuades herself that she is worshipping Satan in the person of Alexander Nogoroff, and cries to him in an orgasm: 'Love me, because you are a murderer; love me, because you are a poisoner. . . .' 'She had a kind of foam on her parched and bitten lips, and her eyes spoke of monstrous fantasies, of sanguinary orgies, of tortures, spasms, nameless sins, &c.' Vera is in brief the type described in Section 29 of this chapter. [Add. 1950]

There was also *Mafarka le Futuriste*, by F. T. Marinetti (which was written in French and then translated into Italian by Decio Cinti), of which Rachilde wrote, in the *Mercure de France* of July 1st, 1910: '*Mafarka* m'a produit l'effet des *Chants de Maldoror*, le personnage qui joue du piano les doigts gantés de sang.'

[82] *Gazzetta Letteraria*, Jan. 4th, 1896.   [83] p. 46.
[84] p. 353.   [85] p. 475.   [86] pp. 273–4.   [87] p. 475.
[88] pp. 237–8.   [89] p. 203.   [90] p. 216.   [91] p. 29.

⁹² G. A. Borgese, *Gabriele D'Annunzio* (Naples, Ricciardi, 1909), especially pp. 63 et seq.; F. Flora, *D'Annunzio* (Naples, Ricciardi, 1926).

⁹³ pp. 476–7.

⁹⁴ See for this as for other sources E. Thovez, *L'Arco d'Ulisse* (Naples, Ricciardi, 1921), in which are collected the well-known lists of sources which appeared in the *Gazzetta Letteraria* of the years 1895 and 1896.

⁹⁵ It may be worth recording here that in 1886 there had appeared from the 'Pléiade' Press a dramatic poem by Pierre Quillard, *La Fille aux mains coupées*, in which the heroine had her hands cut off because they were contaminated by the 'caresses incestueuses et brutales' of her own father. This poem by Quillard merely recounts a very ancient legend (see note 1 of chap. iii), of which versions are to be found also in *Il Cunto de li Cunti*, by G. B. Basile (*La Penta Manomozza*) and in the fables of Grimm (*Das Mädchen ohne Hände*; see ed. Bolte and Polívka, vol. i, pp. 295–311).

⁹⁶ *Le Vergini delle Rocce*, pp. 221 et seq.: 'I reconstructed in my mind the essential moment which had brought about the death of Pantea; and that nocturnal crime assumed in my eyes a beauty of profound import. . . . He must have experienced a wonderful thrill in his innermost self.' Umbelino, as he accompanies his sister to her last devotions, says to her: ' "O Pantea, how blessed you are! Your soul's place is in the lap of Our Lord Jesus Christ". But silently he was saying to her things unspeakable, which she could not hear.' (The inevitable profanation which accompanies sadistic desire.) The fountain in which Umbelino drowns Pantea bears the inscription (p. 256): 'Spectarunt nuptas hic se Mors atque Voluptas— Unus [fama ferat], quum duo, vultus erat: Here Desire and Death, joined together, gazed at each other; and their two faces made one face.'

⁹⁷ *Forse che sì*, p. 442.

⁹⁸ pp. 381–2.

⁹⁹ The words of Nicolò d'Este, Act iii, *ad fin.*

¹⁰⁰ See the interpretation of *Tristan* in the *Trionfo della Morte*: 'Passion inspired her (Isolda) with a homicidal will, and awoke in the roots of her being an instinct hostile to existence, a need of dissolution, of annihilation' (p. 441). See also note 60 of chap. v.

¹⁰¹ *Gabriele D'Annunzio* (Naples, Perrella, 1912), p. 333.

¹⁰² See above, pp. 226–7.

¹⁰³ D'Annunzio's Swinburnian sources will be found to a great extent catalogued in *Critica*, vol. viii, no. 1, vol. x, no. 6, vol. xi, no. 6, vol. xii, no. 1. The first to compare the *Fedra* of D'Annunzio with Swinburne's *Phaedra* was G. P. Lucini, in the article 'L'indimenticabile risciacquatura delle molte "Fedre" ' in *La Ragione*, June 27th, 1909, an article which was reprinted in *Antidannunziana* (Milan, Studio Editoriale Lombardo, 1914), pp. 260 et seq.

¹⁰⁴ *La Gloria*, pp. 106 and 194.

¹⁰⁵ *La Critica*, vol. viii, no. 1, p. 27; communication from Vittorio Lombardini.

106 Cf.:

> . . . and over her shines fire.
> She hath sown pain and plague in all our house,
> Love loathed of love, and mates unmatchable,
> Wild wedlock, and the lusts that bleat or low.
>
> (*Phaedra*)

Elle a été l'Hélène des Troyens. . . . Elle a été Dalila, qui coupait les cheveux de Samson. Elle a été cette fille d'Israël qui s'abandonnait aux boucs. Elle a aimé l'adultère, l'idolâtrie, le mensonge et la sottise. Elle s'est prostituée à tous les peuples. Elle a chanté dans tous les carrefours. Elle a baisé tous les visages, &c.

> (*La Tentation de Saint-Antoine*).

Elsewhere (*La Nave*, p. 104) it is Swinburne's Faustine who serves as model: 'And who can ever say that I was not sent by God as a scourge for the nations?':

> . . . Or did God mean
> To scourge with scorpions for a rod
> Our sins, Faustine?

107 Quoted above, p. 263.

107A This passage has been suggested by Swinburne's *Anactoria*:

> Like me shall be the shuddering calm of night
>
> . . . .
>
> Like me the one star swooning with desire
> . . . and like me
> The land-stream and the tide-stream in the sea
>
> . . . .
>
> And by the yearning in my veins I know
> The yearning sound of waters; and mine eyes
> Burn as that beamless fire which fills the skies
> With troubled stars and travelling things of flame . . .
>
> [Add. 1950]

108 pp. 118 et seq. Compare, for example, the following with the passage quoted above on p. 237:

'Ah, to shake thy life at thy lips . . . and not to take it from thee, but to leave it there in endless torment, to stifle it without extinguishing, to change it into an ill that may wring thy soul and yet not destroy it. . . .'

Nor is *Anactoria* the only poem so used here. As usual, D'Annunzio's lines are an anthology of several of Swinburne's poems (*Hesperia, Dolores, Phaedra, Laus Veneris*. . . .).

109 Flora, op. cit., p. 69:

'In this tragedy [*La Gloria*] the woman is strong, the man weak, cowardly and mean; but this is a not infrequent characteristic in D'Annunzio—Anna Comnena, Gioconda, Mila di Codro, Basiliola, Mortella, Isabella, Gigliola, Fedra and others of his women are stronger and more vehement than the men: the women of D'Annunzio have more will-power even when they are defeated, because their will is reduced to sex, which is always D'Annunzio's ultimate and ruling idea.'

110 *Tragedia, madre d'incesto* and *La lussuria del sacrilegio*.

111 In *Forse che sì* 'criminal sensuality' communicates itself both to

persons and landscapes, and affects even vocabulary and images. 'Flog me!'—shrieks Isabella Inghirami to her lover (p. 437). But it is not only the union of the two which is described as though it were a form of torture (pp. 439–41):

'And in the livid twilight . . . took place the fierce wrestling of two enemies joined together by the middle of their bodies, the growing anguish of the neck with its arteries swollen and crying out to be severed, the frenzied shake of one who strives to drag from the lowest depths the red roots of life and to fling them beyond the possible limit of man's spasm.

'The man cried out as though his virility were being torn from him with the utmost cruelty; he raised himself, and then fell back. The woman quivered, with a rattling sound which broke into a moan even more inhuman than the man's cry. And both remained exhausted on the floor, in the purple half-light, feeling themselves alive, befouled, but with something lifeless between them, with the remains of a dark crime between their bodies—which were now detached from each other, but remained pressed together at the point where that dark crime had been committed, prostrate and silent, overcome by a love which was greater than their love and which perhaps came to them from the place of lacerated, abandoned beauty.'

Torture is to be found not only here; everything in the novel takes on a semblance of 'lacerated beauty', from the landscape of Volterra to the fate of Vana, the girl who kills herself in aesthetically arranged circumstances, and this is a case in which the very superficial critical method of reading the first and the last pages gives an exact indication of the content. On the first page are to be found these words: 'horrible', 'an almost brutal cruelty', 'a ghastly offence against body and soul', 'an inhuman slight against love', 'desperate', 'mad'; and on the last: 'the pain of the deep burn drew forth a cry from him', 'he could not bear the agony'. On the first page, at the very beginning, is also to be found the word 'heroic'.

A sadistic temperament not unlike Isabella Inghirami's is that of Paolina Pandolfi, sadist, mystic, and murderess, in Pierre-Jean Jouve's *Paulina 1880*, Paris, Gallimard, 1925. [Add. 1950]

[112] This passage may be appositely commented upon with Colette's opinion of such a trinity (*Ces plaisirs . . .*, Paris, Ferenczi, 1932, p. 247):

'Le vice prétentieux qui s'intitule "harmonie ternaire de l'amour" est un piège triste. Sa monotonie, ses aspects cirque et "pyramide humaine" ont bientôt fait, je pense, de rebuter les plus grossiers.'

[113] pp. 434–5, 449, 451.

[114] D'Annunzio, in describing Isabella's state of mind, interweaves the songs of the 'Pazzo di Cristo' [Jacopone da Todi] with the lines of *Anactoria*. *Forse che sì*, pp. 345 et seq.:

'Now like the "Passo del Signore", like the "Libro dell' Ardore". . . . she implored an alleviation of her voluptuous martyrdom. . . . The passion of those songs, that "Pazzia non conosciuta", that "Pazzia illuminata", filled her nights with the delirium of their music. The throbbing of her soul stretched forth its pain to the stars, and poured out its lightless fire towards things eternally in travail, whence dropped, now and then, fugitive tears, as though to touch her soul before they vanished. The Lover "with soul expanded" sang in her for love of love, like those tireless nightingales which sing till the whole Universe sings with them.'

Cf. *Anactoria*:

> . . . And fierce reluctance of disastrous stars,
>
> .   .   .   .   .   .
>
> With sorrow of labouring moons, and altering light
> And travail of the Planets of the night,
> And weeping of the weary Pleiads seven
>
> .   .   .   .   .   .
>
> Fierce noises of the fiery nightingales.

The last image in the passage from D'Annunzio just quoted is taken from Shelley.

[115] Cf. *Anactoria*: 'Is not his incense bitterness, his meat—murder?' &c.

[116] p. xlvi.

[117] A. Eulenburg, *Sadismus und Masochismus* (*Grenzenfragen des Nerven- und Seelenlebens*, vol. xix; Wiesbaden, 1902), pp. 18 et seq.

[118] The actual development of meaning in the word *libertin* shows the connexion between the idea of vice and that of revolt against the Divinity: *libertin* and *esprit fort* are synonymous. See F. Perrens, *Les Libertins en France au XVIIᵉ siècle* (Paris, 1896) *passim*, especially pp. 8 et seq., 170 et seq.

[119] 'I see that my poetical secret lies in a sensuality dragged free of the senses'—D'Annunzio.

[120] We need merely mention that the type of cruel, sphinx-eyed woman is dominant in the series of novels called *Grausame Frauen* by Leopold von Sacher-Masoch, who gave his name to the sexual tendency illustrated in this chapter.

[121] On Rachilde, see chap. v, § 14.

[122] Cf. *Trionfo della Morte*, p. 353: 'He believed that she had shown a morbid taste for an exactly similar form of irritation in some of the cases which had occurred, &c.'

[123] *Le Jardin des supplices*, pp. 114, 121, 158, 159.

[124] Cf. note 111.

[125] p. 275.

[126] p. 155.

[126A] The kind of eroticism which forms the subject of these novels could be defined with another phrase by Mirbeau (*Le Calvaire*, p. 123 of the Ollendorff edition):

'Ce n'était plus l'Amour frisé, pommadé, enrubanné, qui s'en va pâmé, une rose au bec, par les beaux clairs de lune, racler sa guitare sous les balcons; c'était l'Amour barbouillé de sang, ivre de fange, l'Amour aux fureurs onaniques, l'Amour maudit, qui colle sur l'homme sa gueule en forme de ventouse, et lui dessèche les veines, lui pompe les moelles, lui décharne les os.' [Add. 1950]

CHAPTER V
BYZANTIUM

Ayez pitié de mon absence
Au seuil de mes intentions!
Mon âme est pâle d'impuissance
Et de blanches inactions.

MAETERLINCK, Oraison (Serres chaudes).

Flat-chested, crop-headed, chemicalized women, of
indeterminate sex,
and wimbly-wambly young men, of sex still more
indeterminate.

D. H. LAWRENCE.

BYZANTIUM

1. Delacroix, as a painter, was fiery and dramatic; Gustave Moreau strove to be cold and static. The former painted gestures, the latter attitudes. Although far apart in artistic merit (after all, Delacroix in his best work is a great painter), they are highly representative of the moral atmosphere of the two periods in which they flourished—of Romanticism, with its fury of frenzied action, and of Decadence, with its sterile contemplation. The subject-matter is almost the same—voluptuous, gory exoticism. But Delacroix lives inside his subject, whereas Moreau worships his from outside, with the result that the first is a painter, the second a decorator.

Moreau advocated two principles, in opposition to the emotional qualities which he held to be an infiltration of literature into painting—the principle of the Beauty of Inertia and the principle of the Necessity of Richness. The Beauty of Inertia was the particular quality which he professed to find in the Prophets, the Sibyls, and the allegorical sepulchral figures of Michaelangelo:

'Toutes ces figures [he said] semblent être figées dans un geste de somnambulisme idéal; elles sont inconscientes du mouvement qu'elles exécutent, absorbées dans la rêverie au point de paraître emportées vers d'autres mondes.'

Moreau believed that he was following the teaching of Michaelangelo as regards this Beauty of Inertia, and of the Flemish, Rhenish, Umbrian, and Venetian Primitives as regards the principle of redundant decoration: 'Consultez les maîtres. Ils vous donnent tous le conseil de ne pas faire d'art pauvre'; he believed also that he was realizing pure art as formulated by Baudelaire, that is, that his 'Beauty of Inertia' conformed to the following rule:[1]

'La passion est chose *naturelle*, trop naturelle même, pour ne pas introduire un ton blessant, discordant, dans le domaine de la Beauté pure; trop familière et trop violente pour ne pas scandaliser les purs Désirs, les gracieuses Mélancolies et les nobles Désespoirs qui habitent les régions surnaturelles de la Poésie'.

And that his 'Necessity of Richness' conformed to this second rule:[2]

'Comme un rêve est placé dans une atmosphère colorée qui lui est propre, de même une conception, devenue composition, a besoin de se mouvoir dans un milieu coloré qui lui soit particulier. Il y a évidemment un ton particulier attribué à une partie quelconque du tableau qui devient clef et qui gouverne les autres. . . . Tous les personnages, leur disposition relative, le paysage ou l'intérieur qui leur sert de fond ou d'horizon, leurs vêtements, tout enfin doit servir à illuminer l'idée générale et porter sa couleur originelle, sa livrée pour ainsi dire. . . . Un bon tableau, fidèle et égal au rêve qui l'a enfanté, doit être produit comme un monde.'

The amusing thing is that Baudelaire, in speaking here of Delacroix, made use of the Master's own expressions. So true is it that the same aesthetic principle may be quoted in support of diametrically opposed kinds of inspiration.

Baudelaire also added:[3]

'L'art du coloriste tient évidemment par de certains côtés aux mathématiques et à la musique.'

Following the example of Wagner's music, which was then in fashion, Moreau composed his pictures in the style of symphonic poems, loading them with significant accessories in which the principal theme was echoed, until the subject yielded the last drop of its symbolic sap.

Though the aesthetics of Baudelaire and the music of Wagner may have been the theoretical premises of Moreau's painting, it is quite obvious that in other respects these theories would not of themselves have sufficed to endow his painting with certain of its peculiar qualities, since it was possible for them to be—since, in fact, they actually were—brought into use in support of extremely different ideas. Moreau's figures are ambiguous; it is hardly possible to distinguish at the first glance which of two lovers is the man, which the woman; all his characters are linked by subtle bonds of relationship, as in Swinburne's *Lesbia Brandon*; lovers look as though they were related, brothers as though they were lovers, men have the faces of virgins, virgins the faces of youths;

the symbols of Good and Evil are entwined and equivo-
cally confused. There is no contrast between different
ages, sexes, or types: the underlying meaning of this
painting is incest, its most exalted figure the Androgyne,
its final word sterility.[4]

It is precisely in such painting, at the same time sexless
and lascivious, that the spirit of the Decadent movement
is most vividly expressed. Nor was it for nothing that the
discoverer of Moreau should have been Huysmans,
creator of the character of des Esseintes, the monster of
decadence of whom d'Aurevilly wrote:[5]

'Des Esseintes n'est plus un être organisé à la manière d'Ober-
mann, de René, d'Adolphe, ces héros de romans humains, passion-
nés et coupables. C'est une mécanique détraquée. Rien de plus. . . .
En écrivant l'autobiographie de son héros, il [Huysmans] ne fait
pas que la confession particulière d'une personnalité dépravée et
solitaire, mais, du même coup, il nous écrit la nosographie d'une
société putrifiée de matérialisme. . . . Certes! pour qu'un décadent
de cette force pût se produire et qu'un livre comme celui de M.
Huysmans pût germer dans une tête humaine, il fallait vraiment
que nous fussions devenus ce que nous sommes, — une race à sa
dernière heure.'

Let us for a moment leave aside this idea of the *fin de
siècle* and the *finis Latinorum*: these were things in which
people believed at the time, but all that it is necessary to
emphasize here is that this was actually a widespread
feeling. Huysmans' remarks on the subject of Moreau
are evidence of what such painting meant to his contemporaries, and they bring us back to the discussion of
the Fatal Woman.

2. Huysmans imagines des Esseintes as having acquired the two masterpieces of Gustave Moreau, the
artist above all others 'dont le talent le ravissait en de longs
transports'[6]—the oil-painting called *Salomé* (in the Mante
Collection) and the water-colour *L'Apparition* (now in the
Luxembourg Museum), both of which were exhibited at
the 1876 Salon, which marked the success of this painter
in the same way in which the Pre-Raphaelite Exhibition
of 1856 had marked the success of D. G. Rossetti. Huysmans' faithful description helps one to trace the type of

literature to which Moreau's *soi-disant* anti-literary painting was related. He describes *Salomé* as follows:

'Un trône se dressait, pareil au maître-autel d'une cathédrale,
sous d'innombrables voûtes jaillissant de colonnes trapues ainsi
que des piliers romans, émaillées de briques polychrômes, serties
de mosaïques, incrustées de lapis et de sardoines, dans un palais
semblable à une basilique d'une architecture tout à la fois musul-
mane et byzantine.

'Au centre du tabernacle surmontant l'autel précédé de marches
en forme de semi-vasques, le Tétrarque Hérode était assis, coiffé
d'une tiare, les jambes rapprochées, les mains sur les genoux. . . .

'Autour de cette statue, immobile, figée dans une pose hiératique
de dieu Hindou, des parfums brûlaient, dégorgeant des nuées de
vapeurs que trouaient, de même que des yeux phosphorés de bêtes,
les feux des pierres enchâssées dans les parois du trône; puis la vapeur
montait, se déroulait sous les arcades où la fumée bleue se mêlait
à la poudre d'or des grands rayons de jour, tombés des dômes.

'Dans l'odeur perverse des parfums, dans l'atmosphère sur-
chauffée de cette église, Salomé, le bras gauche étendu, en un geste
de commandement, le bras droit replié, tenant, à la hauteur du
visage, un grand lotus, s'avance lentement sur les pointes, aux
accords d'une guitare dont une femme accroupie pince les cordes.'

In Flaubert's *Tentation* we read:[7]

'Et Antoine voit devant lui une basilique immense.

'La lumière se projette du fond, merveilleuse comme serait un
soleil multicolore. . . . Et il [Hilarion] le pousse vers un trône d'or
à cinq marches où . . . siège le prophète Manès — beau comme un
archange, immobile comme une statue, portant une robe indienne,
des escarboucles dans ses cheveux nattés, à sa main gauche un livre
d'images peintes, et sous sa droite un globe. . . . Manès fait tourner
son globe; et réglant ses paroles sur une lyre d'où s'échappent des
sons cristallins . . .'

Huysmans is describing Salome's appearance:

'La face recueillie, solennelle, presque auguste, elle commence la
lubrique danse qui doit réveiller les sens assoupis du vieil Hérode,
ses seins ondulent et, au frottement de ses colliers qui tourbillonnent,
leurs bouts se dressent; sur la moiteur de la peau les diamants,
attachés, scintillent; ses bracelets, ses ceintures, ses bagues, crachent
des étincelles; sur sa robe triomphale, couturée de perles, ramagée
d'argent, lamée d'or, la cuirasse des orfèvreries dont chaque maille
est une pierre, entre en combustion, croise des serpenteaux de feu,
grouille sur la chair mate, sur la peau rose thé, ainsi que des insectes

splendides aux élytres éblouissants, marbrés de carmin, ponctués de jaune aurore, diaprés de bleu d'acier, tigrés de vert paon.'

This Salome is sister of the Queen of Sheba in the *Tentation*:[8]

'Sa robe en brocart d'or, divisée régulièrement par des falbalas de perles, de jais et de saphirs, lui serre la taille dans un corsage étroit, rehaussé d'applications de couleur, qui représentent les douze signes du Zodiaque. . . . Ses larges manches, garnies d'émeraudes et de plumes d'oiseau, laissent voir à nu son petit bras rond. . . . Une chaîne d'or plate, lui passant sous le menton, monte le long de ses joues, s'enroule en spirale autour de sa coiffure, poivrée de poudre bleue; puis, redescendant, lui effleure les épaules et vient s'attacher sur sa poitrine à un scorpion de diamant, qui allonge la langue entre ses seins, etc.'

Huysmans sees in Moreau's Salome the type of Fatal Woman described in the last chapter:

'Ce type de Salomé si hantant pour les artistes et pour les poètes, obsédait, depuis des années, des Esseintes. . . . Ni saint Mathieu, ni saint Marc, ni saint Luc, ni les autres évangélistes ne s'étendaient sur les charmes délirants, sur les actives dépravations de la danseuse. Elle demeurait effacée, se perdait, mystérieuse et pâmée, dans le brouillard lointain des siècles, insaisissable pour les esprits précis et terre à terre, accessible seulement aux cervelles ébranlées, aiguisées, comme rendues visionnaires par la névrose. . . incompréhensible pour tous les écrivains qui n'ont jamais pu rendre l'inquiétante exaltation de la danseuse, la grandeur raffinée de l'assassine.

'Dans l'œuvre de Gustave Moreau, conçue en dehors de toutes les données du Testament, des Esseintes voyait enfin réalisée cette Salomé surhumaine et étrange qu'il avait rêvée. . . . Elle devenait, en quelque sorte, la déité symbolique de l'indestructible Luxure, déesse de l'immortelle Hystérie, la Beauté maudite, élue entre toutes par la catalepsie qui lui raidit les chairs et lui durcit les muscles; la Bête monstrueuse, indifférente, irresponsable, insensible, empoisonnant, de même que l'Hélène antique, tout ce qui l'approche, tout ce qui la voit, tout ce qu'elle touche. . . . Le peintre semblait d'ailleurs avoir voulu affirmer sa volonté de rester hors des siècles, de ne point préciser d'origine, de pays, d'époque, en mettant sa Salomé au milieu de cet extraordinaire palais, d'un style confus et grandiose, en la vêtant de somptueuses et chimériques robes, en la mitrant d'un incertain diadème en forme de tour phénicienne tel qu'en porte la Salammbô, en lui plaçant enfin dans la main le sceptre d'Isis, la fleur sacrée de l'Égypte et de l'Inde, le grand lotus.'

Des Esseintes dilates upon the meaning of this emblematic flower: is it a phallic symbol, or an allegory of fertility, or was the painter thinking of 'la danseuse, la femme mortelle, le Vase souillé, cause de tous les péchés et de tous les crimes', or was he remembering the embalming custom of ancient Egypt by which lotus-petals were inserted in the sexual organs of corpses for the purpose of purification?

However, even more disquieting than this to des Esseintes was the water-colour called *L'Apparition*, in which the severed head of the Saint appears, after the crime, to a half-naked, terrified Salome, less majestic and proud 'mais plus troublante que la Salomé du tableau à l'huile':[8A]

'Ici, elle était vraiment fille; elle obéissait à son tempérament de femme ardente et cruelle; elle vivait, plus raffinée et plus sauvage, plus exécrable et plus exquise; elle réveillait plus énergiquement les sens en léthargie de l'homme, ensorcelait, domptait plus sûrement ses volontés, avec son charme de grande fleur vénérienne, poussée dans des couches sacrilèges, élevée dans des serres impies.'

He concludes with a comprehensive appreciation of the art of Moreau, in which he discovers only a vague affinity with Mantegna, Jacopo de' Barbari, Leonardo, Delacroix, but above all a unique originality:[9]

'Remontant aux sources ethnographiques, aux origines des mythologies dont il comparait et démêlait les sanglantes énigmes; réunissant, fondant en une seule les légendes issues de l'Extrême Orient et métamorphosées par les croyances des autres peuples, il justifiait ainsi ses fusions architectoniques, ses amalgames luxueux et inattendus d'étoffes, ses hiératiques et sinistres allégories aiguisées par les inquiètes perspicuités d'un nervosisme tout moderne; et il restait à jamais douloureux, hanté par les symboles des perversités et des amours surhumaines, des stupres divins consommés sans abandons et sans espoirs.

'Il y avait dans ses œuvres désespérées et érudites un enchantement singulier, une incantation vous remuant jusqu'au fond des entrailles, comme celle de certains poèmes de Baudelaire. . . .'

3. In direct opposition to Huysmans' interpretation, which was later developed by Lorrain, Ary Renan, in his study of this painter,[10] speaks of the 'littérature adventice' which had exalted and commented upon Moreau's two pictures 'avec le parti pris d'y découvrir des dépravations

occultes': 'Il est nécessaire', says this critic, 'de les purifier
de ces paraphrases suspectes et, pour ainsi dire, de les
exorciser.'[10A] However, the interpretation that he suggests
comes to the same conclusion:

'... Moreau vivant de longues années sous l'obsession de ce nom
de femme, hanté par la vision d'un geste impitoyable, par l'horreur
de ce sang de juste versé pour la grâce d'un être fatal et beau; car,
ce qu'il demande à l'amer récit de l'Évangile, c'est encore un
monstre à peindre, un monstre femelle encore, dont la force réside
à la fois dans sa beauté charnelle, dans la pratique d'artifices maudits,
dans une malignité spontanée ou suggérée. La syrienne Salomé
devient ainsi, par le désir qu'elle a conçu ou par la vengeance qu'elle
sert, l'incarnation d'une harmonieuse et navrante énergie du Mal,
l'ouvrière d'un de ces crimes démesurés qu'il appartient à l'art de
magnifier.'

The favourite theme of Moreau, which he never tires
of treating in his pictures, is that of Fatality, of Evil and
Death incarnate in female beauty. These are the words
with which he himself commented upon the picture he called
Les Chimères, with the sub-title of 'Décaméron satanique':[11]

'Cette Île des rêves fantastiques renferme toutes les formes de
la passion, de la fantaisie, du caprice chez la femme.

'La Femme, dans son essence première, l'être inconscient, folle
de l'inconnu, du mystère, éprise du mal, sous la forme de séduction
perverse et diabolique. Rêves d'enfants, rêves des sens, rêves monstrueux, rêves mélancoliques, rêves transportant l'esprit et l'âme
dans le vague des espaces, dans le mystère de l'ombre, tout doit
ressentir l'influence des sept péchés capitaux, tout se trouve dans
cette enceinte satanique, dans ce cercle des vices et des ardeurs
coupables, depuis le germe d'apparence encore innocente jusqu'aux
fleurs monstrueuses et fatales des abîmes. Ce sont des théories de
reines maudites venant de quitter le serpent aux sermons fascina-
teurs; ce sont des êtres dont l'âme est abolie, attendant, sur le bord
des chemins, le passage du bouc lascif, monté par la luxure qu'on
adorera au passage. Des êtres isolés, sombres, dans un rêve d'envie,
l'orgueil inassouvi, dans leur isolement bestial; des femmes en-
fourchant des chimères, qui les emportent dans l'espace d'où elles
retombent éperdues d'horreur et de vertige. . . . Au loin, la Ville
morte, aux passions sommeillantes; Ville du Moyen Âge, âpre et
silencieuse, etc.'

Moreau sought the theme of satanic beauty in primitive
mythology and treated it in his pictures of the so-called

'Sphinx' series; this began with the painting which was the success of the 1864 Salon, in which the cruel beast with the face of an imperious woman plants her claws on the breast of the languid youth Oedipus, and ended with the water-colour exhibited in 1886 at the Goupil Galleries, *Le Sphinx vainqueur*, in which the Sphinx reigns supreme over a promontory bristling with bleeding corpses; he treated it also in the *Hélène*, exhibited in the Salon of 1880, in which the Fatal Woman, glittering with jewels, stalks, as though entranced, among the dying:

'Un enlacement de victimes navrées à mort se dénoue à ses pieds. . . . On dirait qu'ils se sont rués sur un bûcher volontaire. L'hommage de leur vie que ces guerriers, ces princes, ces poètes, adressent en vain à l'idole errante se lit sur leurs fronts; un vague sourire passe sur leurs traits blêmis; leurs membres paralysés se détendent, leurs lèvres s'amollissent, et de l'hécatombe où ces étranges victimes se sont offertes s'exhalent, non des imprécations ni d'amères paroles mais des soupirs apaisés, une plainte d'enfants qui s'endorment sous la consolation d'une caresse aimée. . . . Le tableau . . . respire le carnage et la volupté.'

Thus Ary Renan,[12] who goes even farther here in his sinister interpretation of Moreau than Huysmans himself, who confined himself to saying:[13]

'A ses pieds gisent des amas de cadavres percés de flèches, et, de son auguste beauté blonde, elle domine le carnage, majestueuse et superbe comme la Salammbô apparaissant aux mercenaires, semblable à une divinité malfaisante qui empoisonne, sans même qu'elle en ait conscience, tout ce qui l'approche ou tout ce qu'elle regarde et touche.'

It was this Helen, obvious prototype of D'Annunzio's Basiliola, who afterwards inspired Samain with the following sonnet (from *L'Urne penchée*, in *Le Jardin de l'Infante*, 1897 edition):[14]

L'âcre vapeur d'un soir de bataille surnage.
L'Argienne aux bras blancs a franchi les remparts,
Et vers le fleuve rouge, où les morts sont épars,
Solitaire, s'avance à travers le carnage.

Là-bas, les feux des Grecs brillent sur le rivage;
Les chevaux immortels hennissent près des chars. . . .
Lente, elle va parmi les cadavres hagards,
Et passe avec horreur sa main sur son visage.

Qu'elle apparaît divine aux lueurs du couchant! . . .
Des longs voiles secrets, qu'elle écarte en marchant,
Monte une odeur d'amour irrésistible et sombre;

Et déjà les mourants, saignants et mutilés,
Rampant vers ses pieds nus sur leurs coudes dans l'ombre,
Touchent ses cheveux d'or et meurent consolés.

The vision of Helen which appears in Giovanni Pascoli's
Anticlo (in *Poemi Conviviali*) is similar:

'And so, as Anticlo was already dying, there came to him, as
in the mute vision of a dream, Helena. Hotly around her burned
the blaze, above the blaze shone the full moon. She passed, silent
and serene, like the moon, through the fire and the blood. The
flames writhed higher at her passing; men's veins pressed forth a
subtler stream of blood. And the last walls crashed down, and the
last sobs were heard. . . .'

In Pascoli, however, the vision is more chaste, and his
Anticlo, who wishes only to remember Helen, is nearer to
the spirit of the Trojan ancients who considered the war
for such beauty to be a just one, than to the dark sensuality
of the dying men of Samain.

But Salome, Helen, and the Sphinx are not the only
incarnations of eternal feminine cruelty in the work of
Moreau, whose *delectatio morbosa* in subjects of sensual
cruelty and suffering beauty is testified by the innumerable
canvases which cover the walls of the museum he be-
queathed to the State. The Athenians delivered to the
Minotaur, slaves given as food to lampreys, the young man
conquered by the fascination of Death, Diomede torn by
horses, the Thracian maiden half-fainting as she gazes at
the severed head of Orpheus, Saint Sebastian, the heap of
beautiful bodies at the feet of the Hydra,[15] the slaughter of
the Suitors . . . Moreau justified his predilection for such
subjects by an ethical-religious theory—he claimed that
he was celebrating 'la glorification des sacrifices et
l'apothéose des rédempteurs'.

Other pictures illustrate tremendous, monstrous loves
—Pasiphae waiting for the bull, Semele, palpitating
victim on the knee of the Titanic god, Leda, Europa, subjects whose sensuality has become frozen in the visionary
symbolism of languid and lascivious forms. The painter

lingers in this world of his like a child who never tires of listening to terrible and mysterious stories, and his figures have exactly that suggestion of the abstract and epicene which is characteristic of the childish imagination. One has the impression in Moreau, as in Swinburne, of an ambiguous, troubled sexuality. We have travelled far from Delacroix' Sardanapalus, who contemplates with a satisfied air the hecatomb of lovely slave-girls: this is a massacre of youths who burn for a kiss from cruel Helen, the majestic Fatal Woman.

Delacroix was descended from Byron, Moreau is a forerunner of Maeterlinck.

4. It was, in fact, from the plays of Maeterlinck (particularly *La Princesse Maleine*, 1889, and *Les sept Princesses*, 1891: Maeterlinck became famous as the result of an article by Mirbeau in the *Figaro* of August 24th, 1890) that Oscar Wilde derived the childish prattle employed by the characters in his *Salomé* (written in French in 1891, published in 1893),[16] which reduces the voluptuous Orient of Flaubert's *Tentation* to the level of a nursery tale. It is childish, but it is also humoristic, with a humour which one can with difficulty believe to be unintentional, so much does Wilde's play resemble a parody of the whole of the material used by the Decadents and of the stammering mannerism of Maeterlinck's dramas—and, as a parody, *Salomé* comes very near to being a masterpiece. Yet it seems that Wilde was not quite aiming at this, either in the play or in the poem *The Sphinx*, which was discussed in the last chapter.

It was Wilde who finally fixed the legend of Salome's horrible passion. There is no suggestion of this to be found in Flaubert's tale (*Hérodias*), in which Salome is merely the tool of her mother's vengeance and after the dance becomes confused in repeating the instructions of Herodias:

En zézayant un peu, [elle] prononça ces mots, d'un air enfantin:
— Je veux que tu me donnes dans un plat, la tête . . .
Elle avait oublié le nom, mais reprit en souriant:
— La tête de Iaokanann!

Wilde repeats this repartee on the part of Salome, but

in quite a different sense. Salome denies that she has made the request at her mother's instigation. 'C'est pour mon propre plaisir que je demande la tête de Iokanaan dans un bassin d'argent.' And, having obtained the head, she fastens her lips upon it in her vampire passion. Yet not even here can Wilde be given credit for originality.[17] He did not take the idea of Salome's monstrous passion from Flaubert, where it did not exist, nor yet from the pages of *A rebours* devoted to the paintings of Moreau—pages and pictures which certainly had their influence upon the play, but in an incidental manner: in them, in any case, the idea of sensual cruelty remained vague. Heinrich Heine, in *Atta Troll* (written in 1841), had been the first to introduce into literature this theme, which he derived from popular tradition.[18] Herodias appears in the cavalcade of spirits seen from the witch Uraka's window (Caput XIX):[19]

And the third of those fair figures,
Which thy heart had moved so deeply,
Was it also some she-devil
Like the other two depicted?

If a devil or an angel,
I know not. With women never
Knows one clearly, where the angel
Leaves off and the devil begins.

O'er the face of glowing languor
Lay an Oriental magic,
And the dress recalled with transport
All Sheherazade's stories.

Lips of softness like pomegranates,
Lily-white the arching nose,
And the limbs, refreshing, taper,
Like a palm in some oasis.

High she was on white steed seated,
Whose gold rein two Moors were holding,
As along the way they trotted
At the Princess' side afoot.

Yes, she was indeed a princess,
Was the sovereign of Judaea,
Was the beauteous wife of Herod,
Who the Baptist's head demanded.

For this deed of blood was she too
Execrated; and as spectre
Must until the day of Judgement
Ride among the goblin hunt.

In her hands she carries ever
That sad charger, with the head of
John the Baptist, which she kisses:
Yes, the head with fervour kisses.

For, time was, she loved the Baptist—
'Tis not in the Bible written,
But there yet exists the legend
Of Herodias' bloody love—

Else there were no explanation
Of that lady's curious longing—
Would a woman want the head of
Any man she did not love?

Was perhaps a little peevish
With her swain, had him beheaded;
But when she upon the charger
Saw the head so well beloved,

Straight she wept and mad became,
And she died of love's distraction—
Love's distraction! Pleonasmus!
Why, love is itself distraction!

Rising up at night she carries,
In her hand, as now related,
When she hunts, the bleeding head—
Yet with woman's maniac frenzy

Sometimes, she, with childish laughter,
Whirls it in the air above her,
Then again will nimbly catch it,
Like a plaything as it falls.

As she rode along before me,
She regarded me and nodded,
So coquettish yet so pensive,
That my inmost soul was moved.

Heine's Herodias had a success in France. Banville was inspired by it to write one of the sonnets in his *Princesses* (1874), of which the epigraph is the passage from *Atta Troll*: 'Car elle était vraiment princesse: c'était la reine de Judée, la femme d'Hérode, celle qui a demandé

la tête de Jean-Baptiste'; he had already described the
Salome of the picture by Henri Regnault[20] (now in the
Metropolitan Museum, New York) in a sonnet, called *La
Danseuse* (January, 1870, in *Rimes dorées*)—'l'œil en-
chanté par les orfèvreries—du riant coutelas vermeil et du
bassin', concluding:

> . . . Comme c'est votre joie, ô fragiles poupées!
> Car vous avez toujours aimé naïvement
> Les joujoux flamboyants et les têtes coupées.

In *La Forêt bleue* (1883), Jean Lorrain also was inspired
by Heine's lines for his medallions of Diana, Herodias,
and Dame Habonde. Lorrain, however, merely described
'la chasse Hérodiade', without spending any time over the
details of the legend.

A reflection of Heine's poem seems to be visible in
Wilde, when he makes Herod say:

'Voyons, Salomé, il faut être raisonnable, n'est-ce pas? . . . Au
fond, je ne crois pas que vous soyez sérieuse. La tête d'un homme
décapité, c'est une chose laide, n'est-ce pas? Ce n'est pas une chose
qu'une vierge doive regarder. Quel plaisir cela pourrait-il vous
donner? Aucun. Non, non, vous ne voulez pas cela. . . .'

One thinks of the witty lines:

> Anders wär' ja unerklärlich
> Das Gelüste jener Dame—
> Wird ein Weib das Haupt begehren
> Eines Manns, den sie nicht liebt?

In one of the *Moralités légendaires* (published in *La
Vogue* for June-July, 1886, then, with alterations, in the
Revue indépendante edition, 1887), Jules Laforgue im-
proved upon Heine's ironical attitude by presenting an
exquisite caricature of Salome—almost as she might be
presented in a musical comedy by another Offenbach bent
on toying with suggestions of the sinister, or as she actually
appears in the illustrations which Beardsley later devised
for Wilde's play. This is Laforgue's Salome:

'Ses épaules nues retenaient, redressée au moyen de brassières de
nacre, une roue de paon nain, en fond changeant, moire, azur, or,
émeraude, halo sur lequel s'enlevait sa candide tête, tête supérieure
mais cordialement insouciante de se sentir unique, le col fauché, les

yeux décomposés d'expiations chatoyantes, les lèvres découvrant d'un accent circonflexe rose pâle une denture aux gencives d'un rose très pâle encore, en un sourire des plus crucifiés. . . . Elle vacillait sur ses pieds, ses pieds exsangues, aux orteils écartés, chaussés uniquement d'un anneau aux chevilles d'où pleuvaient d'éblouissantes franges de moire jaune. . . . Qui pouvait bien lui avoir crucifié son sourire, la petite Immaculée-Conception? . . .

'Salomé, ayant donné cours à un petit rire toussotant, peut-être pour faire assavoir que surtout fallait pas croire qu'elle se prenait au sérieux, pince sa lyre noire jusqu'au sang, et, de la voix sans timbre et sans sexe d'un malade qui réclame sa potion dont, au fond, il n'a jamais eu plus besoin que vous ou moi, improvisa à même. . . .

'— Et maintenant, mon père, je désirerais que vous me fassiez monter chez moi, en un plat quelconque, la tête de Iaokanann.[21] C'est dit. Je monte l'attendre.

.   .   .   .

'Or là, sur un coussin, parmi les débris de la lyre d'ébène, la tête de Jean (comme jadis celle d'Orphée) brillait, enduite de phosphore, lavée, fardée, frisée, faisant rictus à ces vingt-quatre millions d'astres.

'Aussitôt l'objet livré, Salomé, par acquit de conscience scientifique, avait essayé ces fameuses expériences d'après décollation, dont on parle tant; elle s'y attendait, les passes électriques ne tirèrent de la face que grimaces sans conséquence.'

Finally Salome 'baisa cette bouche miséricordieusement et hermétiquement, et scella cette bouche de son cachet corrosif (procédé instantané)', and died, as a result of losing her balance while throwing the head of Iaokanann from a promontory into the sea, 'moins victime des hasards illettrés que d'avoir voulu vivre dans le factice et non à la bonne franquette, à l'instar de chacun de nous'.

Therefore, even before Wilde made use of the story of Salome, both Heine and Laforgue had emptied it of all tragic content by their ironical treatment of it. Yet, as generally happens with specious second-hand works, it was precisely Wilde's Salome which became popular.[21A] In 1896 the play, originally written for Sarah Bernhardt— who had been prevented from performing it by the censor —had a moderate success at the Théâtre de l'Œuvre; in 1901, a year after Wilde's death, it was given in Berlin, and since then—thanks also to the music of Richard

Strauss—it has continued to figure in the repertories of European theatres. In Germany it has held the boards for a longer period than any other English play, including the plays of Shakespeare. It has been translated into Czech, into Dutch, Greek, Hungarian, Polish, Russian, Catalan, Swedish, and even Yiddish. In Italy it became part of the repertory of Lyda Borelli, and I still remember with what enthusiasm the gentlemen's opera-glasses were levelled at the squinting *diva*, clothed in nothing but violet and absinthe-green shafts of limelight. The Salomes of Flaubert, of Moreau, Laforgue, and Mallarmé are known only to students of literature and connoisseurs, but the Salome of the genial comedian Wilde is known to all the world.

5. I have left to the last what is perhaps the most significant picture of Salome—significant not only artistically but also as a psychological interpretation—the *Hérodiade* of Mallarmé. Though it became known to the public only in 1898, the poet's friends were already acquainted with it a long time before, and naturally Huysmans' des Esseintes had a copy of the dramatic fragment in a precious manuscript of verse by this abstruse poet in his possession: 'Un fragment de l'*Hérodiade* le subjuguait de même qu'un sortilège, à certaines heures.' Contemplating at the same time Moreau's water-colour, which was hung on a wall of his library, enveloped in the shadows of twilight, des Esseintes sips the lines which Mallarmé put into the mouth of the painter's bewitching creature:

'Ces vers, il les aimait comme il aimait les œuvres de ce poète qui . . . vivait à l'écart des lettres . . . se complaisant, loin du monde, aux surprises de l'intellect, aux visions de sa cervelle, raffinant sur des pensées déjà spécieuses, les greffant de finesses byzantines, les perpétuant en des déductions légèrement indiquées que reliait à peine un imperceptible fil.'[22]

There is more in Mallarmé's lines than the mere horror of the episode of the beheading of St. John the Baptist; they present, so to speak, a synthetic portrait of the whole Decadent Movement in the figure of the narcissist-virgin (narcissist to such an extent that Valéry's *Narcisse* actually takes its impulse from here); and even the French language, in the hands of Mallarmé, becomes coloured with 'virginité anubile et ravissante'.[23]

It is true that this Salome is bejewelled and fatal like that of Moreau, but the poem expresses not so much the external aura of preciosity which surrounds her as the anguish of a sterile, lonely soul, troubled with diseased imaginings:

Nourrice. Triste fleur qui croît seule et n'a pas d'autre émoi
Que son ombre dans l'eau vue avec atonie.

     . . . .

Hérodiade. Oui, c'est pour moi, pour moi, que je fleuris, déserte!

     . . . .

J'aime l'horreur d'être vierge et je veux
Vivre parmi l'effroi que me font mes cheveux
Pour, le soir, retirée en ma couche, reptile
Inviolé sentir en la chair inutile
Le froid scintillement de ta pâle clarté
Toi qui te meurs, toi qui brûles de chasteté,
Nuit blanche de glaçons et de neige cruelle!

Et ta sœur solitaire, ô ma sœur éternelle,
Mon rêve montera vers toi: telle déjà
Rare limpidité d'un cœur qui le songea,
Je me crois seule en ma monotone patrie
Et tout, autour de moi, vit dans l'idolâtrie
D'un miroir qui reflète en son calme dormant
Hérodiade au clair regard de diamant. . . .
Ô charme dernier, oui! je le sens, je suis seule.

     . . . .

Des ondes
Se bercent et, là-bas, sais-tu pas un pays
Où le sinistre ciel ait les regards haïs
De Vénus qui, le soir, brûle dans le feuillage;
J'y partirais.

Mallarmé's Herodias, like Flaubert's Salammbô, is a hysterical woman steeped in hieratic indolence: she also, wasting away in the expectation of 'une chose inconnue', can be imagined wandering in the silence of her vast apartments, or ecstatic in a corner, 'tenant dans ses mains sa jambe gauche repliée, la bouche entr'ouverte, le menton baissé, l'œil fixe', tortured by 'obsessions d'autant plus fortes qu'elles étaient vagues';[24] she also is a devotee of the

Moon, and addresses her speech, as though to a sister, to
the cold heavenly sphere which Salammbô had adored and
prayed to as a Mother; in fact Herodias, too, is, like
Salammbô, 'un astre humain' ('Nourrice, suis-je belle?—
Un astre, en verité'; 'ma pudeur grelottante d'étoile').

6. Huysmans, speaking of the erotic works of Félicien
Rops, the artist who, together with Moreau, held the
field among the Decadents, makes the following observations:[25]

'Au fond . . . il n'y a de réellement obscènes que les gens chastes.

'Tout le monde sait, en effet, que la continence engendre des
pensées libertines affreuses, que l'homme non chrétien et par con-
séquent involontairement pur, se surchauffe dans la solitude surtout,
et s'exalte et divague; alors, il va mentalement, dans son rêve éveillé,
jusqu'au bout du délire orgiaque.

'Il est donc vraisemblable que l'artiste qui traite violemment des
sujets charnels, est, pour une raison ou pour une autre, un homme
chaste.

'Mais cette constatation ne semble pas suffisante, car, à se scruter,
l'on découvre que, même en ne gardant pas une continence exacte,
même en étant repu, même en éprouvant un sincère dégoût des
joies sensuelles, l'on est encore troublé par des idées lascives.

'C'est alors qu'apparaît ce phénomène bizarre d'une âme qui se
suggère, sans désirs corporels, des visions lubriques.

'Impurs ou non, les artistes dont les nerfs sont élimés jusqu'à
se rompre, ont, plus que tous autres, constamment subi les insup-
portables tracas de la Luxure. . . . Je parle exclusivement de l'Esprit
de Luxure, des idées érotiques isolées, sans correspondance matérielle, sans besoin d'une suite animale qui les apaise.

'Et presque toujours la scène rêvée est identique: des images se
lèvent, des nudités se tendent; — mais, d'un saut, l'acte naturel
s'efface, comme dénué d'intérêt, comme trop court, comme ne
provoquant qu'une commotion attendue, qu'un cri banal; — et, du
coup, un élan vers l'extranaturel de la salauderie, une postulation
vers les crises échappées de la chair, bondies dans l'au-delà des
spasmes, se déclarent. L'infamie de l'âme s'aggrave, si l'on veut,
mais elle se raffine, s'anoblit par la pensée, qui s'y mêle, d'un idéal
de fautes surhumaines, de péchés que l'on voudrait neufs.

'A spiritualiser ainsi l'ordure, une réelle déperdition de phosphore
se produit dans la cervelle, et si, pendant cet état inquiétant de
l'âme qui se suggère à elle-même et pour elle seule, ces visions
échauffées des sens, le hasard veut que la réalité s'en mêle, qu'une

femme, en chair et en os, vienne, alors l'homme, excédé de rêve, reste embarrassé, devient presque frigide, éprouve, dans tous les cas, après une pollution réelle, une désillusion, une tristesse atroces.

'Cette étrange attirance vers les complications charnelles, cette hantise de la saloperie pour la saloperie même, ce rut qui se passe tout entier dans l'âme et sans que le corps consulté s'en mêle, cette impulsion livide et limitée qui n'a, en somme, avec l'instinct génésique, que de lointains rapports, demeurent singulièrement mystérieux quand on y songe.

'Éréthisme du cerveau, dit la science. . . .'

However Huysmans, who professed Catholicism (a kind of Catholicism to which I shall return shortly), recognized as the only satisfactory explanation that afforded by the Church, which sees a temptation of the Evil One in *delectatio morosa*, in mental onanism.

'En art, cette hystérie mentale ou cette délectation morose devait forcément se traduire en des œuvres et fixer les images qu'elle s'était créées. Elle trouvait, là, en effet, son exutoire spirituel. . . . C'est donc à cet état spécial de l'âme que l'on peut attribuer les hennissements charnels, écrits ou peints, des vrais artistes.'

Of real artists? That may be doubted, but this is not the place to discuss it: our concern here is only to establish how the state of mind just described by Huysmans is fundamental in all the literature of the Decadence, beginning with the work of Huysmans himself.

In a state of mind conditioned thus, sadism finds its natural soil:

'Il semble, en effet, que les maladies de nerfs, que les névroses ouvrent dans l'âme des fissures par lesquelles l'Esprit du Mal pénètre.'[26]

7. Sadism, however, as Huysmans himself also remarks, is a 'bastard of Catholicism',[27] and presupposes a religion to be violated:

'Cet état si curieux et si mal défini ne peut, en effet, prendre naissance dans l'âme d'un mécréant; il ne consiste point seulement à se vautrer parmi les excès de la chair, aiguisés par de sanglantes sévices, car il ne serait plus alors qu'un écart des sens génésiques, qu'un cas de satyriasis arrivé à son point de maturité suprême; il consiste avant tout dans une pratique sacrilège, dans une rebellion morale, dans une débauche spirituelle, dans une aberration toute idéale, toute chrétienne; il réside aussi dans une joie tempérée par

la crainte, dans une joie analogue à cette satisfaction mauvaise des
enfants qui désobéissent et jouent avec des matières défendues, par
ce seul motif que leurs parents leur en ont expressément interdit
l'approche ...

'La force du sadisme, l'attrait qu'il présente gît donc tout entier
dans la jouissance prohibée de transférer à Satan les hommages et
les prières qu'on doit à Dieu; il gît donc dans l'inobservance des
préceptes catholiques qu'on suit même à rebours, en commettant,
afin de bafouer plus gravement le Christ, les péchés qu'il a le plus
expressément maudits: la pollution du culte et l'orgie charnelle.

'Au fond, ce cas, auquel le marquis de Sade a légué son nom,
était aussi vieux que l'Église; il avait sévi dans le xviiie siècle,
ramenant, pour ne pas remonter plus haut, par un simple phénomène d'atavisme, les pratiques impies du sabbat au moyen âge.'

Des Esseintes recognizes in the Witches' Sabbath
'toutes les pratiques obscènes et tous les blasphèmes du
sadisme'.

Sadism and Catholicism, in French Decadent literature,
become the two poles between which the souls of neurotic
and sensual writers oscillate, and which can definitely be
traced back to that 'épicurien à l'imagination catholique'[28]
—Chateaubriand. This phenomenon was noticed by,
among others, Anatole France, apropos of Villiers de l'Isle-
Adam:[29]

'Il était de cette famille de néo-catholiques littéraires dont
Chateaubriand est le père commun, et qui a produit Barbey
d'Aurevilly, Baudelaire, et, plus récemment, M. Joséphin Péladan.
Ceux-là ont goûté par-dessus tout dans la religion les charmes du
péché, la grandeur du sacrilège, et leur sensualisme a caressé les
dogmes qui ajoutaient aux voluptés la suprême volupté de se perdre.'

Anatole France's list is not complete: Huysmans, Verlaine, Barrès, Léon Bloy,* and, more recently, Montherlant
are other well-known examples of this type of confused
Christianity.[30] Dostoievsky offers an analogous case.
Given the extremely equivocal basis on which the religion
of such writers is founded, one may reasonably suspect
that in them, even in its most seemingly innocent manifestations, this religion is merely a disguised form of
morbid satisfaction: repentance may be nothing more than
a mask for algolagnia. Such a suspicion comes into one's
mind, for instance, in the case of Verlaine's prayer: 'Ô

mon Dieu, vous m'avez blessé d'amour.' And algolagnia is quite obvious in passages such as that of Huysmans on the Virgin of the Maître de Flemalle at Frankfurt:[31] 'Cette Madone, si tendrement dolente, on peut lui prêter toutes les angoisses, toutes les transes, &c.'[31A]

8. Huysmans' analysis fits the chief exponents of French Decadence like a glove—beginning, as I have already said, with Huysmans himself. Let us take a rapid glance at this portrait-gallery. Each of the persons represented in it might well repeat the phrase which comes at the beginning of Diderot's *Neveu de Rameau*: 'Mes pensées ce sont mes catins.'

This is an original portrait of J.-K. Huysmans by Paul Valéry:[32]

'Il était le plus nerveux des hommes... grand créateur de dégoûts, accueillant pour le pire et n'ayant soif que de l'excessif, crédule à un point incroyable,[33] recevant aisément toutes les horreurs qui se peuvent imaginer chez les humains, friand de bizarreries et de contes comme il s'en conterait chez une portière de l'enfer; et d'ailleurs les mains pures. . . . Il émanait de lui des reflets d'une érudition vouée à l'étrange.... Il flairait des salauderies, des maléfices, des ignominies dans toutes les affaires de ce monde; et peut-être avait-il raison. . . . Quand il se mit à la mystique, il joignit avec délices, à sa minutieuse et complaisante connaissance des ordures visibles et des saletés pondérables, une curiosité attentive, inventive et inquiète de l'ordure surnaturelle et des immondices suprasensibles. . . . Ses narines étranges flairaient en frémissant ce qu'il y a de nauséabond dans le monde. L'écœurant fumet des gargotes, l'âcre encens frelaté, les odeurs fades ou infectes des bouges et des asiles de nuit, tout ce qui révoltait ses sens excitait son génie. On eût dit que le dégoûtant et l'horrible dans tous les genres le contraignissent à les observer, et que les abominations de toute espèce eussent pour effet d'engendrer un artiste spécialement fait pour les peindre dans un homme créé spécialement pour en souffrir.... L'état des choses pieuses et celui des esprits anxieux entre 1880 et 1900 sont peints en partie et définis dans les trois principaux ouvrages d'Huysmans.'

Among these works, *A rebours* (its very title implies a programme of sadistic constraint of nature) is the pivot upon which the whole psychology of the Decadent Movement turns; in it all the phenomena of this state of mind

are illustrated down to the minutest details, in the instance
of its chief character des Esseintes. 'Tous les romans que
j'ai écrits depuis *A rebours* sont contenus en germe dans
ce livre', Huysmans remarked. Not only his own novels,
but all the prose works of the Decadence, from Lorrain to
Gourmont, Wilde and D'Annunzio, are contained in embryo in *A rebours*. This book is so well known that a few
remarks only may suffice here.

Its descent from Baudelaire is obvious, beginning from
the actual title:

'Appliquer à la joie, au se sentir vivre, l'idée d'hyperacuité des
sens, appliquée par Poe à la douleur. Opérer une création par la
pure logique de contraire. Le sentier est tout tracé, à rebours.'[34]

The taste of des Esseintes, who values works of art,
precious stones, perfumes, flowers, food, &c., all at the
same rate—as instruments of epicurean sensation—is in
conformity with the most orthodox doctrines of Baudelaire:

'Que la poésie se rattache aux arts de la peinture, de la cuisine
et du cosmétique par la possibilité d'exprimer toute sensation de
suavité ou d'amertume, de béatitude ou d'horreur, par l'accouplement de tel substantif avec tel adjectif, analogue ou contraire.'[35]

Again, in his programme of systematic, erudite exploita-
tion of all possible sensations, des Esseintes resembles
Poe's Usher[36]—an Usher who follows in the footsteps of
Bouvard and Pécuchet, though in a tragic vein, whereas
Flaubert had embarked upon the undertaking in the spirit
of parody.

Enthusiasm for monstrous flowers and tropical plants,
for contorted shapes, in fact for 'Medusean' beauty in its
most paradoxical forms—all this was presented by Huysmans with the minuteness of a Dutch still-life painter.
But he did not make the discovery: the credit of that—if
credit it deserves—belongs to Baudelaire and Flaubert.
The same may be said of the enthusiasm for debased Latin,
and in general of the attraction towards everything corrupt
and impure, whether in men, in works of art, or in things.
Even Zola, as early as 1866, had said:[37] 'Mon goût, si
l'on veut, est dépravé. J'aime les ragoûts littéraires
fortement épicés, les œuvres de décadence où une sorte de

sensibilité maladive remplace la santé plantureuse des époques classiques.' Huysmans liked the Latin of the Decline because of its decayed flavour, he liked landscapes distorted by brutal violence, the *banlieue* that seems as if it 'relève toujours d'un mal épuisant qui la mine, et que son côté populaire s'atténue et s'effile dans une attitude alanguie, dans une mine dolente'.[38] The most remarkable pages that he wrote on this theme are to be found in the essay on *La Bièvre* (1898), in which, contemplating the contamination of the little river, befouled by industry, he sees the torture of the river-nymph, whose agony he describes with sadistic satisfaction. But the honour of having discovered the fascination of this particular *faisandé* spot belongs to the Goncourts. In *Manette Salomon* (1867) the painter Crescent finds his inspiration in the 'rachitisme mélancolique de ces prés râpés et jaunis par place'.[39]

Des Esseintes does not merely delight in sadistic fantasies, but, in the manner of *La Philosophie dans le boudoir*, makes a timid attempt at militant sadism by initiating a poor young man into a mode of life which is bound to lead him to crime.

In *Là-bas* (1891) the author explores the darkest and most distant regions of satanism and sadism ('les là-bas, si loin dans les vieux âges!'),[40] and describes the life of a des Esseintes of the Middle Ages, the monster Gilles de Rais, and the modern Black Masses which recall the Witches' Sabbath.[41] It is possible that an interest in Joan of Arc's satanic contemporary was aroused in modern times not only by Sade, who mentions him several times,[42] but also by Stendhal, who, in a correspondence from Nantes (in the *Mémoires d'un touriste*),[43] dwells upon the passion of this strange monster for liturgical ceremonial and sacred music (was it from this musical taste on the part of Gilles that Huysmans derived the idea of placing several of the scenes of his novel in the abode of a music-mad bell-ringer?'), and he more or less invites the writing of a Life of Gilles:

'Quels furent les motifs, quelles furent les nuances non seulement de ses actions atroces, mais de toutes les actions de sa vie qui ne furent pas incriminées ? Nous l'ignorons. Nous sommes donc bien loin d'avoir un portrait véritable de cet être extraordinaire. . . . C'est toujours un libertinage ardent mais qui ne peut s'assouvir qu'après avoir bravé tout ce que les hommes respectent. . . . Toujours on le voit obéir à une imagination bizarre et singulièrement puissante dans ses écarts.'

The Life of Gilles was not written until 1886, by the Abbé Eugène Bossard and René de Maulde;[44] and it was from this that Huysmans got his information. Gilles de Rais was, apparently, also the forerunner of a particular kind of exoticism, if it is true, as one tradition has it, that he derived his impulse from the crimes of the Emperors as related by Suetonius; but this tradition seems unwarrantable.[45]

Parallel to the almost mythical character of Gilles de Rais, Huysmans presents a living woman who resembles him. Gilles is divided, as she is, into three distinct personalities:

> D'abord le soudard brave et pieux.
> Puis l'artiste raffiné et criminel.
> Enfin, le pécheur qui se repent, le mystique.

Hyacinthe is a *diabolique*, a younger sister of the perverse and murderous women whom Huysmans had encountered in the pages of Barbey d'Aurevilly. In moments of crisis her eyes become sulphurous, she has the mouth of a vampire, a will of iron: 'J'ai une volonté de fer, et je ploie ceux qui m'aiment.'[46]

9. Barbey d'Aurevilly, another Holy Father of the Decadent Movement, is the connecting link between two generations, the 'frénétique' of 1830 and the 'decadent' of 1880.[47] The following portrait is from the pen of Anatole France,[48] and has a strong family likeness to that of Huysmans:

'Il affirmait sa foi en toute rencontre, mais c'est par le blasphème qu'il la confessait de préférence. L'impiété chez lui semble un complement à la foi. Comme Baudelaire, il adorait le péché. Des passions il ne connut jamais que le masque et la grimace. Il se rattrapait sur le sacrilège et jamais croyant n'offensa Dieu avec tant de zèle. N'en frissonnez pas. Ce grand blasphémateur sera sauvé. . . . Saint Pierre dira en le voyant : "Voici M. Barbey d'Aurevilly. Il voulut avoir tous les vices, mais il n'a pas pu, parce que c'est très difficile et qu'il y faut des dispositions particulières; il eût aimé à se couvrir de crimes, parce que le crime est pittoresque; mais il resta le plus galant homme du monde, et sa vie fut quasi monastique. Il a dit parfois de vilaines choses, il est vrai; mais, comme il ne les croyait pas et qu'il ne les faisait croire à personne, ce ne fut jamais que de la littérature, et la faute est pardonnable. Chateaubriand qui, lui aussi, était de notre parti, se moqua de nous dans sa vie beaucoup plus sérieusement.'' '

Barbey also, then, provides an illustration to the old saying: 'Lasciva est nobis pagina, vita proba'—an old saying which, however, must be interpreted in the light of Huysmans's explanations quoted above (§ 6). In point of voluptuous imagination des Esseintes classifies Barbey immediately below the Marquis de Sade:[49]

'S'il n'allait pas aussi loin que de Sade, en proférant d'atroces malédictions contre le Sauveur; si, plus prudent ou plus craintif, il prétendait toujours honorer l'Église, il n'en adressait pas moins, comme au moyen âge, ses postulations au Diable et il glissait, lui aussi, afin d'affronter Dieu, à l'érotomanie démoniaque, forgeant des monstruosités sensuelles, empruntant même à la *Philosophie dans le boudoir* un certain épisode qu'il assaisonnait de nouveaux condiments, lorsqu'il écrivait ce conte: *le Dîner d'un athée.* [sic]

'. . . Ce volume [*Les Diaboliques*] était, parmi toutes les œuvres de la littérature apostolique contemporaine, le seul qui témoignât de cette situation d'esprit tout à la fois dévote et impie, vers laquelle les revenez-y du catholicisme, stimulés par les accès de la névrose, avaient souvent poussé des Esseintes.'

D'Aurevilly's preface to the *Diaboliques* is curious:

'L'auteur de ceci, qui croit au Diable et à ses influences dans le monde, n'en rit pas, et il ne les raconte aux âmes pures que pour les en épouvanter.'

It is the usual moral excuse of all licentious writers, from Marino onwards. The moral is attached to the fable in the opposite way to that enunciated in Tasso's lines (*Jerusalem Delivered*, c. 1, st. 3): the 'sweet liquor' is actually contained within the vessel and the brim is smeared with wormwood for the sake of decency.

Pleasure and horror are closely intertwined throughout the six stories. In the first (*Le Rideau cramoisi*) a young woman with 'the forehead of a Nero' takes a horrible

pleasure in going every night stealthily through the room
in which her parents sleep to her lover's room: one night
the emotion is so strong that she dies of it. The title of
the third story, *Le Bonheur dans le crime*, has an obviously
sadistic sound. The women described by d'Aurevilly have
something of the wild beast in them; the stronger sex, as
so often in writers of this period, is really the weaker. The
man, in *Le Bonheur dans le crime*, even goes so far as to
wear ear-rings, while the woman, dressed in black:

'faisait penser à la grande Isis noire du Musée Égyptien, par l'am-
pleur de ses formes, la fierté mystérieuse et la force. Chose étrange!
dans le rapprochement de ce beau couple, c'était la femme qui avait
les muscles, et l'homme qui avait les nerfs. . . .'

The woman's eyes are green ('les deux étoiles vertes de
ses regards'), as is usual in such cases (the eyes of sadistic
characters in popular Romantic literature are, as a rule,
green). When put face to face with a panther, the
'panthère humaine' (i.e. the woman) magnetizes the
'panthère animale'. The story of this handsome couple
discloses a poisoning perpetrated in romantic circumstances upon the wife of the man with the ear-rings.

In *Le Dessous de cartes d'une partie de whist* the company
is even more sinister. A mother who poisons her sons for
the pleasure of sadistic pollution, a nondescript Scotsman
who dabbles in Indian poisons. . . . The woman has green
eyes ('la comtesse portait le sinople, étincelé d'or, dans
son regard comme dans ses armes'; 'ces deux émeraudes,
striées de jaune, . . . étaient aussi froides que si on les
avait retirées du ventre et du frai du poisson de Poly-
crate'; 'ce regard d'ondine, glauque et moqueur'). Her
hands 'ressemblaient à des griffes fabuleuses, comme
l'étonnante poésie des Anciens en attribuait à certains
monstres au visage et au sein de femme'. The man is 'du
pays où se passe la sublime histoire de Walter Scott, cette
réalité du Pirate que Marmor allait reprendre en sous-
œuvre, avec des variantes, dans une petite ville ignorée des
côtes de la Manche'. Again, the ear-rings of the man in
Le Bonheur dans le crime make the narrator think of the
emerald ear-rings of Jean Sbogar. It is a case, therefore,
of belated descendants of the Byronic hero, but dominated

by the woman whom their original ancestor at the beginning of the century was accustomed to subjugate. The
woman is athirst for mystery, for the impossible, for
darkness:

'Mais, quand on y pense, ne comprend-on pas que leurs sensations
aient réellement la profondeur enflammée de l'enfer? Or l'enfer
c'est le ciel en creux. Le mot *diabolique* ou *divin*, appliqué à
l'intensité des jouissances, exprime la même chose, c'est-à-dire des
sensations qui vont jusqu'au surnaturel.'

In this story there is a poisoned ring, in the next, *A un
Dîner d'athées* (the atheists show off to the fullest meaning
of the term: 'ils crachèrent en haut leur âme contre Dieu')
there is a certain Major Ydow who looks like one of the
busts of Antinous—the one in which, through the caprice
or the bad taste of the sculptor (says d'Aurevilly), two
emeralds are set in the marble of the eyeballs. This detail,
too, became later a *cliché* of popular Romanticism:
Antinous and the emeralds are to be found, for instance, in
Lorrain's *Monsieur de Phocas*. The woman in *A un Dîner
d'athées* is 'la plus fascinante cristallisation de tous les
vices' that has ever existed. She belongs to the family of
Carmen.[50] The culminating point of the story is the
profanation of a child's dead body by its parents, the
sealing up, with burning wax, of the *pudenda* of Rosalba
la Pudica, and the killing of the man who perpetrated such
abominations.

In the last of the stories, *La Vengeance d'une femme*, the
wife of a Spanish grandee avenges herself on her husband
by dragging his name in the dirt and exercising so little
control of her own passions that she dies a horrible death
in the Salpêtrière. This 'diabolique' is of Italian origin—
Turre-Cremata, of the family of the Inquisitor Torquemada, who however 'a infligé moins de supplices, pendant
toute sa vie, qu'il n'y en a dans ce sein maudit'. The
heroine of *Le Dessous de cartes*, also, is proclaimed as being,
for her crimes, 'digne de l'Italie du seizième siècle'. As
can be seen, the ancient spectre of the Italian Renaissance,
which had exerted so strong an attraction on the Elizabethan dramatists and the earliest of the Romantics ('cette
fatale et criminelle Italie', said Hugo's Lucrezia Borgia),[51]

continues to provide material for Romanticism in its
latest period.

10. The third portrait in the gallery of the Decadents
is that of Villiers de l'Isle-Adam. He also was a Catholic—
or so he liked to proclaim himself—with a devotion considerably tempered with impiety, and he also was attracted
by sexual monstrosities and sadistic horrors, and moved
about amongst men like a somnambulist, 'ne voyant rien
de ce que nous voyons et voyant ce qu'il ne nous est pas
permis de voir'[52]—a kind of visionary of the pavement,
upheld only by the cheap wit of his luxurious, cruel fantasies. Though prompt to object to foreign manifestations
of sadism,[53] he cultivated a domestic 'jardin des supplices'
where he grafted the metaphysical American vines of
Edgar Allan Poe on to the worn-out stumps of French
Romanticism.

This combination of Poe's speculative ingenuity with
frenzied French Romanticism led Villiers to complicated
inventions such as *Claire Lenoir* (*Revue des Lettres et des
Arts*, October 1867; it appeared again in 1887 with the
title of *Tribulat Bonhomet*), a story which turned upon a
straightforward adultery, but concluded with a spectacle
of horror such as would out-Poe Poe even at his most unbridled: Bonhomet, introducing monstrous probes into
the eyes of the dead Claire, sees there, distinctly reflected
as though in a photographic plate, a picture of her husband
(re-incarnated as a vampire in the form of a Polynesian
pirate, an 'Ottysor-vampire') in the act of brandishing the
severed head of her lover and accompanying the gesture
with an inaudible war-song![54]

The *Contes cruels*, as a whole, show an exploitation of the
same themes as were treated by Pétrus Borel in the *Contes
immoraux*. A leprous Englishman; a German baron with
a passion for playing the executioner;[55] a French queen,
Queen Ysabeau, who punishes her lover by putting him in
the position of being accused of a crime he has not committed, and then rejoicing at his terror when she tells him,
holding him in her arms, of the trick she has played him;
Torquemada, who orders two lovers to be bound together
for forty-eight hours, so that they 'ne s'embrassèrent

jamais plus—de peur . . . de peur que cela ne recommençât'; a cruel Chinese sovereign who threatens a bold young man with a terrible form of torture (one of the tortures upon which, later, Mirbeau dwells so minutely); Queen Akëdysséril, who commands that the death of a young royal couple who were an obstacle to her plans should take place at the moment when they are tasting supreme happiness—all these characters occupy, as it were, a new wing in the museum of fearful wax figures inaugurated by the Romantics about 1830. But the different tone of this period is clearly shown in a story such as *Véra*, which deals with a sepulchral subject in the manner of Poe:[56]

'Les deux amants s'ensevelirent dans l'océan de ces joies languides et perverses où l'esprit se mêle à la chair mystérieuse! Ils épuisèrent la violence des désirs, les frémissements et les tendresses éperdues. Ils devinrent le battement de l'être l'un de l'autre. En eux, l'esprit pénétrait si bien le corps, que leurs formes leur semblaient intellectuelles, et que les baisers, mailles brûlantes, les enchaînaient dans une fusion idéale.'

Under the influence of Poe's tales, lust strives to become intellectualized, the concrete operations of the flesh are blended with decorous abstractions, human loves tend towards the impossibilities of angelic embraces. Magic and pseudo-mysticism *à la Parsifal* become so many spices which are used to give a new taste to the well-known feast of the senses.

11. A comic-heroic treatment (heroic in intention, comic in effect) of the subject-matter which constitutes, more or less, the common background of the whole of Decadent literature, is to be found in Joséphin Péladan, who is the subject of the fourth portrait in our gallery. It is hard to remain serious in front of this picture. Sar Mérodack J. Péladan (in giving a magic sound to his name this eccentric author was thinking of Merodach-baladan, King of Babylon, Isaiah, xxxix) is a figure with a mass of beard and long hair, draped in an old blanket which comes right down to his feet. One gets the impression of a performance of a cheap and homely charade, with the hearthrug to give a touch of Oriental local colour, the

aunt's blouse used as a surplice, and a little perfumed
paper burning, to tickle the nostrils of the spirits of Earth
and Air, as personified by the cat and the pet parrot.
Among the various objects scraped together for this farce
Péladan has also placed the crucifix taken down from the
head of the bed, forgetting the proverb 'Scherza coi fanti
e lascia stare i santi'.

'Barbey D'Aurevilly fut un catholique très compromettant.
M. Joséphin Péladan est plus dangereux encore pour ceux qu'il
défend. Peut-être blasphème-t-il moins que le vieux docteur des
Diaboliques, car le blasphème était pour celui-là l'acte de foi par
excellence. Mais il est encore plus sensuel et plus orgueilleux. Il
a plus encore le goût du péché. Ajoutez à cela qu'il est platonicien
et mage, qu'il mêle constamment le grimoire à l'Evangile, qu'il est
hanté par l'idée de l'hermaphrodite qui inspire tous ses livres; et
qu'il croit sincèrement mériter le chapeau de cardinal!'

Thus Anatole France,[57] who, nevertheless, gave Péladan the credit of being an artist—mad, to any extent, but
still an artist. However fantastic and absurd it may sound,
Péladan devoted himself very seriously to the practice of
magic. In 1888, together with the Marquis Stanislas de
Guaita and Oswald Wirth, he founded the 'Ordre Kab-
balistique de la Rose-Croix', which had among its chief
objects that of ruining the practitioners of Black Magic
and of revealing 'à la théologie chrétienne les magnificences ésotériques dont elle est grosse à son insu'. Various
literary men in the public eye, such as Paul Adam,
Laurent Tailhade and the poet Édouard Dubus, joined
the circle of the Rose-Croix.

Though the supernatural effects of these occult practices may be wrapt in mystery, there is no doubt about
their natural effects: Dubus went mad, and Guaita died
young, at the age of thirty.[58] The book by Bricaud[59]
should be consulted on the subject of these Rosicrucian
clubs and their relations with the practitioners of Black
Magic, as described in *Là-bas*.

In the preface to *Le Vice suprême* (1884), the first
volume of *La Décadence latine, éthopée*, Barbey d'Aurevilly
says of Péladan:

'Je ne sache personne qui ait attaqué d'un pinceau plus ferme et plus résolu ces corruptions qui plaisent parfois à ceux qui les peignent ou qui épouvantent l'innocente pusillanimité de ceux qui craignent les admirer. . . . Il peint le vice bravement, comme s'il l'aimait et il ne le peint que pour le flétrir et pour le maudire. Il le peint sans rien lui ôter de ses fascinations, de ses ensorcellements, de ses envoûtements, de tout ce qui fait sa toute-puissance sur l'âme humaine, et il en fait comprendre le charme infernal avec la même passion d'artiste intense que si ce charme était céleste!'

Péladan's work—pompously called by the author himself 'L'Œuvre Péladane'—although of very slight artistic interest (though D'Annunzio, who, as is well known, borrowed phrases and subjects from it, found it interesting)[60] and, in any case, very little read in France,[60A] nevertheless provides, as often happens with the work of lesser writers, composed, as it is, of *clichés* and commonplaces, an interesting account of Decadent circles and of the taste of the period.

The author himself figures among the characters of the 'éthopée': he is Mérodack, the magician who has read 'toute la littérature de la chair—de Martial à Meursius et à de Sade', since his method is to 'se créer une obsession de ce qu'il voulait vaincre'. Mérodack is 'd'une continence monstrueuse'. He is, in fact, the usual case of the chaste man besieged by lecherous fantasies, a prey to mental erethism.

The chief obsession of Péladan, as Anatole France observes, is the Hermaphrodite. This subject had already been dallied with by Latouche in his undeservedly famous *Fragoletta* (1829); by Balzac (*Séraphita*, *La Fille aux yeux d'or*); and more particularly by Gautier,[60B] who went into ecstasies over the classic marble statue of the Hermaphrodite:

'C'est. . . une des plus suaves créations du génie païen que ce fils d'Hermès et d'Aphrodite. . . . Le torse est un composé des monstruosités les plus charmantes: sur la poitrine potelée et pleine de l'éphèbe s'arrondit avec une grâce étrange la gorge d'une jeune vierge. . . .'

This is from *Mademoiselle de Maupin*, that *apologia* of Lesbian love which Sainte-Beuve called one of the 'Bibles of Romanticism', and which was certainly the Bible of

the Decadence. (Swinburne called it 'holy writ of Beauty'.)
And in *Émaux et camées* (*Contralto*) he says:

> Est-ce un jeune homme? Est-ce une femme?
> Une déesse ou bien un dieu?
> L'amour, ayant peur d'être infâme,
> Hésite et suspend son aveu. . . .
>
> Pour faire sa beauté maudite,
> Chaque sexe apporta son don. . . .
>
> Chimère ardente, effort suprême
> De l'art et de la volupté,
> Monstre charmant, comme je t'aime
> Avec ta multiple beauté!
>
> Rêve de poète et d'artiste,
> Tu m'as bien des nuits occupé,
> Et mon caprice qui persiste
> Ne convient pas qu'il s'est trompé. . .

Baudelaire also (*Les Bijoux*):

> Je croyais voir unis par un nouveau dessin
> Les hanches de l'Antiope au buste d'un imberbe,
> Tant sa taille faisait ressortir son bassin.

Lesbian love was celebrated by Baudelaire not only in
Lesbos and *Femmes damnées*, but was actually intended to
furnish the title for the collected edition of his poems—*Les
Lesbiennes*—as the announcement on the cover of *Salon
de 1846* shows. It moved Swinburne to write *Anactoria*
and *Lesbia Brandon*, and Verlaine wrote some lines on the
subject which are worthy of the licentious paintings of
Fragonard ('L'une avait quinze ans, l'autre en avait
seize . . .'; 'Tendre, la jeune femme rousse . . .');
Beardsley and Conder illustrated Balzac's *La Fille aux
yeux d'or.*[61]

During the years just after 1830, thanks especially to
George Sand, the vice of Lesbianism became extremely
popular:[62]

'En ce temps-là [relates Arsène Houssaye[63]] Sapho ressuscita
dans Paris, ne sachant pas si elle aimait Phaon ou Érinne. Pourquoi ne pas le dire? Ce fut des hautes régions de l'intelligence que
descendirent les voluptés inavouées.'

In the Paris of the *fin de siècle* there were certain haunts

of Lesbians which attracted artists, particularly the 'Rat
Mort', a restaurant in the Place Pigalle:

'The Rat Mort by night had a somewhat doubtful reputation
[says Rothenstein],[64] but during the day was frequented by painters
and poets. As a matter of fact it was a notorious centre of Lesbianism. . . . This gave the Rat Mort an additional attraction to Conder
and Lautrec.'

In the occult circles of which Péladan was *magna pars*
the figure of the Androgyne possessed a recondite significance into which it is not necessary to enter here. It was
this fact which enabled Guaita to say of Péladan's
Curieuse:[65]

'*Curieuse* fait songer à *Séraphîtus-Séraphîta*, mais ce mystère
que Balzac balbutiait d'intuition, M. Péladan le formule avec la
hardiesse et l'autorité sereine de celui qui sait, non plus avec le
fiévreux entraînement de celui qui devine.'

Part of the seventh treatise in Péladan's *Amphithéâtre des
sciences mortes* expounds the theory of the Androgyne under
the title of *Érotologie de Platon*: here the female androgyne
is defined as Martha and Mary in one, combining the
active with the contemplative faculty, a perfect fusion of
intelligence and voluptuousness. Péladan recognizes that
'the number of women who feel themselves to be men
grows daily, and the masculine instinct leads them to
violent actions, in the same proportion as that in which the
number of men who feel themselves to be women abdicate
their sex and, becoming passive, pass virtually on to a
negative plane'.

The Androgyne is the artistic sex *par excellence*, realized
in the creations of Leonardo:

'Léonard a trouvé le canon de Polyclète, qui s'appelle l'androgyne. . . . L'androgyne est le sexe artistique par excellence, il confond
les deux principes, le féminin et le masculin, et les équilibre l'un
par l'autre. Toute figure exclusivement masculine manque de
grâce, toute autre exclusivement féminine, manque de force.

'Dans la *Joconde*, l'autorité cérébrale de l'homme de génie se confond avec la volupté de la gentille femme, c'est de l'androgynisme
moral.

'Dans le *Saint-Jean* la mixture des formes est telle, que le sexe
devient une énigme. . . .

'Le réalisateur de l'éphèbe, de l'adolescent a trouvé le clair-obscur. . . .

'Le *Saint-Jean* du Louvre manifeste ce procédé dans sa pléni-tude: mais au lieu d'un clair-obscur physique, extérieur, d'un jeu de lumière et d'ombre, Léonard découvrit le clair-obscur animique.'[66]

The women of Péladan's novels are generally of the androgynous type. A few examples will suffice, for variety of type is not the strong point of this mystagogic novelist. The Princess d'Este (*Le Vice suprême*)[67] is of an 'éphébisme à la Primatice':[68]

'On dirait l'Anadyomène de ces primitifs qui, d'un pinceau encore mystique, s'essayent au paganisme renaissant, un Botticelli où la sainte déshabillée en nymphe garde de la gaucherie dans la perversité d'une plastique de stupre.'

In another passage a perverse interpretation of Primi-tive painting, in which Péladan emulates Huysmans,[69] supplies the terms of comparison:

'Un ange de missel dévêtu en vierge folle par un imagier pervers; telle semblait Léonora. . . . Sur sa poitrine plate, les seins petits mais précis s'attachaient brusquement, sans transition de modelé, distants et aigus. La ligne de la taille se renflait peu aux hanches, se per-dant dans les jambes trop longues d'une Ève de Lucas de Leyde. L'élancement des lignes, la ténuité des attaches, la longueur étroite des extrémités, le règne des verticales immatérialisaient sa chair déjà irréelle de ton: on eût dit une de ces saintes que le burin de Schongauer dénude pour le martyre; mais les yeux verts[70] au regard ambigu, la bouche grande au sourire inquiétant, les cheveux aux flavescences de vieil or, toute la tête démentait la mysticité du corps.'

These are the ancestors of the Princess d'Este, criminals and weaklings:

'Les fils d'Obizzon étranglèrent leur frère qui le méritait. Al-berto fit brûler vive sa femme et tenailler Jean d'Este. Nicolas III décapita sa femme Parisina pour inceste avec son propre bâtard Hugues. Ce même Nicolas III eut vingt-six bâtards. Hercule coupa les poignets et creva les yeux à deux cents de ses ennemis. Le cardinal Hippolyte fit arracher les yeux à son frère en sa pré-sence. Alphonse fut le bourreau du Tasse. . . . Tous les vices, tous les crimes, voilà vos ancêtres.

The Princess is a 'diabolique', a hobgoblin:

'Les œuvres d'art où la femme triomphe de l'homme l'attiraient invinciblement. A Pitti, à la Loggia, la Judith d'Allori[70A] et celle de Bandinelli l'arrêtaient dans une contemplation souriante et réfléchie.'

The type of man that this woman desires is, naturally, Antinous:

'Sa sidérale nudité rayonne; ses pectoraux semblent lumineux et la princesse, dans son hallucination volontaire, prête ce discours à l'affranchi d'Hadrien:

' "Princesse, tu es belle comme je suis beau. Ne crois pas aux calomnies de l'histoire. L'empereur brûla de feux inutiles. Je suis vierge, je le suis resté pour toi dont le front haut comme celui de Minerve contient la pensée." '

The roles are inverted. Péladan never tires of insisting upon Lesbian and androgynous themes throughout the whole of his monumental 'éthopée'; and any one who has the desire and the patience may gather in this work a very abundant crop of more or less monstrous flowers of evil. In *Typhonia* (1892), for example, the *Journal d'une vierge protestante* is a story of Lesbian loves, and the love-affair of Nebo with the Princess Riazan, in *Curieuse*, is also characteristic.

The Princess Riazan is a Russian. For in 1886—the year in which *Curieuse* was published—the Russian novel (the first French translation of Dostoievsky came out in 1884) was making its triumphal entry into the French intellectual *salons*, thanks to the book by E. M. de Vogüé (*Le Roman russe*), in which some saw the beginning of a neo-mystical era. The Vicomte de Vogüé was saluted as 'the Chateaubriand of a new religious Renaissance'. Light had come from the East, and Péladan hastened to modify the plan of his Twilight of the Gods. 'Ohé! ! ! Ohé! ! ! les races latines!'—the magician Mérodack had exclaimed at the end of the first volume, *Le Vice suprême*, when present at a performance of an opera dealing with a Lesbian subject, orchestrated in the Wagnerian manner, and with scenery imitating the pictures of Gustave Moreau. In *A cœur perdu* (1888) Péladan sees salvation for Europe in the westernization of Russia:

'Elle fut divine cette comédie latine! Voilà les slaves en scène; mais on ne succède ni aux latins, ni aux grecs, ni aux juifs; on les continue, si l'on est de taille à faire suite à ces géants de gloire. L'œuvre politico-économique de l'Occident reste russe. Cependant, cet aigle pour deux têtes n'a qu'une seule couronne; il recevra l'autre au double gironnement romain et latin. Tout l'avenir de la civilisation est suspendu aux lèvres de la femme slave. Aura-t-elle le baiser intelligent?

'La slave latinisée est deux fois femme; seule, elle se donne absolument dès qu'elle aime, et ne reculera jamais devant les conséquences, même tragiques; véritable fille de Shakespeare, qu'un sang plus vermeil et des nerfs de fauve font redoutable autant qu'enivrante. Si l'androgyne pouvait être fréquent, ce serait parmi les Polonaises et les Russes.'

As for the Princess Paule Riazan, she is sufficiently westernized to resemble one of Gustave Moreau's figures. Like these, she is a collection of fragments selected from the Old Masters: she is built *à la* Mantegna; 'Pastorino de Sienne eût médaillé ce profil volontaire, apparenté avec celui de Salaïno, l'éphèbe lombard'. Her breast, however, is worthy of a sphinx by Rops, it is 'une gorge aiguë'. She has masculine characteristics, 'jarret dur, mollet ferme, toutes les virilités compatibles avec la grâce'. She is obsessed by the ideal which is incarnate in Mademoiselle de Maupin.

Nebo, Mérodack's disciple, a painter-aesthete with whom the Princess is in love, is, on the other hand, feminine. 'Sous le frac on devinait que ses seize ans avaient été apolloniens et des fémininités de corps, choquantes chez un homme.' In painting, Nebo is a disciple of Moreau:

'Ce n'étaient que des membres isolés, les torses des filles de la *Nuit*, les jambes frêles et nerveuses de Mantegna; des mains stupéfiantes de race, des bras d'une maigreur restée forte; des embonpoints sveltes; et tout cela modelé avec une telle préoccupation androgyne que la princesse rougit.'

We shall not stop here to follow this couple in their explorations of the 'enfer Parisien', after the style of the *Mystères de Paris*, nor in their gradual coming together (*L'Initiation sentimentale*, 1887), but will pause a moment at *A cœur perdu*, which tells of the seduction of Nebo as undertaken by Paule:

'Résistant au désir de la femme au lieu de le provoquer, Nebo

inversait les rôles et prévoyait que la jeune fille, en sa qualité
d'androgyne, oserait comme un homme, puisqu'il se dérobait comme une femme. Ce phénomène fut aidé par la mise de Nebo, mise
féminine qui dotait de mâleté le désir de la princesse.... Il se faisait
faire la cour et désirer comme une coquette et son but, cependant,
était de retarder la sexualisation.'

For another quality in Péladan is contemplative sensuality. When the moment arrives, Nebo stages his surrender with all the would-be Oriental luxury of a picture
by Moreau. He begins by steeping his own body in
balsams, and arranges to yield himself in accordance with
an elaborate ritual. The woman must be dressed in an
armour of jewels—artificial jewels—like a Salome by
Moreau, only even better:

'Ce n'était pas le vêtement d'orfèvrerie que Gustave Moreau
a donné à ses figures mythiques; ici, la monture de pierres ne se
voyait pas; c'étaient, non des bijoux, des foyers lumineux de toutes
couleurs, harmonieusement disposés.'

Nebo's studio, transformed for the occasion, is lit by
dazzling copper lamps, and filled with perfume from a
tripod in which scented substances burn. Hebrew-
Phoenician phallic symbols are painted on the walls, to
bear witness to 'cet amer souci de la nécessité phallique'.
Nebo wears a Chaldean tiara and, swinging a censer, approaches Paule who is dressed as an idol; when she feels
her nostrils titillated by the incense, the Russian woman
imagines herself 'la grande Istar, l'Aphrodite de Kaldée'.
Canticles form an accompaniment to the gestures of the
ritual, canticles extremely similar to those written later by
Remy de Gourmont (in *Le Pèlerin du silence*). Finally
Nebo tears asunder the purple curtain concealing the
nuptial couch, which is composed of the petals of roses
and lilies mixed with daphne and myrtle.

'Elle le ceintura de ses bras et avec une force de femme énervée,
elle l'enleva de terre, l'affaissa sur elle, l'étreignant comme si elle
eût été le mâle et qu'elle violât.... Un cri fut-il étouffé? ce fut presque insaisissable; les flammes des trépieds étaient près de s'éteindre.
Ô l'analyse des contraires; aux boudoirs et aux chambres de torture,
grésille mêmement un effluve charnel et flotte une odeur de peau
émue; l'appareil de la volupté et son émanation voisinent incroyable-

ment celui des supplices et leur exhalaison. Serait-ce que nous sommes dupes d'une catégorisation traditionnelle, et suggestionnés par nos prédécesseurs de déterminer les sensations en agréables et douloureuses comme si une sainte possédée par Antinoüs ne souffrirait pas plus qu'à l'empalement d'un épieu rougi?'

This remark takes one back to Baudelaire and Sade. But alas! the sexual drama so cunningly arranged by Nebo ends in a fiasco. In the silence is heard the voice of a woman, deluded, almost ironical: 'Ô pontife, c'est tout ce que t'inspire ton idole?'

'L'androgyne expliqué par l'impuissance, et la vertu, effet de débilité!... impuissant, ou du moins insuffisant.'

Péladan saw quite correctly in this, but his lascivious imagination cannot resign itself to the pathetic truth, and for the nights which follow he prepares unspeakable joys and angelic loves for the youthful couple with the Leonardo smile ('le sourire de Léonard, le divin sourire de l'intelligence plissa leur bouche'):

' "Vivants, ces Joconde et ces Saint-Jean s'aimeraient comme nous nous aimons!... c'est-à-dire d'une allure de sphinx à chimère et de sainte à archange, avec une douceur d'éternité dans la résorption du désir inapaisable." '

Péladan's work is a veritable encyclopedia of the taste of the Decadents—Pre-Raphaelitism, the Primitives, the Leonardo smile, Gustave Moreau, Félicien Rops, the Russian novel, the music of Wagner . . . and it is all permeated by his ineffectual sexual obsession, by his Hymn to the Androgyne (in *L'Androgyne*, 1891, a novel the content of which is defined by the author as a 'restitution d'impressions éphébiques grecques à travers la mysticité catholique'):

'Éros intangible, Éros uranien, pour les hommes grossiers des époques morales tu n'es plus qu'un péché infâme; on t'appelle Sodome, céleste contempteur de toute volupté. C'est le besoin des siècles hypocrites d'accuser la Beauté, cette lumière vive, de la ténèbre aux cœurs vils contenue. Garde ton masque monstrueux qui te défend du profane! Los à toi!...

'Anges de Signorelli, S. Jean de Léonard . . . vrais anges du vrai ciel, brûlants Séraphs et Kerubs abstracteurs, tenants des trônes de Iavhé. Seigneurie et essence Déiforme! — Prince du Septenaire, qui tour à tour commandes et obéis. Ô sexe initial, sexe définitif, absolu de l'amour, absolu de la forme, sexe qui nies le sexe, sexe d'éternité! Los à toi, Androgyne.'

Samas, the hero of this novel,

's'étonne que l'amour ne se greffe pas sur l'attrait subi, et cet esclavage de la chair si doux ne le pousse pas au désir de posséder.... Il n'est charmé que par le non-acte, le demi-rêve de ses impressions.'

The last novel of the 'éthopée', *La Vertu suprême* (1900), deserves mention not for its customary parade of sexual monstrosities (there is even a regiment of Lesbians called the 'Royal-Maupin', and the inevitable English sadist),[71] but for its curious ethical-religious ideology. Tammuz makes use of love instead of the dagger, 'ayant de beaux jeunes hommes et de captivantes femmes à lancer comme des faucons sur les ennemis du Vrai, du Beau et du Juste'. Sacred prostitutes are employed to bring back the vicious to the path of virtue. For instance Davèze, 'le poète délicat et tendre . . . le Watteau littéraire' (an obvious portrait of Verlaine) 'est, hélas, un sodomite'. The lovely Bélit tries to normalize 'pauvre Lélian', but still cannot succeed in overcoming her own repulsion: Davèze 'paraissait insauvable'. A priest threatens to throw aside his habit to marry a Protestant woman. To avoid such a scandal the solution is to give him 'une maîtresse intelligente, le soulageant de sa sexualité, le gavant de luxure; dégrisé, il resterait à l'Eglise et à sa mission'. The idea of a similar utilization of vice for humanitarian purposes goes back to Sue,[72] and actually, side by side with aestheticism, Péladan cherished an equally strong passion for the 'thriller': hence his dream of a secret society with an aesthetic ceremonial.[73]

The crowning moment of the novel is a replica of *Parsifal*. Mérodack journeys on a pilgrimage to the Abbey of Montségur, which is dedicated to the cult of the Rosicrucians—a copy of Monsalvat with aesthetic refinements, Flemish tapestries, Renaissance seats . . . but the Grand Cross of the Great Rose is made of artificial rubies, and in its centre, to hold the Host, is a chemical diamond. A Holy Grail of pinchbeck—in fact, an epitome of the whole of Péladan's pathetic 'éthopée'. Images of various divinities adorn the pilasters round the altar: 'l'Oannès de

Kaldée, le Dieu mitré à la queue de poisson, l'Ammon Râ du Nil, la Mayâ de l'Inde et l'Athéné grecque . . . une décoration panthéonique des religions.' Parsifalism is mixed up with Legitimism: the Rosicrucians cultivate the dream of 'the last of the Bourbons'. Inside the temple the organ gives forth the notes of *Parsifal*. But even this superb *décor*, like that which Nebo prepared for his angelic love-affair, is the scene of a fiasco. The companions of Mérodack refuse to pronounce the vow of chastity. Méro-dack 'avait voulu réaliser la Vertu suprême; et Monsalvat, sous le souffle passionnel, s'écroulait'. *Parsifal* changes rapidly into the *Twilight of the Gods*.

12. Among the most characteristic works of this period must be mentioned the novel by Élémir Bourges[74] which actually took its title from Wagner's opera, *Le Crépuscule des dieux* (1884, second edition 1901; the novel was written between 1877 and 1882). Bourges, a member of the Académie Goncourt since its foundation, recounts the vicissitudes of a German ducal family undermined by lust and madness, founding his story partly on actual fact (especially upon the extravagances of August Wilhelm Duke of Braunschweig-Luneburg), and partly colouring it with ideas taken from the *Diaboliques* of d'Aurevilly and from the Elizabethan tragedies. The Duke belongs to a branch of the notorious family of Este, and has several bastards. Foremost among the various Italian adventurers at his court is the singer Giulia Belcredi:

'La Belcredi, point galante et de cerveau mâle, autant que les Laura de Dianti et les Vittoria Accorambona du seizième siècle, c'était une femme faite exprès pour vivre dans ces temps sanglants, dominer sur quelque cour italienne, s'occuper de guerres, de politique, d'intrigues, de poisons, de sonnets, avec un Vinci qui l'eût peinte.'

She has, in fact, a 'sourire dérobé et noir de Joconde', 'ce sourire de sphinx, doux et glacé en même temps, dont elle couvrait et masquait ses plus terribles résolutions'. And also, like one of d'Aurevilly's viragos, Giulia is greedy 'd'émotions nouvelles, inconnues, violentes, surhumaines'. The following reflection is worthy of d'Aurevilly (p. 249 of the second edition):

'Ah! vieille idole de l'amour, qu'importe comment on t'adore!

Dans les dérèglements du corps, c'est toujours notre âme qui agit, et tourmentée de l'infini où elle voudrait s'amalgamer, entraîne, de bourbier en bourbier, son misérable compagnon.'

Giulia, 'cette insolente Joconde', to further her sinister design of getting rid of the Duke's children, so that she, as favourite, may concentrate all the power and wealth in her own hands, drags forth from the twilight of the sub-conscious the incestuous love of two of the Duke's chil-dren, the melancholy Hans Ulric and the ethereal Chris-tiane, and leads it forward to catastrophe. She reads them Byron's *Manfred*, Ford's play *'Tis Pity she 's a Whore*, in which is presented the guilty passion of Giovanni and Annabella, and finally succeeds in making them take the parts of Siegmund and Sieglinde in the *Valkyrie*. Drunk with Wagner's music, the brother and sister, refined and music-mad as characters in Poe, consummate their in-cestuous love, after which Ulric kills himself and Chris-tiane becomes a nun. Finally Giulia becomes the mistress of Otto, another son of the Duke's, violent and a libertine, and together they plot to poison the Duke. The scene in which Giulia prepares the poison, and then combines the sense of sin with that of pleasure by lying with Otto, comes very near to the art of the *Diaboliques*; while the melodramatic catastrophe at Paris, in the Duke's bathroom, when the latter, having discovered the plot, replies to his son's revolver-shot by firing back at him, and Giulia poisons herself upon the body of Otto whom she believes to be dead—and all this while a storm rages out-side, and the French troops mobilized against Prussia (we are in 1870) are passing through the street—is cleverly modelled upon the turbid, bloodstained dramas of the Elizabethans. The novel ends in a remarkably Decadent key. The debauched Duke, weighed down by his excesses, attends a performance at Bayreuth of *Götterdämmerung* and sees in it a symbol of the end of an entire world: 'Tous les signes de destruction étaient visibles sur l'ancien monde, comme des anges de colère, au-dessus d'une Gomorrhe condamnée.' The Duke dies, leaving extravagant disposi-tions in his will as to his tomb. The decay of the German courts, and particularly the madness of Ludwig of

Bavaria, inspired also other writers in France, for example
Toulet in *Monsieur du Paur*. Bourges quotes certain lines
of Agrippa d'Aubigné to serve as motto to his novel:

> Si quelqu'un me reprend que mes vers eschauffez
> Ne sont rien que de meurtre et de sang estoffez,
> Qu'on n'y lit que fureur, que massacre, que rage,
> Qu'horreur, malheur, poison, trahison et carnage,
> Je lui respons: . . .
>
> . . . .
>
> Ce siècle, autre en ses mœurs, demande un autre style.
> Cueillons des fruicts amers desquels il est fertile.
> Non, il n'est plus permis sa veine desguiser;
> La main peut s'endormir, non l'âme reposer.

13. The novels of Catulle Mendès constitute another
éthopée of Latin Decadence. Of all the preachers of misfortune, Mendès was certainly the most voluminous and
the blackest. Speaking of one of his novels,[75] Barbey
d'Aurevilly remarked upon its derivation from the 'frénétique' Hugo of *Han d'Islande* and *Bug Jargal*, and upon the
accentuation of the monstrous side, both of vice and virtue,
in his work:

> 'Tous, sans exception, dans le livre de M. Mendès, ce pandémo-
> nium de chimères où les monstres alternent avec les plus difformes
> caricatures, qui ne sont pas la vérité non plus; tous sont tellement
> pétris et tripotés dans l'hyperbole et dans l'impossible, que Victor
> Hugo lui-même, malgré ses fameux yeux qui grossissent tout ce
> qu'ils regardent, déconcerté par un tel spectacle, serait bien capable
> de dire à la fin qu'une telle société de monstres n'existe pas. Et, de
> fait, Victor Hugo est plus sobre de monstres, lui, dans l'intérêt
> de quelques-uns d'entre eux, tandis que ce diable exaspéré de
> M. Catulle Mendès en met partout, comme de la moutarde.'

Mendès, as we have already had occasion to mention,
brought into actual being certain novels such as Baudelaire had planned in order to *épater le bourgeois*, accompanying his pageant of ghastly wax figures with passages of
moral uplift in the style of Baudelaire's conclusion to the
dialogue between Delphine and Hippolyte:

> Descendez, descendez, lamentables victimes,
> Descendez le chemin de l'enfer éternel!

Jamais vous ne pourrez assouvir votre rage,
Et votre châtiment naîtra de vos plaisirs. . . .

. . . .

Loin des peuples vivants, errantes, condamnées,
A travers les déserts courez comme les loups;
Faites votre destin, âmes désordonnées,
Et fuyez l'infini que vous portez en vous.

Among the novels of Mendès the most typical are
Zo'har (1886) and *La première maîtresse* (1887). The
first tells a story of incest, complicated by an inverted
sexual relationship in which the woman is virile and the
man feeble: it exaggerates the colours used by Barbey
d'Aurevilly, by Villiers de l'Isle-Adam, by Rachilde in
Monsieur Vénus, and Bourges in *Le Crépuscule des dieux*.
In Mendès' novel the characters move convulsively: it is
all hallucination, hysteria, so deliberately, rhetorically
frenzied (one is reminded of Guerrazzi) that it becomes a
veritable parody. When Léopold discovers that his sister
Stéphana is with child by him:

'Il frémit de la tête aux pieds, livide, l'œil fou.

'Qu'était-ce donc? Que voyait-il? Quelle terreur nouvelle, plus
violente que toutes les autres, le secouait? Il allongeait un bras, il
étendait une main, droit devant lui, vers elle; et sa main tremblait,
comme celle d'un homme qui désigne quelque épouvantable apparition. Elle frissonna, livide aussi, à cause de la direction de cette
main. Pourtant, elle dit: — Qu'avez-vous, Léopold?

'— Oh! . . . oh! . . . oh! . . . ton ventre! bégaya-t-il, la main
toujours étendue.'

The following passage describes Léopold's subsequent
hallucination, which is worthy of the brush of a Hierony-
mus Bosch:

'S'il s'était retourné, s'il avait regardé — il fuyait, les yeux clos,
la tête entre ses épaules levées! — il aurait vu d'abominables vivants,
hommes nains, bêtes naines, celles-ci sans tête, ceux-là sans jambes
et se traînant; il aurait vu, comme dans la cour des miracles de
l'enfer, tous les estropiements, tous les inachèvements, toutes les
difformités, toutes les purulences; il aurait vu, en une farandole de
sabbat, des enfants-crapauds[76] et des enfants-araignées, de petites
hyènes et de jeunes loups faits de nœuds de vipères, et des sautèle-
ments de macaques sur leurs ignobles fesses bleues, et, courant aussi,
des nourrices poilues, chèvres debout sur leurs pattes de derrière,

qui, au lieu du lait d'un sein, donnent à boire à des nouveaux-nés
pareils à de très petits vieillards, le pus, goutte à goutte, d'une plaie
qu'elles pressent. Et il savait que tout ce pullulement sortait du
ventre incestueux, là-bas! Il accouchait, il accouchait, le ventre
gros de monstres!'

Mendès carries on his frantic scene against a background of terrifying Norwegian mountains (the same
mountains that had served as *décor* to the impossible love-
affair of Balzac's *Séraphita*), with a waterfall which flames
in the Aurora Borealis like a 'quadruple niagara d'incendie
et de sang'! Léopold flings himself over a precipice and
his sister buries herself alive with his corpse (like the Véra
of Villiers de l'Isle-Adam)—with the usual necrophilistic
details.[77] When they open the tomb, they find an ex-
cessively revolting spectacle (there is even the little corpse
of an unborn child, 'le néant de ce qui n'avait pas été'), and
the horror of the discoverer is such that he hurls the
corpses into the sea and leaves on a journey to the North
Pole, where he hopes to bury his ghastly secret among the
ice-floes. Thus also in *Monsieur Vénus*, of which we shall
speak shortly, de Raittolbe, the eye-witness of the horrible
loves of Raoule and Jacques, leaves for darkest Africa
where he is expected to finish his life. This type of ending
—a sort of geographical catharsis—is common in novels
of this period.

There is an even more pronounced moral pose (this also
is to be found in Guerrazzi) in *La première maîtresse*,
where the preface, printed all in capital letters, gives a
warning of the dangerousness of women, and quotes the
example of the mummy of Psammetichus which was found
after a thousand years intact except at one point in the
neck 'qui était une plaie grouillante de vers, et d'ou sortait
une petite flamme de pourriture', because in that particular place Psammetichus, 'jeune encore, ignorant des caresses
de la femme, avait été baisé par une courtisane'. In this
novel the man is raped by a diabolical woman, who makes
him the slave of her ghastly vampire degeneracy which
makes havoc with men.

'Évelin, si joli, si frêle, Évelin, cet enfant qu'elle avait voulu
parce qu'il ressemblait à tout ce qui est frais et fragile, parce qu'il

était à peine un homme avec des gracilités de fillette, qu'elle avait
pris, elle, l'horrible éducatrice, parce qu'il était, malgré les mauvais
rêves, ignorant et ingénu, Évelin, dans les bras, sous la bouche,
sous les dents, sous les ongles d'Honorine, tremblait comme une
faible proie qui saigne et qui a peur, et qui voudrait fuir, et qui
succombe. . . . Elle connaissait l'épouvantable ravissement d'un
démon qui a conquis l'âme d'une vierge!'

Another devilish woman, this time a Lesbian, is the
central figure in _Méphistophéla_ (1890). Of all the monstrosities which pullulate in the fiction of this period,
Lesbians are among the most popular: there is no need to
do more than mention the grisly episode of Gilonne de
Bonisse and Gabrielle de Vignes in _Saint-Cendre_, by
Maurice Maindron (1898). It was the period of _Les
Amours défendues_ by René Maizeroy, of novels such as
Monsieur Jocaste and _Monsieur Vénus_, the _Marquise de Sade_
and the _Monstres parisiens_—a kind of mythical age of
pornographic literature, with sexual ichthyosauri and
palaeosauri, caprices _à la_ Goya and incubi _à la_ Rops.[77A]

14. The androgyne ideal was the obsession not only of
Péladan, but of the whole Decadent Movement. The first
volume of the _Décadence latine_ had not yet seen the light
when the ideal of the androgyne was proclaimed by a
woman—a girl of twenty—Rachilde (her real name was
Marguerite Eymery), in _Monsieur Vénus_ (in the Brussels
edition of 1884 it is stated as having been written in
collaboration with F. Talman).

Barbey d'Aurevilly immediately became enthusiastic
about the book. Barrès, in the preface which he wrote for
the 1889 edition, with the title of _Complications d'amour_,
described the content of the book as a 'spectacle d'une
rare perversité'—not really so rare at that time—and—
exquisite connoisseur of the human soul as he was—
added:

'Ce qui est tout à fait délicat dans la perversité de ce livre, c'est
qu'il a été écrit par une jeune fille de vingt ans. Le merveilleux
chef-d'œuvre! . . . toute cette frénésie tendre et méchante, et ces
formes d'amour qui sentent la mort, sont l'œuvre d'une enfant, de
l'enfant la plus douce et la plus retirée. . . . Ce vice savant éclatant
dans le rêve d'une vierge, c'est un des problèmes des plus mystérieux
que je sache. . . .'

He also quoted the description of the authoress which Jean Lorrain had written ('Mademoiselle Salamandre', in the *Courrier français* of December 12th, 1886):

'Une pensionnaire d'allures sobres et réservées, très pâle, il est vrai, mais d'une pâleur de pensionnaire studieuse . . . une vraie jeune fille, un peu mince, un peu frêle, aux mains inquiétantes de petitesse, au profil grave d'éphèbe grec ou de jeune Français amoureux . . . et des yeux — oh! les yeux! des yeux longs, longs, alourdis de cils invraisemblables et d'une clarté d'eau, des yeux qui ignorent tout.'

Lorrain began his article in this way: 'Couche-t-elle?— Non, chaste, mais elle a dans son cerveau une alcôve. . . .'

This portrait clearly forms a pendant to the portraits of men which we have been studying in this chapter. Women, too, had started to practise the precept 'lasciva est nobis pagina, vita proba'. Rachilde herself defined *Monsieur Vénus* as 'le plus merveilleux produit de l'hystérie arrivée au paroxysme de la chasteté dans un milieu vicieux'. A remark which de Gourmont once made should perhaps be remembered in this connexion: 'La perversion d'une jeune fille est une preuve de son innocence.'

No analysis of the novel could be better, than that of Barrès, and we shall therefore quote it here:

'Mlle Raoule de Vénérande est une fière jeune fille, très nerveuse; avec des lèvres minces, d'un dessein assez désagréable. Dans l'atelier de sa fleuriste, elle remarque un jeune ouvrier. Couronné de roses qu'il tortille lestement en guirlande, ce garçon, d'un roux très foncé, l'enchante par son menton à fossette, sa chair unie et enfantine, et le petit pli qu'il a au cou, le pli du nouveau-né qui engraisse; et puis il regarde, comme implorent les chiens souffrants, avec une vague humidité dans les prunelles. . . . Raoule installe dans un intérieur fort romanesque ce joli garçon si gras; elle le surprend qui, fou d'une folie de fiancée en présence de son trousseau de femme, lèche jusqu'aux roulettes des meubles à travers leurs franges multicolores. Avec un cynisme de très spirituelle allure, elle le déconcerte quand il imagine d'être aimable; elle le pousse dans un cabinet de toilette, elle le fait rougir par son audace à l'examiner et le complimenter, lui, le rustre qu'elle a recueilli sous prétexte de charité. Et le pauvre mâle humilié s'agenouille sur la traîne de la robe de Raoule, et sanglote. Car, Rachilde le dit excellemment, il était fils d'un ivrogne et d'une catin, son honneur ne savait que pleurer. Ce M. Vénus, absolument désexué de caractère par une suite de procédés ingénieux, devient *la maîtresse* de Raoule. Je veux dire qu'elle l'aime, l'entretient et le caresse, qu'elle s'irrite et s'attendrit auprès de lui, sans jamais céder au désir qui la ferait aussitôt l'inférieure de ce rustre, près de qui elle se plaît à frissonner, mais qu'elle méprise. Elle définit son goût d'une façon admirable: "J'aimerai Jacques comme un fiancé aime sans espoir une fiancée morte.". . . . Raoule de Vénérande, cette insensée au teint pâle et aux lèvres minces, qui lave le corps équivoque de Jacques Silvert, fait songer, avec toutes les différences de climat, de civilisation et d'époque, au vertige de Phrygie, quand les femmes lamentaient Attis, le petit mâle rosé et trop gras. Ces obscures complications d'amour ne sont pas seulement faites d'énervation; à leur luxure se mêle un mysticisme trouble. La Raoule de Vénérande du roman a pour directrice une parente de toute piété, et qui ne cesse de stigmatiser l'humanité fangeuse. Rachilde écrit: "Dieu aurait dû créer l'amour d'un côté et les sens de l'autre. L'amour véritable ne se devrait composer que d'amitié chaude. Sacrifions les sens, la bête." Ces rêves tendres et malgré tout impurs ont toujours tenté les cerveaux les plus fiers. Un romancier catholique, Joséphin Péladan, a cru pouvoir s'abandonner à ces vertiges malsains sans offenser sa religion. . . . La maladie du siècle, qu'il faut toujours citer et dont Monsieur Vénus signale chez la femme une des formes les plus intéressantes, est faite en effet d'une fatigue nerveuse excessive et d'un orgueil inconnu jusqu'alors. . . . On verrait, avec effroi, quelques-uns arriver au dégoût de la grâce féminine, en même temps que M. Vénus proclame la haine de la force mâle. Complication de grande conséquence! le dégoût de la femme! la haine de la force mâle! Voici que certains cerveaux rêvent d'un être insexué. Ces imaginations sentent la mort.'

It could not be better put. Is it necessary, after this, to insist upon the details of the novel? Upon the virility of Raoule, who keeps in her bedroom a panoply of weapons 'de tous genres et de tous pays'? Upon the sadistic complications, which Barrès says are ingenuous, but which, for all that, have their significance, for wherever there is conscious and pleasurable violation of the normal, there the shade of the Divine Marquis is present?[78] Upon Raoule's panther-roar at the sight of the equivocal nudity of Jacques? Upon the evocation of the legendary figure of Antinous, whose bust, with eyes of enamel 'luisants de désirs', adorned Raoule's room? Raoule gives hashish to Jacques:

'Mon amour, murmura-t-elle si bas que Jacques entendit comme on entend au fond d'un abîme, nous allons nous appartenir dans un pays étrange que tu ne connais point. Ce pays est celui des fous, mais il n'est pas pourtant celui des brutes. . . . Je viens de te dépouiller de tes sens vulgaires pour t'en donner d'autres plus subtils, plus raffinés. Tu vas voir avec mes yeux, goûter avec mes lèvres. Dans ce pays, on rêve, et cela suffit pour exister. . . . Jacques, la tête renversée, tâchait de ressaisir ses mains. Il croyait rouler peu à peu, dans une ondée de plumes. . . . A son oreille, bruissaient les chants d'un amour étrange n'ayant pas de sexe et procurant toutes les voluptés.'

In her later work, Rachilde seeks to emphasize the sadistic aspects of her inspiration. In *A Mort* (1886) a dandy, Maxime de Bryon, tortures the delicate Madame Soirès and kills her by inches. Finally, this authoress had no hesitation in exploiting the commercial value of her own speciality by boldly flaunting the sensational title *La Marquise de Sade* (end of 1886), of which Lorrain said: 'Roman à fracas, dont les éditions volent et disparaissent comme emportées dans un tourbillon de curiosité exaspérée et malsaine', but about the competence of which he, who was an authority on that point, declared sceptically: 'C'est ardemment rêvé, d'accord, mais pas du tout vécu . . . oh! pas du tout'; and concluded by describing the writer in her own words:

'Son être d'une chair incorruptible passait au milieu des hystéries de son temps comme la salamandre au milieu des flammes; elle vivait des nerfs des autres plus encore que des siens propres.'

We need not be concerned here with Rachilde's subsequent production. Incredible though it may seem, this writer has continued imperturbably, right down to the present day, to pour forth novels, some more, some less sensational, and even as I write these pages there may be seen in the windows of certain bookshops a book of hers called *L'Homme au bras de feu*, which, as the wrapper, decorated with the mature likeness of the lady who was once Mademoiselle Salamandre, promises, 'hantera fatalement tous les cerveaux épris de rêves d'une mystérieuse sensualité'. Times have changed, and to-day Rachilde employs themes of rough sensuality in the Spanish manner, as is fitting in a period which has produced Montherlant, D. H. Lawrence, and others.

15. The strange passion, sexless and lustful, which was described in *Monsieur Vénus*, was the obsession of the period. It is predominant in the paintings of Moreau, in the novels of Péladan, but is visible everywhere.

Even as early as 1862, the heroine of *Isis*, by Villiers de l'Isle-Adam, had 'l'énigmatique contenance d'une Bradamante mâtinée d'une Circé antique'; the hero of *Valbert*, by T. de Wyzewa (1893), loathes the violent appetites of nature and tries the impossible experiment of a voluntarily chaste marriage. Poe had introduced metaphysical moods into love; the influence of the Russian novel merely developed the tendency. Dostoievsky, especially, gave a more profound treatment to certain of Poe's themes; compare *The Double* with the American writer's *William Wilson*, and observe the preponderance of the 'imp of the perverse' in the characters of Dostoievsky. The French found, or thought they found, in the novels of Dostoievsky a sadism which had become more mystical and more subtle,[79] no longer limited to the grossness of physical torture, but penetrating like a worm-hole into all moral phenomena (which of Barbey's 'diabolical' women had arrived at the perfection of Nastasia Filippovna, who felt a horrible, unnatural joy in the tormenting knowledge of her own dishonour?)';[80] they found also a thirst for the impossible, and impotence elevated to the height of a mystical ecstasy (in Myshkin, the hero of *The Idiot*). Dostoievsky seemed to speak the very language of Baudelaire, not in aphorisms, but with a profusion of introspective eloquence:

'Beauty is a terrible and awful thing! It is terrible because it has not been fathomed and never can be fathomed, for God sets us nothing but riddles. Here the boundaries meet and all contradictions exist side by side. . . . What's still more awful is that a man with the ideal of Sodom in his soul does not renounce the ideal of the Madonna. . . . What to the mind is shameful is beauty and nothing else to the heart. Is there beauty in Sodom? Believe me, that for the immense mass of mankind beauty is found in Sodom. Did you know that secret? The awful thing is that beauty is mysterious as well as terrible. God and the devil are fighting there and the battlefield is the heart of man. . . . I loved vice, I loved the ignominy of vice. I loved cruelty; am I not a bug, am I not a noxious insect? In fact a Karamazov!'[81]

In Sade and in the sadists of the 'frénétique' type of Romanticism it is the integrity of the body which is assaulted and destroyed, whereas in Dostoievsky one has the feeling—to use a phrase from *Letters from the Underworld*—of the 'intimacy of the soul brutally and insolently violated'.[82] Actually Dostoievsky did nothing more than make use, but with profounder understanding, of certain themes used by the 'frénétique' French Romantics, and of the method of the passionate monologue as used in the *Confession d'un enfant du siècle*; and the fact that he was such a belated manifestation of the Romanticism of 1830 made him, by a curious combination of circumstances, particularly vital to the Decadents of the end of the century, who renewed the taste for the 'frénétique' (in a certain sense the case of Dostoievsky is similar, on a larger scale, to that of Barbey d'Aurevilly). The relations of the sexes, in the novels of Dostoievsky, are often the same as in the Decadents: the man is reduced to playing the woman's part, the woman, on the other hand, is wilful and domineering—the Fatal Woman.[82A] Nastasia Filippovna in *The Idiot*, Grushenka in *The Brothers Karamazov*, Natalia Vassilyevna in *The Eternal Husband*. . . .

16. It is a Russian Woman, therefore, Madame Livitinof, in Jean Lorrain's *Très russe* (1886), who represents the type of the *allumeuse*:

'Elle était à la fois l'Attirance et à la fois la Chasteté, triste et mélancolieuse comme une pudeur brisée, pure, adorable et désirable comme l'incarnation même de la Pudeur.'

This Russian woman (naturally she is called Sonia) refuses to give herself to Mauriat when he meets her again. Why? "Pourquoi?" [she repeats] 'et un mauvais sourire, un sourire inquiétant de Joconde [one expected that], à la fois douloureux et cruel, écartait ses lèvres minces: "Parce que la chasteté est l'extrême désir".' Thus she takes delight in tormenting her lover (a weak man, 'cruel comme une femme, doux comme un enfant').

'Elle surexcitait et exaspérait les sens de Mauriat, comme elle eût fait fouetter un de ses serfs, là-bas, dans ses terres, par désœuvrement, caprice, une envie qu'il lui prenait de se prouver à elle-même sa puissance et de voir couler un peu de rouge ... humain. Mauriat était sa propriété comme ses moujiks; elle se l'était affermé en se donnant à lui: c'était l'application du droit féodal dans toute sa splendeur.'

Madame Livitinof is a reincarnation of Marguerite de Bourgogne, of Cleopatra: she, also, dreams of the kiss of a man who will never love again after he has once possessed her. This the author calls 'très russe', and it is in conformity with the psychology of Dostoievsky. For in *The Idiot* (of which the first French translation was in 1887), Gania actually says to Myshkin, about Nastasia:

'You know, I believe she also loves me—in her own way, you understand. You know the proverb: "Whom I love, him I chastise". All through life she will see in me a person to be despised (and perhaps that is what she wants); but in spite of everything she will love me in her way; she prepares herself for that, such is her character. I tell you, she is profoundly Russian.'

In order to bring home his point, Lorrain gives a version of a Russian ballad in which is described the appalling punishment meted out to the son of a king, by a duke's daughter, whom he espied naked in her bath: the king's son, blinded and thrown into a deep dungeon, still goes on loving the lady, whom he sees always young and beautiful as on the fatal day.

A *fumiste* of quite deplorable taste, Jean Lorrain (his real name was Paul Duval), practised only one of the vices which he loved to parade before the public, but that a more than sufficient one—etheromania. His perversity, as some one wrote of him,[83] 'ne descend pas plus bas que le cerveau. Ou si d'aventure une fois elle s'y hasarde, c'est une expérience en vue de la littérature.' Monsieur de Phocas, a character into which Lorrain put more of himself than into any other, declaims the lines from Valéry's *Narcisse*, which are no less characteristic of the 'decadent' state of mind than the lines from Mallarmé's *Hérodiade* which Huysmans made des Esseintes admire:

> Ô frères, tristes lys, je languis de beauté
> . . . . . .
> Que je déplore ton éclat fatal et pur!

Lorrain's fixation, as a theoretical sadist, was to give himself the airs of a murderer: he combed his hair forward (he had dyed his hair red, as Baudelaire had dyed his green) to make his forehead look lower and to bring into greater prominence what Bataille described as 'les maxillaires assassins'; he was also attracted by the spectacle of the underworld and did his best to frequent it as much as possible; and he kept always in his sitting-room a livid and bloody truncated head . . . made of wax. It was a case of 'virility complex' in a being of feminine sensibility, a hysterical, with homosexual tendencies. Assisted by an affectionate mother, this chronic invalid crawled about in the sunshine of Provence, disguised as a werewolf.

It is possible that I may be accused 'de me faire la partie trop belle', as the French say, in looking for illustrations of the atmosphere of the Decadence in the works of Jean Lorrain. For Lorrain carried the fashions of the period to the degree of paroxysm—the passion for unhealthy, perverse young men (he, too, was attracted by the Androgyne),[84] for the satanic Primitives (Botticelli's *Primavera* was at that time considered 'satanique, irrésistible, et terrifiante'),* for Gustave Moreau and the Pre-Raphaelites, for flowers of strange and equivocal shapes (cf. the phallic flowers of des Esseintes),[85] for *faisandage* and all kinds of combinations of lust and death. The exotic perversions which were the vogue of the *fin de siècle* were sadism *à l'anglaise* and the Slav soul: Lorrain quickly became a passionate student of both.

In *Les Noronsoff* (*Le Vice errant*) he tells the story of an ancestral crime in a Russian family, in virtue of which its women become Messalinas and its men Heliogabali. The hero of the tale combines this unenviable heredity with the heredity of the Borgias, since his mother, an Italian, has in her veins the ancient blood of Alexander VI! 'Nul doute que de ces deux sangs princiers, Borgia et Noronsoff, quelque redoutable fleuron n'eût jailli . . . . . le fleuron suprême d'une lignée de crimes, de folies et de sang.' It is a fine combination:

'Les Russes ont des âmes d'enfant. Instinctif et impulsif avec une naïveté candide, nul peuple ne se pourrit plus facilement au contact des vieilles civilisations. . . . Le prince Wladimir était bien un fils de cette race sauvage et tendre, hâtée dans sa décomposition facile par cette goutte de sang florentin, apportée là par les San Carloni.'

So we find ourselves in the full flood of the 'décadence latine', but it can hardly be said that the new Europe was to arise, as Péladan hoped, from this crossing of Slav and Latin. The more or less sadistic orgies of this tiresome descendant of Neros, Trimalchios, and Heliogabali may easily be imagined. In the end, after an access of vampirism (he tries to cut the throat of one of his moujiks in order to drink 'son jeune sang, son sang frais de force et de santé'), 'dans un hoquet suprême il crachait enfin la vieille âme de Byzance trop longtemps attardée en lui'. Though Lorrain put something of his own character into that of Noronsoff and laid on the colours pretty thick (even the Russian prince is, among other things, a kind of invalid ogre, pampered by his mother), he put much more of himself into the hero of *Monsieur de Phocas* (1901), a novel which partly imitates Wilde's *Picture of Dorian Gray*, but surpasses its model in the intensity of the obsessions it displays.

17. It is rather surprising that a critic as serious as Charles du Bos should announce that Wilde's work 'n'a jamais reçu le traitement qu'elle mérite: en ce qui concerne *The Picture of Dorian Gray*, j'estime que l'on a toujours témoigné d'une grande injustice'.[86] I do not wish to enter here into the question of the artistic value of Wilde's novel, but merely to consider its interest as an illustration of the period.

The aesthetic ancestry of *Dorian Gray* has been exhaustively studied;[87] it is traceable mainly to *Mademoiselle de Maupin* and *A rebours*. The work itself, then, though written in English, belongs really to the French school and must be considered as a curious exotic reflection of it.[88]

At the risk of fatiguing the reader with one parenthesis inside another, like so many Chinese boxes, I should like to point out in passing how Swinburne's influence introduced into England the French literary tendencies to which he had paid homage. Through Swinburne, the

younger generation was initiated into the Decadent Movement, and continued the discovery on its own account in
defiance of the initiator himself who, grown more temperate
with age, wrote a parody (*The Statue of John Brute*, unpublished) of that same *Dorian Gray* which indirectly he had
rendered possible.

A contemporary of Swinburne, Arthur O'Shaughnessy
(1844–81), in his *Epic of Women* (1870), parades before
us a procession of Fatal Women, instruments of perdition
to mankind—Eve, the wife of Hephaestus, Cleopatra,
Salome, Helen. And following the example of Baudelaire
and Swinburne, he wrote a poem *To a Young Murderess*, in
which recur the delirious accents of Swinburne's sadistic
maniacs.

> Will you not slay me? Stab me, yea, somehow
> Deep in the heart: say some foul word at last
> And let me hate you as I love you now.
> Oh, would I might but see you turn and cast
> That false fair beauty that you e'en shall lose,
> And fall down there and writhe about my feet,
> The crooked loathly viper I shall bruise
> Through all eternity!—
>
>   Nay, kiss me, Sweet!

In another passage he professes his love for the 'passion
of purple Nero'—a Romantic 'purple patch' which has
now become commonplace.

Water Pater, the forerunner of the Decadent Movement in England (particularly in his conclusion to *Studies
in the Renaissance* (1873), the book from which we have
quoted the famous passage where the 'Medusean' type of
beauty is found incarnate in La Gioconda) shows himself
as being 'ready to indulge in the luxury of decay, and
amuse himself with fancies of the tomb'—to use a phrase
from *Duke Carl of Rosenmold*—in his tales of the muffled
lives of exquisitely meditative youths (see *A Child in the
House*, and the characteristic fate of all these youths,
Marius the Epicurean, Flavian, Watteau, Duke Carl of
Rosenmold), and of beauty devastated by cruelty (Denys
l'Auxerrois).[89]

The feminine souls of Pater's 'frail androgynous beings'

are already open to all the influences of the Decadence; Duke Carl of Rosenmold is a sensual dilettante in the manner of Ludwig II of Bavaria or of des Esseintes. It was not therefore astonishing that Pater should have crowned with his approval the *Confessions of a Young Man* (1888), in which George Moore finally succeeded, after various unsuccessful attempts (early verse imitated from Baudelaire, *Flowers of Passion*, 1878, *Pagan Poems*, 1881; the novels *A Mere Accident*, 1887, and *Mike Fletcher*, 1889) in presenting to the younger generation in England, already saturated with Pater's aestheticism, a version—which was somewhat superficial, it is true—of the gospel of *Mademoiselle de Maupin* and *A rebours*.[90] Later, in *Evelyn Innes* (first edition 1898, revised edition, 1908) Moore wrote a novel which is just as typically *fin de siècle* as D'Annunzio's *Il Piacere*, with aesthetic Hellenism *à la* Gautier (Sir Owen's favourite passage in literature is the one in *Mademoiselle de Maupin*: 'Je suis un homme des temps homériques. . . .'), with the music of Wagner (*Tristan*), aesthetic backgrounds, and pseudo-mysticism.

Themes of a decadent and perverse nature, at second hand, recur in several minor poets of the time—Arthur Symons, Richard Le Gallienne, John Gray, Theodore Wratislaw, Lionel Johnson, Olive Custance, Ernest Dowson,[91] and, in more recent times, J. E. Flecker, author of the sadistic fantasy *Hassan*.*

The essence of the English Decadent school is contained in the forty odd pages of Aubrey Beardsley's 'romantic novel', *Under the Hill* (published in part in *The Savoy*, and as a posthumous volume in 1904, but it must be remarked that the accessible version is very much expurgated),[92] in which a precious style resembling that of the *Hypnerotomachia* (from the famous illustrations of which Beardsley's drawings derived not merely ornamental *motifs* but actual technical suggestions)[93] moves with an eighteenth-century rhythm and is full of voluptuous Gallicisms: it is a *faisandé* style, after the aesthetic theory of des Esseintes. It may be remembered, incidentally, that Thomas Griffiths Wainewright, of whom Wilde speaks in *Intentions*, the subtle, perverse aesthete of the beginning of the nineteenth century who handled pen, pencil, and poison, adored the *Sogno di Polifilo*.

In *Under the Hill* the exquisite Abbé Fanfreluche, the Poliphilus of this slight adventure, enters into the mysterious hill where dwells Helen, and is there invited to a magnificent orgy. The story is simply an uninterrupted description of *décors* before which Fanfreluche goes, Poliphilus-wise, into ecstasies—dresses, hair 'floral with red roses'; decorative 'Terminal Gods' abound, quotations from books rare or imaginary (*A Plea for the Domestication of the Unicorn, The Ineffable and Miraculous Life of the Flower of Lima*, &c.) and from the operas of Wagner.[94] There is also a description of a ballet with satyrs and shepherdesses, *The Bacchanals of Sporion*, Sporion being 'a tall, slim, depraved young man with a slight stoop, a troubled walk, an oval impassible face with its olive skin drawn tightly over the bone, strong, scarlet lips, long Japanese eyes, and a great gilt toupet'. The work is oddly dedicated to the Cardinal Poldi Pezzoli, 'Nuncio to the Holy See in Nicaragua and Patagonia', by the convert Beardsley, a Catholic of the French Decadent type. In the *Ballad of a Barber*, also published in *The Savoy*, Beardsley gives expression to a perverse caprice; the barber Carrousel, excited by the youthful freshness of a little princess of thirteen years old, 'as lyrical and sweet As one of Schubert's melodies', cuts her throat:

> He snatched a bottle of Cologne,
> And broke the neck between his hands.
> The Princess gave a little scream,
> Carrousel's cut was sharp and deep;
> He left her softly as a dream
> That leaves a sleeper to his sleep;
> He left the room on pointed feet,
> Smiling that things had gone so well.
> They hanged him in Meridian Street.
> You pray in vain for Carrousel.

But the classic of the Decadence in England is *The Picture of Dorian Gray* (first published in *Lippincott's Monthly Magazine*, July 1890), in which the hero, depraved by the reading of French books, professes the principles of pagan hedonism of Gautier's d'Albert, refined by the more recent recipes of des Esseintes. The novel, from the moment of its appearance, was attacked in the *St. James's Gazette*, where 'The New Voluptuousness' which 'always leads up to blood-shedding' was stigmatized. Although Wilde affirms in his book that 'behind every exquisite thing that exists, there is something tragic', speaks of 'sorrows' which 'stir one's sense of beauty' and of 'wounds . . . like red roses', and altogether tries to surround the figure of the hero with sinister shadows of mystery and death, he never succeeds in creating an atmosphere of anguish. He may well borrow from Poe (*The Oval Portrait*), from Rossetti (*Saint Agnes of Intercession*, *The Portrait*), possibly from Maturin,[95] the idea of the enchantment of the portrait, and again from Poe (*William Wilson*), and from Stevenson (*The Strange Case of Dr. Jekyll and Mr. Hyde*, 1886, and *Markheim*, 1885) the alarming idea of the hero's double personality;[96] but he is capable of introducing, right into the midst of a scene which he wishes to make horrifying, an opium-tainted cigarette, a pair of lemon-yellow gloves, a gold-latten match-box, a Louis Quinze silver salver, or a Saracenic lamp studded with turquoises, which brings the whole edifice to the ground by revealing the fact that the author's real interest is in the decorative. Thus he speaks of events which 'crept with silent blood-stained feet into his brain', of death, whose 'monstrous wings seem to wheel in the leaden air around me'. . . . I must not be accused of indulging in the aesthetic analysis from which I agreed to refrain: these inopportune decorative images are proof of a lack of seriousness in Wilde's conscience and of the superficiality of his hedonism, and show him to be greedy and capricious as an irresponsible child. He accepted even scandal not unwillingly (it has been pointed out that he might easily have left England between the first and the second trial), not so much because of the fascination of disaster—though that undoubtedly contributed—but because of the tragic completeness which it conferred upon his career—for an objective and decorative, rather than a subjective, reason.[96A] The style of *Dorian Gray* alternates between the

fanciful and the witty: in the dialogue Wilde on the whole
proves himself a late descendant of the eighteenth-century
playwrights, making one pun after another, and in his
descriptive passages assuming the false *naïveté* and picturesque bombast of an adult who wishes to appear ingenuous and surprising to the children whom he is trying
to amuse. Wilde's point of view, in fact, is always scenic;
he sees things as in stage-perspective; he is all the time
arranging his characters, his landscapes, his events, and
making them pose. When all is said, the whole significance
of *Dorian Gray* may be considered to have been expressed
in the little set of Latin verses (*In honorem Doriani
creatorisque ejus*) which Lionel Johnson dedicated to
Wilde, who had sent him a copy of the novel:[97]

> Amat avidus amores,
> Miros, miros carpit flores,
> Sævus pulchritudine:
> Quanto anima nigrescit,
> Tanto facies splendescit,
> Mendax, sed quam splendide!

Granted Wilde's imitative capacity, his work is less
characteristic of the period than it seems at the first
glance, less characteristic, at any rate, than Lorrain's
Monsieur de Phocas, which for all its Decadent ornamenta-
tions and its monotonous wheezing of pathetic interjection
(what a number of 'Oh!s' it contains!), bears witness to a
profoundly troubled and painful state of mind.*

In *Monsieur de Phocas*, instead of the frivolous Epicurean, Lord Henry, there is the sadistic English painter
Ethal to play the part of corruptor, and the dilettante
Dorian Gray becomes the obsessed Freneuse. Detailed
comparisons might also be made between the secondary
characters and the episodes of the two books. For example,
the killing of Ethal was suggested by the murder of Basil
Hallward, and the Duc de Freneuse, like Dorian Gray,
frequents sordid taverns, the haunts of criminals, disguis-
ing himself for the occasion, and so on. Besides this,
Lorrain, who was acquainted with English artistic circles,
combined incidents which really happened with his own
fictitious ones. Claudius Ethal, 'le fameux Ethal qu'un

procès retentissant avec Lord Kerneby [in connexion with
the price of a portrait] vient d'éloigner d'Angleterre et
d'amener à se fixer à Paris' is, at least in this respect, taken
from Whistler, whose lawsuit with an English journalist
over a portrait for which he had asked a thousand guineas
had been talked about by Robert de Montesquiou in
Lorrain's house.[98]   Claudius Ethal, in other respects, was
modelled upon the living Toulouse-Lautrec and James
Ensor,[99] and upon the imaginary Georges Selwyn of Goncourt's *La Faustin*.[100]

Dorian Gray, like des Esseintes, was a collector of
jewels; Freneuse is obsessed by jewels, 'envoûté, possédé
d'une certaine transparence glauque' for which he searches
in vain, both in precious stones and in the eyes of human
beings. It is the limpid, green clearness of the aquamarine
in the eyes of Astarte 'qui est le Démon de la Luxure et
aussi le Démon de la Mer', of which he catches a glimpse
in 'la dolente émeraude embusquée comme une lueur dans
les orbites d'yeux des statues d'Herculanum', in the liquid
green eyes of certain busts of Antinous, 'la prunelle ex-
tasiée et féroce, implorante pourtant', in the glance of the
infernal bride in the picture called 'The Three Brides' by
the turbid Catholic painter Toorop,[101] and in the look in
the eyes of the tortured, 'la divine extase effarée, sup-
pliante, la volupté épouvantée des yeux des sainte Agnès,
des sainte Catherine de Sienne et des saint Sébastien'[102]—
the look which Freneuse eventually discovered, portrayed
to perfection, in the face of the wounded youth who opens
the front of his tunic with a gesture of offering, in Gustave
Moreau's picture, *Les Prétendants*.

'Gustave Moreau, l'homme des sveltes Salomés ruisselantes de
pierreries, des Muses porteuses de têtes coupées et des Hélènes aux
robes maillées d'or vif, s'érigeant, un lys à la main, pareilles elles-
mêmes à de grands lys fleuris, sur un fumier saignant de cadavres!...
Salomé, Hélène, l'Ennoia fatale aux races, les Sirènes funestes à
l'humanité! A-t-il été assez hanté, lui aussi, de la cruauté symbolique
des religions défuntes et des stupres divins adorés autrefois chez les
peuples!

'Visionnaire comme pas un, il a régné en maître dans la sphère
des rêves, mais, malade jusqu'à en faire passer dans ses œuvres le

frisson d'angoisse et de désespération, il a, le maître sorcier, envoûté
son époque, ensorcelé ses contemporains, contaminé d'un idéal
maladif et mystique toute cette fin de siècle d'agioteurs et de ban-
quiers; et, sous le rayonnement de sa peinture, toute une génération
de jeunes hommes s'est formée, douloureuse et alanguie,[103] les yeux
obstinément tournés vers la splendeur et la magie des jadis, toute
une génération de littérateurs et de poètes surtout nostalgiquement
épris, eux aussi, des longues nudités et des yeux d'épouvante et de
volupté morte de ses sorcières de rêve.

'Car il y a de la sorcellerie dans les pâles et silencieuses héroïnes
de ses aquarelles.

'C'est extasiantes et extasiées qu'il fait toujours surgir ses princesses dans leur nudité cuirassée d'orfèvrerie; léthargiques et comme
offertes dans un demi-ensommeillement, presque spectrales tant
elles sont lointaines, elles ne réveillent que plus énergiquement les
sens, n'en domptent que plus sûrement la volonté avec leurs charmes
de grandes fleurs passives et vénériennes, poussées dans les siècles
sacrilèges et jusqu'à nous épanouies par l'occulte pouvoir des
damnables souvenirs![104]

'Ah! celui-là peut se vanter d'avoir forcé le seuil du mystère,
celui-là peut revendiquer la gloire d'avoir troublé tout son siècle.
Celui-là, avec son art subtil de lapidaire et d'émailleur, a fortement
aidé au faisandage de tout mon être.'[105]

Lorrain was a friend of E. de Goncourt, and it is not
unlikely that the magic of this 'transparence glauque' in
painting was first pointed out by him. We read, for instance, in the *Journal* of the Goncourts:[106]

'Chez la jeune fille au type de Memling, les yeux dans le plaisir,
au lieu de se voiler et de mourir, vous regardent comme des yeux
de rêve. C'est une clarté, une lucidité étrange, un regard somnam-
bulesque et extatique, quelque chose d'une agonie de bienheureuse
qui contemplerait je ne sais quoi au delà de la vie. Ce regard singulier et adorable n'est pas une lueur, ni une caresse, il est une paix, une
sérénité. Il a un ravissement mort et comme une pâmoison mystique.
J'ai possédé dans ce regard toutes les vierges des primitifs allemands.'

In *Buveurs d'âmes* (1893)[107] Lorrain had already developed the pseudo-mystical type of the Goncourts (which
also resembles the type of Hyacinthe in *Là-bas*) in the
following way:

'La femme [Madame Lostin] surtout est extraordinairement
curieuse avec ses regards d'au-delà, noyés d'eau et comme en allés
dans le bleu intense des prunelles, tandis que la bouche à la fois

sensuelle et sauvage lui fait un sourire de bacchante mystique; et puis j'aime son art, un art visionnaire et morbide, et la couleur dolente et le faire précieux et somptueusement rare de ses pastels; j'aime les navrantes têtes de décollées et de martyres qu'elle évoque, inévitablement posées sur le revers d'un plat ou baignant, comme des fleurs coupées, dans l'eau sanglante d'un verre en forme de calice; j'adore enfin le bleu transparent et froid des yeux de ces pitoyables têtes, ces yeux pardonnants et las, où je retrouve ses prunelles à elle, pareilles à deux translucides émaux, et puis il se dégage de leur intérieur un tel parfum de simplicité et de foi.'[108]

These eyes, in which 'luit et sommeille une eau si verte, l'eau morne et corrompue d'une âme inassouvie, la dolente émeraude d'une effrayante luxure',[109] were precisely the eyes of Jean Lorrain himself, which Normandy describes thus: 'des prunelles glauques, caressantes, exténuées et comme défaillantes en une interminable agonie'.

The obsession of homicidal lust is actually described by Lorrain in such precise and vivid terms that one cannot help thinking that he must have found his inspiration in his own etheromaniac nightmares.[110] The customary allusion to the cruelties of Nero is, with him, very much more than a mere literary subject or pose:

'Oh! Néron buvant avec délices les larmes des martyrs, la volupté sinistre des Augustans jetant aux prétoriens la pudeur et l'effroi des vierges chrétiennes, les éclampsies de joie forcenée et féroce, dont s'emplissaient les lieux infâmes avant les jeux sanglants du cirque, et les jeunes filles, les enfants et les femmes livrées deux fois aux bêtes, au tigre et à l'homme!'

A very appropriate epitaph on Jean Lorrain, and indeed on all Decadent literature, is to be found in Colette's *Ces Plaisirs* (1932, pp. 106–7):

'Je la connus [la Cavalière], en effet, férue des prunelles transparentes, et quand je lui dis qu'elle partageait avec Jean Lorrain l'obsession des yeux verts ou bleus, elle se fâcha:

'Oh, mais ce n'est pas du tout la même chose. Jean Lorrain, il s'embarque sur des yeux verts, pour aller... nous savons où. C'est un homme à qui l'abîme n'a jamais suffi. . . .

'Le mot vaut mieux que son époque et que la littérature de dix-neuf cent, boursouflée d'envoûtements et de masques, de messes noires, de décapitées bienheureuses dont le chef vogue parmi des narcisses et des crapauds bleus.'

18. In *Monsieur de Phocas* there occur, among other quotations, some lines from the *Oraisons mauvaises* of Remy de Gourmont which are filled with sadistic profanity:

Que ta bouche soit bénie, car elle est adultère,
Elle a le goût des roses nouvelles et de la vieille terre,
Elle a sucé les sucs obscurs des fleurs et des roseaux;
Quand elle parle, on entend comme un bruit lointain de roseaux,
Et ce rubis impie de volupté, tout sanglant et tout froid
C'est la dernière blessure de Jésus sur la croix. . . .

In *Princesses d'ivoire et d'ivresse* (1902) Lorrain romances in the manner of Gourmont, Wilde, and, above all, of his friend Marcel Schwob (cf. *Le Livre de Monelle*). Incidentally all these writers came under the same influences and had remarkable affinities of temperament and a conspicuous preference for sadistic themes. In Lorrain's *Princesses* is to be found the usual combination of pseudomysticism and cruelty, with Pre-Raphaelite subjects carried to extremes, for the author felt strongly the fascination of a certain kind of bejewelled painting, stylized and more or less perverse, which was then in the height of fashion—Moreau, Toorop (who had a good excuse for appearing exotic, since he was the son of a Dutch governor of Java and a Javanese princess), Khnopff, and the English Pre-Raphaelites, particularly Burne-Jones. There was a reflection of this type of painting in Italy with Cellini, Costetti, and in general the artists who moved within the orbit of the 'Cronaca Bizantina' and the influence of D'Annunzio.

La Princesse aux lys rouges is a curious translation into terms of Decadent art of Flaubert's *Légende de saint Julien l'hospitalier*. The virgin princess Audovère, by the act of destroying flowers destroys at the same time, by witchcraft, the princes and warriors who are her father's enemies:[111] each lily that, smiling, she tears to pieces in her lovely, cruel fingers is the body of a young man who falls in battle, each foxglove that she kisses is an open wound. But one evening, after a battle which has been fought near the cloister where this murderous princess conducts her operations, there comes to her a wounded fugitive; then

from the flowers there begin to come forth groans and
sighs, and the petals become like human flesh, and as the
princess continues to break the stalks all round her,
suddenly, from a taller cluster of flowers, 'une transparence
bleuâtre, un cadavre d'homme émergea': it is the image
of the Crucified One, in which the princess recognizes the
wounded fugitive. In his agony he reproves her: 'Why
did you strike me? What had I done to you?' Next morning the princess is found dead in the garden, and around
her the lilies bloom again, everlastingly red. This idea of
the mingling of flowers and tortures is extremely common
in the work of the Decadents.

La Princesse des chemins is simply a prose interpretation
of Burne-Jones's picture, *King Cophetua and the Beggar-
Maid*, with a special insistence upon the 'ivoire taché de
sang' of the girl's naked feet; her eyes have in them 'une
flamme bleue vigilante et triste'.[112] In the story *La Princesse au sabbat* there is a princess 'tenaillée par des griffes,
baisée, mordue, léchée et chevauchée par mille bêtes
invisibles', like her sister, the *Princesse aux miroirs*—
obviously echoes of Lorrain's etheromaniac delirium.

After the princesses come the princes, *Princes de nacre
et de caresse*, and here also there are flowers and tortures.
Narkiss, Prince of Egypt, so beautiful that his mother
worships his cradle, 'et des crimes avaient aussitôt entouré
sa naissance', is a youth in the manner of Wilde. One night
he goes to a temple where bloody sacrifices are performed:
'une atmosphère pestilentielle y régnait, lourde d'odeurs
de sang et de charogne, lourde de parfums de fleurs et de
parfums d'aromates aussi', an atmosphere so attractive to
Narkiss that he 'eût toujours voulu demeurer là . . . dans
ces parfums de meurtre, de lotus et d'encens'. The young
prince, as can be seen, is a typical Decadent, and comes to
a thrilling end: he sees the reflection of his own face like
a magic flower in the putrid waters of the Nile, and dies
there, among carrion and luxuriant flowers.[113] It is a Greek
myth interpreted with Oriental gorgeousness, a prose
translation of a Moreau picture. Moreau also suggested the
luxurious, blood-stained setting of *La Fin d'un jour*, which
tells of a rebellion at Byzantium, and has the severed head

of an Empress, crowned with jewels, as *cul-de-lampe*; also, partly, of *La Marquise de Spolète*, who is the usual type of praying mantis, murdering her own lovers. A gruesome tale is told of her——how she danced before the court dressed as Salome, how the aged Duke changed the performance into a real tragedy by having his wife's three lovers, who were acting in the play, decapitated, and how he finally immured his wife in a cell, together with the three heads, having put poison upon their lips. The portrait of the Marquise is taken from a certain picture of the school of Leonardo which hangs in the Uffizi, and which Lorrain describes in the style of Huysmans:

'La mort de saint Jean-Baptiste, la décollation du Précurseur, la légende de luxure et de sang dont toute la Renaissance italienne a eu comme l'obsession, Hérode et Salomé, les terribles figures qui ont tenté tous les peintres de cette époque et dont les musées nous ont légué la dangereuse hantise. . . .'[114]

In the last story, *La Princesse sous verre*, we read of a gipsy's violin which brings a curse with it (as in *Les Noronsoff*), and of a princess enclosed in a glass coffin, who slips suddenly during its transport 'de son lit de soie pâle dans la boue grasse du chemin' and has her hands devoured by Prince Otto's pack of hounds. (In Italy Corrado Govoni (born 1884) made similar excursions into gloomy, algolagnic fantasies of this kind.) The portion of the book which goes under the title of *Masques dans la tapisserie* is dedicated to D'Annunzio. It has been observed[115] that D'Annunzio took his *Sonetti de le Fate* and other lines in the *Chimera* from Lorrain's second book, *La Forêt bleue* (1883).

The reader may be surprised that I have devoted so much space to an examination of the work of a mannerist like Lorrain. My reply is that this work, precisely because it is so hopelessly ruined by mannerisms, provides an excellent illustration of the common background of the Decadents and of themes which were repeated at the time with a sort of mechanical detachment.

19. These same themes, enlivened, however, by an ironical imagination and by a surer critical taste, are to be found also in the fictional works of Remy de Gourmont,

another of those writers 'lascivious in word but pure in life' so typical of the Decadence, an intellectual whose dislike for action was rendered chronic by leprosy, which gave his face the repulsive appearance known as *facies leontina*.[116] Gourmont was a Decadent nourished upon the spirit of the *Encyclopédistes*. His *Physique de l'amour*—in which he sets out to demonstrate from the example of the animal world that those sexual practices which man considers perverse represent so many virtues among the innocent insects, and that in nature 'tout n'est . . . que vol et assassinat: ce sont des actes normaux'—is conceived in the spirit which caused Diderot to write his *Rêve de d'Alembert* (with its *Suite de l'entretien*) and the *Supplément au voyage de Bougainville*,[117] with the addition of a good dose of sadistic theories. Belated *Encyclopédiste* as he is, Gourmont mocks at religious superstition; but he is also a Decadent, and as such makes use of religion in order to extract sensations from it. It is from this twofold nature that his particular half-humoristic, half-serious tone is derived.

However much disgust Gourmont may have shown later (in *Épilogues*)[118] for Sade, 'le bourreau extravagant, le fou sanguinaire et stercoraire', he made consummate use, at one period, of the litany of sacrilege, the sadistic mingling of obscene and religious themes.[119] Thus, in the *Litanies de la rose* (1892, reprinted in *Le Pèlerin du silence*, 1896) he evokes false, cruel women under the image of various kinds of roses; in the *Correspondances* he twists the phraseology of mysticism to lascivious meanings, and in the *Fantôme-duplicité* (written from September to November 1891, published in 1893) he provides a detailed initiation into the Black Mass. The woman in the latter story is called Hyacinthe, like the corresponding character in Huysmans' *Là-bas* (which came out actually in 1891).[120] A few passages will suffice to give an idea of the flavour of profanity which emanates from almost every image in the *Fantôme*:

> *Damase* — Sois la fécondité des adorations et des sourires et réjouis-toi du supplice d'être écrasée au pressoir, pour être bue, vin pur, dispensatrice des ivresses

royales. Tout entière, ô vierge double — oui: et
sois spiritualisée, beauté charnelle, et sois réalisé,
intellectuel fantôme.

Le Chœur —   Procul recedant somnia
                     Et noctium phantasmata.

Gourmont went further than any one in this employ-
ment of sacred and mystical texts for the purpose of adding
a new flavour to erotic adventure, but as he was not a believer like Huysmans, his pages lack that sense of revolt
and horror which breathes in all the sadistic abandonments
of *Là-bas*. *Le Fantôme* constitutes, as it were, a *jeu à côté*,
a distraction from the erudite philological labours of this
extremely learned connoisseur of texts.

'La curiosité la soutint dans cette épreuve, et nous épuisâmes
avec méthode tous les articles de l'évangile gnostique, sans que
notre santé eût notablement fléchi. . . .

'En notre étude de la théorie mystique, si parfois des mots
scandalisaient mon amie, je les interprétais à son intelligence avec
toute la déférence due aux textes des grands saints. Elle apprit que
les caresses de la main gauche, ce sont les premières souffrances,
preuve du sacrifice accepté; et les caresses de la main droite, tout
le manuel sanglant de l'amour: le baiser des épines, l'attouchement
des lanières plombées, la morsure adorable des clous, la pénétration
charnelle de la lance, les spasmes de la mort, les joies de la putridité.

'Un soir, comme je lisais la vie de sainte Gertrude, la vierge aux
ingénieuses dilections qui eut le divin caprice de remplacer par des
clous de girofle les clous de fer de son crucifix — et j'en étais à la
page où Jésus lui-même, pour charmer sa bien-aimée, descendit
vers elle, et, la tenant embrassée, chanta:

> Amor meus continuus,
> Tibi languor assiduus,
> Amor tuus suavissimus
> Mihi sapor gratissimus. . . .

'Je cherchais la signification seconde des ces quatre vers — lorsque
Hyacinthe m'apparut toute nue, me priant de la flageller. Elle
tenait à la main une discipline de chanoinesse, sept cordelettes de
soie en détestation des sept péchés capitaux, et sept nœuds à chaque
corde pour remémorer les sept manières de faillir mortellement
dans le même mode sensationnel.

' "Les sept cordes de la viole!" dit-elle en souriant étrangement. "Les roses, ce seront les gouttes de sang qui fleuriront ma chair".

. . . .

'Je suis sûr qu'elle eut l'illusion d'un grave martyre, d'une fustigation digne d'Henri Suso ou de Passidée, qu'on trouvait dans leurs cellules évanouis parmi un ruisseau de sang et des lambeaux de chair attachés à la ferraille et aux molettes du solide martinet tombé de leurs doigts las, malgré leur volonté de souffrir jamais lasse — mais j'avais été clément, voulant bien contenter un caprice, mais non souiller de cicatrices une peau dont l'intégrité m'était chère.

. . . .

'Ses bras s'abattirent autour de mon cou et elle tomba, m'entraînant avec elle dans le plus mémorable abîme de divagations voluptueuses. . . .'

The ironical conclusion of this course of sacrilegious and sadistic experiments is that, whereas the man intends to make use of them in order to elevate his mistress 'en intelligence et en amour', she, on the other hand, 'avait l'art et l'audace de clore tous les élans vers en haut par un élan dernier vers en bas, suivant la logique de sa nature, évidemment plus lourde que l'air spirituel'. Her life had merely been an imitation, a reflection of the man's, and the conclusion, while showing the complete childishness of this game of sadism and sacrilege, reaches a degree of bitterness which is the one thing genuinely felt in the whole of this learned exercise.

'Je quittai la fenêtre. Hyacinthe jouait toujours avec ses bagues. Elle était toute pâle: il me sembla que des rais de lumière passaient au travers de son corps — de ce corps qui venait pourtant de témoigner à mes mains son évidence charnelle et sa véracité.

'J'avais froid, j'avais peur — car je la voyais, sans pouvoir m'opposer à cette transformation douloureuse — je la voyais s'en aller rejoindre les groupes des femmes indécises d'où mon amour l'avait tirée — je la voyais redevenir le fantôme qu'elles sont toutes.'

20. Another scholar among the Decadents, 'une sorte d'encyclopédiste du xixe siècle, un Diderot plus moderne, moins spontané peut-être, mais plus artiste', as Henri Bérenger calls him,[121] was Marcel Schwob. The art of Schwob is much superior to that of many of the Decadents, but his sensibility and the themes which inspired him are

just the same. Varying estimates might be made of the
sharpening effect upon his sensibility of the tuberculosis
which was to bring his career to an untimely end, and of
the importance of the influence upon his inspiration of his
great passion for a consumptive girl, Louise (Vise), which
is unforgettably recorded in *Le Livre de Monelle* (1894).
The love-letters of Schwob are reminiscent of those of
Keats in the quality of their anguished sensuality, mingled
with ideas of death and drunken with self-surrender. One
of these letters was described by Pierre Champion[122] as 'le
plus grand trait de lumière qu'un homme puisse projeter
sur lui-même'. In it Schwob turns upon himself in this
way, addressing his future wife:

'Crois que je ne suis pas faible — mais tu es trop forte pour moi —
tu m'as terrassé. Que ce ne soit pas un jeu, ou que toi-même, tu
me joues contre la mort. Entends-tu? Tes petites paroles sous tes
cheveux sont les degrés tendres de l'escalier par où je descendrai
sous la terre. Je ne peux pas te dire que je t'aime. — Ce n'est pas
assez fort; je meurs de toi, et tu me fais mourir de toi. Écrase-moi
sous tes pieds.'

Edmond de Goncourt immediately detected a kindred
spirit in Schwob:

'Vous êtes l'évocateur magique de l'antiquité, de cette antiquité
héliogabalesque à laquelle vont les imaginations des penseurs et les
pinceaux des peintres, de ces décadences et de ces fins de vieux
mondes, mystérieusement perverses et macabres.'

In his capacity of scholar, Schwob made passionate researches into certain *faisandé* periods and aspects of the
past; he, too, like Gourmont, was interested in the Latin
of the Decline; he made a study of the slang of the medieval criminal bands, and of the career of that strange poet
of the underworld, François Villon; he disinterred from
old texts and archives the figures of vagabonds, eunuchs,
brigands, criminals; he had a strong feeling for what
Flaubert had called 'la vieille poésie de la corruption et de
la vénalité', and an adoration for certain historic prostitutes
—Theodota, the youthful concubine of Alcibiades, Anne,
the prostitute who helped De Quincey, the 'petite prostituée' whom Napoleon, at the age of eighteen, met at the
Palais Royal, and little Nelly who consoled the convict

Dostoievsky; he felt the charm of the medieval *fillettes com-munes*, 'celles qui hantent à l'entour des villes de France, assises sur les pierres des cimetières, pour donner du plaisir à ceux qui passent'; he translated *Moll Flanders*; he investigated grisly, mysterious episodes of the Middle Ages, the Crusade of the Innocents, stories of lepers, of victims of the plague, of beggars, folklore of a ghastly kind; and he followed with interest the criminal trials of his own day. The story of the incest of Annabella and Giovanni in Ford's *'Tis pity she's a Whore* found in him a fervent admirer.[123]

Schwob's tales, written under the influence especially of Poe, might, with more reason than those of Villiers de l'Isle-Adam, be called *Contes cruels*; as with Villiers, in close conjunction with monstrous and gruesome themes there are to be found others which have a sinister humour (in these his influence was Mark Twain). The fundamental tone of his work is decidedly sadistic, and visions of an algolagnic character abound. Examples of this are to be found in the volume *Cœur double*, his first collection of tales (1891), in *Arachné*; *L'Homme double* (in which reappears the decapitated woman of Baudelaire's *Une Martyre*); in *La Vendeuse d'ambre*; *Le 'papier rouge'*; *Fleur de cinq-pierres* (the love-affair of the daughter of an executioner with a murderer, in the very storehouse in which the guillotine is kept—a similar theme to that treated by Janin in the chapter entitled *Le Baiser* in *L'Âne mort*); in *Le Roi au masque d'or* (1892), in which, as well as the influence of Poe and of Flaubert can be seen that of the fables of Wilde:[124] this is the tale which gives its name to the volume and which presents in mythical form a profoundly personal theme; also in the other tales in this volume, *L'Incendie terrestre*, *Les Embaumeuses*, *Les Faulx-visaiges*, *Les Milésiennes*, *Le Sabbat de Mofflaines*, *Blanche la sanglante*. Just as the *Légende des gueux* in *Le Cœur double* is a kind of 'légende des siècles' exemplified in episodes of crime in every century, so *Les Vies imaginaires* (1896) evokes, throughout history, the lives of abnormals, of prostitutes, of pirates. In *Cratès, cynique*, the central theme is one of coprophily, in *Septima, incantatrice*, of

necrophily, in *Clodia* and in *Cyril Tourneur*, of incest, in
Pétrone, of homosexuality, in *Nicolas Loyseleur*, in *Alain le
gentil*, and in *MM. Burke et Hare, assassins*, of sadism, and
in *Katherine la dentellière, fille amoureuse*, of prostitution.
Many of the protagonists of these lives end by being barbarously murdered, for the sake of money, by their own
lovers. Clodia:

'Un ouvrier foulon l'avait payée d'un quart d'as; il la guetta au
crépuscule de l'aube dans l'allée, pour le lui reprendre et l'étrangla.
Puis il jeta son cadavre, les yeux grands ouverts, dans l'eau jaune
du Tibre.'

Petronius:

'Un grassateur ivre lui avait enfoncé une large lame dans le cou,
tandis qu'ils gisaient ensemble, en rase campagne, sur les dalles
d'un caveau abandonné.'

Katherine:

'Une nuit un ruffian qui contrefaisait l'homme de guerre, coupa
la gorge de Museau pour lui prendre sa ceinture. Mais il n'y
trouva pas de bourse.'

Many of the characters renounce a life of ease, in order
to give themselves up, intoxicated with humiliation and
degradation, to vagabondage, low debauchery, and the
voluptuous joys of squalor.

The story entitled *Les Faulx-visaiges*, in which the
writer piles up into a dazzling whole various passages
taken from the chroniclers (particularly Mathieu d'Escouchy) relating to massacres and rapine, gives a picture
of the Middle Ages as the morbid imagination of Schwob
saw them:

'Les Écorcheurs, Armagnacs, Gascons, Lombards, Écossais,
revenaient par bandes de la terrible bataille de Saint-Jacques, et ils
avaient rôti les jambes des paysans tout le long de la route. ... Tra-
versant les villes le plus rarement qu'ils pouvaient, ils se ruaient aux
étuves, bâillonnaient la maîtresse, jetaient la paille par les fenêtres,
forçaient les fillettes sur les bahuts, et, tordant les clefs des portes
dans leurs serrures obscènes, partaient en tumulte à la lueur des
falots. ... D'ordinaire ils préféraient les fillettes communes assises
aux portes des bonnes villes, le soir, à l'orée des cimetières. Elles
n'avaient qu'une cotte et une chemise. ... Elles couchaient à l'air,
entre les fosses, dans l'eau croupissante. Elles rêvaient le sol jonché

de paille des étuves, dans quelque rue noire. Les guetteurs de chemins, batteurs à loyer, épieurs et fausses gens de guerre, les emmenaient un peu de temps, et parfois ne leur coupaient pas la gorge.... Venaient aussi quelques vagabonds qui avaient été clercs... ils menaient un ou deux pauvres enfants dont ils avaient scié les jambes près des pieds et arraché les yeux, qu'ils montraient pour apitoyer les passants tandis qu'ils jouaient de la vielle.... Puis, dans le mois de novembre, arrivèrent à la suite de ces traînards de mystérieuses figures nocturnes.... Ces hommes de nuit se distinguaient des autres par une habitude terrifiante et inconnue: ils avaient leurs visages couverts de faux-visages.... Ces Faulx-Visaiges tuaient cruellement, éventrant les femmes, piquant les enfants aux fourches, cuisant les hommes à de grandes broches pour leur faire confesser les cachettes d'argent, peignant les cadavres de sang pour appâtir les métairies et les réduire par la peur. Ils avaient avec eux des fillettes prises le long des cimetières, qu'on entendait hurler dans la nuit. Personne ne savait s'ils parlaient. Ils surgissaient du mystère et massacraient en silence.'

In *Le Livre de Monelle* Schwob sketches, in short fables, the portraits of young girls 'tourmentées d'égoïsme et de volupté et de cruauté et d'orgueil et de patience et de pitié': they are like younger sisters, like so many different aspects of the one and only Monelle, the dead love whom Schwob exalts to the proportions of a symbolic figure of the ideal courtesan—a decadent Beatrice, almost, sublimation of the theme of the little prostitute by which he was obsessed. Among these portraits of young girls, which he surrounds with a light that is melancholy and often perverse (for example *La Voluptueuse*, *La Perverse*), *L'Insensible* must be mentioned here because it deals with a theme which is characteristic of the Decadence, the theme of Salome.

In this fable the Princess Morgane goes to a distant country of the East in search of a 'véritable miroir', and after a pilgrimage through countries inhabited by men with monstrous customs (like some of those which are illustrated in Flaubert's *Tentation*), arrives at an inn which in old times had been 'la demeure d'une reine cruelle'. This queen, who is not named in the story, is none other than Salome, and as soon as the Princess Morgane has looked at herself in the copper charger which is still filled with the blood of the decapitated saint, she becomes cruel and voluptuous, instead of, as till then she had believed herself to be, insensible:

> 'Personne ne sait ce que la princesse Morgane vit dans le miroir de sang. Mais sur la route du retour ses muletiers furent trouvés assassinés, un à un, chaque nuit, leur face grise tournée vers le ciel, après qu'ils avaient pénétré dans la litière. Et on nomma cette princesse Morgane la Rouge, et elle fut une fameuse prostituée et une terrible égorgeuse d'hommes.'

21. Gourmont's Hyacinthe, 'si jeune encore, toute frêle d'une pureté athénienne et si pleine de la grâce des inconscientes Èves', who came of a 'race morte au monde depuis des siècles — Fleur d'automne et la dernière ... rose penchée sur une rivière d'ombre', is an adolescent with 'chair d'ostensoir' such as one frequently meets in the works of the Decadents. She is like Bérénice in *Le Jardin de Bérénice*, by Barrès (1891), an author who is even more fond than Gourmont of metaphysical subtleties and refinements of sadism—a sadism more ethereal and more highly concentrated, but no less obvious.[125]

Bérénice is one of those 'révoltées dont l'âcreté et la beauté piétinée serrent le cœur'; Barrès delights in seeing her suffer and languish, and surrounds her 'd'une désolation incomparable', in the malarial region of Aigues-Mortes—a young girl, 'harmonique à ce pays', dying against a background of fever-swamps. Then he devises a further torture by transporting her to Toledo:

> 'Si la rudesse de Tolède ne suffisait pas pour opprimer Bérénice et pour nous la faire attendrissante, ainsi qu'il est nécessaire, par un dernier trait nous saurions l'affliger: dans cette ville cuite et recuite, où l'odeur de benjoin qui vient des rochers rejoint l'odeur des cierges qui sort de l'immense cathédrale, nous montrerions l'enfant affamée.'[126]

At the end he displays 'cette petite libertine' in her death-agony, and then dead:

> 'Mon inclination ne sera jamais sincère qu'envers ceux de qui la beauté fut humiliée: souvenirs décriés, enfants froissées, sentiments offensés. . . . Quand Bérénice était petite fille, dans mon désir de l'aimer, j'avais beaucoup regretté qu'elle n'eût pas quelque infirmité physique. Au moins pour intéresser mon cœur avait-elle sa misère

morale. Une tare dans ce que je préfère à tout, une brutalité sur un faible, en me prouvant le désordre qui est dans la nature, flattent ma plus chère manie d'esprit et, d'autre part, me font comme une loi d'aimer le pauvre être injurié pour rétablir, s'il est possible, l'harmonie naturelle en lui violée.'[127]

The excuse he offers is a specious one, but the feeling for tainted beauty is profound in Barrès. To make the *faisandage* even more subtle, Bérénice is 'toute ramassée dans l'amour d'un mort', her dead lover, and Philippe is like a *voyeur* who spies into the interior life of this melancholy girl, longing to share in it, to 'promener' his hands 'sur son âme passionnée'. In certain respects Barrès anticipates the Proust of the *liaison* with Albertine. In *Un Homme libre* (1889) we read:[128]

'Peut-être serait-ce le bonheur d'avoir une maîtresse jeune et impure, vivant au dehors, tandis que moi je ne bougerais jamais. Elle viendrait me voir avec ardeur; mais chaque fois, à la dernière minute, me pressant dans ses bras, elle me montrerait un visage si triste, et son silence serait tel que je croirais venu le jour de sa dernière visite. Elle reviendrait, mais perpétuellement j'aurais vingt-quatre heures d'angoisse entre chacun de nos rendez-vous, avec le coup de massue de l'abandon suspendu sur ma tête. Même il faudrait qu'elle arrivât un jour après un long retard, et qu'elle prolongeât ainsi cette heure d'agonie où je guette son pas dans le petit escalier. Peut-être serait-ce le bonheur, car, dans une vie jamais distraite, une telle tension des sentiments ferait l'unité. Ce serait une vie systématisée.

'Ma maîtresse, loin de moi, ne serait pas heureuse; elle subirait une passion vigoureuse à laquelle parfois elle répondrait, tant est faible la chair, mais en tournant son âme désespérée vers moi. Et j'aurais un plaisir ineffable à lui expliquer avec des mots d'amertume et de tendresse les pures doctrines du quiétisme: "Qu'importe ce que fait notre corps, si notre âme n'y consent pas!" Ah! Simon, combien j'aimerais être ce malheureux consolateur-là.'

There is also the inevitable mingling of sacred and profane:

'Elle serait pieuse. Elle et moi, malgré nos péchés, nous baiserions la robe de la Vierge.'

And an insistence on the melancholy side of this sensuality of a *buveur d'âmes*:

'Elle serait jeune, belle fille, avec des genoux fins, un corps ayant une ligne franche et un sourire imprévu infiniment touchant de sensualité triste. Elle serait vêtue d'étoffes souples et un jour, à peine entrée, je la vois qui me désole de sanglots sans cause, en cachant contre moi son fin visage.'

Among the devices which he imagines[129] in order to 'aiguillonner' his erotic sensations are the following 'spiritual exercises':

'1º. Se représenter l'Objet, de chair délicate et de gestes caressants, aux bras d'un homme brutal, et pâmée de cette brutalité même, embellissant ses yeux de misérables larmes de volupté, qu'elle n'eût dû verser que sainte et honorant Dieu à mes côtés. . . .

'2º. Se représenter qu'ayant fait le bonheur de beaucoup d'indifférents qui tous l'abîmeront un peu, elle deviendra vieille et dédaignée, sans revanche possible.[130]

'M'abandonnant à une bonté triste et sensuelle, je souffrais de cette fatalité où son beau corps engrené était chaque jour froissé, etc.'

These characteristics, and the necessity of representing 'the Object' to himself as an abnormal, infamous being

('Seule son infâme ingéniosité m'intéressait à elle, et je la lui reprochais, me plaisant à lui détailler tout haut, combien elle violait les lois ordinaires de la nature et de la bienséance')

have an exact parallel in the works of Sade.

Resembling Chateaubriand, perhaps, more closely than any other writer (Chateaubriand who, as Gourmont remarked,[131] 'plane invisible sur toute notre littérature'), Barrès dwells upon the subject of incest in *Un Amateur d'âmes* (1893):[132]

'[Delrio] en vint à songer à une fille que son père avait eue d'un amour adultère.

'Sa sœur! et dans sa dix-neuvième année! Ce souvenir répandit en lui un sentiment de fraîcheur et de volupté. . .

'Elle [Simone] était toujours vêtue de jaune et de violet, couleurs violentes qu'il préférait à toutes et dont les combinaisons le baignaient d'un plaisir sensuel. Par une bizarrerie d'imagination, il l'avait priée de ne porter comme lingerie que de rudes et grossières toiles; il lui plaisait que cette façon de cilice atténué le liât constamment, dans l'esprit de la jeune fille, à une gêne d'ordre si intime.'

Simone recalls the image of Dante's Pia, and, like her, pines away in the febrile atmosphere of Toledo, which at the same time has a refining effect upon her:

'Delrio la caressait et la consolait, jusqu'à ce qu'elle eût sous les paupières des larmes qu'il baisait avec une telle compassion que son cœur se brisait délicieusement. "Il me semble", lui disait-il, "que j'ai plus de plaisir à te presser dans mes bras que n'en eut notre père à te donner la vie".'

Simone kills herself:

'Comme elle était belle, sa sœur, brûlante, puis glacée de fièvre, dessinant sous les draps son jeune corps révolté par la mort!.....
'Par un sentiment de pudeur et d'amour, elle lui disait:
' — N'es-tu pas dégoûté de m'embrasser malade comme je suis?....
'Mais d'un ton tel qu'il lui répondait:
' — Ô mon bel œillet qui n'es plus la mélancolique Pia. Depuis ton éclatante et surprenante décision, combien je t'aime ainsi sanglante! et que je te désire sous ce pâle et sous ce rouge de la mort!
'Et les tendres gémissements que lui imposait sa blessure se mêlant à leurs aveux demi-étouffés, elle mourut en pressant contre ses petits seins éclaboussés de sang les mains de l'ami de son cœur.'

The following passage occurs in the *Cahiers* of Barrès:[133]

'C'est le martyre qui a fourni à la poésie les combinaisons les plus diverses. Il y a dans ces imaginations de supplices, je ne sais quelle sombre et étrange volupté que l'humanité savourera avec délice pendant des siècles.'

In *Les Déracinés* (1897) the beautiful Armenian Astiné Aravian, who is an incarnation of the Oriental, pagan type of love, in the manner of the courtesan in Flaubert's *Novembre* ('Elle vient d'Asie et de régions mystérieuses et parfumées comme de belles esclaves voilées'), and who bears in herself the exotic charm of Tiflis, the city 'de même infecte et parfumée, c'est-à-dire sentant la mort et les roses', is murdered in a sadistic fashion by two degenerates:

'Ce cadavre, ce sang et ces beautés découvertes, dans ce tragique abandon, c'est l'éternelle Hélène "tant admirée, tant décriée" qui une fois encore est venue du rivage homérique, avec le trésor augmenté sans cesse de sa fabuleuse beauté, attiser dans notre sein une ardeur que rien ne satisfera. Hélène! mais du moins, cette fois, pour que soit complète son atmosphère de volupté, il ne manque pas au tableau l'appareil du carnage.... Une telle vie, à moins d'être incomplète et même contradictoire, ne supportait que ce dénouement où il y a du vice, de l'horreur et des accents désespérés.'

In spite of all the elaborate and meritorious structures

with which, as an intellectual, Barrès sought to cover up the primitive sources of his feeling, these latter are no less obvious than in Swinburne: it is an algolagnic sensibility which embraces both human beings and inanimate objects. There is perhaps food for thought in the short note which is to be found in Barrès' *Cahiers*, and which seems to recall a similar passage in Flaubert:[134]

'Enfant élevé dans un hospice, parmi de jeunes femmes à opérer, j'ai aimé la douleur.'[135]

Even in the first of his novels, *Sous l'œil des barbares* (1888), this feeling is proclaimed in perfectly plain terms:

'Lourds soirs d'été, quand sorti de la ville odieuse pleine de buée, de sueur et de gesticulations, j'allais seul dans la campagne et, couché sur l'herbe jusqu'au train de minuit, je sentais, je voyais, j'étais enivré jusqu'à la migraine d'un défilé sensuel d'images faites de grands paysages d'eau, d'immobilité et de *santé dolente*, doucement consolée parmi d'immenses solitudes *brutalisées* d'air salin.'[136]

Later (in *La Mort de Venise*) he says of Venice:

'Désespoir d'une beauté qui s'en va vers la mort. Est-ce le chant d'une vieille corruptrice ou d'une vierge sacrifiée? Au matin, parfois, dans Venise, j'entendis Iphigénie, mais les rougeurs du soir ramenaient Jézabel. . . . Ceux qui ont besoin de se faire mal contre la vie, de se déchirer sur leurs pensées, se plaisent dans une ville où nulle beauté n'est sans tare.'

Aigues-Mortes and Venice are for Barrès the land of heart's desire—places where beauty pines away in the imminent shadow of death. Siena also: [137]

'Cette rude petite ville de Sienne, si pleine de volupté, apparaît à l'imagination comme la recéleuse chez qui le Sodoma vint entasser les trésors qu'il composait selon les conseils de Vinci et selon son propre cœur, qui était trouble. . . .

'Le Sodoma! c'est la volupté du Vinci: mais le trouble qui nous inquiétait dans le sourire lombard, ici gagne tout le corps. . . . Il transforme dans son esprit les réalités du monde extérieur pour en faire une certaine beauté ardente et triste.'

He feels this also for Spain, the thirsty land which he explores 'ne laissant perdre aucune occasion d'être froissé', Spain with its churches full of that odour of decomposition which is the breath of life to him, in which he especially admires 'ces poupées faisandées, ces corps déshabillés et

saignants, ces genoux et ces coudes écorchés du Christ',
and El Greco's strange pictures, in which he sees hidden
profanities and problematical incests: for example he
imagines one of the painter's models to be his daughter,
'cette émouvante fiévreuse' whom El Greco 'divinise
mieux chaque jour'.

Again, in *Mes Cahiers*, he says:[138]

> 'Mais surtout qu'ai-je tant aimé à Venise, à Tolède, à Sparte;
> qu'ai-je désiré vers la Perse? des cimetières.'

Certain of his titles, moreover, are eloquent enough,
such as *Du Sang, de la volupté, de la mort*, or *Amori ac
dolori sacrum*, which he justifies as follows:

> 'La mort et la volupté, la douleur et l'amour s'appellent les unes
> les autres dans notre imagination.   En Italie, les entremetteuses, dit-
> on [one would like to know where! Cf. above, p. 370] pour faire voir
> les jeunes filles dont elles disposent les asseoient sur les tombes dans les
> églises.   En Orient les femmes prennent pour jardins les cimetières.
> A Paris, on n'est jamais mieux étourdi par l'odeur des roses que si l'on
> accompagne en juin les corbillards chargés de fleurs.   Sainte Rose
> de Lima . . . pensait que les larmes sont la plus belle richesse de la
> création.   Il n'y a pas de volupté profonde sans brisement de cœur.
> Et les physiologistes s'accordent avec les poètes et les philosophes
> pour reconnaître que, si l'amour continue l'espèce, la douleur la
> purifie. . . .
>
> 'Il en va ainsi des roses et des fleurs de magnolia qui n'offrent
> jamais d'odeur plus enivrante, ni de coloration plus forte qu'à
> l'instant où la mort y projette ses secrètes fusées et nous propose ses
> vertiges.'

Later on Barrès sought either to smother or to sublimate
these spontaneous impulses, though in *Un Homme libre*[139]
he had said: 'Il faut que je respecte tout ce qui est en moi;
il ne convient pas que rien avorte.'   There was never a more
passionate Wagnerite than he, but in *La Mort de Venise*
(1903) he issues a warning against the morbid influence of
Tristan.   There was never a more unbridled exotic, and
yet, though in *L'Ennemi des lois* (1892) he exalted the
value of Maltère's love for the Russian, Marina ('ainsi le
sentiment qu'il gardait de Marina avait permis à André de
ne pas s'enfermer, comme dans une côterie, dans sa
race'), in *Les Déracinés* (1897), on the other hand, he

adopted the opposite point of view, and speaks of exoticism as 'un virus . . . un principe par lequel devait être gâté' the 'sens naturel de la vie' of Sturel. The idyll with Astiné is a recantation of the idyll with Marina (who was probably suggested by the same person).[140] A Romantic by instinct, Barrès longed to be a Classic: 'Mon amour de l'ordre, amour auquel je m'oblige'.[141] And again:[142]

'Engagés dans la voie que nous fit le xixᵉ siècle, nous prétendons pourtant redresser notre sens de la vie. J'ai trouvé une discipline dans les cimetières où nos prédécesseurs divaguaient, et c'est grâce peut-être à l'hyperesthésie que nous transmirent ces grands poètes de la rêverie que nous dégagerons des vérités positives situées dans notre profond sous-conscient.'

From sadism to the cult of sublimated energy, placed at the service of country or humanity—the same parabola can be seen in Swinburne, in Barrès, and in D'Annunzio. And even if, on final analysis, the very fact of this deliberate aiming at energy shows an absence of any source of spontaneous energy, even if a 'virility complex' denotes a lack of virility, that is still no reason for underrating the moral value of the effort which these artists made towards sublimation. As to the aesthetic value of the works produced by the painful method which they chose to adopt, that is another matter. 'Amour auquel je m'oblige.' Love—Manzoni's Don Abbondio might reply—is not a thing with which one can endow oneself. No more is inspiration.

22. André Gide was saved 'par gourmandise', as he expresses it, from adopting a rigid doctrine like Barrès, and from crystallizing into an attitude which was unnatural to him. It has always been his chief preoccupation to avoid any fixed anchorage: whether this inability of his to be consistent, this restlessness as of some one who is always on the point of undertaking a new journey, is not a form of anxiety-neurosis caused by a confused sexual attitude, is a conjecture of which I do not feel inclined to take the responsibility.

Gide, with his own 'fond noir à contenter', came under the dominant influence of Nietzsche and Dostoievsky and the more special influence of Wilde. 'Être ondoyant et divers', du Bos[143] has described him—and perhaps one might add without further ado, a moral hermaphrodite, suspended among various potentialities and, in consequence, negative, sterile. A confession such as the following is symptomatic:[144]

'Non, dis-je enfin, désireux de bien prendre position, l'action ne m'intéresse point tant par la sensation qu'elle me donne que par ses suites, son retentissement. Voilà pourquoi, si elle m'intéresse passionnément, je crois qu'elle m'intéresse davantage encore commise par un autre. J'ai peur, comprenez-moi, de m'y compromettre. Je veux dire de limiter par ce que je fais, ce que je pourrais faire. De penser que parce que j'ai fait *ceci*, je ne pourrai plus faire *cela*, voilà qui me devient intolérable. J'aime mieux *faire agir* que d'agir.'

He has, on the one hand, a fear of committing himself, and, on the other, as du Bos remarks, a violent desire to commit himself.[145] In the former is reflected his psychological ambiguity, in the latter the sadistic pleasure of the sensation of pride in one's own humiliation, and of violating and shocking the modesty of others, such as made Dostoievsky and his heroes burst forth into devastating confessions, and caused Gide to write *Si le grain ne meurt*. (One might quote as a more immediate source Wilde's attitude to scandal,[146] except that there is more seriousness in Gide than in Wilde.) The result of this complex psychological formation was that Gide took up the attitude of a 'martyr of pederasty',[147] thus satisfying his homosexual and his algolagnic desires at the same time. It is scarcely necessary to mention that the 'Prometheus' pose and the taste for satanism, the 'ricanement intérieur',[148] which are to be found in Gide, are sadistic qualities.

Certain passages from *L'Immoraliste* may be quoted in illustration of this. Michel, when he discovers that the Arab boy Moktir is a thief, instead of being angry, is delighted, and makes the thief his favourite; he is fascinated by the corrupt peasant, Bute,[149] and by the poachers whom he accompanies in their nocturnal expeditions; at Syracuse he delights in the 'société des pires gens'; he finds pleasure —even a 'savoureux bonheur'—in telling lies; he possesses Marceline after a violent struggle in which he subdues and binds a drunken coachman ('Ah! quels regards après, et

quels baisers nous échangeâmes . . .'); he admires that
miniature Heliogabalus, King Atalaric, who, suborned by
the Goths, rejected his Latin education, gave himself up
to debauchery 'avec de rudes favoris de son âge', and died,
after a short life 'violente, voluptueuse et débridée', at the
age of eighteen; he proclaims that his merit consists in
'une espèce d'entêtement dans le pire'. The influence of
Wilde, whom Gide had met in Algeria, is obvious; Wilde
is to a certain extent the character of Ménalque, the corruptor, who preaches the cult of the Greek world and in-
sinuates the Nietzschean principle of the right of might.
And like Sibyl Vane in *The Picture of Dorian Gray*—of
which an echo can be discerned in this book—Marceline
is sacrificed to the brutal egotism of the man. What, in
fact, could be more reminiscent of Wilde than this idea:

'Chaque jour croissait en moi le confus sentiment de richesses
intactes, que couvraient, cachaient, étouffaient les cultures, les
décences, les morales.

'Il me semblait alors que j'étais né pour une sorte inconnue de
trouvailles; et je me passionnais étrangement dans ma recherche
ténébreuse, pour laquelle je sais que le chercheur devait abjurer et
repousser de lui culture, décence et morale.'

The same themes recur in the *Faux-monnayeurs* (1925).
Little Georges is surprised in a theft, and becomes, for
this reason, of special interest to Édouard (the character
who represents the author himself), and all the more exciting when he is discovered to be his nephew. The
incident which gives the title to the novel—that of the
schoolboys who lend themselves to the circulation of false
coin—is a sign of the same idiosyncrasy: the author enjoys the contemplation of the moral corruption of these
seductive youths. One of them, Ghéridanisol, sets an
infernal trap for the weak, feminine Boris, with the intention of leading him to commit 'un acte monstrueux': this
act is the suicide of Boris under the eyes of his grandfather, who, in his desperation, develops theories of
diabolical mysticism:

'Et savez-vous ce que Dieu a fait de plus horrible?. . . . C'est de
sacrifier son propre fils pour nous sauver. Son fils! son fils! . . . la
cruauté, voilà le premier des attributs de Dieu.'

In this remark old M. La Pérouse seems to speak like a character from Dostoievsky; and very much in the manner of Dostoievsky also are the characters of Armand and of Strouvilhou—Armand who, like the hero of *Letters from the Underworld*, finds a bitter pleasure in degradation, abets and at the same time denounces the prostitution of his sister Sarah, contracts a venereal disease, and refuses to have it attended to in order to 'pouvoir se dire, quand on commence à se soigner: "il est trop tard!" '; and Strouvilhou whose nihilistic ideas, instilled into the mind of his young cousin Ghéridanisol, culminate in the sacrifice of Boris. Armand commits incest with his sister by proxy; in the morning he comes into the room where Bernard has slept with Sarah with his consent, and—

's'avance vers le lit où sa sœur et Bernard reposent. Un drap couvre à demi leurs membres enlacés. Qu'ils sont beaux! Armand longuement les contemple. Il voudrait être leur sommeil, leur baiser Il sourit d'abord, puis, au pied du lit, parmi les couvertures rejetées, soudain s'agenouille. Quel dieu peut-il prier ainsi, les mains jointes? Une indicible émotion l'étreint. Ses lèvres tremblent.... Il aperçoit sous l'oreiller un mouchoir taché de sang; il se lève, s'en empare, l'emporte et, sur la petite tache ambrée, pose ses lèvres en sanglotant.'

Here Armand is modelled on Dostoievsky's Idiot; in another place he is possessed by that same 'imp of the perverse' upon which Poe, Baudelaire, and Dostoievsky had all dilated, and tortures his sister Rachel, who is going blind, by his revelation of Sarah's guilt:

'Armand avait une main sur la poignée de la porte; de l'autre, avec sa canne, il maintenait la portière soulevée. La canne entra dans un trou de la portière et l'agrandit.

'Explique ça comme tu pourras, dit-il, et son visage prit une expression très grave. — Rachel est, je crois bien, la seule personne de ce monde que j'aime et que je respecte. Je la respecte parce qu'elle est vertueuse. Et j'agis toujours de manière à offenser sa vertu. Pour ce qui est de Bernard et de Sarah, elle ne se doutait de rien. C'est moi qui lui ai tout raconté. ... Et l'oculiste qui lui recommande de ne pas pleurer! C'est bouffon!'

The women in this novel, Laura, Pauline, Rachel, sacrificed and tortured, are remote descendants of Sade's virtuous Justine. (Actually, here, not even Juliette could have escaped, for Lilian, who is by no means virtuous, ends by being barbarously murdered by her lover Vincent.) Rouveyre[150] makes the following remark on Gide's female characters:

'Ses sacrifiées religieuses, Gide les traite *con amore*, et pourtant, cruel tourmenteur, il va jusqu'à refuser à la dernière et à la plus significative de ses héroïnes (Gertrude de la *Symphonie*) la joie même de la lumière du jour, et c'est une aveugle que l'Amour voudrait bercer dans ses bras adorables. Gide imagine que, une opération lui donnant la lumière, cette âme, étrangement défaite, en est livrée naturellement au suicide.'

Although Gide's work extends to our own times, it is in the Decadent Movement that it has its roots. We must now turn back in order to complete our account of Decadent literature.

23. Rops, together with Moreau, is the artist most representative of the Decadent Movement. His importance is testified in the *Journal* of the Goncourts as early as 1868:[151]

'Rops est vraiment éloquent, en peignant la cruauté d'aspect de la femme contemporaine, son regard d'acier, et son mauvais vouloir contre l'homme, non caché, non dissimulé, mais montré ostensiblement sur toute sa personne.'

We have already quoted the passage from Huysmans upon the chastity of artists with licentious imaginations, which was written about Rops.[152] We must again quote from Huysmans' essay, because at the present day it is impossible to see in Rops's mediocre drawings the 'terrible' qualities which his contemporaries discerned in them:

'M. Félicien Rops, avec une âme de Primitif à rebours, a accompli l'œuvre inverse de Memlinc; il a pénétré, résumé le satanisme en d'admirables planches qui sont comme inventions, comme symboles, comme art incisif et nerveux, féroce et navré, vraiment uniques.'

His object, like that of Moreau, was to portray Evil incarnate in woman—a portrayal which Rops intended to be satirical, but which, owing to his excessive complaisance with the subject, he could not raise above the level of mere illustration, often pornographic.

Rops portrayed the triumph of woman as 'démoniaque et terrible . . . le grand vase des iniquités et des crimes, le charnier des misères et des hontes, la véritable introductrice des ambassades déléguées dans nos âmes par tous les vices . . . maléficiée par le Diable et vénéficiant, à son tour, l'homme qui la touche.'

'Il a restitué à la Luxure si niaisement confinée dans l'anecdote, si bassement matérialisée par certaines gens, sa mystérieuse omnipotence; il l'a religieusement replacée dans le cadre infernal où elle se meut et, par cela même, il n'a pas créé des œuvres obscènes et positives, mais bien des œuvres catholiques, des œuvres enflammées et terribles. . . .

'Il a, en un mot, célébré ce spiritualisme de la Luxure qu'est le Satanisme, peint, en d'imperfectibles pages, le surnaturel de la perversité, l'au-delà du Mal.'

In the case of Rops also, the literary antecedent is to be found in Flaubert. For the whole of this Belgian artist's work seems bent upon representing the symbolic figure of Lust and Death which is described in the *Tentation* as follows:

'Il aperçoit au milieu des ténèbres une manière de monstre devant lui.

'C'est une tête de mort, avec une couronne de roses. Elle domine un torse de femme d'une blancheur nacrée. En dessous, un linceul étoilé de points d'or fait comme une queue; — et tout le corps ondule, à la manière d'un ver gigantesque qui se tiendrait debout.'

In fact, when Lorrain tries to describe the art of Rops,[153] he gives the impression of paraphrasing the passage just quoted:

'Et devant tous ces spectateurs à groin de porc et ces spectatrices à face convulsée de goule, le souvenir d'une eau-forte de Rops s'imposait, une effroyable et justicière eau-forte, où la Luxure, la Luxure impératrice du monde, est stigmatisée sous les traits d'un squelette couronné de fleurs, mais un squelette on peut dire sirène, car au-dessous des vertèbres du torse s'épanouit une croupe charnue, et deux jambes fusent, deux jambes rondes de statue ou de danseuse, qui épousent les reins en forme de beau fruit.'[154]

24. Moreover, may we not now apply to Rops the judgement of Laforgue upon the poetical disciples of Baudelaire? 'Tous ses élèves ont glissé dans le paroxysme, dans l'horrible plat comme des carabins d'estaminet.'

Maurice Rollinat, a sort of diluted Baudelaire, a methodical collector of horrors, is Rops translated into verse. As Maurras justly says,[155] 'où Baudelaire écrit vampire, Rollinat met sangsue'. But the source of inspiration is always the same, the vampire-woman and the masochistic pleasure of her victim. Rollinat's *Névroses* (1883) contains innumerable 'succions convulsives', innumerable Mesdemoiselles Pieuvre and Mesdemoiselles Squelette and Mesdames Vampire, and putrefactions, shudders, and profanities without end. It will more than suffice to quote *Le Succube*, which, though it does not reach the frenzy of certain other poems (there are dizzy plunges into the depths of the repulsive and macabre, for example in *La belle fromagère* and *Les deux poitrinaires*), gives an idea of the predominant flavour of his work:

> Toute nue, onduleuse, et le torse vibrant,
> La fleur des lupanars, des tripots et des bouges
> Bouclait nonchalamment ses jarretières rouges
> Sur de très longs bas noirs d'un tissu transparent,
>
> Quand soudain sa victime eut un cri déchirant:
> 'Je suis dans un brouillard qui bourdonne et qui bouge!
> Mon œil tourne et s'éteint! où donc es-tu, ma gouge?
> Viens! tout mon corps tari te convoite en mourant!'
>
> A ces mots, la sangsue exulta d'ironie:
> 'Si tu veux jusqu'au bout râler ton agonie,
> Je t'engage, dit-elle, à ménager ta voix!'
>
> Et froide, elle accueillit, raillant l'affreux martyre,
> Ses suprêmes adieux par un geste narquois
> Et son dernier hoquet par un éclat de rire.

In another poem (*A la Circé moderne*) the lover calls upon the vampire-woman: 'Harcèle-moi de ta malice, — salis-moi de tes trahisons! — insulte-moi!' and so on.

Rollinat used to recite these verses at the *cabaret* of the 'Chat Noir', accompanying himself on the piano, his mouth twisted into a frightful grin, his face convulsed with terror and agony. By dint of repeating—

> Mon crâne est un cachot plein d'horribles bouffées. . . .
>
> . . . .
>
> Le meurtre, le viol, le vol, le parricide
> Passent dans mon esprit comme un farouche éclair,

he ended by making himself really fit for the asylum, and died there in 1903.[156]

Rollinat's house, as described by Bourget to Goncourt,[157] gives an idea of his surroundings:

'Un hôtel étrange, un hôtel donnant l'impression d'une localité choisie par Poe pour un assassinat, et au fond de cet hôtel, une chambre, où parmi les meubles traînaient des vers écrits sur des feuilles à en-têtes de décès, et dans cette chambre une maîtresse bizarre, et un chien rendu fou, parce qu'on le battait quand il se conduisait en chien raisonnable, et qu'on lui donnait du sucre, quand il commettait quelque méfait, — enfin le locataire fumant une pipe Gamba, à tête de mort.'

'Les malheurs de la vertu' and 'les prospérités du vice' applied to a pet dog! With rather more suitability, Rollinat also represented cats as being sadistic, as may be seen in his *Jalousie féline*, in which a cat that had become hydrophobic from jealousy 'déchiquète les seins' of a beautiful woman![158]

Rollinat saw life in terms of a macabre etching by Rops, Albert Samain as a languid *décor* by Moreau. He, too, insists on the voluptuous pleasure of tears, as had Rollinat in *Les Plaintes*:

> Sous l'archet sensitif où passent nos alarmes
> L'âme des violons sanglote, et sous nos doigts,
> La harpe, avec un bruit de source dans les bois,
> Égrène, à sons mouillés, la musique des larmes.

In Samain we read:

> La Vie est comme un grand violon qui sanglote. . . .

In Samain are to be found the usual subjects—Salome, Helen, the Hermaphrodite (whose eyes are, of course, green: see *L'Hermaphrodite* in *Au jardin de l'Infante*), Lesbianism (see *Les Vierges au crépuscule* in *Aux flancs du vase*), the Black Mass ('Le Bouc noir passe au fond des ténèbres malsaines'), *faisandé* Spain, 'du sang, de la volupté, de la mort', the litanies of Lust (written in 1889):[159]

> Luxure, fruit de mort à l'arbre de la vie . . .
>
> · · · · · · ·
>
> Luxure, avènement des sens à la splendeur.
> Diadème de stupre et manteau d'impudeur.

· · · · · · ·

Je te salue, ô très occulte, ô très profonde,
Luxure, Idole noire et terrible du monde.

Luxure, Tiare des Césars pâles et fous.
Collier des grandes hétaïres aux crins roux.

Luxure, nerfs des nerfs, acide de l'acide,
Luxure, ultime amour damné qui se suicide.

Vierge d'or et de sang, vierge consolatrice,
Vierge vierge à jamais, vierge dévoratrice.

Cité de feu — Philtre d'oubli — Vrille de fer.
Vierge damnée et Notre-Dame de l'Enfer.

Je te salue, ô très occulte, ô très profonde,
Luxure, Impératrice Immortelle du monde.

This sacrilegious hymn is a French reflection of Swinburne's *Dolores*. Again:

> Tes yeux verts, ô ma Bien-Aimée,
> Rêvent dans l'ombre parfumée
> D'affreux supplices pour les cœurs;
>
> Et ton nez irrité respire
> Dans l'étouffement des odeurs
> Des fêtes sanglantes d'empire![160]

It is not necessary to quote *Le Fouet* (in *Au jardin de
l'Infante*), and the dramatic poem *Poliphème* (published
posthumously in *Aux flancs du vase*, 1901) in order to
prove the close relationship of Samain's particular sensibility to that of Swinburne. Samain, who lived an almost
monastic life ('La vie est une fleur que je respire à peine')
and was an affectionate son, died of consumption in 1900.

There was the same type of inspiration, the same
manner of death also, in the case of Ephraïm Mikhaël, of
whom Mendès wrote:[161]

'Chacun de ses poèmes est comme un bûcher de trésors flambants
où rêve un Sardanapale environné de nudités parées de gazes et de
perles, mais un Sardanapale qui aurait écrit l'*Ecclésiaste*. D'autres
fois, il fait penser à un royal affligé qui aurait versé, pleur à pleur,
tout le sang de ses veines, dans un lacrymatoire d'or incrusté de
rubis et de chrysoprases.'

When they have nothing better to do, these poets em-
bark upon subjects of profanation. It may be doubted

whether the Jew Mikhaël found as much enjoyment in writing his poem *Impiétés* as the Catholic Robert de Montesquiou in comparing his heart to a ciborium [162] or to a shrine. Of Montesquiou, who was the model for Huysmans' des Esseintes[163] and for Proust's Charlus, it will suffice to record the following anecdote, related by E. de Goncourt:[164]

'Whistler demeure, dans ce moment, rue du Bac, dans un hôtel qui donne sur le jardin des Missions Étrangères. Montesquiou, invité dernièrement à dîner, a assisté à un spectacle qui a laissé chez lui la plus grande impression. C'était dans le jardin des Missions Étrangères, la nuit presque tombée, un chœur d'hommes chantant des *Laudate*, un chœur de mâles voix s'élevant — Montesquiou suppose que c'était devant de mauvaises peintures, représentant les épouvantables supplices dans les pays exotiques — s'élevant et s'exaltant en face de ces images de martyre, comme si les chanteurs du jardin étaient pressés de leur faire de sanglants pendants.'

An amateur of gems and of handsome gymnasts of the *éphèbe* type, Montesquiou kept portraits of Swinburne, Baudelaire, and the Goncourts as the tutelar geniuses of his library.[165]

Sappho is reborn in the dress of Baudelaire and Swinburne in the Lesbian poems of Renée Vivien (her real name was Pauline Tarn, and by origin she was partly Anglo-Saxon),[166] but sincerity of tone succeeds nevertheless in ennobling the worn-out perverseness of their content. The image of white lilies crushed by cruel hands recurs with painful insistence all through her work (about fifteen volumes of verse published between 1901 and 1910), together with other themes which make up the repertory of the Decadent Movement—green eyes, cruel faces of Amazons and Bacchantes, seductive corpses of women who have been strangled or drowned, scenes of the Black Mass, Spain in its guise of 'le sang, la volupté, la mort', the Gioconda smile ('Ah! ton sourire aigu de Dame florentine!'), the charm of the Androgyne.[166A] The following, from *La Vénus des aveugles* (1903), is an example of perverse Pre-Raphaelitism, entitled, in the manner of Dante, *Donna m'apparve*:

> Lève nonchalamment tes paupières d'onyx,
> Verte apparition qui fus ma Béatrix.

Vois les pontificats étendre, sur l'opprobre
Des noces, leur chasuble aux violets d'octobre.

Les cieux clament les De profundis irrités
Et les Dies irae sur les Nativités.

Les seins qu'ont ravagés les maternités lourdes
Ont la difformité des outres et des gourdes.

Voici, parmi l'effroi des clameurs d'olifants,
Des faces et des yeux simiesques d'enfants,

Et le repas du soir sous l'ombre des charmilles
Réunit le troupeau stupide des familles.

Une rébellion d'archanges triompha
Pourtant, lorsque frémit le paktis de Psappha.

Vois! l'ambiguïté des ténèbres évoque
Le sourire pervers d'un Saint Jean équivoque.

The theme of sterile, cruel love, emphasized from the
very first lines (*A la femme aimée*):[167]

. . . De longs lys religieux et blêmes
Se mouraient dans tes mains, comme des cierges froids.
Leurs parfums expirants s'échappaient de tes doigts
En le souffle pâmé des angoisses suprêmes.
De tes clairs vêtements s'exhalaient tour à tour
L'agonie et l'amour —

works itself up sometimes in echoes of Swinburne's
Dolores (*Notre-Dame des fièvres, Tolède*):[168]

. . . Vierge qui souris à la mort des vierges,
Qui demeures sourde à l'obscur appel,
Madone vers qui matines et vêpres
Montent en grelottant, Notre-Dame des Lèpres!

Ta cathédrale . . .
Sur les lits souillés de hideux hymens,
Suinte la moiteur des mains de malade.
Les ladres squameux et les moribonds
Mêlent leur soupir au cri des orfraies
Et baisent tes genoux, Notre-Dame des Plaies!

Tes tragiques élus ont incliné leurs fronts
Sous le vent divin de tes litanies.
Et, parmi l'encens et les chants sacrés
Et l'écoulement des âcres sanies,
S'exhale un relent de pestiférés.
Le pus et le sang et les larmes pâles
Ont béni tes pieds nus, Notre-Dame des Râles!

Swinburne's influence is evident in many of her poems, for example, in the one which has the English title *To the Sunset Goddess*,[169] which may be compared with *Anactoria*:

> L'odeur des lys fanés et des branches pourries
> S'exhale de ta robe aux plis lassés: tes yeux
> Suivent avec langueur de pâles rêveries. . . .
> Tu ressembles à tout ce qui penche et décline.
> Passive, et comprimant la douleur sans appel
> Dont ton corps a gardé l'attitude divine,
> Tu parais te mouvoir dans un souffle irréel.
> Ah! l'ardeur brisée, ah! la savante agonie
> De ton être expirant dans l'amour, ah! l'effort
> De tes râles! — Au fond de la joie infinie,
> Je savoure le goût violent de la mort. . . .

The artificiality of the themes is occasionally redeemed by some cry which appears, as it were, to be echoed from the depths of one of John Webster's tragedies: 'Tu te flétriras un jour, ah! mon lys!' That she was really aware of this artificiality was shown by Renée Vivien in her pathetic end,[170] for she allowed herself to die of starvation when she was only thirty-two (in 1909), but not without first being converted to Catholicism. The hermaphroditism which was characteristic of the *fin de siècle* could find no better illustration than that afforded by the close affinity between the inspiration of Samain and that of Renée Vivien. Apropos of this poetess Le Dantec[171] says: 'Son énergie de femme est comparable à la langueur souvent mièvre et féminine de Samain: ce n'est qu'affaire de dosage, et le résultat est identique.'

A very successful parody of all the poetry of this period is to be found in *Les Déliquescences d'Adoré Floupette, poète décadent*, by Gabriel Vicaire and Henri Beauclair (A Byzance, Lion Vanné, 1885). The fundamentally sadistic quality of this poetry is here stressed in the grotesque dialogue of the Decadents. The ideal of the Decadent is:

'Une belle tête exsanguë avec de longs cheveux pailletés d'or, des yeux avivés par le crayon noir, des lèvres de pourpre ou de vermillon coupées en deux par un large coup de sabre, le charme alangui d'un corps morbide, entouré de triples bandelettes comme une momie de Cléopâtre. Voilà l'éternelle charmeuse, la vraie fille du diable!'[172]

One of the speakers praises the *Imitation of Christ* and confesses that he prefers it even to Sade's *Justine*. But it must be admitted that the attempted parodies of Decadent poems given in the *Déliquescences* are much less frenzied than the lines which were written in all seriousness during that period. How, indeed, would it be possible to write a parody of *Névroses*?

Feebler still is the parody in the lines *The Decadent to his Soul* by Richard Le Gallienne (in *English Poems*, 1892).[173] He, too, stresses the taste for contamination and profanity which is typical of the period:

> His face grew strangely sweet—
> As when a toad smiles.
> He dreamed of a new sin:
> An incest 'twixt the body and the soul
>
> .   .   .   .   .
>
> Then from that day, he used his soul
> As bitters to the over dulcet sins,
> As olives to the fatness of the feast—
> She made those dear heart-breaking ecstasies
> Of minor chords amid the Phrygian lutes,
> She sauced his sins with splendid memories,
> Starry regrets and infinite hopes and fears;
> His holy youth and his first love
> Made pearly background to strange-coloured vice.
>
> Sin is no sin when virtue is forgot.
> It is so good to sin to keep in sight
> The white hills whence we fell, to measure by—
> To say I was so high, so white, so pure,
> And am so low, so blood-stained and so base;
> I revel here amid the sweet sweet mire
> And yonder are the hills of morning flowers:
> So high, so low; so lost and with me yet;
> To stretch the octave 'twixt the dream and deed,
> Ah, that's the thrill!
> To dream so well, to do so ill—
> There comes the bitter-sweet that makes the sin.[174]
>
> First drink the stars, then grunt amid the mire,
> So shall the mire have something of the stars,
> And the high stars be fragrant of the mire.
>
> .   .   .   .   .   .

> Let's wed, I thought, the seraph with the dog,
> And wait the purple thing that shall be born.
>
> And now look round—seest thou this bloom?
> Seven petals and each petal seven dyes,
> The stem is gilded and the root in blood. . . .
> I light my palace with the seven stars,
> And eat strange dishes to Gregorian chants.

Here the old subject of the Miltonic Lucifer is no longer heroic, as in Byron, but has become elegiac.

The most celebrated poet of the Decadent Movement in France, Verlaine, is a faithful mirror of his times. Open to all possibilities of depravity, he celebrates love in all its phases, from the most ingenuous to the most perverse. Coulon[175] very aptly calls attention to an early poem on the actress Marco,[176] which touches all the chords of the poet's 'integral sensuality':

> Quand Marco passait, tous les jeunes hommes
> Se penchaient pour voir ses yeux, des Sodomes
> Où les feux d'Amour brûlaient sans pitié
> Ta pauvre cahute, ô froide Amitié;
> Tout autour dansaient des parfums mystiques
> Où l'âme, en pleurant, s'anéantissait;
> Sur ses cheveux roux un charme glissait;
> Sa robe rendait d'étranges musiques
>   Quand Marco passait.
>
>   .   .   .   .
>
> Mais quand elle aimait, des flots de luxure
> Débordaient, ainsi que d'une blessure
> Sort un sang vermeil qui fume et qui bout,
> De ce corps cruel que le crime absout:
> Le torrent rompait les digues de l'âme,
> Noyait la pensée, et bouleversait
> Tout sur son passage, et rebondissait
> Souple et dévorant comme de la flamme,
>   Et puis se glaçait.

Just as there are hints of sadism in Verlaine, so there are also to be found in him the taste for sacrilege and profanation (no poet ever made so much use of the words *chaste*, *chasteté*, *chastement* as this faun who was expert in every kind of lust), homosexuality, even if only sporadic ('Nous ne sommes pas l'homme — pour la docte Sodome — quand

la Femme il y a!'),[176A] and, finally, the 'fatal' conception of
woman:[177]

> Ô la Femme! Prudent, sage, calme ennemi,
> N'exagérant jamais ta victoire à demi,
> Tuant tous les blessés, pillant tout le butin,
> Et répandant le fer et la flamme au lointain,
> Ou bon ami, peu sûr, mais tout de même bon,
> Et doux, trop doux souvent, tel un feu de charbon
> Qui berce le loisir, vous l'amuse et l'endort,
> Et parfois induit le dormeur en telle mort
> Délicieuse par quoi l'âme meurt aussi!

In *Extrêmes-onctions*, one of the *Histoires comme ça*,[178]
the various themes of perversion also occur. Verlaine
describes the beauty of the body of 'un jeune homme du
plus grand monde' ('Nu, c'était Hercule à vingt ans,
Antinous à trente. Très poilu, etc.'), which contrasts with
the horrible disfigurement of his once handsome face
caused by a formidable 'coup de poing américain': he
describes also this young man's affair with a girl whom he
had started in life:

'Il semblait que la passion de la femme eût crû en raison directe
de l'épouvantable laideur actuelle de l'homme; laideur épouvantable,
nous le répétons, mais, insistons-y, laideur qui s'imposait. Il
semblait aussi que l'homme, par quelle loi fatale sinon infernale, ou
divine! et qu'Edgar Poe eût appelée: *Perverse*, et par quel vertige!
s'abîmât dans son étrange attraction vers cette femelle qu'il avait
perdue.'

The conclusion is extremely *fin de siècle*:

'Un jour, ou plutôt, une nuit, comme ils revenaient de souper
du cabaret, à peine au lit la fille eut un de ces caprices dont elle
était, au reste, assez coutumière.

'La chambre tendue et tapissée de bleu avec un lustre d'opale,
l'immense lit, aux plus immenses rideaux clairement sombres,
étaient engageants vers ces manœuvres. Leurs splendides nudités,
comme lactées dans ce milieu lunaire, d'abord s'étreignirent, puis
s'éteignirent, puis s'étreignirent à nouveau, pour, après, l'homme
s'agenouiller. . . .

'Alors, elle, tel le prêtre catholique, dans le sacrement de l'ex-
trême-onction, console tous les sens, rassure l'âme, asséna son frêle
poing naguère armé d'une arme immonde contre un simple visage

séducteur qu'elle avait déformé et qui l'avait éblouie, tua, dans cette
génuflexion de lui, la tête qui avait conçu ce déshonneur-là.'

Verlaine (who counted Swinburne among his masters)[179]
had intended to do great things with this type of subject,
if he had been able. On May 16th, 1873, he wrote:[180]

'Je fourmille d'idées, de vues nouvelles, de projets vraiment
beaux. . . . Un roman féroce, aussi sadique que possible et très sèche-
ment écrit.'

25. There remains the question as to why, during that
period, the limits of which are variously defined between
the early 'eighties and the opening of the twentieth century,
there should have been, in France especially, such an
abundance of writers characterized by the specialized form
of sensuality of which we have been speaking. For even if
fashion and influences both indigenous and foreign can
account for a large number of works of a specific tendency,
they still do not suffice to explain the original native
qualities visible in the writers themselves. In writers such
as Huysmans, Lorrain, and Barrès, sadism is more deeply
ingrained than can be accounted for by the mere influence
of a cultural atmosphere.[180A]

Moreover this tendency is also to be found in eccentric
writers such as P. J. Toulet, who, in the few but exquisite
works which he left, deals with themes of cruelty in a
decorous and elegant style rather reminiscent of the eighteenth century, a little like that of Diderot or Restif en-
riched with the wit of a Voltaire (if one wishes to find a
contemporary affinity, one cannot help thinking of Anatole
France). In *Monsieur du Paur* (1898) the subject of
English sadism provides a few extremely prurient
moments; in *Le Mariage de Don Quichotte* (1902) we
meet Elycias the Inquisitor 'dont les traits délicats
semblaient trahir vingt ans à peine', a sadistic epicure who
tells his own story, starting from his youth, to which a
flavour of pleasure was given by frequent beatings, to his
adventure with the perverse Gladie, who loves him all the
more after he has killed her lover and who, after being
sold out of jealousy to a cruel Turk, dies under torture.

One is forced to the conclusion that perhaps the un-
limited licence to deal with subjects of vice and cruelty,

which was introduced into literature together with
Romanticism, created an atmosphere favourable to the
expression of individual feeling, which, in different circumstances, would have remained latent and repressed.
It must also be remembered that literary fashion and
specialized sensibility reacted upon each other, like
burning-glasses, with multiplied intensity, with the result
that, between the writer who set about to make the most
of certain fashionable themes, and the one who found in
the fashion of the moment an encouragement to his own
native téndencies, and who, in disclosing them, increased,
by his personal contribution, the intensity of the fashion,
there sprang into existence that extraordinary conflagra-
tion of cerebral lechery which occupied the end of the
century and gave the impression of a genuinely imminent
catastrophe. Even as early as 1866 the Goncourts, who
were always interested in manifestations of vice,[181] had
observed:[182]

'La méchanceté dans l'amour, que cette méchanceté soit physique
ou morale, est le signe de la fin des sociétés.'

And twenty years later, apropos of a crime which had
been committed, Edmond de Goncourt noted:[183]

'Ces neuf voyous qui, après avoir violé cette malheureuse mar-
chande, lui ont mis le feu au ventre, ça fait peur. Voici les Gugusse
venant des marquis de Sade. Ce n'est plus un cas particulier, c'est
tout le bas d'une nation atteint de férocité dans l'amour.'

His conclusion is an arbitrary one, but it shows to what
a degree attention was focused upon certain aspects of
vice. The oft-repeated lament over the downfall of Latin
civilization, the 'Ohé! ! ! Ohé! ! ! les races latines!' of
Péladan, the conviction of d'Aurevilly that the race had
arrived 'à sa dernière heure', Verlaine's 'Je suis l'Empire
à la fin de la décadence'—such things show not so much
the terror, as the attraction, of disaster: the very ideas of
Decadence, of imminent Divine punishment like the fire
of Sodom, of the 'cupio dissolvi', are perhaps no more than
the extreme sadistic refinements of a *milieu* which was
saturated to excess with complications of perversion.

In process of time it has become possible to see that it
was a question of mental attitude, of a momentary dizziness

el mal y su rutina.

on the brink of a precipice, which, epidemic as it was, soon wore itself out into a monotonous *routine du gouffre* (to use Colette's expression), rather than a real decay of society: the year 1900 no more marked the date of a cataclysm than did the year 1000. The philosophy of Schopenhauer, the music of *Götterdämmerung*,[184] the Russian novel, the plays of Maeterlinck—all these were absorbed and digested, after doing no more than create an impression of a delicious death-agony.

From about 1880 till the beginning of the present century the idea of Decadence was the turning-point round which the literary world revolved:

'Se dissimuler l'état de décadence où nous sommes arrivés serait le comble de l'insenséisme. Religion, mœurs, justice, tout décade. . . . La société se désagrège sous l'action corrosive d'une civilisation déliquescente. L'homme moderne est un blasé. Affinement d'appétits, de sensations, de goûts, de luxe, de jouissances, névrose, hystérie, hypnotisme, morphinomanie, charlatanisme scientifique, schopenhauérisme à outrance, tels sont les prodromes de l'évolution sociale.'

This is from a paper called *Le Décadent*, April 10th, 1886. A little later Huysmans wrote:[185] 'Les queues de siècle se ressemblent. Toutes vacillent et sont troubles.' And Marcel Schwob wrote of this period (in the story *Les Portes de l'opium*, in *Cœur double*):

'Nous étions arrivés dans un temps extraordinaire où les romanciers nous avaient montré toutes les faces de la vie humaine et tous les dessous des pensées. On était lassé de bien des sentiments avant de les avoir éprouvés; plusieurs se laissaient attirer vers un gouffre d'ombres mystiques et inconnues; d'autres étaient possédés par la passion de l'étrange, par la recherche du quintessencié de sensations nouvelles; d'autres, enfin, se fondaient dans une large pitié qui s'étendait sur toutes choses. . . . J'éprouvais le désir douloureux de m'aliéner à moi-même, d'être souvent soldat, pauvre ou marchand, ou la femme que je voyais passer.'

In this confession some of the characteristic aspects of the period are passed in review—schizoidism, disintegration, sadism behind a mask of pity ('Ces modernes saint Vincent-de-Paul du sentiment, toujours à la recherche d'âmes souffrantes . . .' wrote Lorrain in *Buveurs d'âmes*:

'Cette passion de charité un peu effrayante n'est, au fond, qu'un sadisme délicat et pervers de raffiné épris de tortures et de larmes').[185A] 'Tout décade . . .'—there were some who really felt this, others who sweated to add fuel to the flames and thus increase the impression that they were the fires of Hell.

The period of antiquity with which these artists of the *fin de siècle* liked best to compare their own was the long Byzantine twilight, that gloomy apse gleaming with dull gold and gory purple, from which peer enigmatic faces, barbaric yet refined, with dilated neurasthenic pupils. The writers of the first part of the nineteenth century, filled with nostalgia, had re-evoked the Imperial orgies of the Orient and of Rome, dominated by some monstrous superhuman figure such as Sardanapalus, Semiramis, Cleopatra, Nero, Heliogabalus; but on the threshold of the present century even this virile personal element seemed to disappear. The Byzantine period was a period of anonymous corruption, with nothing of the heroic about it; only there stand out against the monotonous background figures such as Theodora or Irene, who are static personifications of the female lust for power.

The Flaubert of *Salammbô* had outlined the method, the necessary historical erudition was supplied by Diehl; and the Decadents devoted themselves to living over again the gory annals of the Eastern Empire, torn by dissensions and court hatreds, hemmed in on all sides by barbarian conquerors, a body full of bruises and decay enveloped in the symmetrical folds of a mantle of heavy gold.

Attempts were also made to write popular novels on Byzantine subjects. The publisher Edoardo Perino of Rome, for instance, announced in the *Cronaca Bizantina* of December 13th, 1885, '*Teodora*, a Byzantine historical novel, written by I. Fiorentino, illustrated by Giuseppe Pigna', with the following seductive 'puff', the syntax of which, in the Italian, is truly barbaric:

'Theodora—A woman who, starting from the lowest ranks of the people, rose to occupying the seat of an empress on the greatest throne in the world, who presents in herself a strange mixture of abjectness and grandeur, of cruelty, magnificence and magnanimity, is a subject not less worthy of study than of admiration. Byzantine society of thirteen centuries ago, with its theological disputes, its fierce pleasures, its strange crowd of eunuchs, bishops, captains and charioteers, thronging and intermingling round the Imperial throne, forms a most fitting circle round this fantastic figure.'

Apart from differences of style, Paul Adam and Gabriele D'Annunzio said exactly the same things in their descriptions of Byzantium. *Décor* is everything in these works, but it must be noted that the value of the *décor* is not purely scholarly. The meticulous catalogues of trappings, of objects, of acts, do not aim merely at giving an atmosphere. The ferment of impure, violent deeds which these *décors* have witnessed underlies the descriptions of them. Objects become so many symbols of wickedness, lust, or cruelty. The *décor* in itself is already an enunciation of a spiritual and moral atmosphere. The essence of this civilization is well expressed in a few words which Paul Adam puts into the mouth of the ambassador of the Franks, in *Irène et les eunuques*:[186]

'Pour la quatrième fois, je reviens à Byzance. Il y a plus de langues coupées, plus d'yeux crevés, mais le reste ne change pas.'

The scene evoked is usually the same, a mixture of carnage, of precious, exotic objects, and of the profanation of sacred things. Adam gives the tone of his book in its first pages:

'Avant qu'il eût frappé trois fois l'image, elles se ruèrent, le déchirèrent après l'avoir décortiqué de sa cuirasse et de ses cuissards. Ensuite elles traînèrent la masse de ces chairs effrangées le long des étalages où ceux d'Arménie exposent les soies de Chine et les objets venus par les caravanes des Nestoriens. . . .

'Le sang et les pleurs souillèrent les sanctuaires dévastés. Les chiens avides emportèrent des mains tranchées dont les doigts gardaient les bagues en laiton. . . .

'Les soldats s'armèrent de tridents et le (Étienne) mirent en pièces avec sa dalmatique en fils d'or. Vers les eaux immondes, ils traînèrent, dans le tissu précieux et saigneux, tout le poids inerte de l'apôtre. . . .

'La plèbe militaire . . . se plut à voir promener sous le soleil, autour de la Spina, dans le stade, des moines et des courtisanes liés ensemble.'

Great choreographic movements seek to disguise under
a false sparkle of picturesqueness the absence of any real
thinking. The following passage, a kind of long stage-
direction, may be taken as an example of the final development attained by a form of art which had not lacked a
certain nobility in the *Salammbô* of Flaubert:[187]

'Quand on eut ôté les tapis suspendus aux balcons de Byzance;
quand on eut retiré des façades les fleurs déjà flétries, les draps d'or et
d'argent, les coffrets d'émaux, les emblèmes et les insignes; quand on
eut abattu les arcs de triomphe, et ramassé en tas les pétales de roses
semés deux jours avant sous les pas du cortège; quand les tavernes,
sur le port, se furent vidées de leurs derniers ivrognes ahuris; quand
la foule des pécheresses vint s'accuser dans les églises en se proster-
nant sous la galerie de l'ambon devant l'iconostase dépeuplée de ses
images; quand les palefreniers de l'Hippodrome recommencèrent
à promener par la ville les chevaux parés pour la vente, et les moines
à vanter les médecines élaborées dans les couvents célèbres par leurs
miracles, puis à les troquer, au coin des rues, contre des légumes
frais, des œufs, des volailles grasses; quand les chameaux persans
chargés de marchandises s'agenouillèrent à nouveau devant les
boutiques des Arméniens et tendirent vers les enfants amusés les
grosses lèvres de leurs museaux dignes; quand les maçons se remirent
à gâcher du ciment rose, en haut des échafaudages, et les commères
à babiller en se signant mille fois sur leurs voiles graisseux mais
honnètement croisés; quand les fonctionnaires du Palais eurent
quitté leurs allures d'empressement pour musarder à pas mous le
long des colonnades, et se saluer avec des révérences hiérarchiques;
quand les eunuques du Gynécée impérial se furent remis à compter
les dépenses avec les billes multicolores de leurs tringles et les jetons
d'étain jetés sur les coffres; quand les esclaves alertes eurent apporté,
le surlendemain des noces, les confitures de gingembre et les gâteaux
d'anis aux jeunes époux éveillés, épuisés encore par les ébats voluptueux, Irène ne se reconnut point.'

26. The most monumental figure of the Decadent
Movement, the figure in which the various European
currents of the second half of the nineteenth century con-
verged, was given to the world not by France but by Italy,
and by a part of Italy in which, more than in any other,
the general level of life is instinctive and primitive, a real
'Italia barbara'—the 'remota e inculta'[188] province of the
Abruzzi.

Certain salient characteristics in D'Annunzio may be

due to peculiarities of origin and culture; indeed he is always and before everything the child of a semi-barbarous race, who, coming into contact with a more than mature civilization, assimilated it rapidly and summarily, with the inevitable discords which result from such a process of imperfect adaptation.[189] Beneath the veneer appears from time to time the *spirito crudo* (raw nature).

The veneer, however, is thick and shining, and at the first glance may create the impression of a *parvenu* of culture—like a barbarian who, exalted all at once to the throne of Byzantium, covers himself with all the jewels he can lay hands on. But his original attitude impresses its own character on his genius: D'Annunzio is primarily an Abruzzese who has made his second home in Tuscany, secondarily an Italian who has made his second home in Paris. But neither Tuscan nor French culture was native to him, nor an essential part of him: he had to acquire them from the outside, since he was not able, by natural familiarity with them, to understand them thoroughly from the inside. He absorbed those aspects of them which could be most easily assimilated by his *spirito crudo*.

'From far, far away there came to him a troubled yearning, from the most distant sources, from the primitive bestiality of sudden unions, from the ancient mystery of sacred lusts.'

It is Stelio Effrena speaking:[190] the 'mystery of sacred lusts', though it seems to be mere rhetorical emphasis, is actually a very good description of the raw nucleus of semi-barbaric sensuality which was D'Annunzio's natural inheritance. At the contact with French Decadence, the feeling for profanation, for taboo, which was innate in D'Annunzio, found a propitious soil in which to develop; cruelty in love, which served the French Decadents as stimulant to a naturally feeble instinct, was also an essential part of the 'primitive bestiality' of a semi-savage stock such as the Abruzzese, since primitive people are just as cruel as the ultra-civilized, the former from instinct, the latter from mental erethism.

A mind still clouded by the sediment of brutality which permeates the extravagant rites of primitive religions is more open than any other to possibilities of abnormal

development. The lack of humanity which is usually remarked upon in a very large proportion of D'Annunzio's
work may be attributed, I think, to a meeting of extremes
in the same person: D'Annunzio is a barbarian and at the
same time a Decadent, and there is lacking in him the
temperate zone which, in the present period of culture, is
labelled 'humanity'. The twofold nature of this extremism
explains why D'Annunzio has been a warrior as well as a
voluptuary.

Many people, especially outside Italy, have not yet been
able to realize how it is that a Decadent, such as D'Annunzio is believed to be, was able to conduct himself in
arms in a manner so daring as to have made him one of the
war-heroes of Italy. A Decadent, an aesthete, is, as a rule,
nervous, a bad soldier. They forget that D'Annunzio is a
primitive as well as a Decadent.

The stages by which this son of the Abruzzi became
urbanized are well known. Literary fashions, at the end
of the last century (I wonder if things are very much
changed to-day) arrived in Italy by way of France. Keeping in mind the dates of certain events in France—1880,
the apotheosis of Schopenhauer; 1886, the appearance of
the Russian novel, thanks to the efforts of the Vicomte
E.-M. de Vogüé; 1885, the foundation of the *Revue
Wagnérienne*, which canonized the latest musical craze
('Le dieu Richard Wagner irradiant un sacre', wrote
Mallarmé in his *Hommage*); remembering also that precisely at this same period English Pre-Raphaelitism and
the gospel of Ruskin were received into high favour in
France; and then comparing the dates of *L'Invincibile*
(1890), of *Giovanni Episcopo* and *L'Innocente* (1892), of
Il Fuoco (1900)—one can see D'Annunzio ready to welcome all the latest novelties, his attention strained outwards, anxious to receive themes, philosophies, tastes from
outside. As was to be expected, he fixed upon the most
specious aspects of these movements, and on the showiest
artists. Lorrain and Péladan were his first models: he
borrowed certain of their most obvious characteristics
from Swinburne and Nietzsche, without penetrating into
their subtleties or shades of meaning. The delicate

qualities of the more refined of the Decadents, such as Barrès, Remy de Gourmont, Mallarmé, were entirely alien to him. The proof that D'Annunzio's mind remained persistently rudimentary, in spite of his repeated experiments in culture, is his entire ignorance of humour. His humour is pedantic, verbal, Rabelaisian in character, never syntactic or Voltairean. Look at the description of the college years in *Le Faville del Maglio*, where the pedantic language is supposed to generate the *vis comica*: it is the most primitive of all comic expedients, the purely linguistic.

D'Annunzio's habit of building up his own individuality from outside, of searching for himself in others, of appropriating his various sources and reducing them to a common denominator—in the same way as those clever Southern Italian painters of the seventeenth century, of whom Luca Giordano is the most typical—has caused his work as a whole to have the appearance of a monumental encyclopedia of European Decadence. Wilde had attempted something of the same kind, but Wilde, passive imitator as he was, did not possess D'Annunzio's power of giving unity to his vast machine. This power of D'Annunzio's, which, in fact, constitutes his genius, is simply 'carnality of thought',[191] the gift of being able to endow every thought with 'a weight of blood', the gift of the Word, which D'Annunzio has in a degree at least equal to the great French writer who corresponds to him in the preceding period—Victor Hugo. To put it briefly —Victor Hugo is the D'Annunzio of Romanticism, D'Annunzio the Victor Hugo of Decadence.

Late in his life D'Annunzio, passionate lover of the 'diversity of creatures', of the 'Siren of the world', has solemnly reasserted his faith in the world of the senses, seeking to hold it tightly in his weakening grasp by realizing it, no longer in the form of words, but of walls and furniture, in the vast Pantheon of the Vittoriale. Usually the great spirits of the earth, once they have entered the shadow of old age, divest themselves of material things and regard as mere trifles the worldly possessions with which they have delighted to surround themselves in the fulness of life. D'Annunzio, on the other

hand, seems to have tried to give an exact shape and form
to his memories and longings by collecting round him a
veritable museum of curiosities and precious objects, and
by crystallizing in the form of emblems, devices, and
hieroglyphics the diversity of a world which once he com-
manded by the sound of words. This lust for possession—
the lust which made him write at the bottom of a page of
proofs: '(1927) Printer! I shall be young again! (1882)'
—produced, at the beginning of the century, the *Laudi*;
to-day, grown rigid but no less tenacious, it produces the
poem of precious stones, metals, tapestries, in which
Narcissus may see his own image exalted and multiplied
and may have the illusion that he feels the warmth of life
beating in his pulses, as in his younger years.

Like Faust, D'Annunzio began by stamping his im
pression on the world of thought, to finish by leaving it on
nothing more than a small material world. This is the
pathetic involution of a sensualist who, as Poet, Lover,
Condottiere, had a greater share of the good things of the
earth than has been granted to any one. The friend of the
Muses ends as custodian of a Museum—as D'Annunzio's
seventeenth-century brother, the Cavaliere Marino, lover
of conceits, might have expressed it.

In the Vittoriale the Decadent Movement seems to have
achieved a final monumental expression. It is Péladan's
Montségur, Lorrain's Noronsoff Palace, translated into
actuality: at the Vittoriale, also, there is a 'décoration
panthéonique des religions', a combined atmosphere of the
shrine of Parsifal, of a princely palace, and of an aesthete's
paradise, with casts of Greek statues, emblematic trappings,
Franciscan symbols, objects of worship and of war; a vast
collection of *bric-à-brac* to which many different cultures
and periods, arts, religions, and nature herself, have contributed.[192] All these innumerable and varied things, rare
and curious, played an important part in the world of
Gautier, the Goncourts, des Esseintes, Dorian Gray,
Lorrain, and in that century which made use of every kind
of exoticism and eclecticism to distract the restlessness of
its exasperated senses and to make up for its lack both of a
profound faith and of an authentic style.

NOTES AND ADDENDA TO CHAPTER V

[1] *L'Art romantique*, apropos of Th. Gautier (p. 168 of the Calmann-Lévy edition), but the quotation is there taken from another text.

The principle thus formulated offers a certain affinity with Winckel-mann's 'Stillness and calm, as they suit the sea, so they suit beauty', &c. See M. Praz, *Gusto neoclassico*, pp. 43, 44, 45. Moreau's two principles may be compared also with those of 'conspicuous waste' and 'conspicuous leisure' applied to fashions by Thorstein Veblen in his *Theory of the Leisure Class*, New York, 1934, and further developed by Quentin Bell, in *On Human Finery*, London, Hogarth Press, 1947. [Add. 1950]

[2] Id., pp. 11–12. I give the quotation in the order in which it is found in the volume by A. Renan, *Gustave Moreau* (Paris, ed. Gazette des Beaux-Arts, 1900), p. 48.

[3] Id., p. 11. Pater supports this: 'All art constantly aspires towards the condition of music.' Angelo Conti also illustrates this principle, in his book on Giorgione, and from there it was taken by D'Annunzio (*Il Fuoco*, Stelio's speech); he had already commented on it in his review of Conti's book in *Convito*, vol. i, p. 73 ('Note su Giorgione e su la Critica', later repeated as part of the preface to Angelo Conti's *Beata Riva*, Milan, Treves, 1900).

[4] Cf. the essay on Moreau by A. Symons in *From Toulouse Lautrec to Rodin* (London, Lane, 1929), pp. 159–69; and especially a passage of Huysmans (*Certains*, 1889, pp. 18–19) where he is speaking of the exhibition of Moreau's water-colours at the Goupil Galleries:

'Une impression identique surgissait de ces scènes diverses, l'impression de l'onanisme spirituel, répété, dans une chair chaste; l'impression d'une vierge, pourvue, dans un corps d'une solennelle grâce, d'une âme épuisée par des idées solitaires, par des pensées secrètes, d'une femme, assise en elle-même, et se radotant, dans de sacramentelles formules, de prières obscures, d'insidieux appels aux sacrilèges et aux stupres, aux tortures et aux meurtres'.

The painting of the Pre-Raphaelite Simeon Solomon is of the same character, upon which see Swinburne's essay (now in *Complete Works*, Bonchurch ed., vol. xv), which finds Solomon's epicene figures to be expressive of the 'cunning and cruel sensibility' of Sade, *et pour cause*! (cf. Lafourcade, op. cit., vol. i, pp. 214–17.)

See also W. Gaunt, *The Aesthetic Adventure*, London, Cape, 1945, pp. 45–8, 126–8. Also W. Pater noticed the ambiguous character of Solomon's art: his *Bacchus*, exhibited at the Royal Academy in 1868, seemed to him a complete realization of the melancholy and troubled figure of Dionysus Zagreus: 'the god of the bitterness of wine, "of things too sweet"; the sea-water of the Lesbian grape become somewhat brackish in the cup' ('A Study of Dionysus', in *Greek Studies*, p. 37). [Add. 1950]

On the minor poets of the English Decadent Movement H. Jackson (quoted below, note 91) says:

'There was an unusual femininity about it; not the femininity of women, nor yet the feminine primness of men; it was more a mingling of what is effeminate in both sexes. This was the genuine minor note, and it was abnormal—a form of hermaphroditism' (p. 163).

⁵ Barbey d'Aurevilly, *Le Roman contemporain* (Paris, Lemerre, 1902), pp. 274, 275, 278. The essay on Huysmans appeared originally in the *Constitutionnel* of July 28th, 1884.

⁶ *A rebours*, v.

⁷ *Œ. compl.*, op. cit., pp. 50–1. Ary Renan, in his apologia (op. cit.) of the art of Moreau, strives to point out differences between Flaubert and Moreau: in the latter there is to be found, not an historical reconstruction, but a fantastic conception based on Oriental models. He concludes:

'Il n'y eut, entre les deux artistes, aucun échange direct d'influence; mais il y a souvent parité dans leur optique, dans la percée qu'ils ouvrent sur le passé reculé … Dans *Salammbô*, qui parut en 1863, l'écrivain ne s'abandonnait-il pas tout à l'orgie plastique de la richesse nécessaire, et n'a-t-il pas fait de sa Carthage le fabuleux magasin de tous les *mirabilia* du monde antique ? Puis, dans la *Tentation* (1874) ne fait-il pas défiler, au son de vocables rarissimes, l'idéale caravane des dieux abolis ?'

It seems difficult to deny the influence of Flaubert or at least of that type of exoticism, cultivated by Gautier and Leconte de Lisle, which was then in the air. At any rate certain of Flaubert's descriptions, such as those of the Hindu Trimurti and of Artemis of Ephesus, in the *Tentation*, are unmistakably verbal anticipations of pictures by Moreau.

⁸ Nevertheless Huysmans says in *La Cathédrale* (p. 331) that the Queen of Sheba

'n'a pu s'incorporer dans la *Tentation de Saint Antoine* qu'en une créature puérile et falote, en une marionnette qui sautille, en zézayant; au fond, il n'y a que le peintre des Salomés, Gustave Moreau, qui pourrait la rendre, cette femme vierge et lubrique, casuiste et coquette, &c.'.

⁸ᴬ Moreau's *Apparition* has also inspired Juliette Lermina Flandre in her 'Salomé, reine de Chalcis', published in *Les Œuvres Libres*, July 1924, pp. 211–12:

'Elle dansait follement comme dans le délire et elle inventait les pas les plus lascifs. Tout à coup, elle cria. Tout tournait autour d'elle. Le mur de mosaïque s'enfonçait, disparaissait. A sa place surgissait une vision effroyable où du sang ruisselait, où des cris d'agonie hurlaient. Elle s'arrêta net, la main tendue. Elle avait rattrapé sa robe merveilleuse qu'elle serrait contre elle craintivement de son autre main:—Oh! dit-elle, là. . . . Une chose affreuse! Une tête d'homme . . . avec du sang! . . .' [Add. 1950]

⁹ The figure of Salome in the sketch for the oil picture (in the Moreau Museum) repeats a classical pose seen in the Spartan dancer in a bas-relief by Callimachus acquired in Italy (at Florence) by the Berlin Museum in 1892 (described in the *Jahrbuch des K. Deutschen Archäologischen Instituts*, vol. viii, 1893, p. 77)—a classical pose also illustrated in the triangular base at the Villa Albani (a figure described as one of the Hours by Winckelmann, *Opere*, Prato, Giachetti, 1830, vol. iv, pp. 504–5, atlas pl. lxxxix, no. 226 on the left).

¹⁰ Op. cit., p. 62.

¹⁰ᴬ On the impression made by Moreau's paintings see also L. Deshairs,

Gustave Moreau, Paris [1931], p. 7, where he says that his friends 'rient quand on voit en ses tableaux des imaginations de fumeur d'opium, ou quand un docteur, après une rapide inspection, conclut gravement: "C'est du sadisme" '. Other attempts to clear Moreau of the accusation of morbid sensuality were made by L. Bénédite in *Deux idéalistes: G. Moreau et E. Burne-Jones*, Paris, Ollendorff, 1889 ('Non, certes, Gustave Moreau ne fut point une sorte de sensualiste étrange et troublant, lubrique et névrosé, fasciné par le vertige de l'érotisme, hanté par les symboles des perversités et des dépravations. Son œuvre n'a pu produire cette impression inattendue que sur l'hystérie morale, la déséquilibration morbide de notre temps'); and by G. Rouault, *Souvenirs intimes*, p. 42 ('Gustave Moreau n'était pas intérieurement si inquiet ni si tourmenté'). [Add. 1950]

11 This comment by Moreau (November 1897) is quoted in the essay by R. de Montesquiou, *Le Lapidaire*, read at the Galerie Georges Petit, May 26th, 1906, and included in *Altesses sérénissimes* (Paris, Juven, 1907): see p. 7 of this latter volume, and on pp. 55–7 Montesquiou's comment on *Hélène* and *Salomé*.

12 Op. cit., p. 78.

13 In *L'Art moderne*, 1883, pp. 136–7 (*Le Salon officiel de 1880*).

14 It must be observed that the interpretation of A. Renan was influenced by Samain's sonnet. *La Lyre héroïque et dolente*, by Pierre Quillard, also dating from 1897, contains a poem on *Les Yeux d'Hélène* dedicated to Marcel Proust, in which the poet imagines Helen as a young girl already burdened with the horror of her future destiny:

> L'effroi religieux issu de ses prunelles
> Ardentes d'incendie et de fauves clartés
> Saisit étrangement les cœurs épouvantés
> Et pleins de visions sombres et solennelles.
>
> Passe, vierge, terrible au col souple et nerveux;
> L'inexpiable sang pour les siècles macule
> Ton front clair comme un jour d'été sans crépuscule
> Et la mort des héros surgit de tes cheveux.
>
> Passe, reine d'amour, semeuse de désastres,
> Dans ta robe de gloire et de sérénité,
> Et vois fleurir les deuils autour de ta beauté,
> Sous tes regards pareils aux froids rayons des astres......

Also Paul Bourget composed a *Hélène* in the style of Moreau (in *Revue indépendante*, no. 11, p. 254), and Henri de Régnier, in one of the poems (*La Barque*) of *Hélène de Sparte* (in *Les Médailles d'argile*, Paris, Mercure de France, 1900), shows the shadows crowding round Helen when she descends to the nether world, the shadows of all those who suffered because of her beauty, but who do not curse her now:

> Non. Tous, debout, les bras tendus vers la Beauté,
> Au lieu de la maudire, eux qui sont morts pour elle,
> D'une bouche muette où nul cri n'est resté
> Acclament en silence Hélène toujours belle.

[Add. 1950]

Samain also wrote three poems inspired by the *Salomé* of Moreau, as seen through the pages of Huysmans: 'Des soirs fiévreux et forts comme une venaison—mon âme traîne en soi l'ennui d'un vieil Hérode', in *Le Jardin de l'Infante*; 'Mon cœur est comme un Hérode morne et pâle' (cf.: 'Tel que le vieux roi, des Esseintes demeurait écrasé, anéanti, pris de vertige devant cette danseuse'), and *Hérode*, in *Le Chariot d'or* (1901).

[15] This picture obviously suggested *La Diana d'Efeso e gli schiavi*, by A. Sartorio.

[16] *Salomé* was translated into English by Lord Alfred Douglas and published with illustrations by Beardsley in 1894, at The Bodley Head. The influence on *Salomé* of Maeterlinck's plays was remarked by M. Arnauld in 'L'Œuvre d'O. Wilde', in *La Grande Revue*, May 10th, 1897, and was the subject of particular study in E. Bendz, 'A propos de la *Salomé* d'Oscar Wilde', in *Englische Studien*, vol. li (1917–18), pp. 48–70. There is also a dissertation on the subject (Munich, 1913) by F. K. Brass, *O. Wildes Salome. Eine kritische Quellenstudie.*

[17] Bendz says: 'L'amour de Salomé, voilá l'idée originale de Wilde, voilà son coup de maître !'

[18] On the tradition followed by Heine cf. Reimarus, *Stoffgeschichte der Salome-Dichtungen* (Leipzig, Wigand, 1913), pp. 46 et seq., 101–5.

[19] Quoted from *Atta Troll and Other Poems by Heinrich Heine*, Translated by T. S. Egan (London, Chapman and Hall, 1876).

[20] In his picture entitled *Capital Execution under the Moorish Kings*, Regnault treated the blood of the victims in the same spirit in which he had treated the jewels in *Salomé*, like the 'hail of rubies' to which a seventeenth-century poet had compared the blood of a chastised courtesan. See chap. i, p. 37.

[21] Note that the way in which the name is written is that of Flaubert. In fact, Laforgue's *Salomé* (which the author had conceived as early as 1882) is partly a parody of Flaubert's story. See F. Ruchon, *Jules Laforgue* (Geneva, Editions Albert Ciana, 1924), p. 110. But the figure of Salome is barely seen in Flaubert and he gives it the suggestion of an artless urchin, so that it could scarcely account for Laforgue's fantasy.

[21A] In 1894 a drama by Antoine Sabatier was performed, *Le Baiser de Jean*, in which Salome is presented in the same way as in Wilde as a hysterical woman, with demoniacal and macabre traits, mad with sadistic love. Salome has inspired also the Russian poet Alexander Blok (the second poem on *Venice*, in his *Italian poems*, 1909), and the Portuguese Eugenio de Castro (*Salomé e outros poemas*, 1896), the author of *Belkiss* (see addition to note 34 of chap. iv of this book).

[22] *A rebours*, pp. 259–60.

[23] A. Rouveyre, *Le Reclus et le retors, Gourmont et Gide* (Paris, Crès, 1927), pp. 55–6.

[24] *Salammbô*, chap. iii.

[25] *Certains*, p. 78.

[26] *A rebours*, Preface, p. xi.

²⁷ Id., pp. 211 et seq. Perhaps not only of Catholicism, if one may interpret as a ceremony similar to the Black Mass the profanation of the Eleusinian Mysteries of which Thucydides speaks (VI. xxviii: 'καὶ τὰ μυστήρια ἅμα ὡς ποιεῖται ἐν οἰκίαις ἐφ' ὕβρει'—'and also that the mysteries were being performed in private houses in mockery'.)

²⁸ This is Sainte-Beuve's definition, *Chateaubriand et son groupe*, op. cit., vol. i, p. 89. On the subject of Chateaubriand's inspiration, the same critic wrote (id., vol. i, p. 246) that this inspiration may be said to be 'infernale et satanique . . . dans toute sa franchise, dans tout son blasphème', in a passage of the letter of René to Céluta (see chap. iii, § 7): 'Mais elle ne se produit ailleurs qu'à demi voilée et comme dans un faux jour, en se mêlant frauduleusement à un rayonnement d'en haut.'

²⁹ *La Vie littéraire*, Troisième Série, p. 121.

* *p. 321, line 32, add:* That very same Léon Bloy, who, as we have seen (addition to note 191 of chap. iii), shuddered with horror while reading Lautréamont, professed to be a follower of Barbey d'Aurevilly (cf. L. B. Martineau, *Souvenirs d'un ami*, Paris, Librairie de France, 1924, pp. 95–6) and, under the influence of *Les Diaboliques* (see Section 9 of this chapter), wrote *Histoires désobligeantes*, Paris, Dentu, 1894, which are a literary counterpart of Wiertz's pictures (see chap. iv, note 80): we find there a husband who asks his wife's lovers to dinner in order that they should eat her heart, a son whom covetousness of the inheritance causes to leave in the crematory furnace the coffin with his father who, being still alive, tries to get out of it; mothers who poison their children in order to please their lovers, wretched fathers blackmailed into yielding their daughters to old boon companions, revellers who throw bread into lavatories under the eyes of hungry beggars, babies killed in the cradle because the expression of their faces stirs hateful memories in a father. One of the characters of *La Femme pauvre* (Paris, Mercure de France, 1897) bursts out into these words 'impies, exécrables, venues de l'Abîme':

'Cette Antoinette avec qui tu as couché, triste cochon, et que j'ai fait élever moi-même, avec tant de soin, par une vieille cafarde, pour qu'un jour elle devînt mon petit succube le plus excitant, sais-tu qui elle est? Non, n'est-ce pas? tu ne t'en doutes guère, ni elle non plus. J'étais informé, heure par heure, de ce qui se passait entre vous deux. Mais *il ne me déplaisait pas que l'inceste préparât l'inceste*, car JE SUIS SON PÈRE ET TU ES SON FRÈRE.'

And soon after: 'Cette histoire vous fait peur, Clotilde. Elle est banale, cependant.' [Add. 1950]

³⁰ One aspect of this, in relation to Spanish picturesqueness, was dealt with by me in a chapter of *Unromantic Spain* (London and New York, Knopf, 1929), 'Du Sang, de la volupté, de la mort.' See also F. Paulhan, *Le Nouveau mysticisme* (Paris, Alcan, 1891) pp. 90 et seq., in the chapter 'L'amour du mal'.

Of the Spanish authors who have mixed the sacred with the profane, themes of lust and death, Ramón del Valle-Inclán, is worth mentioning: in what is perhaps his masterpiece, the *Sonata de primavera* (in *Sonatas—Memorias del Marqués de Bradomín*, 1902–7), he creates a magical atmosphere which reminds us at the same time of Hoffmann's whims and of the decadent languor of D'Annunzio's *Vergini delle rocce*. Macabre and monstrous hints (incest is 'el magnifico pecado de las tragedias antiguas'), the excitement deriving from committing sin in a convent, from attending mass after sinning, recur in the other *Sonatas*, chiefly in those *de estío* and *de invierno*. Notwithstanding all this, the protagonist declares that he has always preferred to be the marquis of Bradomin rather than 'ese divin Marqués de Sade', and that the bloody rose of perversion has never opened in his own love-affairs. [Add. 1950]

[31] *Trois Primitifs* (Paris, 1905).

[31A] An indictment of all these 'neo-Catholic' writers from an orthodox point of view will be found in the chapter 'De sensuali mysticismo recentioris cuiusdam scholae pseudo-catholicae' of Father Laurence Janssens's *Summa Theologica*, Rome, Tipografia poliglotta vaticana, 1929, vol. viii, Appendix iii, Sect. ii, Membr. ii, Cap. ii, R. lxxxii, pp. 649–67. 'Sed et aliud vitium in hac "esthétique délicate" est severe corripendum: realismus scilicet impudentissimus, quo omnia, etiam pessima, ita describuntur, ut inter Jammismum et Zolismum vix aliquid intersit, nisi falsus iste mysticismus qui priorem altero reddit quasi peiorem.' [Add. 1950]

[32] *Variété II* (Paris, Nouvelle Revue Française, 1930), pp. 235 et seq. An important study is Helen Trudgian's *L'Esthétique de J.-K. Huysmans*, Paris, Conard, 1934.

[33] On this subject see J. Bricaud, *J.-K. Huysmans et le satanisme*, d'après des documents inédits (Paris, Chacornac, 1913), especially pp. 67 et seq.

[34] Baudelaire, *Œuvres posthumes*, p. 411.

Babbitt, *Rousseau and Romanticism*, op. cit., p. 332, footnote, sees the title of Huysmans's book anticipated in Seneca (*To Lucilius*, ep. cxxii), where he speaks of those who try to be original at all costs and do everything differently from the others: 'ut ita dicam, *retro* vivunt'. [Add. 1950]

[35] Draft of the preface to *Les Fleurs du mal* in *Œ. post.*

[36] The analogy was noted by Seylaz (op. cit., note 9 of chap. i, pp. 171 et seq.) who calls des Esseintes 'réplique parisienne de Roderick Usher'. Des Esseintes also compares himself in one point with Usher (*À rebours*, pp. 254–5): 'se sentant ainsi que la désolant Usher, envahi par une transe irraisonnée, par une frayeur sourde.'

[37] *Mes haines*, p. 66. As for Zola's further affinities with the Decadents, see in ch. xv of *Thérèse Raquin* the passage culminating in the sentence: 'Le crime leur semblait une jouissance aiguë,' &c.

[38] *Pages retrouvées*, p. 182.

[39] *Manette Salomon*, pp. 286–8. Quoted by H. Bachelin, *J.-K. Huysmans* (Paris, Perrin, 1926), pp. 83–84. See, in Bachelin's book, chaps. v ('Le Parisien enthousiaste de Paris') and vi ('Les Faubourgs et la Bièvre lépreux et charmants'). Cf. chap. i of the present volume, p. 45.

[40] *Là-bas*, p. 301.

⁴¹ On Huysmans in respect to satanism, see the book of J. Bricaud (op. cit., note 33, pp. 10 et seq.):

'Un astrologue parisien, Eugène Ledos, le Gevingy de *Là-bas* — et un ancien prêtre habitant Lyon, l'abbé Boullan (Docteur Johannes in *Là-bas*), achevèrent de le documenter — faussement parfois . . . sur le satanisme moderne (Boullan attributed his own satanic practices to the Rosicrucians, p.65) . . . La correspondance entre Huysmans et l'abbé Boullan est volumineuse; elle date du 6 février 1890 au 4 janvier 1893.'

See pp. 13 et seq. for the identification of certain of the characters in *Là-bas*; and pp. 19 and 20 of Bricaud's sequel, *Huysmans occultiste et magicien*, 'Avec une Notice sur les Hosties magiques qui servirent à Huysmans pour combattre les envoûtements' (Paris, Chacornac, 1913).

'La vérité est que si certains détails de la Messe Noire sont empruntés à des documents anciens tirés soit des Archives de Vintras, soit des pièces du procès de la fameuse voyante diabolique Cantianille, Huysmans avait bien assisté à une des messes noires dites assez fréquemment dans le quartier même qu'il habitait, la rue de Sèvres'.

See also further on, p. 317, for his relations with the Rosicrucians. 'Huysmans disait encore, parlant de Guaita et de Péladan, qu'ils avaient tout tenté contre lui, avant et surtout après son roman *Là-bas*'. (Bricaud, *Huysmans et le satanisme*, p. 37). He would have us believe that he received 'coups de poing fluidiques', &c.! The practices of the Abbé Boullan contained every sort of thing—'du mysticisme délirant, de l'érotomanie, de la scatologie, du sadisme et du satanisme' (p. 66). In this connexion Bricaud refers one to the book by S. de Guaita, *Le Serpent de la Genèse*, chap. vi, dedicated to the 'Modernes Avatars du Sorcier'. The volume forms the second part of *Essais de sciences maudites* by Guaita, who was a disciple of Éliphas Lévi (Paris, vol. i, Carré, 1890; vol. ii, Librairie du Merveilleux, 1891; vol. iii, Bibl. Chacornac, 1897). Guaita deals with *Là-bas* on pp. 504-5 of vol. ii.

On Huysmans's Satanism see also R. Schwaeblé, *Le Satanisme flagellé: Satanistes contemporains, incubat, succubat, sadisme et satanisme*, Paris, R. Dutaire (later H. Daragon) [1912], chap. v, p. 67 (a slight work, for all its high-sounding title; it is worth quoting only because its author knew Huysmans intimately). [Add. 1950]

⁴² e.g. *Justine*, vol. ii, p. 171, vol. iv, p. 290; *Philosophie dans le boudoir*, vol. i, p. 153.

⁴³ Paris, Crès, 1927, vol. i, pp. 318 et seq.

⁴⁴ E. Bossard et R. de Maulde, *Gilles de Rais, maréchal de France, dit Barbe-bleue* (1404–1440) (Paris, Champion, 1886).

⁴⁵ Bossard, pp. 10 and 12; E. Gabory, *La Vie et la mort de Gilles de Raiz dit — à tort — Barbebleue* (Paris, Perrin, 1926), p. 135. Gilles stated clearly: 'Ces voluptés abjectes, ces crimes atroces, j'en ai conçu seul la pensée. J'ai tué par plaisir, pour ma propre délectation et sans le conseil de qui que ce soit.' Gabory's confutation of the tradition that sees in Gilles the prototype of Bluebeard is incontestable (pp. 228 et seq.). In the popular imagination, however, the two characters were mixed up together. See

also L. Hernandez, *Le procès inquisitorial de G. de Rais* (Paris, Bibliothèque des Curieux, 1921), p. lxxxviii, and E. Richard, 'La Constance du satanisme; la vraie histoire de Gilles de Rais', in the *Mercure de France* for November 1st, 1921.

⁴⁶ *Là-bas*, pp. 210–11.

⁴⁷ The sadistic theme of at least one of the *Diaboliques* (*A un dîner d'athées*) had already been used by d'Aurevilly in an early tale, *Le Cachet d'onyx* (1831), which shows all the characteristics both of sensibility and of style, with which d'Aurevilly appeared to be endowed half a century later. This author provides one of the most obvious illustrations of the close relationship between the Romanticism of 1830 and the Decadence. Cf. *Le Cachet d'onyx, Léa, Fragment* (Paris, La Connaissance, 1921), with a short essay by R. L. Doyon on 'Du Marquis de Sade à Barbey d'Aurevilly'. Cf. also chap. i, § 5.

⁴⁸ *La Vie littéraire*, vol. iii, pp. 44–5.

⁴⁹ *A rebours*, p. 213.

⁵⁰ See chap. iv, p. 209.

⁵¹ Act 1, sc. 2.

⁵² France, *La Vie littéraire*, vol. iii, p. 122. Cf. also J. de la Varende, 'Villiers de l'Isle-Adam', in the *Revue des Deux Mondes* for November 1st, 1938, pp. 175–89.

⁵³ See the chapter 'Swinburne and "le vice anglais" '.

⁵⁴ Chapitre xx, *Le Roi des épouvantements*.

The idea may have come from D. Boucicault's drama *The Octoroon*, 1859. See Allardyce Nicoll, *Late Nineteenth Century Drama*, Cambridge University Press, 1946, vol. i, p. 88.

⁵⁵ *Le Convive des dernières fêtes*. It seems that this character actually existed. Dühren, *Das Geschlechtsleben in England*, op. cit., vol. iii, p. 76, tells of an English baronet, Sir Claude de Crespigny, well known in the county of Essex as the 'Amateur Hangman', who used to take delight in performing the functions of an executioner, especially when it was a case of hanging women, when a horrible *rictus* used to contract his face. See also H. France, *En 'Police Court'* (Paris, Charpentier, 1891) pp. 249–50.

⁵⁶ See Seylaz, op. cit., p. 136.

⁵⁷ *La Vie littéraire*, vol. iii, pp. 237–8.

⁵⁸ On Guaita, the curious offshoot of a crossing of German, Italian and Lorrain blood, see M. Barrès, *Un Renovateur de l'occultisme, Stanislas de Guaita* (1861–1898) (Paris, Chamuel, 1898); also *Amori et dolori sacrum*, pp. 115–46.

In 1883 Guaita had published (chez Lemerre) a small volume of verse dedicated to Leconte de Lisle, *La Muse noire*, in which the usual Decadent themes recur. The Muse invoked by the poet is 'une négresse aux formes opulentes', an image which is derived from Baudelaire and Rops:

> Ange de la Douleur qu'on ne peut consoler
> Elle avait dans le Ciel deux ailes étendues.

De son corps ruisselait l'effluve des luxures
Et des rares désirs inassouvis toujours.
Sa gorge palpitait, où saignaient des morsures
Ouvertes sous la dent féroce des amours.

Pleins d'étoiles, des pleurs roulèrent de ses yeux
Où flamboyait l'orgie en sa splendeur païenne . . .

Her kiss is 'sinistre, enivrant, infernal'. As for pagan orgies, the poem *Fantaisie césarienne* presents a *blasé* emperor who imagines himself burning a victim over a slow fire:

Que ce soit une femme — et qu'elle soit fort belle.

Oh! supplice très doux à voir, digne d'un dieu!
De douleur jaillira le lait de sa mamelle
Sous le regard du ciel ironiquement bleu;

Puis son petit enfant la verra, toute nue,
Par la flamme léchée abominablement, &c.

There are not lacking the usual maledictions against the 'Nature Mère', the Promethean challenge and the hymn to Lucifer (*Les Paroles d'un maudit*) who has taught the poet 'le charme de l'Enfer'. Lucifer himself succumbs to the charm of an impure woman 'aux grands yeux gris de fer' (*L'Impure*). The poet celebrates the 'buveurs d'opium, de haschisch et d'absinthe' who absorb 'le vertige extatique du Crime', and fathom 'les arcanes suprêmes—de la Perdition et de la Volupté'. To Maurice Rollinat, whose *Névroses* were at that time having a terrific success, Guaita dedicated a little piece of vampire poetry called *Les Spectres*.

59 *Huysmans et le satanisme*, quoted in note 33; and *Huysmans occultiste et magicien*, quoted in note 41. On the occultist movements in France see the latter volume, p. 9.

Similar currents of satanism also manifested themselves among the English Decadents, especially in Aleister Crowley, founder of the review *The Equinox, the official organ of the A ∴ A ∴ : the review of scientific illuminism* (1909–13). Crowley started his career by writing poems which were a slavish imitation of Swinburne and later devoted himself to the practice of black magic. In order to get some idea of Crowley's poetry it is only necessary to read his *Jezabel*, in which are to be found effusions of this kind:

Now let me die, at last desired,
    At last beloved of thee my queen.
Now let me die, with blood attired,
    Thy servant naked and obscene;
To thy white skull, thy palms, thy feet,
Clinging, dead, infamous, complete.

Now let me die, to mix my soul
    With thy red soul, to join our hands,
To weld us in one perfect whole,
    To link us with desirous bands.
Now let me die, to mate in hell
With thee, O harlot Jezabel.

See also the poems *Madonna of the Golden Eyes* (in *The Temple of the Holy Ghost*), *Messaline* (in *Alice: an Adultery*), an imitation of Swinburne's *Faustine*, collected in *The Works of Aleister Crowley* (Foyers, Society for the Propagation of Religious Truth, 1905). In *Gargoyles* (*being strangely wrought images of Life and Death*, Foyers, id., 1906), the poem *Kali*, a hymn to the sanguinary goddess who breaks the poet 'on the wheel of woe', is modelled, like *Jezabel*, on *Dolores*. Among the innumerable works of Crowley may be mentioned the play *Tannhäuser* (London, Kegan Paul, &c., 1902) in which the accents of Swinburne are imitated in a disconcerting manner. Crowley also, naturally, goes into ecstasies over the Hermaphrodite. The following is taken from a sonnet 'for E. F. Kelly's drawing of an Hermaphrodite':

> O body pale and beautiful with sin!
> O breasts with venom swollen by the snakes
> Of passion, whose cold slaver slimes and slakes
> The soul-consuming fevers that within
> Thy heart the fires of hell on earth begin!

Note the curious Swinburnian alliteration in the third line.

Another English satanic occultist is Austin Osman Spare, who wrote *The Book of Pleasure* (*self-love*), *the Psychology of Ecstasy* (London, published by the Author, 1913), with curious symbolic illustrations.

[60] See E. Thovez, *L'Arco d'Ulisse* (quoted in chap. iv, note 94) chapters 'I fondi segreti del Superuomo e il Mistero del nuovo Rinascimento', and 'Le briciole del Superuomo', already published as articles in the *Gazzetta Letteraria* of Jan. 18th and Feb. 29th, 1896.

Especially noteworthy is the derivation of the Wagnerian parenthesis in the *Trionfo della Morte* from Péladan's *Victoire du mari*, in which, during a performance of *Tristan and Isolde* at Bayreuth, the two lovers Adar and Izel, bewitched by Wagner's 'satanic' music, abandon themselves to erotic excesses.

'Jusqu'à Bayreuth, la volupté était leur recherche, depuis le sort jeté par l'œuvre de Wagner, les spasmes ne servaient plus que de moyens à leur plaisir; le but c'était l'ivresse de la mort' (p. 98).

For Péladan 'une Wagnererie' (p. 102) is practically synonymous with a Witches' Sabbath.

'Ce finale inouï, où le rut de la chair se mêle au rut de l'âme, où l'ithyphallie domine le désespoir; cette provocation à la mort et ces malédictions au soleil faisaient entrevoir au penseur le grand mystère de la seconde mort. Wagner, comme Balzac, a pentaculé avec l'adorable divination du génie, l'arcane de l'amour suprême' (p. 94).

'Ô le dommage que Wagner ait ignoré la Kabbale!' exclaims Péladan. However, Doctor Sexthental, who commits a 'stupre sidéral' with Izel (pp. 146 et seq.) was not ignorant of it. These curious pages of Péladan's novel, and others similar (110–111) may be read as a complement to the volumes of Bricaud.

[60A] After D'Annunzio's borrowings became known, Marcel Schwob wrote (in *Le Phare de la Loire* for January 28th, 1896, an article reprinted in *Œuvres Complètes*, *Lettres Parisiennes*, Paris, Bernouard, 1929, p. 101):

'On ne peut constater qu'une chose: c'est que bien peu de gens apparemment lisaient en France les "éthopées péladanesques", puisqu'il a fallu que le cri "au voleur" nous vînt d'Italie, pour nous ouvrir les yeux. . . . C'est peut-être que les éthopées étaient ennuyeuses, et que nous n'avons pas de goût pour les "sareries". Autrement il faut convenir qu'elles étaient bien à notre portée, et, de plus, décorées d'androgynes alléchantes pour les faire vendre. Mais on ne les lisait guère. Soyons donc reconnaissants à M. D'Annunzio d'en avoir tiré de belles pages et laissons crier les ratés dont les livres ne se vendront ni plus ni moins.' [Add. 1950]

60B Gautier was enraptured by the delightful, exciting ambiguity of the dancer Fanny Elssler ('the outline of her arms has something both soft and nervy which recalls the shape of an extraordinary handsome and slightly effeminate youth, like Bacchus and Antinous', &c.: a sentence which betrays acquaintance with Winckelmann). [Add. 1950]

61 *La Fille aux yeux d'or* (*The Girl with the Golden Eyes*), by Balzac, translated by E. Dowson, with illustrations by Ch. Conder and cover-design on back by Aubrey Beardsley, 1896. Cf. W. Rothenstein, *Men and Memories*, vol. i, p. 244:

'When Lane dropped Beardsley after the Wilde scandal, Beardsley at once found a patron in Smithers. Smithers was a bizarre and improbable figure—a rough Yorkshireman with a strong local accent and uncertain *h*'s, the last man, one had thought, to be a Latin scholar and a disciple of M. le Marquis de Sade. Smithers had a bookshop in Bond Street, where he dealt in fine editions and in erotic art and letters . . '. He commissioned Conder to illustrate *La Fille aux yeux d'or*. This was Conder's favourite story. The subject appealed to him strongly, as did certain parts of *Mademoiselle de Maupin*.'

In *La Fille aux yeux d'or* Lesbian love is however presented rather discreetly, and only towards the end of the novel does it reveal its volcanic fury. [Add. 1950]

62 In this connexion see R. Jasinski, *Les Années romantiques de Th. Gautier* (quoted in chap. iii, note 85), pp. 288 et seq. See also the note on *Gamiani*, chap. iii, note 109.

Jules-Robert Auguste was the painter of this 1830 Lesbian love; he delighted in representing two beauties, a white daughter of the North and a negress, melting in each other's arms in a tropical scene (gouache in the Alfred Beurdelay Collection, pastel in the Orléans museum); he gave thus a lascivious version of the blonde—brunette *motif* which was a favourite with the Romantics. See Charles Saunier, 'Monsieur Auguste', in the *Gazette des Beaux-Arts*, 1910, vol. i, 441; vol. ii, pp. 51, 229. The contrast between two opposite types of beauty, already dealt with by Greuze in *The Two Friends* (Louvre), and in *The Two Sisters* (or *The Comparison*, Georges Petit sale, 1912, no. 156); by Mme Vigée-Lebrun in *The Two Sisters* (Sedelmeyer sale, i–ii, Paris, 1912), by William Owen in *The Sisters*, is taken up again and again by the painters of the eighteen-forties (for instance Dubufe's *Blonde and Brunette*, Overbeck's *Italy and Germany*, &c.); in literature, we have the sisters Minna and Brenda in Scott's *Pirate*, Rebecca and Rowena in *Ivanhoe*, &c. Courbet's *Les Dormeuses* (reproduced in Ch. Léger, *Courbet*, Paris, Crès, 1929, pl. 44) is particularly interesting because of its lascivious implications. Oriani, in *Al di là*, Bologna, Cappelli, 1927, vol. ii, p. 197, causes Elisa di Monero to say in an ardent confession of Lesbian love to Mimy: 'Why did Courbet, in a moment of genius, paint Venus and Psyche? You are sleeping, blonde, and the brunette cannot steal like a wolf into your room. . . .' [Add. 1950]

[63] *Les Confessions*, op. cit., vol. ii, p. 13, chap. 'Où il n'est pas question du rocher de Leucade'. The subject of Lesbian love during the second Empire is treated by P. Petruccelli della Gattina in the *Cronaca Bizantina* of 1883 (series of articles entitled 'Grandi Etere').

[64] Rothenstein, op. cit., p. 59. On *fin-de-siècle* Lesbianism see also Colette, *Ces plaisirs . . .* , pp. 97 et seq., and p. 107 on the fascination of the Androgyne.

[65] *Essais de sciences maudites*, op. cit., vol. i, p. 71. See pp. 124 et seq.: 'Analyse de l'Androgyne d'Henry Khunrath', especially p. 134, 'L'Androgyne de Khunrath représente *Adam-Ève*, ou l'Homme Universel éparpillé dans la matière et sombré dans le devenir'. On p. 248 of vol. ii, part 2 ('La Clef de la Magie Noire') it is maintained that the Androgyne represents the synthesis, 'la plenitude ontologique', &c.

[66] 'Épilogue' in *Leonardo da Vinci; conferenze fiorentine* (Milan, Treves, 1910; course of lectures held in the spring of 1906 at Florence, under the auspices of the Società Leonardo da Vinci), p. 308. Moreau had in his vestibule a photograph of the *Saint John*, 'dont le mystère le devait séduire' (Montesquiou, op. cit., p. 13.)

And Renée Vivien, in the novel *Une Femme m'apparut . . .* (Paris, Lemerre, 1904), p. 1: 'Par un soir indécis, l'Annonciatrice vint vers moi. Le visage de l'Annonciatrice était mystérieux et troublant comme celui du San Giovanni de Léonard.' [Add. 1950]

[67] I have already said (p. 254) that the figure of the Princess d'Este was partly modelled on the Princess Belgiojoso (1808–71), who was one of the *lionnes* of Paris from 1835 to 1842. Péladan's Princess is an 'allumeuse d'hommes'; Princess Belgiojoso is described as follows in the *Confessions* of Houssaye:

'Cette grande dame, qui avait tout pour elle, n'était pas bien sûre d'avoir un cœur, car elle n'avait que la passion de l'esprit; elle voulait bien qu'on se donnât à elle, mais elle ne se donnait pas. Elle servait avec une grâce adorable le festin de l'amour; puis elle s'envolait au moment de se mettre à table.'

The furnishing of the Princess d'Este's rooms recalls that of the rooms of the Princess Belgiojoso, especially of her study, which was adorned with Primitive paintings with gold backgrounds and filled with the tomes of the Church Fathers. Princess Belgiojoso was busy writing a work upon the dogma of the Catholic Church (which she published at Paris in 1842), and used to have conferences with fashionables preachers, particularly with the Abbé Cœur. Of this book, Sainte-Beuve wrote to Madame Juste Olivier (quoted by A. Augustin-Thierry, *La Princesse Belgiojoso*, op. cit., p. 28):

'Il a paru un livre encore inachevé; c'est sérieux, catholique d'intention, semi-pélagien et origénien de fond, d'un style très ferme, très simple, enfin une très précieuse curiosité, venant d'une Italienne galante, d'une Trivulce.'

Princess Belgiojoso also appeared in public and at the theatre in the squalid ash-coloured robe·of the Grey Sisters, with—supreme coquetry—a garland of white flowers on her head. These and other details, recorded by the contemporaries of the Princess, are to be found echoed in Péladan. The Princess d'Este, also, is a painter (like the Princess Belgiojoso), takes an interest in mysticism, and tries to seduce the priest Alta under the pretext of religious conversations. The husband of Péladan's Princess is an unbridled libertine, as was Prince Belgiojoso: in both cases the union was of short duration.

If, on the one hand, the presence of the Princess Belgiojoso in Paris helped to make popular the cause of Italian independence, it served, on the other hand, to revive in the minds of the Romantics the sinister legend of the Italian Renaissance (the Princess d'Este is 'l'Italienne vindicative et féroce') with the addition of a new macabre significance.

On Princess Belgiojoso, see also pp. 123, 178, 254, 293, and the book by Barbiera, op. cit., especially pp. 115 et seq., 136 et seq., 147 et seq., 151, 188. It can hardly be said that the Princess Belgiojoso is portrayed in the character of Laura Piaveni in Meredith's *Vittoria*, as is suggested by A. Luzio, *Garibaldi, Cavour, Verdi* (Turin, Bocca, 1924) p. 443. Laura Piaveni is a very abstractly described type of patriotic lady.

[68] Primaticcio had perhaps been brought into fashion by the Goncourts. Cf. *Manette Salomon*, p. 32:

'Le corps de Caroline Alibert, le corps d'une Ourania du Primatice, allongé, effilé, avec des extrémités si souples qu'elle faisait, d'un mouvement, passer tous les doigts d'une de ses mains l'un sous l'autre.'

[69] See, in *Certains* (1889) the essay on Bianchi (i.e. Francesco Bianchi Ferrari, the fifteenth-century painter) whose 'singulière personnalité' Huysmans contrasts with the 'sourdes médiocrités de Raphaël'. 'Le Louvre possède un seul tableau de Bianchi et de cette toile s'exhalent pour moi des émanations délicieuses, des captations dolentes, d'insidieux sacrilèges, des prières troubles.' (G. Moore, speaking of the taste of the decadents in *Mike Fletcher*, 1889, p. 39, gives a translation of this passage.)

Huysmans is speaking of a picture which is not by Bianchi Ferrari, but by Alessandro Araldi (Venturi, *Storia dell'Arte Italiana*, vol. vii, part 3, pp. 1121–4, fig. 845). Before reading his divagations, it may be of interest to see how the picture appears to a real art critic, B. Berenson (*The Italian Painters of the Renaissance*, Oxford University Press, 1932, p. 272):

'A still higher place belongs to the author of the Louvre altar-piece ascribed to him [Bianchi]. Its severely virginal Madonna, its earnest yet sweet young warrior saint, its angels, so intent upon their music, the large simplicity of its arrangement, the quiet landscape seen through slender columns, the motionless sky, all affect one like a calm sunset, when one is subdued, as by ritual, into harmony with one's surroundings.' [Add. 1950]

Huysmans dwells upon the androgynous charm of the figure of San Quintino (the true forerunner of the warrior-saints of Burne-Jones). See especially:

'L'aspect entier du saint fait rêver. Ces formes de garçonne, aux hanches un peu développées, ce col de fille, aux chairs blanches, ainsi qu'une moelle de sureau, cette bouche aux lèvres spoliatrices, cette taille élancée, ces doigts fureteurs égarés sur une arme, ce renflement de la cuirasse qui bombe à la place des seins et protège la chute divulguée du buste, ce linge qui s'aperçoit sous l'aisselle demeurée libre entre l'épaulière et le gorgerin, même ce ruban bleu de petite fille, attaché sous le menton, obsèdent. Toutes les assimilations éperdues de Sodome paraissent avoir été consenties par cet androgyne dont l'insinuante beauté, maintenant endolorie, se révèle purifiée déjà, comme transfigurée par la lente approche d'un Dieu. . . . Un chevalier qui, après avoir été affamé de tracas luxurieux, agonise sous le poids de ses peines.'

Huysmans describes minutely the various tortures to which this beautiful youth was subjected. Then he passes on to another insidious form of sacrilege. The various figures in the picture resemble each other:

'On dirait du Saint Benoît, le père, de Marie et du saint Quintin, la sœur et le frère, et du petit ange vêtu de rose jouant de la viole d'amour, l'enfant issu du diabolique accouplement de ces Saints. Le vieillard est un père qui a resisté aux aguets d'épouvantables stupres, et dont le fils et la fille ont cédé aux tentations de l'inceste et jouent la vie trop brève pour expier les terrifiantes délices de leur crime; l'enfant implore le pardon de son origine, et chante de dolentes litanies pour détourner la souveraine colère du Très-Haut.'

He imagines the painter to have 'travesti en de religieux costumes des podestats usés par les déboires du bonheur et les joies du vice'.

In the portrait of a girl by Bartolomeo da Venezia, in the Städelsches Kunstinstitut in Frankfurt (Venturi, vol. vii, part 4, p. 699, calls the portrait *La Cortigiana*) Huysmans also discovers a delicious, wicked air. The woman is offering a bunch of flowers and seems to be saying: 'Prends garde si tu acceptes; la menace est visible; l'offre est comminatoire, l'amour est sans lendemain; le spasme se prolonge en un râle d'agonie près d'elle.'

'Qu'est-ce que cet être énigmatique, cette androgyne implacable et jolie, si étonnamment de sang-froid quand elle provoque ? elle est impure mais elle joue franc jeu; elle stimule, mais elle avertit; elle est tentante mais réservée; elle est la pureté de l'impureté, "puritas impuritatis", selon l'expression de Juste Lipse; elle est en même temps l'instigatrice de la luxure et l'annonciatrice de l'expiation des joies des sens. . . . Les plus belles œuvres du Musée ne paraissent que des peintures, au sens strict du mot, en comparaison de celle-là qui va plus loin, qui est autre chose, qui pénètre, pour tout dire, dans le territoire de cet au-delà blâmable dont les dangereux anges de Botticelli entrebâillent parfois les portes.'

Then, enlarging upon the significance of the picture, he adds:

'Un fait est certain, elle vécut, pendant la Renaissance, dans cette Italie qui fut alors l'auge de toutes les luxures, le réservoir de tous les crimes; l'état des minuscules provinces régies par des despotes dont le sadisme s'exerçait en d'amoureux supplices, était effroyable, etc. . . . L'amour paraissait fade s'il restait naturel et ne franchissait pas le degré permis des parentés; et encore fallait-il, pour en relever le goût, le faire macérer dans une saumure de poisons, dans une sauce de sang. . . . À rêvasser devant cette fillette de Francfort, si prête à délibérément méfaire, je songe forcément au Pape Alexandre VI, à cet espagnol, père de nombreux enfants dont un né de son accouplement avec Lucrèce Borgia, sa fille.'

He imagines the portrait to be that of Giulia Farnese, the mistress of Pope Borgia, who 'avec son corps de garçonne pouvait prétendre aux alibis et varier, tout en restant femme, les menus du Pape.'

'Quelle qu'elle soit, elle n'en a pas moins l'âme d'une Giulia et elle en est une parente plus ou moins éloignée, avec sa mine pas bonne, son air défiant, son corps gracile et ses seins brefs; elle est charmante et elle est malsaine; elle dégage l'odeur vireux des plantes à fleurs vertes, des plantes à craindre; elle est de coupe-gorge et elle est de vénéfice. Avec ses prunelles si glacialement claires et sa petite moue méchante, elle surgit, telle qu'une Circé, ne laissant aux amoureux qu'elle provoque que deux alternatives, celle de l'étable et celle de la tombe.'

Péladan also evokes Circe, apropos of the Princess d'Este: 'Elle fut la fée mauvaise de Virgile, et aux rayons de ses yeux verts, s'opéra soudain l'immonde métamorphose.'

Huysmans concludes with this final ejaculation:

'La pseudo Giulia résume, à elle seule, toute la férocité de la luxure et tous les sacrilèges de la Renaissance. Cette créature qui tient, je le répète, de la sibylle et de la sorcière, de la courtisane et de la bayadère, concentre dans sa tenue, dans son regard, les infernales manigances des principats Italiens et de la Rome païenne des Papes. Elle est réellement plus qu'une femme, plus même que l'illusoire Papesse Jeanne, l'incarnation de l'Apostoline à laquelle Lucifer, parodiant l'Évangile, a dit par trois fois: 'Pais mes boucs'. Elle est celle qu'assistait dans les consistoires des cardinaux simoniaques, L'Esprit du Mal; elle est un symbole, le symbole des hontes de la Papauté, le symbole échoué à Francfort, dans la ville même qui sonne aujourd'hui la curée de l'Église, entre les mains des Juifs.'

It is easy to discern in this portrait by Huysmans the influence of Pater's Gioconda.

It is noteworthy that G. Swarzenski considers the picture to be actually an idealized portrait of Lucrezia Borgia ('Bartolomeo Veneto und Lucrezia Borgia', in *Staedeljahrbuch*, vol. ii, 1922, pp. 63–72: Swarzenski quotes Huysmans's passage). [Add. 1950]

70 On green eyes, see p. 327 of this chapter, also the chapter 'Swinburne and "le vice anglais" '.

70A Already Musset had been impressed by Allori's picture:

Mais qui peut oublier cette fausse Judith,
Et dans la blanche main d'une perfide amante
La tête qu'en mourant Allori suspendit?

(*Contes d'Espagne et d'Italie*) [Add. 1950]

71 See the chapter cited in note 70.

72 See above, chap. iv, § 6. It was the idea of sexual pleasure as a weapon of religious propaganda that caused Péladan to write, in his *Réponse à Tolstoi* (Paris, Chamuel, 1898, p. 211): 'C'est dans les bras nus des reines que ce sont convertis les rois barbares.'

73 A curious application of the method of Sue to certain fictitious doings at the Vatican may be seen in the thirteenth (the last but one) of the novels of the 'éthopée', *Finis Latinorum*, in which the Jesuits, according to custom (cf. Sue's *Le Juif errant*), represent the Spirit of Evil which is finally put to shame. Cf. p. 377:

' "La Compagnie de Jésus va mourir: car elle n'a plus rien de Jésus, elle n'est plus qu'une secte de mahométans. . . . .

' "Assassin, empoisonneur, monstre pervers, honte de toute religion, je te dégrade au nom de l'Agneau".

'Et le mage arracha le crucifix qui pendait au cou du jésuite et l'en souffleta.'

74 The work of Bourges had a certain degree of success in its own time and was not without influence on Lorrain, who was also a friend of E. de Goncourt (see especially *Les Noronsoff*, of which I speak on pp. 353 et seq.; *Monsieur de Phocas*, for a criminal suggestion conveyed by the corruptor through a work of art; *La Princesse sous verre*, &c.), and also on Mendès (*Zo'har*, see above, pp. 344 et seq.).

75 'La vie et la mort d'un clown' in the *Constitutionnel* of Aug. 25th, 1879; the article was published later in the volume *Le Roman contemporain*.

76 Pascoli indulges, but more soberly, in a similar macabre fantasy in *L'Etèra* (*Poemi di Ate*, in *Poemi Conviviali*).

77 It is possible that Mendès was here remembering a tale from the *Thousand and One Nights*, in which a prince is buried in the vault of a necropolis with his sister, and both are found burnt to ashes by the same divine fire which destroyed Gomorrha.

77A Among the sadistic demons in Mendès's Chamber of Horrors we may mention also the drunken dwarf Alas Schlemp in *Luscignole*, Paris, Dentu, 1892, who blinds with white-hot irons his little niece Luscignole in the same way as he had blinded nightingales to improve their song. The novel concludes with the words:

'Jamais, quand ses yeux étaient ouverts, elle n'a aussi mystérieusement, aussi tendrement, aussi éperdument chanté! et elle s'extasie d'elle-même! ... résignée, inconsciemment, à l'implacable loi qui impose comme condition à la parfaite beauté du chant, la douleur, l'ombre, et, au milieu de toute la vie, l'exil.'

Thus the gist of the novel is a repulsive variation of the theme: 'Les plus désespérés sont les chants les plus beaux.' (See Chap. I, Section 2.) There is in the novel also a young German ruler, Frederick, king of Thuringia, famous for his musical enthusiasm, for the construction of castles in the mountains, no less than for his disinclination to women, in short a thin disguise of Ludwig II of Bavaria (his favourite musician, Hans Hammer, is, of course, Wagner). [Add. 1950]

78 *Monsieur Vénus*, 1902 edition, p. 42:

'Son père (Raoule's) avait été un de ces débauchés épuisés que les œuvres du Marquis de Sade font rougir, mais pour une autre raison que celle de la pudeur.'

79 On Dostoievsky's psychic state, see S. Freud, 'Dostoievsky and Parricide', translated by D. F. Tait in *The Realist*, July 1929. Freud describes Dostoievsky as a 'sadomasochist'. The episode of the little girl of twelve years old in *Stavrogin's Confession* is the most clearly symptomatic, and, in the same fragment, the joy of being despised, cuffed, ill-treated, is described in no doubtful terms. Stavrogin marries a lame, weak-minded servant-girl: the idea of marriage with an extremely abject being thrills him. He decides to circulate his confession by scattering the pages broadcast, to send it to the newspapers and to have it published abroad in translations. Here there are all the appearances of masochism and exhibitionism. Profanation follows. Stavrogin smashes a crucifix. 'You honour the Holy Spirit without knowing it', Bishop Tikhon says to him. It seems to be a similar story to that of Baudelaire's Catholicism. In *The Brothers Kara-*

mazov Dmitri says that he is ready to marry Grushenka if she wishes: when her lovers come, he will retire into the next room, he will polish their boots, attend to the samovar, 'fag' for them. This situation was adopted by Western writers, following the example of the Russian novel, e.g. by Frank Wedekind in the *Büchse der Pandora*, Act III.

⁸⁰ Another of Dostoievsky's women, a certain countess in *Insulted and Injured*, 'was so voluptuous that the Marquis de Sade might have taken lessons from her'. One cannot help wondering whether Dostoievsky was here speaking from real knowledge of Sade's work. Vogüé, op. cit., hints at sadism in Dostoievsky (1910 edition, p. 251).

⁸¹ Translation by Constance Garnett (London, Heinemann, 1912), pp. 109–10. It must be noted, however, that the word 'Sodom' in Russian does not exactly evoke the image of a sin against nature: in Russian the word 'sodòm' is used for 'hubbub', 'confusion' (cf. Italian 'far bordello') (communication from L. Ginzburg). So that a Western reader may easily come to exaggerate the significance of the passage quoted.

⁸² The Russian soul, according to Dostoievsky, is *naturaliter* inclined to sadism : 'I believe that the fundamental need of the Russian soul is a thirst for suffering, a constant thirst in everything and from all time' (*Diary of an Author*). It may well be that he is here speaking particularly of that sort of suffering and pain which constitutes a catharsis, but any one can see how short a step it is from this to the application to suffering of the principle of 'art for art's sake'. It suffices to quote as an illustration the necrophilo-algolagnic orgy which concludes *The Idiot*, and the character of the invalid Lisaveta in *Karamazov*.

The habit, when generalized, has no more moral significance than the murderous marriage of the praying mantis. In *Karamazov* (p. 137) Fyodor Pavlovitch describes a tradition of Mokroe:

'At Mokroe I was talking to an old man, and he told me: "There's nothing we like so much as sentencing girls to be thrashed, and we always give the lads the job of thrashing them. And the girl he has thrashed to-day, the young man will ask in marriage to-morrow. So it quite suits the girls, too", he said. There's a set of de Sades for you !'

In another place Ivan says:

'With us blows are a natural thing, the rod and the whip, all that is a national characteristic . . . Rods and whips are something that belongs to us, that cannot be taken away. . . We have the ready and immediate pleasure that accompanies the historic torture of the rods.'

See the whole chapter.

A further illustration is supplied by Maxim Gorky's short story *Red* (1900), on the relations between Vaska, the flogger of prostitutes, and the girl Aksinya (see Maxim Gorky, *A Book of Short Stories*, ed. by A. Yarmolinsky and Baroness Moura Budberg, with a Foreword by A. Huxley, London, Cape, 1939). [Add. 1950]

⁸²ᴬ There is only a partial affinity between the aspects of sensibility and taste we are analysing, and the work of A. Strindberg, whose occasionally sadistic accents (for instance in *Miss Julia*, 1888, in *Simoom*, 1890, in *Sir Bengt's Lady*, &c.) are not the main feature of the complex picture

of exasperated and very personal revolt, both sexual and social, which is presented by this writer. The hyperbolical horrors described by him in plays and novels such as *The Spook Sonata* and *Black Flags* remind us of Pétrus Borel's *Contes immoraux*; the figure of the woman in *The Father* and in *Le Plaidoyer d'un fou* may appear to us of the same kind as the Fatal Woman we have seen in chap. iv; and Strindberg's qualms and dabbling in magic (he believed in Péladan's prophetic mission) may seem to possess a family likeness with Huysmans; but the atmosphere, the *tempo* of Strindberg are different from those of the decadents we are studying. Suffering from a schizophrenic process of a paranoiac type, Strindberg offers in any case a fit study for a psychoanalyst (see K. Bachler, *A. Strindberg, eine psycho-analytische Studie*, Vienna, 1931, and the chapter 'Il dramma dell' erotismo decadente' in M. Gabrieli's *August Strindberg*, Göteborg, 1945). Strindberg next to the Russian novelists has been the paramount influence on German literature of the *fin de siècle*. [Add. 1950]

83 Édouard Conte, quoted on p. 137 of G. Normandy's book on Lorrain referred to in note 12 of chap. i. See also Normandy's later volumes on *Jean Lorrain* (Paris, Rasmussen, 1927), and *Jean Lorrain intime* (Paris, Michel, 1929). On p. 73 of the former see the following quotation from a letter of Lorrain's:

'. . . Mes sens ont fait naufrage dans la bataille, et je sors de la lutte ruiné physiquement, mais moralement affiné, délié, reposé, avec des aspirations bleuâtres vers les sveltesses et les longues, les fines, les émaciées de la beauté spiritualiste . . . des amours d'archanges avec des chérubs, monstrueux à force d'être purs! . . . Je ne suis pas coquet comme une femme, mais comme un homme, ce qui est pis, et Georges Selwyn n'aurait pas été embarrassé de deviner que là où il n'y a rien, rien ne peut être. . . . Pourquoi voulez-vous qu'il y ait quelque chose? Tous, depuis le Salis-Burlesque jusqu'à votre Hautesse, en passant par le grand maître d'Aureville, veulent qu'il y ait quelque vice affreux, séduisant, repoussant, abject et divin à la fois, puisqu'il nous vient des dieux, dans ce malheureux Lorrain, composé d'un cerveau sensuel et d'un corps chaste . . . mais absolument, et cela par paresse et par propreté surtout.'

84 In *Monsieur de Phocas*, p. 47, for example, a Greek dancer is called a 'Vénus Alcibiadée'. 'Le fait est qu'elle est à la fois Aphrodite et Ganymède, Astarté et Hylas.'

* p. 353, *line 22, add*: See also the Goncourts, *L'Italie d'hier, Notes de voyages*, 1855–56, Paris, Charpentier, 1894, pp. 78–9, where the Angel of Memmi's *Annunciation* is found 'déconcertant, presque satanique . . . avec son long cou de serpent . . . avec l'étrangeté de sa beauté perverse'. [Add. 1950]

85 In *Monsieur de Phocas* the following lines on black irises are ascribed to the hero:

Thyrses de crêpe éclos en calices funèbres

. . . . .

Ô douloureuses fleurs de lune et de velours

Mon âme trouve en vous des sœurs et des complices
Turgides floraisons d'un jardin de supplices,
De son rêve obsédé d'effarantes amours!

Mirbeau's *Jardin des supplices* was published in 1899. The page of the diary of *Monsieur de Phocas* which contains these lines was supposed to have been written in April 1899. On Botticelli's *Primavera* see the short story *Ophelius* in *Buveurs d'âmes*.

[86] *Le Dialogue avec André Gide* (Paris, Au Sans Pareil, 1929), p. 228.

[87] B. Fehr, 'Das gelbe Buch in Oscar Wildes Dorian Gray', in *Englische Studien*, vol. lv, pp. 237–56; W. Fischer, 'The poisonous book in O. Wilde's Dorian Gray' (id., vol. li, pp. 37–47). See also: E. J. Bock, 'Walter Paters Einfluss auf O. Wilde' (*Bonner Studien zur englische Philologie*, Nr. 8, Bonn, 1913); E. Bendz, *The Influence of Pater and Matthew Arnold in the Prose-writings of O. Wilde* (Diss., Lund, 1914).

[88] H. Jackson justly observes (p. 58, op. cit. note 91 below) with regard to the Decadent Movement in England:

'The chief influences came from France, and partially for that reason the English Decadents always remained spiritual foreigners in our midst; they were not a product of England but of cosmopolitan London.'

[89] See A. J. Farmer, *Le Mouvement esthétique et 'décadent' en Angleterre* (1873–1900) (Paris, Champion, 1931, Bibliothèque de Littérature Comparée), chap. ii, especially pp. 73–5; M. L. Cazamian, *Le Roman et les idées en Angleterre: l'anti-intellectualisme et l'esthétisme* (1880–1890), Paris, Les Belles Lettres, 1935 (Publications de la Faculté des Lettres de l'Université de Strasbourg, fasc. 73); W. Gaunt, *The Aesthetic Adventure*, op. cit., pp. 48–58; Bertram Newman, 'Walter Pater: a Revaluation', in *The Nineteenth Century* for May 1932, pp. 633–40. Close in spirit to Pater is the work of J. A. Symonds on the Greek poets (1873) and on the Italian Renaissance (1875–86).

Pater's literary pedigree is to be traced not only to Ruskin but also to Winckelmann and Swinburne, whose lives are full of sinister shadows; and as we read the pages in which Pater stresses beauty and sorrow as the dominant impressions in his portraits of youths, as we see him dwelling on the decay of beautiful things, either buildings or human beings—with an occasional macabre or cruel note, as in *Denys l'Auxerrois* and *Apollo in Picardy*, which jars in the otherwise suave page, we cannot help thinking that at the bottom of that attraction to Winckelmann and Swinburne there was an unconfessed kinship of peculiar sensibility. But Pater's life has no such sensational episodes as Swinburne's, nor, as in Winckelmann's case, does a tragical end give the lie to an apparent serenity—apparent only in the written work, because whoever, like Bartolomeo Cavaceppi, had intercourse with Winckelmann, knew what a black sediment of neurasthenia was at the bottom of the soul of the worshipper of Greek serenity. Pater's life flowed monotonously in his neat and severe rooms at Brasenose College and then in London, with social contacts disciplined by his flawless sense of ritual; unless we want to find, as some have found, a slight clue in Pater's friendship with the painter Simeon Solomon, a tragical figure, or an artist, known to Swinburne, destined to end in vice and poverty after brilliant beginnings. While deep earnest religiousness and an almost ascetic temperance ennoble the personality of Pater, on the other hand the climate of his work contains already the very essence of decadence. His inspiration remains motionless throughout his life, as if spellbound by the image of some rich and melancholy adolescence: 'He would think of Julian, fallen into incurable sickness, as spoiled in the sweet blossom of his skin like pale amber, and his honey-like hair; of Cecil, early dead, as cut off from the lilies, from golden summer days, from women's voices; and then what comforted him a little was the thought of the turning of the child's flesh to violets in the turf above him.' A pathetic pageant of Ovidian metamorphoses keeps passing before the greyish-green eyes of the thick-set man with a pale face—almost an Asiatic mask—to whom the heavy jaw and bushy whiskers give the air of a retired officer. A mixture of manliness and languor hints at a vague kinship with the physical type of a Flaubert, even of a Jean Lorrain. A curious anecdote about Pater is reported by Frank Harris: 'He seemed at times half to realise his own deficiency [low pressure]: "Had I So-and-so's courage and hardihood," he cried once, "I'd have——". Suddenly the mood changed, the light in the eyes died out, the head drooped forward again, and with a half smile he added, "I might have been a criminal—he, he", and he moved with little careful steps across the room to his chair, and sat down.' See B. Newman, 'Walter Pater: A Revaluation', in *The Nineteenth Century and After*, vol. cxi, no. 663 (May 1932). In one of his earliest essays, on *Aesthetic Poetry*, written in 1868, he showed himself fully awake to the charm of William Morris's *Defence of Guenevere*, where 'as in some medicated air, exotic flowers of sentiment expand, among people of a remote and unaccustomed beauty, somnabulistic, frail, androgynous, the light almost shining through them'; he recoiled from the fascination of this decadent world, and cancelled the essay after it had reappeared in the first edition of *Appreciations* (1889) (reprinted in R. Aldington's *Selected Works of Walter Pater*, London, Heinemann, 1948). In *Marius the Epicurean* Pater stemmed his decadent tendency and chastened it within the frame of an ascetical classicism, whose formula he had found in Winckelmann.

The essay on *Sandro Botticelli* (August 1870) already struck Pater's keynote, a note of dreamy and melancholy frustration. All Pater's characters belong to transition periods or else are born outside their time, find themselves in the midst of circumstances with which they are unable to cope, or else wander in a maze of possibilities in which they disperse their energies. (See my introductions to *Le più belle pagine di Walter Pater*, Milan, Garzanti, 1944, and to my translation of *Il Rinascimento*, Naples, Edizioni scientifiche italiane, 1946.) Later on history no longer suffices Pater in order to give incarnations of his tormented ideal of creatures of transition, and he invents 'imaginary portraits' (1887). A poet of divided and weary souls and of enchanted places heavy with sadness—'delightful, tumbledown old places'—for him, as for all the great Romantics, Beauty was ever allied with decay and death.

Symonds printed privately two small books on sexual inversion, one on Greek paiderastia, and another on the modern aspects of the question; he came into touch through correspondence with Havelock Ellis, and proposed to join forces with him towards the production of a book on homosexuality.

Symonds's death put an end to the project, but Ellis utilized part of the material supplied by Symonds in a work which at first appeared in German *Das konträre Geschlechtsgefühl* (1896); the English version (1898) was, bought up on the eve of publication by Horatio Brown, Symonds's executor, in the interest of the family. Ellis (*My Life*, London, Heinemann, 1940, pp. 295–6) did not complain of the suppression, believing that 'the significance of a book on inversion would have been greatly discounted by the fact that one of the writers was known to many as personally concerned in the question of homosexuality'.

A typical decadent poem of Symonds is his Keatsian ode to *The Genius of the Vatican*.

Round the Italian Renaissance there crystallized also the exotic aspirations of Frederick William Rolfe (Baron Corvo), author not only of the curious *Chronicles of the House of Borgia* (1901) but also of a novel, *The Desire and Pursuit of the Whole* (posthumously published in 1934), in which the peculiar sensibility of the writer finds an outlet; see my essay on 'Baron Corvo' in *Studi e svaghi inglesi*, pp. 311–12. [Add. 1950]

⁹⁰ See Farmer, op. cit., pp. 101 et seq. In the French version, made by the author himself, *Confessions d'un jeune anglais* (Paris, Savine, 1889), are to be found certain new passages, among which is the following:

'Jamais auparavant l'âme d'un homme n'avait été aussi embrouillée avec celle de la femme; et pour expliquer l'anormal de cette sympathie sexuelle, je ne puis qu'imaginer qu'il y avait avant ma naissance quelque hésitation de sexe.' And also: 'Je suis efféminé, maladif, pervers. Mais avant tout pervers. Tout ce qui est pervers me fascine.'

⁹¹ See G. Turquet-Milnes, *The Influence of Baudelaire in France and England* (London, Constable, 1913); O. Burdett, *The Beardsley Period* (London, Lane, 1925); Farmer, op. cit., and especially Holbrook Jackson, *The Eighteen-Nineties* (London, Cape, 1913; new edition 1927).

* *p. 356, line 26, add:* Arthur Machen's *The Hill of Dreams* has been called 'the most decadent book in English literature'. [Add. 1950]

⁹² H. Jackson, p. 101, says of the complete edition: 'There are passages which read like romanticised excerpts from the *Psychopathia Sexualis* of Krafft-Ebing.'

⁹³ If the vicious faces of Beardsley's figures are compared with those of the figures in Francesco Colonna's book, it will be seen that the English artist has merely loaded the latter with moral (or rather, immoral) content, by means of slight perversions of feature. The following description of a fountain will serve as an example of the 'Poliphilesque' style:

'In the middle was a huge bronze fountain with three basins. From the first rose a many-breasted dragon and four little loves mounted upon swans, and each love was furnished with a bow and arrow. Two of them that faced the monster seemed to recoil in fear, two that were behind made bold enough to aim their shafts at him. From the verge of the second sprang a circle of slim golden columns that supported silver doves with tails and wings spread out. The third, held by a group of grotesquely attenuated satyrs, was centred with a thin pipe hung with masks and roses and capped with children's heads.

From the mouths of the dragon and the loves, from the swans' eyes, from the breasts of the doves, from the satyrs' horns and lips, from the masks of many points, and from the children's curls, the water played profusely, cutting strange arabesques and subtle figures.'

Cf. the description of the fountain in the garden of Eleuterillide in *Hypnerotomachia*. Very likely Beardsley read Poliphilus in Claudius Popelin's French version, *Le Songe de Poliphile*, Paris, Lisieux, 1883, vol. i, p. 141. See my article on 'Some Foreign Imitators of the "Hypneroto-machia Poliphili" ' in *Italica*, vol. xxiv, p. 1 (March 1947). [Add. 1950]

⁹⁴ Beardsley was a Wagner enthusiast. 'Seldom, when he was in London, did he miss a "Wagner night" ' (H. Jackson, op. cit., p. 96). Among his drawings there is one called *The Wagnerians*.

⁹⁵ See H. Richter, *Geschichte der englischen Romantik* (Halle, 1911), vol. i, p. 294; and D. Scarborough, *The Supernatural in Modern English Fiction* (New York and London, 1917), p. 32. When Wilde came out of prison, he lived for a time under the name of Sebastian Melmoth, obviously suggested by Maturin.

As for the theme of the transfusion of a soul into a portrait, see also *The Portrait* in N. Gogol's *Tales of St. Petersburg*, in which an usurer survives in the terrible eyes of his portrait. [Add. 1950]

⁹⁶ Railo, op. cit., pp. 188 and 306–7. See Ralph Tymms, *Doubles in Literary Psychology*, Cambridge, Bowes and Bowes, 1949.

⁹⁶ᴬ On Wilde's trial see W. Gaunt, *The Aesthetic Adventure*, pp. 141–64, and Montgomery Hyde, *The Trials of O. Wilde*, London, Hodge, 1948.

⁹⁷ Burdett, op. cit., p. 179.

* *p. 359, line 27, add:* Lorrain has taken over from Zola this mannerism of interjections, of 'Ah!s'; see for instance *Rome* (Charpentier ed., 1896), p. 228: 'Ah, les bouches de Botticelli, ces bouches charnelles, fermes comme des fruits, ironiques ou douloureuses, énigmatiques en leurs plis sinueux sans qu'on puisse savoir si elles taisent des puretés ou des abominations!' (see incidentally the whole passage for the typically *fin-de-siècle* interpreta-tion of Botticelli); p. 241: 'Ah! ce pape qu'on ne rencontre plus . . .'; p. 282: 'Ah! cette foule énorme de concert monstre . . .'; p. 300: 'Ah! ces misères du pays froid . . .'; p. 376: 'Ah! la villa Mattei, sur la pente du Cœlius, avec son jardin en terrasses . . .'; p. 395: 'Ah! cette colossale demeure . . .'; p. 484: 'Ah! ces bords noirs qui s'enfonçaient, ce lac morne et noir qui gisait, là-bas, au fond!' [Add. 1950]

⁹⁸ *Journal* of the Goncourts, vol. ix, pp. 78–9 (Oct. 19th, 1892).

⁹⁹ Henri de Toulouse-Lautrec, an aristocrat 'égaré dans la pègre par masochisme', as Théodore Duret said, had a monstrous appearance, similar to that which Lorrain attributed to Ethal. The latter resembles the dwarf of the Duke of Alba painted by Anton Mor (in the Louvre), with a phy-siognomy 'malfaisante et sensuelle', a sarcàstic mouth, 'la tête énorme, l'encolure épaisse, le torse trop long, comme dévié sur les jambes trop courtes, je ne sais quoi d'oblique et de tortu'. Toulouse-Lautrec's con-

temporaries have handed down a similar portrait of him. For example W. Rothenstein, *Men and Memories*, vol. i, p. 63:

'He had suffered arrest in the growth of his arms and legs, while his head and body were disproportionately large. With a broad forehead, fine and extremely intelligent eyes, he had lips of a startling scarlet, turned as it were outwards, and strangely wide, which gave a hideous expression to his face—a dwarf of Velasquez with the genius of a Callot.'

The characteristic of the sadistic painter Ethal was 'de dégager immédiatement le masque de tout visage humain', to see the animal physiognomy which is hidden in every face: his portraits were fierce caricatures.

'It amused Lautrec to find formulas for a person's appearance, which he reduced to the simplest expression. . . . For some perverse reason his drawings of Yvette (Guilbert) were among the most savage he ever made.'

(Rothenstein, op. cit., p. 66). With regard to Lautrec's sadistic tastes Rothenstein writes:

'He wanted to take me to an execution, he was enthusiastic about operations performed before clinical students, and pressed me to join him at the hospital.'

With Toulouse-Lautrec Ethal has also in common 'le goût des bouges'. Other qualities in Ethal are borrowed from Whistler, among others the preference for Empire furniture. (Cf. Rothenstein, p. 83.) Ethal's mania for masks finds a parallel in the Anglo-Belgian artist James Ensor (E. Verhaeren, *James Ensor*, Bruxelles, Van Oest, 1908). (See *La Plume*, 1899, special issue dedicated to Ensor; and A. H. Cornette, 'James Ensor' in *La Revue de l'Art*, tome lxii, no. 337, June 1932, pp. 17–32.)

There was after all a vogue for masks at the time. The collector Albert Goupil, for instance, decorated with two human masks a piece of armour (see *Gazette des Beaux-Arts*, 1885, vol. ii, p. 297), in the same way as Ethal decorates an Empire cheval-glass with masks. [Add. 1950]

¹⁰⁰ See the chapter 'Swinburne and "le vice anglais" '.

¹⁰¹ In the chapter 'L'Emprise':

'Et la fiancée de l'Enfer, avec ses deux serpents se tordant sur ses tempes et retenant son voile, a le masque le plus attirant, les yeux les plus profonds, le sourire le plus vertigineux qu'on puisse voir. Si elle existait, comme j'aimerais cette femme! Comme je sens que ce sourire et ces yeux dans ma vie, ce serait la guérison! . . .

Lorrain's books, like those of many other erudite Decadents, teem with reminiscences. Among the less obvious ones I trace that of Isis' apparition to Lucius in Apuleius' *Metamorphoses* (xi. 3), in the apparition of Astarte which concludes *Monsieur de Phocas*. Both figures wear a diadem of light and a black robe; the passage: 'Palla splendescens atro nitore, quae circumcirca remeans . . . ad ultimas oras nodulis fimbriarum decoriter confluctuabat' may have suggested: 'Un voile de gaze noire, une vapeur de crêpe qui dérobait le sexe et s'enroulait aux hanches pour se nouer comme un lien autour des deux chevilles, aggravant le mystère de la pâle apparition' (Apuleius says: 'palla . . . quae longe longeque etiam meum confutabat obtutum').

¹⁰² See Barrès' remarks on Sodoma's saints in 'Les beaux contrastes de Sienne', in the volume *Du Sang, de la volupté, de la mort* (1894).

[103] A typical case is that of Barrès (*Mes Cahiers*; Paris, Plon, vol. i, 1929, p. 31):

'On allait à la vitrine du marchand du boulevard Saint-Germain admirer la *Vieillesse du roi David* gravée par Bracquemont, d'après le tableau de Gustave Moreau et que Gabriel Sarrazin admirait si fort que ses amies se cotisèrent pour le lui offrir. J'ai beaucoup aimé cela et les préraphaélites que je découvris successivement dans des revues d'art, dans des recherches assez difficiles chez les photographes et au cours de voyages à Londres. Puis je sentis que je me nourrissais de sucreries, et cette sensation fut si forte qu'elle me dégoûta des primitifs italiens que les esthètes avaient copiés et dont je ne sus pas sentir la vigueur ni les mystérieuses ambitions.'

[104] Cf. *A rebours*, p. 78, on the subject of Moreau's *Salomé*:

'Elle réveillait plus énergiquement les sens en léthargie de l'homme, ensorcelait, domptait plus sûrement ses volontés, avec son charme de grande fleur vénérienne, poussée dans des couches sacrilèges, élevée dans des serres impies.'

[105] *Monsieur de Phocas*, pp. 348 et seq.

[106] Vol. i, p. 339, Sept. 8th, 1860.

[107] The expression is found in D'Annunzio's *Piacere*, p. 402: 'The mouth of the tireless and inexorable drinkers of souls (*bevitrici d'anime*).'

[108] p. 67. Lorrain must have been thinking of Solario's *Head of Saint John*, in the Louvre (Venturi, vol. vii, part 4, pp. 971 et seq., fig. 657). See also the chapter 'Les Yeux glauques', and see on pp. 80–1 the description of the 'buveur d'âmes', one of those

'modernes Saint Vincent-de-Paul du sentiment, toujours à la recherche d'âmes souffrantes, prêts à tous les dévouements pour les guérir et consoler. . . . Cette passion de charité un peu effrayante n'est, au fond, qu'un sadisme délicat et pervers de raffiné épris de tortures et de larmes'.

[109] *Monsieur de Phocas*, p. 22.

[110] Id., p. 66:

'Que de fois me suis-je éveillé au milieu de la nuit, défaillant à tous les râles et à tous les cris devenus tout à coup perceptibles de la ville endormie, les cris de rut et de volupté qui sont comme la respiration nocturne des cités! . . . Oh! mes cruelles et interminables nuits de révolté et d'impuissant sur le rut de Paris endormi, ces nuits où j'aurais voulu étreindre tous les corps, humer tous les souffles et boire toutes les bouches, et qui me trouvaient, le matin, affalé sur le tapis et l'égratignant encore de mes mains inertes, ces inutiles mains qui n'ont jamais saisi que du vide et dont les envies de meurtre crispent encore les ongles, vingt-quatre heures après mes crises, ces ongles que je finirai par enfoncer quelque jour dans la chair satinée d'une nuque et. . . . Vous voyez bien qu'un démon me possède . . . un démon que les médecins traitent avec du bromure et de la valérianate d'ammoniaque comme si les médicaments pouvaient avoir raison d'un tel mal!'

[111] This was a piece of witchcraft attributed in the *Volksbuch* to Faust, who, in order to prove his power as a necromancer, decapitated a lily, and at the same instant the head of another miracle-worker who had dared to oppose him detached itself from his body and rolled on the ground.

[112] These bare feet and aquamarine eyes were an obsession of Lorrain; we find them in other stories in this volume, in *Mélusine enchantée*, in *Le Prince dans la forêt*. . . . In a letter of Nov. 9th, 1901, to Jules Bois, Lorrain relates how, when he was living in the Rue de Courty, he was

haunted by hallucinations of 'pieds nus' which 'surgissaient dessous les portières' (Normandy, op. cit., p. 107). See also note 56 of chap. iv.

[113] Cf. the passage from *Mademoiselle de Maupin* quoted in chap. iii, p. 161.

[114] Cf. Huysmans, *Certains*, p. 90: 'La Luxure, devenue plus tard un péché chrétien, se symbolisa dans la danse carnassière des Hérodiades.'

Among Italian paintings inspired by Salome attention may be drawn to a particularly morbid one by Francesco del Cairo at the Turin Picture Gallery, in which Salome appears as if swooning before the Baptist's head. If we follow the subject down to modern times, we should find a similarly deliquescent expression on the face of Gustav Klimt's Judith (*Judith and Holophernes*, a picture sold at the Moos Galleries, Geneva, in April 1920, reproduced in the catalogue of the sale of the Collection de feu M. le Dr. L.). [Add. 1950]

[115] See the article by Thovez in the *Gazzetta Letteraria* of Apr. 25th, 1896.

[116] On the curious physical life of Gourmont, see Dr. P. Voivenel, *Remy de Gourmont vu par son médecin*, Essai de physiologie littéraire (Paris, Éditions du Siècle, 1924) (p. 99: 'C'est un sensuel à la fois pervers et chaste, les deux choses étant complémentaires') and A. Rouveyre, already quoted in note 23.

[117] See chap. iii, § 2.

[118] Première Série, Paris, Mercure de France, 1903, p. 313.

[119] Rouveyre, p. 61:

'Gourmont . . . fut initialement frappé par Mallarmé et par Huysmans. Ses premières œuvres sont, vers ou proses, poèmes ou essais, une véritable débauche de sacrilèges religieux, où sont mêlés l'Alcôve et l'Autel, avec une grande excitation de l'auteur, dont on devine l'agitation, à ces imaginations attemptatoires.'

On sadism in Gourmont, see P. Delior, *Remy de Gourmont et son œuvre* (Paris, Mercure de France, 1909, p. 18; Collection 'Les Hommes et les Idées').

[120] The influence of *Là-bas* was noted by Delior, op. cit., p. 17.

[121] In *L'Hermitage*, Jan. 1892, p. 51.

[122] Pierre Champion, *Marcel Schwob et son temps* (Paris, Grasset, 1927) p. 114. On Marguerite Moreno, Schwob's wife, see Colette, *Ces plaisirs*, pp. 88 et seq.

[123] The lecture on *Annabella et Giovanni*, printed by the Mercure de France in Dec. 1894, is now included in *Œuvres complètes de M. Schwob* (Paris, Bernouard, 1927–30), vol. ix (*Chroniques*).

[124] Schwob was an admirer of Wilde, to whom he dedicated the fable *Le Pays bleu*, which first appeared in the *Écho de Paris* of Dec. 6th, 1891, and whose *The Selfish Giant* (from *The Happy Prince and other Tales*) he translated in the Supplément Littéraire of the same paper, Dec. 27th, 1891.

[125] A. France wrote of him, with regard to *Le Jardin de Bérénice* (La *Vie littéraire*, vol. iv, pp. 223 et seq.): 'Il n'a point d'instincts, point de passions. Il est tout intellectuel, et c'est un idéaliste pervers.'

[126] *Du Sang, de la volupté, de la mort*, p. 172 (*Excuses à Bérénice*).

127 Cf. *L'Âne mort*, discussed in chap. iii, § 14.

128 Ed. Émile-Paul, 1912, pp. 147–8.

129 *Un Homme libre*, pp. 214 et seq.

130 Similarly, in *L'Ennemi des lois*, p. 235:

'Marina ... je ne te reconnais que dans deux attitudes, ou fiévreuse et souffrant à cause de moi et me blessant de telle façon que tu rends de plus en plus impossible ton bonheur, ou contente, mais acceptant une domination qui te souille'.

Typical Russian as she is (see above, p. 337) Marina says (p. 106): C'est si bon, quand on adore quelqu'un, de lui faire du mal !' See also p. 238:

'Et tous ces mystères déchirants emplissaient l'âme d'André et la conquéraient comme le souffle si rauque d'Othello devant Desdémone innocente et assassinée, comme les cris d'amour de Juliette si impure dans son ardeur.'

131 *Le Livre des masques*, vol. i, p. 186.

132 Reprinted in *Du Sang, de la volupté, de la mort*.

133 Vol. ii, p. 27.

134 See chap. iii, p. 162.

135 Vol. i, p. 134. According to the note (p. 290):

'Peu après la naissance de Maurice Barrès, sa mère, malade, dut séjourner pendant de longues années au couvent de la Toussaint, à Strasbourg. Tour à tour l'un des deux enfants, Marie ou Maurice, restait auprès de leur mère.'

136 The italics are mine.

137 *Du Sang*, &c., pp. 280, 285–6. In connexion with Venice—when the Campanile di San Marco collapsed, Barrès declared himself opposed to its reconstruction: 'In this collapse Barrès pointed out to all the world the striking proof of his interpretation of Venice: *désespoir d'une beauté qui s'en va vers la mort*' (Ojetti, *Cose viste*, vol. v, Milan, Treves, 1931, p. 243).

138 Vol. ii, p. 216: on El Greco, see also J. Lorrain, *Monsieur de Bougrelon* (1897):

'Le plus merveilleux de tous, peut-être, le sublime dans l'horrible, El Greco, infernal et céleste à la fois, car l'enfer c'est le ciel en creux ... le Greco ... peignait avec le sang des plaies des anatomies dessinées avec un charbon ardent, et ce charbon, il l'avait pris au bûcher de la sainte Inquisition.'

139 p. 205.

140 In *L'Ennemi des lois*, p. 127, Marina makes a brief mention of Tiflis, 'beau pays sensuel', and of its beautiful women, a mention which was further developed by Astiné in *Les Déracinés*.

141 *La Mort de Venise*, p. 19 of *Amori et dolori sacrum*.

142 Id., p. 6.

143 In the *Dialogue* cit., p. 130. The expression is Montaigne's, and E. Colburn Mayne, whose book was well known to du Bos, had already applied it to Byron (*Byron*, 1924 edition, p. 403).

144 From *Conversation avec un Allemand quelques années avant la guerre*; the passage is quoted by du Bos, p. 148.

145 Barrès, in *Un Homme libre*, p. 213, had said:

'En moi grandit avec rapidité, conformément à mon rôle, cet appétit de se détruire, cette hâte de se plonger corps et âme dans un manque de bon sens, cette sorte de haine de soi-même qui constituent la passion! Ah! l'attrait de l'irréparable, où toujours je voulus trouver un perpétuel repos. . . .'

146 See above p. 359.

147 Du Bos, op. cit., p. 247.

148 The definition is from Rouveyre, op. cit., p. 154.

149 *L'Immoraliste*, pp. 194 et seq.:

'De ses récits sortait une trouble vapeur d'abîme qui déjà me montait à la tête et qu'inquiètement je humais. . . . Et j'appris peu à peu bien d'autres choses qui faisaient de la maison Heurtevent un lieu brûlant, à l'odeur forte, autour duquel, quoi que j'en eusse, mon imagination, comme une mouche à viande, tournoyait.'

150 Op. cit., pp. 153–4.

151 Vol. iii, p. 195.

152 This essay on Rops (from the volume *Certains*), together with other articles on this artist (one of them by Péladan) and poetical tributes to his work, was reprinted in the June 15th, 1896 number of *La Plume*, a special number dedicated to Rops.

153 In *Monsieur de Phocas*, in the chapter called 'Cloaca Maxima'.

154 This is evidently a description of the frontispiece to Péladan's *Initiation sentimentale*.

155 *Barbarie et poésie* (Paris, Nouvelle Librairie Nationale, 1925) p. 179: 'Maurice Rollinat ou le macabre incongru', first published in the *Gazette de France*, Nov. 1st, 1903.

156 Statistics of the deaths of Decadent artists would show as great a proportion of premature deaths as among the *Stürmer und Dränger* of a century before. Statistics of this kind are hinted at by H. Jackson (op. cit., p. 130) in the case of English artists.

157 *Journal*, vol. vii, p. 116, Mar. 24th, 1886.

158 The Italian 'Byzantines', 'Byzantine' though they were, could not swallow the *Névroses*. See G. Salvadori's damning review of *Les Névroses* in *Cronaca Bizantina*, Mar. 16th, 1883 (Anno III, vol. i, no. 6).

159 In *Monsieur de Phocas* these lines are recited at a *soirée* of depraved people (chapter: 'Quelques monstres'). Samain's *Au jardin de l'Infante* is called there: 'Ce livre si chargé d'orage et de luxure, d'un charme si opprimant et malsain.'

160 *Au jardin de l'Infante*, p. 20.

161 In *Rapport sur le mouvement poétique français de 1867 à 1900* (Paris, Fasquelle and Imprimerie Nationale, 1903).

162 The comparison of the heart to a ciborium is common among the Decadents. See, for example, J. Lorrain, *La Forêt bleue*, p. 25, *Le Ciboire*: 'De mon cœur vide et froid j'ai fait un grand ciboire, etc.'

163 See W. Rothenstein, op. cit., vol. i, p. 95:

'Montesquiou, it was generally supposed, was Huysmans' model for des Esseintes. Montesquiou too had a tortoise whose shell he inlaid with jewels; the tortoise's retort on this outrage was direct and emphatic—it died. . . . I met him one day on his way to hear Weber's music, when he told me that one should always listen to Weber in mauve!'

[164] *Journal*, vol. ix, p. 120, Apr. 5th, 1893: Montesquiou's supposition was, after all, warranted by the actual practice of the Jesuits in the XVIIth century. See E. Mâle, *L'Art religieux après le Concile de Trente*, Paris, Colin, 1932, pp. 110 et seq.

[165] *Journal*, vol. viii, p. 252.

[166] On Renée Vivien, see the essay by Charles Maurras, in *L'Avenir de l'intelligence* (Paris, Fontemoing, 1905), pp. 157 et seq. ('Le Romantisme féminin, I'); the study by Y. G. Le Dantec, *Renée Vivien, femme damnée, femme sauvée* (Aix-en-Provence, Aux Éditions du Feu, 1930), and the illuminating pages (pp. 113 et seq.) of Colette's *Ces plaisirs* (pp. 127 and 137 bear on Renée Vivien's sadistic experiences). The collected poems have been published in two volumes, *Poèmes de Renée Vivien* (Paris, Lemerre, 1923–4).

[166A] In the novel *Une Femme m'apparut* . . . (Paris, Lemerre, 1904; see also the addition to note 66 of this chapter), we find, for instance, p. 2: 'Undine elle-même ne fut point aussi cruellement et suavement blonde. Lorély a des yeux d'eau glacée . . .'; p. 5: 'J'attendais Lorély dans un boudoir glauque. . . . Des fleurs éclataient partout en gerbes, en fusées, en masses touffues. . . . C'étaient des lys tigrés . . .'; p. 7: 'elle me sourit d'un sourire florentin'; p. 8: 'l'exquise pâleur un peu verte qui méprisait le fard'; p. 49: 'S'éloigner le plus possible de la nature, là est la fin véritable de l'art'; p. 145: 'Et je me trouvai devant le cadavre de Lorély. . . . Lorély flottait sur un marais stagnant. Les seins blêmes étaient deux nénuphars. Les yeux révulsés me regardaient. . . . Elle flottait, les cheveux mêlés d'iris et de roseaux, comme une perverse Ophélie.' Nothing could be more 'modern-style' than this last picture. [Add. 1950]

[167] *Poèmes*, vol. i, p. 1.

[168] *Poèmes*, vol. ii, p. 1.

[169] *Poèmes*, vol. i, p. 129. For other echoes of Swinburne cf. i, p. 87, 'Et les lys ont gardé . . .' (in the poem *Water Lilies*) with *The Garden of Proserpine*; p. 100, *Souveraines*, with *The Masque of Queen Bersabe*; p. 139, 'J'épouserai la mer, la souveraine amante . . .' (in *A Venise*) with *The Triumph of Time*; vol. ii, p. 114 (*Le Monde est un jardin*) with *The Garden of Proserpine*. On p. 67 there is a version of *Erotion* 'd'après Swinburne'. Maurras' difficulty about the lines:

> Et le vin des fleurs et le vin des étoiles
> M'accablent d'amour . . .
> Déesse à qui plaît la ruine des roses . . .

would have been lessened if the Swinburnian origin of these expressions had occurred to him. Instead of this he observes (op. cit., p. 167):

'La vraie Sappho . . . ferait des objections à la 'ruine des roses', eu égard au génie de notre idiome: une rose ne fait pas figure de vieille tour; et, quant au vin des fleurs, c'est une chose, et le vin des étoiles en est une autre, fort éloignée.'

[170] There is a curious resemblance between the death of Renée Vivien and that of Swinburne's imaginary Lesbia Brandon, who, in the last chapter (*Leucadia*) of the novel, poisons herself slowly with flowers and eau de Cologne.

171 Op. cit., p. 112. See the whole interesting parallel between the two poets, pp. 115–20.

172 For this taste for the cadaverous, see chap. i, § 5.

173 Other English parodies of the Decadent movement and of *Fin-de-Siècleism* (as it was called) are to be found in *A Full and True Account of the Wonderful Mission of Earl Lavender*, by John Davidson (London, 1895); *Baron Verdigris: a Romance of the Reversed Direction* (cf. *A rebours*), by Jocelyn Quilp (1894), both with frontispieces by Beardsley, the first representing a scene of flagellation (cf. Appendix); *The Green Carnation*, by R. Hichens (1894), and *The Autobiography of a Boy*, by G. S. Street (1894). In the last two books, which are both similar in content, the hero is an effeminate youth (a caricature of Wilde) who provokes every one's laughter by his exquisite and vicious poses. None of these parodies has for us to-day the *vis comica*, all the more intense because involuntary, of certain authentic works of the Decadence.

Compare with the theme of Le Gallienne's poem what the decadent character, Walter Hamlin, says in Vernon Lee's *Miss Brown* (London, 1884), a novel in which the circles of English decadents and aesthetes are described (a poet, Cosmo Clough, is a thin disguise of Swinburne, whereas Postlethwaite adumbrates Wilde), vol. iii, pp. 108–9; and Anne's reply: 'I thought your indecision between the bog and the stars rather contemptible', and p. 124 Clough's words: 'A poet must know the stars, and know the mud beneath his feet.' [Add. 1950]

174 Cf. Barrès, *Un Homme libre*, p. 244:

' Je ne déteste pas que des parties de moi s'abaissent quelquefois: il y a un plaisir mystique à contempler, du bas de l'humiliation, la vertu qu'on est digne d'atteindre. . . .'

175 M. Coulon, *Verlaine, poète saturnien* (Paris, 1929; Collection 'La Vie de Bohème'), pp. 35 et seq.

176 In *Poèmes saturniens, Œuvres complètes* (Paris, Messein, 1919), vol. i, pp. 62 et seq. On Marco, cf. Musset, *Confession d'un enfant du siècle*, Deuxième Partie, ch. iv (ed. *Œuvres complètes*, Garnier, vol. vii, pp. 119 et seq.)

176A See the following lines with the title *Le Bon Disciple*:

> Je suis élu, je suis damné;
> Un grand souffle inconnu m'entoure.
> O terreur! *Parce Domine!*
>
> Quel ange dur ainsi me bourre
> Entre les épaules, tandis
> Que je m'envole au paradis?
>
> Fièvre adorablement maligne,
> Bon délire, benoît effroi,
> Je suis martyr et je suis roi,
> Faucon je plane et je meurs cygne!
>
> Toi, le Jaloux qui m'as fait signe,
> *Tout* me voici, voici tout moi!
> Vers toi je rampe encore indigne!
> —Monte sur mes reins, et trépigne!

See F. Porché, *Verlaine tel qu'il fut*, Paris, Flammarion, 1933, pp. 414 and 235; also p. 98: 'Il est fort probable que Verlaine était tout autre chose qu'un "homosexuel accidentel" ', and the details given there, chiefly the evidence offered by the book of verse *Hombres* (original title *D'aulcuns*) privately printed in 1904. [Add. 1950]

177 *Lucien Létinois*, ii, in *Amour*; *Œ. compl.*, vol. ii, p. 77.

178 *Œuvres posthumes*, vol. i.

179 *Correspondance de Paul Verlaine* (Paris, Messein, 1902), vol. i, p. 319.

180 Id., vol. i, p. 97.

180A An influence of the cultural atmosphere can be traced also in the work of writers who in other respects soar above decadentism, for instance in the work of Thomas Mann. Thus in his story *Tobias Mindernickel* we find a Dostoievskian type of outcast, who finds shelter from the world which laughs at him, and from his own fearful loneliness, in the company of a fox-hound, whom he ill-treats and fondles by turns, until, one day, when the dog is livelier than usual, he sadistically stabs him in order to be able to pity him; in *Der Tod in Venedig* we have Aschenbach deriving a painful pleasure from his impossible passion for a beautiful Polish youth, in the oppressive atmosphere of cholera-stricken Venice (see note 45 to Chap. I of the present book); in *Der Zauberberg* (1924) the sanatorium offers ideal surroundings for themes of love and death in the morbid passion of Hans Castorp for Madame Chauchat. [Add. 1950]

181 On the attitude of the Goncourts, see P. Sabatier, *L'Esthétique des Goncourt* (Paris, Hachette, 1920), and E. Seillière, *Les Goncourt moralistes* (Paris, Nouvelle Revue Critique, 1927), Deuxième Partie, Ch. IV, iii, 'La crainte de la femme', iv, 'L'amour interdit à l'artiste.'

In Sabatier's book see especially chap. xxiii, ' La recherche des sentiments morbides', and chap. iv, 'Absence du sentiment de l'amour chez les Goncourt'. On p. 124 we read:

'Les Goncourt, si défiants à l'égard de la femme, avaient par certains côtés un tempérament très féminin, ce qui n'a rien de contradictoire. Cet herma-phrodisme intellectuel . . . n'est pas sans précédent aux époques de décadence.'

Rather it is, as we have seen, one of its conspicuous characteristics.

'Au XIXᵉ siècle, les Goncourt furent, pensons-nous, les premiers à réunir des tendances que la nature a séparées. Leur esthétique . . . se ressentira de cette dualité de goûts. Bornons-nous ici à la constater, tout en y trouvant une explication vraisemblable de cette surprenante anaphrodisie qui les caractérise. Ils étaient trop semblables à l'autre sexe pour être de vrais amants.'

182 *Journal*, vol. iii, p. 14.

183 *Journal*, vol. vii, p. 136 (July 15th, 1886).

184 Another work which illustrates the *fin-de-siècle* taste for Wagner is *La Lueur sur la cime*, by Jacques Vontade (the pseudonym of Madame Bulteau, the friend of Toulet and of the archaeologist Boni) (Paris, Calmann-Lévy, 1904). A certain Albert Marlette (p. 13) claims that 'Lorsqu'il écoute le grand duo du second acte du *Tristan*, (il) éprouve d'une façon complète tous les agréments de l'amour.' Another character, the writer Étienne Marken (pp. 89–90) weeps during the whole performance of

Parsifal. André says to Jacqueline (pp. 97–8): 'Je puis résumer aisément l'impression générale que me fait la musique de Wagner: elle me donne une envie excessive de vous embrasser à fond.' Marken speaks to Jacqueline of the love of Tristan (p. 335): 'Cet amour qui garde le masque de l'épouvante et où le baiser doit avoir le goût de la mort.' (Cf. p. 354: 'le désir meurtrier de Tristan.') The furore for *Tristan and Isolde* at the end of the century is also witnessed by Mark Twain (see A. B. Paine, *Mark Twain, A Biography*, vol. ii, p. 922): 'I know of some, and have heard of many, who could not sleep after it, but cried the night away. I feel strongly out of place here. Sometimes I feel like the one sane person in the community of the mad.'

185 *Là-bas*, p. 252.

185A A passage from a letter of Rimbaud (publ. in the *Revue européenne* for October 1928) could be quoted in order to illustrate Schwob's analysis:

'Maintenant je m'encrapule le plus possible. Pourquoi? Je veux être poète, et je travaille à me rendre *voyant*; vous ne comprendrez pas du tout, et je ne saurais presque vous expliquer. Il s'agit d'arriver à l'inconnu par le dérèglement de tous les sens. Les souffrances sont énormes, mais il faut être fort. . . .' [Add. 1950]

186 p. 276 of the ninth edition (Paris, Ollendorff, 1907). Another novel with a Byzantine background (VIIIth century) is *Byzance* by Jean Lombard, Paris, Savine, 1890, written in a glittering and oppressive style. Lombard wrote another novel on the decline of the Roman Empire, *L'Agonie*, whose subject was thus summed up in the press (*Polybiblion*, October 1889): '*L'Agonie* est une évocation historique de la Rome d'Héliogabale. M. Lombard a dépensé un immense talent à décrire brutalement et sans réserve les orgies sans nom, les monstrueuses impudicités, les stupres effrénés, les vices immondes auxquels se livraient alors et le prêtre du soleil qui gouvernait l'Empire et sa mère Soemia, et ses favoris et ses prétoriens.' The Dutch poet and novelist Louis Couperus (1863–1923) wrote a novel on the Rome of Heliogabalus, *De Berg van Licht*.

187 Id., pp. 37–9. Similar examples of excessive piling-up of the picturesque occur in the *Vies imaginaires* of M. Schwob. As an example see the beginning of the life of *Pétrone, romancier*.

188 *Le Faville del Maglio*, vol. ii, p. 211.

189 Something similar has already been said by Borgese, in his volume already quoted, p. 163, where he sums up the personal tragedy of D'Annunzio in this 'definitive formula': 'Barbarousness burdened and oppressed with culture.' But the explanation which Borgese gives of this formula is different from that attempted in these pages.

190 *Il Fuoco*, p. 188.

191 See chap. iv, note 59.

192 On the Vittoriale, see M. Barilli, *Al Vittoriale con Gabriele D'Annunzio* (Florence, Bemporad, 1930). See also the poet's significant message attached to the deed of gift of the Vittoriale, reported in the *Corriere della Sera* of Oct. 5th, 1930, in the article 'Il Vittoriale donato al popolo italiano'.

APPENDIX
SWINBURNE AND 'LE VICE ANGLAIS'

SWINBURNE AND 'LE VICE ANGLAIS'

1. It seems to be an assured fact that sexual flagellation has been practised in England with greater frequency than elsewhere—if, at least, we are to believe Pisanus Fraxi[1] and Doctor Dühren,[2] who have made special researches into the subject. Their conclusion appears also to be confirmed by the fact that literature on this subject comes mainly from Anglo-Saxon sources. The type of English algolagnic became fixed, once and for all, towards the end of the eighteenth century, in the person of George Augustus Selwyn (1719–91), one of the most conspicuous figures of society under George III, who seems, in some respects, almost to anticipate Swinburne. In him also a morbid attraction for sights of suffering went hand in hand with a pronounced affection for children:

'With a thorough enjoyment of the pleasures of society, an imperturbable good humour, a kind heart, and a passionate fondness for children, he united a morbid interest in the details of human suffering, and, more especially, a taste for witnessing criminal executions. Not only was he a constant frequenter of such scenes of horror, but all the details of crime, the private history of the criminal, his demeanour at his trial, in the dungeon, and on the scaffold, and the state of his feelings in the hour of death and degradation, were to Selwyn matters of the deepest and most extraordinary interest. Even the most frightful particulars relating to suicide and murder; the investigation of the disfigured corpse, the sight of an acquaintance lying in his shroud, seem to have afforded him a painful and unaccountable pleasure.'[3]

This taste on the part of Selwyn gave rise to a great many anecdotes, the majority of which are related by Horace Walpole in his *Letters*. 'George', says Walpole, among other things, 'never thinks but *à la tête tranchée*.' On the occasion of the ghastly execution of Damiens, who had made an attempt upon the life of Louis XV, Selwyn went specially to Paris, on January 5th, 1757, 'mingled with the crowd in a plain undress and a bob-wig', and 'when a French nobleman, observing the deep interest

which he took in the scene, asked him: "Vous êtes bourreau?" he replied: 'Non, non, monsieur, je n'ai pas cette
honneur; je ne suis qu'un amateur".' A different version
of the incident is given by Sir Nathaniel Wraxall:[4]

'Selwyn's nervous irritability and anxious curiosity to observe
the effect of dissolution on men, exposed him to much ridicule, not
unaccompanied with censure. He was accused of attending all
executions; and sometimes, in order to elude notice, disguised in a
female dress. I have been assured that, in 1756, he went over to
Paris expressly for the purpose of witnessing the last moments of
Damiens. . . . Being among the crowd, and attempting to approach
too near the scaffold, he was at first repulsed by one of the executioners; but having informed the person, that he had made the
journey from London solely with a view to be present at the punishment and death of Damiens, the man immediately caused the people
to make way, exclaiming at the same time: "Faites place pour
monsieur; c'est un Anglois, et un amateur".'

I have no doubt that this anecdote gave rise to the
French legend of the Englishman whose greatest pleasure
was to attend executions, a legend which was developed
during the Romantic period and received a new stimulus
from the Goncourts. The sadistic Englishman in Edmond
de Goncourt's *La Faustin* (of which I shall speak shortly)
is, in fact, actually called Georges Selwyn. The name of
the eighteenth-century sadist must have been well known
to the Goncourts, who were keen students of that particular period.[5] Another historic episode of English sadism is
closely connected with Italy: I refer to the well-known
story of Lady Hamilton's behaviour during the executions
at Naples in 1799.

2. In Pétrus Borel (*Contes immoraux*, 1833, *Monsieur de
l'Argentière, l'accusateur*) there is an Englishman who
pays five hundred francs for a window from which to
watch an execution.

In Féval's *Mystères de Londres* (1844) a certain Doctor
Moore and a chemist called Rowley carry out lethal experiments on a young woman, Clary Mac-Farlaine. The
unfortunate girl is shut up in a padded room, so that her
shrieks may not be heard from outside. The chemist has
a craze for poisons; every evening, before going to bed,

he reads a chapter of Doctor Veron's *Toxicological Amusements*. He shows a refinement of cruelty in his treatment of Clary. Apart from this, Féval keeps on the whole to generalities: 'Nous en avons dit assez pour que le lecteur comprenne ou devine quelle dut être la conduite du docteur Moore auprès du lit de Clary Mac-Farlaine.' Apropos of London he says:

'L'homme fort s'indigne et se retourne contre le monstre qui pollue ainsi sa propre race, contre ce peuple pourri jusqu'à la moelle, contre cette capitale, grande prostituée experte à toutes hontes, dont la corruption colossale, mise à nu quelque jour, épouvantera le monde, et qui finira par s'écrouler, abîmée comme Sodome ou Ninive, sous le fardeau trop lourd de son ignominie.

Les Mystères de Londres caused a certain stir. The American papers reviewed it with headlines of this kind: *Awful revealing! ! ! Capital discoveries! ! ! Unveiled England! ! !* It must be observed that Féval had never set foot in England.

3. A description which was destined to be widely echoed occurs in the *Journal* of the Goncourts, under the date April 7th, 1862. It is worth quoting this description almost in full, since it served as a source to various writers:

'Aujourd'hui j'ai visité un fou, un monstre, un de ces hommes qui confinent à l'abîme. Par lui, comme par un voile déchiré, j'ai entrevu un fonds abominable, un côté effrayant d'une aristocratie d'argent blasée, de l'aristocratie anglaise apportant la férocité dans l'amour, et dont le libertinage ne jouit que par la souffrance de la femme.

'Au bal de l'Opéra, il avait été présenté à Saint-Victor un jeune Anglais, qui lui avait dit simplement, en manière d'entrée en conversation, "qu'on ne trouvait guère à s'amuser à Paris, que Londres était infiniment supérieur, qu'à Londres il y avait une maison très bien, la maison de Mistress Jenkins, où étaient des jeunes filles d'environ treize ans, auxquelles d'abord on faisait la classe, puis qu'on fouettait, &c. ... Dans le temps, j'ai loué, avec un ami, une fenêtre, pour une grosse somme, afin de voir une assassine qui devait être pendue, et nous avions avec nous des femmes pour leur *faire des choses* — il a l'expression toujours extrêmement décente — au moment où elle serait pendue, &c. ..." Donc aujourd'hui Saint-Victor m'introduit chez ce terrible original. C'est un jeune homme d'une trentaine d'années, chauve, les tempes renflées comme une orange, les yeux d'un bleu clair et aigu, la peau extrêmement fine et laissant voir le réseau sous-cutané des veines, la tête—c'est bizarre—la tête d'un de ces jeunes prêtres émaciés et extatiques, entourant les évêques dans les vieux tableaux. Un élégant jeune homme ayant un peu de raideur dans les bras, et les mouvements de corps à la fois mécaniques et fiévreux d'une personne attaquée d'un commencement de maladie de la moelle épinière, et avec cela d'excellentes façons, une politesse exquise, une douceur de manières toute particulière.

'Il a ouvert un grand meuble à hauteur d'appui, où se trouve une curieuse collection de livres érotiques, admirablement reliés, et tout en me tendant un Meibomius, *Utilité de la flagellation dans les plaisirs de l'amour et du mariage*, relié par un des premiers relieurs de Paris avec des fers intérieurs représentant des phallus, des têtes de mort, des instruments de torture, dont il a donné les dessins, il nous dit: "Ah! ces fers... non, d'abord il ne voulait pas les exécuter, le relieur.... Alors je lui ai prêté de mes livres.... Maintenant il rend sa femme très malheureuse.... Il court les petites filles..., mais j'ai eu mes fers". Et nous montrant un livre tout préparé pour la reliure: "Oui, pour ce volume j'attends une peau, une peau de jeune fille, &c.".[6] Et tout en contemplant, d'un regard de maniaque, les ongles de ses mains tendues devant lui, il parle, il parle continuement, et sa voix un peu chantante et s'arrêtant et repartant aussitôt qu'elle s'arrête, vous entre, comme une vrille, dans les oreilles ses cannibalesques paroles.'

In 1868 Maupassant made the acquaintance of Swinburne at Étretat, and went to dine at the little villa which he occupied with his friend George Powell. Swinburne had given the villa, which he described in a letter to his mother as 'the sweetest little old farmhouse', a name taken from a novel by the Marquis de Sade—*Chaumière de Dolmancé*, and to the avenue in the garden the name *Avenue de Sade*.[7] The account of this visit which Maupassant gave to Edmond de Goncourt—and which is certainly analogous to the one which he wrote as a preface to the French translation by G. Mourey of *Poems and Ballads* (Paris, Savine, 1891)—was used by Goncourt for his portrait of the imaginary Georges Selwyn in *La Faustin* (1881–2). Maupassant describes Swinburne thus:

'Le front était très grand sous des cheveux longs, et la figure allait se rétrécissant vers un menton mince ombré d'une maigre touffe de barbe. Une très légère moustache glissait sur les lèvres

extraordinairement fines et serrées, et le cou qui semblait sans fin
unissait cette tête, vivante par les yeux clairs chercheurs et fixes, à
un corps sans épaules, car le haut de la poitrine paraissait à peine
plus large que le front. Tout ce personnage presque surnaturel
était agité de secousses nerveuses. Il fut très cordial, très accueillant;
et le charme extraordinaire de son intelligence me séduisit aussitôt.
Pendant tout le déjeuner on parla d'art, de littérature et d'humanité;
et les opinions de ces deux amis [Swinburne and Powell] jetaient
sur les choses une espèce de lueur troublante, macabre, car ils avaient
une manière de voir et de comprendre qui me les montrait comme
deux visionnaires malades, ivres de poésie perverse et magique. . . .
Mais MM. Swinburne et Powell furent délicieux de fantaisie et
de lyrisme.'

The following is Maupassant's criticism of Swinburne
as a poet—given from hearsay, since he could not read
him in the original:

'Une sorte d'Edgar Poe idéaliste et sensuel, avec une âme d'écrivain plus exaltée, plus dépravée, plus amoureuse de l'étrange et du
monstrueux, plus curieuse, chercheuse et évocatrice des raffinements
subtils et anti-naturels de la vie et de l'idée.'[8]

The *Honorable* Georges Selwyn in *La Faustin* has
many points in common with Maupassant's Swinburne:
'la séduction de son intelligence' mixed with 'un tas de
riens indéfinissables qui déplaisaient: . . . c'était surtout
au-dessous d'un front d'hydrocéphale, une figure qui ne
semblait pas de son sexe, une figure de vieille femme, dans
laquelle allait et venait un ricanement perpétuel, pareil à
un tic nerveux.' Selwyn shows great erudition and speaks
of various subjects 'sur un mode enthousiaste . . . tirant de
sa mémoire des citations interminables, montrant une connaissance extraordinaire de toutes les littératures d'Europe,
&c.' Georges Selwyn leaves Lord Annandale's castle and
betakes himself to the 'petite maison sur les côtes de la
Bretagne, la Chaumière de Dolmancé', a name which
brings a 'terrible sourire énigmatique' to his lips.

In this portrait, Goncourt was also thinking of the
young Englishman described in the *Journal* of 1862, as it
appears from Selwyn's 'mains desséchées d'une manière
curieuse', in which the nails of the little fingers were notice-
able (Selwyn grows them long in the Chinese manner,

'enfermés dans un onglier d'or'); also from his nervous symptoms which were due to an affection of the spinal cord, and from the 'aigu vibrant de sa voix de fausset en joie'. But Goncourt also endowed Georges Selwyn with certain of Baudelaire's characteristics: he dressed in a pretentious fashion, and 'ne portait pas de cravate; le décolletage descendait jusque sur la poitrine'. Baudelaire, as he is described in the *Journal* of the Goncourts (October 1857), was 'sans cravate, le col nu . . . en vraie toilette de guillotiné'. He gives him also certain characteristics of Barbey d'Aurevilly. Selwyn drinks brandy 'à pleines lampées', just as E. de Goncourt had seen Barbey d'Aurevilly do; the latter has a 'teint boucané' (*Journal*, May 5th, 1875), so also Selwyn 'avait une peau qu'on aurait dite boucanée et que seules tannent ainsi les existences mauvaises, fatales, criminelles'; just as d'Aurevilly has 'une longue mèche de cheveux lui balafrant la figure', so Selwyn 'prenait encore un caractère étrange de ce qu'au milieu de ses cheveux, très noirs, une mèche blanche . . . était arrangée et mise en évidence avec une certaine affectation'.[9] And just as the elegance of d'Aurevilly was 'frelatée', so Selwyn was 'prétentieusement mis avec des vêtements tachés.' D'Aurevilly, who also loved to describe sexual perversions, had presented, in one of the *Diaboliques* (*Le Dessous de cartes d'une partie de whist*, 1874), a sadistic couple—the Scottish captain Marmor de Karkoël and the Comtesse de Tremblay de Stasseville. A fusion of the various characters (the anonymous Englishman, Swinburne, Baudelaire, d'Aurevilly) would easily occur to the mind of Goncourt owing to the qualities which they had in common—disproportionate forehead, lordliness of manner, elegance of conversation, perversity of imagination, &c.[10]

The sinister Englishman in *La Faustin* created a certain impression at the time. Goncourt tells how Bourget accompanied him a good way in the street 'pour s'entretenir avec *lui* du personnage de l'honorable Selwyn, dont sa cervelle semble grisée'; he even went so far, in his megalomania, as to suppose it possible 'qu'il se créât, dans une vingtaine d'années, une école autour de *la Faustin*.'[11] *La*

Faustin was 'un des volumes les plus caressés par des Esseintes'.[12]

4. Certain scandals about London which were revealed by the *Pall Mall Gazette* in 1885 seemed at the time to prove that the attribution of sadism as an English characteristic was by no means merely arbitrary. In its issues of July 6th, 7th, 8th, and 10th, 1885, there was published in this paper a series of articles entitled 'The Maiden Tribute of Modern Babylon', in which were exposed the results of an inquiry into youthful prostitution in London. The moving spirit of this campaign, which was intended to provoke Government measures for the protection of minors, was the journalist W. T. Stead. In his excess of zeal he did not hesitate to undertake on his own initiative an experiment which, when the scandal came out, brought him to justice and caused him to be condemned to three months' hard labour. The articles in the *Pall Mall Gazette* made a considerable stir not only in England but also on the Continent, especially in France, where they were quoted in the *Temps* and the *Figaro*, and published in book form by Dentu, in a literal translation, in the same year (*Les Scandales de Londres dévoilés par la Pall Mall Gazette*: there were also Portuguese and German translations). The paragraphs which made the greatest impression on the French were those which dealt with sadism—'Why the cries of the victims are not heard', and 'Strapping girls down': these paragraphs were considerably abridged when the collected articles were put on sale by the *Pall Mall Gazette* (August 22nd, 1885), but were reproduced from the original version in the French translation. The English paper declared that 'padded rooms for the purpose of stifling the cries of the tortured victims of lust and brutality are familiar enough on the continent', but to continental eyes these 'chambres matelassées pour assourdir les cris des victimes' (victims who were sometimes less than thirteen years old!) appeared to be a conspicuously English phenomenon. In the issue of September 18th of the paper *Le Succès* Villiers de l'Isle-Adam dealt with *Le Sadisme anglais* (an article which was reprinted later in *Histoires insolites* and in *Nouveaux Contes*

cruels, 1888). The articles in the *Pall Mall Gazette* had reminded Villiers de l'Isle-Adam of a conversation which he had had in the spring of the same year 'avec deux jeunes et célèbres littérateurs anglais' whom he met in the Champs-Élysées. The two Englishmen, like the monster of the same kind described in the *Journal* of the Goncourts, affected to despise the frivolous nature of French libertinism:

'Ils s'étendirent en savantes variations sur le viol et sur les moyens dont on se sert, là-bas, pour l'accomplir commodément, soit en certaines demeures de Londres, soit en certains vieux châteaux anglais perdus dans les brumes. Chambres matelassées, oubliettes perfectionnées, anesthésiques et voitures de sûreté défilèrent sur leurs langues avec une verve sinistre. . . .'

One of the two Englishmen concluded:

'Au fond... pour connaître et comprendre les préférences passionnelles d'un peuple, la *nature*, enfin, des sens dont son organisme, en général, est pénétré, je dis qu'il n'est pas inutile de méditer, d'approfondir les impressions dominantes que laissent dans l'esprit, à cet égard, les œuvres de son *exprimeur* favori, de son Poète national. . . . Notre poète vraiment national est Algernon Charles Swinburne. . . . La dominante de ce qu'il exprime, en ses rêves sensuels, correspond le mieux à celle des sens de la majorité des Anglais.'

And, in order to give an example of the inspiration of the poet most representative of England, he declaimed the most perverse passage of *Anactoria* 'd'une voix féline et caressante: *Je voudrais que mon amour te tuât*', &c. Then:

'Ces milliers d'enfants et de toutes jeunes filles enlevés, achetés, et exportés chez nous, servent, je vous l'atteste, à nous procurer le genre de délices voluptueuses dont parle notre poète national; nous épuisons, parfois, sur leurs personnes, la série des plus douloureux raffinements, faisant succéder aux tortures des tortures plus subtiles. Et, si la mort survient, nous savons faire disparaître ces restes inconnus.'

If the meeting described by Villiers de l'Isle-Adam really took place, one of the 'jeunes et célèbres littérateurs anglais' who spoke to him may perhaps have been that great admirer of Swinburne—Wilde.

5. It was from the French translation already mentioned of the *Pall Mall Gazette* articles that D'Annunzio

derived Andrea Sperelli's knowledge of English libertinism (*Il Piacere*, 1889 edition, pp. 404–6):

'All the horrors of English libertinism rose up in Sperelli's mind—the exploits of the "Black Army" of the London pavements, the implacable pursuit of "filles vertes"; the brothels of the West End, of Halfousn (*sic*) Street, the elegant houses of Anna Rosemberg (*sic*) and of Mrs. Jefferies; the secret rooms, hermetically sealed, padded from floor to ceiling, where the shrill cries which torture wrings from its victims are deadened. . . .'

It was the French translation, *Les scandales de Londres*, which had 'Halfsoon Street' and 'Rosemberg', instead of 'Half Moon Street' and 'Rosenberg', as in the original; and in it was also to be found the expression 'filles vertes'. Also D'Annunzio was easily enabled to quote an English term such as *black army*, because the French translator, in his anxiety to give the literal meaning, often gives the original text in parenthesis, as for instance on p. 92: '. . . ce mode de recrutement de "l'armée noire (black army)" des trottoirs.' The French translation of *Il Piacere* repeats the mistakes, while the English omits the whole passage.

The Marquis of Mount Edgcumbe described in the same chapter of *Il Piacere* is none other than the double of the perverse Englishman described in the *Journal* of the Goncourts (second volume, published in 1887, which the author of *Il Piacere* had recently read).[13] Elena's husband is introduced to Sperelli at the theatre (p. 325), Goncourt's Englishman was introduced to Saint-Victor at the Opera. Like him, Elena's husband has 'a voice very curious in tone, rather shrill, &c.' and talks continuously (p. 400), ('il parle, il parle continuement'); he is 'bald on the temples' ('chauve'), has 'light-coloured eyes beneath the large convex brow' ('les tempes renflées comme une orange, les yeux d'un bleu clair et aigu'), 'those eyes which sometimes had dead, glassy reflections, or became animated with an indefinable glare, rather like the eyes of a madman' ('et tout en contemplant d'un regard de maniaque . . .'), 'veins in the forehead' which 'swelled' ('la peau . . . laissant voir le réseau sous-cutané des veines . . .'), 'a step which was rather jerky and unsteady, as of a man who suffers from the first stages of paralysis, from an

incipient disease of the spine, the . . . torso . . . rigid, not
responding to the movement of the legs, like the torso of
an automaton' (p. 402), 'the elbows . . . stiff, with the
stiffness of paralysis' (p. 404) ('un . . . jeune homme ayant
un peu de raideur dans les bras, et les mouvements de
corps à la fois mécaniques et fiévreux d'une personne
attaquée d'un commencement de maladie de la moelle
épinière'). The English sadist whom the Goncourts met
stares with the eyes of a maniac at 'les ongles de ses mains
tendues devant lui', and Georges Selwyn, in *La Faustin*,
had curious hands with pointed little-finger nails, as has
been already mentioned; the Marquis of Mount Edgcumbe, also, has 'sadistic' hands, but in certain of their
characteristics ('those soft, whitish hands, sprinkled with
very fair hairs') they remind one more of the well-known
hand of Lacenaire described by Gautier ('en même temps
molle et féroce . . . cette chair froide au duvet roux'). The
'grand meuble à hauteur d'appui' in which the sadistic
Englishman of the Goncourts kept his 'curieuse collection
de livres érotiques' becomes 'the large secret cupboard' of
the sadistic Englishman of D'Annunzio, who, however, is
not content with quoting only one of the rare books, but
makes use of the occasion to show off his knowledge of
pornography. The 'curious bindings stamped with phallic
emblems' correspond to the binding of Meibomius
described by the Goncourts 'avec des fers intérieurs représentant des phallus', &c. For the Meibomius described
by the Goncourts D'Annunzio substitutes Maclisius, but
the quotation was not made in vain in the *Journal*.[13A]

6. The sadistic English surgeon Welkinson, described
by Toulet in *Monsieur du Paur* (1898), actually called himself Meibomius ('Savez-vous ce que signifie M.? Non;
eh bien, ça veut dire Meibomius: un prénom que je me
suis donné et que je mérite, au moins'). This surgeon is
the brother of the *soi-disant* head-mistress of a college, at
gloomy Sambridge: the pupils are 'des filles de douze à
seize ans, presque toutes maladives, pâles'—in fact it is an
English version of the school directed by the surgeon
Rodin and his sister Célestine in the country town of
Saint-Marcel near Paris, as described by the Marquis de

Sade in *Justine*.[14] For this English version Toulet naturally had recourse to the *Scandales de Londres dévoilés par la Pall Mall Gazette*: from it he derived the method of quoting here and there, in parenthesis, the imaginary English text of a detective's report on the horrible discoveries made at Miss Welkinson's college; and, finally, the details of the report itself from two particular paragraphs already quoted, 'Why the cries of the victims are not heard' and 'Strapping girls down'. Doctor Welkinson has in his house in Regent Street 'un cabinet hérissé des plus barbares panoplies qui se puissent voir: partout l'acier luisant qui perce, scie et taillade la douloureuse chair de l'homme y étincelle et rampe sur les murs. . . .'

'Vous regardez mes bijoux, fit-il avec un rire âcre et retentissant qui éclatait au fond de sa gorge en laissant tous ses traits immobiles. Et mes fleurs, qu'en dites-vous? — Je ne m'en étais pas aperçu tout d'abord, mais en effet ce musée de tortures était ensanglanté çà et là des pivoines et des roses les plus magnifiques, et des bottes de lilas embaumaient dans les coins.'

It is unnecessary to add that, though the Doctor's face is immobile, 'son corps était agité sans cesse comme du linge sous le vent': he, also, has some serious nervous disease, like his antecedents, whether real (Swinburne) or imaginary (Goncourt's Selwyn). The mixture of flowers and instruments of torture is to be found also in O. Mirbeau's *Jardin des supplices* (written in 1898–9); but in this the English sadist is a woman instead of a man, a woman with eyes 'verts, pailletés d'or', like her 'diabolical' sister described by Barbey d'Aurevilly in the *Dessous de cartes*, the Comtesse de Stasseville ('ces deux émeraudes, striées de jaune . . .'). Eyes of this type seem to be a regular characteristic of the sadists described in the works we are discussing.[14A] Baulelaire, in the poem *Le Poison*, saw in green eyes an indication of cruelty:

> Tout cela ne vaut pas le poison qui découle
> De tes yeux, de tes yeux verts,
> Lacs où mon âme tremble et se voit à l'envers. . . .
> Mes songes viennent en foule
> Pour se désaltérer à ces gouffres amers.

> Tout cela ne vaut pas le terrible prodige
> De ta salive qui mord,
> Qui plonge dans l'oubli mon âme sans remord,
> Et, charriant le vertige,
> La roule défaillante aux rives de la mort!

Major Ydow, too, in Barbey d'Aurevilly's *A un dîner d'athées*, has green eyes which bring to mind the emerald eyes set in the head of a certain bust of Antinous.[15] This is a detail which was remembered by Jean Lorrain in *Monsieur de Phocas* (1901), in which, as in the *Jardin des supplices*, all the perverse elements of the literature of the *fin de siècle* seem to converge. Lorrain's Duc de Freneuse belongs to the family of Huysmans' des Esseintes, of Wilde's Dorian Gray, and has something of the real Montesquiou (as we have seen); but the type of corruptor, the sadistic English painter Ethal, the *voyeur* of the phenomena of physical and moral degeneration, is a reincarnation of Goncourt's Georges Selwyn. Ethal's poisoned ring, however, is not so much copied from the Œil d'Eboli, as the author states, as from the ring of Barbey d'Aurevilly's Marmor de Karkoël, and the ladies painted by him die of mysterious maladies like those in the *Dessous de cartes*. Freneuse, alarmed by the fatal influence of Ethal, exclaims:

'Pour qui me prend-il? Est-ce que par hasard il me rangerait au nombre des sadiques et des violeurs d'enfants, que sont presque tous ses compatriotes, ces puritains anglais aux faces congestionnées de porto et de gin ... qui, le soir, trouvent l'apaisement de leurs sens surchauffés dans les bureaux de placement des servantes irlandaises ... les pauvres petites impubères aux larges yeux de fleurs que la misère de Dublin envoie tous les mois au Minotaure de Londres?'

Here again is an echo of the *Maiden Tribute of Modern Babylon*, where the Minotaur of London is spoken of and the systems used for 'entrapping Irish girls' are denounced:

'Oh, la froide et cruelle sensualité anglaise — [continued Monsieur de Phocas] — la brutalité de la race et son goût du sang, son instinct d'oppression et sa lâcheté devant la faiblesse, comme tout cela flambait dans les yeux d'Ethal pendant qu'il s'attardait, avec une joie de félin, à me raconter l'agonie voulue de son petit modèle.'

The diary of the Duc de Freneuse opens with a quotation from Swinburne's *Laus Veneris*, which serves more or less as an indication of the content of the whole volume; further on he quotes other passages from the same poem, commenting upon it in the light of personal experience.

Among the minor characters of *Les Noronsoff* in *Le Vice errant* (1902) appears the poet Algernoon (*sic*) Filde, 'le lauréat anglais dont le récent divorce avait bouleversé Londres'; Algernoon Filde, 'l'auteur de *Vénus et d'Adonis* (*sic*) et du *Masque de la reine Bethsabée* . . . l'écrivain quasi scandaleux et partant illustre d'Hadrien au bord du Cydnus'. This poet had come into contact with the law on account of certain 'accès de tendresse un peu répétés pour des petites mineures, mais sait-on jamais exactement l'âge de ces bairmaids (*sic*) irlandaises dont le pullulement encombre la Cité?' (p. 266).

The following is a description of the personal appearance of this hybrid cross between Swinburne, Wilde[16] and Byron (pp. 280–1):

'(Noronsoff) d'instinct détestait cet Anglais maigre et glabre, à la face rusée de mauvais prêtre. Avec son menton accusé, ses joues creuses, et son sourire amer, ses yeux surtout, ses yeux gris à la fois perçants et troubles, profondément enfoncés sous l'entablement d'un ample front de penseur, Filde évoquait assez la ressemblance de Dante, mais d'un Dante qui se serait attardé et complu dans les cycles d'un équivoque Enfer. Il y avait du mystère dans ce profil émacié de l'École florentine, mais il y avait encore plus de sarcasme; et sous la noblesse du front les yeux ardaient d'un mauvais désir. Il y avait une cruauté dans l'ironie de ces prunelles mouvantes, et l'impression était plus gênante encore quand les prunelles demeuraient fixes.'

The sadistic Englishmen described by the Goncourts are not forgotten in this sketch, nor yet the portrait of Swinburne given by Maupassant.

A short time before (in 1900) Péladan, in *La Vertu suprême*, had described minutely a case of 'vice anglais'—'Dans le vice', he declares, 'cette race a un chapitre spécial, horrible'. Péladan too had obviously obtained his information from the *Scandales de Londres*:

'La seule ville au monde, où il y ait des maisons de torture, comme il y a des maisons de joie patentées, c'est Londres. Là, on peut monter dans un cab qui s'arrête à une maison tranquille: on vous introduit dans une cave aux parois matelassées et on vous pose ces questions: "Quel sexe? Quel âge? Bâillonnée ou non? Chloroformée ou non? De la charpie et des éponges?" Car une table de chirurgie est le lit de ces épouvantables débauches.'

The reason given by Péladan is curious:

'Le Latin regarde la femme à la gorge . . . L'Anglo-Saxon ne sait pas ce que c'est qu'un sein: de là, sa grossièreté et sa férocité en luxure.'

In Péladan's novel an elderly sadist, Sir Arthur Glocester (*sic*) exacts certain abnormal forms of compliance from a poor but beautiful governess, Nannah, whom he has married. He consents to her demand for a divorce on the condition that for twelve days she shall submit to certain of the horrible practices of the Black Mass. Sir Arthur decides to kill her by torture, and for the scene of his crime he selects a lonely farmhouse in Cotentin (Normandy) called Mimort, obviously a reminiscence of the *Chaumière de Dolmancé* of Swinburne and the imaginary Selwyn. Sir Arthur dresses up as an Inquisitor and treats his victim as though she were guilty of horrible crimes and sacrileges; he subjects her to tortures, at first in pretence, but afterwards becoming each day more real, until some of her friends, who have rushed to liberate her, rescue her from him, kill him, and burn down the sinister hovel. Sir Arthur conforms in every possible respect to the type that we know already. For instance—'Sir Arthur a vieilli, en quelques mois; ses tics, un mouvement spasmodique des doigts faisant griffe et le rictus nerveux qui lui sabre la figure d'un sourire de fou, se sont accrus.' Péladan does not fail to drag in Swinburne:

'Je pense à Swinburne qui a osé chanter le même penchant de férocité qui tient sir Arthur . . . Des gens bien intentionnés et peu occupés, comme on chasse à la vipère, devraient chasser au vice anglais . . . Swinburne a chanté le sadisme et toujours l'Anglo-Saxon incarnera la honte humaine: la race qui ensanglante la volupté, qui cache le couteau de l'assassin dans le lit de l'amour!'

7. This rapid review makes obvious the connexion between the various books in which the type of English

sadist is described, a connexion sometimes just as close as that which runs through the Elizabethan dramas in which the part of villain is entrusted to a disciple of Machiavelli.[17]   Though Swinburne may show up in sinister fashion against the background of the Decadent Movement, as did Machiavelli against the background of the Elizabethan age, it would be a mistake to regard him as a monster in the way in which the English, until a comparatively recent time, regarded Machiavelli.   The figures of both were distorted by legends to which their works gave credence: round their names crystallized analogous elements which already existed and which became coloured with a decided tinge of national quality.   After all, in the whole series of descriptions of English sadists which we have quoted, there are to be found only three persons who actually existed—the real George Selwyn of the eighteenth century, the anonymous gentleman whose acquaintance the Goncourts made in 1862, and Swinburne, whom Maupassant met in 1868.   All the others are derived, with amplifications, from them.   It must, however, be recorded that in the Introductory Note to the *Full and True Account of the Wonderful Mission of Earl Lavender* (1895) John Davidson spoke of a genuine 'recrudescence of flagellation', and saw in it 'an indication of a critical turn in the history of the world':

'The Flagellant society to which the Lady of the Veil introduced Earl Lavender may therefore be taken as a sign of the times —a sign of an age of effete ideals.   At least, the existence of such a sect among the wealthy classes is a proof of the existence of widespread contempt of the great commonplaces of life—love, marriage, and the rearing of children.'

¹ *Index Librorum Prohibitorum* (London, privately printed, 1877) especially pp. xl–xli.

² E. Dühren, *Das Geschlechtsleben in England*, vol. ii (Berlin, Lilienthal, 1903), pp. 336 et seq., 'Die Flagellomanie'.

³ J. H. Jesse, *George Selwyn and his Contemporaries* (London, Bentley, 1843), pp. 4–5.

⁴ Jesse, op. cit., p. 11.

⁵ Selwyn is spoken of in *Nocturnal Revels: or, the History of King's Place, and other modern Nunneries*, by a Monk of the Order of St. Francis (London, Goadby, 1779); translated into French as *Les Sérails de Londres ou les Amusements nocturnes* (Paris, Chez Barba, 1801). That Selwyn was not the only one of his kind seems to be assumed by a contemporary English authoress, Lady Eleanor Smith, who, speaking of the change of manners which took place in England about 1837, observes (*Flamenco*, 1931, p. 133):

'Gone were rakishness and lawlessness and wild carousing, and those mighty bucks and beaux who bullied night watchmen, and swooned with delight at the Opera, and who, drenching themselves with scent, sauntered forth of a morning to watch women burnt at the stake.'

Lady E. Smith was probably thinking of the clubs known as the 'Hellfire' and the 'Bold Bucks' (see R. Nevill, *London Clubs*, London, Chatto & Windus, 1911, p. 17, and De Quincey, *Works*, Edinburgh, 1863, vol. xiii, p. 124).

See also E. Beresford Chancellor, *The Hell-Fire Club*, London, Philip Allan & Co., 1925 (in the series *The Lives of the Rakes*); R. Fuller, *Hell-Fire Francis*, London, Chatto & Windus, 1939; Van Wyck Brooks, *The World of Washington Irving*, London, Dent, 1946, p. 349, footnote, where he speaks of the Medmenham Monks, a club whose members indulged in the most reckless sexual licence, with criminal practices which possibly suggested what is narrated in George Lippard's *The Quaker City, or The Monks of Monks' Hall*. See also the pages of *The Hardman Papers* (op. cit., on note 41 to chap. iv) concerning the harsh treatment to which Thomas Day, the author of the famous educational book *The History of Sandford and Merton* (1783–89), in which he exalted the prosperities of virtue, submitted the women he intended to marry: 'In some aspects of his mentality, the virtuous and high-minded Thomas Day came perilously near to his contemporary, the Marquis de Sade, though of course their aims were widely different.' In the First Series of R. H. Barham's *Ingoldsby Legends* (published in book form in 1840) there is, in the style of Coleridge's *Christabel*, a parody of the English lord (My Lord Tomnoddy) who attends capital executions (*The Execution*). As for the cruelty of the eighteenth and previous centuries' English towards animals (cock-fighting, bear-baiting), see Pope's articles in *The Guardian* for 1713, quoted by E. Audra, *L'Influence française dans l'œuvre de Pope*, Paris, Champion,

1931, p. 468. As for the ferocity of the dramas, which caused foreigners to consider the English a nation which delighted in gruesome spectacles, see no. 44 of *The Spectator*. [Add. 1950]

⁶ Something similar is related of Barbey d'Aurevilly: 'C'est classique de raconter, dans les bureaux de rédaction, que d'Aurevilly avait fait tanner une peau de femme pour des reliures.' (J. Péladan, *La victoire du mari*, 1889, p. xxxiii.)

There lived in Paris about 1840 an Englishman whose characteristics are curiously similar to those described by the Goncourts. This was Frederick Henkey, described as 'un homme si maigre qu'il devait marcher avec des béquilles à cause de sa grande faiblesse, et si amateur de livres sotadiques qu'il mériterait d'être appelé le Don Quichotte des obscènes', &c. See G. Apollinaire, preface to the *Tableau des mœurs de ce temps* by Crébillon fils, reprinted in Paris in 1921 in the Bibl. des Curieux, and preface to the *Œuvre du Chevalier de Nerciat*, p. 41, in the same collection, 1927. [Add. 1950]

⁷ Lafourcade, *Swinburne*, p. 197.

⁸ It is curious how certain characteristics of Swinburne, which later became fixed in the *cliché* of the sadist, should also belong to Usher in Poe's tale, *The Fall of the House of Usher*—thin, very pale lips, excessive development of the forehead, habitual trembling. Among Usher's favourite books was the *Directorium inquisitorium* of the Dominican, Eymeric de Gironne. With Maupassant's account of Swinburne cf. H. Taine's (*H. Taine, sa vie et sa correspondance*, Paris, Hachette, 1905, vol. iii, p. 145, letter from Oxford, June 4th, 1871):

'Hier, chez M. Jowett. Présenté à M. Swinburne le poète; ses vers sont dans le genre de Baudelaire et de Victor Hugo: petit homme roux en redingote et cravate bleue, ce qui faisait contraste avec tous les habits noirs et cravates blanches; il ne parle que raidi, rejeté en arrière avec un mouvement convulsif et continu des membres comme s'il avait le delirium tremens — très passionné pour la littérature française moderne, Hugo, Stendhal, pour la peinture.— Son style est d'un *visionnaire malade* qui, par système, cherche la sensation excessive.' (The italics are mine.)

Maupassant also relates, among other strange things which he saw and heard at the *Chaumière*, that 'des ossements traînaient sur des tables, parmi eux une main d'écorché, celle d'un parricide, paraît-il, dont le sang et les muscles séchés restaient collés sur les os blancs.' This appears to be a whim inspired by Gautier's poem on the hand of Lacenaire.

Maupassant must have relished such eccentricities, if, as Paul Morand maintains (*Vie de Maupassant*, pp. 199 and 202), he was himself 'un sadique né', and in the shadow of the Divine Marquis. [Add. 1950]

⁹ It will be seen shortly how D'Annunzio made use of the *Journal* of the Goncourts. It is therefore possible that the 'white lock among the dark hair, which . . . grew from the middle of the forehead' of Giorgio Aurispa's mysterious uncle (*Il Trionfo della Morte*) is derived from here. The points of relationship between the art of D'Annunzio and that of

the Goncourts have been studied by P. Sabatier (op. cit., chap. v, note181), pp. 595–9.

'M. D'Annunzio s'est imprégné de la lecture de la *Faustin* et de *Chérie*, de la *Maison d'un artiste* aussi, et c'est ce qui explique les rapports qu'on retrouve entre la *Faustin*, le *Feu* et l'*Enfant de Volupté*.'

According to Sabatier *Il Trionfo della Morte* derives from *La Faustin* by way of Rosny's *Daniel Valgraive*; La Foscarina, in *Il Fuoco*, has several of the characteristics of La Faustin (p. 342). Sabatier, however, gives no exact comparison of particular passages; he does not note, for instance, that the episodes of the virgin Orsola, who looks at herself naked in the mirror, and of the death-agony of the dog Sancio, in the *Novelle della Pescara*, are adaptations of episodes in *Manette Salomon* (Manette in front of the mirror, and the death agony of the monkey Vermillon), that certain Roman landscapes in *Il Piacere* (such as, in part, the famous passage of 'Rome under snow'), of the *Elegie Romane*, of the *Chimera*, are borrowed from passages in *Madame Gervaisais*, and so on. As regards the influence of Rosny, however, it must be noted that *L'Invincibile* (the first version of the *Trionfo della Morte*) appeared in the *Tribuna Illustrata* in 1890, whereas *Daniel Valgraive* was not published by Lemerre till 1891: I do not know if it appeared first in some paper in which D'Annunzio might have read it.

10 Granted the system of documentation which forms the basis of the novels of the Goncourts, the fact that it should be possible to quote a source for each detail in the characters of these novels is not surprising. Thus the episode of La Faustin's giving up the stage in order to retire to a lonely villa with Lord Annandale. is taken from the actual life of the celebrated tragic actress of the eighteenth century, Clairon, who did the same thing for a German prince. See E. Seillière, *Les Goncourt moralistes*, p. 87.

11 *Journal* of the Goncourts, vol. vi, Jan. 20th and Feb. 8th, 1882. See also above, note 9.

12 Huysmans, *A rebours*, p. 241.

13 This source was pointed out by G. P. Lucini, in *Antidannunziana*, op. cit., pp. 218–19, under the heading *Mastro* (a list of D'Annunzio's plagiarisms), which, together with much useful information, contains very curious oversights. D'Annunzio may have found the name of his character in the Bibliography to Vernon Lee's book of *Studies of the Eighteenth Century in Italy* (1880), which appeared in 1882 in an Italian translation (*Il Settecento in Italia*): there is to be found the quotation of *Musical Reminiscences from 1773* by the Earl of Mount Edgcumb (1834). Elena calls her husband by the affectionate nickname of 'Mumps'. Whether this is deliberate imitation or pure coincidence, Mrs. Figgup, Snarl's 'whore' in the *Virtuoso* of Thomas Shadwell (1676), uses this same nickname in a scene in Act III which is an illustration of the British love of flagellation:

Snarl. Ah poor little Rogue! in sadness, I'll bite thee by the Lip, i' faith I will. Thou hast incens'd me strangely, thou hast fir'd my Blood, I can bear it no longer; i' faith I cannot. Where are the Instruments of our Pleasure? Nay, Pr'ythee do not frown; by the Mass, thou shalt do't now.

Fig. I wonder that should please you so much, that pleases me so little?

Snarl. I was so us'd to 't at *Westminster* School, I could never leave it off since.

Fig. Well: look under the Carpet then, if I must.

Snarl. Very well, my dear Rogue. But dost hear? thou art too gentle. Do not spare thy Pains. I love Castigation mightily—So, here's good Provision. (*Pulls the Carpet, three or four Rods fall down*).

A similar scene, as we have noticed (see addition to p. 36, Section 3 of Chap. I), is to be found in Otway's *Venice Preserv'd*. [Add. 1950]

¹³ᴬ The sadist described here is again found, with a different nationality (Russian instead of English), in the character of Tushchievich of Diego Angeli's *L'Orda d'oro* (Milan, Treves, 1906); see pp. 45 and 217. The Russian has faded eyes which seem fixed on some indefinite shape in the void; when recollecting a capital execution in France (of a shepherd who had ripped women), he remains motionless, absorbed in himself, and 'only his fingers' tips shook imperceptibly'; he loves flowers and certain special smells; compels his beautiful wife (who has 'bright blue eyes in the perfect oval of her face, and a great halo of auburn hair round her pure forehead') to do infamous things. Also in Leandro's (Giustino Ferri's) *L'ultima notte* (see addition to note 81 of chap. iv) we find a Russian woman, Vera, who is a sadist and a worshipper of the devil. [Add. 1950]

¹⁴ Vol. i, chap. vi. Examples of similar schools in England are not lacking. See that of Elizabeth Brownrigg described by Dühren, op. cit., vol. ii, p. 425.

Also Squeers's school, described in Dickens's *Nicholas Nickleby*, supplies an outlet to the cruelty of its director. From this and from the general tone of the novel (which well might bear as a title *Nicholas Nickleby ou les malheurs de la vertu*) G. Lafourcade derived a hint for his curious article on Dickens's sadism: 'Charles Dickens ou le Rose et le Noir', in the review *Marsyas*, vol. iv, 162 (June 1934), pp. 760–2 ('Il coiffait de charité et de philanthropie des curiosités qui n'avaient en elles-mêmes rien de charitable ni de philanthropique'). See also G. Katkov, 'Steerforth and Stavrogin, On the Sources of *The Possessed*', in the *Slavonic Review*, 1949, pp. 469–88; and what Alexander Blok says of Dickens's novels in *The Collapse of Humanism*. [Add. 1950]

¹⁴ᴬ Already in *The Arabian Nights* (Nights 861–5; trans. by Mardrus, Paris, Fasquelle, 1903, vol. xiv, pp. 19–20) the vampire woman, who was a marvellous blonde girl 'of the islands of the farthest North', had blue eyes and a look 'as sweet as the sea'. This vampire woman had been the model of the Aurelia of Hoffmann's *Serapionsbrüder*, Book IV (Part viii, Berlin edn., Reimer, 1821, p. 427 et seq.). Gérard de Nerval had this story at the back of his mind when he called Aurelia the most fascinating incarnation of the ghost of a woman: see A. Marie, *Gérard de Nerval*, Paris, Hachette, 1914, p. 129.

On the other hand Carmilla, the vampire woman of Sheridan Le Fanu's story (in the volume *In a Glass Darkly*, 1872), a kind of fairy transposition of a Lesbian love-affair, not unlike Coleridge's *Christabel*, has black eyes: 'large, dark, and lustrous'. [Add. 1950]

¹⁵ Thin lips are another characteristic. See above, note 8. The lips of the Comtesse de Stasseville are 'ténues et vibrantes comme la cordelette d'un arc': 'la rigidité de cette lèvre étroite et meurtrière'. Irina Mouravieff, 'la Marquise de Sade de la Russie rouge', in the *Madone des Sleepings* by M. Dekobra (a probable allusion to the exploits of Rosa Luxembourg), has blue eyes and thin lips: 'Sa petite bouche mince n'exprimait pas la bienveillance et ses prunelles de lazulite pâle n'étaient rien moins qu'angéliques.'

The female sadists portrayed in the works of the Decadents are generally blondes. For instance, Clara, in the *Jardin des supplices*, is a blonde. And Swinburne, speaking of a picture by Simeon Solomon, made the following observation in an article which appeared in the *Dark Blue Magazine* of 1871, and which was later republished in vol. xv of the Bonchurch Edition of the *Complete Works* (*Simeon Solomon: Notes on his 'Vision of Love' and other Studies*):

'. . . . the admirable picture of Roman ladies at a show of gladiators, exhibited in 1865, which remains still his masterpiece of large dramatic realism and live imagination. All the heads are full of personal force and character, especially the woman's with heavy brilliant hair and glittering white skin, like hard smooth snow against the sunlight, the delicious thirst and subtle ravin of sensual hunger for blood visibly enkindled in every line in the sweet fierce features. Mr. Solomon apparently has sufficient sense of physiology to share the theory which Mr. Alphonse Karr long since proposed to develop at length in a systematic treatise 'sur la férocité des blondes'.

Cf. also E. de Goncourt, *La Faustin*, p. 253, apropos of Lord Annandale 'C'était dit d'une voix très douce, mais avec un visage sur lequel, tout à coup, était montée l'aiguë cruauté des blonds'. And J. Lorrain, *Ophelius* in *Buveurs d'âmes*, p. 164: 'Terribles, ces femmes de race anglo-saxonne, de race blonde. La cruauté aiguë des blonds n'est pas une invention littéraire. Le Nord est plein de ladies Viane.'

¹⁶ Lorrain's favourite system seems to be to change slightly certain well-known names by altering the initial letter, without bothering about the linguistic absurdity which results. Thus Filde does not exist, though Wilde does, Noronsoff does not exist, but there is a name Woronsoff (a Princess Woronsoff lived in Florence at the end of the nineteenth century). In the same way, in *L'Écho de Paris* for June 27, 1895, there appeared a gossipy chronicle, *Esthéticité* (*Scènes de la vie anglaise*) by Raitif de la Bretonne (a pseudonym of Lorrain), where Swinburne is introduced under the fictitious name of Algernon Isburne.

¹⁷ Other echoes of English sadism are to be found in *Naja Tripudians*, by Annie Vivanti (Florence, Bemporad, 1920; upon which see Benedetto Croce's note in *La Critica*, Jan. 20th, 1931, pp. 73–5, 'Riscontri curiosi'), and in *Au coin des rues*, by Francis Carco (op. cit., in note 45 of chap. i), pp. 142 et seq., *Le Possédé*. In this last story the English painter Willy Bing, whose face is 'marqué d'une singulière vieillesse' and who has

enormous hands covered with yellow hairs, says in his exotic French that he feels 'une espèce dégoûtante de curiosité avant les exécutions capitales vers l'aube', and relates a certain visit of his to the 'petites rues infectes et les manières de brasseries où étaient assises les femmes mutilées', a horrible sight which fills him with a 'bonheur secret'.

INDEX

Abercrombie, L., on Romanticism, 18–19

Accoramboni, V., 200, 341

Achillini, C., his *Bellissima Spiritata*, 37, 39; his *Bellissima Mendica*, 40, 41

Adam, P., 331; and Byzantium, 398–9

Adimari, A., 3; and the beauty of defects, 36, 38, 39, 41, 50; and negresses, 44

Adulteresses, sonnets on, 262–3

Aeschylus, 57, 282; and the Fatal Woman, 199, 200

Aestheticism, and the Fatal Woman, 210; and female beauty, 212–13; and the exotic, 213

Agoult, Mme d', on the Princess Belgiojoso, 124

Aikin, J. and A. L., and the pleasure from Terror, 27

Alcibiades, 295, 369

Alcman, 3; not a Romantic, 4

Aldington, R., 423

Algolagnia, 48, 156; in Cleopatra, 215; Swinburne and, 225, 226, 231, 236; in Rossetti, 228; in D'Annunzio, 268; in the Decadents, 321, 322, 365; in Schwob, 370; in Barrès, 377; in England, 437 *et seq.*

Alison, A., 20

Allan, Frances, 46

Allori, C., 336, 418

Althea, 199

Amadis de Gaule, the 'noble bandit' and, 85

Amestris, 240, 250

Ampère, A. M., 1

Ancient world, nostalgia for, in Gautier, 213–14; in Stendhal, 285; as a source of the Fatal Woman, 216, 222, 240; the Decadents and, 397

Androgyne, the, 182–3, 216, 414; Moreau and, 305; Péladan and, 334–40; the Decadent Movement and, 346, 350, 415; Rachilde and, 346–9; Pater and, 355–6; Vivien and, 388; Colette and, 415; Lorrain and, 421; *see also* Hermaphroditism

Anet, C., his *Ariane*, 209

Angeli, Diego, 455

Angiolieri, C., 5

Annunzio, G. d', 6, 47, 296, 297, 356, 409, 413–14, 427; and the relationship between Beauty and Death, 31–2; and the Medusa-Gioconda smile, 52; and the regenerated prostitute, 111; his debt to Flaubert, 188, 262; and the Fatal Woman, 210, 258, 261–5; and Swinburne, 238, 259, 269, 272, 273, 290, 291, 297–8; as a sadist, 264–5, 274–7, 298–300; his 'libido', 265; his obsession with bloodshed, 266–8, 281; his plagiarism, 269–72, 298; and the tragic poets, 291; and Moreau, 310; influenced by Huysmans, 323; and Péladan, 332; his influence, 363, 365; Barrès compared with, 379; and Byzantium, 398; the chief figure of the Decadent Movement, 399–403; as a barbarian, 401, 434; his first models, 401–2; his humour, 402; compared with Hugo, 402; and the Vittoriale, 402–3; and art and music, 404; and English libertinism, 444–5; and the Goncourts' *Journal*, 446, 453–5

Anthology (Greek), 202

Antigonus Carystius, 4

Antinous, 328, 360, 393, 414, 448; the Androgyne, 336, 348

Apollinaire, G., 453

Apuleius, 426

Arabian Nights, 120, 213, 419, 455

Araldi, A., 416

Arioso, L., 1

Arlt, G. O., 175

Arnaud, Baculard d', on the taste for the Horrid, 46

Arnauld, M., 407

——, Mère M.A., 174

Arnold, M., 422

Art, its interpretation, 2–3; and the use of formulas, 3

Arthurian Romances, 8

Artist, the, and the history of culture, 2; an exoticist, 211

Atalaric, 381

Atkinson, N., 178

Aubigné, A. d', 343

Aubry, A., 133

Aucassin et Nicolette, 8

Audra, E., 452

Auger, P. S., on the Byronic fashion, 82, 165

August Wilhelm, Duke of Braunschweig-Luneburg, 341

Auguste, Jules-Robert, 414

Augustin-Thierry, A., 124, 178, 415

Aurevilly, Barbey d', 72, 131, 341, 350, 395, 408, 421, 448, 456; his *Léa*, 39, 51; Flaubert's early work compared to, 158; and the Fatal Woman, 209, 277; and Huysmans' Des Esseintes, 305, 405; France and, 321, 325–7; and the Decadent Movement, 325–9; on Péladan, 331–2; and Mendès, 343, 344; and Rachilde, 346; compared with Dostoievsky, 351; a model for Goncourt's Selwyn, 442; and green eyes, 447, 448; and flagellation, 453

Austen, Jane, 175

Ayres, Ph., 50, 51

Babbitt, I., 18-19, 50, 85, 172, 183, 284, 409

Bacchiacca, 292

Bachelin, H., 409

Bachler, K., 421

Bachofen, J. J., 17

Bacon, F., 21, 47

Baird-Smith, Mrs., 179

Baldensperger, F., 175, 189, 205

Balzac, H. de, 119, 181, 236, 334, 345, 414; and the 'frénétique' type of novel, 122; his Jane la Pâle, 287; and the Hermaphrodite, 332; Beardsley and Conder and, 333, 414

Bandinelli, B., 336

Banville, Th. de, 40; his sonnets on adulteresses, 262–3; inspired by Cleopatra, 286; and Heine's Herodias, 314–15

Barbari, J. de', 308

Barbé-Marbois, Sophie de, 178

Barbier, A., his Liberty likened to Swinburne's, 248

Barbiera, R., 178, 416

Barham, R. H., 452

Barilli, M., 434

Baronio, 272, 273

Baroque, use of the term, 3, 5, 6, 12

Barrès, M., 32, 50, 169, 291, 402, 411, 426, 427, 429; on Byron, 93; and Delacroix, 143; and the exotic, 210; and the Leonardo smile, 294; his confused Christianity, 321; and Rachilde, 346–8; his Bérénice, 373–5; other works of, 375–9, 429; Sadism in, 376–7, 379, 394; and Venice, 377, 429; France and, 428; on himself, 429–30, 432

Bartoli, D., 161

Bartolomeo da Venezia, Huysmans and, 417–18

Basile, G. B., 297

Bataille, H., 353

Baudelaire, Ch., 3, 17, 21, 47, 78, 83, 112, 125, 133, 182, 239, 255, 288, 308, 321, 350, 353, 355, 356, 370, 382; on beauty, 23, 53; and the connexion between Beauty and Pain, 29–30, 31; and the strange, 38–9; and the beauty in deformities, &c., 40–5; and Hugo, 47; and *Les Liaisons dangereuses*, 103–4, 169; influence of de Sade on, 108, 128–9, 148, 157; and Maturin, 119; influence of Borel on, 134–5, 136, 138; early influences on, 139, 182; and Delacroix, 141, 142, 144, 153, 184, 304; as he appeared to his contemporaries, 144–5; his Decadence, 145; and Poe, 46–7, 51, 146–8, 153, 155, 186, 192; his type of love, 147–8; and Jeanne Duval, 151–2; sadism in, 152, 185; his reputed impotence, 153, 187; proposed titles of his novels, 153–4; compared with Flaubert, 157, 160, 163; and Ducasse, 165; and Janin, 180; compared with Swinburne, 223, 226, 237; his influence on Swinburne, 228, 256, 257; D'Annunzio and, 269, 276, 277; and the Fatal Woman, 277, 281; and the fetishism of naked feet, 290; his rules of

Beauty, 303–4; his influence on Huysmans, 323, 325; and Mendès, 343–4; disciples of, 384–5, 388, 411, 419, 453; the Goncourts and, 442; and green eyes, 447–8

Bäumler, A., 8

Beardsley, A., 315, 407, 432; and Balzac's *La Fille*, &c., 333, 414; and Decadence in England, 356–7; and Colonna, 424–5; and Wagner, 425

Beauclair, H., and parody of the Decadents, 380–1

Beaumont, F., 291

Beauty, in the Medusa conception, 25–7; and the Horrible, 27; and Melancholy, 28–31; and Death, 31–2; in disease and decay, 36–40; in defects and abnormalities, 40–5; the Romantics and, 82; Baudelaire and, 186; The Pre-Raphaelites and, 228; of Inertia, 303; Moreau and, 303–9; Dostoievsky on, 350–1; Barrès and, 374, 377

Beauvoir, R. de, 139

Beckford, W., 86, 211, 284

Belgiojoso, Princess, 123–5, 178, 254, 294; Péladan's Princess D'Este based on, 416

Bell, Quentin, 404

Bendz, E., 407, 422

Benedetto, L. F., and Flaubert, 191, 205, 283

Bénédite, L., 406

Bérenger, H., on Schwob, 368

Berenson, B., 292, 416

Berlioz, 123; and the macabre, 139–40

Bernanos, G., 277

Bernhardt, Sarah, 316

Berni, F., 36

Bernini, L., 19

Bertaud, J., 51, 187, 290

Bianchi, *see* Ferrari

Bibliophile Jacob, *see* Lacroix, P.

Birkhead, E., 86

Black Mass, the, 276, 278, 324, 366, 386, 388, 408

Blake, W., 18; and Milton, 58, 148; Swinburne and, 233, 247; and de Sade, 290

Blessington, Lady, 73

Blind, K., 247

Bloch, I., *see* Dühren, Dr.

Blok, Alexander, 407, 455

Bloodshed, Delacroix's obsession with, 141, 143; D'Annunzio's obsession with, 266–8; Flaubert's obsession with, 156, 160, 190, 265

Bloy, Léon, 194, 321, 408

Bluebeard, 410

Bock, E. J., 422

Bois, J., 427–8

Boito, A., 295

Bonal, F., 51

Bonaparte, Marie, 46

Boni, G., 433

Borel, P., 181, 182, 296; Janin and, 128, 138; and the 'tale of terror', 133; his *Contes Immoraux*, 133–6, 421; his *Madame Putiphar*, 136–8, 195; Baudelaire on, 138–9; likened to Flaubert, 158–9; and Lautréamont, 165–6; compared with Sue, 208, 283; de l'Isle-Adam compared with, 329; and English sadism, 438

Borelli, Lyda, 317

Borgese, G. A., 266, 297, 434

Borgia (family), 60, 353, 417, 424

——, Lucrezia, 115, 226, 328, 417, 418; as the Fatal Woman, 200, 227

Borromini, F., 19

Bortone, G., 175

Bosch, H., 344

Bossard, Abbé E., 195, 325, 410

Botticelli, 335, 353, 417, 422, 423, 425

Boucher, F., 202

Boucicault, D., 411

Bouilhet, L., inspired by Cleopatra, 286

Boulay-Paty, E., his *Élie Mariaker*, 39–40

Boulenger, J., 183

Boullan, Abbé, and Satanism, 410

Bourdin, P., and de Sade, 129, 171, 180

Bourges, É., his *Le Crépuscule des Dieux*, 341–3, 344, 419

Bourget, P., 169, 406; on Rollinat's house, 386; Goncourt and, 442

Brantôme, 48, 230

Brass, F. K., 407

Brawne, Fanny, 249, 285

Bremond, H., 211

Breton, A., and Lautréamont, 194

Bretonne, Restif de la, 171, 394; and de Sade, 109–11, 171; his influence on Sue, 209

Bricaud, J., and Black Magic, 331, 410, 413

Brie, F., 191, 285, 288; and exoticism, 210, 211, 213, 260

Brignole-Sale, A. G., on the Whipped Courtesan, 37; some facts of his life, 50

Brissot, on the beauty of the Horrid, 46

Brooks, Van Wyck, 452

Brosses, Président de, on *Thérèse Philosophe*, 100–1

Brown, 'Capability', 21

——, Horatio, 424

——, Dr. J., 20

Browning, Robert, 49

Brummel, 191

Brunetière, F., 7

Bulteau, Mme, 433

Bulwer-Lytton, 93

Burchiello, 165

Burdett, O., 424, 425

Burke, E., 20

Burnand, F., and Adah Menken, 292

Burne-Jones, E., 228, 416; Lorrain and, 363, 364

Butt, J., 17

Buxton-Forman, H., 249

Byron, Lord, 85, 87, 91, 93, 103, 392; as the rebel type, 63–8, 85; the relation of his heroes to Zeluco, 68, 74; his debt to Chateaubriand, 69–71, 89; and Mrs. Radcliffe's Schedoni, 71; as the Fatal Man, 72, 80–3; and incest, 73, 75, 90–1; his treatment of his wife, 73–6; and vampirism, 78, 80, 81; in the *Cahiers* of Barrès, 93; and the persecuted maiden, 120, 121, 122; his influence on French writers, 137, 138, 141, 312, 327; Flaubert and, 164; Ducasse and, 165; and Swinburne, 234–5; a satanist, 277; and exoticism, 285; his influence on Guerrazzi, 296

Byron, Lady, Byron's treatment of, 74–6, 91

Byzantium, Chapter V, *passim*; introduction of this fashion into Italy, 430; D'Annunzio and, 272; the Decadent Movement and, 397–9; Adam and, 398–9

Cabanès, Dr., on Baudelaire, 185

Calderón de la Barca, P., 118

Caligula, 168

Callimachus, 405

Camerana, G., 295

Campbell, Th., and the 'picturesque', 20, 22

Cantianille, 410

Carcano, Giulio, 176

Carco, F., on the attraction of vice, 52; and English sadism, 456

Carducci, G., his idea of Liberty likened to Swinburne's, 259, 268; Nencioni and, 259

Carlisle, Lord, 247

Casanova, 170

Castelvetro, L., 167

Castiglione, B., 20

Castro, Eugenio de, 288, 407

Cat, the, Poe and, 146; Wilde and, 256–7; Rollinat and, 386

Catherine II, 221

Catholicism, Huysmans and, 320, 408; in French Decadent literature, 321

Catiline, 59, 60

Cavaceppi, Bartolomeo, 422

Cazamian, L., 422

Cazotte, J., his *Le Diable amoureux*, 202, 282

Cellini, B., 294, 363

Cenci, Beatrice, 116–18, 176, 296

Cendrars, B., 193

Cervantes, 120; Schiller and, 85

Challant, Comtesse de, 200

Chambers, E. K., 17

Chamfort, 73

Champion, P., on Schwob, 369, 428

Chancellor, E. Beresford, 452

Chantepie, Mlle Leroyer de, 162

Chapman, George, 230

——, Guy, 284

Charles IX of France, 229

Charpentier, J., 183

Chastel, A., 288

Chastelard, 230–2

Chateaubriand, 103, 172, 282, 284, 326, 336; and the pleasure from melancholy, 30–1; his René, 77, 93, 172; Byron's debt to, 69–70, 89; and the appearance of *Atala*, 88; and incest, 111–12; and exoticism, 191–2; and the Fatal Woman, 201, 204, 219; and French Decadent Literature, 321, 408; Barrès' resemblance to, 375

Chatterton, Th., 123

Chênedollé, Ch. P. de, 172

Chevalier, E., Flaubert and, 164, 180, 193

Christianity, and the appreciation of landscape, 19

Cinderella, as the persecuted maiden, 167

Cinthio, G. B. Giraldi, 48

Cinti, D., 296

Clairon, 454

Claretie, J., 181, 182

Classic, as an approximate term, 1; the classic–romantic antithesis, 6–11; Barrès and, 379

Clemm, Virginia (Mrs. E. A. Poe), 46

Cleopatra, as a Fatal Woman, 213–16, 222, 230, 231, 240, 254, 283, 285, 352, 355, 397; the Romantic poets and, 219, 229, 286; Swinburne and, 250, 251–2, 256

Clytemnestra, 199

Cœur, Abbé, 415

Coleridge, S. T., 5, 11, 452, 456; and the Eternal Feminine, 213, 285

Colet, Louise, Flaubert and, 161–2, 192

Colette, 299, 428, 431; and Decadent literature, 362, 396, 415

Collins, W., 27

——, W. Wilkie, 173

Colonna, F., 289, 425; Beardsley and, 356–7, 424

Comnena, La, 268, 271

Conder, Ch., 333, 334, 414

Cons, L., 182

Constant, B., his *Adolphe*, 305

Conte, E., 421

Conti, A., and Decadence, 261; and art and music, 404

Coprophily, Schwob and, 370–1

Cornette, A. H., on J. Ensor, 426

Corvo, Baron, *see* Rolfe

Costetti, G., 363

Coulon, M., 392, 432

Couperus, Louis, 434

Courbet, 414–15

Courtenay, William, 284

Cozens, Alexander, 284

Crashaw, R., his rendering of Marino on Satan, 56–7

Crébillon (fils), 453

Crépet, E., 184, 186, 187, 290

——, J., 184

Crespigny, Sir Claude de, 411

'Criminal sensuality', in D'Annunzio, 298–9

Croce, B., 171, 295; and the use of approximate terms, 1, 8; and the classic-romantic antithesis, 10–11, 17; and Flaubert, 188, 193, 283; on Kleist, 282; on A. Vivanti and English sadism, 456

'Cronaca Bizantina', the, 363, 397, 430

Crowley, A., and satanism, 412–13

Culture, history of, 2

Curling, J., 213, 293

Custance, O., 356

D'Alembert, 100

Dalton, J., 21

Damiens, R. F., 437, 438

Dante, 1–2, 15, 20, 255, 285, 449; Milton and, 57; and the Fatal Woman, 200, 375, 388

Danton, G. J., 110

Dargenty, G., and Delacroix, 142, 184

Davidson, J., 432, 451

Davies, Sir John, 289

Day, Thomas, 452

Death, Beauty and, 31

Decadence, and Romanticism, 83, 108, 154; Conti and, 261; Moreau as a representative of, 303; exponents of, in France, 322–65; the literary world and, 396

Decadents, the, and de Sade, 128; Wilde and, 312; Péladan and, 339; and the 'frénétique', 351; their obsession with green eyes, 360; and Wagner, 433–4

Decadent Movement, the, paintings of, 305; Mallarmé and, 317; Rops and, 319, 383; literature of, 320;

d'Aurevilly and, 325–8; de l'Isle-Adam and, 329–30; Péladan and, 330–1; Mendès and, 343; and the Androgyne, 336, 350; and the 'frénétique', 351; Lorrain and, 353, 359–65; in England, 355–9, 412–13, 422; de Gourmont and, 366–8, 373; Schwob and, 368–73; Gide and, 383; Vivien and, 388–90; parodies of the poetry of, 390–2, 432; Verlaine and, 392; causes of the Movement, 394 *et seq.*; and Byzantium, 397; D'Annunzio and, 399 *et seq.*; its relation to Romanticism of 1830, 411

Decameron, 69

De Foe, D., 5, 110

Dekobra, Maurice, 210, 456

Delacroix, E., his macabre style, 141–2, 143; compared with Swinburne, 142, 144, 247; Baudelaire on, 184, 304; compared with Baudelaire, 153, 184; likened to Flaubert, 155, 158, 161–2; as a painter, 303, 308, 312

del Cairo, F., 428

Delilah, 222, 272

Delior, P., 428

Denham, J., 19

Denison, Albert, 178

De Quincey, Th., 127, 129, 179–80, 193, 369, 452; and murder, 126, 179; his Mater Lachrymarum, 212

de Roy, E., 41

Deshairs, L., 405–6

Deutsch, N. Manuel, 32

Deutschbein, M., on 'romantic' and 'romanesque', 17–18

Diamond, W., 17

Dianti, L. de, 341

Dickens, Charles, 455

Diderot, 127, 167, 322, 368, 394; and beauty and morality, 32; on Richardson's Lovelace, 99; as a forerunner of de Sade's *Justine*, 99; and the justification of perversion, 99–100; and the persecuted maiden, 99, 174; Maturin's debt to, 121, 177; de Gourmont compared with, 366

Diehl, Ch., 397

Diodorus Siculus, 286

Don Quixote, the bandit of, 85

Donadoni, E., on Tasso, 33

Donne, J., and the beauty of maturity, 37, 40

Dostoievsky, 108, 147, 290, 370, 433; profanation, 157; and *Thérèse Philosophe*, 168; and the Fatal Woman type, 209; his confused Christianity, 321; in France, 336, 350; and 'frénétique' Romanticism, 351; his influence on Lorrain, 352; his influence on Gide, 379, 380, 382; his psychic state, 419–20; as a sadist, 419, 420

Douglas, Lord Alfred, 407

Dowden, E., 294

Dowson, E., 356, 414

Doyon, R.-L., 411

Drake, N., 27

Drama, 'monastic', 122, 173

Dryden, John, 49

Du Bos, Ch., on Byron as an 'outlaw', 72–3, 91, 92, 429; and Wilde, 354; and Gide, 380

Dubufe, 414

Dubus, É., 331

Ducasse, I., *see* Lautréamont

Ducray-Duminil, 209

Dufay, P., and Baudelaire's impotence, 187

Du Fresnoy, Ch. A., 19

Dühren, Dr., 289, 411, 437, 452

Dumas, A. (père), 141, 182, 289; his Antony as a 'fatal' rebel, 77; and the recognition scene, 115; and the *roman-feuilleton*, 122; and the horrible, 133; de Sade's influence on, 139; and Orientalism, 215

Dumesnil, R., and Flaubert, 154, 155, 163, 188

Duplan, J., 192

Duret, Th., 425

Duval, Jeanne, 44, 151–2, 182

——, P., *see* Lorrain, J.

Dyer, J., and the 'picturesque', 19

Eaton, H. A., 179

Eckermann, J. P., 17

Ecstasy, in the exotic, 211, 212

Egan, T. S., 407

Eggli, J. E., 87, 93

El Greco, Barrès on, 378

Eliot, T. S., 17

Elizabethan dramatists, 49, 68; and beauty, 28; and delight in pain,

36; influenced by Italian Renaissance, 200, 328; their influence on Swinburne, 228, 230, 291; Bourges and, 341, 342; and Machiavelli, 451

Ellis, Havelock, 423–4

——, S. M., 289

Elssler, Fanny, 414

Empedocles, 169

Encyclopédistes, 111, 366, 368

England, the Fatal Woman in, 223; Decadent Movement in, 355–9, 412–13, 422; flagellation in, 437–51; sadism in, 437–8, 443–51, 456–7

Englishman, the, 134, 181–2

Englishwoman, the, as a Fatal Woman, 210

Ensor, J., 350, 426

Ernst, Max, 194

Escholier, R., 184

Escouchy, M. d', 371

Este (d') (family), 297, 335, 341

Estève, E., 82, 86–7, 94, 173, 174

Eternal Feminine, Swinburne and, 240, 273

Eton, its influence on Swinburne, 249, 251

Eulenburg, A., 300

Euripides, 8, 250

Evil, as a part of beauty, 309

Exoticism, 5, 19, 284; in Flaubert, &c., 191; and the erotic, 207; and the Fatal Woman, 210; and mysticism, 210–11; the Romantics and, 211; in Gautier, *Une Nuit de Cléopâtre*, 213; true and false, 285–6; Delacroix, &c., and, 303; de Rais and, 325; Barrès and, 378–9

Eymery, Marguerite, *see* Rachilde

Falk, B., 292

Farmer, A. J., 422, 424

Farnese, Giulia, 417–18

Farnie, H. B., 292

Fatal Man, the, descendant of the Byronic hero, 77–8, 80, 216; as a vampire, 79–80; his metamorphosis, 281

Fatal Woman, the, 154, 421; in Flaubert, 156, 220–3; in mythology and literature, 199–200; the Romantics and, 201 *et seq.*; Lewis's Matilda as, 202–4; in Chateaubriand, 204–5; in Mérimée, 205–7; in Sue, 207–9;

as a Russian woman, 209–10, 351; in Gautier, 213–16; sexual cannibalism in, 215–16; the archetype, 219–20, 288; in Swinburne's Mary Stuart, 229–33; in Dolores, &c., 238–46, 249; in Monna Lisa, 253–4; her change in Wilde's *The Sphinx*, 256–7; in Wilde's *Salome*, 258; in D'Annunzio, 258, 261–5, 269; in Nencioni, 258–60, 261; in Italy, 261; her noble origin, 271; studied from life, 277–9; in Gilkin, 279–80; her metamorphosis, 281; Huysmans and, 305, 307; Moreau and, 310; in Dostoievsky, 209, 351; in O'Shaughnessy, 355; Verlaine and, 393

Fatality, as a part of beauty, 309

Faulkner, Jane, Swinburne and, 246, 254, 260, 264, 298

Faust, 403, 427

Faustine, Swinburne and, 239–40, 254, 260, 264, 298

Fehr, B., 288; and Wilde's sources, 294, 422

Ferrari, F. Bianchi, 416

Ferri, G. (Leandro), 296, 455

Féval, P., and the *romans-feuilleton*, 80; his Rio-Santo as Byron, 80–1; and English sadism, 437–8

Fiorentino, I., 397

Fischer, W., 422

Flagellation, in Swinburne, 225–7, 251, 289; in literature, 289; in England, 437, 438, 449, 454–5

Flandre, J. L., 405

Flaubert, G., 295, 423; *Bouvard et Pécuchet*, 21, 141, 372; and Romantic sensibility, 28, 31; and the Beauty of Pain, 45; his analogy with Baudelaire, 154; and de Sade, 154–7; profanation in, 157, 188; his feminine ideal, 157–8; his taste for the Orient and Rome, 158–9, 191; exoticism in, 159–61, 207; his letters to Louise Colet, 161–2; one of his letters to Mlle Chantepie, 162; and Byron, 164; his sadistic temperament, 163–4; on Janin, 180; and incest, 188; and Borel, 189–90; and the Fatal Woman, 201, 205, 210, 254, 277–8, 283; Vampirism in, 220–1; inspired by Cleopatra, 222; compared with Swinburne,

229, 235, 244, 277; compared with D'Annunzio, 262, 265, 272, 274; and the fetishism of naked feet, 290–1; Wilde's debt to, 294, 312, 313; compared with Huysmans, 306–7, 325; his Salome, 317, 407; his Salammbô, 251, 310, 318, 319, 399; his influence on Lorrain, 363; and Schwob, 369, 370; Barrès and, 376, 377; the literary antecedent of Rops, 384; and Byzantium, 397, 399; compared with Moreau, 405

Flecker, J. E., 356

Flemalle, Master of, 322

Fletcher, J., 291

Flora, F., and D'Annunzio, 266, 275, 297, 298

Flottes, P., and Baudelaire's religion, 184–5; and Baudelaire's impotence, 187

Ford, J., 49, 291, 342, 370

Foscolo, 168

Fragonard, 333

Fraisse, A., Baudelaire and, 184

France, use of word 'romantique' in, 13; and the 'noble brigand', 63, 86; the 'tale of terror' in, 122; the Russian novel in, 336, 350 et seq.; literary fashion in, 401

France, A., 129, 180, 394; and Baudelaire, 185; and sadism and Catholicism in Decadent literature, 321; on d'Aurevilly, 325; on Péladan, 331; and Barrès, 428

——, H., 411

François, A., 17

Fraxi, Pisanus, 437

Freud, S., and Dostoievsky's psychic state, 419

Fuller, R., 452

Futurism, 6

Gabory, E., 410

Gabrieli, M., 421

Gall, F. J., 130

Gallienne, R. Le, and the Fatal Woman, 281; and Decadence, 356; his parody of the Decadents, 391–2, 432

Gamiani, de Musset and, 183

Gargiulo, A., on D'Annunzio, 269, 270, 297

Garnett, C., 420

Gattina, P. Petruccelli della, and Lesbianism, 415

Gaunt, W., 293, 404, 422, 425

Gautier, Judith, 47

——, Th., 94, 124, 133, 180, 191, 222, 251, 281–2, 283, 295, 358, 403, 404, 446, 453; and the roman-charogne, 125, 128; de Sade's alleged influence on, 139, 182–3; and Delacroix, 141; his exoticism compared with Flaubert's, 158, 159–60, 197; and the Fatal Woman, 210, 213; and female beauty, 212; as a founder of aesthetic exoticism, 205, 405; his Nuit de Cléopâtre, 213–16; his Roi Candaule, 217–18, 292; and the Vampire woman, 218–19; and the archetypal Fatal Woman, 219–20, 254, 279, 281, 282; and Swinburne, 223, 227, 228, 229, 231, 236, 244; inspired by Cleopatra, 252; and the Hermaphrodite, 332–3, 356, 414, 428

Gavarni, Goncourt on, 169

Géricault, 142

Germany, and the 'tale of terror', 122

Gide, A., 28, 169, 290; his influences, 379–80, 381; characteristic of, 380; sadism in, 380–1, 382–3

Gilkin, I., his Fatal Woman, 279–80

Gilpin, W., 20, 21

Ginzburg, L., 420

Gioconda, La, 3, 294, 341, 342, 351; her mysterious smile, 45, 52, 281, 293; Walter Pater and, 253–4, 281, 418; Huxley and, 256; Wilde and, 257; Conti and, 261; the Goncourts and, 293; the Androgyne and, 334, 339

Giordano, L., 402

Giorgione, Conti on, 261, 404

Girardin, Marquis de, and the word 'romantique', 13

Gironne, E. de, 453

Godwin, W., his St. Leon, 177; his Caleb Williams, 282

Goethe, 10, 94, 121, 259, 282; his Wilhelm Meister and Hamlet, 2, 17; and the Medusa legend, 26, 27; and the Vampire legends, 78, 79, 81–2, 219; and the persecuted maiden, 98, 112, 113, 119, 120, 167,

172, 205; and the regenerated prostitute, 111

Gogol, N., 425

Goncourt, J. and E. de, 184, 291, 293, 324, 403, 416, 419, 421, 425, 453; on the beauty of corruption, 45; on the influence of the *Confession* of de Musset, 140–1; and Flaubert, 155; on *Justine*, 169; and the Gioconda, 293; and Moreau, 361–2; and Schwob, 369; and Rops, 383; and Rollinat, 386; and de Montesquiou, 388; and vice, 395, 433; *hermaphrodisme intellectuel* of, 433; and sadism in England, 438, 439–40, 441, 444, 445–6; and Baudelaire, 442; E.'s Georges Selwyn, 447, 448, 449, 451; D'Annunzio and, 453–4; and the *cruauté des blonds*, 456

Gorer, G., 290

Gorky, Maxim, 420

Gosse, E., 224; and Swinburne, 247

Goupil, Albert, 426

Gourmont, R. de, 108, 338, 347, 369, 402; on Louÿs' *Aphrodite*, 284; influenced by Huysmans, 323; quoted by Lorrain, 363; compared with Lorrain, 365; as a sadist, 366–7; sacrilege in, 367–8; compared with Barrès, 373; on Chateaubriand, 375; his physical life, 428; Rouveyre on, 407, 428

Govoni, C., and the Fatal Woman, 209; his algolagnic fantasies, 365

Goya, 60, 174, 346

Gozzano, G., 111

Gracq, Julien, 194

Graves, R., 21

Gray, J., 356

——, T., 17, 20

Greece, and the 'tale of terror', 115, 176; and the Fatal Woman, 199, 216; Leonardo's Gioconda compared with its sculptures, 253

Greuze, J.-B., 414

Grien, H. Baldung, 32

Grierson, H. J. C., on the classic–romantic antithesis, 7–8, 9, 17, 84

Grillparzer, F., his debt to *The Monk*, 114, 175

Grimm, J. and W., 297

Guaita, Marquis S. de, 331, 410, 411; on Péladan, 334; his works, 410

Guastalla, R., 296

Guerrazzi, F. D., 176, 296, 344, 345; and the horrible, 261, 295–6; influence of Mrs. Radcliffe on, 296

Hadrian, 19

Haferkorn, R., 17

Halpérine-Kaminsky, E., and *Thérèse Philosophe*, 168

Ham, Roswell Gray, 49

Hamilton, Lady, 438

Hardman Papers, 289, 292, 452

Hardy, T., Tess as a persecuted maiden, 173

Harris, Frank, 423

Hartland, R. W., 178, 181

Hauff, W., 180

Hawthorne, N., 168, 173

Heine, H., Nencioni and, 259; and the fascination of women already dead, 287; and the Princess Belgiojoso, 293–4; Herodias, 313–14, 316, 407

——, M., on de Sade, 170, 173

Heinse, J. J. W., 211

Helen, 229, 253, 357, 376, 406; as an inspiration, 216, 222, 258, 259, 355; D'Annunzio and, 261, 262; Samain and, 310–11, 386; Pascoli and, 311

Heliogabalus, 159, 179, 191, 214, 353, 381, 397, 434

Hellenism, and the 'picturesque', 19; and the 'tale of terror', 115, 176

Hell-fire Club, the, 452

Henkey, Frederick, 453

Hermaphroditism, Wainewright and, 213; Swinburne and, 236; the Decadents and, 332 *et seq.*, 390, 404; in Gide, 380; in Samain, 386; Crowley and, 413; the Goncourts and, 433; *see also* Androgyne

Hernandez, L., 411

Herodias, in Heine's *Atta Troll*, 313–14, 407; *see* Salomé

Hichens, R., 432

Hippodamia, 31

Hock, S., 94

Hoffmann, E. T. W., 409, 455; his debt to *The Monk*, 113–14

Hofmannsthal, Hugo von, 50, 294

Hölderlin, 4, 10, 11

Homer, 199, 215, 259

Homosexuality, in Gide, 380; in Verlaine, 392; in Schwob's characters, 371

Horror, the cult of, 26–45, 46; Guerrazzi and, 261, 295–6; its attraction in woman, 278–9

Hospital, the, as a background, 279

Houghton, Lord, see Monckton Milnes

Houssaye, A., and J. Janin, 124, 179; and the Princess Belgiojoso, 254, 415–16; and Lesbianism, 333

Howard, W. M., 20

Howell, Ch. A., 292

Hughes, Randolph, 289

Hugo, V., 141, 175, 328, 453; and the relationship between Beauty and Death, 31, 32, 47; his debt to The Monk, 114; and the recognition scene, 115; the 'frénétique' type of novel, 122, 135; de Sade's alleged influence on, 139; and Baudelaire, 144; his debt to Mérimée, 205, 206; inspired by Cleopatra, 286; Mendès' debt to, 343; D'Annunzio likened to, 402

Humanism, 211

Hussey, C., and the 'picturesque', 19–20

Huxley, A., and the Gioconda smile, 256

Huysmans, J. K., 135, 179, 191, 296, 335, 352, 410, 416, 418, 421, 428; and the Fatal Woman, 277, 278; and Moreau, 305, 306–8, 310, 404, 405, 406, 427; and Mallarmé's Salomé, 317; on chastity in art, 319–20, 326, 383; and sadism, 320–1, 367, 394; and neo-Catholicism, 321, 322; Valéry on, 322; his A Rebours, 322–3, 354; his Decadent taste, 324; and de Rais, 324–5; his Hyacinthe, 325, 361, 366; Lorrain and, 365, 448; and Rops, 383; and de Montesquiou, 388, 430; and Decadence, 396; and Satanism, 410; and Bianchi Ferrari, 416–18

Hyde, H. Montgomery, 425

Iamblichus, 176

Idman, N., 177

Imitation of Christ, 391

Imperia, 220, 226

Incest, 408, 409; its place in the 'tales of terror', 71; Byron and, 71, 73, 75, 89–90; the Romantics and, 111; Chateaubriand and, 111–12; in Shelley, 118; in Flaubert, 188; in Swinburne, 236–7; in D'Annunzio, 265, 267, 275, 297; in Quillard, 297; in Mendès, 344; in Schwob, 371; in Barrès, 375–6, 379; in Gide, 382

Inertia, Moreau and the Beauty of, 303

Intrigues monastiques, 173

Irene, 397

Irving, W., 27, 136, 182, 452

Isle-Adam, Villiers de l', 321, 344, 345, 370, 411; and the Decadent Movement, 329–30; and the Androgyne, 350; and sadism in England, 443–4

Italian Renaissance, its influence, 328, 416

Italy, erotic invention in, 260, 294; the Fatal Woman in, 261 et seq.; and the Decadent Movement, 399, 401; France and her literary fashion, 401; and the Byzantines, 430

Jackson, H., on the minor poets of the Decadent Movement, 404, 422, 425, 430

Jacopone da Todi, 299

Jammes, F., 409

Janin, J., 168; his L'Ane Mort, 124–7, 131, 132, 133, 134, 155, 179, 290, 370, 429; and de Sade, 127–30; and Borel's Madame Putiphar, 128, 138; likened to Flaubert, 158; his Honestus, 179, 189

Jansenists, 51

Janssens, Father Laurence, 409

Jasinski, R., 180, 414

Jesse, J. H., 452

Jesuits, the, 418

'Jeunes-France', the, 124, 139

Jezebel, 250, 272, 377; Crowley's Jezabel, 413

Joan, Pope, 418

Johnson, L., 356, 359

Johnson, S., and the word 'romantic', 12–13

Jouve, P.-J., 299
Jowett, B., 453

Karr, A., 456
Keats, 197; and romanticism, 5, 11, 15; and the beauty of melancholy, 30, 31, 135; exoticism in, 211–13; Swinburne and, 238, 249, 292; Wilde and, 257, 258; and the Belle Dame, 285; his Lamia, 250; Schwob compared with, 369
Khnopff, F. E. J. M., 363
Khunrath, H., 415
Kierkegaard, S., 169
Killen, A. M., 177–8
Kleist, H. von, his Penthesilea, 10, 204; Croce on, 282
Klimt, Gustav, 428
Klopstock, F. G., 59, 60
Knight, R. Payne, 20
Krafft-Ebing, R., 94, 424
Kräger, H., and Byron's love of fatality, 85, 90

Lacenaire, 164, 453
Laclos, Choderlos de, his Les Liaisons dangereuses, 101–3, 110, 168, 170, 284; de Tilly on, 102–3; Baudelaire and, 103–4
Lacroix, P. (Bibliophile Jacob), 128, 139, 180
Laforgue, J., 281; and Salomé, 315–17, 407; and the disciples of Baudelaire, 384
——, Dr. R., 185
Lafourcade, G., 455; and Swinburne, 224, 227, 231, 232, 233, 236, 243, 244, 247, 248, 288–9, 290, 292, 404, 453
Lamartelière, J. H. F., 63
Lamartine, A. de, 17
Lamb, Lady Caroline, Byron and, 75; her Glenarvon, 77
Lambert, Sir John, anecdote of, 51
Lamia, 250
Landscapes, Chateaubriand on, 30–1; D'Annunzio on, 47; in the novels of D'Annunzio and Mirbeau, 279
Langdon, S. H., 282
Larat, J., on the origin of the 'noble bandit', 85
Lassailly, Ch., 182

Lasserre, P., his Le Romantisme français, 172, 183
Latouche, H. J. A. Thabaud de, 332
Latréaumont, N. du Hamel de, 193
Lautréamont, Comte de (Ducasse, I.), 137, 165–6, 194, 408; Sue and, 193; the Surrealists and, 193–4; a specimen of, 194–5
Lawrence, D. H., 301, 349; and Poe, 147, 185–6
Leandro, see Ferri, G.
Le Dantec, Y. G., on Vivien, 390, 431
Ledos, E., 410
Lee, N., 49
——, Vernon, 432, 454
Le Fanu, J. S., 173, 456–7
Leigh, Augusta, Byron and, 75, 90–1
Lenclos, Ninon de, 172
Lenz, J., and the persecuted maiden, 173
Leopardi, G., 290
Leroyer de Chantepie, Mlle, see Chantepie
Le Sage, 132
Lesbianism, 189, 414, 455–6; the Decadents and, 332–4, 415; in Paris, 333 et seq.; in Mendès, 346; in Samain, 386
Lessing, 172
Letourneur, P., and the word 'romantique', 13
Levaillant, M., 172
Lévi, E., 410
Lewis, M. G., 78, 86, 173, 174, 282; his The Monk, 62–3, 113, 121, 132, 175, 287; his sources, 173, 188–9; and the Fatal Woman, 201, 202–5, 207; his Bleeding Nun, 121; influence on Flaubert, 157
Libertin, meaning of the word, 300
Liberty, Swinburne as the Bard of, 247–8
Lilith, legend of, 199, 282
Lippard, George, 452
Lipsius, J., 417
Lisle, Leconte de, 405, 411
Literary criticism, and the history of culture, 2; its false interpretations, 2–6
Littré, on 'romantique', 7
Livy, 172
Lombard, Jean, 434

Lombardini, V., 297
Lombroso, C., and Baudelaire, 185
Longiano, S. F. da, 16
Lorrain, C., and the 'picturesque', 19
——, J., 423, 425; and Hugo, 47; and the Gioconda, 254; and Huysmans, 308, 323, 365; inspired by Heine, 315; compared with d'Aurevilly, 328; and Rachilde, 347, 349; and the Russian Woman, 351-2; as a sadist, 353-4, 363-5, 394; compared with Wilde, 359-60; and Moreau, 360-1; and the Goncourts, 361-2; his etheromania, 362, 427; Colette on, 362; Rops and, 384; and the Decadent Movement, 386; D'Annunzio and, 401, 403; Bourges and, 419; his perversities, 421-2; his reminiscences, 426, 427, 428, 430; and English sadism, 448, 456
Louÿs, P., and the Fatal Woman, 201, 209; compared with Sue, 283-4
Lovelace, R., 19, 38, 50
——, Earl of, his Astarte, 63-4, 87
——, Richardson's, 68, 98-9, 101, 104, 109
Lucas van Leyden, 335
Lucini, G. P., 297, 454
Ludwig II of Bavaria, as an inspiration, 342-3, 356, 419
Luther, 148
Luxembourg, Rosa, 456
Luzio, A., 178, 416

Macchia, G., 184
Machen, Arthur, 424
Machiavelli, the Elizabethans and, 60, 62, 86, 451; and exoticism, 286
McIntyre, C. F., 86
Maclisius, 446
Maeterlinck, M., 15, 95, 301; D'Annunzio's debt to, 266; Moreau as a forerunner of, 312; and the Decadent Movement, 396; his influence on Wilde's Salomé, 407
Magalotti, L., 5
Magnasco, 32
Maigron, L., 51, 171; and the 'Jeunes-France', 124
Maindron, M., 346
Maizeroy, R., 346

Mâle, E., 431
Malfi, Duchess of, 200
Mallarmé, S., 283, 352, 402, 428; his Salomé, 317-19; and Wagner, 401
Malmesbury, William of, 287
Malvezzi, A., 178
Mander, C. van, 20
Mandeville, Sir John, 230
Mandiargues, A. P. de, 194
Mann, T., 433; his Tod in Venedig, 52
Mantegna, 308, 337
Manwaring, E. W., 20
Manzoni, A., 379; his Nun of Monza, 174; and the 'tale of terror', 175-6
Margaret of Burgundy, 115, 158, 214, 221, 230, 352
Marie, A., 182, 288
Marinetti, F. T., his Mafarka le Futuriste, 296
Marino, G. B., 6, 326, 403; and the element of surprise in poetry, 38; his negress slave, 44; and Satan, 55-6, 58, 71
Marlowe, C., 49, 289, 291; and the delight in pain, 36, 48-9; his Dr. Faustus, 121; and the Orient, 191
Marsollier, see Vivetières
Martial, 332
Martineau, L. B., 408
Martino, P., 182
Marvell, A., 20
Mary Stuart, 221; Swinburne and, 227, 229-32
Masoch, see Sacher-Masoch
Masochism, in Rousseau, 289; in de Musset, 183; in Flaubert, 156; in the nineteenth century, 216; in Swinburne, 227, 289; in D'Annunzio, 273
Massinger, P., 291
Maturin, C. R., 114, 138, 177; his Melmoth the Wanderer, 78-9, 118-22; his debt to Diderot's Religieuse, 177; Wilde and, 358, 425
Maulde, R. de, 195, 325, 410
Maupassant, G. de, 453; on Swinburne, 291; meets Swinburne, 440-1, 449, 451, 453
Maurois, A., and Byron, 73, 91
Maurras, Ch., 385; and Vivien, 431
Mayer, Mlle Constance, 293

Mayne, E. C., and Byron's Life, 73, 74, 89, 429

Mazzini, G., and Swinburne, 247

Medmenham Monks, 452

Medusa, cult of, 43, 281; Shelley on, 25–6; the Romantics and, 25–45; in Flaubert, 156–7; Huysmans and, 323

Meibomius, 440, 446

Meinhold, W., 228

Melbourne, Lady, 74

Melville, Herman, 176

Memling, 361, 383

Memmi, L., 421

Mendès, C., 131, 419; and Baudelaire, 153–4; a preacher of misfortune, 343; his novels, 344–6, 419; and Lesbianism, 346; on Mikhaël, 387–8

Menken, Adah, Swinburne and, 246–7, 292

Meredith, G., 178; and Swinburne's Cleopatra, 251; and the Princess Belgiojoso, 416

Mérimée, P., 129, 286; his Vampire, 79, 94; and the Fatal Woman, 201, 205–7, 217, 218, 219, 283

Messalina, as the Eternal Feminine, 221, 240, 260, 353, 413

Meursius, 332

Michaelangelo, Swinburne on, 249–51; and the Fatal Woman, 254, 287; Moreau and, 303

Michelangelo, Andrea di, 292

Mickiewicz, A., 165

Middle Ages, Schwob and, 370, 371–2

Mikhaël, E., Mendès on, 387–8

Miller, H. M., 90

Milton, 20, 84, 90, 149, 165; his conception of Satan, 56–9, 88, 392; his Satan as the original of the rebel type, 59–60, 61, 68, 71, 85, 86, 203; Byron and, 63

Mimnermus, 215

Mirbeau, O., 46, 154, 225, 300, 326, 422; and the Fatal Woman, 210, 277, 278, 279; and Maeterlinck, 312; and English sadism, 447, 456

Molènes, Madame de, Baudelaire and, 43

Moll Flanders, 370

'Monastic Drama', see Drama

Monckton Milnes, R., 91; and Swinburne, 225–6, 234–5; and flagellation, 289

Monglond, A., 48, 89, 91, 169, 171

Monk, Samuel H., 46

Monna Lisa, Pater on, 253–4

Monselet, Ch., 182

Montaigne, 429

Montano, L., and Magalotti, 5

Montesquiou, R. de, 360, 406, 415; anecdote of, 388; Huysmans and, 388, 430; Lorrain and, 448; Proust and, 388

Montherlant, H. de, 321, 349

Monti, V., 4

Montigny, Darles de, his Thérèse Philosophe compared with Clarissa, 100–1; Dostoievsky and, 168

Montijo, Comtesse de, 206

Monvel, Boutet de, his Les Victimes cloîtrées, 173

Moore, G., 416; and the Decadent Movement in England, 356

——, J., his Zeluco, 68–9, 74

——, O. H., 84

——, Thomas, 182

Mor, A., 425

Morand, Paul, 453

Moreau, G., 154, 213, 404, 405, 406, 415; and the Fatal Woman, 216; his principles as a painter, 303–4; and Wagner's music, 304; characteristics of his figures, 304–5; Huysmans and, 305–8, 317, 404; compared with Flaubert, 302–3, 405; his conception of female beauty, 309, 311, 406; his 'Sphinx' pictures, 310; subjects of his pictures, 311–12; a forerunner of Maeterlinck, 312; Wilde and, 313; artist of the Decadents, 319, 383, 386; his influence on Péladan, 336, 337, 338, 339; and the Androgyne, 350; Lorrain and, 353, 360–1, 363, 364–5; his Salomé, 427

Morelli, D., 292

Moreno, M., 428

Morley, Lord, 253

Mornet, D., 46

Morris, W., 228, 423

Mottini, E., 174

Mount Edgcumb, Earl of, 454

Mouquet, J., 187

Mourey, G., 270, 271, 291, 440
Müller, W., 177
Murger, H., 139
Murillo, 122
Murry, J. Middleton, 285
Music, relation of painting to, 304, 404
Musset, A. de, 28, 165, 183, 418; and the regenerated prostitute, 111; de Sade's influence on, 139, 140, 183; his *Confession d'un enfant du siècle*, 140–1, 351, 432
Mysticism, 284; and exoticism, 210–11, 212

Nadar, and Baudelaire, 153, 187
Napoleon I, 137, 369
Nature, Baudelaire on, 148; Swinburne on her laws, 233–4, 235, 290; Leopardi on, 290
Necrophily, 3, 219; in the Princess Belgiojoso, 123, 178; in Berlioz, 123; in Flaubert, 157; in Schwob, 371
Negresses, 44, 52
Nencioni, E., 271; his Fatal Woman derived from Swinburne, 258–60, 261
Nerciat, Chevalier de, 453
Neri, F., 295
Nero, 159, 164, 179, 190, 229, 355, 397; de Sade on, 190; Flaubert and, 190; Lorrain and, 362
Nerval, Gérard de, 288, 455
Nevill, R., 452
Newman, B., 420, 423
Nicoll, Allardyce, 411
Nicolson, H., and Swinburne, 223–4, 248
Nietzsche, 10, 128; D'Annunzio and, 269, 401; a sadist, 290; Gide influenced by, 379, 381
Noble bandit, *see* Rebel type
Nocturnal Revels, 452
Nodier, Ch., 27; his *Jean Sbogar*, 63, 77, 80, 85, 327; and the vampire, 79; his *Hélène Gillet*, 181, 208
Normandy, G., on Lorrain, 47, 362, 421, 428
Novalis, 14; and the relation between pain and desire, 28

Ode to Consumption, 27

Offenbach, 315
Ojetti, U., 429
Olivier, Mme Juste, 415
Onions, C. T., 17
Oriani, Alfredo, 189, 295, 415
O'Shaughnessy, A., his Fatal Women, 355
Otway, T., 49–50, 175, 455
Ourousoff, Prince Alexander, 186
Overbeck, F., 414
Ovid, 289, 423
Owen, William, 414
Ozy, Alice (Pilloy, Julie-Justine), 187

Paganini, N., 43
Paget, V. (Vernon Lee), 432, 454
Pain, Keats's conception of love as, 285; its connexion with desire, 28
Painting, its relation to music, 304, 404
Pall Mall Gazette and sadism in England, 443–7
Pan, as an inspiration of sadists, 277
Parini, 168
Pascoli, G., 216, 419; his vision of Helen, 311
Pastorino, G. M., 337
Pater, W., 3, 46, 223, 261, 286, 293, 404, 422–3; and the Fatal Woman, 210, 254, 288; and Monna Lisa, 253–4, 257, 287, 418; a forerunner of the Decadent Movement, 355–6; and art and music, 404; and the Androgyne, 355–6
Paulhan, F., 408
Peacock, T. L., 21
Péladan, J., 154, 209, 321, 354, 395, 410, 418, 421; and the Fatal Woman, 254–5, 268; and the Decadent Movement, 330, 332; France on, 331; d'Aurevilly on, 331–2; and the Hermaphrodite, 332, 333, 334–9, 350, 414; and Russia, 336–9; D'Annunzio and, 401, 403; and Wagner, 341, 413; and the Princess Belgiojoso, 415–16; and Rops, 430; and sadism in England, 449, 453
Pepys, S., 12
Perceau, L., on *Gamiani*, 183
Perino, E., 397
Perrens, F., 300

Persecuted maiden, the, Reybaud on, 97; Clarissa as a type of, 97–9; in *Faust*, 98; in Diderot, 99; de Sade and, 109; development of the theme in Europe, 112–14; in Mrs. Radcliffe, 114–15; in other women writers, 115–16; in Shelley's *Cenci*, 116–18; in Borel, 134; Wesselowsky on, 167

Perversion, its justification by materialism, 99–100; Baudelaire and, 146; in Swinburne, 224–5; Monckton Milnes and, 225–6; in D'Annunzio, 267

Petrarch, 6, 15, 230, 255; and the 'picturesque', 19; and the Eternal Feminine, 213

Petronius, 371

Phillips, W. C., 93

Picturesque, the, use of the term in France, 13–14; in England, 19–20; in Hellenistic civilization, 19; of Italian origin, 19; in landscape painting, 20–1; in garden designs, 21

Pierre-Quint, L., 193–4, 195

Pilloy, Julie-Justine, *see* Ozy, Alice

Pindar, 4

Piranesi, 19

'Pittoresque', *see* Picturesque

Planche, G., 193

Plato, 8, 9, 334

Pleasure, its connexion with pain, 28

Poe, E. A., 46, 91, 121, 136, 342, 386, 393, 441; and the beauty of strangeness, 47, 51; and Delacroix, 144; on Perversity, 146–7, 185, 382; Baudelaire and, 146–8, 149, 153, 154, 182, 184, 192; and Flaubert, 157; D. H. Lawrence on, 185–6; Rossetti and, 228; Nencioni and, 258; Huysmans compared with, 323; his influence on de l'Isle-Adam, 329, 330; Dostoievsky and, 350; Wilde's debt to, 358; his influence on Schwob, 370; Swinburne and, 453

Poetry, and mysticism, 211

Polidori, Dr. G. G., his *The Vampire*, 78

Polo, Marco, 5

Polycleitus, 334

Pope, A., 452; and romanticism, 12, 14

Popelin, C., 425

Porché, F., 187, 433

Portigliotti, G., 50

Powell, G., 440, 441

Prarond, E., and the synthetic Fatal Woman, 288

Pre-Raphaelites, 211, 212, 260; their influence on Swinburne, 227–8, 238; the Decadents and, 339, 353, 363; Vivien and, 388; in France, 401; paintings of, 404

Pre-Raphaelite Exhibition, 305

Prévost, Abbé, 90; and the regenerated prostitute, 110, 111, 179

——, M., 175

Price, Uvedale, 20

Primaticcio, 335, 416

Primitives, the, 415, 427; Moreau and, 303; Decadents and, 339, 353; the Goncourts and, 361; and Rops, 383

Prina, Count, 168

Procopius, 272

Prometheus, Satan's likeness to, 56; D'Annunzio and, 276; Guaita and, 412

Prostitutes, Flaubert and, 158; the Goncourts and, 45; Schwob and, 369–70, 371

Proust, M., 107, 406; anticipated by Barrès, 374; and de Montesquiou, 388

Psammetichus, 345

Pushkin, and Orientalism, 215

Quillard, P., 297; his poem on Helen, 406

Quilp, J., 432

Rachilde, 178, 296, 344, 345, 350; and the Fatal Woman, 277; and the Androgyne, 346–7; Barrès on, 347–8; sadism in, 348, 349

Racine, 126

Radcliffe, Mrs. Ann, 121, 173, 174; her romantic criminals, 60–1, 62, 86, 87–8; Byron's debt to, 66, 68, 85; her sources, 173; Manzoni and, 175; and the persecuted maiden, 114–15, 123; her influence on Guerrazzi, 176

Railo, E., his *Study of the Elements of English Romanticism*, 86, 88, 90, 173, 175, 177, 188, 282, 287, 425

Rais, Gilles de, 100, 108, 129, 194–5, 249; Huysmans and, 324; Life of, 325, 410–11

Ranieri, Antonio, 176

Raphaël, 416

Räuber-, Ritter-, and Schauer-romantik, 122

Raya, Gino, 176

Raynaud, E., 182, 187

Realism, 18

Rebel type, the, a descendant of Milton's Satan, 59–60, 63, 71, 85; in Schiller's *Räuber* (Karl Moor), 59–60, 77; in Mrs. Radcliffe's Schedoni, 60–2, 66, 87, 88; in Lewis, *The Monk*, 62–3; in Zschokke's Abellino, 63; brought to perfection in Byron, 63–8; in Moore's Zeluco, 68–9; in Chateaubriand's René, 77, 93

Reed, A. L., 17

Regnault, H., his Salome, 315, 407

Régnier, Henri de, 406

Reichart, W. A., 182

Reik, T., 155, 188

Reimarus, 407

Religion, the sadist and, 109; the Decadent writers and, 320–2, 366, 418

Rembrandt, 85

Renan, Ary, 190; and Moreau, 308–9, 310, 406

Reni, Guido, 176

Rensselaer, W. Lee, 20

Repton, Humphrey, 21

Reybaud, L., on the persecuted maiden, 97

Reynaud, L., 70; and Richardson, 167; and Romanticism, 167

Reynolds, Sir Joshua, 20

Ribera, 85

Richard, E., 411

Richardson, S., 68, 167, 170, 172; Clarissa as the type of persecuted maiden, 97–8; his background of sensuality, 98–9; *Clarissa* compared with Montigny's *Thérèse Philosophe*, 100; his influence in France, 101–2; derivatives of, 113, 119, 167, 169, 181

Richness, Moreau and the Necessity of, 303, 304

Richter, H., 89–90, 425

——, Jean Paul, 14, 180

Ricketts, Ch., 256

Rimbaud, 434

Ripamonti, G., 174

Robespierre, 133

Rochester, 2nd Earl of, 49

Rohde, E., 85

Rolfe, F. W. (Baron Corvo), 424

Rollinat, M., a literary Rops, 385; and vampirism, 385–6; his house, 386; Guaita and, 412

Romanesque, distinguished from 'romantic', 13, 17–18

Romantic, as an approximate term, 1; false applications of the term, 4–5; the classic–romantic antithesis, 6–11; history of the word, 11–16; its use in France, 13; its meaning, 14–15; distinguished from Romanesque, 17–18

—— Literature, erotic sensibility and, 38

—— Movement, in European literature, 8

Romantics, the, and Milton, 58–9; their Fatal Men, 60, 76–83; and Vampirism, 78–80, 219; perversities, 108; and the regenerated prostitute, 110–11; and incest, 111; and the recognition scene, 115; and de Sade, 128; and the story of the Bleeding Nun, 174; and the Fatal Woman, 200–2; and exoticism, 211; and Orientalism, 215

Romantics, French, and Swinburne, 228; and the 'frénétique', 351

Romanticism, distinguished from Romanesque, 17–18; in the Medusa conception, 25–7; and the Pleasure in Pain relationship, 28; Borel and, 138; Baudelaire and, 145–6; its turning-point with Baudelaire and Flaubert, 154; Reynaud's theory of, 167; Delacroix as a representative of, 303; and its liking for green eyes, 327, 328; de l'Isle-Adam and, 329, 330; and the 'frénétique', 351; and sadism, 394–5; its relation to Decadence, 411

Rops, F., 157, 183, 337; Huysmans and, 319–20, 383, 430; the Decadents and, 339, 346, 386; the artist of the Decadent Movement, 383–6; and woman as Evil, 383–4; Guaita and, 411

Rosa, Salvator, and the 'picturesque', 18, 19, 20, 60, 122

Rosamond, 227, 228

Rosicrucians, Péladan and, 331, 340, 410

Rosny, J. H., 454

Rossetti, D. G., 119; his preference for the sad and the cruel, 228; and Swinburne, 246–7; and Pater, 253; and D'Annunzio, 267; his success, 305; Wilde's debt to, 358

Rothenstein, W., 334, 415; on Lautrec, 426; and Montesquiou, 430

Rouault, G., 406

Rousseau, J. J., 93, 95, 169, 171; and the word 'romantique', 13; anticipated by de Montigny, 101; his ethical theory, 104; and the regenerated prostitute, 111; masochism in, 289

Rouveyre, A., on Gide, 383, 407; on de Gourmont, 428, 430

Rowe, N., his *Fair Penitent*, 97

Royère, J., and Baudelaire, 185, 187

Rubens, 296

Ruchon, F., 407

Rudwin, M., 282

Ruskin, J., 401, 422

Russia, the Fatal Woman in, 207, 209–10; and Orientalism, 215; influence of Russian novels in France, 336, 339, 340–4, 396, 401; Dostoievsky, 419, 420

Sabatier, A., 407

——, Madame, Baudelaire and, 153, 187

——, P., and the Goncourts, 433, 454

Sacher-Masoch, Leopold von, 224, 300

Sade, Marquis de, 112, 113, 125, 131, 132, 137, 147, 168, 169–71, 173–4, 175, 194, 284, 290, 293, 321, 391, 409, 414, 452; his influence on literature, 99; his likeness to Byron, 82–3; and the customs of savage tribes, 100; and de Montigny, 101; the justification of vice as expressed in *Justine* and *Juliette*, 104–8; Restif de la Bretonne and, 109; his characters compared with Shelley's Cenci, 116–18; his influence on the *roman-charogne*, 125; Janin and, 127–30, 138, 179; his influence on Baudelaire, 139, 148, 153; Flaubert and, 154, 155, 156, 163–4, 193; his growing influence, 164–5; on public executions, 177; De Quincey and, 179; France on, 180; on Nero, 190; and Sue, 209; Swinburne and, 91–2, 224, 225, 228, 232–4, 242–4, 247, 249, 290, 440; D'Annunzio compared with, 269, 276; and Stendhal, 285; and de Rais, 324; Péladan and, 332; Rachilde and, 348; de Goncourt and, 169, 395; de Gourmont and, 366; Gide and, 382–3; compared with Solomon, 404; the Russian novel and, 419–20; in England, 448–9

Sadism, the basis of, 107–8; the inversion of values and, 108; and virtue, 108–9; and religion, 109; in Shelley's *The Cenci*, 116–18; Maturin on, 119–22; lycanthropy and, 139; de Viel Castel and, 139, 182–3; in Delacroix, 143–4; and ennui, 146; in Flaubert, 156, 163–4; in Baudelaire, 149 *et seq.*, 185; in Swinburne, 233–5, 236–7, 242; in D'Annunzio, 264–9, 274–7, 299; in Kleist, 282; literary, in Italy, 296; in French Decadent literature, 320, 321; in Huysmans, 324; in d'Aurevilly, 327, 411; in de l'Isle-Adam, 329; in Rachilde, 348, 349; in Dostoievsky, 350; Lorrain and, 353–4, 363; in de Gourmont, 366–8; in Schwob, 370; in Barrès, 373; in Gide, 380; in Verlaine, 392; in the Decadent Movement, 394; the Russian soul and, 420; in Lautrec, 426; in England, 437–8, 443–51

Sadists, Promethean attitude of, 277; female, of the Decadents, 456

Sadleir, M., 175

Sainte-Beuve, C. A., 139, 153, 180; and Baudelaire, 43, 145, 149; on

Byron's debt to Chateaubriand, 70, 88; on Byron and de Sade, 82–3, 124; and Flaubert, 155, 163; on de Sade's influence, 164–5, 235; and Sue, 183, 208, 209; and the Fatal Woman, 201, 205; on Chateaubriand, 408; on *Mademoiselle de Maupin*, 332; and the Princess Belgiojoso, 415

Saint Gertrude, 367

Saint-Just, 130

Saint Paul, 8, 293

Saint Peter, 151

Saint-Pierre, Bernardin dé, 112; his *Paul et Virginie*, 221

Saint Rose of Lima, 357, 378

Saint-Victor, P. de, 187, 439

Saint Vincent de Paul, 209, 396, 427

Salaino (Salai, A.), 337

Salomé, 144, 405, 407, 428; as the Fatal Woman, 216, 258, 259, 272, 277; of Moreau, 305–9, 405; Wilde and, 312–15, 316–17; Laforgue and, 315–16, 317, 407; O'Shaughnessy and, 355; Lorrain and, 365; Schwob and, 372–3; Samain and, 386; *see* Herodias

Salvadori, G., 430

Samain, A., and the Fatal Woman, 216; inspired by Cleopatra, 286; inspired by Moreau's Helen, 310, 386–7, 406–7; and Lust, 386–7; his affinity with Vivien, 390, 432

Sand, George, 104, 139, 276; her debt to *The Monk*, 114; de Musset and, 183; and Lesbianism, 333

Sandys, F., Swinburne and, 251

Sappho, 236, 240, 260, 261

Sardanapalus, 143, 155, 159, 191, 387, 397; Byron and, 90; Gautier and, 214

Sarrazin, G., 427

Sartorio, A., 407

Satan, 103–4, 131, 132, 172, 173; Milton's conception of, 53, 56–9, 71, 88; Tasso and, 55; Marino on, 55–6; as the sublime outlaw, 59–63, 68, 81; and Byron's rebel type, 63, 75; Baudelaire and, 104; in Maturin, 119–20; Lewis and, 203; Mérimée and, 205; Swinburne and, 240; Péladan and, 255; in Soulié's *Mémoires du Diable*, 130 *et seq.*

Satanism, Baudelaire and, 103–4, 145; de Sade and, 104; Chateaubriand and, 112, 408; in D'Annunzio, 276; Moreau and the beauty of, 309–10; sadism and, 321; in Huysmans, 324, 410; in Gide, 380

Satanists, Promethean attitude of, 277

'Satrapism', 213

Saunier, Charles, 414

Scandales de Londres, see *Pall Mall Gazette*

Scarborough, D., 425

Schiller, 6, 90, 93; on *Paradise Lost*, 58–9; his sublime outlaw in *Die Räuber*, 59–60, 63, 68, 77, 85, 87; and the Fatal Man, 80; and the regenerated prostitute, 111; and profanation of the Madonna, 188

Schlegel, F. von, 9, 14

Scholten, W., 177

Schongauer, M., 335

Schopenhauer, 261, 396, 401

Schubert, 357

Schwaeblé, R., 410

Schwob, M., 188, 413, 434; Lorrain and, 363; and the Decadent Movement, 368–73, 396; his researches, 369–70; as a sadist, 370; his perverse themes, 370–1, 372; and Salome, 372–3; and Wilde, 428

Scott, Sir Walter, 86, 178, 327, 414; and the rebel type, 87–88; his debt to *The Monk*, 114, 175; and the 'tale of terror', 122

Séché, A., 51, 187, 290

——, L., 183

Seillière, E., 17, 85, 433, 454

Selwyn, G. A., 360, 421; as a sadist, 437–8, 451, 452

Semiramis, 200, 214, 230, 240, 260, 397

Seneca, 49, 143, 183, 294, 409

Sensibility, approximate terms, 5; its development in 18th century, 11, 27

Seventeenth-century writers, their approach compared with the Romantics', 38, 40

Sex, and the exotic, 207

Seylaz, L., 47, 182, 409, 411

Shadwell, T., 49, 454

Shaftesbury, 454

Shakespeare, 13, 17, 28, 49, 60, 62, 113, 152, 174, 291, 337, 429; interpretation of, 2–3; his characters as a source of Fatal Man, 61–2, 86, 89; Shelley's *Cenci* and *King Lear*, 117; the suffering of virtue in, 167; Swinburne on, 251; Taine and, 291

Sheba, Queen of, 288

Shelley, P. B., 4, 11, 31, 46, 78, 92, 176, 259; and the Medusa, 25–6; and pain and pleasure, 28; on the conception of Good and Evil, 59, 85; his feminine ideal, 90; the persecuted maiden in *The Cenci*, 116–18; and incest, 118; D'Annunzio and, 300

Shelley, Mrs., her *Frankenstein*, 78, 115–16, 130; her *Valperga*, 116

Sidney, Sir Philip, 19

Signorelli, L., 339

Sitwell, S., 284

Smith, Lady Eleanor, 452

——, Horace, 182

——, L. Pearsall, 87; on 'romantic', 11, 13

Smithers, and Beardsley, 414

Sodoma (il), 377, 426

Solario, A., 427

Solomon, S., 422; painting of, 404, 456

Song of Solomon, 44

Soulié, F., 158, 181, 296; and de Sade, 130, 139; his *Mémoires du Diable*, 130–3, 138

Soupault, P., 193

Southey, R., 165

Spain, the Fatal Woman in, 207, 209; Barrès and, 377–8; Samain and, 386; Vivien and, 388

Spare, A. O., 413

Sphinx, Moreau's pictures of, 306

Spiers, Chr. H., his *Das Petermännchen*, 113

Staël, Madame de, on Goethe's *Bride of Corinth*, 81–2; Chateaubriand and, 88–9

Stampa, S., 175

Stannard, Mrs., 46

Stead, W. T., 443

Stelzi, G., 123, 178

Stendhal, 19, 124, 169, 286, 453; and necrophily, 178; his nostalgia for the ancient world, 286; and de Rais, 324

Sterne, L., 127

Stesichorus, 222

Stevenson, R. L., 358

Strauss, R., 317

Street, G. S., 432

Strich, F., and the 'classic–romantic' antithesis, 9–10

Strindberg, A., 284, 420–1

'Sturm und Drang', Lewis and, 63; and incest, 90; and the Gretchen tragedy, 172–3; death statistics of, 430

Sublimation, Barrès and, 379

Sue, E., 183, 191, 195, 340, 418; and the *romans-feuilleton*, 63, 80, 122, 178; and the regenerated prostitute, 111; and the recognition scene, 115; influence of de Sade on, 139, 183; his *Latréaumont*, 193; and the Fatal Woman, 172, 201, 207–9; Louÿs compared with, 209, 283

Suetonius, 325

Suffering, Maturin on, 119

Summers, Montague, 86, 175, 177, 282

'Superwoman', the, in D'Annunzio, 269, 271–4; of Gilkin, 279

Surrealists, the, 194; and Ducasse, 165, 193

Suso, H., 368

Swarzenski, G., 418

Swinburne, A. C., 116, 176, 181–2, 186, 291, 293, 388, 413, 422, 432, 447; and the Elizabethan dramatists, 36, 48–9; Byron's influence on, 91; and de Sade, 91, 225, 232–4, 242–3, 290; Delacroix compared with, 142, 144, 153; and the persecuted maiden, 173; and the Fatal Woman, 210, 223, 235–6, 238–46, 249, 251, 254, 264; and female beauty, 213; compared with Baudelaire, 223; his artistic personality, 223–5; and flagellation, 225–7; and the relation of man to woman, 227; his Mary Stuart, 227, 229–33; and tainted beauty, 228–39; on nature and crime, 233–4, 235; sadism in, 235–8, 241; and incest, 236; his *Anactoria*, 237–8, 298; his Dolores,

241–6; and Jane Faulkner, 246; and Adah Menken, 246–7; and Liberty, 247–8; his influence on Literature, 249–53; Wilde's debt to, 256; Nencioni's debt to, 258–60, 261; his influence on D'Annunzio, 265, 266, 267, 269–77, 297, 298, 299–300, 401; and Moreau, 304, 312; and Lesbianism, 333; his influence in England, 354–5; compared with Barrès, 377, 379; compared with Samain, 387; his influence on Vivien, 389–90, 431; Verlaine and, 394; and Simeon Solomon, 404; anticipated by Selwyn, 437; meets de Maupassant, 440–1; portrayed by E. de Goncourt in *La Faustin*, 441, by J. Lorrain in *Esthéticité*, 456, by V. Lee in *Miss Brown*, 432; and Poe, 441, 453; his national estimation, 444, 451; Lorrain and, 449; Péladan and, 450; and female sadists, 456

Symbolism, 211, 212

Symonds, J. A., 422, 423–4

Symons, A., 356, 404

Tailhade, L., 341

Taine, H., on Milton's Satan, 58; and the Elizabethan dramatists, 291

'Tale of terror', the, 60–3, 86, 89, 175; its invention, 114; in Greece, 176; in Maturin, 118; in France, 122–3, 124; its translation into real life, 123; in Meinhold, 228

Talma, 95

Talman, F., 346

Tarn, Pauline, *see* Vivien, Renée

Tasso, T., 6, 32, 33, 37, 48, 49, 204, 236, 326, 335; and Beauty and Death, 32–6; his idea of Satan, 55, 56; Chateaubriand and, 205

Telleen, J. M., 90

Terms, literary, use of, 1, 3, 5–7, 12, 16

Thackeray, 93, 181

Theodora, 191, 221, 272, 397

Thérèse Philosophe, Clarissa compared with, 100–1; de Sade and, 104; Dostoievsky and, 168

Thomson, J., 19

Thovez, E., 262, 297, 413, 428

Thucydides, 408

Tiberius, 168

Tilly, P. A. de, 51, 102

Tillyard, E. M. W., 84

Tolstoy, L., 418

Tommaseo, N., 178

Toorop, J., 360, 363, 426

Torquemada, 328, 329

Toulet, P. J., 290, 343, 433; and sadism in England, 126, 446; sadism in, 394

Toulouse-Lautrec, H. de, 334, 360; his appearance, 425–6

Tourneur, C., 371

Trevelyan, R. C., 282

Tréogate, Loaisel de, his *Comtesse d'Alibre*, 175

Tristan l'Hermite, 50

Trompeo, P. P., 174

Trudgian, Helen, 179, 409

Turquet-Milnes, G., 424

Twain, Mark, 434; Schwob influenced by, 370

Tymms, Ralph, 425

Ustick, W. Lee, 17

Valerini, A., 295

Valéry, P., on 'classic' and 'romantic', 8–9; and Mallarmé, 317, 352; on Huysmans, 322

Valle-Inclán, R. del, 171, 192, 286, 408–9

Vampirism, 284, 455–6; Byron and, 78; the Romantics and, 78–80; Poe and, 147; in Baudelaire, 152; in Gautier, 217–20; in Flaubert, 220; in Swinburne, 230–1; Rollinat and, 385

Vanbrugh, Sir John, and the 'picturesque', 19

Van Dyck, and Brignole-Sale, 50

Varende, J. de la, 411

Vasari, G., 20

Vathek, 203, 211

Vauvenargues, Marquis de, 32, 48, 73

Veblen, Thorstein, 404

Velasquez, 426

Veneto, Bartolomeo, 418

Venturi, A., 416

Verhaeren, E., 426

Verlaine, P., 340, 433; his confused Christianity, 321–2; and Lesbianism, 333; and the Decadent Movement, 392-4, 395

Vicaire, G., and parody of the Decadents, 390-1

Viel Castel, Comte H. de, on de Sade's influence, 139, 182

Vigée-Lebrun, Mme, 414

Villon, F., 214, 219; Schwob and, 369

Vinci, Leonardo da, 25, 46, 415; and the Gioconda smile, 52, 253-6, 294, 341; Pater on, 253-4; Barrès on, 294, 377; Moreau and, 308; and the Androgyne, 334-5, 339; school of, 365

Virgil, 34, 204, 205, 226, 418

Virtue, its place in tragedy, de Sade's opinion of, 101; in Les Liaisons dangereuses, 101, 102; sadism and, 108-9

Visiak, E. H., 58, 84

Vittoriale, the, D'Annunzio and, 402-3, 434

Vivanti, A., 456

Vivetières, B. J. Marsollier de, his Camille, 173

Vivien, Renée, her Lesbian poems, 388-90; studies of, 431

Vogüé, E. M. de, 336, 401, 420

Voivenel, P., 428

Volland, Sophie, 32

Voltaire, 179, 394

Vontade, J., 423

Wackenroder, W. G., 211

Wagner, 141, 172, 185, 261, 269, 297, 336, 419; Moreau and, 304; the Decadents and, 339-41, 342, 356, 357, 396, 401, 433-4; Barrès and, 378; Péladan and, 413; Beardsley and, 425

Wainewright, T. G., 293; an alleged forerunner of Wilde, 213, 356

Walpole, H., 86; his Castle of Otranto, 27, 86; and George Selwyn, 437

Warton, J., 12

Watt, W. Whyte, 175

Watts-Dunton, T., and Swinburne, 249

Weber, C. M. von, Delacroix compared with, 142, 144, 184; and de Montesquiou, 430

Webster, J., 291, 390; and the delight in pain, 36; and the Fatal Woman, 200

Wedekind, F., 420

Welby, T. Earle, and Swinburne, 224, 225, 248, 251, 293

Wesselowsky, on the persecuted maiden, 167

Whistler, J. M., 360, 388, 426

Wiertz, A., 296, 408

Wilde, O., 291, 356, 403, 407, 414, 425, 432, 444; and the Fatal Woman, 210, 223, 256-8; Wainewright a forerunner of, 213; and the Gioconda smile, 257; and Salome, 258, 312-13, 316-17, 407; and the 'superwoman', 273; his sources, 294; and Maeterlinck, 312; influenced by Heine, 315; influenced by Huysmans, 323; his Dorian Gray, 354, 357-60, 422; compared with Lorrain, 359-60, 363, 364, 448, 449; his influence on Schwob, 370, 428; his influence on Gide, 379-80, 381; compared with D'Annunzio, 402; as Sebastian Melmoth, 425

Wilkinson, Miss S., and the persecuted maiden, 115

Willoughby, L. A., 85, 86

Wilson, J. Dover, 17

Winckelmann, 47, 404, 405, 414, 422, 423

Wirth, O., 331

Wise, T. J., 225

Wolff, S., 20

Wölfflin, H., 9, 10

Woodbridge, B. M., 90

Wratislaw, T., 356

Wraxall, Sir Nathaniel, 438

Wyzewa, T. de, 350

Yeats, W. B., 14

Young, A., 21

Yovanovitch, V. M., 94

Ysabeau, Queen, 329

Zola, E., 175, 283, 409, 425; on his taste in literature, 323-4; and sadism, 409

Zschokke, H., his Aballino, 63, 80, 86

OXFORD

MORE OXFORD PAPERBACKS

Details of a selection of other books to follow. A complete list of Oxford Paperbacks, including The World's Classics, Twentieth-Century Classics, OPUS, Past Masters, Oxford Authors, Oxford Shakespeare, and Oxford Paperback Reference, is available in the UK from the General Publicity Department, Oxford University Press (JH), Walton Street, Oxford, OX2 6DP.

In the USA, complete lists are available from the Paperbacks Marketing Manager, Oxford University Press, 200 Madison Avenue, New York, NY 10016.

Oxford Paperbacks are available from all good bookshops. In case of difficulty, please order direct from Oxford University Press Bookshop, 116 High Street, Oxford, Freepost, OX1 4BR, enclosing full payment. Please add 10% of published price for postage and packing.

THE ROMANTIC IMAGINATION

Maurice Bowra

This is a classic, illuminating study of the major poets of the Romantic movement and their followers; Blake, Coleridge, Wordsworth, Shelley, Keats, Byron, Poe, Christina and Dante Gabriel Rossetti, and Swinburne. Originally delivered as a series of lectures at a time when the Romantics were to some extent in critical opprobrium, *The Romantic Imagination* sought to reassess the literary values of these poets.

SHELLEY

Poetical Works

Edited by Thomas Hutchinson
New edition, corrected by G. M. Matthews

This edition by Thomas Hutchinson (1905), corrected and updated by G. M. Matthews (1970), contains every poem and fragment of Shelley's verse that had hitherto appeared in print. The text, based on Mary Shelley's own editions of 1839 has been freshly collated by Thomas Hutchinson, who had indicated in footnotes every material departure from the originals. Shelley's antiquated or eccentric spellings have been modernized except where required by rhyme or metre. The original pointing has been retained except where it tends to obscure or distort the poet's meaning.

There are also headnotes to each poem, detailing its composition and publication, and a list of the principal editions of Shelley's works.

COLERIDGE

Poetical works

Edited by Ernest Hartley Coleridge

This edition by Ernest Hartley Coleridge, grandson of the poet, contains a complete and authoritative text of Coleridge's poems. Here are his earliest extant teenage poems, his masterly meditative pieces, and the extraordinary supernatural poems—'The Rime of the Ancient Mariner', 'Kubla Khan', and 'Christabel'.

The text follows that of the 1834 edition, the last published in the author's lifetime. The poems are printed, so far as is possible, in chronological order, with Coleridge's own notes as well as textual and bibliographical notes by the editor.

WORDSWORTH

Poetical Works

Revised by Ernest de Selincourt

This edition of Wordsworth's poems contains every piece of
verse known to have been published by the poet himself, or of
which he authorized the posthumous publication. The text,
which Thomas Hutchinson based largely upon the 1849–50
standard edition—the last issued during the poet's lifetime—
was revised in 1936 for the Oxford Standard Authors series by
Ernest de Selincourt.

ROMANTICS, REBELS AND REACTIONARIES

English Literature and its Background 1760–1830

Marilyn Butler

This book takes a fresh look at once of the most fertile periods in English literature, a half-century which produced writers of the stature of Blake, Keats, Coleridge, Wordsworth, Byron, Scott, and Jane Austen. Marilyn Butler questions the validity of grouping such diverse talents and personalities under the critical label 'Romantic', and instead presents them to the reader both as individuals and as part of a larger cultural landscape.

This is a highly original book which is sure to enlighten and stimulate students of the period as well as the general reader.

'Dr Butler is brilliantly acute . . . at restoring to literary works the subdued political ticks and rumblings which the alarmed ears of their first readers would have picked up.' John Carey, *Sunday Times*

'Why has it not been done before? one asks of Marilyn Butler's excellent new book, which analyses the diverse writers of the Romantic period exclusively—but also exhaustively and subtly—in political and ideological terms.' *Listener*

An OPUS book

OXFORD

THE ROMANTIC AGONY
MARIO PRAZ

'*The Romantic Agony* is now a classic in a sense which places it among such books as have, in the depth of their insights, power to alter a reader's understanding of the history of his society, and perhaps of his own history.'
Frank Kermode

In his remarkable study, *The Romantic Agony*, Mario Praz has described the whole Romantic literature under one of its most characteristic aspects, that of erotic sensibility. This 'exceedingly learned, informative and curious book' (*New Statesman*) is, in effect, an analysis of a mood in literature—one which, however transient, was widespread. Expressed in dreams of 'luxurious cruelties', 'fatal women', corpse-passions, and sinful agonies of delight, the mood—as seen in the influence of Byron and De Sade—had a major effect on poets and painters of the nineteenth century. And the affinities between them and their twentieth-century counterparts make Professor Praz's account of the Romantic-Decadents 'one of the indispensable guides', as Frank Kermode observes, 'to the study of our own literature and our own epoch'.

First published in 1933, *The Romantic Agony* was reissued in 1951 in a second edition containing much new material, and was further revised in 1970, when Frank Kermode's Foreword was also included for the first time. It has been translated from the Italian by Angus Davidson.

ISBN 0-19-281061-8

Cover paintings: *Vanity, Death, Purgatory*, by Memling.
Courtesy of the Musées de la Ville de Strasbourg.

9 780192 810618